Mombasa
30-35
126-2...
296

S0-ARM-129

Fielding's
LITERARY
AFRICA

Norfolk Hotel
P 155

Karen B
p. 171 →

Kenya →
p. 292

Current Fielding Titles
_____

Red Guides—updated annually
_____

FIELDING'S BERMUDA AND THE BAHAMAS 1988
FIELDING'S CARIBBEAN 1988
FIELDING'S ECONOMY EUROPE 1988
FIELDING'S EUROPE 1988
FIELDING'S MEXICO 1988
FIELDING'S PEOPLE'S REPUBLIC OF CHINA 1988
FIELDING'S SELECTIVE SHOPPING GUIDE TO EUROPE 1988

Blue Guides—updated as necessary
_____

FIELDING'S AFRICAN SAFARIS
FIELDING'S EUROPE WITH CHILDREN
FIELDING'S FAMILY VACATIONS USA
FIELDING'S FAR EAST
FIELDING'S HAVENS AND HIDEAWAYS USA
FIELDING'S LEWIS AND CLARK TRAIL
FIELDING'S LITERARY AFRICA
FIELDING'S MOTORING AND CAMPING EUROPE
FIELDING'S SPANISH TRAILS IN THE SOUTHWEST
FIELDING'S WORLDWIDE CRUISES 3rd revised edition

Fielding's
LITERARY
AFRICA

by
Jane and Leah Taylor

Fielding Travel Books
% William Morrow & Company, Inc.
105 Madison Avenue, New York, N.Y. 10016

Copyright © 1988 by Jane and Leah Taylor

All rights reserved. No part of this book may be reproduced or utilized in any form or by any means, electronic or mechanical, including photocopying, recording or by any information storage and retrieval system, without permission in writing from the Publisher. Inquiries should be addressed to Permissions Department, William Morrow and Company, Inc., 105 Madison Ave., New York, N.Y. 10016.

Library of Congress
Library of Congress Cataloging-in-Publication Data

Taylor, Jane.
    Fielding's literary Africa : 7 great itineraries based on 7 great
books / Jane and Leah Taylor.
    p. cm.
    ISBN 0-688-05071-9
    1. Africa—Description and travel—1977–   2. Literary landmarks-
Africa. I. Taylor, Leah. II. Title.
DT12.25.T39   1987
960—dc19   87-30516
                                                            CIP

Printed in the United States of America
First Edition

1 2 3 4 5 6 7 8 9 10
BOOK DESIGN BY BERNARD SCHLEIFER

To the memory of Nirmal Singh Roopra, who deeply loved his family and country. "Kaka" gave us an appreciation of Kenya that only knowing him could provide.

Jane and Leah Taylor, the authors of *Fielding's African Safaris,* have lived, worked, and traveled in Africa for the past 15 years. They live in Washington, DC.

CONTENTS

INTRODUCTION

Fielding's Literary Africa is intended for *amateur* historians like ourselves, and in the African context the word *Africanist* is freely used to describe all those seriously interested in African history, culture, or languages. Professional Africanists may resent amateur intrusion, but the field is, at this writing, small enough to contain both academicians and buffs. The common denominator between us is a fascination with that which is Africa south of the Sahara and a love for the peoples of that region. To say, without having been to Africa, that one is an Africanist is one thing. The reality of Africa upon arrival on the continent can be unnerving, especially so for Afro-Americans. Some orientation is required if time after arrival is not to be lost in frustration, exasperation, and possibly disillusionment.

As historians we are obliged to take a historical perspective to contemporary situations. Most amateur Africanists can work only with world history from about 3000 B.C. Before that date, we know intellectually of cavemen, dinosaurs, ice ages, and molten lava, but to conceptualize these drives us into the realm of fantasy. It isn't necessary to go back in history that far to find a useful measuring tool as an aid in understanding ourselves and the problems confronted in Africa. When looking at Africa's assimilation of a Western lifestyle in the past 100 years it is interesting to parallel it with that of the ancient Romans in the British Isles. The Romans invaded Britain in 54 B.C., stayed 400 years, and left behind sophisticated plumbing and the art of gracious dining. Immediately upon their departure for Rome the "native Britons" inaugurated the Dark Ages, and for the next 1000 years threw the contents of their chamberpots out their windows; believed bathing to be injurious to their health, conveyed water to their hovels and castles from polluted rivers and wells in buckets instead of pipes, and found Henry VIII's table manners admirable.

The Victorians (1837) were just emerging from a century of wanton privilege and feudal serfdom when they set about adding Africa to their Indian conquest. The self-righteousness of Albert and Victoria; her widowhood; the personalities of her prime ministers and the "jumped-up" tradesmen operating the East India, the East Africa, and the Royal Niger companies brought a pomposity to their interaction with indigenous peoples yet to be excelled in the conduct of international relations.

This pomposity and the preoccupation with white skins crossed the Atlantic and Pacific, and this Victorian heritage is one of the monkeys riding on many peoples' shoulder now, at the end of the 1980s, as we approach Africa and the wider vision of one world.

The other monkey is the lack of technological progress. Withstand becoming judgmental when you travel to Africa. The East and Central Africans have been known to us for less than 100 years. It took them some time to decide if

ix

they wanted us. (Some may say we forced ourselves on them. True. But then, life in general is forced on all of us with less opportunity to reject or accept than the Africans have had to accept westernization. The Masai said no. Rejection of the White invader was and is a possible and attainable alternative.) Having made the decision to come along, they are daily confronted with the process of accepting or rejecting our introductions on a one-by-one basis. Each individual African makes the choice. That such time for decision making imparts itself onto the conduct of everyday life and manifests itself in improbable bureaucracies and hopelessly slow waiters is to be expected. But by comparison to the ancient Britons, the Africans have assimilated the Western lifestyle at greased-lightning speed.

Because of technological advances and because this is the close of the 20th century, we tend to think our civilization is the most advanced. Technology is only one facet of civilization. We, in the West, have unmanageable social problems that would make participants of ancient cultures shudder.

However, to justify our assertion, statistics are employed to prove that a greater percentage of us have a higher standard of living than have had citizens of any other civilization. This is not statistically accurate. Measuring equality of access into the wealth of a society does not necessarily mean an access to materialism. (That is a parochial definition.) Nor does access necessarily mean equality and nondiscrimination.

The historian can recognize that there is much to be said for knowing one's place in a society as opposed to living under pressure to excel, and the stress of "exercising one's potential."

The human motivators of greed and envy have been minimized by some societies more effectively than they have by most Christian societies despite the fact that these are named among the seven deadly sins. Minimizing greed and envy diminishes competitiveness: the very foundation of most Christian democracies. (How contradictory we are!) Imperialism had such a stronghold on the imagination that most Victorians were unable to harbor any feeling but disgust or pity for noncompetitive social structures such as those they found in Africa.

Withstand these two monkeys who would continue to ride on our non-African shoulders.

No book, no pictures, can adequately convey Africa south of the Sahara. The written word can only provide conceptions and misconceptions. Film can only reflect. Neither can come into the soul and into the heart and bring even a splinter of understanding of that which is Black Africa. But Africa can capture the mind and ultimately the heart.

Africa is where that elusive *it* in life is at.

Nothing mystic.

Nothing supernatural.

Just the cradle of man.

. . . so does a voyage mark the change and renewal of the human being to the extent of making him a "resuscitated" person. The distance between someone who has traveled and someone who has never left his native soil is immeasurable. The latter always belong to the strictures in force in his cultural setting, and the elements constituting his destiny may always be revealed in spite of their multiple possibilities for ordering. The former destroys "the order of things" which existed at his birth and he also modifies the network of units which make up his destiny. Society and the diviner possesses a firm hold over the one who remains at home—they know him or can at any moment know him—but this hold becomes ineffectual over the one who leaves, for he has become something other.

—From *The Religion, Spirituality, and Thought of Traditional Africa* by Dominique Zahan, The University of Chicago Press, Chicago and London, 1979.

OVERVIEW OF THE SEVEN GREAT ITINERARIES

Prelude: *The Lost Cities of Africa* by Basil Davidson

To say that before the coming of the Whites to Africa, Africa had no history, is to demonstrate one's ignorance. As the great Africanist Mary Kingsley wrote, Africa and Europe are like two mountains whose peaks are of equal height yet which are two different entities.

There is more justification to be on the defensive concerning European history than African history—the mayhem and massacres of Europe turn African tribal wars into spats by comparison; the neglect of the elderly, child abuse, and sexual deviancy in Western societies force the definition of traditional African societies to be Utopia. The comparisons could go on and on.

And yet, the absence of cathedrals built at the expense of the poor, the substitution of grass mats for self-aggrandizing debating chambers, the dearth of factories and mines where men and women become drones and moles, have, up to now, led the international community who take it upon themselves to judge Africa, say she has no history.

In developing itineraries for the amateur Africanist we start at the beginning with the lost cities of Africa which provide tangible proof of her valid cultures and history.

Encounter: *Livingstone* by Tim Jeal

There were Europeans in Africa before Livingstone, but no other single figure had as much influence on that continent during the latter half of the 19th century as Livingstone. It was he who took up the cry for commerce and conversion that had been muted by those who worked toward the abolition of African slavery. And we have chosen *Livingstone* in particular because of Tim Jeal's brilliant drawing of a man who exemplifies the character virtues and failings typical of the men and women who were to follow him in the latter half of the last century. Business and conversion combined to take Africa to the juncture where we find her today. Well-meaning, crass, muddled Europeans judged Africa, found her wanting, and started to recreate their own image in a Black world.

The Maze: White Nile by Alan Moorehead

Before commerce and conversion could be undertaken the age-old maze of the rivers Nile and Niger had to be traced and in the process a distant-from-Africa public opinion began to form based on tales of adventure, hardships for the teller of the tales, and distortions of African societies, provoking sensational, righteous tongue-wagging in the brownstones of New York, where the *Tribune* graced the drawing rooms, and in kerosene-lit back kitchens of Midland company-owned terrace houses.

Having discovered the source of the Nile and traced the Niger, the information had to be put to practical use, and thus opened the next phase of recent African history: development, imperialism, call it what you will; we call it *Step #1* in turning simple commerce into economies that could sustain consumer-oriented African communities.

Pandora's Box: Lunatic Express by Charles Miller

Nothing is ever simple in Africa, and the building of a railroad to open up East Africa was a Pandora's box, full of surprises and lessons about Africa still not fully grasped today by those who would change the basis of African life.

Lunatic Express is more than an itinerary for railroad buffs—it is a story that contains much of value to those who would work in Africa now, not the least of which is that despite computer banks and high technologies, most entrepreneurs start projects in total ignorance of African conditions, just as the railroad engineers and surveyors started on the "lunatic express."

Anglophilia: Flame Trees of Thika by Elspeth Huxley

Englishmen and South Africans swarmed to take up the invitation to push Africans aside and farm the rich, virgin lands of Kenya Colony. They brought what they considered to be the White man's culture and in doing so ingrained the materialism that was their lifestyle on their hosts and hostesses. Much of Africa has yet to rise above such indoctrination: Mercedes automobiles have replaced communual approbation as status symbols, and the desire for the good life motivates Africans to leave their humble homes at dawn to chase the brass ring Europeans set before them.

Empathic Interlude: Out of Africa by Karen Blixen

Interspersed with the great forces demonstrated by the other itineraries, there occasionally arises on the African scene a spiritual marriage between the soul of the African and the soul of an outsider. For the participants the experience is enduring. This is what happened to Karen Blixen, and it has happened to many less well-known outsiders. Seldom do the contractuals in such empathic marriages have a voice in the unfurling of Africa's future. They—the African and the outsider—carry on their separate lives, keeping the experience something very personal; standing, on the sidelines as the future comes roaring, propelled by unsympathetic forces both African and foreign, to a climax.

The Juncture: The Africans by David Lamb

It has been 100 years since White men and women first set about putting East and Central Africa to rights, and the continent is at a juncture. Having endangered a continental identity during that century, the crossroads have arrived in which a decision must be made to continue or to revert.

The crisis point has been reached because African economies have crumbled in their imitation of White economic patterns—capitalist, socialist, or communist. Donor nations go to the conference table, not always with vested interests, but neither do they consider the alternative of allowing Africa to become Africa again, and go her own way. In the hearts and minds of Black African leaders who sit at the conference tables opposite their patrons, the desire to adopt White economic systems is stronger today than ever. Returning to their own mountain is the furtherest option from their consideration.

In following the itinerary for *The Africans* the irony of David Lamb's humor should not cloud his remarks concerning African character and personality, which is unlike some other societies. Africans cannot with predictability be motivated.

David Lamb, in his closing chapter, urges that Africans go forward following the pattern of industrialized nations. He believed, at the time he was writing, that were South Africa to dismantle apartheid that nation could lead and assist the continent. We, writing now in 1987, feel South Africa has left it too late, and we can see nothing ahead for all of *southern* Africa than chaos in the foreseeable future.

Nor do we believe that Africa north of Zambia/Zimbabwe is necessarily tied to South Africa, and the point of crisis north of southern Africa remains, regardless of what happens in southern Africa. There is a need for decision making, we feel, to be predicated on what is right for Africa—not for anyone else—least of all world opinion, if they choose not to follow the pattern of industrialized nations or pay off loans that funded the implementation of a lot of bad advice. This past 100 years is only a fractional part of African history; a resumption of traditional life could not be more devastating to the happiness of the people than continuing on the path set by their invaders.

Fielding's
LITERARY
AFRICA

PRELUDE:
THE LOST CITIES
OF AFRICA

BY
BASIL DAVIDSON

**LITTLE, BROWN &
COMPANY, BOSTON
1959**

*Above, a detail from the pylon at Meroe, Sudan, inscribed with the lion-god,
whose body is that of a snake.*

Basil Davidson knew nothing of Africa before he visited that continent, but on his return to England he became engrossed in African studies.

In preparing for an occupation or profession the candidate usually begins by studying the subject in an academic or trade environment. After a number of years of mastering the basics and perhaps serving an internship or apprenticeship, the trained mind enters the profession at the bottom of the ladder. Not so Basil Davidson.

On that first trip Davidson caught Africanitis. There is a certain advantage to this back-door entry. If you've visited a place, reading its name can spark associative recall: "Oh yes, that's the place where we got a flat tire." A visual image is immediately conjured up, a personal contact is made, and what would be nothing more than another sterile new word takes on meaning.

The disadvantage of this firsthand educational process is that you may be totally unaware of the significance of a nearby pile of ancient rocks while you are preoccupied with changing the flat tire. Nor, under this back-door system, do you necessarily appreciate the confused, disjointed information about the local people's home as they help change the tire. However, once into academia, on reflection and with creative recall, such idle patter can be worked up into an A paper to impress undergraduate professors with your thorough grasp of African history, anthropology, etc.

Before the publication of Davidson's many titles, people who should have known better believed Africa had no history. It was not until Davidson rephrased the information he found in scholarly studies, making it palatable to a wider audience, that the richness of African history began to be appreciated. In popularizing African history his back-door entry occasionally shows: The discipline of an early academic environment and the humbleness the Ph.D. process ensures is sometimes noticeably absent. It is wise to exercise caution when quoting Davidson against professional Africanists on certain points.

It is our sincere hope that among the younger people who purchase *Fielding's Literary Africa* there will be, whether coming in through the front door or the back, those who will become Africanists, and in their careers will build on work that interprets African history for the general public.

Lost Cities Routing from North America

To do the entire itinerary in one trip:
Royal Air Maroc-Montreal/New York-Casablanca-Cairo
Kenya Airways-Cairo-Khartoum
Kenya Airways-Khartoum-Nairobi
Kenya Railways-Nairobi-Mombasa

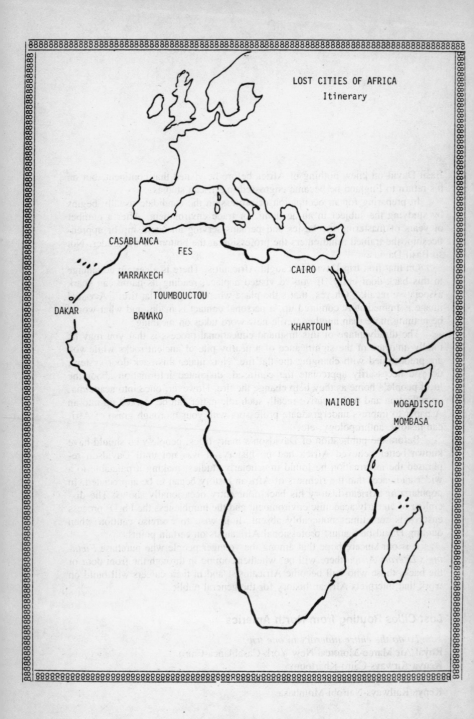

LOST CITIES OF AFRICA
Itinerary

CASABLANCA
FES
MARRAKECH
CAIRO
TOUMBOUCTOU
DAKAR
BAMAKO
KHARTOUM

NAIROBI
MOGADISCIO
MOMBASA

Kenya Airways-Mombasa-Mogadiscio
Kenya Airways-Mogadiscio-Nairobi-Cairo
Royal Air Maroc-Cairo-Casablanca
Avis-Rent-a-Car with driver-Casablanca-Marrakech-Fes-Casablanca
Air Afrique-Casablanca-Dakar
Air Afrique-Dakar-Bamako
Train-Bamako-Koulikoro
Steamer-Koulikoro-Toumbouctou (mid-July to mid-Dec. only)
Air Mali*-Toumbouctou-Bamako
Air Afrique-Bamako-Dakar-New York/Montreal

To do the eastern Africa itinerary only:
Royal Air Maroc-Montreal/New York-Cairo
Kenya Airways-Cairo-Khartoum
Kenya Airways-Khartoum-Nairobi
Kenya Railways-Nairobi-Mombasa
Kenya Airways-Mombasa-Mogadiscio
Kenya Airways-Mogadiscio-Nairobi-Cairo
Royal Air Maroc-Cairo-New York/Montreal

To do the Moroccan cities and Toumbouctou only:
Royal Air Maroc-Montreal/New York-Casablanca
Avis-Rent-a-Car with driver-Casablanca-Marrakech-Fes-Casablanca
Air Afrique-Casablanca-Dakar-Bamako
Train-Bamako-Koulikoro
Steamer-Koulikoro-Toumbouctou (mid-July to mid-Dec. only)
Air Mali-Toumbouctou-Bamako
Air Afrique-Bamako-Dakar-New York/Montreal

To do the Toumbouctou itinerary only:
Air Afrique-Montreal/New York-Dakar-Bamako
Train-Bamako-Koulikoro
Steamer-Koulikoro-Toumbouctou (mid-July to mid-Dec. only)
Air Mali-Toumbouctou-Bamako
Air Afrique-Bamako-Dakar-New York/Montreal

As these routings and carriers are unfamiliar to most travel agents, you may want to make your reservations for airline tickets through Merikani Hotel Reservations Service, Inc. (P.O. Box 53394, Temple Heights Station, Washington, DC 20009, tel. (USA) 301–530–1911).

Lost Cities Routing from the United Kingdom

To do the entire itinerary:
Kenya Airways-London-Cairo
Kenya Airways-Cairo-Khartoum
Kenya Airways-Khartoum-Nairobi
Kenya Railways-Nairobi-Mombasa

*For information on this carrier please see "Transportation."

Kenya Airways-Mombasa-Mogadiscio
Kenya Airways-Mogadiscio-Nairobi-Cairo
Royal Air Maroc-Cairo-Casablanca
Avis-Rent-a-Car with driver-Casablanca-Marrakech-Fes-Casablanca
Royal Air Maroc or Air Afrique-Casablanca-Dakar
Air Afrique-Dakar-Bamako
Train-Bamako-Koulikoro
Steamer-Koulikoro-Toumbouctou (mid-July to mid-Dec. only)
Air Mali*-Toumbouctou-Bamako
Air Afrique-Bamako-Dakar
Royal Air Maroc or Air Afrique-Dakar-Casablanca
Royal Air Maroc-Casablanca-London

To do the eastern African itinerary only: Same as above, but instead of changing in Cairo for a flight to Casablanca, stay on the Kenya Airways flight, which continues to London.

To do the western African itinerary only:
Royal Air Maroc-London-Casablanca
Avis-Rent-a-Car with driver-Casablanca-Marrakech-Fes-Casablanca
Royal Air Maroc or Air Afrique-Casablanca-Dakar
Air Afrique-Dakar-Bamako
Train-Bamako-Koulikoro
Steamer-Koulikoro-Toumbouctou (mid-July to mid-Dec. only)
Air Mali-Toumbouctou-Bamako
Air Afrique-Bamako-Dakar
Royal Air Maroc-Dakar-London

To do Toumbouctou only:
Royal Air Maroc-London-Dakar
Air Afrique-Dakar-Bamako
Train-Bamako-Koulikoro
Steamer-Koulikoro-Toumbouctou (mid-July to mid-Dec. only)
Air Mali-Toumbouctou-Bamako
Air Afrique-Bamako-Dakar
Royal Air Maroc-Dakar-London

Lost Cities Routing from Saudi Arabia

To do the entire itinerary:
Saudi Airlines-Jeddah-Mogadiscio
Kenya Airways-Mogadiscio-Mombasa
Kenya Railways-Mombasa-Nairobi
Kenya Airways-Nairobi-Khartoum
Kenya Airways-Khartoum-Cairo
Royal Air Maroc-Cairo-Casablanca
Avis-Rent-a-Car with driver-Casablanca-Marrakech-Fes-Casablanca
Royal Air Maroc or Air Afrique-Casablanca-Dakar

*For information on this carrier, see "Transportation."

Air Afrique-Dakar-Bamako
Train-Bamako-Koulikoro
Steamer-Koulikoro-Toumbouctou (mid-July to mid-Dec. only)
Air Mali*-Toumbouctou-Bamako
Air Afrique-Bamako-Dakar
Royal Air Maroc-Dakar-Jeddah via Casablanca

To do the eastern African itinerary only: Same as above, but at Cairo
return to Jeddah using Saudi Airlines.

To do the western African itinerary only:
Royal Air Maroc-Jeddah-Casablanca
Avis-Rent-a-Car with driver-Casablanca-Marrakech-Fes-Casablanca
Royal Air Maroc or Air Afrique-Casablanca-Dakar
Air Afrique-Dakar-Bamako
Train-Bamako-Koulikoro
Steamer-Koulikoro-Toumbouctou (mid-July to mid-Dec. only)
Air Mali-Toumbouctou-Bamako
Air Afrique-Bamako-Dakar
Royal Air Maroc-Dakar-Jeddah via Casablanca

To do the Toumbouctou itinerary only:
Royal Air Maroc-Jeddah-Dakar via Casablanca
Air Afrique-Dakar-Bamako
Train-Bamako-Koulikoro
Steamer-Koulikoro-Toumbouctou (mid-July to mid-Dec. only)
Air Mali-Toumbouctou-Bamako
Air Afrique-Bamako-Dakar
Royal Air Maroc-Dakar-Jeddah via Casablanca

Lost Cities Routing from Australia or New Zealand

To do the entire itinerary:
Singapore Airlines-Auckland/Sidney-Bombay
Kenya Airways-Bombay-Nairobi
Kenya Railways-Nairobi-Mombasa
Kenya Airways-Mombasa-Mogadiscio
Kenya Airways-Mogadiscio-Nairobi
Kenya Airways-Nairobi-Khartoum
Kenya Airways-Khartoum-Cairo
Royal Air Maroc-Cairo-Casablanca
Avis-Rent-a-Car with driver-Casablanca-Marrakech-Fes-Casablanca
Royal Air Maroc or Air Afrique-Casablanca-Dakar
Air Afrique-Dakar-Bamako
Train-Bamako-Koulikoro
Steamer-Koulikoro-Toumbouctou (mid-July to mid-Dec. only)
Air Mali*-Toumbouctou-Bamako
Air Afrique-Bamako-Dakar

*For information on this carrier, see ''Transportation.''

Air Afrique or Royal Air Maroc-Dakar-Casablanca
Royal Air Maroc-Casablanca-Cairo
Singapore Airlines-Cairo-Auckland/Sidney

To do the eastern African itinerary: Same as above, but at Cairo take the Singapore Airlines flight home.

To do the western African itinerary:
Singapore Airlines-Auckland/Sidney-Cairo
Royal Air Maroc-Cairo-Casablanca
Avis-Rent-a-Car with driver-Casablanca-Marrakech-Fes-Casablanca
Royal Air Maroc or Air Afrique-Casablanca-Dakar
Air Afrique-Dakar-Bamako
Train-Bamako-Koulikoro
Steamer-Koulikoro-Toumbouctou (mid-July to mid-Dec. only)
Air Mali-Toumbouctou-Bamako
Air Afrique-Bamako-Dakar
Air Afrique or Royal Air Maroc-Dakar-Casablanca
Royal Air Maroc-Casablanca-Cairo
Singapore Airlines-Cairo-Auckland/Sidney

To do the Toumbouctou itinerary only:
Singapore Airlines-Auckland/Sidney-Cairo
Royal Air Maroc-Cairo-Dakar
Air Afrique-Dakar-Bamako
Train-Bamako-Koulikoro
Steamer-Koulikoro-Toumbouctou (mid-July to mid-Dec. only)
Air Mali-Toumbouctou-Bamako
Air Afrique-Bamako-Dakar
Royal Air Maroc-Dakar-Cairo via Casablanca
Singapore Airlines-Cairo-Auckland/Sydney

The Lost Cities of Africa Itinerary

We have selected the following lost cities for the itinerary: Meroe in Sudan; the Swahili city states of Mombasa and Mogadiscio and the island of Zanzibar, as well as the smaller sites of Jumba la Mtwapa, Mnarani, and Gedi; and Toumbouctou in Mali. We would have liked to include the Zimbabwe Ruins, a trip to Benin and Nigeria, and, of course, Ethiopia. However, political conditions in those countries make encouraging travel to them irresponsible. The government of Zimbabwe publicizes the ruins and invites tourists, but there have been incidents that, in our opinion, make travel in Zimbabwe unacceptable. Both Benin and Nigeria have excessively high street crime figures, and after our experience in the communist Seychelle Islands we have vowed never to recommend/travel to a communist country for pleasure; this eliminates Ethiopia.

Reservations for the entire itinerary can be made, without charge, through

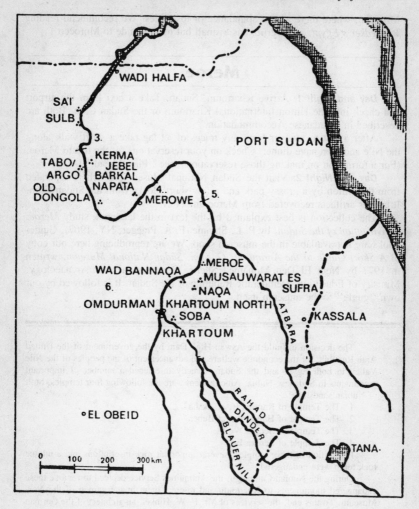

The River Nile in northern Sudan showing archaeological sites and the cataracts (numbered).

Merikani Hotel Reservations Service, Inc. (P.O. Box 53394, Temple Heights Station, Washington, DC 20009, tel. (USA) 301–530–1911). Merikani will also obtain the necessary visas for our readers for the cost of the visas—there is no service charge.

We have written the itinerary by country so that all of it can be done, or only parts undertaken. With the loss in February 1987 of Pan Am's flight from West to East Africa, the complete itinerary is not as easily accomplished as it would be if that flight were operating. However, there is always a plus to every minus, and the airline routing we have given allows for stops in Egypt and in

Morocco, where there are an abundance of lost cities. We recommend reading *Baededker's Egypt,* and Berlitz has a small but useful guide to Morocco.

Meroe

Day and Night 1: Arrive Khartoum, Sudan. Take a taxi from the airport and check into the Hilton International Khartoum or the Sudan Club. Both are described in "Sudanese Accommodation."

After a rest to recover from any traces of jet lag take a short walk along the Nile and then have dinner. Check on your reservations for the trip to Meroe. (For information on making those reservations, see "Plan Ahead.")

Day and Night 2: Visit the Sudan National Museum, which is separated from the Hilton by a grassy park and a few short blocks from the Sudan Club. It houses artifacts recovered from Meroe and Nuri.

The collection is best explained by the text in the landmark study *Meroe: A civilization of the Sudan,* by P. L. Shinnie (F. A. Praeger, NY, 1967). Guidebooks are not available in the museum shop. We are reproducing here our copy of *A Short Guide to the Antiquities Garden, Sudan National Museum,* written in 1977 by Nem El Den Mohamed Sherif, Commissioner for Archaeology, Ministry of Education, Democratic Republic of the Sudan. It is followed by our own "guide" to the museum itself.

The decision to build the Aswan High Dam by the government of the United Arab Republic for the economic welfare and advancement of the peoples of the Nile Valley in both Egypt and the Sudan, directly threatened a number of important monuments in Sudanese Nubia. Among them were the following four temples, built of Nubian sandstone:

1. The Temple of Ramses II, at Aksha
2. The Temple of Hatshepsut at Buhen
3. The Temple of Semna West
4. The Temple of Semna East

In addition to these temples, several important rock inscriptions and a unique rock tomb were endangered.

During the Nubian Campaign, the Antiquities Service decided to remove these endangered monuments to Khartoum and re-erect them in the garden of the New Museum. To this end, the services of Mr. F. W. Hinkel, an architect of the German Democratic Republic Academy of Sciences, were obtained. These monuments were originally located along the Nile and in order to give the visitor some idea of how there were originally placed, an artificial lake was dug as a symbol of the Nile. The monuments have been sited along the sides of the lake with the same orientation that they originally had. Mr. Hinkel not only supervised the dismantling, transportation, and re-erection of all the monuments, but he also designed the lay-out of the garden and the special moveable structures which protect the temples from the rains during the summer in Khartoum.

This short guide will describe the monuments of the garden in the following order:

1. The Lake and Frogs
2. Faras Columns
3. Aksha Temple

CULTURAL TIME CHART: NORTHERN SUDAN

Historical Period	Location along the Sudanese Nile	Time
Pre-historical		
Palaeolithic	Faras, Khor Abu Anga (Omdurman)	
Mesolithic	Khartoum	4400 B.C.
Neolitic	Faras, Omdurman Shanhein Ab	4000 B.C.
Nubian. The semi-nomadic peoples domesticated sheep/goats/cattle.	Gezira Dabarosa, Halfa Degheim, Jebel Sheikh Suliman, Melik El Nasir, Saras	3000 B.C.
Nubian established between the 1st and 3rd cataract	Ambikole, Argin, Debeira, Duweishat	2100 B.C.
Kerma Culture established between the 2nd and 4th cataract	Kerma, Saras, Ukma	1700 B.C.
Middle Egyptian Kingdom at the 2nd cataract	Argo, Buhen, Kerma, Mirgissa, Semna, Uronarti	1500 B.C.
New Egyptian Kingdom at the 4th cataract	Abusir, Aksha, Amara, Buhen, Debeira, Faras, Kawa, Mirgissa, Semna, Sesibi, Sulb, Uronarti	1300 B.C.
Napatan Period (capital at Napta)	Amentago, Jebel Barkal, Jebel Moya, Kadakol, Kawa, Kurru, Meroe, Nuri, Tabo	900 B.C.
Meroitic Period (Capital at Meroe)	Argin, Attiri, Basa, Buhen, Eddamer, Faras, Gemai, Kawa, Kurru, Matuga, Meinarti, Murshid, Musauwarat es Sufra, Nuri, Sedenga, Serra, Semna, Singa, Tabo, Wad Bannaqa	600 B.C.
- - - - - - - - - - - - - - - - - - -	- - - - - - - - - - - - - - - - - -	0
A Culture arose in the north which incorporated certain Meroitic i.e. their architecture, agriculture with Byzantine influences.	Argin, Faras, Firka, Kosma, Meinarti	300 A.D.

Christian Period
  Nobatia with the capital at Faras
  Makuria with the capital at Dongola
  Alodia with the capital at Soba
	Abdel Gadir, Ambikole, Argin, Attiti, Buhen, Debeira, Difinarti, Kulubnarti, Meinarti, Melik el Nasir, Old Dongola, Saras, Semna, Songi, Ukma	600 A.D.

Islamic Period
  Funj Kingdom with the capital at Sennar
  Fur Kingdom with the capital at Darfur
	Abugeili, Airi, Meinarti, Singa, Taya	1300 A.D.

Modern or contemporary period		1800 A.D.

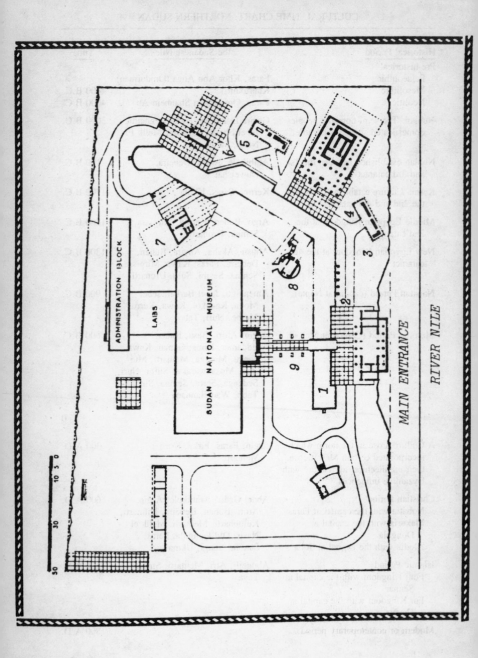

Grounds of the Sudan National Museum

4. Buhen Temple
5. Inscriptions Shed
6. Semna West Temple
7. Semna East Temple
8. The Tomb of Djehuty-hetep
9. The Avenue of Lions

1. The Lake and Frogs

The artificial lake in the garden of the Sudan National Museum is 200 metres long, 10 metres wide, and .80 metres deep. A colossal sandstone statue of a frog, resting on a solid base, is placed at each end of the lake. These statutes date to the Meroitic period (sixth century B.C. to fourth century A.D.) and have been brought from Basa, an ancient site east of Shendi in the Northern Province.

The frog was the symbol of the ancient Egyptian goddess "Heket", and these two were placed at an ancient rain water reservoir, where they were probably regarded as charms to ensure an abundant rainfall.

2. Faras Columns

On the border between Egypt and the Sudan lay Faras on the west bank of the Nile, some thirty-eight kilometres north of Wadi Halfa Town. This was the "Ibshek" of the pharaonic Egyptians and the "pachoras" of the Christian era, when it was the capital of the Christian Kingdom of Nobatia, which extended from the first Cataract to the Third.

At Faras were found archaeological remains of all periods from the A-Group (3,100 B.C. down to the nineteenth century.) They included cemeteries, forts, temples, and churches with magnificent paintings on their walls.

The five granite columns, beside the lake to our right as we come out of the main entrance to the museum grounds, are from one of the Faras churches. Noteworthy are the Maltese Crosses near the tops of the columns. The columns were removed from Faras to Khartoum by the Antiquities Service in 1964.

3. The Temple of Aksha

Twenty kilometres north of the town of Wadi Halfa, on the west bank of the Nile, lay Aksha. Here, Ramses II (1290–1224 B.C.) built a temple of sandstone dedicated to the living image of himself. When excavated, in 1961, the temple was found to be in very bad condition and it was decided to salvage only the best preserved and most important part of it. This was the west wall of the temple forecourt.

This wall was removed from Aksha in 1963 and re-erected here in 1968. The reliefs on the wall are of considerable interest. On the northern part (to our right) is a list of the northern countries conquered by Ramses II and the southern part list the southern countries he conquered. The ovals beneath each figure contain the names of the countries or localities, and the figures, which are prisoners with their hands behind, represent the captives from each locality.

4. Buhen Temple

The site of the well known ancient town of Buhen was on the west bank of the Nile, some 25 kilometres south of Aksha. It was one of the military colonies founded in Nubia by the pharaohs of the Twelfth Dynasty (1991 to 1778 B.C.). It was a rectangular, walled town planned as a trading station and to guard the southern end of the trade route to Egypt.

The earliest mention of Buhen is on a stela found there, which dates to the reign of Sesostris I. Next, the name occurs in a late Middle Kingdom papyrus, discovered in a tomb under the Ramesseum at Luxor, which names all the seventeen Nubian forts between Semna in the south and Shellal in the north.

The situation of Buhen, at the southern end of the long navigable stretch of

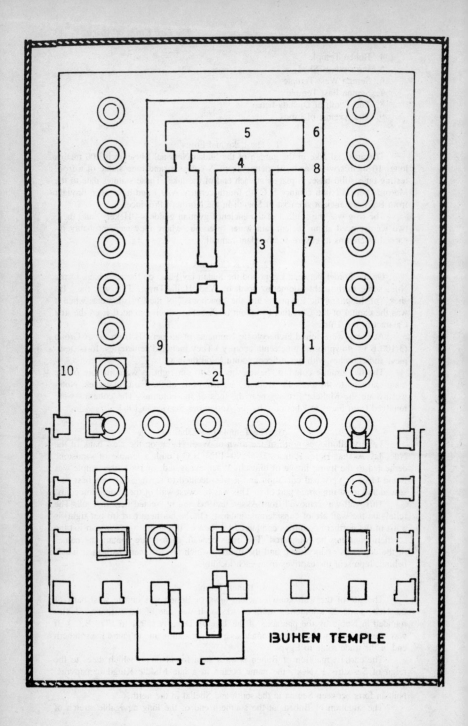

BUHEN TEMPLE

river between the First and Second Cataracts, gave it great importance not only as a trading centre, but also as an administrative centre for the area. Here, as its quays, boats from Egypt discharged their cargo and were reloaded with the luxury products of the south. There is no doubt that such a centre played an important role in the cultural exchanges between the two countries.

Following the collapse of the Middle Kingdom and the Hyksos invasion, the Egyptians lost their power in Nubia. Buhen was sacked and burnt by the Kushities. But, when the Hyksos were driven out of Egypt by the warrior Kings of the Eighteenth Dynasty, Buhen was reoccupied and its fortifications were rebuilt and rehabilitated. It was again a flourishing centre and contained two temples, public buildings, garrison quarters, workshops for the gold trade, etc. As an Egyptian colony, Buhen remained secure until the final collapse of the Egyptian power at the end of the Twentieth Dynasty (1085 B.C.). As a settlement, however, it had a continued occupation right down to the Christian era.

The formidable Middle Kingdom fortress at Buhen, the best preserved in Nubia before it was flooded by the waters of the High Dam, consisted of an elaborate series of fortifications built on a rectangular plan measuring 172 metres by 160. The defense system consisted of a brick wall, 4.85 metres thick and at least 10 metres high with towers at regular intervals. At the bottom of this main wall was a brick-paved rampart, protected by a series of round bastions with double rows of loopholes. The whole was surrounded by a dry ditch cut into bed rock, 6.50 metres deep. The ditch was 8.40 metres wide and the outer scarp was heightened by brickwork. There were two gates on the east side, facing the Nile, and a third, heavily fortified, gate on the west side, facing the desert.

At a later date Buhen was enlarged and the older structure probably became a citadel, surrounded by the buttressed main wall, a wide, brick-paved terrace and a sunken roadway. The new outer defensive wall consisted of a number of irregular salients with projecting towers, and was a mile around. This wall was surrounded by a dry ditch.

Of the two Eighteenth Dynasty temples, the one built inside the Middle Kingdom citadel walls by Queen Hatshepsut (1490 to 1468 B.C.) is a magnificent monument. It was dedicated to Horus, the falcon-headed god, "Lord of Buhen". The importance of this temple, the most noteworthy of her reign in Nubia, lies in its great historical and artistic interest. Here one finds reliefs of the finest Eighteenth Dynasty style and execution, and the colors on the walls are still well preserved. Later, the temple was usurped by Thutmosis III who distorted the original design and systematically and ruthlessly defaced the cartouches and the portraits of Queen Hatshepsut.

The temple is built of Nubian sandstone and consists of two principal parts: a forecourt, and a rectangular building with a row of columns on its north, south and east sides.

The entrance:

On the jambs of the entrance door we see the standing figure of King Thutmosis III, with his right arm extended as though in the act of presenting the temple to the god to whom it is dedicated.

The forecourt:

Through the entrance, which does not coincide with the axis of the temple, we pass into the forecourt, which was certainly the work of Thutmosis III. On the columns of the forecourt are found cartouches and inscriptions dating from the time of Thutmosis III and later. The square pillars contain fine reliefs, depicting the King receiving the symbol of life from the great gods and goddesses. Numerous records of officials, viceroys of Kush and prominent people are seen on the pillars of the forecourt below the principal scenes.

On the column to the left, immediately after entering the forecourt, are carved the cartouches of Ramses III, IV, and V. On the west face of the pillar just to the left of this column is a large triumphal stela of Thutmosis III. It records the military achievements of this King in Lybia and Syria. It was engraved under the direction of Nehi, Viceroy of Nubia at that time, and is dated to the twenty-third year of Thutmosis's reign.

The temple proper:

Beyond the forecourt lies the temple proper, with several columns on each of the northern and southern sides and six across the east front. This is the original temple built by Queen Hatshepsut, but her figures have been mutilated and altered in many places. This building consists of a Transverse Hall, the Sacred Barque Chamber, two subsidiary rooms, one on each side of the Sacred Barque Chamber, and, at the rear of the building, the Sanctuary.

The Transverse Hall, the first room inside the doorway of the temple building, was the coronation hall. On the north wall, to our right, (marked 1 on the plan), is a scene showing a King Kneeling before a god, who is seated on a throne and who is laying one hand on the King's shoulder. In front of them stands a priest wearing a leopard skin. On the wall to the south of the doorway. (2) We find one of the finest reliefs of the temple. The scene is one in which a bull and a pair of cows are being offered. Notice how the lowest cow is licking her calf while a boy rides between her horns.

In the west wall of the Transverse Hall are two doorways. The northern one leads to a sort of chamber, above which was probably another small room. The other door, in the centre of the west wall, opens directly into the Sacred Barque Chamber. The figures in this doorway are thought to represent the Nubian King Taharka (688 to 663 B.C.).

On the north wall of the Scared Barque Chamber (3), only the pedestal on which the barque stood, with the cartouches of Thutmosis III inscribed on it, remains to be seen. The figure of Thutmosis III is in front of the barque and there are sacrificed cattle before him. On the west wall (4) the King offers two vases of wine and also food to a god seated on a throne.

The southern subsidiary chamber is entered from the Sacred Barque Chamber and leads to the Sanctuary.

The walls of the Sanctuary bear a fine series of ceremonial scenes (5). Here, the alterations which Thutmosis III carried out to replace the figures of Hatshepsut are clearly noticeable. In every alternative figure the portrait of Hatshepsut has been scraped out and an inferior painting substituted. On the north wall of the Sanctuary (6) we see the god ''Horus of Behen'' facing Thutmosis III.

The exterior walls are also decorated. The northern exterior wall (7) has a series of representations of the King and Queen alternately making different offerings to gods and goddesses. But the blocks which originally bore the figures of Queen Hatshepsut have been cut out of the wall and new blocks with fresh figures inserted in their place. One of these inserted blocks is still in place (8), just opposite the second column from the west.

The southern exterior wall also bears scenes of rulers making various offerings to deities. For example, in the most eastern scene (9) the King is offering birds and cattle to a god.

King Taharka:

A number of sculptured relief blocks will be seen built into the southern mud brick wall of the temple enclosure. These pieces date to the reign of King Taharka, who made some minor additions to Buhen Temple.

5. The Inscriptions Shed

The Inscriptions Shed lies a few yards to the south of Buhen Temple and houses an exhibition of some important inscriptions which were rescued from Nuba.

The first of these (9) is at the north end of the pavillion. It is a stela which was originally engraved on the north wall of a grotto in an isolated rock at Faras. It depicts Setau, Viceroy of Nubia under Ramses II, standing with both hands raised in adoration. Behind him stands his wife, Nefer-mut, holding a papyrus stem and a sistrum in her right hand, her left hand raised in adoration. In front of Setau we find the name of Ramses II in a cartouche and in fact the couple are worshipping the King.

To the left of the inscription of Setau is another (2), which is from the famous Rock of Abusir. This rock was a large cliff on the west bank of the Nile at the foot of the Second Cataract where passers-by have cut their names from the most ancient times down to the present century. This particular inscription is dated to "year 16 under the Majesty of the Good God, Menkheperre (Thutmosis III), given life", and mentions the name of a scribe called Amen-hetep.

The next inscription to the left (3) is a very important historical document. This was a scene originally engraved on a sandstone slab on the top of a small hill, known as Jebel Sheikh Suliman, about seven miles south of Wadi Halfa on the west bank of the Nile. It is the earliest record of Egyptian conquest in Nubia and is also one of the earliest hieroglyphic inscriptions in the Nile Valley. It dates to the reign of King Jer (about 3000 B.C.), the third King of the First Dynasty. The scene records a battle in the Nile waged by King Jer against the Nubians.

At the right of the scene there is a First Dynasty style boat, with its vertical stern and high prow. Below the boat float many corpses, while from the prow hangs a figure. To the left of this are two wheel-like designs, which are the hieroglyphic signs portraying a village with cross-roads, which signify a town. To the left of the town signs we see the ripple sign for water, after which is a man with his arms tied behind his back and holding a bow (Egyptian Zeti), personifying "Ta-Zeti," land of the Bow, meaning Nubia. Behind this figure is the name of King Jer on what is probably a palace facade.

The final piece (4) in the pavillion is an altar of the famous King Taharka (688 to 663 B.C.), which was found in his temple at Semna West, some 60 kilometres south of Wadi Halfa. A nicely cut hieroglyphic inscription appears on the front of the altar. It reads, "King of Upper and Lower Egypt, Takarka, may he live forever, has made his monument to his father, the Good God Kha-Kau-Re (Sesostris III). This altar is about 4 feet high, 2 feet 7½ inches square at the top, and its sides are slightly concave.

6. Semna West

To the right (south) of the Inscriptions' Shed, is the Temple of Semna West.

In the twentieth century B.C., during the Twelfth Dynasty, the expansion of the Egyptians southwards reached above the Second Cataract when Nubia was subjugated as far as Semna, some sixty kilometres south of Wadi Halfa. This strategic point, the narrowest point on the Nile, was made the southern frontier of the Egyptian Middle Kingdom. It was here that the remarkable stela of Sesostris III was set up to mark the boundary, in the eighth year of his reign. It forbade any Nubian to pass Semna except if on diplomatic business or on his way to trade at *Iken* (now known to be Mirgissa, 40 kilometres north of Semna on the west bank of the Nile).

To control the trade route and protect the frontier, two fortresses were built on the west bank and one on the east bank. The northernmost fort on the west bank, which was the largest and strongest of the three, was named "Sekhem-Khakaure." It was a remarkable structure, surrounded by a dry ditch, and shows the high level of proficiency the Egyptian military architects had attained in the art of constructing

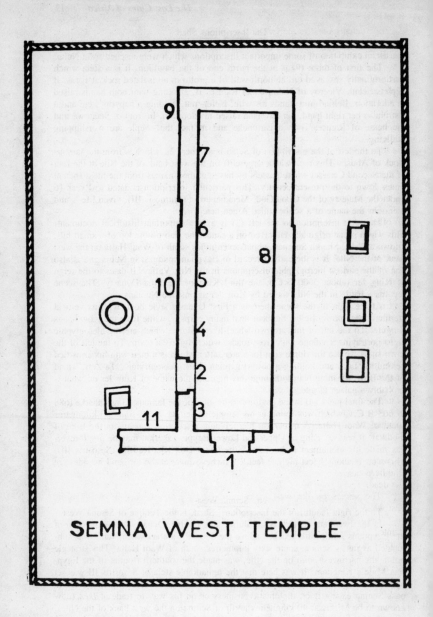

SEMNA WEST TEMPLE

effective defences and in the selection of a site. This fortress and the one opposite it on the east bank were both reoccupied in the New Kingdom, particularly under the Eighteenth Dynasty.

In the sixteenth century B.C., Thutmosis I built in each fort, a small temple, partly of brick and partly of stone. A couple of generations later, both temples were replaced by fine sandstone temples.

The Semna West Temple was erected by Thutmosis III. It was dedicated to the Nubian god Dedwen and to the deified Sesostris III. This temple ranks among the best preserved free-standing temples of pre-ptolemaic date in the whole Nile Valley. Virtually every inch of this temple, save the outer face of the north wall and the tops of the roofing blocks, is covered with scenes in relief, hieroglyphic inscriptions and painted work. The texts and scenes are undoubtedly the work of first-class craftsmen. The temple is of a single chamber, with the remains of covered colonnades on the east and west sides. On the east side there are three square pillars and on the west, one polygonal.

On the exterior of the south wall (1), above the main door, we see Thutmosis III offering milk to Khnum, the ram-headed god on the right, and to Dedwen on the left. The inscriptions on the right jamb of the door state that Thutmosis III made this monument for the King of Upper and Lower Egypt, Sesostries III while the left jamb tells us that the monument was made for Dedwen, the chief god of Nubia. On the wall to the left of the doorway is an interesting text of a certain Queen Katimala. Here we notice that a sufficient erasure of the original was made to provide a surface for the scene and text of this queen. Katimala is an unknown sovereign, and this text is the only evidence we have of her existence. She is thought to have been one of the Meroitic Queens. Like Hatshepsut, she styles herself King of Upper and Lower Egypt. This record consists essentially of a picture of the queen in conversation with the goddess Isis, and a long inscription in thirteen columns.

Entering the temple chamber by the door in the south wall, we see, over the door opening to the west on the left (2), a list of offerings which were made in the temple. Just on the left of that door (3) Thutmosis III can be seen dedicating these offerings. On the other side of the door (4), Sesostris III, in the form of Osiris, is seated in the sacred barque. After the barque, Dedwen is seen, embracing the King (5). Next to this is Thutmosis III making offerings (6). This scene is followed by another sacred barque (7) in which a coffer rests. On the last part of this wall Dedwen is depicted giving life to Thutmosis III.

The scene on the north or end wall is badly preserved, but originally Thutmosis III was making offerings to Amon-Re, "Lord of the Thrones of the Two Lands." The headless, seated statue in front of the end wall is that of Osiri, King or god of the dead.

The scenes on the west wall are more or less mirrored in the opposite east wall.

Before leaving the room, note the ceiling, where the roofing slabs have been painted to represent the night sky, with a dark blue ground and yellow five-pointed stars.

The scenes on the exterior of the west wall of the temple are interesting. At the north end of the wall (9) Thutmosis III, "the good god, the Lord who achieves, son of Re, beloved of Him, of His body" offers a pectoral to Dedwen, who says, "O my son, of my body, King of Upper and Lower Egypt, Lord of the Two Lands, I give you all life, welfare, Prosperity and all joy". Beside this scene is (10) Dedwen, seated on a throne with one hand stretched out over the crown and the other over the shoulder of the King, who is kneeling before him. In front of the King stands the priest of Dedwen who is praying the god to reward the King for building this temple for Him. On the inside of the south wall (11) we see Dedwen embracing Thutmosis III.

7. Semna East

The second Eighteenth Dynasty temple at Semna was on the east bank of the river in another fortress, and can now be seen on the opposite side of the artificial lake.

The Temple of Semna East, or Kumma, as it stands, is the work of Queen Hatshepsut, Thutmosis II and Amenophis II and their architects and artists during the period between 1490 and 1410 B.C. The temple was dedicated to the ram-headed god Khnum, the chief diety of the First Cataract and whose cult was widespread throughout Nubia. The temple is built of Nubian sandstone which was brought, according to the temple inscriptions, from the region called "Shaat," which is known to be the quarries of Sai Island, some 112 kilometres south of Semna.

The three sides of the Semna East temple were originally embedded in mud brick walls and so were never carefully finished or decorated. These walls have been reconstructed with mud bricks of the original size, up to the height that remained at the time the temple was removed to Khartoum.

The approach to the temple building is through a colonnaded court, the remains of which are two monolithic columns and two square pillars, which were half-embedded in the surrounding mud brick wall. At the extreme left of the outside of the west wall (1) "the Good God, Lord of the Two Lands, Menkheperre, son of Re, of His body, Thutmosis III" stands, receiving life from Dedwen, Lord of Nubia. Behind Dedwen stands the ram-headed Khnum. To the right of this scene (2), Thutmosis III makes offerings to Khnum. Between the two doors is a scene in which the ibis-headed god, Thoth, marks on a palm branch held by Khnum, the number of the year of life of a sovereign.

Entering the temple by the door at the extreme right, we find, on the inside of the west wall (4), Thutmosis III sitting between Khnum and deified Sesostris III, who is granting him life. To the right of this scene and immediately after the door (3) a figure is seen offering wine to Khnum. The figure was originally Queen Hatshepsut, but her names have been erased. Continuing to the right along the south wall, the next scene is of Thutmosis III performing a religious dance before the goddess Hathor and presenting a bird to her (5).

The scene at the left end of the opposite, north wall of this chamber (6) depicts the King offering something in two vases to Khnum and Sesostris III. Next to this, we see (7) the King making food offerings to Sesostris III. The third scene (8), on this wall is of the King offering food to Khnum, who is seated on a throne, and burning incense before him.

The doorway in the northeast corner of the first chamber (9) leads to a small, square courtyard (10), the walls of which are decorated with scenes of the Pharaoh with various gods and goddesses.

The east door of this court gives way to a small chamber, where there are three scenes on the south wall. The first (11), on the left, show the deified Sesostris III embracing a sovereign. The middle scene (12) is of Amenophis II making offerings to Khnum, who says, "I give all life, dominion and health to my beloved son". The right scene (13) is again Amenophis II, who holds out a jar to Khnum, who says to him, "I give all health, all joy to the King of Upper and Lower Egypt Lord of the Two Lands". On the west wall of this chamber (14) Amenophis II makes food offerings to Khnum, who is seated on a throne.

The two small doors in the north side of this chamber lead to two small cells (15, 16). These are the penetralia of the temple. On their walls are religious scenes of different kinds. A certain amount of the original paint is preserved on the reliefs of these rooms.

8. The Tomb of Djehuty-hetep

The tomb of Djehuty-hetep is situated on the same side of the artificial lake as Semna East, at the bend opposite the Faras Columns.

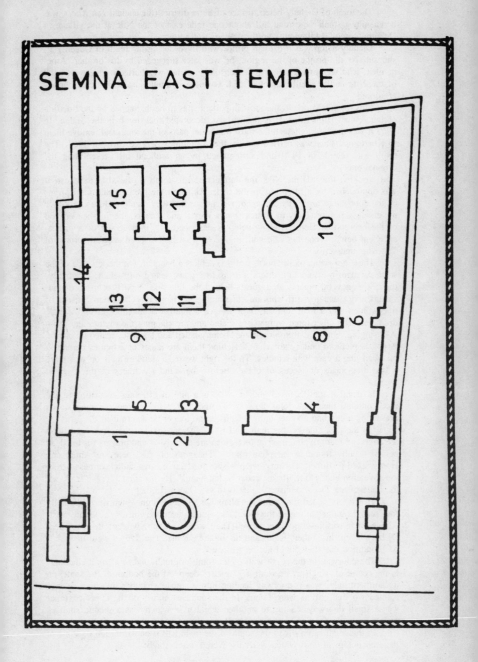

SEMNA EAST TEMPLE

The tomb of Djehuty-hetep, prince of Serra district (the ancient *Teh-Khet*), was hewn into a small sandstone hill about one mile east of the Nile at the village of Debeira, some 20 kilometres north of Wadi Halfa town.

Djehuty-hetep was a Nubian prince who lived during the reign of Queen Hatshepsut. As the prince of the region, he was later succeeded by his brother, Amenemhet, who was first a scribe at Buhen. Amenemhet was buried on the west bank of the Nile at the small hamlet of Sidi Oweis el Qurani, just opposite his brother's tomb.

This tomb was one of the most important sites to be threatened by the flooding of the Aswan High Dam. It is the earliest, decorated rock tomb in the Sudan. In 1962 it was decided to detach the most important parts of the tomb and remove them to Khartoum. This was carried out by the Antiquities Service early in 1963. The tomb was rebuilt in 1970 and surmounted by an artificial hill, resembling the original one.

Looking towards the Nile, the entrance to this tomb (1) faced to the west. It was approached by a ramp cut in the rock. Although the hieroglyphic inscriptions on the door jambs are badly damaged, we can see that they mention Horus, probably the goddess Hathor, Lady of Ibshek (Faras West), and Anubis, the dog-headed god of the necropolis. Here, Djehuty-hetep is described as "Prince, son of a prince, excellent heir", "one not idle with regard to what he has been ordered, prince of Teh-Khet and scribe".

The other scene on the north wall (5) depicts a banquet. On the left side of the scene, a man in a loincloth offers a drink to a guest seated on a chair. Originally, there were several other seated guests behind the first one. Next is a group of musicians and a dancing girl who are entertaining the banquet. The group consists of five women and a man. On the right we see a flautist, a dancing girl and a male drummer. The other three women are seated and are clapping the rhythm and probably singing. On the extreme right are Djehuty-hetep and his wife, seated on chairs. A dog is pictured under their chairs. Behind them are traces of a figure, perhaps a man carrying a vase with handles. To the right we see a stand or table on which are a five drab vases or pieces of bread. Below the stand are traces of three seated women.

In front of the deceased and his wife is a pile of offerings consisting of the usual onions, meat and lotus flowers. To the left of the offerings a man stands presenting a cup and another thing which can no longer be determined.

On the east side of this main hall is a doorway (6). On the jambs and lintel are engraved hieroglyphic inscriptions which are the wishes and prayers for the dead person usually found in Egyptian tombs. The gods invoked here are Amun and Horus, Lord of Buhen. Djehuty-hetep wishes for "favor, love and cleverness before the sovereign and a long life as leader of the King". He is called, "brave leader of the Lady of the Two Countries", that is to say Queen Hatshepsut.

This doorway led into a small rectangular shrine, within which were originally four seated figures cut out of the rock. The figures faced the entrance, looking west. Above each was inscribed his name. They were Tentnub, wife of the deceased; Djehuty-hetep; his father, Ruiu; and his mother, Runa. The figures were in such a bad condition that they could not be removed.

The doorway in the south wall of the tomb originally led to a small chamber, in the centre of which was a shaft 4.75 metres deep. At the bottom of the shaft, on its northern side, was a doorway leading into a square chamber in which several painted wooden coffins were found. In the southeast corner of the upper chamber was a small doorway leading to another chamber in which was a second shaft, 3 metres deep, descending to another small chamber.

In the small room off to the south of the main hall is an exhibition of some of the archaeological finds which were discovered in this tomb.

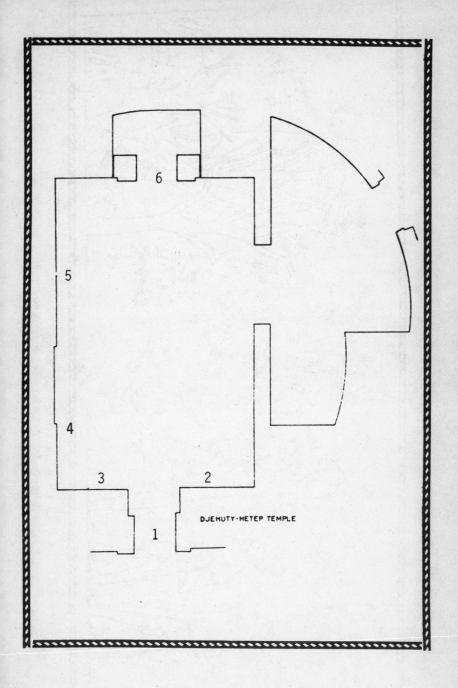

6

5

4

3

2

1

DJEHUTY·HETEP TEMPLE

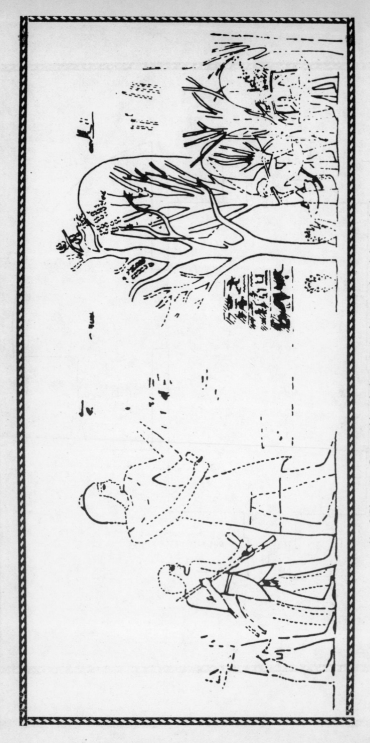

No. 3 Plantation Scene. Although the centuries have weathered the mural, the lush fertility of the Nile valley during ancient times is evident.

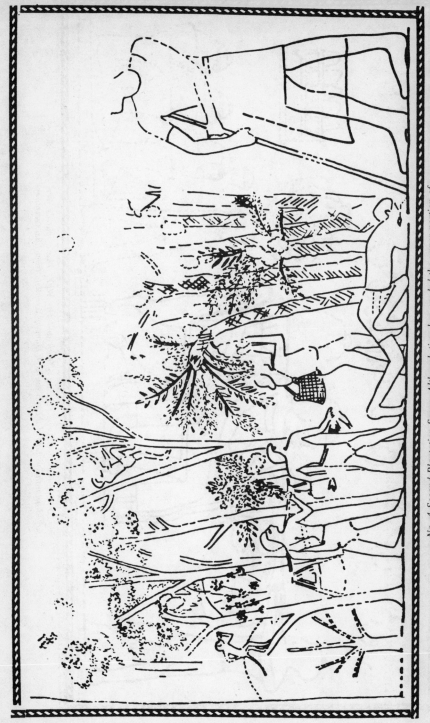

No. 4 Second Plantation Scene. Although time has eroded the upper portion of the mural the liveliness of the people and animals is still apparent.

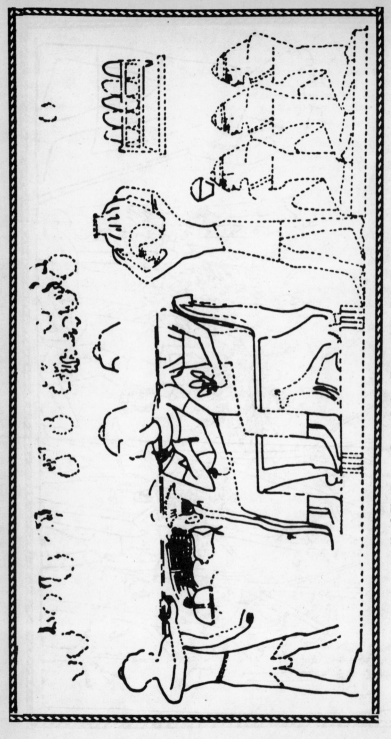

No. 5 The Banquet Scene. Djehuty-Hetep and His Wife. These murals were saved from the waters of the Aswan High Dam by scientists from East Germany.

9. The Avenue of Lions

The path leading from the bridge over the artificial lake to the main museum building is flanked on both sides with statues of Lions.

These Lions, which are made of sandstone, like the frogs, were brought from Basa, the site which lies in the Wadi Hawad, east of Shendi. Some of the Lions were found at the entrance to a temple there, while others were placed around the edge of a *hafir* (water reservoir). The Lion nearest the bridge on the left bears the name of the Meroitic King Amanikhable (70 to 50 B.C.). The last Lion on the same side is devouring a man who is the symbol of the King's enemies.

On the steps leading to the door of the museum are two statues in granite dating to the reign of King Taharqa. The rams are the symbol of the god Amun and are protecting the king who stands between the forelegs of the god. These two statues stood in front of the great temple of Amun at jebel Barkal.

The spelling of proper nouns in the guide is reproduced as given; these may vary from other transliterations.

From this lengthy description of the Museum Garden it might seem that it is very large—this is not the case. If the map of the garden, which is given as the first illustration in the text, is studied, it will be realized that the plot for the entire museum building and the garden is approximately 650 feet by 500 feet. Yet an air of spaciousness prevails, enhanced by the open Sudanese sky and the sunlight casting shadows as it plays among these ancient objects. To Leah and I, the opportunity to study the exhibits alone, without mobs of tourists and harsh-voiced tour guides made the Sudanese Museum one of the most memorable museums we have visited.

A visit to the Sudan National Museum is an absolute necessity in connection with the *Lost Cities of Africa* itinerary as the exhibits testify that in all probability a vital key to African history will be discovered by future research and archaeological digs in the area of Meroe.

Although they lack the gold of Egypt's National Museum displays, we found the Sudanese exhibits absorbing.

The second floor of the museum contains exhibits from the Christian and Islamic periods, and, again, holds much of interest.

Day 3: Travel to Meroe for a one-day trip. Meroe consists of small pyramids and is located between Atbara and North Khartoum. The pyramids can be seen from the railroad; to the left when coming from Atbara.

Readers should realize that the situation in Sudan—that is, the availability of gas (petrol) and transportion to Meroe—is unpredictable. We feel the situation is settling down and life for both Sudanese and tourists is becoming more stable than it has been. Promises are sometimes made by local travel agents or tour operators in Khartoum with the best of intentions that cannot be kept. In "Plan Ahead" we give the name of a person whom we feel can be relied on to keep his word, and who can find gas if anyone in Khartoum can—and he has the vehicles. If for some reason he is unable to arrange the trip and you are at the Hilton, ask to speak *directly* to the general manager and get his thoughts on how to get to Meroe; if you're at the Sudan Club—even if you're not British, go to the British Council offices—we found their staff very knowledgeable and helpful with our queries.

It is possible to go to Meroe on the train, to get off at Atbara and hire a taxi back to the site of the pyramids. This can become more expensive than

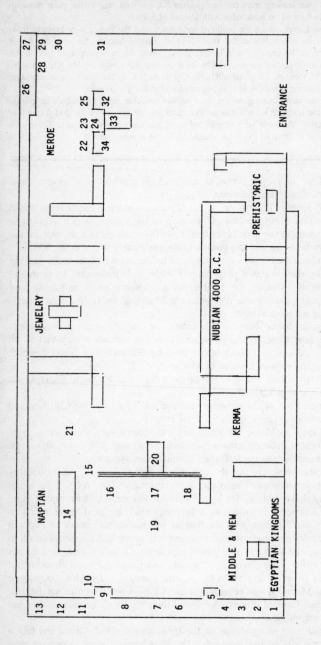

FLOOR PLAN OF THE GROUND FLOOR OF THE SUDAN NATIONAL MUSEUM, KHARTOUM

MEROE

JEWELRY

NAPTAN

MIDDLE & NEW
EGYPTIAN KINGDOMS

NUBIAN 4000 B.C.

PREHISTORIC

KERMA

ENTRANCE

GARDENS

Avenue en Nil

----- to the Khartoum Hilton

-------- to the Sudan Club

Upon entering the museum, visitors are encouraged to turn left and start their visit by viewing the objects in chronological order starting with the prehistoric items. Our map numbers the larger exhibits.

1. Granite statue of King Sebek-hotep IV (XIII Dynasty). Argo.
2. Granite statue of King Sesostris III (XII Dynasty). Uronarti.
3. Granite statue of King Sesostris III. Uronarti.
4. Granite pillar with inscriptions by Amenemhet (XVIII Dynasty). Debeira.
5. Sarcophagus with sandstone cover without inscription. Sulb.
6. Granite sacrificial table of King Siaspiqa, Meroitic Period. Nuri.
7. Statue of King Aminimalel, Napatan Period. Gebel Barkal.
8. Granite sacrificial table of King Senkamanisken, Napatan Period. Nuri.
9. Wooden sarcophagus Djehuty-hetep (XVIII Dynasty). Debeira.
10. Bronze door hinge with the name "Taharqas." Kawa.
11. Unfinished granite pillar with painted decoration. Nuri.
12. Granite statue of King Anlamani, Napatan Period, Gebel Barkal.
13. Granite statue of King Siaspiqa. Nuri.
14. Granite sarcophagus of King Anlamani, Napatan Period. Nuri.
15. Pearl inlay of the four sons of Horus. Nuri.
16. Granite sphinx of King Senkamanisken. Gebel Barkal.
17. Granite sacrificial bowl. Nuri.
18. Granite sphinx sacrificial table.
19. Granite altar of King Atlanersa, Napatan Period.
20. Statue of King Atlanersa, c. 653–643 B.C.
21. Obelisk Piankhis, Napatan Period. Kadakol.
22. Sandstone statue of a woman, Meroitic Period. Meroe.
23. Sculpture of the ram god Amon with the gods Sebiumek and Arensnuphis, Meroitic Period. Musauwarat.
24. Sculpture of the ram god Amon and the lion-headed gods Schu and Tefnut, Meroitic Period. Musauwarat.
25. Sandstone statue of a man, Meroitic Period. Meroe.
26 and 27. Sandstone statue of the god Ba in the form of a falcon. Faras.
28. Coffin lid made of pottery. Argin.
29. Sandstone statue of a prisoner. Tabo.
30. Bronze casting of the head of the Roman Emperor Augustus. Meroe.
31. Container opening in the form of a lion's head. Meinarti.
32 and 34. Large granite pillars of King Taharqa, Napatan Period. Kawa.
33. Colossus of King Taharqa, c. 688–663 B.C.

starting out from Khartoum because gas, when it is available, is even higher priced outside the capital city. To go by rail it would be necessary to have your own tent and camp out, taking the train back to Khartoum a few days later.

For the purpose of our itinerary, we will assume you will take a one-day safari to Meroe. A full description can be found in Shinnie's book.

Night 3: Overnight at the Hilton or Sudan Club.

Day and Night 4: You will need to study the airline schedules to determine if you'll be spending a fourth day in Khartoum. There are only two flights a week to Nairobi—one on Kenya Airways, the other on Sudan Airways. We recommend Kenya Airways. In 1986 the pilots of Sudan Airways went on strike because of operating conditions. While these may have been straightened out, Kenya Airways is preferred. Time can be spent shopping; shopping in Khartoum can produce some very interesting souvenirs. As the stores are difficult to locate, and have only Arabic signs, we have provided details in "Background for Sudan."

The Swahili City States

Mombasa, Lamu, Gedi, Jumba la Mtwapa, Mnarani

The Kenyan section of the Zinj coast (as the Swahili city states were called) is from Kiwayu in northern Kenya to Msambweni on the south coast. By far the most important of the ruins are to be found at Lamu, Gedi, and Jumba. At these sites almost entire settlements can be seen. The remaining sites offer badly deteriorated or, at best, obscured foundations of buildings not yet fully researched by archaeologists.

During the zenith of the Kenyan city states, Pate (near Lamu) and Malindi were the most prosperous, with Mombasa (Mvita) close behind. Yet today, nothing remains of the ancient city of Malindi apart from a tomb near the present post office. The word *Mvita* in Swahili means "war," and Mombasa is reportedly the most fought-over city in history. Much of the Swahili part of the town is still actively inhabited; the Portuguese built Fort Jesus on the promontory of the island, where the most important archaeological finds are likely to be discovered. Some excavation has been done within the walls of the fort, but undoubtedly much more still lies beneath the massive walls and fortifications.

The purist will want to examine each of the known Kenyan sites and to follow closely the descriptions in *Men and Monuments of the East African Coast* by James S. Kirkman (Lutterworth Press, London, 1964) and *East Africa and the Orient: A Cultural Syntheses in Pre-Colonial Times* edited by H. Neville Chittick and Robert I. Rotberg (Africana Publishing Co., New York and London, 1975). However, enthusiastic amateurs like ourselves will be content with the major sites readily accessible to the traveler: Jumba la Mtwapa, Gedi and Mnarani, Lamu, and Mombasa (Fort Jesus and Old Town).

The National Museums of Kenya publish very interesting and well-pre-

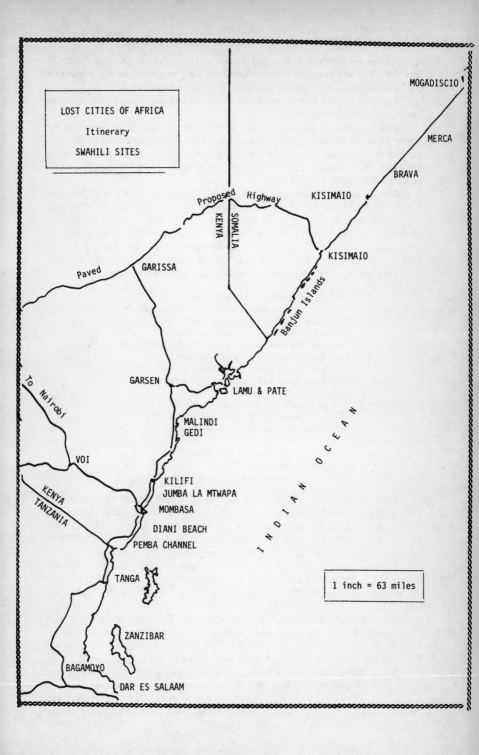

LOST CITIES OF AFRICA
Itinerary
SWAHILI SITES

MOGADISCIO

MERCA

BRAVA

KISIMAIO

Proposed   Highway

KENYA   SOMALIA

Paved   GARISSA

KISIMAIO

Banjun Islands

To Nairobi

GARSEN

LAMU & PATE

MALINDI
GEDI

VOI

KILIFI
JUMBA LA MTWAPA

KENYA
TANZANIA

MOMBASA

DIANI BEACH
PEMBA CHANNEL

INDIAN OCEAN

1 inch = 63 miles

TANGA

ZANZIBAR

BAGAMOYO

DAR ES SALAAM

sented titles on Swahili culture and guides to Gedi, Fort Jesus, and Jumba la Mtwapa. We will not repeat the information here as copies of the museum's publications are always readily available at a very nominal cost.

You will need a map of the coast of Kenya and we suggest you purchase one at a Mombasa bookstore.

Day 1: Arrive in Mombasa. Take a taxi from the station or airport to the Castle Hotel in the city center. Plan to have a restful day orienting yourself to the city and to Kenya. Before turning in, ask that a picnic lunch be ready after breakfast the following day. We suggest an Avis driver be used, but we also provide information for self-drive.

Day 2: Jumba la Mtwapa Ruins, Gedi (Malindi optional), and Mnarani Ruins. When driving out of the Castle parking lot, turn left; take the very next left—remember, as driving is on the left in Kenya, that this will necessitate crossing over the first lane to the far lane. Continue straight—there will be several circles or roundabouts—following the signs to the "New Nyali Bridge." This is a toll bridge, so have some small change ready. Continue on the Malindi road until the sign for Jumba la Mtwapa Ruins is seen on the right.

> Cockroaches rustle in the empty courts,
> Where once men gathered, now the crickets shrill.
> The chatter in the ante-rooms has ceased
> And there remains only dirt and foul decay.
> The courtyards now are choked with weeds and thorns,
> Bushes are canopied over with wild vines,
> Men fear today to pass these yawning doors
> For inside silence and Darkness reign supreme.
> If you believe me not, and say I lie,
> then go yourself and peer about those halls.
> Call out. Your echo will come back, naught else,
> For human voices can be heard no more.

> —*Al-Inkishafi: Catechism of a Soul*
> by Sayyid Abdalla Bin Ali bin Nassir,
> translated by James de Vere Allen

There is an air of gaiety about the Jumba Ruins; bright sunlight filters through the thousand branches of the aged baobob tree that dominates the plot. The guide on duty, a representative of the Museums of Kenya, will take you through the remains of houses and holy places for a small set fee, which is posted with the entrance price. Again, the entrance price is very small.

There are stone picnic benches and tables by the shore opposite the "Mosque by the Sea." No flies or other intruders will disturb your reveries as you much on the fare the chef at the Castle has provided and listen for the "echo [to] come back."

After lunch, there is still time to drive to Gedi. Turn right at the main road after leaving the Jumba Ruins and continue straight until the sign for Gedi is seen on the right. You will have passed Kilifi Ferry and followed the signs for Malindi, but Gedi is 8 km (about 5 m) south—before Malindi.

If you are tempted to see Malindi, by all means go into the town. There is, as we have said earlier, very little to see of historical interest apart from the Vasco da Gama monument, and even this is not on its original site. Malindi has become, over the past 15 years, a sleazy tourist town full of cheap tour groups who responded to the slogan "Kenya for Sun, Sand, and Sex" (a European advertising slogan now banned by the Kenyan government). The result is the seamier side of both Kenyan and European lifestyles.

A Museums of Kenya guide is available at Gedi, and there is a bookshop; do purchase the guide to the site. *Al-Inkishafi: Catechism of a Soul* can also be purchased here. You will probably want to take along a tripod to photograph Gedi; unlike the Jumba Ruins, much of Gedi is in deep shadow. The tripod will, of course, allow for slower shutter speeds. Even so, open up your lens a stop lower.

There is more to see at Gedi than at the Jumba Ruins and, for the serious student of ancient Swahili cities, Gedi is a well-documented, carefully excavated, and well-maintained site well worth several hours' study.

The Mnarani Ruins are at the southeastern-most point of Kilifi Creek. Leave Gedi as you came, and turn left at the main road. Just after the Kilifi Ferry— and we mean *just* after—is the turning to the right for Mnarani Ruins. It is really a wise precaution to wear rubber boots when walking down this path as it is overgrown, there are no Museums of Kenya personnel in charge, and there is a small stream to cross, which means there may be snakes. The path winds down and the ruins are beside the southeastern shore of the creek.

(Park—and lock—your car, leaving it on the highway. If you like, you can give a few shillings—when you return—to a local person for watching the car. There is always someone standing around this side of the ferry to look after cars.)

Having seen the Mnarani Ruins, drive on a few yards to a dirt road on the lefthand side leading to the Mnarani Club. Drive down and have afternoon tea or a soft drink. The view of the Indian Ocean and Kilifi Creek from the club's terrace is magnificent.

Be sure to leave before 5 p.m. in order to arrive back in Mombasa just before dark at 6:15.

Night 2: Overnight at the Castle Hotel.

Day 3: A one-day tour of Lamu. Readers wishing to go to Lamu can easily do so by air on a day trip from Mombasa or Malindi. We suggest going from Mombasa. The route can also be driven, but the road after Garsen—it is necessary to drive inland and then toward the ocean via that town because the coastal area is very swampy—is very poor. After November the river is often in flood, and the small ferry is incapable of successfully fording the strong currents. There is very little to see, in any case. For many years I had been longing to see the village of Witu because of its historic connection with German explorer Karl Peters. One year we drove up to Lamu and stopped at Witu. There is little of interest there and hospitality seemed to be an unknown word to Wituites.

Reservations for the flight to Lamu can be made in the lobby of the Castle Hotel. The plane leaves at about 8 a.m. and returns in the afternoon.

Leah hated Lamu from the moment she looked down from Petley's Hotel porch and saw one of the loitering men below kick a half-starved kitten 15 feet. The stinking, open drains and the body of a dead kitten outside an expensive store the next day did nothing to change her mind, nor did my remonstrations that such things and such conditions were to be found throughout much of the Third World. The meowing of a kitten throughout dinner that evening led to a search by flashlight. To no avail; no kitten was to be found.

Cats are much respected in Egypt and Morocco but, generally speaking, animals in Africa fare badly. A case in point being Morocco where, apart from cats, the treatment afforded to farm animals almost ruined our stay in the country. The British Sunday newspapers regularly, for 35 years to my personal knowledge, run a small display advertisement asking for donations to care for the old, infirm donkeys of North Africa. Humane treatment and compassion for animals in Africa is not the norm, except among the peoples of the Sahara. In Somalia and Mali the people love their camels and horses—and Egyptian horses are beautifully kept—but these are exceptions.

Not letting Leah's opinions unduly sway me, I must admit that I found myself reluctant to eat anywhere in Lamu other than at Petley's Inn. Flies journeyed from the open sewers, which empty directly onto the beach, to the food and people's diseased eyes. Open sewers can be acceptable if toilet debris travels with free-flowing sluice water, but this is not the case in Lamu. Of late, the Municipal Council of Lamu has had trouble collecting taxes, and sanitation work, once subsidized by the central government from Nairobi, is now the responsibility of local authorities. Ordinarily business people would join together to keep the city clean, but this is not the case in Lamu.

We hope that by the time this is published Lamu will have put its house in order and be back to the clean little tourist center for the study of Swahili culture that it was several years ago. During our visit the lack of sanitation detracted from the beautiful Lamu Historical Society Museum, which is next door to Petley's. The museum is housed in the former (British) District Commissioner's offices, and exhibits objects found in Lamu during archaeological digs and private restorations of Lamu homes in a manner that reflects the tutelage of the curator under Roland Hower of the Natural History Museum of the Smithsonian Institution. The exhibits are creatively displayed, most particularly the Chinese porcelain collection, which is hung on whitewashed walls so that the sunlight, as the day progresses, plays upon and illuminates the still vivid colors of the ancient pieces. Apart from the glass-encased exhibits and graphic explanations, two rooms have been furnished in the Swahili manner for a wedding day's festivities: a groom's room and a bride's room. The sunlight floods the beamed high-ceilinged rooms through windows with walls that are 18–24 inches thick.

Incidentally, British and Europeans have bought and restored many of the old Swahili houses in both Lamu and Shela, and many of these contain some excellent antiques. When the owners are away some houses can be rented on a daily or weekly basis. Reservations can be made by writing to the Lamu Historical Society (P.O. Box 45916, Nairobi, Kenya). Or, if the curator is at the museum on the day you are in Lamu and you wish to arrange a rental, this can be done from the museum. Tour operators also handle rentals, but they add a service charge. It is cheaper to make arrangements through the society. The usual charge through the society is about US$20 a day. This includes a servant who will do the cooking, although the cost of food is in addition to the rent.

Between the society and the Museums of Kenya a very comprehensive list of titles on Swahili culture have been printed. Many of these are available at the Lamu Museum Shop, as are some nice crafts.

A great deal of tender loving care has gone into establishing the Lamu Museum—the exhibits are excellent and the visit is another "must" for students of Swahili culture. If time permits, spending more than just a few hours in

Lamu is certainly worthwhile. We stayed at Petley's Inn, which we describe in "Kenyan Accommodation." If time presses, return to Mombasa by the afternoon flight.

Don't visit Lamu during the Moslem month of Ramadhan. This month-long holiday begins on April 18, 1988, and April 8, 1989 (subtract 10 days from the previous year's starting date). Lamu experiences severe water shortages during Ramadhan and life is a hardship for local and visitor alike.

Night 3: Overnight at the Castle Hotel, Mombasa.

OLD TOWN MOMBASA NIGHT

The moon rises over the Indian Ocean,
—the Milky Way is her veil, covering
what should not be seen.

A smuggler's lamp winks in the night to
Arab dhows, bringing gold, ivory and
Persian carpets;

The smell of perfume blows in the wind
as Swahili women in darkened alley
homes burn gum Arabic to scent
themselves;

Storekeepers drink spiced coffee and talk
loudly, piercing the silence of the
night;

And finally, when all but a few are fast
asleep, the wind whispers stories of
a thousand and one nights, until the
sun chases Shererazade away.

Memories of childhood by Leah Taylor

Day 4: Fort Jesus and Old Town, Mombasa. We have deliberately placed Fort Jesus at the end of the Kenyan Swahili coast itinerary, because after seeing some of the Swahili ruins you'll have an appreciation of what the Portuguese found when they arrived on this coast. We suggest visiting Fort Jesus in the early morning because the fort is especially pleasant then. Even though the fort is within walking distance of the hotel, we suggest you take the car; by the time you're ready to return the sun will be high in the sky and the walk back will be too hot and tiring.

Come out of the Castle Hotel parking lot and go right, then take another right, passing in front of the Castle Hotel as you do so. Continue around the circle (roundabout) and go straight. Fort Jesus will be seen 5 blocks ahead. There is plenty of room to park the car in front of the fort.

The museum, set within the walls of the Portuguese fort, houses not only artifacts from Swahili sites but also recoveries made during the 1970s by a team of divers, funded in part by the University of Texas, from a Portuguese ship sunk in the waters immediately in front of the fort.

Be sure to go to the topmost turrets for a spectacular view of the Indian Ocean. A cool, refreshing—and probably a welcoming—drink of fresh lime juice is available on this level.

During early British colonization of Kenya, Fort Jesus was used as a prison.

For the Swahili scholar, Fort Jesus offers an extensive collection of artifacts and the curator is always interested in meeting the serious student; don't hesitate to go to his office and introduce yourself.

We suggest lunch at the Castle, and a drive back toward Fort Jesus in the late afternoon after a little siesta for a walk through Old Town. The entrance is just after the fort. Avoid the obvious tourist traps, but there is an interesting shop just before the old dhow harbor, on the left.

This evening we suggest dinner at Tamarind Restaurant, overlooking the old harbor. Although we counsel not to drive at night, going out in Mombasa door-to-door in a car is perfectly safe. It is not advisable to walk around the city at night. To get to Tamarind, go over the New Nyali Bridge, but instead of following the signs pointing to the Malindi road, turn to the right immediately after the bridge. The Tamarind is a mile up the road on the right. (On our map of Mombasa, take the road leading to Krapf Memorial.)

Night 4: Castle Hotel.

Zanzibar

Day 5: Fly to Zanzibar for a one-day tour. Zanzibar—what a marvelous name; what exotic images it conjures in the imagination. Yet today Zanzibar is a testament to the egocentricity of former president Nyerre and the despair one man can bring to a once-vital people.

Nyerre was the legitimate president of Tanganika at the time of that territory's independence. He became greedy and engineered the takeover of the island of Zanzibar. The Zanzibaris are ethnically very different from the mainlanders, yet Nyerre imposed an administration on the island staffed by mainlanders who neither understood nor appreciated Zanzibar's long cultural history. The Zanzibaris responded with a Gandhi-like passive resistance. The economy was bankrupted. Nyerre, whose ulterior motive in annexing the island was to divert Zanzibari wealth to the impoverished mainland, admitted defeat in 1985 and relaxed the monetary constraints he had imposed on the island. Whether the Zanzibari business community can revitalize the island's commerce, only time will tell.

We cannot emphasize too strongly the existence in Zanzibar, Dar-es-Salaam, and all of northern Tanzania of a strain of malaria that does not respond to the drugs usually prescribed for the treatment of malaria. Some physicians believe that this strain can be treated with a drug whose trade name is Fansidar, but we have been told on very good authority that Fansidar is not successful in all cases. We are suggesting only a day tour from Kenya to Zanzibar to avoid exposure to this dangerous strain of malaria. Mosquitoes come out at dusk and stay out through the hours of darkness. A day trip, therefore, avoids any possibility of being bitten. We further suggest using only a Kenyan-based, Kenyan-owned tour company so that there will be no danger (as there is when a Tanzanian company is used) of the plane having to refuel in Tanzania or Zanzibar, where fuel shortages are notorious. A lack of fuel could necessitate staying the night in Zanzibar. We recommend using United Touring Service (UTC).

It is not wise to leave the group and wander off during the tour. We remind you that there is a very strict dress code in effect in Tanzania and the government officials are not past arresting women in slacks, tight dresses, or low-cut necklines. This is the place for a safari or shirtwaist dress that hits mid-calf. Men with other than short-back-and-sides haircuts may have a government barber do what their own barber should have done before their visit to Tanzania.

Zanzibar has the remains of some beautiful old historical buildings. These will be worth visiting, but the pleasure is not worth risking one's health.

Kilwa, a southern Tanzanian port, holds some of the most interesting Swahili ruins and is very extensive. Transportation in Tanzania, by rail, road, or air, is hopeless and nothing, absolutely nothing can be depended upon to function. We wrote hoping to get some assistance, but after a prolonged delay the answer came back that there could be no assurances on how to reliably get to Kilwa.

Night 5: Overnight, after returning by air from Zanzibar, at the Castle Hotel, Mombasa.

Day 6: Check out of the Castle Hotel. Kenya Airways flight to Mogadiscio, Somalia.

Mogadiscio, Brava, Merca, Kismaio

Few archaeological digs have been done in Somalia. However, the sites are accepted by archaeologists, historians, and geographers to be earlier than those in Kenya. There is a natural reluctance to positively date them because thorough, modern, scientific on-location research has not been conducted. Instead, citation is made to the mention of cities or towns along the coast of the land of Punt, as Egyptians called present-day northern Somalia.

Indeed, it may be centuries—as it was in the case of certain sections of the City of London, where Roman ruins were only recently discovered—before access can be gained to original Somali locations, presently inaccessible because of continuous habitation over the past thousand years—at Merca, Mogadiscio, and Brava.

As our reference we have used the work of Neville Chittick, "An Archeological Reconnaissance of the Southern Somali Coast," which appeared in the journal *Azania,* IV-1969 (Nairobi: British Institute in East Africa). Most major universities, and certainly those with departments of African studies may have *Azania,* or your local library may obtain it on inter-library loan. Failing this, there are a limited number of reprints available by writing to the British Institute in East Africa (P.O. Box 30710, Nairobi, Kenya), enclosing US$5 or its equivalent to cover the cost and airmail postage.

Day 1: Arrive in Mogadiscio. Don't expect the airport formalities in Somalia to be like any airport formalities you've experienced before, unless you've been to Madagascar. Somali airport formalities are better than the latter country's, but it's a matter of degree. Chaos reigns. Absolutely nothing dangerous is going to happen to you. Keep your dignity, don't get flustered, dress well, and despite the pushing and shoving, you will be well treated.

Take a taxi to the Juba Hotel. (See our description under "Somali Accommodation.") Once in Mogadiscio, you'll have to determine what the gas (petrol) supplies are like before deciding if you can go to Brava. If there's a shortage, be content with visiting the excellent museum and the Sheikh Abdulaziz Mosque.

At the time of our visit a new museum was under construction. When it

Sheikh Abdulaziz Mosque in Mogadiscio, Somalia, which is believed to date from the year 1000.

will open is not known. Assuming the old one is still in use—life moves slowly in Africa—you'll find that it is within walking distance of the Juba Hotel. The new site is a short taxi ride away.

We found an interesting bit of information about the museum when conducting in-depth research on it that appeared in *Bildende Kunst* (German Democratic Republic, vol. 23, part 11, 1975):

> The "Museo Dello Somalia" was one of the first museums founded in Africa, containing jewelry, furniture, and manuscripts bought from old families along the coast of Magadishu. After the declaration of independence in 1960, the Italian government handed the museum over to the Somalis and after nine years a great part of the art works had disappeared. The museum's collections are now being rebuilt and in 1973, with the development of the Somali written language, the labels for the objects were changed from English and Italian to Somali. This was the first opportunity for all parts of the population to develop an understanding of the works. Today the National Museum in Mogadishu plays an increasingly important role in the social life of the country.

From our experience in Somali, we would not place the blame entirely on the local people for any disappearance of the museum's exhibits. Taking advantage of the innocence of the Somalis has constituted a full-time career for certain expatriates in the country. One such grave robber sent a young Englishman to see us at the hotel to warn us not to go south—because of the danger. The only danger was that we might carry off (as they were) artifacts from the Swahili ruins to sell in Europe.

The Swahili archaeological sites were studied when the Italians were in Somalia, and there is literature dating from the 1920s. However, only Neville Chittick (who has since died) had conducted even a preliminary survey south of Mogadiscio in the recent past. The Commissioner of Antiquities of the government of Somalia is not unaware of the thefts being perpetrated in his country, and readers experiencing difficulties in traveling to more remote areas of Somalia should be sensitive to his concern. Scientists, after their credentials have been verified, are conducting research, but Somali does not have enough scientists of her own to supervise their activities. Beyond doubt, once a large number of archaeological digs have been made in Somalia, like Sudan, much of African history will need to be revised. For instance, there are *prehistoric* sites from northern Somalia down through the country. How will this tie in with Leakey's work at Lake Turkana?

Janet Stanley, chief librarian at the Smithsonian Institution's National Museum of African Art Library has called our attention to *Somalia in Word and Image,* edited by Katheryne S. Loughran, et al. (Bloomington: Indiana University Press, 1986), which includes photographs of some of the exhibits in the present museum in Mogadiscio. We also want to thank Ms. Stanley for her immeasurable assistance to us in researching material for the *Lost Cities of Africa* itinerary.

Artifacts in the old museum are housed in the palace of the former Sultan of Mogadiscio. The building is a genuine Swahili palace and more authentic than Lamu Museum, which was formerly a British administrative headquarters. The artifacts housed in the Magadiscio museum are, for the most part, nomadic Somali items and Italian colonizer records. However, the Swahili architecture is well worth the visit, especially to study the use of light and shadow in Swahili rooms. There is a domed skylight of colored glass by which the Sultan's advisers foretold his fortune from astrological readings. It was possible to bring boats up under the main floor to secrete slaves, ivory, and gold into the house.

Photo permits must be obtained from the Somali government, and if you tell the Merikani Hotel Reservations Service that you would like a permit, they will try to get one for you before you leave home.

We took a taxi to the very old section of Mogadiscio, then got out and walked while the driver waited. This original site of the port of Mogadiscio is very densely populated and undoubtedly holds many archaeological treasures beneath the active street life of today's citizens.

The Sheikh Abdulaziz Mosque is located in Mogadiscio and reportedly dates from the year 1000 A.D. It can be seen from the outside, but non-Moslems are not permitted to enter. Any taxi driver can take you to see it.

If a trip to Brava is possible, the ancient mosque, which is shown in Neville Chittick's book, is now painted Neopolitan colors and quite unrecognizable from the picture Chittick showed in his article. Brava is a very interesting town, and beautiful when first seen after turning off the main Mogadiscio-Kismaio highway.

It is possible, at low tide, to drive back to Mogadiscio along the beach.

Before turning inland there is a Swahili ruin at Gondershe. The ruin is not terribly old, according to Chittick not more than 150 years, and we suggest readers not visit it since we had an unpleasant experience here. A small mosque behind the ruin is still in use. We were allowed to go in and this should have alerted me that all was not as it should be. A man had run down from the village to show us through the mosque. After seeing it we drove up through the village to join the highway. An older man stopped us and became very insistent that we give him more than we had given the guide. The young women gathered around the Land Rover and wanted our bracelets and hung on to the doors, refusing to let us move on, adamant that we would not, could not leave without parting with our luggage. We had a Somali driver, but even he had difficulty in getting us out of the situation. This location has been visited by tourists and the villagers have become spoiled—or corrupted. It just might be that those expatriates whom we made reference to earlier were part of the problem.

We went all the way down to the Bajun Islands, south of Kismaio. We will be going again and are prepared to have readers who are interested in joining us come along. A very great deal of advance planning is necessary. We were lucky and as the guests of the Ministry of Tourism were given a car and driver, but such are not commercially available. Then, too, it was torture not to have a boat to explore the beautiful islands, and we plan to make up for this deficiency. Readers who want to take us up on our invitation are asked to write us at P.O. Box 53394, Washington, DC 20009. In *Fielding's African Safaris* we extended the same invitation to campers and the two purposes will be combined and offered by us until Somalia offers more services in the south for her tourists.

There is no need to return to Mombasa at the conclusion of the visit to Somalia, although departure for Mogadiscio was from that city. There is a flight on Kenya Airways that goes directly to Nairobi; also a flight on Air Somali.

If you have a day or two to spend in Nairobi, the National Museum of Kenya is well worth a visit, although there are very few Swahili exhibits worthy of note; but you may find the British Institute of East Africa of interest. Also the MacMillan Library, in downtown Nairobi, has an excellent Africana collection.

Although seldom mentioned in standard texts, the Comoro Islands and the north-northwest shore of Madagascar were also sites of Swahili cities. The French have recorded oral history from the Comoroes. Pierre Verin, under the auspices of the Wenner Gren Foundation, has authored *Les Echelles Anciennes du Commerce sur les Cotes Nord de Madagascar,* tome I, describing the presently known archaeological Malagasy sites.

Toumbouctou

Here is adventure! Exotic, hospitable, humble Mali! The Swahili itinerary should, we feel, be done before the Toumbouctou itinerary. The contrasts are overwhelming, but the extremes put African history in balance.

We discuss in detail the airport at Dakar, Senegal, which will be the base from which readers will change flights for Bamako, Mali, in the itinerary for *The Africans*. That airport, is an education in itself.

Reservations for the entire itinerary to Toumbouctou can be made, without charge, through Merikani Hotel Reservations Service (P.O. Box 53394, Temple Heights Station, Washington, DC 20009, tel. (USA) 301–530–1911). We also invite readers to join us; we tell you how below.

Day 1: Arrive Bamako on the Air Afrique flight from Dakar, Senegal. The sky is open and the air dry; the contrast between Bamako and Dakar is immediately apparent. Passengers with reservations at the Sofitel l'Amitie are met by a hostess from the hotel who sits behind a kiosk before immigration and customs. She is dressed in national costume and her coiffure would make any New York hairdresser who specializes in African styles green with envy. She is elegant, intelligent, multilingual, and welcomes you with a smile as she takes your passports. Baggage comes in, by hand, and is quickly chalked by trained officials; no questions asked.

The hostess, having met all the passengers, comes through and leads you to a waiting Mercedes bus. Driving into Bamako, the air becomes dusty as vehicles ahead of the bus disturb the sand that lightly covers the tarmacked road. Small mud buildings are passed: some are stores, some homes. Everywhere there is activity; a paced activity—the intensity of Dakar Airport has been left behind in Senegal.

The bridge comes into view—not a suspension bridge, just an ordinary low-lying, unassuming bridge, but it crosses the river Niger and beyond is the city of Bamako.

The bus pulls in under the portico of the Sofitel l'Amitie, making the temperature drop not less than 15 degrees. The desk clerks are, again, multilingual, and a room is quickly assigned.

The rooms look out over the bridge and now the River Niger can be seen for long stretches in either direction. Small home gardens are tended by its banks just beyond the hotel boundary, which encloses a simple garden and an azure swimming pool. The air-conditioned room is cool and dim. Bamako is a destination that does not disappoint.

Let the afternoon and evening of this first day be one of orientation and relief; relief because to know that you have made it to Mali and that Toumbouctou lies ahead surely is a great victory.

Dinner and overnight in the Sofitel l'Amitie.

Day 2 and 3: Preparing for Tombouctou. No more self-indulgence today; today is the day to start obtaining the necessary travel documents for the journey north. Your passport will be carrying only a 7-day visa for Mali, and undoubtedly you're going to want to take pictures. This means a visa extension and a permit to photograph must be obtained. We give all the details on how to do this in "Travel Documents." The process is going to take today, and probably tomorrow. Intersperce your comings and goings with cool drinks and conversations in the Sofitel bar. Many fascinating people frequent this lounge, and hopefully, you'll strike up a conversation with one or more of them to add to the enjoyment of the day. The key is to take it easy in getting your papers in order.

How you travel to Toumbouctou will depend on the time of year you visit Mali, your personal time constraints, and whether or not Air Mali is flying again. There is also an overland route by car or bus.

Train and steamer: A rail line runs from Dakar in Senegal to Bamako, with a branch line to Koulikoro. This town is the embarkation point for the steamer. The steamer calls at a number of small ports, one of which is Kabara, the disembarkation city for Toumbouctou. The steamer continues on to Gao, turns around, and returns on the same route it followed on the outward voyage. Complete details can be found in "Transportation."

The steamer can only operate when the River Niger floods, which is usually from the end of July to the first week in December. Depending upon the rains in the Guinee mountains, this time frame can vary from year to year. However, except during a *severe* drought, the July-December time frame is reliable. There are two steamers, one a weekly "packet boat," meaning one that carries mail, small parcels, and passengers and operates on a regular schedule. Then there is the fortnightly steamer, which carries cargo and passengers.

There are several luxury cabins and a larger number of first-class cabins on the steamers. When all of the first-class cabins are not sold the captain allows other passengers to use the first-class deck. They sleep, cook, and spend the day on the deck; there is virtually no privacy. When all first-class and luxury-class cabins are sold to one buyer the deck is used only by that group.

The voyage to Kabara (for Toumbouctou) takes 4 nights; boarding is on a Tuesday evening; arrival is very early Saturday morning. The voyage to Gao takes 6 nights, arriving on Sunday evening. Passengers can, if they wish to

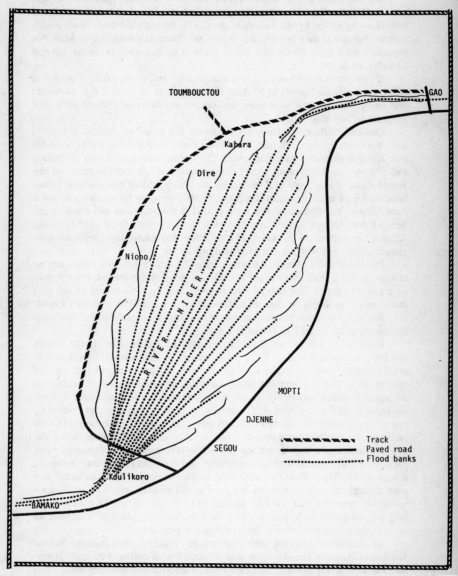

Sketch map indicating the flooding of the River Niger between Bamako and Toumbouctou. (In the dry season it is possible to drive through the river bed).

return to Koulikoro (for Bamako) by steamer, pick up the steamer on her return journey on a Wednesday.

We had a long conversation with an American who had organized a voyage taking all of the first-class and luxury-class cabins. We plan to follow suit and extend an invitation to our readers to contact us through Merikani Hotel Reservations Service if they would like to join us. There is no agency in Mali that organizes such trips; that's why we've taken it upon ourselves, as we have in Somalia, to do so.

If you plan to take your chances and go 2nd, 3rd, or 4th class, a great deal of advance planning needs to be done if the trip is to be made a real adventure and enjoyable, and not something that simply needs to be endured. We give suggestions in "Plan Ahead."

Domestic airline: The only mark against the record of African airlines is that of a crash by Air Mali (see "Transportation"). From what we have heard, this accident shouldn't have happened. The airline was immediately disbanded and is now, at this writing, being reorganized through the assistance of the World Bank. It may very well be that by the time you decide to take the Toumbouctou leg of the *Lost Cities* itinerary, flights will again be operating between Bamako and Toumbouctou. We have provided the addresses and phone numbers of Air Afrique offices and you should check with them—although Air Afrique has nothing to do with Air Mali, they may know about services operating in Mali, and whether Air Mali is flying again.

Private charters: Across the street from the Sofitel l'Amitie Hotel are the offices of two private charter airlines. One is government-owned, but operates as a private charter. We wasted two days getting their rates only to discover that it would probably be cheaper to charter Air Force 1 or the Queen's Flight.

We heard a rumor that sometimes a missionary aircraft can be hired, but this seems to be on an "as available" basis.

Overland by car or bus: Two factors inhibit travel by car: (1) the lack of reliable rental vehicles, and (2) the erratic supply of gas (petrol). Avis does not, at this writing, have an agency in Mali, and only the government department of tourism (S.M.E.R.T.) operates tourist vehicles or rents cars. Maintenance on the rental vehicles, reportedly, is not good, and breakdowns are frequent. Joining other tourists in a S.M.E.R.T. minibus, or participating in a tour offered by one of two local travel agencies, is not wise. On the way back from Mali we met a group who had been involved in a crash while using such services. The tour operator really had no inkling of how to take care of the situation. Most passengers had escaped with severe bruises and cuts, but one woman sustained a back injury. There were no pain killers in the hospital at Bamako, and it was only through the intervention of the American Embassy and SOS Insurance's immediate response that she was evacuated to Europe within 48 hours. For a long trip we prefer to be in control of the vehicle we're riding in or to have an Avis driver whom we know to be a responsible person.

At some time or other there was a bus operating from Bamako-Segou-Nampara-Goundam-Toumbouctou that connected with another bus from Toumbouctou to Gao via Bourem. Another route, Gao-Mopti, connecting with a bus to San and Segou, also operated. We know that a bus operates from Bamako to Segou, but could uncover no information about the other routes.

Joining a reliable overland tour operated by Encounter Overland from London, England, or contacting our friend, Malcolm Gascoigne, who does custom safaris, is the best method to travel across Mali. We give the addresses of both contacts in "Transportation."

While it might appear when looking at a Michelin map that it's a fairly simple matter to drive from Segou-Nampara-Goundam-Toumbouctou-Bourem-Gao, in reality it is not. We have tried to show on our map of the River Niger as it flows between Bamako and Gao what we did not previously understand when using Michelin. There can never be any certainty about how high the river will climb when it is in flood, or how long it will take to recede. As the roads, or tracks, shown between the points mentioned, cross flooded areas, major problems arise. If the river is up or stays up longer than usual, the road is underwater. If the river has been slow in receding, the roadbeds remain saturated, making for stretches of unbelievably sticky, deep mud. Driving during the dry season does not eliminate problems as the tracks are obscured by blowing sand and the heat is intolerable.

Days 4–10: Check out of the hotel and take the train to Koulikoro. Board the steamer to Toumbouctou. We visited Mali during the dry season, when the River Niger was not in flood, and traveled to Toumbouctou by road. We can do little to describe the steamer voyage, except to say that we very much look forward to making it.

Day 11: Arrive Toumbouctou. There are taxis available for the 10-mile trip from Kabara to the town.

As we have written in *Fielding's African Safaris,* the getting to Toumbouctou is more interesting than arriving. The town is small and the hotel disappointing (see "Malian Accommodation"). Nevertheless, there is a thrill of accomplishment in having arrived and we felt very elated. There is little to see: the market was very dusty and dirty, and we preferred the markets we had seen traveling up through the countryside. Reportedly the ports at which the boat stops en route are very near the local markets, and by the time a multitude of these have been visited, Toumbouctou market will probably hold little interest. However, souvenirs are of vital interest. There is a shop in the hotel, but outside there are a number of young men, all of whom claim their father brought the object he is trying to sell you "across the Sahara in a caravan." They ask you to go to their tents, which are some 500 yards from the hotel. Once there, the original host is joined by his relatives and neighbors. You are asked to sit on a carpet and the entrepreneurs sit opposite. Items of various quality and authenticity are then laid on the rug separating you from them. Absolutely astronomical prices are asked. We ended up with a few trinkets, but found the T-shirts at US$10 in the hotel shop would probably be more appreciated than some of the items offered in the tent.

The old mosque will, of course, be high on the list of things readers will want to see, as well as Caillie's house. A government guide will go with you to the town; we got fed up waiting for him—he was late—and went on our own. If you do plan to use the guide, plan on his being 30 to 40 minutes late. He caught up with us in town and we got the impression he was annoyed that we had gone on without him more for pecuniary reasons than for the fact that we were not enjoying the asthetics of Toumbouctou as much as we might have with him. There is supposed to be a set fee—we believe it may be padded; a few hours later, when I took Leah's picture in front of the hotel while he was sitting in a chair at the front gate, he asked for money for letting us take his picture. We told him that, in fact, he had marred the picture; what we really wanted was a picture of ourselves, not him, in front of the hotel. A certain amount of corruption seems to have filtered through the Saharan sand due to Toumbouctou's popularity with tourists.

As a matter of interest, we were told that almost 1500 tourists make the trek to Toumbouctou annually, most of them coming overland across the Sahara in tour groups such as those operated by Encounter Overland. Details of such groups are given in "Transportation."

Readers will have to decide how they will return to Bamako, taking into consideration the availability of air services; if they are not operating, the trip will have to be made either by rejoining the steamer on its next trip and going on to Gao and from there finding some means of public transportation—which is very iffy—to Bamako via Mopti, or simply taking the boat back to Bamako when it sails south.

Return to Bamako and overnight at the Sofitel L'Amitie—you'll feel like you've come home.

PLAN AHEAD: All reservations can be made, without charge, through Merikani Hotel Reservations Service. Nor do they charge for obtaining visas; they only charge for the actual cost of the visa plus registered return-receipt postage, if hotel reservations are made through them. They will also send along the recommended maps with the confirmation of your hotel reservations. These are charged at the price quoted on the maps. Merikani also offers this service to non-North American readers. Their address is P.O. Box 53394, Temple Heights Station, Washington, DC 20009, tel. (USA) 301–530–1911. However, we have provided all the necessary information to make your own reservations.

The following needs to be done before departure: Check the "Basic Information Checklist" in the "Background Information" section for necessary travel documents; make hotel reservations—numbers and addresses are given in the headings preceding the hotel descriptions; make airline reservations for international flights using the routings we have suggested at the beginning of the itinerary; reserve an Avis car where needed; write UTC (United Touring Service) and reserve a tour to Zanzibar (P.O. Box 42196, Nairobi, Kenya); for the trip to Meroe, contact Thomson Travel (Attention: Graham Thomson, Street 15, New Extension, Khartoum, Sudan); purchase SOS insurance (see "Travel Documents"); purchase traveler's checks; write, but do not send money, to Kenya Railways for a reservation on their overnight sleeper train Nairobi-Mombasa return (details in "Transportation").

Clothing for Sudan, Somalia, and Kenya should be nothing out of the ordinary. We believe you will be better treated if you dress conservatively. Except for the one-day trip to Zanzibar Island you will not experience dress code restrictions. The Tanzanians require that women refrain from wearing shorts, miniskirts, and shoulderless dresses, and that men have short back-and-sides haircuts. For the steamer trip in Mali, absolutely only 100% cotton garments, as the heat can get pretty fierce. Despite the heat, the body should be protected from the intense rays of the sun by loose clothing. If you purchase some kangas when you're in Kenya (the sarong-type length of fine printed cotton worn by many women at the coast), you'll find this can be a versatile protector from the sun. The loose kanga can be worn as a shawl, draped over the legs when sitting down to protect the ankles and feet, and even madonnalike over the head. A kanga allows air to circulate under the fabric while providing shade from the sun. A wide-brimmed hat for both men and women that will protect the back of the neck as well as the face is another necessity. Contradictory as it may seem, a kanga can be a warm garment when held tightly against the body; two kangas worn as a shawl will ward off the chill that comes over the desert after the sun goes down. Sandals will be the most practical and comfortable shoes.

Decaffeinated coffee is not available in any of the countries visited on the *Lost Cities* itinerary; if you prefer it, bring a supply. Bottled mineral water should be taken along on the steamer in Mali. It may or may not be available on the ship. In any case, it will be cheaper if you buy it in the Bamako supermarket than from the stewards on the steamer. Prices in the Bamako supermarket are a quarter of the ones charged in hotels and restaurants. Try the brand-name AWA, which is bottled in Senegal and is every bit as good as the more expensive mineral waters imported from France. Those traveling luxury and first class will have the cook on board prepare their meals. They will, however, want to supplement these meals with snack foods. These can be purchased at the supermarket in Bamako at fairly reasonable prices. Those traveling second class and below will need to take all their food as the cook will not prepare their meals. While it is possible to purchase fresh fruits and vegetables when the steamer docks in the various ports, it should be remembered that these may be in limited supply and must be cooked before eating. A few compact picnic foods brought from home and supplemented by Bamako supermarket purchases would ensure you don't go hungry. We caution against accepting food from fellow passengers in second class and below. Undoubtedly, it will be offered, but it is unlikely that your digestive system is prepared to peacefully accept the possible contamination a meal may harbor. Try to make yourself self-sufficient. Food everywhere in Mali will be found to be very expensive for those traveling on a tight budget. Use the supermarket while in town, and plan on picnic meals. Meal prices at the hotel in Toumbouctou are outrageously high, and there's very little to buy in the market. There is no supermarket in Toumbouctou. If you find your grocery supply is large enough to require a box to carry them in, remember there are plenty of men looking for the opportunity to earn a few francs; you can always get someone to carry them onto the ship for you.

Start taking malaria tablets two weeks before your intended departure date. A first-aid kit should be taken. Only if you are in the very best of health should you contemplate the Mali leg of the itinerary; medical services are almost non-existent, although, in case of emergency, there is an Italian-staffed hospital at Dire and the steamer docks at this port just before the port for Toumbouctou. The health information contained in "Bye-the-By" should be read and reread by those traveling second class and lower on the steamer.

Plain, boiled hard candy (sweets) will be nice to have to give to the children in rural areas and at the various River Niger ports. You may want to bring a few inexpensive souvenirs from your hometown to give to those who are kind to you as you travel. These need be nothing elaborate: postcards, ballpoint pens with your city's name imprinted; and for very special kindnesses, a T-shirt with your city's logo.

Take plenty of film, and read our suggestions on how to care for your camera and film in extreme temperatures in "Bye-the-By." Keep your camera on your person at all times in Zanzibar.

Obtain your maps from Forsyth Travel Library (9154 West 57th St., P.O. Box 2975, Shawnee Mission, KS 66201-1375, tel. (USA) toll-free 800–367–

7984 or, if busy, 913–384–3440). Maps will be available in Kenya, although not the exact ones we recommend, and in Bamako you'll have to make time to go to the Institut Geographique National, where maps of the River Niger can be purchased.

For those traveling on the steamer second class or below, it will be necessary to take a bed roll, as only deck space is provided. Bedding is provided in first and luxury class. Insect repellent will be needed by all passengers and should be applied just at sunset before the mosquitoes come out.

Lastly, take along a few good books for the steamer voyage; look over our annotated bibliography. *The Great Brown God,* if not read before your vacation, will be of particular interest.

If you find you've accumulated too many books and souvenirs in Kenya, there is a very reliable "left luggage" room at Dakar International Airport where you can package and leave the items you don't want to take literally all the way to Toumbouctou. You'll be passing back through Dakar on your way home.

Once in Africa, reconfirm flight reservations 24 hours ahead of scheduled departures (Kenya Airways); 12 hours ahead (Air Afrique). This can present a real problem when flying from east to west Africa. Ask if you can telex ahead to the Air Afrique office in Dakar from the Royal Air Maroc counter or office in either Cairo or Casablanca (assuming you're using our suggested routing) to reconfirm your Dakar-Bamako flight. When reconfirming for the return flight (Bamako-Dakar) it's best to go personally to the Air Afrique office (a block from the Sofitel l'Amitie Hotel) to ensure that it's done. The first day in Mombasa, make the reservation for the one-day flight to Lamu and reconfirm the UTC tour to Zanzibar.

Accommodation recommended in the *Lost Cities of Africa* itinerary: *Sudan*—Khartoum Hilton International or Sudan Club (economy); *Kenya*—Castle Hotel, Mombasa; *Somalia*—Juba Hotel, Mogadiscio; *Kenya*—Hilton International Nairobi (if required to connect with the flight to Cairo); *Egypt*—Ramses Hilton International, Cairo (if required to connect with the flight to Casablanca); *Morocco*—Casablanca Hyatt Regency, Casablanca (if required to connect with the flight to Dakar); *Senegal*—Dakar Aerogare Hotel (if required to connect with the flight to Bamako); *Mali*—Sofitel l'Amitie, Bamako; Relais Azalai Hotel, Toumbouctou; Sofitel l'Amitie, Bamako (on arrival back in that city from Toumbouctou).

Estimated Budget

Lost Cities of Africa Itinerary

Sudan—Meroe portion (4 days)
Does not include airfares unless otherwise stated

	US$	
	1 person	2 people
Arrive Khartoum: Taxi to Hilton or Sudan Club	$ 7	$ 7
Select option (a) or (b)		

	US$	
	1 person	2 people
(a) Hilton International Khartoum, 4 nights, $158 single, $182 double, includes all taxes = $632 and/or $728		
Meals: breakfast $6, lunch $10, dinner $15 = $15 = $31 + 15% tips × 4 days = $142.60 and/or $285.20		
Total for 4 nights at Hilton and taking meals in hotel: $774.60 and/or $1013.20		
(b) Sudan Club, 4 nights, $25 single, $50 double, includes taxes = $100 and/or $200		
Meals: (slightly less but not significantly less than Hilton considering the difference in quality) breakfast $5, lunch $8, dinner $10 = $23 + 15% tips × 4 days = $105.80 and/or $211.60		
Total for 4 nights at Sudan Club and taking meals at club: $205.80 and/or $411.60		
One-day Land River trip to Meroe (these are outside figures but expect to pay a high price). Gas (petrol) was $30 a gallon when we were in Khartoum and a Land Rover does about 10 mpg.	400	800
Taxi to airport $7 (allow $3 for city taxis)	10	10
Entrance fee to museum, allow	1	2
Tips to porters and bellmen	12	12
Gratuity to housekeeping staff, $1 a night for 1 or 2 people	4	4
NOTE: SOS Insurance is added at the end of the complete estimated budget		
Total option (a):	$1201.60	$1841.20
Total option (b):	$ 632.80	$1239.60
Cost per person sharing option (a):	$ 920.60	
Cost per person sharing option (b):	$ 619.80	

Kenya—Swahili Ruins including Zanzibar (6 days)

	1 person	2 people
Arrive Mombasa: taxi to Castle Hotel	5	5
Castle Hotel, 6 nights, bed and breakfast, includes all taxes, $47 single, $74 double	282	444
Meals: lunch $6 (including packed picnic lunches prepared by the hotel's chef), dinner $10 = $16 a day × 6 days	96	192
Avis car with driver for trip to Jumba-Gedi-Mnarani (1 day), and driving around Mombasa seeing Fort Jesus, etc. (1 day), allow 350 km, including full insurance	149	149
Driver $20 a day × 2 days	40	40
Gas (petrol)	22	22
One-day guided tour to Lamu by air from Mombasa (airfare included)	200	400
One-day guided tour to Zanzibar (airfare included)	200	400
Taxi to airport	5	5
15% tips to waiters/waitresses on all meals	18.90	37.80

	US$	
	1 person	2 people
Tips for bellmen and porters	16	16
Gratuity to housekeeping staff, $1 a night for 1 or 2 people	6	6
Total:	1039.90	1761.80
Cost per person sharing:	$858.40	

Somali—Swahili Ruins (3 days)

	1 person	2 people
Arrive Mogadiscio: taxi to Juba Hotel	$ 12	$ 12
Juba Hotel, 3 nights, $84 single, $108 double	252	324
Meals: breakfast $5, lunch $8, dinner $15 = $28 a day × 3 days	84	168
Taxi fares around city, approximately $5 a trip, 4 round trips (museum, mosque, beach, etc.)	40	40
Tips to bellmen and porters	8	8
15% tips to waiters/waitresses on meals	12.60	25.20
Gratuity to housekeeping staff, $1 a night for 1 or 2 people	3	3
Taxi to airport	12	12
Total:	423.60	592.20
Cost per person sharing:	$296.10	

Kenya—overnight in Nairobi if required

	1 person	2 people
Taxi from airport to hotel	15	15
Nairobi Hilton International, 1 night, includes all taxes	89	110
Meals: breakfast $6, lunch $8, dinner $12 = $26 a day	26	52
Allow $4 on average for city taxi fare (figure is given for 2 round trips, and 1 trip to railroad station)	20	20
15% tips to waiters/waitresses on meals	3.90	7.80
Gratuity to housekeeping staff, $1 a night for 1 or 2 people	1	1
Total:	$154.90	$205.80
Cost per person sharing:	$102.90	

Senegal—overnight at Dakar Airport, if required

Although in some instances the airline will pick up the cost of overnight accommodation, it may be necessary to pay for this yourself. In which case the following information for Yoff International Airport, Dakar, Senegal may be helpful.

	1 person	2 people
Overnight at Airport Hotel	$44	$44
Meals in the airport restaurant: breakfast (continental) $3, lunch $8, dinner $10	21	42
Taxi to beach hotels or into town (fares, regardless of distance, seem to be about the same)	28	28

	US$	
	1 person	2 people
15% tips to waiter on meals	3.15	6.30
Gratuity to housekeeping staff	1	1
Total:	97.15	121.30
Cost per person sharing:	$60.65	

Mali—Toumbouctou (10 or 15 days)

	1 person	2 people
Arrive Bamako: Sofitel bus to hotel (no charge)	—	—
Sofitel l'Amitie, 3 nights, $89 single, $98 double	$ 267	294
Meals: breakfast $6, lunch $10, dinner $15 = $31 a day × 3 days	93	186
Visa extension and permit to photograph	10	20
Taxis around town to extend visa, obtain permit to photograph, and pick up train and steamer tickets, allow $3 a trip, 10 trips	30	30
Groceries for picnic meals on the steamer, and mineral water	50	100
Train fare to Koulikoro	20	40
Steamer ticket to Toumbouctou	313	626
Taxi from Kabara to hotel in Toumbouctou	15	15
Hotel Relais Azalai, Toumbouctou, 2 nights, @ $54 single, $62 double	108	124
Meals: (take some picnic foods if possible) breakfast (continental) $8, lunch $20, dinner $25 = $51 × 2 days	102	204

Select option (a) or (b)

	1 person	2 people
(a) Taxi to the airport if using Air Mali or Mission Aviation if returning to Bamako by air, $8 for 1 or 2, and airfare to Bamako $156 + $8 = $164	_____	_____
(b) Taxi to Kabara to reboard steamer back to Bamako, $15 for 1 or 2, and steamer fare $313 = $328 or $641	_____	_____

Note: If planning to return on steamer, 3 nights must be spent at Toumbouctou (see Toumbouctou schedules in "Transportation" section). Add another night and meals at Toumbouctou, or $54 + $51 = 105 single, or $62 + 102 = 164 double

	1 person	2 people
Sofitel l'Amitie, 1 night	89	98
Meals: 1 day (see Bamako above)	31	62
Sofitel airport bus to airport, no charge	—	—
15% tips to waiters/waitresses on meals	33.90	67.80
Tips to bellmen and porters	26	26
Gratuity to housekeeping staff, $1 a night for 1 or 2 people, includes steamer's cabin steward option (a) $20; option (b) $15	—	—
Total option (a):	$1361.90	$2066
Total option (b):	1635.90	2712.80
Cost per person sharing option (a):	1033	
Cost per person sharing option (b):	1356.40	

Budget totals for the *Lost Cities of Africa* Itinerary
(US$)

	1 person	2 people	per person sharing	cost per day per person 1 person	cost per day per person sharing
Sudan (Meroe) 4 nights					
(a) Hilton	1201.60	1841.20	920.60	300.40*	230.15
(b) Sudan Club	632.80	1239.60	619.80	158.20	154.95
Kenya (6 nights)					
(Swahili city states)	964.90	1566.80	783.40	160.81	130.56
Somalia (3 nights)					
(Swahili city states)	423.60	592.20	296.10	142.20	98.70
Kenya (1 night)					
(layover)	154.90	205.80	102.90	—	—
Senegal (1 night)					
(layover)	97.15	121.30	60.65	—	—
Mali (Toumbouctou)					
(a) 10 nights	1048.90	1440.80	720.40	104.89	72.04
(b) 15 nights	1322.90	2086.80	1043.40	88.19	69.56

*This figure is inordinately high due to the current foreign exchange rate for Sudanese pounds. Hilton rates should be reconfirmed nearer departure time as it is very likely their tariff will have dropped.

Estimated Budget for Paupers: *Lost Cities of Africa* Itinerary

We mentioned that if you use an overlanding tour truck you may see more lost cities and costs for the trip would be reduced—depending on the number of travelers.

A second thought is that by making up a group, but following the means of transportation we have suggested, airfares may also be reduced.

We discuss in the pauper's estimated budget for the *Lunatic Express* itinerary the options for cheaper accommodation in Mombasa, Kenya, as well as in Nairobi. Readers following the *Lost Cities* itinerary can consider these. It is unlikely that the hotels in Khartoum or Mogadiscio would give reductions for group travel, although it is possible to sleep three to a room in the Hilton Khartoum for only a slightly higher charge. The hotels in Mali, we believe we're safe in saying, will not give reductions for groups. Many times these hotels are the only ones in town, and competition doesn't exist. Nor is there likely to be a discount for the UTC one-day tour to Zanzibar for a group, or the one-day flight to Lamu. However, it's worth a try.

Merikani Hotel Reservations Service (P.O. Box 53394, Temple Heights Station, Washington, DC 20009, tel. (USA) 301–530–1911) has brochures describing overlanding itineraries.

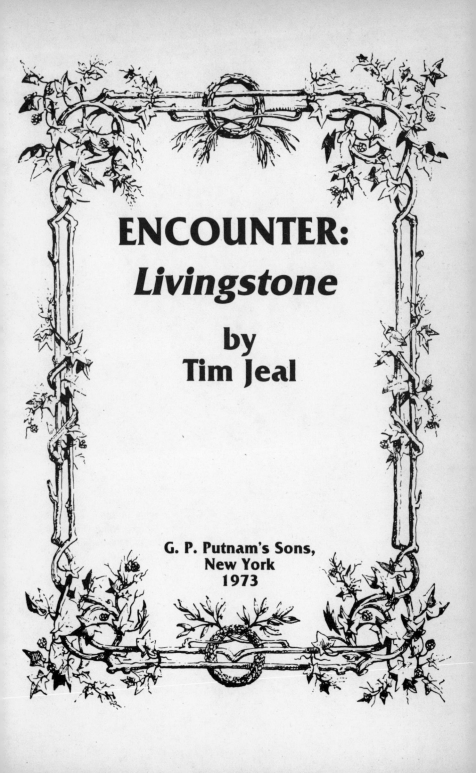

ENCOUNTER:
Livingstone

by
Tim Jeal

G. P. Putnam's Sons,
New York
1973

Tomes have been written about Livingstone.

Hero-worshiping tomes.

Until Tim Jeal, with the courage of youth, wrote his biography, the literature was replete with superlative descriptions of Livingstone's character. Jeal tells us of the man: his inner conflicts, weaknesses, and strengths, but above all else, Jeal shows Livingstone to be as vulnerable as any of us, devoid of the hero's artificiality.

The real heroes of the Livingstone story, the manifestation of "perfect love" in the Christian religious sense, were Susi and Chuma, who wandered behind Livingstone. That they smoked marijuana to pass the time and slept with whatever lovelies happened to be in their beds along the trail does not diminish their character. Their activities are discussed in Livingstone's Diary in the National Library of Scotland, Blantyre, folio number 10734 and quoted in Donald Simpson's *Dark Companions: The African contribution to the European exploration of East Africa* (Paul Elek, Ltd., London, 1975). Livingstone employs very colorful language to describe them. Susi was a poor cook and hopelessly inept at keeping Livingstone's gear in order or away from thieving hands. Chuma was "a boisterous, roaring laughter-provoking boy" *(Dark Companions).* Their singing and giggling was a constant irritant to Livingstone.

Two innocents until the moment "old souls" transmigrated in the hour of need, when the irresponsible Livingstone, hemorrhaging internally, cast the result—his broken body—literally onto the shoulders of his "dark companions," Susi and Chuma.

Victorians overworked the adjective *devotion,* and never more than with reference to Chuma and Susi.

Devotion does not explain their earlier attitude toward Livingstone's leadership. For them the safari had been a game. They followed along up until the moment of crisis, knowing they, unlike Livingstone, could be happy wherever they chose to drop off. In fact they did try to leave. Livingstone had to shoot—he missed—at them to make them come along at one point. He spent many hours coaxing. Susi and Chuma were no blind, devoted followers.

Rather than devotees, they were a *response* to a young soul—Livingstone's soul—now in its last weeks on earth—a soul already in limbo. Confused in his faith, vindictive toward his friends, harboring vices the hymns and chapbooks warned against—until these forces wore down Livingstone's spirit and his soul was humbled. As a small child, he knelt in prayer on his deathbed.

What made Susi and Chuma rise to the level of heroes?

It was not the embittered soul of Livingstone that—somewhere approaching crisis point—transmigrated to Susi and Chuma.

Perhaps into Susi and Chuma came the souls of slaves who had died in

*David Livingstone's porters, Susi and Chuma, who nursed him in his last illness.
After his death they buried his heart in Africa under a tree, then dried his body
and carried it from central Africa to Zanzibar so it could be buried "with his
own people."*

agony along the same route Livingstone followed. Black souls. Old souls, who,
seeing through the tattered abolitionist web Livingstone had woven, now came
to use his physical body. A body that, having shed a young soul, could assume
an old soul and plead their cause in the White world where they could not go.

Ridiculous?

Maybe.

Many things are ridiculous in Africa.

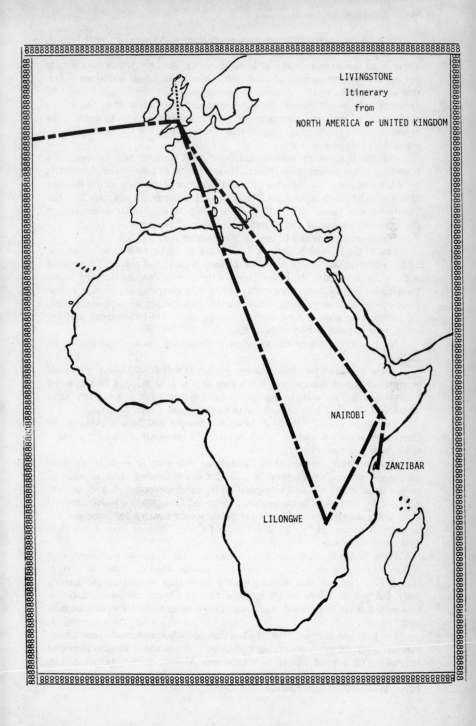

LIVINGSTONE
Itinerary
from
NORTH AMERICA or UNITED KINGDOM

NAIROBI

ZANZIBAR

LILONGWE

You be the judge after you have spent time in Africa. The most logical, scientific of us become less assured, less confident that there is no "other world." There is an indefinable energy at work in Africa. An energy that does not, in our opinion and the opinion of many other Africanists, come within the definition of the words *mystic, occult, telepathy, magic,* or *witchcraft.* It must be experienced to be recognized; having experienced the phenomenon, and having neither read of such an occurrence nor heard a satisfactory term to describe the experience, one is left to simply say that it is an energy—a phenomenon in the literal definition of that word.

Perhaps that energy commanded Susi and Chuma to take Livingstone's body back to his people. John Brown, Harriet Beecher Stowe, no single incident by Whites to prove the injustice of slavery convinced as many as did this one bloodless act by two Black men. Public feeling was emotionally roused in England, and that public ultimately used the power of the British government to put teeth into the law of 1807 banning slavery in their empire.

Why weren't Susi and Chuma at Westminster Abbey?

One of the Nairobi Society of St. Vincent de Paul committeemen—after I, as the volunteer administrator of one of their homes, had regaled the meeting with the latest antics of the beneficiaries of the society's charity (stealing sugar, complaining that meat was served only once a day, intriguing and plotting against those employed to serve them)—commented, "I know we are supposed to help the undeserving poor as well as the deserving poor, but I sometimes wish we could have just one or two of the latter."

So it is with Livingstone, the Church Missionary Society, and the Nassik Boys.

Those to whom we show charity, we hope, will reward us by virtuously being deserving of that charity. When they aren't, as in the case of Jacob and John Wainright, we usually manage to furnish them with a temporary halo, which will glow just long enough for us to save face.

Tim Jeals writes, "Because Jacob Wainwright had been a pupil at the Church Missionary Society's Nassik School, the missionaries paid his passage to England as a fund-raising exercise."

Readers deeply interested in Livingstone will want to read, as we have mentioned above, Donald Simpson's *Dark Companions,* in order to study in greater detail the events that transpired during the five-month trek back to Zanzibar led by Susi and Chuma as they transported Livingstone's body. Simpson gives many authoritative references to prime source material for dedicated Africanists to peruse. He writes that Susi and Chuma thought John Wainwright "ran away" en route.

Jacob Wainwright, being the most literate in the 70-person entourage, kept a diary as they traveled. Yet Simpson tells us that when the editor of Livingstone's *Last Journals* was working on the manuscript he did not use Jacob's diary, but instead "drew on the reminiscences of Chuma and Susi." Later he tells us that when in England, Jacob's "brash manner made a very bad impression."

The halo had dimmed. The Moslem Susi and Chuma, devoid of any Christian sacrament except baptism, were ultimately recognized as those responsible for making the funeral service in Westminster Abbey possible. They traveled, Simpson continues, to England, "at the expense of Livingstone's old friend, James Young," *after the funeral.*

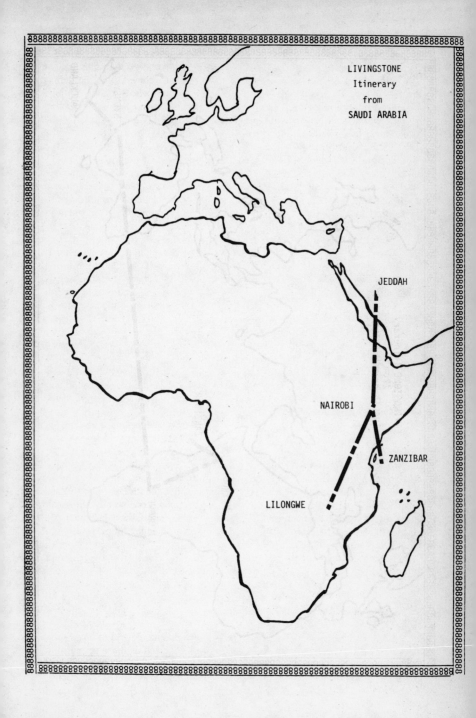

LIVINGSTONE
Itinerary
from
SAUDI ARABIA

JEDDAH

NAIROBI

ZANZIBAR

LILONGWE

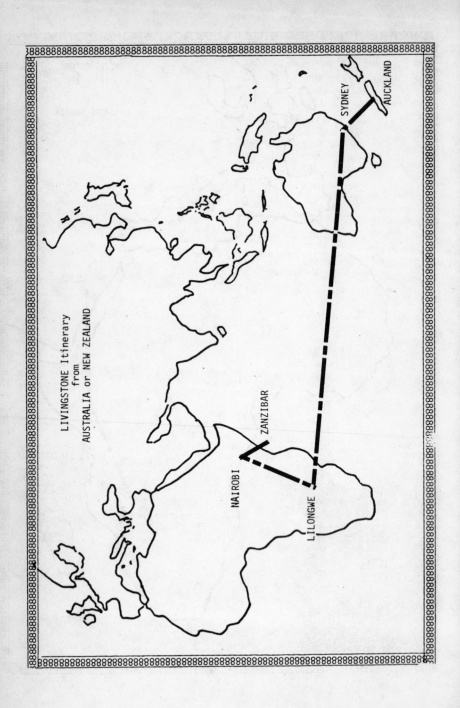

LIVINGSTONE Itinerary
from
AUSTRALIA or NEW ZEALAND

AUCKLAND

SYDNEY

ZANZIBAR

NAIROBI

LILONGWE

The itinerary we have planned includes:

England and Scotland: En route to Kenya, readers living in Canada, the U.S., or the UK may want to see the relevant Livingstone sites in Great Britain: in London, a visit to the Royal Geographical Society (located on the corner of Exhibition and Kensington roads), Westminster Abbey, where his body is buried in the nave, and Room 19 of the National Portrait Gallery (St. Martin's Place), where there is a painting of Livingstone in the Empire Overseas Collection.

You can take a night sleeper train to Scotland and visit Livingstone's home village in Blantyre (about midway between Glasgow and Edinburgh), which is now reconstructed and designated as a national monument. There is an interesting museum connected to the site and the journey is very worthwhile as a point of reference in judging Livingstone.

Readers from Australia and New Zealand may want to continue on to Great Britain for this purpose, finding that routing their itinerary with Malawi first is more economical than starting out in Kenya.

Readers in Saudi Arabia may want to see the Livingstone sites in Great Britain when they are on another trip.

Kenya: Livingstone never set foot in what is now Kenya, but for practical reasons we use Nairobi as the base to take a day trip to Zanzibar.

Tanzania: Livingstone's house is on Zanzibar Island.

Malawi: Lilongwe is the international airline destination city; visit Kusungu National Park, which Livingstone explored; Livingstone traced the Shire

Livingstone, hemorrhaging internally, was carried by Susi and Chuma for many miles during his "last journey."

River through what is now Lindowe National Park; Cape Maclear is the site of the first Universities Mission and the location that Livingstone recommended to them; and spend two days on the Lake Malawi steamer, the *Ilala II* (named for the tribe that inhabited the village, in what is now Zambia, where Livingstone died).

Zambia: only if political conditions have drastically changed from what they are as of this writing; it will be possible to take an Avis car from Lilongwe, Malawi, to Lusaka, Zambia, to visit the Livingstone Memorial erected in the village where he died. Livingstone's heart is buried under a tree near the memorial. A visit to Victoria Falls, also in Zambia near the Zimbabwe border, could form a part of the itinerary *if* political conditions change.

Return to Lilongwe, Malawi, for departure for home.

Livingstone Routing from North America

Pan American—New York-London
Taxi—London
British Railways—London-Glasgow
Avis—Glasgow-Blantyre-Glasgow
British Railways—Glasgow-London
Kenya Airways—London-Nairobi
UTC one-day tour—Nairobi-Zanzibar-Nairobi
Kenya Airways—Nairobi-Lilongwe
Avis—Land travel in Malawi
Kenya Airways—Lilongwe-London
Pan American—London-New York

An illustration of Zanzibar that appeared in H. M. Stanley's How I Found Livingstone.

Pan American can write the entire ticket (except for the UTC tour and rail journeys) and it will read New York-Lilongwe, Malawi, with a stopover in Nairobi on the outward journey.

Livingstone Routing from the United Kingdom

Kenya Airways—London-Nairobi
UTC one-day tour—Nairobi-Zanzibar-Nairobi
Kenya Airways—Nairobi-Lilongwe
Avis—Land travel in Malawi
Kenya Airways—Lilongwe-London

Livingstone Routing from Jeddah

Saudia Saudi Arabian Airlines—Jeddah-Nairobi
UTC one-day tour—Nairobi-Zanzibar-Nairobi
Kenya Airways—Nairobi-Lilongwe
Avis—Land travel in Malawi
Kenya Airways—Lilongwe-Nairobi
Saudia Saudi Arabian Airlines—Nairobi-Jeddah

Saudia can issue the ticket Jeddah-Lilongwe with a stopover on the outward flight in Nairobi.

Livingstone Routing from Australia-New Zealand

Quantas—Sydney-Harare, Zimbabwe
Kenya Airways—Harare-Nairobi
UTC one-day tour—Nairobi-Zanzibar-Nairobi
Kenya Airways—Nairobi-Lilongwe
Avis—Land travel in Malawi
Air Malawi—Lilongwe-Harare
Quantas—Harare-Sydney

The *Livingstone* Itinerary

Readers may make reservations for the entire itinerary, without charge, through Merikani Hotel Reservations Service (P.O. Box 53394, Temple Heights Station, Washington, DC 20009, tel. (USA) 301–530–1911).

Readers can plan their own itinerary for London and Blantyre; we start in Africa.

Zanzibar

Day 1: Arrive Nairobi, Kenya, and check into the Mt. Kenya Safari Club, Nairobi. This elegant hotel, whose Executive Suites (fractionally higher priced than a standard room) offer views of Mts. Kenya and Kilimanjaro off in the distance, will be a hospitable starting point for the itinerary.

Night 1 and Day 2: Recover from jet lag, confirm your reservation for the one-day trip to Zanzibar on day 3, and look through *Fielding's Literary Africa* for anything in Nairobi that might be of interest—tea on the famous Norfolk Hotel porch, lunch in the Tate Room of the New Stanley, a walk around Nairobi City Market, and perhaps dinner in the Hilton International's Amboseli Grill. All these are within a short walking distance from the Mt. Kenya Safari Club, Nairobi. Remember, however, not to walk the streets after 5:30 p.m. There are always taxis in front of the Hitlon to take you back to the club after dinner.

Ask the guest services staff at the club to confirm your reservations on the Kenya Airways flight to Lilongwe for day 4.

Day 3: Keep your room at the club, and take the one-day trip by air to Zanzibar. Livingstone's house can be seen, and although many of his original papers are in the library at Zanzibar, reportedly they have deteriorated badly because the air conditioner donated for the purpose of preserving them has broken. You will have a guide, and it's best to stay with him and not wander off.

Return to Nairobi the same day.

Night 3: Mt. Kenya Safari Club, Nairobi.

Malawi

Day 4: Check out of the club, and take a Kenatco taxi, which will be available in front of the club, to Jomo Kenyatta International Airport. Arrive in Lilongwe, which is a beautiful, well-planned capital city. It is unbelievably perfect, as an architect's model might be. Absolutely no trash or clutter. One area, known as Capital Hill, houses the various government departments in modern, new buildings separated by landscaped lawns. Zomba was the former capital of Malawi, and only since the 1980s has Lilongwe become the nation's center of government.

Kamuzu International Airport, 7 miles or 11.2 km from Lilongwe, is new, everything is squeaky clean, and the few passengers are handled in turn. No turmoil here.

The customs officers meticulously inspect every item of baggage. We noticed the passengers who were obviously Malawi residents did not allow the customs people to satisfy their curiosity as did we initiates. A certain amount of rightful indignation seems to work; when I asked the officer what he was looking for and he replied, "Pornographic materials," we then retorted, "Do we look like the kind of people who would carry such things?" etc., the suitcases were quickly chalked.

The dress code is strictly enforced. No slacks for women and girls, dress hems must cover the knees; men must have short back-and-sides haircuts; and a clean, well-groomed appearance is necessary for both men and women. Malawi is not the place for unkempt travelers.

We want to make a special point here about car hire in Malawi. There are other car hire firms, but in reading their contracts we found them even more unsatisfactory than non-Avis contracts in other countries. One-car accidents are not covered. Although there is very little traffic on Malawi's roads, many sections of roads are treacherous, made more so by the absence of vehicles for

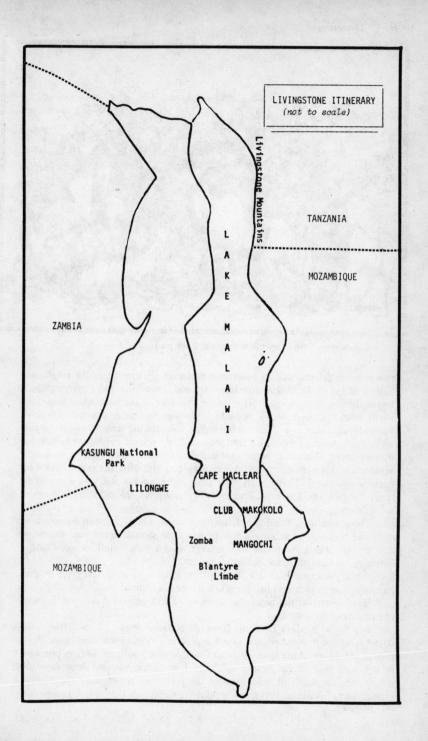

LIVINGSTONE ITINERARY
(not to scale)

TANZANIA

MOZAMBIQUE

ZAMBIA

Livingstone Mountains

L
A
K
E

M
A
L
A
W
I

KASUNGU National
Park

CAPE MACLEAR

LILONGWE

CLUB MAKOKOLO

Zomba   MANGOCHI

MOZAMBIQUE   Blantyre
Limbe

Nyala antelope, rarely seen outside of the game parks of Malawi.

many miles; drivers tend to become complacent. For instance, the single-lane Salima to Lilongwe road is a series of up and down hills; full concentration is required to be ready to pull off onto the shoulder of the road when oncoming traffic is met. It is perfectly possible to damage the car or occupants in what would be regarded as a "one-car accident." Should the renter avoid damaging a fender or bumper by crashing into the oncoming vehicle in order to be covered by insurance? There is also the problem of potholes, which can cause one-car accidents. Avis policies cover one-car accidents and offer the normal Avis insurance coverages. There is an Avis desk at the airport and your car will be ready for pick up. The drive into town is straightforward and there is no need for a driver..

Check into the Capital Hotel and have lunch. The flight from Nairobi is in the same time zone and only a few hours; there should be no need to rest or any jet lag. We drove to the city market, which was in full swing, being a Saturday, and bought some beautiful baskets.

When you come back ask that a picnic lunch with cold beverages be prepared for you to pick up after breakfast the next morning.

Have dinner at the hotel that evening. There generally is some form of entertainment on Saturdays.

Day 5: (a Sunday) Drive to Kasungu National Park, returning the same day. Livingstone visited what is now the park in 1863, approaching from Nkhotakota. He followed the trade route to Chief Mwase's village. This is just west of Kusungu town at the present village of Linngo. He traveled three days (40 miles) into the north of what is now the park. We quote from the Malawi Department of National Parks and Wildlife pamphlet, *Antiquities, Kasungu National Park:*

One of the things which impressed Livingstone most in the Kasungu district was the extent and quality of the local iron-working industry: "Here at every third or fourth village, we see a kiln-looking structure, about six feet high, by two-and-a-half or three feet in diameter. It is a clay, fire-hardened furnace, for smelting iron. No flux is used, whether the specular iron, the yellow haematite, or magnetic iron ore is fused, and yet capital metal is produced. Native manufactured iron is so good, that the natives declare English iron to be 'rotten' in comparison, and specimens of African hoes were pronounced at Birmingham to be as nearly equal to the best Swedish iron. As we passed along, men sometimes ran from the fields they were working in, and offered for sale new hoes, axes and spears of their own workmanship. It is certainly the iron age here. . . ." Livingstone's route took him at least very close to the fine example of an iron smelting furnace, ng'anjo, which is preserved beside the road to Kangwa Camp just north of the Dwangwa crossing. [Shown on the park map, which we mention below.] It is just possible that this ng'anjo is one of the ones he saw. It could be over a hundred years old, adds greatly to the value of the Swangwa ng'anjo as one of the few complete surviving examples of an ancient Malawi craft, which has been practised here since the first Iron Age people settled by the lakeshore in the 3rd century A.D.

Our map is reproduced from a national park map and a larger copy can be purchased at the park. The "Antiquities" pamphlet, which is sold for a few pennies at the park gate, traces Livingstone's probable route in the centerfold map; we have superimposed this route on the park map.

In driving to the park, the destination is Lifupa Lodge, where directions will be given on where to pick up a guide. The route is well marked.

Certainly Zaire national parks are wilder than Kasungu National Park in Malawi, but for "the real Africa" it would be hard to match Kasungu. Kasungu provides both a very natural habitat and a basic infrastructure for tourists. The game-viewing access roads are overgrown down the center because very few vehicles use them. The road was easily driven without four-wheel drive, the only misfortune to the car being that it collected tall grass on the underside, axle wheels, etc.

Elephants, smaller than Kenyan elephants, come close to the road and can be seen in small groups even during an hour-and-a-half drive. Fat, fat zebra are also near the road, not in huge herds but rather in groups of five or six.

During the dry season the game is more concentrated at the artificial waterhole near Lifupa Lodge and the many little streams that flow through the park. More game is seen in the dry season than rainy months.

We tremendously enjoyed the park, even though I personally· am of the school that once you've seen one elephant, you've seen them all. We had good company, perfect weather, a helpful guide, and as ours was the only visitors' car in the park, the safari was unique.

Night 5: Drive back to Lilongwe for another night at Capital Hotel.

Day 6: (a Monday) After breakfast, if you have been unable to obtain the maps from Travel Books Unlimited (we give full information in "Bye-the-By"), drive over to the shopping center, where the Lilongwe Office of the Survey Department will have the maps you will need to get around the country, particularly the southern lakeshore, as well as trace the route of the Shire River. Incidentally, in Malawi that river is pronounced as though there were an *i* instead of an *e* at the end of the word: *Shiri*. Look through the maps and determine which you want. We took: Malawi, scale 1:1 000 000, perfectly useless as a road map but good for overall topography; Nankmba Peninsula, which

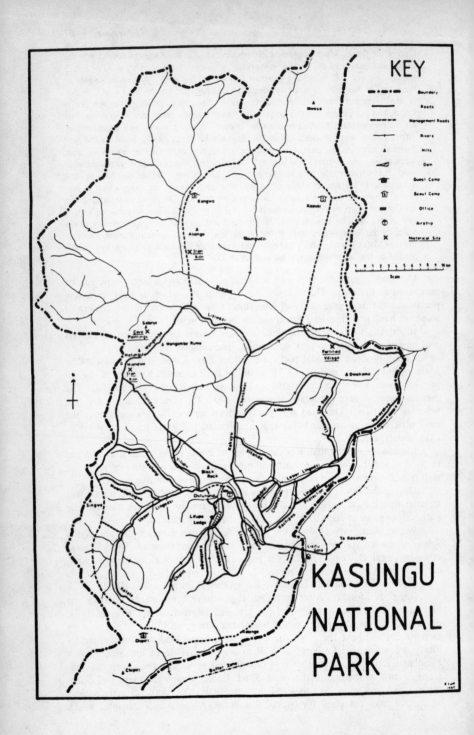

KEY

- ·—·—· Boundary
- ——— Roads
- ---- Management Roads
- ⊢⊢⊢ Rivers
- ▲ Hills
- ◁ Dam
- ⬛ Guest Camp
- 🅂 Scout Camp
- ▬ Office
- 🆁 Airstrip
- ✕ Historical Site

0 1 2 3 4 5 6 7 8 9 10 km
Scale

N

Mwasa

Kangwa

Kapuni

Alongo

Msumgudzi

✕ Iron Kiln

Dzandzu

Salonye
✕ Cave Paintings
Wangombe
△ Wangombe Ruins
Lisiwezi

Natumbe
△ Mwandwe
✕ Iron Kiln

✕ Fortified Village

△ Dwakama

Chankhosi
Limemba

Kehuru

Vitanda

Ndunkha

Black Rock

Lower Lifupa

Singwa

Upper Lifupa
Dzvfunama
🆁
Lifupa Lodge

Kachipwa

Lisitu Gate
To Kasungu

Chipri

Msongo

🅂 Chipri

△ Chipri

Buffer Zone

KASUNGU

NATIONAL

PARK

shows Cape Maclear on Sheet 1434B2; also get Nkope 1435A1 and ask if this goes over to Mangochi; if not, get Mangochi and south to include Liwonde National Park—however, a map of the park may be available at the Park and Wildlife Office (in the same complex, ask directions from the staff at the survey office); Department of Surveys 325, City of Blantyre (includes Limbe) is also helpful; and there are maps of each of the Lake Malawi port towns. The maps are reasonably priced and certainly very helpful to have along, if not always accurate roadwise.

Go back to the hotel, where the Pastry Shop should now (mid-morning) be well stocked. Buy enough to get you through the day, plus a little bit more. The Cornish pasties, meat with thinly sliced potato in a flaky pastry envelope, are delicious. Don't forget to have your Thermos filled with a soft drink from the bar; also a flask of water.

Your destination is now Club Makokolo (see "Malawian Accommodation"). The drive should take about four to five hours. Go east from Lilongwe to Salima, but before that town there will be a turning to the right. Road signs point the way to Mangochi. Twenty miles before Mangochi, the sign for Club Makokolo will be seen.

Check into the club and settle into your room. Although you may be tempted to have a swim in the lake, we advise against it. The Government of Malawi tourist literature states that Lake Malawi is the only African lake free of the disease bilharzia. We made inquiries of Catholic nursing sisters about the incidence of bilharzia in Malawi, and next to malaria, it is the second most common disease.

We also met a Britisher whose 12-year-old daughter contracted the disease from the lake. We are strongly recommending that despite what you read elsewhere, and what locals say, *do not go swimming in the lake*.

Day 7: After breakfast at Club Makokolo, drive to Mangochi. Visit the Lake Museum; although very small and poorly kept, it has several publications that will make the itinerary more interesting. They are: *Cape Maclear* by P. A. Cole-King, 1982, describes the missionary settlement, Livingstone's contacts with Cape Maclear, and continues the history up to 1950. *Mangochi: The Mountain, the People and the Fort* by P. A. Cole-King, 1982, discusses Livingstone in the Mangochi district and has interesting accounts about the British fort built near Mangochi town; *Lilongwe: A Historical Study* by P. A. Cole-King, 1971, describes Livingstone's diary entries when crossing the Lilongwe Plateau and later colonial administration of the district; *The Nkhotakota Lake Shore and Marginal Areas, Malawi: An Archeological Reconnaissance* by K. R. Robinson, 1979, contains interesting text concerning the settlement of ancient potters at Nkope (near Nkopola, which is immediately next door to Club Makokolo).

Drive back to the club and spend the remainder of the day reading the booklets and relaxing.

Night 7: Club Makokolo.

Day 8: (a Wednesday) If you brought food from home (see "Plan Ahead"), take it and a Thermos and water flask with you to the Lindowe National Park. Otherwise, you can ask the chef at Club Makokolo to prepare sandwiches and a picnic lunch. Although there are local cafes, we don't recommend them. Retrace the drive to Mangochi that you took yesterday. Take the turn to the south to the town of Lindowe. Follow the signs to Lindowe National Park.

The Lechwe waterbuck, not found in Africa north of Malawi, spend much of the time submerged in water. They presently inhabit Liwonde National Park along the banks and tributaries of the Shire River.

Following the Shire River by road in other parts of Malawi is almost impossible, although it is crossed several times by black-topped roads. Lindowe National Park abuts the eastern bank of the Shire just south of Lake Malombe. During the rainy season, access is only by boat; and in order to see the most animals in the river, the dry season is, naturally, the best time to make a visit.

Leave the park before 4 p.m., because you'll want to be back before dark. We drove at night and had no problems, but if a breakdown had happened along the long stretches of sparsely populated road, it would have been impossible to get assistance. Help from other motorists is much more difficult at night, and traffic is extremely light on Malawian roads.

It is possible to stay overnight in the park, but there is a problem about the *Ilala II* steamer; it can only be loaded at the southernmost port of Chipoka on a Friday afternoon. If you have plenty of time, and can wait another week, spending the time at the southern lakeshore, then, by all means stay a few days in Lindowe National Park. Information about accommodation in the park is in "Malawian Accommodation."

Night 8: Club Makokolo.

Day 9: (Thursday) If you have read the booklets purchased the day before at the Lake Museum, a visit to Cape Maclear will be more interesting. There are two ways to visit the old mission and the graves of the missionaries. One is to drive. The road is terrible—dirt, with large outcrops of boulders. Please refer to "Cape Maclear" under "Additional Notes on Malawi" at the end of this itinerary, in which the route is described in detail. It can be driven and we did it, but quite frankly, I was so furious by the time we got to the site that I didn't

Dr. Robert Laws of the United Presbyterian Church, who, with the help of his wife, devoted his life to leading the Free Church Livingstonia mission.

enjoy it. Much more enjoyable and more true to the Livingstone experience, although more expensive, is to rent the power boat from Club Makokolo and go around by water. It is a beautiful trip and the true feeling of what Livingstone and the missionaries experienced can best be appreciated by boat.

Night 9: Return to Club Makololo for a final night.

Day and Night 10: Board the *Ilala II*. Night on board. By now you will know your way around the southern shore of the lake and, using the map, can drive to the port of Chipoka.

The Lake Malawi steamer: Two steamers are in service on Lake Malawi, the *Ilala II* and the *Chaucy Maples. Avoid* the latter; it is smaller, antiquated, and vibrates from bow to stern like a brass band. The *Ilala II* is of decent size, and cabin class is comfortable. The six cabins have both single and double berths. There is plenty of deck space to move about and a top deck from which there are unobstructed views of the lake. There is a dining room that serves three meals, tea, and snacks, but the discriminating traveler is advised to bring along a few survival foods as well as bottled water. There is plenty of Coke and Fanta on board and a reasonably priced, adequately stocked bar.

The engine room is midships, and while the diesel-powered engines perform under totally uninsulated conditions, cabin class is far enough away to

An old sketch of the Ilala I; *the* Ilala II, *which now operates on Lake Malawi, is a power steamer.*

deaden the sound somewhat. Third class would be hell: The saloon benches are upholstered after a fashion, but the majority of the seating space comprises metal benches welded to the metal floor above the engine room.

One car or at the most two can be carried on board, and these are parked at *Ilala*'s bow. It is possible to buy a third-class ticket and sleep in the car.

Keep in mind there were actually three Livingstonia Mission sites: first at Cape Maclear, second at Bandawe, and the third where the town of Livingstonia is now.

This is where a choice must be made as to how long a voyage is to be taken on the *Ilala II* and how many mission sites are to be visited. Studying the schedule of the *Ilala II* will help to make those decisions, remembering that not all ports have facilities for disembarking the car.

Whatever you decide, once disembarked drive back to Lilongwe and return the car, then spend your last night at the Capital Hotel before departing for home. The car can, of course, be left at the airport.

Additional notes on Malawi:

Blantyre is the commercial capital of Malawi high up in a misty, oftentimes rainy, climate. The city is comparatively small and has only a few multi-storied buildings. It's pleasant enough, but there is little of interest outside of the National Museum and the original church built by the Reverend D. C. Scott and a group of local workmen between 1888 and 1891. Neither Scott nor his workers were professional architects, and it is interesting to see how they mixed and matched several architectural styles. Unfortunately, the present congregation has seen fit to paint the lovely old weathered brick interior with vinyl paint

Early missionaries in Malawi trading cloth for food. (From Story of the Universities Mission, *Rev. H. Rowley.)*

(please God, don't let them get enough money to paint the exterior) and the cupola is a vibrant cobalt blue. The old hardwood carvings have received a coat of sticky-never-dry shellac. We hurried away before the good reverend could rise from his grave and bring his wrath down on any and all who were near the unintentional desecration of his most beautiful effort.

Limbe is the sister city of Blantyre, and is small also. It was the center for the tobacco and tea auctions during the colonial period. Some still take place, but not on the pre-independence scale.

We enjoyed visiting the workshop for the handicapped in Limbe, where Malawi-grown cotton is woven into table mats and tapestries. These are available at one of the gift shops in the Capital Hotel, and prices there are the same as in the showrooms at the workshops. Ask directions to the handicapped workshops from the Avis staff in Blantyre.

Cape Maclear: Leaving the blacktop road at the place indicated by a sign reading "To Cape Maclear," there follows a road that has not seen a grader's blade for some five years. The day we drove it two Caterpiller graders and a highway roller were parked at the junction. Their drivers were supposedly working on the shoulders of the main tarmacked road, but had succeeded in shoring up earth and mud onto the road surface instead of the shoulders. Admittedly, two days later when we drove back it looked quite good and the dirt was off the tarmac. Just a strange way of operating earthmoving equipment.

This access road to Cape Maclear has been a bone of contention between those who would preserve the site of the first Universities Mission and the colonial—and now independent—government of Malawi for some 50 years. The problem is spelled out in the little booklet you can purchase from the Man-

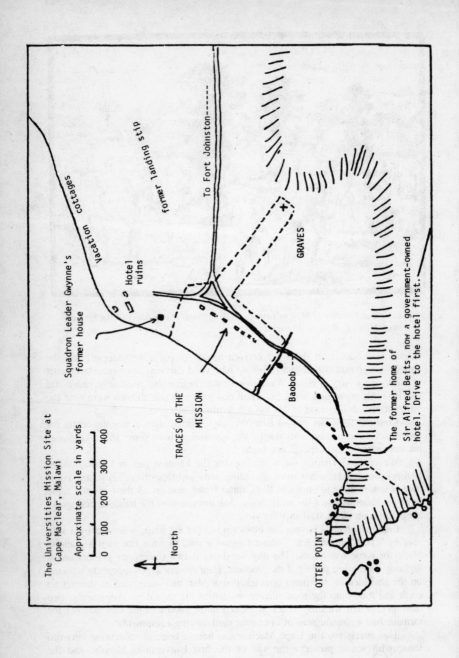

The Universities Mission Site at
Cape Maclear, Malawi

Approximate scale in yards

0   100   200   300   400

North

Squadron Leader Gwynne's
former house

Vacation cottages

Hotel
ruins

former landing strip

To Fort Johnston -----

TRACES OF THE
MISSION

Baobob

GRAVES

The former home of
Sir Alfred Belts, now a government-owned
hotel. Drive to the hotel first.

OTTER POINT

gochi Museum entitled *Cape Maclear*. There seems little point in complaining about it, and after you've successfully driven through the high grass, rocks, and mud—always bearing to the left—go down to the hotel and then use the sketch map to work your way back to the graves and old mission site.

However, we are recommending that visitors spare themselves the frustration of maneuvering the land approach to the graves and instead hire the *Sunbird* power boat from Club Makokolo to make the trip by water.

Livingstone's Other Explorations

Livingstone traveled widely throughout southern and eastern Africa—not simply in Malawi. Unfortunately, much of the territory he covered is impractical to visit today. His last expedition, passing along the Ruvuma River, which forms the boundary between present-day Tanzania and Mozambique, could, we understand, only be done as he did it—on foot. A friend of ours traveled from northern to southern Tanzania by bicycle, along the shores of Lake Tanganyika, and was stripped of all he possessed by the local people. The Livingstone Mountains on the Mozambican shore can be seen from the *Ilala II* steamer.

South Africa, where Livingstone first started his missionary work, is politically unstable, and while Botswana may in itself be travelworthy, the country is like a mouse between fighting bears—South Africa versus Zambia and Zimbabwe.

We had very much wanted to include in the *Livingstone* itinerary a visit to Ujiji, Tanzania, where Stanley found Livingstone, and Tabora, the Arab trading station. Wise counsel has prevailed because of the virulent strain of malaria prevalent particularly in that part of the country.

Malawi, unlike other African countries, has maintained diplomatic relations with South Africa since her independence. Her neighbors, who do not officially have such relations, are heavily dependent on South Africa for access to ports, rail, and employment of their nationals in South African industries and mines. Hopefully, Malawi will be able to maintain her neutrality.

PLAN AHEAD: Hotel, airline, Avis, rail, steamer, UTC tours, and overlanding reservations can be made, without charge, through Merikani Hotel Reservations Service. Nor do they charge for obtaining visas; they only charge for the actual cost of the visa plus registered, return-receipt postage, if hotel reservations are made through them. They will also send along the recommended maps with the confirmation of your reservations. These are charged at the price on the maps. They offer these services to all our readers, irrespective of where they live. Their address is P.O. Box 53394, Temple Heights Station, Washington, DC 20009, tel. (USA) 301–530–1911. However, we have provided all the necessary information for you to make your own reservations.

The following needs to be done before departure: Check the "Basic Information Checklist" in the "Background Information" section for necessary travel documents; make hotel reservations—numbers and addresses are given in the headings preceding the hotel descriptions; make airline reservations for international flights using the routings we suggest at the beginning of the itinerary; reserve an Avis car where needed; purchase SOS Insurance (see "Travel Documents"); purchase traveler's checks; write, but do not send money, to reserve a place on the *Ilala II* steamer (details in "Transportation"); write to UTC (United Touring Company, P.O. Box 42196, Nairobi, Kenya) for the day trip to Zanzibar.

Think about what you're going to wear, keeping in mind Malawi's dress code. We suggest only 100% cotton garments, but apart from that suggestion, Malawi and Kenya require nothing out of the ordinary. In neither country do people "dress" for dinner.

Malawi is full of good bargains and you're going to want plenty of space to carry home souvenirs. Taking food to Malawi, therefore, is not going to be a hardship. Once the food is consumed there'll be room for the bargains. You'll need enough for lunch and a snack while game viewing along the Shire River in Lindowe National Park, and for the days spent on the *Ilala II* steamer. Crackers, to substitute for bread, peanut butter can be a good choice for Americans and Canadians, and for Britishers, Australians, and New Zealanders, crackers and some of their very excellent local cheeses that don't require refrigeration, such as cheddars. Pudding packs, canned pate, little sausages—plan out a menu for the days you'll be picnicking.

Start taking malaria tablets two weeks before your intended departure. Taking along dehydration salts will be a good safeguard if the itinerary is done during Malawi's dry season. (Gatorade crystals are flavored dehydration salts.)

We wished we had a few lengths of mosquito netting to put over the Avis car windows in Kasungu National Park to keep out the tsetse flies. It would be worthwhile to try old-fashioned coils of sticky fly paper in this situation, hanging them with safety pins from the car's interior roof. The cars are not air conditioned and it's not practical to keep the windows closed, although this is what we did since we were not prepared.

Clothes are very expensive in Malawi and if you have a few items in good condition that you normally would be giving to a local charity, run them over with an iron and take them with you. The very conscientious Malawians who clean your hotel rooms will appreciate such clothing—for themselves or their familes—more than cash. Just ensure when it comes time to leave that the person who has been caring for you is the one to receive your gift by giving it to him/her in person—not simply leaving it with a note in the room. The standard of living in Kenya is considerably higher than in Malawi, and we do not suggest this as remuneration for Kenyan housekeeping staffs.

Plain, boiled hard candy (sweets) will be nice to have to give to the children in rural areas.

Take plenty of film, more than you think you'll need, a telescopic lens for the camera, and, although Malawi does not present extreme climatic conditions, the camera should be protected using ordinary safeguards. In Zanzibar keep it on your person at all times.

Obtain your maps from the Survey Office in Malawi when you arrive, or prior to departure from Travel Books Unlimited (see "Bye-the-By").

Once in Africa, reconfirm flight reservations 24 hours ahead of scheduled departures; pay for your steamer ticket when you pick it up at Chipoka.

Accommodation recommended for the *Livingstone* itinerary: *London*—Hilton International at Kensington (near the Royal Geographical Society); *Edinburgh*—Caledonian Hotel; *Nairobi*—Mt. Kenya Safari Club, Nairobi; *Lilongwe*—Capital Hotel; at the lakeshore—Club Makokolo; *Ilala II* steamer; Nkhata Bay Rest House; Mzuzu Hotel.

Estimated Budget

Livingstone Itinerary

Kenya portion (3 nights)
Does not include airfare to Lilongwe, Malawi via Nairobi, Kenya

	US$	
	1 person	2 people
Arrive Nairobi: taxi to hotel	$ 15	$ 15
Mt. Kenya Safari Club, Nairobi, Executive suite, $132, single, $148 double × 3	396	444
Meals: breakfast $6, lunch in the Tate Room of the New Stanley Hotel $10, dinner in Club $15, high tea at the Norfolk Hotel $7; other meals; $6 breakfast, lunch $8, dinner in the Amboseli Grill of Hilton $15, picnic lunch to take to Zanzibar $7, and additional dinner $15 and breakfast $6	95	190
Taxis around Nairobi, $3 a trip in the city center, 4 trips	12	12
One-day tour to Zanzibar, $150 + $50 for Tanzanian government tour guide (airfare is included)	200	400
Taxi to airport	15	15
Departure tax	10	20
Total:	$ 743	$1096
Cost per person sharing:	548	

Malawi portion (12 nights)
Arrive Lilongwe: Avis agent meets flight

Avis car, unlimited mileage, full insurance, 12 days (Nissan Class B)	416	416
Gas (petrol) 1600 km divided by 40 km per gallon × $5 a gallon. Price is pre the drop in oil prices	200	200
Capital Hotel, Lilongwe, $84 single, $94 double, includes breakfast, 2 nights	168	188
Meals: dinner evening of arrival $12, picnic lunch prepared by Capital Hotel chef $6, dinner Sunday evening $12	30	60
Entrance fee to Kasungu National Park	5	10
Tip to park guide	5	5
Capital Hotel pastry shop purchases Monday morning	10	20
Maps, if not purchased from Travel Books Unlimited	20	20
Club Makokolo, 4 nights, $35 single, $44 double, includes breakfast	140	176
Meals: lunch $7, dinner $10 = $17 × 4 days	68	136
Entrance fee to Lindowe National Park	5	10

	US$	
	1 person	2 people
Allow $150 for boat (any number of persons) if visiting park during rainy season	150	150
Charter boat from Club Makokolo and return	135	135
Embark on the *Ilala II* steamer at Chipoka. Note: Consult the *Ilala II* steamer timetable in "Transportation" to determine how many days you wish to stay on board the steamer and at which port you wish to disembark, remembering that only certain ports disembark cars. (These are noted on the timetable.) After making this determination, a more exact figure can be entered in the budget. We are assuming disembarkation will be at Nkhata Bay primarily because we have failed to identify overnight accommodation at Chilumba and the time of arrival is nightfall.		
Fare in the first-class cabins: Chipoka to Nkhata Bay	55	110
Charge for car	100	100
Bar purchases (meals will be picnic foods brought from home or purchased in Kenya)	25	50
Nkhata Bay Rest House, overnight	12	24
Meals: still using picnic foods		
Drive to Mzuzu: check into hotel; drive on to Livingstonia, have lunch there; Mzuzu Hotel, $62 single, $73 double, includes breakfast	62	73
Return to Mzuzu Hotel for dinner	8	16
Drive to Lilongwe and check into Capital Hotel, $84 single, $94 double, includes breakfast	84	94
Meals: lunch $7, dinner $8	15	30
Return Avis at airport		
Departure tax	6	12
To waiters/waitresses 15% on all meals (Kenya and Malawi)	48.15	96.30
Gratuity to housekeeping staff, $1 a night for 1 or 2 persons	15	15
Tips to porters/bellmen/steamer stewards	30	30
SOS Insurance, $15 a week or $45 a month per person	30	30
Grand total:	$1813.15	$2148.30
Cost per person sharing:	$1074.15	

Livingstone Paupers

Malawi portion (10 days)
Does not include airfare to Lilongwe, Malawi

	US$	
	1 person	2 people
Arrive Lilongwe: taxi into town	$ 15	$ 15
overnight, Capital Hotel, $84 single, $94 double, includes breakfast	84	94

	US$	
	1 person	2 people
Meals: dinner evening of arrival $12, pastries and meat pies purchased from hotel shop to eat on train and while waiting to board steamer $10	22	44
Taxi to station	5	5
Train fare to Chipoka, single fare	9	18
Steamer fare Chipoka to Chilumba, return (6 nights on board)	61	122
Allow for soft drinks (and alcoholic drinks) at steamer's bar	40	80
Meals: food brought from home		
Spending money at each port	50	100
Disembark at Chipoka: take train to Blantyre	9	18
Taxi in Blantyre to hotel in Limbe	5	10
Shire Highlands Hotel, 2 nights, $40 single, and $50 double, includes breakfast	80	100
Meals: dinner evening of arrival $9, lunch $6 for following two days, and dinner second day	30	60
Taxis around town to see cathedral, museum, etc.	20	20
Return to Lilongwe on luxury bus	8	16
Overnight Capital Hotel, includes breakfast	84	94
Dinner evening of arrival from Blantyre-Limbe $12	12	24
Taxi to airport	15	15
15% tips to waiters/waitresses on meals	9.60	19.20
Tips to bellmen/porters/steamer crew	10	10
Gratuity to housekeeping staff and cabin steward	10	10
Departure tax	6	12
SOS Insurance, $15 a week	30	60
Total:	$614.60	$946.20
Cost per person sharing:	$473.10	

THE MAZE:
The White Nile

by
Alan Moorehead

Hamish Hamilton,
London
1960

The White Nile was our primer.

In 1970 we knew nothing of Africa. Alan Moorehead opened the door. What a magnificent beginning!

When I volunteered to go to Africa as an agriculture teacher, we were given three choices of countries: Kenya, Ethiopia, or Uganda. Kenya was too colonial British for me. (How we change!) Moorehead had written only slightly of Ethiopia; we had yet to read *The Blue Nile.* Uganda, because of what I had read in *The White Nile,* seemed more for us.

I totally failed to connect with Uganda the reports heard on the BBC that some African general had overthrown some African president. It wasn't until I started teaching (which was the day after we got off the plane) that the penny dropped: Uganda was that African country; the general was Idi Amin Dada; the president was Milton Obote.

Like so many other would-be benefactors, Amin had the right idea in the beginning. Obote is and was an absolute louse. Obote, upon his return to Uganda with the help of Julius Nyerre of Tanzania, got away with things the international media would have had—and did have—a field day over with Amin.

But we were not to know this then, and I am straying from Moorehead and *The White Nile.*

But not really; parts of Uganda, Sudan, and Tanzania are far more dangerous to local and visitor alike today than they were 100 years ago when Moorehead writes of them. Following the sequence of the text in the preface of *The White Nile,* here is a short review of today's conditions in the countries named:

Tanzania today is a Mickey Mouse country, made that way because its citizenry have been worked over a scrub board of administrative systems in the past 100 years. Up until 1985 Julius Nyerre had been president since independence. He was dedicated to creating a social Utopia, having been influenced by the British Labour Party, which was in office when he went to college in the United Kingdom. He has failed miserably.

Earlier, at the beginning of the 19th century, the Arabs opened up the mainland from Zanzibar island; at the Treaty of Berlin in 1886 the Germans were given Tanganyika (the mainland of Tanzania—see below). Their rule lasted until 1945 when, after Germany's defeat, the British were given control. They started some really hair-brain development schemes (for instance, the famous Groundnut Scheme), and, as mentioned, when they gave the country over for independence, Nyerre embarked on, and enforced, national socialism. (He held more than 10,000 political prisoners up to 1979—so much for brotherly love.)

Socialist welfare policies must be financed by taxation and in those countries that can provide tax dollars for social welfare programs, the theory works. There's nothing wrong with the concept, only something wrong with the econ-

Sir Samuel and Lady Baker, the subjects of Richard Hall's Lovers on the Nile
(see "Annotated Bibliography" "Bye-the-By").

omists who implement socialist programs in poor countries. Of course, it's a Catch 22—the poorer the country, the more welfare programs are needed. Money must come from somewhere, and in the case of Tanzania, Julius Nyerre decided to use donations and grants from capitalist economic systems to finance socialism. Unfortunately, donors grow tired and now 25 years after the experiment, financing is drying up. There are severe shortages of even the most commonplace commodities today in Tanzania. The economy is in a shambles, not because donors have signed-off, but because Tanzanians are like most other human beings and want commensurate reward for their labor. Commensurate meaning that if they work harder than their neighbor they expect to get more than their neighbor by way of financial reward. Agriculture has been especially hard hit in Tanzania as farmers were denied, by the socialist projects, from market prices.

Tanzania is not a nice place for tourists despite government-paid advertising to the contrary. A generation of shortages has made for social unrest. Tour operators advertize itineraries that include Tanzania, but we suggest only a one-day trip and strongly urge that a trip to Tanzania be postponed until conditions are better.

Zanzibar was a sultanate, the cradle of Swahili culture, rich from the export of cloves. The island became an independent republic in 1964. Socialist Tanganykan leaders could not tolerate flourishing capitalism on their doorstep. (Kenya was irksome enough.) So they took the island, fabricated the word *Tanzan-i-a*, and installed officials from the mainland and secret police instead of islanders to govern.

The Zanzabaris have conducted a Gandhi-type passive resistance; the clove trees are untended; the island is bankrupt. The Zanzabaris have refused to subsidize Tanganyika. In 1985 the mainland government threw in the towel and now allows business on the island to function as it will—without their control. This jesture appears to have come too late to stimulate a quick turn-around either economically or socially, and Zanzibar island remains in a shambles.

Tanzanian radio broadcasts propaganda to the Comoro Islands and the Seychelles, hoping to form an Indian Ocean socialist archipelago.

Good news for both Tanzania and Zanzibar came in December 1984 with the announcement that Julius Nyerre planned to step down as president. He had made such announcements before, but his potential successor met with an automobile accident. The announcement in December was caged with wording that there are many able men capable of succeeding Julius. However, although a new president was installed, Nyerre has kept control of the country's only political party.

Uganda is the next country discussed in the preface. Leah has maintained for several years that in the years to come Uganda and Nigeria, two countries that have undergone the most damaging political upheavals since their independence, will be the leaders of Africa. Education has played a prominent role in both countries. Like the Welsh and Scots, every Nigerian and Ugandan family sacrifices to produce at least one professional. Coupled with this is the fact that both Nigeria and Uganda are rich in natural resources. If the political problems can be overcome, which they surely will be, there will be a large cadre of dedicated, educated citizenry to develop the resources.

Yoweri Museveni and a ragtag army of countrymen and women who had nothing to lose—things couldn't get much worse—forced Milton Obote from Uganda. The June 1986 issue of *New African* magazine reported that the people under his leadership are demanding, by walkouts and strikes, the removal of corrupt executives in parasitical (the name used for government-owned industries) enterprises. Such spontaneous (as opposed to union-backed) action on the part of average workers is almost unheard of in Africa. President Museveni responded by removing such executives from office. Action at the community level by people who refuse to be intimidated could ultimately lead to New England–style town hall democracy.

Although the Ugandan civil service has continued to function, and function well, throughout the past years of political trauma, readers must realize that it is going to be some time before the entire country is brought under control. The police, although dedicated to law and order, are often helpless to enforce it because so many weapons are still in the hands of the populace. Not even church leaders have authoritative voices. During the years of Amin and Obote, some people settled their scores without recourse to the legal system. These types of "paybacks" filtered down to the most personal level: If you owed me money, and I pressed you to pay, my mother or sister was found murdered. This is the real damage that has been done to the Ugandan people. They have been exposed to massive, massive brutalities from those who ruled them; and many times they employed brutalities to survive.

In the acknowledgments in *Fielding's African Safaris* I cited the encouragement given me by Professor Walter K. Hanak. I can remember submitting a paper to him in our class of Research Techniques in History in which I outlined the British colonial interest in Uganda, i.e., so they could control the headwaters of the Nile. Who controls the Nile, controls Egypt is a time-worn axiom. Who controls Egypt, controls Suez and the passage to India is the second part of that axiom. The old British strategists used to say Suez, Aden, and Afghanistan are the three key areas in containing Russian ambitions. It is with cynical amusement that those old boys remark that in the age of atomic warfare Egypt was iffy for a number of years, and Aden and Afghanistan have gone under, while they were capable of holding these vital points with foot soldiers. Diverting the Nile's waters by military attack remains a possibility; a possibility that could wreck havoc on almost one-quarter of the African peoples.

President Reagan's raid on Libya was not unconnected with Libyan involvement in Sudan today or with the old strategists' axioms.

In the past 70 years Christian missionaries have evangelized southern Sudan and turned many of the people away from paganism. This has been a problem in uniting the country with the Moslem north. Why the British made Sudan one country instead of two can only be explained by their concern to keep the River Nile consolidated.

Many present-day strategists, as is evidenced by the take-over of Aden and Afghanistan, believe in the old axioms. Egypt had been first on the list at the dawn of the cold war, and Egypt came under communist domination. The strategists on our side were frightened for a while—Anthony Eden was so frightened that British forces, egged on by the French, invaded Egypt. Egypt is again her own master, but the threat comes now from Moslem fundamentalists and anti-Zionists.

The president of Sudan, who has now been overthrown (we were in Khartoum three weeks before that event), was a Moslem and attempted to impose Moslem fundamentalist law on southern Sudan. Communist Ethiopia, to the east, has given sustenance and comfort to the southern guerrilla movement;

Libya has given military aid to northern Sudan to repress the guerrillas. Missionaries, oil exploration workers, and donor aid staff have been caught in the crossfire; at one time or another each group has had hostages taken by southern guerrillas, hoping to bring world attention to their cause. Although they attempt to stay neutral, Uganda and Kenya seem sympathetic to the southerners. Those world powers who are against Libya are also with the southerners. Necessity makes strange bedfellows.

At this writing we are not encouraging you to try to make the journey from Khartoum to Juba. Officially, travel is prohibited, but we have known cases where travelers got through. Apart from the danger of being taken hostage, there is the almost total lack of medical services. Even in more tranquil times this is true—there are, apart from missionary clinics, no valid hospital services in the south. When it was possible to fly a patient to Nairobi in a few hours this was not the disaster it might have been. Now, such flights are becoming impossible.

Another consideration is that while President Museveni and the local people of Uganda have been fairly successful in clearing Obote's and Amin's remnant armies out of the Kampala and Jinja areas, the same is not true in the north of the country. These soldiers know they have no future and are desperate. Many of them are armed. They travel back and forth between southern Sudan and northern Uganda.

Napoleon's ambition to bring order and cleanliness out of the chaos that is Egypt remains unattained 200 years after he ordered Carienes to sweep their homes.

"The government tells us in the year 2000 everything will come right," our taxi driver told us.

The antiquities in the National Museum are enclosed in finger-smudged glass cases, many have no descriptive legend, most have dust accumulated on their surfaces. A few of these pieces were shown at the National Gallery of Art in Washington several years ago. There they looked magnificent—cleaned, dramatically lit, each piece cherished. Who knows what happens to the $3 entrance fee charged the thousands of tourists who visit the National Museum of Egypt. Certainly it is not spent entirely on the museum.

Embittering to the tourist is the two-tier system of pricing: one price for locals, another several times greater for tourists—their honored guests.

Money problems in Egypt start at the airport, where we were compelled to exchange a minimum amount of money into Egyptian currency at an artificially low rate of exchange. The regulations governing foreign exchange change like the wind, and we will not go into detail because within six weeks of our visit, the regulations had changed again.

Go to Egypt forewarned, and go with money and a generous heart. Put your credit cards away and don't use them; the Egyptian pound price of an item becomes one-third more when it appears on your monthly statement because of Egyptian currency control.

Conditions—not the currency conditions but the atmosphere and tourist travel—get better after Aswan.

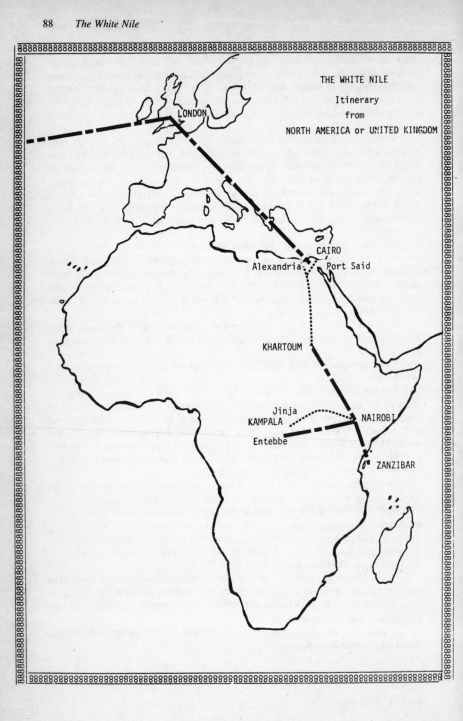

THE WHITE NILE

Itinerary

from

NORTH AMERICA or UNITED KINGDOM

LONDON

CAIRO
Alexandria   Port Said

KHARTOUM

Jinja
KAMPALA   NAIROBI
Entebbe

ZANZIBAR

White Nile Routing from North America

Pan American/Air Canada—New York/Montreal-London
Taxi—visiting Gordon sites in London

White Nile Routing from the United Kingdom

Kenya Airways—London-Cairo
Egyptian Railways—Cairo-Alexandria-Cairo
Egyptian Railways—Cairo-Port Said-Cairo
Egyptian Railways—Cairo-Aswan
Taxi—Aswan-El Sadd el Ali
Lake Nasser steamer—El Sadd el Ali-Wadi Halfa
Sudan Railways—Wadi Halfa-Khartoum
Kenya Airways—Khartoum-Nairobi
Kenya Airways—Nairobi-Entebbe
Airline bus—Entebbe-Kampala
Taxi—Kampala-Kabaka's Tomb, etc.
Airline bus—Kampala-Entebbe
Kenya Airways—Entebbe-Nairobi-London
Pan American—London-New York

Alternate:
Kenya Railways—Nairobi-Jinja-Kampala
Taxi—Kampala-Kabaka's Tomb, etc.
Airline bus—Kampala-Entebbe
Kenya Airways—Entebbe-Nairobi-London
Pan American—London-New York

The Pan American ticket will read New York-Entebbe with a stopover in Cairo on the outward journey and, if desired, a stopover in Nairobi on the return journey. It may be cheaper to forfeit the use of the Cairo-Khartoum ticket to gain the benefit of a return fare New York-Entebbe.

White Nile Routing from Jeddah

Saudia Saudi Arabian Airlines—Jeddah-Cairo
Egyptian Railways—Cairo-Alexandria-Cairo
Egyptian Railways—Cairo-Port Said-Cairo
Egyptian Railways—Cairo-Aswan
Taxi—Aswan-El Sadd el Ali
Lake Nasser steamer—El Sadd el Ali-Wadi Halfa
Sudan Railways—Wadi Halfa-Khartoum
Kenya Airways—Khartoum-Nairobi
Kenya Airways—Nairobi-Entebbe
Airline bus—Entebbe-Kampala
Taxi—Kampala-Kabaka's Tomb, etc.
Airline bus—Kampala-Entebbe
Kenya Airways—Entebbe-Nairobi
Saudia Saudi Arabian Airlines—Nairobi-Jeddah

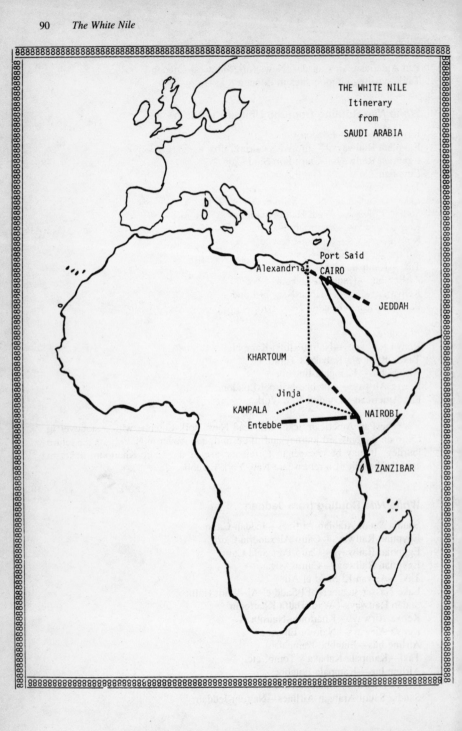

THE WHITE NILE
Itinerary
from
SAUDI ARABIA

Port Said
Alexandria   CAIRO
JEDDAH

KHARTOUM

Jinja
KAMPALA   NAIROBI
Entebbe

ZANZIBAR

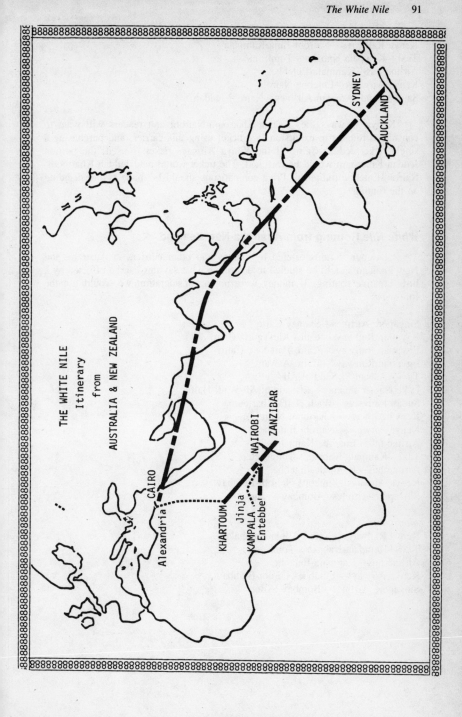

THE WHITE NILE
Itinerary
from
AUSTRALIA & NEW ZEALAND

Alternate:
Kenya Railways—Nairobi-Jinja-Kampala
Taxi—Kampala-Kabaka's Tomb, etc.
Airline bus—Kampala-Entebbe
Kenya Airways—Entebbe-Nairobi
Saudia Saudi Arabian Airlines—Nairobi-Jeddah

Kenya Airways flies Jeddah-Khartoum-Nairobi and readers will want to consider a round-trip excursion fare ticket using this carrier, and purchasing a single ticket Jeddah-Cairo. If the Kenya Airways ticket is used, the portion Jeddah-Khartoum would be forfeited. The ticket would read Jeddah-Khartoum-Nairobi-Entebbe roundtrip. Price comparisons should be made before deciding on the routing.

White Nile Routing from Australia-New Zealand

"Discount" fares offered by Qantas and other carriers in Australia and New Zealand should be studied to determine what savings can be effected by a little creative routing. If money were not a consideration we would use the following:

Singapore Airlines—Sydney-Cairo
Egyptian Railways—Cairo-Alexandria-Cairo
Egyptian Railways—Cairo-Port Said-Cairo
Egyptian Railways—Cairo-Aswan
Taxi—Aswan-El Sadd el Ali
Lake Nasser steamer—El Sadd el Ali-Wadi Halfa
Sudan Railways—Wadi Halfa-Khartoum
Kenya Airways—Khartoum-Nairobi
Kenya Airways—Nairobi-Entebbe
Airline bus—Entebbe-Kampala
Taxi—Kampala-Kabaka's Tomb, etc.
Airline bus—Kampala-Entebbe
Kenya Airways—Entebbe-Nairobi-Bombay
Singapore Airlines—Bombay-Sydney

Alternate:
Kenya Railways—Nairobi-Jinja-Kampala
Taxi—Kampala-Kabaka's Tomb, etc.
Airline bus—Kampala-Entebbe
Kenya Airways—Entebbe-Nairobi-Bombay
Singapore Airlines—Bombay-Sydney

The White Nile Itinerary

The itinerary covers London (England), Cairo, Alexandria (because we were interested in the locals mentioned in Alan Moorehead's *The Blue Nile*, and assume readers will be equally interested), Cairo-Port Said-Cairo, Aswan, (Egypt), Wadi Halfa and Khartoum (Sudan), Nairobi (Kenya), a one-day trip to Zanzibar (Tanzania), and Kampala and Jinja (Uganda).

Reservations for as much of the itinerary as possible may be made, without charge, through Merikani Hotel Reservations Service, Inc. (P.O. Box 53394, Temple Heights Station, Washington, DC 20009). Merikani will obtain the necessary visas for the price of the visas, there is no service charge. Whether through Merikani or not, obtain a visa for Sudan before leaving home.

We recommend this itinerary be done only during the months of January, February, or March. At other times of the year, the heat and flies could make travel along this route miserable.

In order to follow the itinerary several maps are necessary. Unfortunately, we could find no one map that included all the towns and villages discussed in Moorehead's books: Michelin 154 (Africa North East), Carta's Map of Egypt, and Clyde Leisure Map of Egypt & Cairo, together have all of the places he names. Try to obtain them from Forsyth Travel Library (P.O. Box 2975, Shawnee Mission, KS 66201, or call them toll free 800–FORSYTH).

Gordon went across Europe by train and then took a ship to Port Said. It is possible today to take a train to Piraeus in Greece and then to Alexandria, Egypt. Alternately, a flight from London to Cairo will save time and so is more practical for readers who have a time constraint.

For convenience, we start a new day-by-day itinerary in each country so that readers can use the entire itinerary or select only those portions in which they are interested.

Readers from North America or the United Kingdom may like to first visit the Gordon sites in Britain before going on to Africa.

Of general interest will be the National Army Museum (with an excellent display of the evolution of the Enfield rifle), located just before the junction of Royal Hospital Road and Tite Street, in London's Chelsea district.

In the gardens of the Ministry of Defence, facing the Thames River, is a statue of Gordon. In Westminster Abbey along the north aisle of the nave there is a bust of Gordon, and at St. Paul's Cathedral there is another bust located not far from the Kitchener Memorial Chapel in the west end of the north nave aisle.

A bus trip to Greenwich will be rewarding for several reasons: Gordon was baptized at St. Alfege's Church, located a few short blocks from the Maritime Museum; Gordon spent several years at Woolwich; and the buildings of the Royal Artillery will be of interest. Returning to London, stop at Rotherhithe to see Orchard House, located on the same road that the bus uses (Lower Road). This is where King Freddie, the last kabaka of Uganda, whom we discuss later, died in 1969.

Take the 188 bus, which can be boarded at Waterloo, Aldwych, Kingsway, or Euston (the latter is its starting point), to Greenwich. After seeing Greenwich, take the 177 bus to Woolwich. Returning, take the 177, changing to the

188—get off at Rotherhithe at one of the local pubs for a drink or a sandwich, then continue to London on the 188.

Egypt

Day 1: Arrive in Cairo, Egypt. Check into the Ramses Hilton International. Visit the National Museum of Egypt, which is just a few short blocks away from the hotel. The museum certainly was not in Cairo at the time of Gordon; the items from King Tut's tomb were awaiting discovery some 50 years later. The Citadel was important to Gordon—we took an American Express tour to see it. Frankly, it was a great disappointment as it was dirty and unswept, but it is probably something readers will want to see for themselves.

Of course, the Pyramids were as they are, but when I first saw them in 1950 they were on the outskirts of Cairo. Today, there are commercial buildings almost immediately adjacent to the base of the Sphinx. Certainly they are nothing like the scenes painted by the Orientalist School of European and American artists, which have shaped our preconceptions of these ancient wonders.

American Express also does a tour to the Pyramids, both during the day and an evening sound-and-light show. The sound is broadcast in various languages and you will want to be sure that it is in English the night you decide to go.

American Express, in the lobby of the Ramses Hilton International, can also obtain a railroad ticket for your journey to Alexandria. There is an additional service charge, which is compensated for by what the taxi driver would charge you to take you to the station to stand in line to buy a ticket.

In Alexandria we stayed at the El Mehrek Hotel (see "Egyptian Accommodation").

You will want to see Qaitbai and El-Sad forts—both are shown on the Clyde's map. Qaitbai Fort is open but under renovation. There is a small, interesting collection of Napoleonic exhibits. These exhibits will be supplemented by recoveries from Abu Kir Bay (immediately to the east of Alexandria). Egyptian deep-sea divers have been sent to France for training in the recovery of submerged relics. When they return to Egypt they will mount an operation to recover the remnants of Napoleon's flotilla, sunk by British Admiral Lord Nelson. There is a charge of 10 Egyptian pounds to take your camera inside Qaitbai Fort, or it can be left with the ticket taker at the gate.

Upon leaving Qaitbai Fort, drive to Abu Kir Bay. A sewerage system is being laid under the supervision of an American engineering company funded by USAID. This will succeed where Czechoslovakian engineers failed 20 years ago in ridding the area of pollution. The work is anticipated to take eight years, and it will be interesting to see how the Egyptian divers and American engineers manage to dovetail their efforts. Overnight and one day is enough for Alexandria; plan to take the evening train back to Cairo.

We drove, using a Thomas Cook car and driver, across the delta from Alexandria to Port Said. The driver insisted on bringing his wife so she could shop in the duty-free port of Port Said; he did not know the roads, although he had been with Thomas Cook many years; he refused to drive along the Suez Canal, which was our purpose in going to Port Said. For this pleasure we were charged $270. Par for the course in Egypt. By returning to Cairo and going to Port Said by train, you'll be more than $150 better off than we were, plus—as the train follows the canal—you'll be sure to see it.

Night 4 and Day 5: Overnight at the Ramses Hilton International, Cairo. Make an early start the next morning for the train journey to Port Said.

As the Cairo-Port Said train, unlike the train to Alexandria, does not have a restaurant car, take along something to drink and snack on. The tracks go parallel to the canal and the train ride is really what you've come to see. There is very little of interest in Port Said, although we found the people friendly. It is possible to go up and return to Cairo in one day. Lunch at the roof restaurant of the Holiday Hotel provides a good view of the town, although the port can't be seen.

Night 5 and Day 6: Another night at the Ramses Hilton, taking the early-morning train to Luxor and Aswan.

We took the famous French Wagon-Lits sleeper train to Luxor and Aswan, and that had to be the most uncomfortable, claustrophobic train in the world. The suspension rationale is logical only to the French engineers who designed them. The sway is back and forth like a dinghy in choppy seas. We suggest taking a day train—ask guest services in the Hilton for the timetable.

We went right on through to Aswan, but if you're interested in the Valley of the Kings at Luxor it is possible to break the train journey there, stay overnight, and take the train on to Aswan the next day. If you prefer not to stay the night, there is an afternoon train that goes to Aswan and you can stop only for a few hours.

At Aswan we experienced the first relief from the hysteria and chaos that we found in "Lower Egypt." Aswan is a quiet, calm town. We stayed at a traveler's class hotel, Happi Hotel. There is also an Oberoi Spa Hotel. Wherever you stay, it's safe to eat only what you buy from the small grocers: packaged foods, bottled water. (See "Bye-the-By: Health Precautions in Remote Areas.")

We took a local sailboat to Kitchener's Island. There's a botanical garden on the island and we liked the machine-made rag rugs the vendors sell. The Oberoi Hotel is located on Elephantine Island and the ferry back and forth is free.

Before you start sightseeing, however, you will want to buy your ticket for the steamer across Lake Nasser. The office for the steamship company is within a very short walking distance from Happi Hotel. Ask anyone where it is.

Nile Valley River Transport will not sell you a ticket unless you have a Sudanese visa. Visas cannot be obtained either in Aswan or at the border. They are very adamant about this.

The boat leaves on a Monday morning from El Sadd el Ali, which is 14 mi south of Aswan. There is a train available, but it's difficult to manage with baggage and groceries; taxis are reasonably priced.

Once at the docks, we were forced to change from the taxi we arrived in from Aswan to a taxi parked at the docks. The driver then drove us a matter of 200 yards to the customs shed. For this we paid 3.50 Egyptian pounds. Our original driver almost came to blows with the drivers at the dock over this enforced change, but to no avail.

Passengers should be at the embarkation point by 8:30–9 a.m. The boat is scheduled to leave at 10 a.m. It does not always do so, but they play by the rules even if the rules don't always work. The customs officers, immigration, etc., pack up as soon as everyone at the dock has been cleared. If you're not there, despite the fact that you've got a ticket and the ship isn't going anywhere for another two hours, you're out of luck.

There are two classes of tickets, first and third—no second. We took first class. (Fares are given in "Estimated Budget.") To say that the third-class passengers are exotic is an understatement. In third class everyone sleeps on the deck, next to one another. First class is air conditioned, which is necessary.

Before departure there is a lot of yelling at the quayside: everything gets sorted out in the end.

Porters are available to carry baggage on board. At night the ship anchors in mid-lake and resumes the journey in the early morning. Mutton stew over rice is available in the dining room, and tea. Meals are not included in the fare. The kitchen is clean, but the dishes are not sterilized, and who knows if the cook ever had a health check. We don't recommend eating on board. Huge Nile Perch circle the ship when it is at anchor. BBC Overseas services comes in after dark. Blankets are provided, plus one sheet. At this writing the mattresses are still in their plastic coverings. At night little insects fly in through the large porthole. Bring along a 4-yard length of mosquito netting and drape this, triple thickness, over the window to prevent their entry. The tiny insects don't bite, they are simply annoying. Mosquitoes do, and they come in as well. Insect spray is helpful, but if you put the net up before dark it's not needed. Movement of the ship is minimal; there are excellent stabilizers.

The temperature in February is cold at 55 degrees at night, daytime 70. It would be hell in summer on an all-metal ship without insulation. The placid lake water reflects the sun, with temperatures to 130°F. Although first class is air conditioned, it could still be very hot. The Southern Cross can be seen during the crossing. Cabins 1 through 8 are on the starboard side, 14 to 18 on port; others are inside cabins. Abu Simbel comes up on the starboard side going south. Smoke detectors are in the cabins. Good firefighting equipment on board. Cabins, while extremely nice, do not have private bathrooms and there is a "ladies" and "gents" washroom and eastern toilet. No toilet paper; bring some Kleenex. No soap and towels. Bring along a washcloth to clean the counter after preparing meals in the cabin.

Cabins have an electrical outlet located immediately behind a small, sliding cover under the ceiling light switch at the cabin door. We made tea using our electric immersion heater. When buying one at home make sure to buy a good brand; it is worth the extra few dollars. We also made dehydrated soups successfully but did not do other cooking. (Remember the smoke detector.)

Sudan

The route across Lake Nasser is jointly administered by Egypt and Sudan. The chairmen rotate every two years from each country. Two steamers operate; one leaves Aswan (just below El Sadd el Ali) for Wadi Halfa every Monday and the other leaves Wadi Halfa on Thursdays for Aswan. The lake is quite still, with only very small waves. Surrounding is dry, parched rock desert. Very peaceful and relaxing. Air dry despite the lake. Sudanese immigration and health formalities are carried out on the ship.

The route across Lake Nasser is jointly administered by Egypt and Sudan. The chairmen rotate every two years from each country. Two steamers operate; one leaves Aswan (just below El Sadd el Ali) for Wadi Halfa every Monday and the other leaves Wadi Halfa on Thursdays for Aswan. The lake is quite still, with only very small waves. Surrounding is dry, parched rock desert. Very peaceful and relaxing. Air dry despite the lake.

There is a problem getting Sudanese money. First, it is illegal for Egyptian banks to pay out Sudanese pounds; second, it is illegal to use Egyptian pounds in Sudan; third, there is no way to legally overcome the problem. No one worries too much about this: Once on the Wadi Halfa side of the lake, the traveler can use Egyptian pounds to pay the boatmen with no problem and to pay the driver of the communal vehicle that takes travelers into town. In Wadi Halfa there is a very efficient bank where money can be changed—foreign currency, not Egyptian pounds.

The steamer leaves on Monday and arrives on the south shore on Wednesday morning. Disembarkation starts at about 10 a.m., although the ship will have been just off shore all night. The rule is that if the ship arrives before 1 p.m. on Tuesday, passengers disembark that afternoon. If not, the ship waits until the following morning.

Sudan Railways—Wadi Halfa to Khartoum waits for the ship's passengers to leave, whenever that is. So don't worry about missing the train.

Disembarking from the ship, the European, American, and Japanese passengers try to act cool, as if they've done this every day of their lives. Inwardly, we're certain, they're terribly excited. This is the dream they have dreamed while pouring over maps for months.

Currency control for Sudan takes place at the disembarkation shed, as does Sudanese customs. List on your currency control forms any cameras and radios. A Sudanese appears and carries your baggage to a very small rowboat powered by an outboard engine. Passengers are motioned to sit on the board that forms a seat about midway between the bow and stern. Baggage is deposited at your feet. Foolishly, you wait for the boatman to push off. No. Cheap suitcases bound with rope, boxes bound with twine, cooking pots and pans pulled up into a sheet, are deposited at your feet alongside your matched luggage. From bow to stern the little boat is heaped with baggage belonging to other passengers who elect to walk the third of a mile to the waiting Land Rovers and matatoos (a Japanese pickup truck, which functions as a bus—see "Transportation: Buses").

The small boat does not sink, and you are unloaded from it by cheerful, helpful hands after the chattels have deadened all sensation in your feet.

Numerous vehicles on the shore wait to transport travelers and baggage. We just stood and waited, indicating our reluctance to pile into the back of a pickup with the men. We were ushered to the front seat of a vehicle to make the journey with the driver. We paid what we were asked; it wasn't much. (The reader should understand that most of the action is performed in pantomime; there aren't too many English-speakers around.)

Into Wadi Halfa you go, across small sand dunes, until the railroad station is reached. We did not realize it at the time but the quite considerable, well-laid-out buildings between the eroded hills and the station are not Wadi Halfa proper. The city lies to the far side of the hills.

The train doesn't depart until 5:15 p.m., so there is plenty of time to get everything done.

Although money is openly changed in front of the station at black-market rates, the currency permit stamped by officially recognized banks and hotels must be shown on departure from Sudan, so it really is not advisable to take advantage of these offers.

There is a very clean, dormitory-style hotel on the left (when one's back is to the station) several hundred yards along the main thoroughfare. It's more than adequate for overnight accommodation or for someone traveling along the Nile northward for a good rest after the train ride from Khartoum.

The Sudan Railways advertises the seating offered on the train to Khartoum as sleeping car, first class, second class, and third class. Do not confuse sleeping car with first class. To the Sudanese they are two different categories. Sleeping car is a compartment that contains one long seat with a bunk above it. The compartment is dark, cramped, and holds an unbelievable quantity of dust and dirt. There seems to be some sort of patronage system operating to obtain sleeping car tickets. We asked for one, were given Car 22, and then told we were wrong and had asked for first class.

Admittedly, while still dust-laden, the first class compartment we were given—with a note in Arabic and English pasted to the window denoting that the occupants were "tourists"—was better than sleeping car. Our compartment contained three once-red, plush, curved-to-fit-the-body-of-a-Bengali seats, and a small folding table. More than three passengers can be squeezed into the compartment, but in our case the little slip of paper on the window protected us from intrusion. Windows are very old and let in the dust from the desert. The electric fan does not work and there is no way to turn off the small, dim, overhead light. The three seats are too narrow to stretch out on. We made a bed for Leah by laying the suitcases on the floor and somehow we got through the night. With ingenuity one could hang a hammock to replace the suitcase bed. Other things necessary to survive the 30-hour journey apart from food are: 12 men's handkerchiefs; 1 roll paper towels; cloths large enough to put over the dirty seats (we used towels that we bought, after we saw the compartment, in Wadi Halfa)—a couple of sheets would work well; a strip of gauze or mosquito netting, 3 by 4 feet, to cover the window, and some heavy plastic tape to put it up. Details in "Plan Ahead."

Water is carried on the train in huge clay pots into which everyone dips their jam jar or cup. There is no ladle. The water is muddy. There is a buffet car, but it is terribly dirty; don't eat from it. Toilets are Eastern and do not appear to have water to flush.

This trip is to be undertaken only by those in excellent health and who are not accident prone. There are absolutely no doctors for miles, and even 2 miles under the desert conditions would be like 40 if a sick person had to be carried to medical help. Wear, if you use glasses, only frame glasses; contact lenses would be impossible. Asthma sufferers may have a problem; the air is extremely dry, repeat, *extremely* dry. It goes without saying that no one with a heart condition should attempt the trip.

At Shendi everyone gets out. There is a market. Don't eat the cooked food or fruits without a peel. Bananas are good.

Everyone is very good-natured. Security is very good. No problems whatsoever with other passengers.

Khartoum

Moving down the Nile, from Egypt into Sudan, for us—and perhaps for Gordon—is like coming out of the darkness into light; comparable to entering the wrong end of a funnel into the full cup of sunlight and space. Cairo, Alexandria, the Delta—tight, constricted, and overpopulated until, at Khartoum, the two Niles meet and a new world begins. Spacious, open, where caravans cross and the White Nile carries the strong inner heart of Africa from Zaire to meet the mountain streams of ancient Abyssinia. A blending of ideologies struggle to take shape. After Khartoum the visions blur, rain forests shade away lofty purpose in mysticism, and dry savannahs stage the interplay of wide animal scenarios.

Khartoum, established, founded, laid out on Britainia's shield of vengeance, prepares for her centennial. By her 200th birthday we predict she shall rival Lagos, Nigeria, and Kampala, Uganda, for the leadership of Africa.

Gordon loved the desert. In fact, riding camelback in the desert had been, before the siege, his only recreation apart from Bible reading. The monument of him on a camel is no sculptor's substitution for a horse. The camel to Gordon was, as it is to all desert people, a symbol of freedom—a freedom for the soul as well as the body.

Khartoum has all of the infrastructure necessary for the visitor. We found security to be absolute; the people are friendly, helpful, and charming; there are good and efficient travel agents and hotels of all categories; a resident expatriate community has familiarized the African citizens with foreign ways, so that one is not a walking curio; and a variety of sites are unique to the city.

What Khartoum and Sudan do not have is a stable economy; however, the new government is making progress. Former President Numeri had justifiably developed a paranoia. Reportedly 14 attempts had been made on his life. His neighbors, Ethiopia to the east and Libya to the west, are envious and greedy; Egypt to the north has historically proven to have an eye on annexing the Sudan; and where those borders end, the chaotic domains of Chad, Central African Republic, and Uganda take up the slack.

Millions of American dollars and Saudi riyals have been poured into Sudan in an effort to stem the tide that seems to push the country ever backward. It is as if one tried to glue together a broken vase only to find that there was no adhesive strong enough to bind the fragments together. Yet the Sudanese people live on.

As we write, and for the past few years, no travel has been permitted south of Khartoum. The situation can change. Readers will want to check with their state department or foreign office for current travel conditions. Those living in Saudi Arabia will find up-to-date reports in he English-language-daily, *Arab News*.

We liked Khartoum very much, and for the adventurous, mature Africanist (mature meaning knowing how to take care of one's health and maintain a low-key character) the city has much to offer.

Upon arrival in Khartoum, take a taxi and check into either the Hilton International or the Sudan Club. A good soak in a hot bath will help you recover from the train journey.

We hesitate to provide a day-by-day itinerary for Sudan as you may want to spend more time than it takes simply to see the museum, and it may be that

General Charles George Gordon, "Chinese Gordon," the hero of Khartoum surely one of the most romantic of Victorians. His stand at Khartoum when the city was encircled by the Maadi's forces kept Queen Victoria and the British public mesmerized. (Reprinted by permission of National Portrait Gallery, London.)

you'll have time on your hands between flights—the flights to Nairobi are not daily ones.

Khalifa's House Museum, Omdurman: Having come so far in search of Gordon it would have been appropriate to encounter some type of prelude, fanfare, or at minimum, a ceremonial drive upon approaching the Maadi's tomb. As it is, approximately 200 yards after crossing the bridge over the Nile, the silver dome is seen almost immediately on the right—shining in the African sun and across the road—the Khalifa's House Museum.

A low wall separates the house from the street and the visitor passes through an archway shaded by a low-branched tree.

Inside the anteroom, the ticket seller—sitting at a desk beside a glass showcase of ancient postcards and locally printed paperbacks in Arabic—charges a few (25) piastas for entry.

A boat, a small boat for so grand an enterprise, fabricated of heavy metal, corroded with holes along its keel, is just past the entrance. This is the actual boat that the French used to cross the Nile and stake their claim to Equatoria (southern Sudan); a claim that would have joined their African empire from the Atlantic to the Red Sea. The British put an end to this dream and confiscated the little boat at Fashoda. Horse-drawn carriages made in France and used in Khartoum, and General Wingate's automobile, custom-made for Sudanese conditions, are also on display, along with rifles—handmade by the Maadi's gunsmiths—battle flags, uniforms, letters.

A small room dedicated specifically to Gordon exhibits his leather water canteen, notes and cards, and a curious complete set of Dervish chain mail, which was found in a metal footlocker at Sukain. The metal footlocker was packed with his dress uniform by a junior officer (the donor of the exhibit) in Cairo before Gordon's departure for Khartoum. There is no explaining of how the Dervish uniform replaced the British general's clothing.

Followers of the White Nile itinerary may want to read Michael Barthrop's *War on the Nile: Britain, Egypt and the Sudan 1882–1898* (published by Blandford Press, Poole, Dorset, England; distributed in the United States by Sterling Publishing Co., Inc., 2 Park Ave., New York, NY 10016). The photographs, many of them never before published, are marvelous, and the text is extremely knowledgeable. The foreword to the book is of particular interest:

> Neither a nationalist military revolt in Egypt nor an enslaved people's uprising in the Sudan directly threatened, by armed might, the security of the British Empire but, as always, waiting in the wings were those other two great expansionist Powers of the period: Russia, eager for an outlet into the Levant at the expense of the Sultan of Turkey (Egypt's nominal overlord); and France, then building her African empire and with a long tradition of influence in Egypt.

Although the *modus operandi* has changed—terrorists replacing foot soldiers—the name of the game is the same a hundred years later. The Soviets now covertly keep the kettle boiling; the British have been joined by the Americans; the French sell arms to the highest bidder; and Libya adds pepper to the stockpot that is Sudan.

The Khalifa's house is large, and the sunken bath, supplied with hot water, reflects the culture of the Italian, identified only as Petro, who designed it for the Khalifa.

If you came to the museum by taxi, your driver may encourage you to visit the market. We tried it and got a good case, a few days later, of sand fly fever from the countless carriers that live in the dusty sand dividing the market stalls. Wear a pair of boots or at least knee-high socks.

Gordon's Headquarters: The general's offices are now the Presidential Palace, and visitors are not allowed inside. It can only be seen through the iron gates.

Sudan National Museum is located next door to the Hilton and well worth a visit, although there is little to connect the exhibits with the text of *The White Nile*. A short description is given in our itinerary for *The Lost Cities of Africa*.

How long readers will want to stay in Khartoum will be a personal decision, but we are allowing three nights with a departure by air for Nairobi on the fourth day. We discuss making your onward (to Nairobi) reservations in "Plan Ahead."

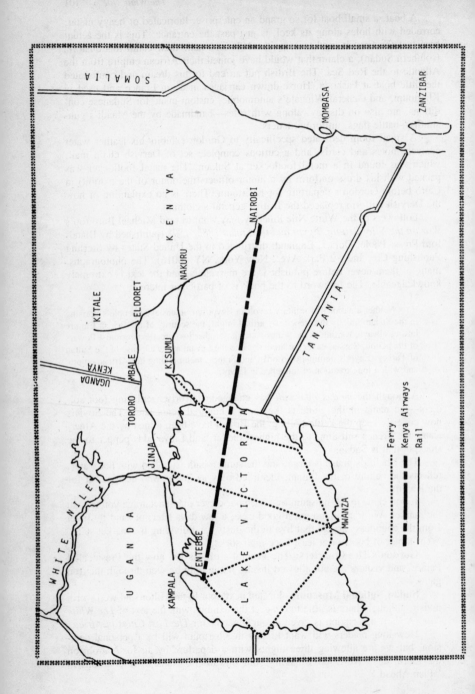

Zanzibar Island

The one-day tour to Zanzibar will be by air through United Touring Company. There are two ways to travel to Uganda: (1) by plane to Entebbe, which is the international airline destination city for Kampala and (2) by train, which will permit you to see the Rift Valley explored by Joseph Thomson (mention is made of him in *The White Nile*). Thomson opened a new route to Uganda that was disastrously followed by Bishop Hannington. The previous route had been through northern Tanzania, starting at Zanzibar Island (see Chapter 16, "Paradise Reformed," *The White Nile*). Descriptions of this section of Kenya (Nairobi to Kisumu) are given in the *Lunatic Express* itinerary.

If the option to travel by train from Nairobi to Kampala is taken, then a stop can be made on the way at the city of Jinja to see the Source of the Nile. Make a one-day layover at Jinja, then continue the next day by train to Kampala. However, if you decide to go by air it will be necessary to take the train to Jinja, stay one night, then return to Kampala.

Day 1 of the Kenya stopover: Arrive Nairobi. Take a taxi to the Hilton International or any of the Nairobi hotels we recommend; however, it is interesting to use the Hilton to compare it to the previous Hiltons—each has a separate, distinct character that adapts to the culture of the country.

Day 2: Make arrangements through UTC (United Touring Company) to take the one-day tour to Zanzibar, which you have previously reserved. Having done so, go to the Kenya Railways station and pick up and pay for your tickets to Kampala if you are going by train. Purchase a one-way ticket as you will want to return to Nairobi by air. If you have decided to fly to Uganda both ways, reconfirm your flight with Kenya Airways.

Day 3: Take the one-day tour of Zanzibar. (Our comments on Tanzania are to be found in the *Lost Cities of Africa* itinerary and may be of interest).

Day 4: Depart from Nairobi for Uganda. The itinerary will be flexible after this point as the time frame will depend upon your choice of transportation. Allow one day to get to Jinja from Nairobi. When flying the time is only 45 minutes, with an additional 2 hours to clear Ugandan customs and take the airline bus into Kampala.

Uganda

Passengers arriving by air can take the airline bus that makes the 21-mi journey to the capital. The train, of course, leaves passengers in the heart of Kampala.

For accommodation there are two choices—the International Hotel or the Kampala Sikh Gurdwara; both are described in "Ugandan Accommodation."

After a day of rest and orientation—and particularly, after seeing how the land lies for travel—plan to visit the Kasubi Tombs, which is the reason for coming to Uganda. It may also be possible to visit the Shrine of the Uganda Martyrs at Namungongo, just outside Kampala following the Pope Paul VI Road. Alan Moorehead touches on the Kabaka Mwanga's persecution of the pages at his court who refused to engage in sodomy in the closing pages of chapter 16 of *The White Nile*. We have provided additional suggested reading in 'Bye-the-By." These martyrs are the only ones jointly shared by both Protestants and Catholics.

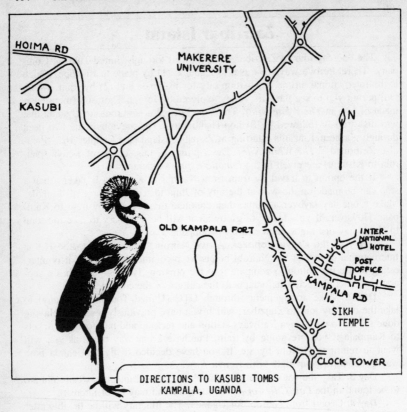

HOIMA RD

MAKERERE
UNIVERSITY

KASUBI

N

OLD KAMPALA FORT

INTER-
NATIONAL
HOTEL

POST
OFFICE

KAMPALA RD

SIKH
TEMPLE

CLOCK TOWER

DIRECTIONS TO KASUBI TOMBS
KAMPALA, UGANDA

The Crested Crane is the national emblem of Uganda.

The following definitions may be helpful (root word: *ganda*):

Tribal land belonging to the tribe	Buganda
Singular form	Muganda
Plural form	Baganda
Their language	Luganda
Adjective	Kiganda as in Kiganda society
Independent country comprising the tribal lands of many tribes	Uganda includes all land within the official boundary including Buganda

We take the following information on the Kasubi Tombs from Uganda's Ministry of Culture and Community Development, Department of Antiquities publication written in 1972 by our former neighbor in the Kampala suburb of Bugalobi, Hamo Sassoon. Mr. Sassoon was at that time Conservator of Antiquities and is well known throughout East Africa for his work in archaeology. His wife supplied the drawings. We doubt that the guide is presently available and believe readers will find the information useful.

Cover, Guide to Kasubi Tombs, *Hamo Sasson, Conservator of Antiquities, Ministry of Culture and Community Development, Department of Antiquities, Government of Uganda, 1972.*

The Tombs of the Kabakas

The significance of Kasubi Tombs cannot be fully appreciated without some knowledge of the historical background. The kingdom of Buganda probably had its origins in the fifteenth century or even earlier; although the earliest rulers, or kabakas, who founded the kingdom are surrounded by a somewhat mythical aura, there is no doubt that the Baganda still know and venerate the shrines of at least thirty-four kabakas. The last five important kabakas were:

Suna II	circa 1836–1856	
Mutesa I	1856–1884	
Mwanga II	1884–1897	(but interrupted by the short reigns of two usurpers)
Daudi Chwa II	1897–1939	
Mutesa II	1939–1966	(when the kingdom was absorbed into the modern Republic of Uganda).

It was the custom for each of the earlier kabakas to choose a hill and to build himself a new capital when he took over the kingdom. Many of the kabakas also changed their capital sites every year or two during their reigns, but most of the capitals seem to have been in the area to the northwest of Kampala which is known as Busiro.

One of the reasons for the frequent changes of capitals must have been the need for firewood; early illustrations of the royal enclosures show that the surrounding countryside was almost treeless. Another reason was undoubtedly epidemic diseases, such as plague and smallpox; consequently, when a capital was deserted, it was often destroyed by burning—which was easy enough as all the buildings were made from wood and grass and reeds.

Until the death of Mutesa I in 1884, it had always been the custom for the Kabakas to be buried in two shrines, one of which contained the body, and the other, usually some miles distant, which contained the jawbone. Possession of the jawbone was important in confirming the new kabaka's claim to the throne, with the result that the jawbone shrines had much more attention paid to them than the body shrines.

Mutesa I, however, had become a Muslim, and was also interested in Christianity; when he died, the age-old custom was broken and he was buried complete with his jawbone. Not only this, but he chose to be buried in his own palace, which at the time of his death in 1884 was on Kasubi hill.

Mutesa was succeeded by Mwanga II in 1884, and he was followed by Daudi Chwa in 1897. Both of these kabakas followed the example of Mutesa and were buried beside him at Kasubi.

The burial of Mwanga II was delayed because he had been exiled to the Seychelles in 1897, and he died there in 1903. His remains were brought back to Uganda in 1910, and he was buried at Kasubi. Mutesa II was in exile in London at the time of his death on 22 November 1969. His body was flown back to Uganda on 31 March 1971. After lying in state in Namirembe Cathedral, the body was finally laid to rest beside his grandfather, Mwanga, on 4 April 1971.

The Great House, or Muzibu Azaala Mpanga

The traditional palace of the kabaka was a great, round structure made of wooden posts and reeds, with the thatched roof coming right down to the ground. Suna II had his last capital at Kasubi, and his palace must have been similar to the present building; being made with such temporary materials, the building could not last very long. Mutesa I rebuilt it as his palace in 1882, only two years before it became his tomb. The building was rebuilt several times between Mutesa's death and 1938. Daudi Chwa II then decided that a permanent foundation and framework should be constructed for the building. This was done to an architect's design in concrete and steel, and the frame was covered with reeds and thatch. The work of reconstruction took almost exactly two years; before it was completed, Daudi Chwa died and was buried beside his father, Mutesa I.

The diameter of the present building is about 15 metres, and it preserves carefully the style and details of the earlier traditional buildings.

Inside the Great House

As you enter the Great House, you will see four groups of insignia which include, copper, brass and iron spears; those in the centre belong to Mutesa I, those on the left are Mwanga's, and to the right are the spears of Daudi Chwa. The new spears on the extreme left belong to the last kabaka, Mutesa II. The posts which support the roof are covered with barkcloth which is made from the bark of wild fig trees; the same material is used for the curtains which screen certain parts of the house. Behind these curtains there is space for the widows of the kabakas to sleep and to keep their belongings when they are on duty guarding the tombs. So that the tombs may never be neglected, these duties are inherited from the original widows. Besides guarding the tombs, they have to look after the inside of the house and make the mats which cover the floor; they also have to keep the ground in front of the tombs tidily strewn with the special type of soft grass which is traditionally used as a floor covering in Buganda.

*Kabaka Mutesa's capital at Rubaga, situated on one of the hills overlooking the
city of Kampala and now the site of a Catholic cathedral. From* Mackay of
Uganda, *1868.*

The Other Buildings

The royal enclosure, or Lubiri, is surrounded by a reed fence 2 kilometers
long; by an ancient custom, the reeds are always used upside down for the fence at
a kabaka's tomb. The traditional entrance hut is called "Bujabukula," which means
that a moment of great significance or danger is approaching. After passing through
Bujabukula, a small thatched hut on the left contained the royal drums. This is in a
small courtyard which leads into the main courtyard containing the Great House.
Around the sides of this courtyard there are other houses, some of which are for the
windows, and some for tombs of members of the royal family.

Hamo Sassoon doesn't, as he is writing a purely academic guide to the
tombs, go into the personal lives of the kabakas.

Mutesa I presents interesting challenges to those who would understand
him. Deliberately he vacillated on the subject of his conversion to Moslem,
Protestant, or Catholic religions, and used his indecisiveness as an instrument
of his foreign policy. His astute, calculating personality is revealed when one
reads the detailed history of the Buganda and missionary journals. He hoped to
gain most favored nation treatment for Bugunda by suggesting his own possible
conversion to the same religious persuasion as the rulers first of Zanzibar, then
of Egypt, and finally of Britain. This was a sophisticated, ego-flattering technique, which the Arabs did not fully buy but which most certainly had the
desired effect on Christian emissaries to his court—they danced to Mutesa's
tune for years hoping to gain his soul. That his policies were successful is

evidenced by the fact that Mutesa kept his throne, retained the center and control of the East African ivory trade at Budo, fought off all neighboring rivals, and died neither circumcised nor baptized. (Although Hamo has said in his guide to the tombs that Mutesa I was a Moslem, that guide was written in 1972. Research since that time, published in *Islam in Uganda: Islamization through a Centralized State in pre-Colonial Africa* by Ayre Oded (Israel Universities Press, Jerusalem, 1974), can find no evidence in the literature translated from Arabic documents in Zanzibar that Mutesa I formally became a Moslem by undergoing circumcision.

Perhaps the life of Mutesa II, "King Freddie," is the most tragic. Upon independence from the British in 1962, the kabaka—who was educated in England at Sandhurst military academy, sophisticated, and elegant—became president of the newly formed republic of Uganda. Milton Obote was made prime minister. Although King Freddie was the kabaka of Uganda, the idea was that he would serve in the ceremonial position as president, representing all the people. Obote, intent on his socialist policies, had no time for royalty and sent soldiers—led by none other than then Colonel Idi Amin—to rout him out of his home in Kampala. The kabaka fled to Britain. There his old friends deserted him; he survived on an infinitesimally small pension earned as a result of service in a company of the Queen's Royal Guards, supplementing the pension with work as a platform porter at Paddington Railway station in London until he died—some say—of alcoholism. Idi Amin brought his body back to Uganda and allowed burial in Kasubi Tombs. For this single act, Amin, although not a Muganda, gained a loyalty among the kabaka's people, which was only diminished as the excesses of his army grew to the unpardonable.

Since 1972 many books have been written about Uganda; most of them have been of a sensational nature. Prior to the 1970s, titles were usually academic or biographical. The U.S. Freedom of Information Act exempts certain records of the CIA from researchers' study if it is "in the interest of national defense or foreign policy" to do so. The British CID records for Uganda during the period 1963–73 would be even more difficult to obtain. As for any pertinent Israeli records, who knows when they may be made public? The Israelis were the first foreigners to be thrown out of Uganda by Amin, and while Amin never actually threw Americans and the British out of the country, he certainly made life very difficult for Americans (Peace Corps volunteers where shot, newspaper correspondents murdered, etc.). It was common gossip in Kampala at the time that the CIA, CID, and Israelis all were playing games with Uganda's politicians. Things did not spontaneously happen in Uganda and today's African leaders have justification for being suspicious of outside interference in their political arenas. Because of the intrigue, both domestic and foreign, contemporary Ugandan history remains one of the most fascinating topics among Africanists. If only one could return to academic writing based on prime source material, doubtless the truth would be stranger than any fiction sensationalists now write.

If you traveled to Uganda by air and wish to go to Jinja to see the Source of the Nile, you will need to make inquiries concerning train times. We urge you to take the train and not go by road (despite the fact that going by train takes longer than by car). Most vehicles will be overcrowded and there may be roadblocks. The train journey is very interesting and as there is only one class you will be able to meet ordinary Ugandans among the other passengers.

Arriving in Jinja there will be taxis at the station. If not, go to the stationmaster's office and they will call one for you. Check into the Crested Crane Hotel, and then take a drive by taxi to see the Source of the Nile.

Speke's famous falls have become Owen Falls Hydroelectric Dam. The dam can be viewed from the bridge, which passes over the Nile, but when we were in Uganda it was not permitted to walk along the banks of the river. There usually policemen at either end of the bridge, and you can ask if this restriction has been lifted.

Jinja is a very pretty town—immaculately clean—tropical, with palm trees bordering the access roads. The people here are the Busoga, who, like the Buganda, had a king.

Return to Kampala the next day. You may have a few days to kill before there's a flight back to Nairobi. You can spend time in the National Museum—the exhibits are excellent. If you want to travel outside of the Kampala-Jinja area we suggest you visit with your embassy personnel and determine just how much traveling is safe to undertake—and act accordingly.

Depart from Entebbe, changing planes in Nairobi for the flight home.

PLAN AHEAD: Reservations for the intinerary can be made through Merkani Hotel Reservations Service (P.O. Box 53394, Temple Heights Station, Washington, DC 20009, tel. (USA) 301–530–1911). However, if you wish to make your own reservations we have supplied all the necessary information.

The following needs to be done before departure: Check the "Basic Information Checklist" in "Background Information" for necessary travel documents; make hotel reservations—numbers and addresses are given in the heading preceding the hotel's description; make airline reservations for international flights using the routings we suggest at the beginning of the itinerary; reserve an Avis car where needed; purchase SOS Insurance (see "Travel Documents"); purchase traveler's checks; decide if you are going to purchase your maps before you leave or wait until you arrive. If the former, order from Forsyth Travel Library (9154 West 57th Street, P.O. Box 2975, Shawnee Mission, KS 66201-1375). Reserve UTC tour to Zanzibar; start taking malaria tablets two weeks before anticipated departure date.

Once in Cairo: After checking into the Ramses Hilton call the American Express office in the lobby asking that they obtain return rail tickets for you to Alexandria, and return tickets to Port Said. Ask them for their brochures of tours to the Citadel and the Pyramids.

In Aswan: Go to the Nile Valley River Transport Office, making sure you have your Sudanese visa in your passport (take it along to show them), and purchase a first-class ticket for the steamer. Purchase groceries for the steamer voyage and the train journey to Khartoum. Allow eight bottles of mineral water per person.

In Khartoum: Confirm your airline reservations for the flight to Nairobi.

In Nairobi: If you decide to go to Uganda by train it will be necessary to go to the Kenya Railways station and get the tickets. If you plan to use the Kisumu-Port Bell steamer, the tickets can be purchased through Kenya Railways as well. If you plan to fly there will be no need to reconfirm your flight as you are simply laying over.

For all but the train trip from Aswan to Wadi Halfa, special clothing is not needed. Travelers are better treated if they dress conservatively, although dress codes are not in effect in any of the countries included in the itinerary except on the island of Zanzibar. Women should not be tempted to wear trousers or slacks on the train. You will be traveling with primarily country people who value femininity. The Sudanese ladies will be very elegantly dressed in national costume. A cotton shirtwaist dress cut fuller in the skirt will be very suitable. Do not wear khaki or any other military-looking clothing. Sandals are perfectly acceptable, if you don't mind your feet getting dirty. It gets very, very cold at night in the compartment and there is no heat. A sweater will be needed, if not a nylon jacket with a lining. The compartments have a pull-down shade and it's possible to dress in privacy. Jeans could be worn at night to sleep in. For men, ordinary conservative clothing will be best. Do not wear a caftan or other "going native" style of clothing; it looks ridiculous to everyone. There are a number of checkpoints to pass through. Officials tend to treat travelers as they are dressed. Conservative, dignified clothing within your own culture elicits courteous dignified treatment. Dress sloppily and you'll be treated disrespectfully. The hippie look definitely encourages officials to search the person and his/her belongings for drugs.

To help keep out the sand that blows through the gaps of the window frames, a four-yard length of mosquito netting is very useful. Press the edges of the netting into the window frame cracks to hold it in place. Even with mosquito netting you're going to be covered in sand by the time you arrive in Khartoum. We don't know where you can purchase mosquito netting in the United States. In London, try Harrods. Failing that, you can get it in Cairo. Do not buy cheap, stiff nylon netting. Effective mosquito netting is soft and resists tearing. Mosquito netting is also useful on the boat to keep out the small insects that come in through the porthole after dark.

Binoculars will add to the enjoyment of the trip. We had a small, cheap radio and were able to listen to the BBC after dark.

Take a first-aid kit and a prescription pain killer—just in case. Dehydration salts are an absolute must and should be taken starting in Aswan—please see "Bye-the-By: Health Precautions in Remote Areas."

Take something interesting to read—have a look through our "Annotated Bibliography." Cigarettes can be purchased in Egypt and Sudan and are reasonably priced—just remember to take along a supply for the train and boat trip as there won't be any place to buy them easily.

Your camera should be carried in something totally dustproof. We suggest readers look through the Voyageur's catalog. This will be sent to readers making reservations for this safari through Merikani Hotel Reservations Service, or readers can write directly to Voyageur's (P.O. Box 409, Gardnar, KS 66030). We used one of their Voyageur Float Totes made from quality 20 ml vinyl, fully lined with protective closed cell foam. The closure is not a usual one and the contents in the bag are absolutely sealed from outside pollutants. At this writing the price is US$17, catalog number 10100 size 12 by 14 feet, 14 ounces.

This same company also sells the All Weather Reflective Blanket. Voyageur does not manufacture these as it does the tote bags, and we understand similar blankets can be purchased in many stores. To quote from the catalog: "This tough, heat-reflective blanket is ideal for many outdoor uses—from a ground cloth to an emergency bivouac shelter. The blanket material is an aluminized plastic film laminated on both sides of a fiber scrim for strength. This insulation material works because of its high heat reflectivity (80%). It can be used equally well to keep heat in. (Put a space blanket, shiny side out, on top of and inside your cooler for a noticeable increase in effectiveness!) The Space Blanket is waterproof, windproof, will not crack, mildew or shrink. Reinforced grommeted corners. Size: 56″ × 82″.'' We have used the same blanket for three years and find it especially useful to throw over our car when it's necessary to park or wait under an African sun. It certainly does keep in body heat, and you can roll up in it and be very warm. (Catalog number A6100, the current price is US$14.) Voyageur's also sells Stick Tight Boat Tape, which could be useful in holding the mosquito netting to the window on the train. We haven't tried this particular tape but it seems sturdier than other plastic tapes. Anything that can be used to keep the desert sand out of the compartment will be a blessing.

When we were in Egypt there was plenty of imported (from Europe) packaged foods. To be on the safe side, however, it might be wise to take along a few camping foods. We find African-manufactured crackers very inferior to American or British crackers and we always take these from home to substitute for bread. There were plenty of Dutch packaged cheeses in Egypt. There is no decaffeinated coffee. Take an immersion heater to make coffee or tea from bottled mineral water, which you can buy in Aswan. Plan out a menu for the two full days and nights on the steamer, and for the 30 hours on the train. Once in Khartoum, the Hilton and Sudan Club have everything.

Accommodation recommended for the *White Nile* itinerary: London, England—Kensington Hilton International; Egypt—Ramses Hilton International (Cairo), El Mehrek Hotel (Alexandria); (optional: in Port Said we recommend the Holiday Hotel); Happi Hotel (Aswan). Sudan—Khartoum Hilton International or the Sudan Club. Kenya—Hilton International Nairobi; in Kisumu the Sunset Hotel. Uganda—the International Hotel or the Kampala Sikh Gurdwara; the Crested Crane in Jinja.

Estimated Budget

White Nile Itinerary

Egypt and Sudan portion (26 nights)
Does not include airfare unless otherwise stated

	US$	
	1 person	2 people
Arrive Cairo: Taxi to Ramses Hilton International	15	15
Ramses HI, 2 nights, $97 single, $123 double	194	246
Meals: breakfast $6, lunch $12, dinner $15 = $33 × 2	66	132
American Express tour to Pyramids	10	20
American Express tour to Citidel	10	20
Entrance fee, National Museum	3	6
Taxi to train station	5	5
Train to Alexandria: return fare plus $5 American Express charge to obtain ticket	12	19
Arrive Alexandria: Taxi to El Meherek Hotel	5	5
El Meherek Hotel, 1 night, includes breakfast	25	25
Meals: lunch $10, dinner $15 (at Ramada Renaissance)	25	50
Taxis around Alexandria: The drivers seem unable to get over a charge of $5 a trip, no matter where you	20	20

	US$	
	1 person	2 people

go. See if you can strike a bargain for all-day use of vehicle and driver as this reportedly is cheaper. Have front desk staff at hotel see if they can negotiate a price. Avis rental cars, with offices situated in the Sheraton, are hopeless.

	1 person	2 people
Taxi to train station next morning	5	5
Arrive Cairo: Taxi to hotel from station	5	5
Ramses Hilton International, 2 nights, $97 single, $123 double	194	246
Meals: breakfast $6, lunch $12, dinner $15 = $33 × 2	66	132
Train to Port Said: return fare plus $5 American Express charge to obtain tickets	13	21
Taxi to train station	5	5
Arrive Port Said: Taxi from station to city center	5	5
Lunch in Port Said, Holiday Hotel	10	20
Return to Cairo: Taxi from city center to station	5	5
Arrive Cairo: Taxi from station to Ramses HI	5	5
Overnight at Ramses (previously charged)		
Taxi to station for train to Aswan	5	5
Train to Aswan: single fare plus American Express charge	30	60
Arrive Aswan: Taxi from station to Happi Hotel	5	5
Happi Hotel, $17 single, $22 double, 2 nights	34	44
Groceries and mineral water for trip to Khartoum, meals in Aswan	60	120
Spending money in Aswan	25	50
Ticket for Lake Nasser steamer, single fare, first class	40	80
Taxi to port to board steamer; no expenses on board	10	10
Arrive Wadi Halfa: rowboat to taxi	5	10
Taxi to Wadi Halfa	5	10
Groceries	8	16
Train ticket: first class or sleeping car to Khartoum; no expenses on the train	60	120
Arrive Khartoum: taxi to Hilton or Sudan Club	5	5
Select option (1) or (2)		
(1) Hilton International Khartoum, 4 nights, $146 single, $170 double, includes all taxes = $584 or $680	——	——
Meals: breakfast $6, lunch $10, dinner $15 = $31 × 4 days = $124 or $248 + 15% tips ($18.60 or $37.20)	——	——
(2) Sudan Club, 4 nights, $25 single, $50 double, includes all taxes = $100 or $200 + 15% tips ($13.80 or $27.60)	——	——
Meals: (slightly less than Hilton considering difference in quality and choice) breakfast $5, lunch $8, dinner $10 = $23 × 4 = $92 and $184	——	——
Taxis around Khartoum, allow $5 a trip and a bit more for Khalifa's House Museum as you will want driver to wait	30	30

	US$	
	1 person	2 people
Taxi to airport to depart from Nairobi, Kenya	5	5
Departure tax	8	16
Total option (1):	$1764.60	$2538.20
Total option (2):	$1243.80	$1984.60
Cost per person sharing option (1):	$1269.10	
Cost per person sharing option (2):	$ 992.30	

Kenya portion (3 days)

Arrive Nairobi: Taxi to hotel	15	15
Hilton International Nairobi, 3 nights, $89 single, $110 double, includes all taxes	267	330
Meals: breakfast $5, lunch $8, dinner $12 = $25 × 3 days	75	150
Zanzibar tour (price includes transportation to the airport and Tanzanian guide's fee)	340	680
Taxis around Nairobi	15	15
Total:	$712	$1190
Cost per person sharing:	$595	

Uganda portion (6 days)

Select option (3) or (4):

(3) Train to Kampala via Jinja, first class, one way	84	168
Stopover 1 night in Jinja: taxi station to hotel	3	3
Crested Crane Hotel, 1 night	66	83
Taxi to Owen Falls and return	5	5
Taxi to station from hotel	3	3
Meals: breakfast $5, lunch $8, dinner $12	25	50
Arrive Kampala: Taxi to hotel or temple	5	5
Return to Nairobi by air	130	260
Airport bus from Kampala to Entebbe	7	14
Total:	$328	$591
Cost per person sharing:	$295.50	
(4) Fly to Uganda, round trip	260	520
Taxi Hilton International Nairobi to airport	15	15
Departure tax	10	20
Airport bus from Entebbe (Uganda) to Kampala	7	14
Return train ticket Kampala-Jinja	20	40
Taxi from station to hotel in Jinja	3	3
Crested Crane Hotel, 1 night	66	83
Taxi to Owen Falls and return	5	5
Taxi to station from hotel	3	3
Arrive Kampala: Taxi to hotel or temple	5	5
Airport bus Kampala to Entebbe	7	14
Total:	$401	$722
Cost per person sharing:	$361	

	US$	
	1 person	2 people
Select option (5) or (6)		
(5) International Hotel, Kampala, single $90, $110 double, × 5 days = $450 or $550		
(6) Kampala Sikh gurdwara, donation of $10 for each night, per person, plus a gift for the gyani's children brought from Nairobi (allow $20 per person for gifts) × 5 nights = $70 or $140		
Meals: (not served in this gurdwara, so price for meals, regardless of which accommodation is used will be the same) breakfast $8, lunch $10, dinner $15 = $33 × 5 days	165	330
Taxis around Kampala and to Kasubi Tombs	40	40
Total option 5:	$655	$920
Cost per person sharing:	$460	
Total option 6:	$275	$510
Cost per person sharing:	$255	
15% tips to waiters/waitresses on all meals (options (1) and (2) excepted, as they are included in the Sudanese totals)	64.80	129.60
Tips to bellmen/porters, stewards/boat crew	56	56
Gratuity to housekeeping staff $1 a night for each night (1 or 2 persons)	· 23	23
SOS Insurance, $45 for one month	45	90
Many permutations of the options are possible, we give as an example the most expensive and the cheapest:		
Hilton Khartoum, International Kampala, fly back to Nairobi from Kampala	$3721.40	$5403.80
Cost per person sharing:	$2701.90	
Sudan Club, Kampala Sikh gurdwara, train both ways	$2747.60	$4574.20
Cost per person sharing:	$2287.10	

Paupers *White Nile* Itinerary

Egypt and Sudan portion (26 nights)
Does not include airfare unless otherwise stated

	US$	
	1 person	2 people
Arrive Cairo: Taxi to Garden City Hotel	15	15
Garden City Hotel, 2 nights, $25 single or double	50	50
Meals: breakfast at Hilton: $6, picnic style from groceries purchased locally, allow $7 = $13	26	52
Bus fares to Pyramids, Citidel, and National Museum	3	6
Bus to train station	.50	1
Train to Alexandria, return fare, 2nd class	4	8

	US$	
	1 person	2 people
El Mehrek Hotel, overnight, includes breakfast, $25 single or double	25	25
Meals: lunch in Alexandria from groceries purchased locally $3, dinner at Ramada Renaissance Hotel $10	13	26
Buses around Alexandria	3	6
Bus to railroad station	.50	1
Return to Cairo; bus to Garden City Hotel	.50	1
Garden City Hotel, 2 nights	50	50
Meals: breakfast at Hilton $6, lunch and dinner picnic style from groceries purchased locally, allow $7 a day ($13 × 2 days)	26	52
Train to Port Said, return fare, second class	6	12
Bus from station to city center	.50	1
Lunch in Port Said at Holiday Hotel	10	20
Return to Cairo same day: bus from station to Garden City Hotel	.50	1
Overnight Garden City Hotel, (previously charged)		
Bus to railroad station for train to Aswan	.50	1
Train to Aswan, single fare, second class	25	50
Bus from station to Happi Hotel	.30	.60
Groceries and bottled water purchased for trip to Khartoum from local grocers and also for meals in Aswan	60	120
Happi Hotel, 2 nights, $17 single or double	34	34
Ticket for Lake Nasser steamer, single fare, first class	42	84
Taxi to port to board steamer (really a necessity as there are groceries and bottled water to carry); no expenses on board steamer	10	10
Arrive Wadi Halfa; Walk to taxi park for taxi to Wadi Halfa	5	10
Groceries	8	16
Train to Khartoum, first class or sleeping car; no expenses on train	66	132
Arrive Khartoum: taxi to Sudan Club (train arrives about 10 p.m.)	6	6
Sudan Club, 4 nights, $25 single, $50 double, includes tax	100	200
Meals: breakfast $5, lunch $8, dinner $10 = $23 × 4 days (though it may be possible to economize with picnic meals, inflation in Khartoum has made prices very high, so use figure as a minimum)	92	184
Buses—although they are few and far between—around Khartoum	4	8
Taxi to airport for flight to Nairobi	5	5
Departure tax	8	16

Total:	$699.30	$1203.60
Cost per person sharing:	$601.80	

Kenya portion

Arrive Nairobi: airport bus to center of town	5	10
Bus from city center to guest house	.75	1.50

	US$	
	1 person	2 people
Methodist Guest House, 3 nights, full board, $17 single, $34 double	51	102
Optional: Zanzibar tour: Price includes transportation to airport from downtown hotels and compulsory guide. It is not recommended that readers attempt independent travel to Tanzania; apart from health considerations, they would eventually pay much more than shown here.	340	680
Buses around Nairobi	5	10
Spending money in Nairobi	15	30
Total:	$416.75	$833.50
Cost per person sharing:	$416.75	

Uganda portion

Depart Nairobi RR station to Kampala, round-trip ticket, 1st class, including bedding and meals	84	168
Stopover 1 night in Jinja. Taxi from station to Sikh Gurdwara. Donation to Sikh Gurdwara, taxi to Owen Falls and return, taxi to station	21	21
Arrive Kampala: Taxi to Kampala Sikh Gurdwara (it is possible to walk the distance)	5	5
Kampala Sikh temple, $10 donation for each night, per person, plus a gift for gyani's children brought from Nairobi (allow $10 for gifts) × 5 nights = $60	60	120
Buses around Kampala and to Kasubi Tombs	5	10
Meals: (meals are not served in this temple, so price for meals, regardless of what accommodation is used, will be about same) breakfast $8, lunch $10, dinner $15 = $33 a day × 5 days. Note: Some economies can be made by buying fresh fruit, etc., but prices are high and these amounts should be set aside.	165	330
Total:	$340	$654
15% tips to waiters/waitresses on all meals	58.35	116.70
Gratuity to housekeeping staff $1 a night for 1 or 2 persons	20	20
SOS Insurance, 1 month	45	90
Total:	$1579.40	$2917.80
Cost per person sharing:	$1458.90	

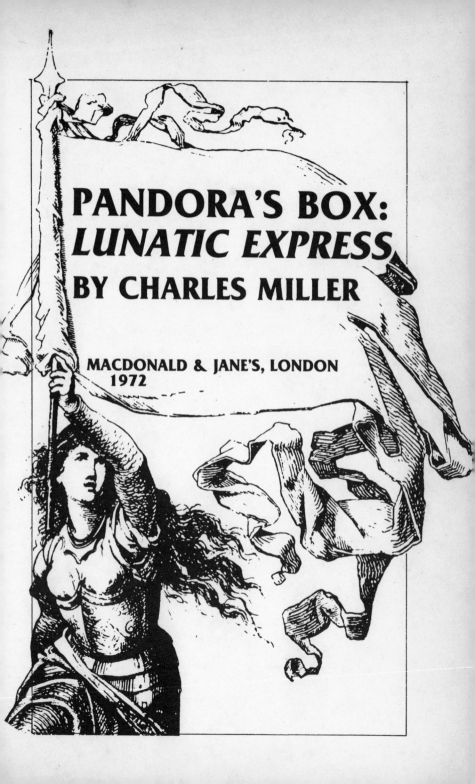

PANDORA'S BOX:
LUNATIC EXPRESS
BY CHARLES MILLER

MACDONALD & JANE'S, LONDON
1972

Building railroads in any new territory is charged with adventure. But building the Uganda Railway, as it was then called, with lions eating plate-layers and engineers, has to be the all-time epic adventure of the world's railway sagas.

Following the itinerary for Lunatic Express can be compared to watching a Eugene O'Neill play. The first act starts off slightly confused: setting the scene, explaining the problem. The theme develops in act two, and act three pulls it all together with the curtain going down on a statement about life. And so the building of the Uganda Railway must have seemed to the men who built it, but they had no O'Neill to forecast what lay ahead.

Lions were a constant threat to the safety of those who would venture into Africa's interior. This Victorian engraving illustrates Livingstone's encounter with one—only a taste of what lay in store for the engineers and plate-layers constructing the Uganda Railway.

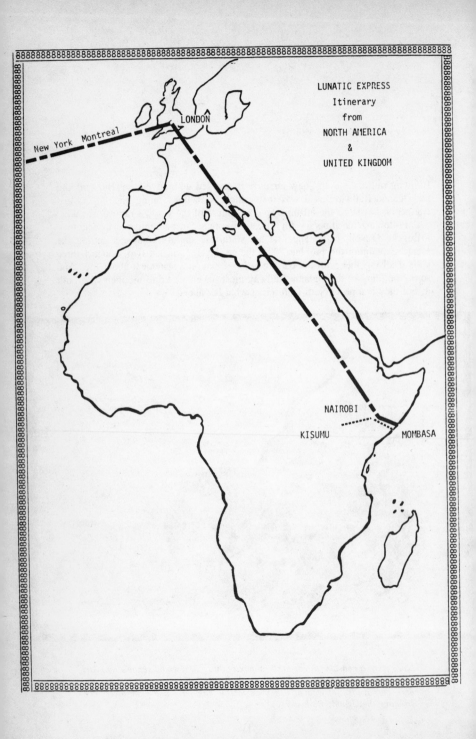

LUNATIC EXPRESS
Itinerary
from
NORTH AMERICA
&
UNITED KINGDOM

Mombasa, the port city where the railroad begins, is a relatively quiet, small town, more exciting when reflecting on its history than walking its streets. The great Swahili ruling families may be gone, yet there is a cosmopolitanism here not to be found in other Kenyan cities. In Old Town, like the greening of black lace on an old mantilla, the buildings speak of a dignity that was.

In the "Annotated Bibliography" we have listed books whose pictures depict Kilindini Docks as they were when the Uganda Railway engineers started construction. The old harbor on the north side of the island was the focal point for shipping as it had been for centuries; the draft of dhow vessels is shallow, easily accommodated on the north shore. British, American, and European merchant vessels had a deeper draft, and the coastal waters of Kilindini on the southern shore were made to order. If large quantities of raw materials from the hinterland were to be exported, these would be the carriers of commerce. Dhows sufficed for the relatively short voyages carrying mangrove poles, ivory, and slaves to Oman and the Persian Gulf. But the factories of the Industrial Revolution in Great Britain were geared to high production, and slaves were not a wanted commodity. Not Black slaves anyway. There was an abundance of landless peasantry streaming into the Midlands in search of piece work. Labor was not a problem.

Street scene in Mombasa, Kenya, sketched after World War II, although this particular area is much the same today.

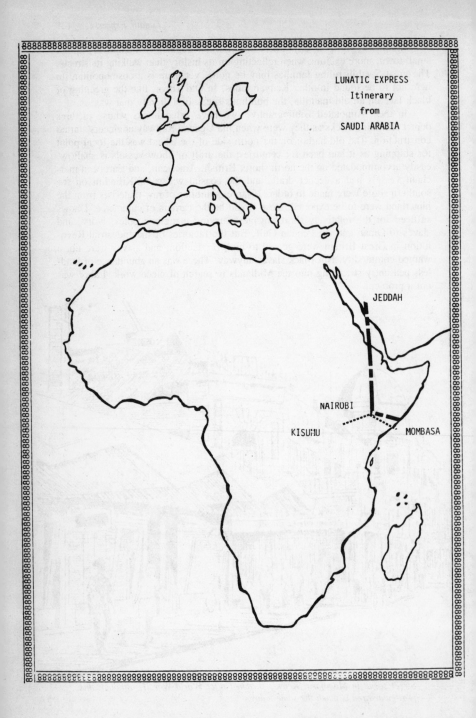

LUNATIC EXPRESS
Itinerary
from
SAUDI ARABIA

JEDDAH

NAIROBI

KISUMU   MOMBASA

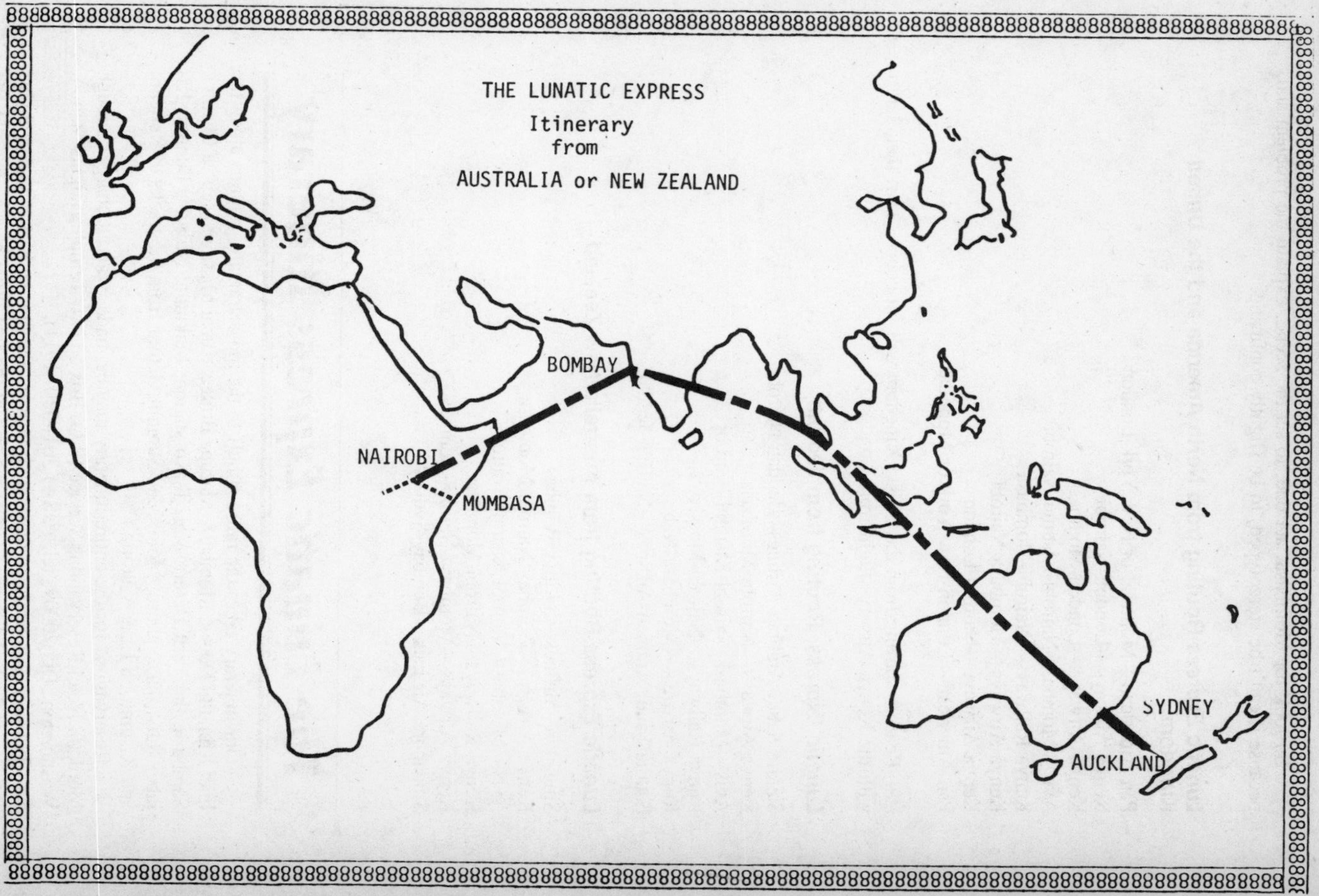

THE LUNATIC EXPRESS
Itinerary
from
AUSTRALIA or NEW ZEALAND

SYDNEY

AUCKLAND

BOMBAY

MUMBASA

NAIROBI

So look for Mombasa, act one, to set the scene, explain the problem and, because it can't be stereotyped, to be slightly confusing.

Lunatic Express Routing from North America and the United Kingdom

Pan American—Montreal or New York-London
Kenya Airways—London-Nairobi
Kenya Airways—London-Mombasa
Avis—Mombasa-Nairobi-Kisumu-Nairobi
Kenya Railways—Nairobi-Mombasa
Kenya Airways—Mombasa-Nairobi
Kenya Airways—Nairobi-London
Pan American—London-New York or Montreal

Readers starting from the United Kingdom will, of course, start their safari with the Kenya Airways flight from London.

Lunatic Express, Routing from Jeddah

Saudia Saudi Arabian Airlines—Jeddah-Nairobi
Kenya Airways—Nairobi-Mombasa
Avis—Mombasa-Nairobi-Kisumu-Nairobi
Kenya Railways—Nairobi-Mombasa
Kenya Airways—Mombasa-Nairobi
Saudia Saudi Arabian Airlines—Nairobi-Jeddah

Lunatic Express Routing from Australia-New Zealand

Singapore Airlines—Sydney-Bombay
Kenya Airways—Bombay-Nairobi-Mombasa
Avis—Mombasa-Nairobi-Kisumu-Nairobi
Kenya Railways—Nairobi-Mombasa
Kenya Airways—Mombasa-Nairobi-Bombay
Singapore Airlines—Bombay-Sydney

The Lunatic Express Itinerary

Our itinerary takes the railroad buff to the most dramatic stations along the line: Kilindini Docks, Mombasa; Macupa Bridge; Rubai Mission; Maji ya Chumvi; Samburu; the Taru Desert; Voi; Tsavo station; Makindu; Nairobi; Limuru; Kijabe; Naivasha; Nakuru; Molo; Mau Summit; detour from the tracks to Kericho; and Kisumu on Lake Victoria.

Reservations for the entire itinerary may be made, without charge, through Merikani Hotel Reservations Service (P.O. Box 53394, Temple Heights Station, Washington, DC 20009, tel. (USA) 301–530–1911).

We suggest readers do the route by car, as the present highways run almost parallel to the railway line, and at the end of the line drive back to Nairobi and take the train to Mombasa. It really isn't feasible to get on and off the train.

There are only two daily departures from Mombasa to Nairobi—5 and 7 p.m., both arriving 8 a.m. The same scheduled times apply to the two Nairobi-Mombasa trains. Passengers can get off at some stations, but often you would be deposited in small villages in the middle of the night where there is no accommodation and you would have to wait 24 hours to resume the journey.

By car, either driving yourself or with an Avis driver, it will be possible to stop not only at the stations we suggest but also to wander off and explore the nearby country—some of which is now national game parks.

So if you are coming to Kenya expressly to follow the *Lunatic Express* itinerary, book your airline ticket through to Mombasa. This will mean a change to Kenya Airways in Nairobi.

Day 1 and 2: Outrigger Hotel, Mombasa. Arrange for an Avis car to meet you at Moi International Airport in Mombasa. When you land, immediately as you enter the waiting room, you will see an Avis driver holding a small blackboard on a stick above his head on which has been written your name.

Let him drive you to the Outrigger Hotel (description in "Kenyan Accommodation"). Spend the remainder of the day resting, looking at the ships from your window as they pass into Kilindini Harbour, or swimming in Outrigger's pool. Decide if you want to drive the next day or if you want the Avis driver. Instruct Avis accordingly.

The next morning, visit Mombasa. We suggest you go to town in the morning when it is cooler and tour Kilindini Docks in the afternoon.

Use our map of Mombasa, because the other maps ignore the fact that north is universally accepted as being the top of a map, and this can be disorienting. However, our map shows only the main streets and a few places that we mention. Use our map, but also purchase the Esso cartoon map. It isn't laid out correctly, but it does show each street.

Drive to Fort Jesus. At the time of the building of the railway, these roads were lined with mango, cashew, and banana trees rather than shops and offices as they are now. One of the old trolleys, which was pushed by Swahili men along the 3-mile road between Old Town and Kilindini Harbour, with two passengers comfortably seated under its shading canopy can be seen at Fort Jesus.

Park and lock the car just in front of Fort Jesus and make your way up the cool, dark, inclined passageway. Charles Miller, author of *Lunatic Express*, gives background on Fort Jesus. There is a small charge to enter and the ticket seller also sells a guide to the fort and many other Museums of Kenya publications. The museum cases in Fort Jesus display relics recovered from archaeological digs within the walls of the fort as well as artifacts recovered by divers from the waters immediately in front of the fort. During one of the many battles for the fort, a Portuguese galleon was sunk. In the late 1970s the University of Texas contributed toward the salvage of these naval treasures.

After touring the fort walk into Old Town, taking the right-hand road. (See the sketch map in the *Lost Cities of Africa* itinerary.) Look in the shops but refrain from buying (they are, for the most part, ripoffs) until you see the stores at the end of the street. They sell an interesting assortment of antiques and crafts from up and down the east African coast. If you go toward the shore, you may be fortunate in seeing one or two of the few dhows that still call into this ancient port.

Return to your car and take Lighthouse Road back into town, noticing the Likoni Ferry as you drive around the first circle (roundabout). Imagining that the ensuing circles are clock faces, you will enter a circle at 6 o'clock and

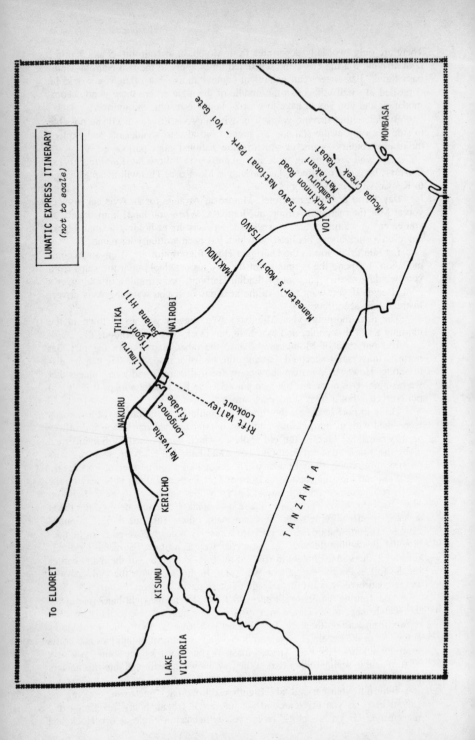

LUNATIC EXPRESS ITINERARY
(not to scale)

should drive out of the circle at 12 o'clock. There are several circles. Continue until, in the center of one circle, you see the sign marked "Nyali Bridge." Turn left—at 9 o'clock. Follow this road and the repeated signs for Nyali Bridge. There is a toll to pay at the bridge. After the bridge take a right-hand turn that follows the coastline. The grave of Mrs. Krapf can be seen by continuing on this road to McKenzie Point. Our map of Mombasa indicates the Krapf monument, and a few steps opposite it is his wife's grave.

Along this same road is perhaps *the* best restaurant in Kenya, the Tamarind. Stop and treat yourself to lunch on the terrace from where you can watch the comings and goings of people on the far shore and little boats in the old dhow harbor.

When you sign up for the Avis car mention that you would like to do the tour of the docks, if you have not previously made your reservations through Merikani Hotel Reservations. Avis will give you the information necessary to do so.

After touring Kilindini, try the Castle Hotel for either a cold beer, Coke, or tea on their famous porch (see "Kenyan Accommodation"). Return to the Outrigger for a shower and rest, and then have dinner in their dining room.

During this day and a half you will gain an appreciation of Mombasa's geographical features. It becomes apparent that Mombasa was the ideal site to develop as a commercial port and railhead to "open up East Africa to commerce." Apart from the trading conducted by MacKinnon's IBEA (Imperial British East Africa company), which had failed to show a profit for its investors, Kenya was virtually unknown. Settling the country with British farmers had not been envisaged. Speke, Burton, Grant, and Stanley had praised Uganda. Missionaries, both Catholic and Protestant, were established around what is now the city of Kampala. However, it was not totally to reinforce the missionaries' efforts that the railroad was built. MacKinnon, as chairman of the British India Steam Navigation Company, had an inordinate interest in promoting commerce to ports where his company might claim a monopoly as the Elder Dempster Line had in West Africa. In the section "Flute Out of Tune," Miller examines the motives of MacKinnon and ultimately the British government. No geological survey had been conducted to identify what resources might produce wealth. Perhaps they thought the odds favored finding another gold strike, as Rhodes had in Zimbabwe, or a valuable crop to rival the palm kernel oil taken from the River Niger. MacKinnon and the British public were ardent anti-slavers, and followed Livingstone's line of reasoning that legitimate trade could put an end to the traffic in human misery. Who was to say that these vast, unchartered regions of East Africa were not destined to be another India once the business acumen of England's merchants were applied to them? All these speculations and more entered into the decision to embark on railroad and port construction at Mombasa—but, as Miller points out, it was as much an emotional as a rational decision.

Day 3: Try to get a good night's rest to make an early start for the second act of *Lunatic Express*—the drive to Nairobi.

Macupa Bridge: Use the map of Mombasa to leave Outrigger Hotel and get onto the Mombasa-Nairobi highway. Try to leave between 9 and 9:30 a.m. The road follows the railroad tracks over Macupa Creek (note your mileage)—through the section known now as Changamwe—to Miritini and then to Mazeras, where the railroad engineers and workers got their baptism of fire as to what was in store for them if they intended to lay tracks across Kenya.

Note the above paragraph reads glibly; the stretch through Changamwe has been under construction for 5 years, as of 1987. The detour road is unbelievably terrible. Know that it becomes a normal road after Miritini.

We stopped at the unmarked entrance on the left-hand side of the road leading to a quarry to take pictures of Mombasa, as the view from this spot was exceptionally good.

Rabai Mission: Plan to stop at the village of Rabai where Johann Krapf made his home. Turn off the highway 6¼ mi past the Macupa Bridge. There is a sign, easily missed, indicating this right turn to Rabai. It is a well-paved road. Drive *about* 5 mi up and down low hills. On the right is the sign "Krapf Secondary School." Turn right toward this sign up a dirt road. Keep going, bearing left, until you reach the compound of Krapf Primary School playground. Park anywhere in the shade.

Krapf—who believed the Galla tribe to be the dominant, most powerful tribe in eastern Africa—determined to concentrate on their conversion to Christianity, believing that by their example conversion of the other tribes would follow.

The text of *Lunatic express,* in describing the numerous tribes encountered during the construction of the railroad, shows that there were many diverse tribes. There would appear to have been no truly dominant tribe in Kenya *at that time*.

So, Krapf, with this goal, was disappointed when he journeyed directly west from Mombasa hoping to find the southern populace of the Galla. Instead of Galla he found the Rabai.

The present population of Rabai is a mixture of many tribes, as runaway slaves, freed slaves, and refugees came to Krapf's mission as a haven. Whatever their origin, they are a delightful people both as adults and as children. Our reason for hoping you can leave Mombasa about 9 to 9:30 a.m. is so you can visit, as we did, with the primary school children during their morning recess.

The children are happy to see visitors; they are very shy, very well behaved as they follow you around smiling and repeating "Good morning! Good morning!" A multitude of dark eyes peer from behind braver eyes whose owners stand courageously in front of their contemporaries, all curious to know what brings you to their village.

The church dominates the compound, and directly opposite is the Rabai post office. We made inquiries there as to the whereabouts of the minister, only to be told he was away. However, the young postal worker was very helpful, hospitable, and gracious as a guide. We have since met Minister Demla, a grandson of James Rossendemla, who was the first African pastor at Rabai.

Krapf set about the task of evangelizing among the Rabai, and his diary *(Travels, Researches and Missionary Labours During an Eighteen Years' Residence in Eastern Africa,* Trubner: London, 1860, reprinted 1968 by Frank Cass, London and Johnson Reprint Corp.) is of extreme interest to those hoping to gain an insight into the development of racism. The attitudes of many Victorians can give a partial clue. Krapf, as we read him, is pompous, frustrated, and contemptuous of the Africans around him. He is also self-satisfied and displays an ethnocentricity that blinds him to any hope of understanding his hosts. His attitude contrasts dramatically with the uninhibited curiosity and readiness of the Rabai to objectively study and observe strangers, to assess what they see, and to adopt what they deem of value and tolerate what they reject.

From Rabai, Johann Rebmann, who joined Krapf in 1846, explored the west and became the first European to see, on May 11, 1848, the snows of Kilimanjaro.

Krapf's major contribution has been the writing in Roman script (it was previously written in Arabic) of the Swahili language and the compilation of a dictionary and grammar. There is a Krapf Society, sponsored by the West German government with headquarters in Kenya, whose members—of many nationalities, including Swahili scholars from the coast—build on the work he started. More about the society can be had by writing the German Embassy (P.O. Box 30180, Nairobi, Kenya).

The church at Rabai is actually Rebmann's doing. The site is serene and the climate temperate in contrast to the higher humidity of sea-level Mombasa. The present-day inhabitants have a reputation for scholarship among their youth, and although it is wrong to play favorites, we find them the most engaging people in Kenya, except, perhaps, for the Swahilis!

Leaving Rabai, return to the main Nairobi-Mombasa highway (this will be a right turn at the end of the Rabai road). If you have a particular interest in *Mariakani,* where so many railroad workers contracted their first of many bouts with African diseases, stop in and see the station.

Maji ya Chumyi: The next station, which stradles a stream, Maji ya Chumvi ("maji" meaning "water" and "Chumvi" meaning "salt"), is where Preston "had only a few crowbars, several hundred wooden sleepers (ties) and his own ingenuity" to lay a 40-foot girder across its banks.

Samburu: Manjewa station is followed by Samburu. Apart from Samburu being their first encounter with tsetse flies, whose bite killed the majority of transport animals brought for use in building the railroad, Samburu is not a station of outstanding interest in the building of the Lunatic Express. However, while driving the Nairobi-Mombasa road we had a flat tire and "limped" into the village, which is no more than a collection of small shops on either side of the highway. Everyone in the village gathered around to see the puncture and assist in changing the tire. They refused our offer of payment. In January 1984 a tragic car accident near Samburu killed four of the occupants. The generous help of the people of Samburu was acknowledged by their relatives in a paid advertisement in the press. If you can make up an excuse to stop—to buy a Coke or cigarettes—and can find a way to strike up a conversation, we think you'll find the people charming. (The name of their town should not be confused with the nomadic tribe of the same name who live in northern Kenya.) Samburu is also known for a pink-orange-cream sandstone quarried nearby, and as you drive toward Nairobi you'll see piles of the stone displayed for sale. They make beautiful fireplaces.

Taru: Next come Mwembeni and Taru stations; the latter is the beginning of what Preston calls the Taru Desert. Flying over and driving through this area today, it is difficult, using our contemporary definition of the word "desert," to understand his use of this term. The land is hard and dry most of the year, except during the short rainy season, but hardly a desert in the sense of sand and dunes. Miller agrees that it is not a desert, "but something more like a dense forest of wire-bristled, man-high, scrubbing brushes." The density of the thorn bush today, 80 years later, must be less than it was when the railroad was being built. The bushes are a few feet apart now, and it would be possible to pick a path through them without too much danger of being cut by their thorns. This was not the case at the turn of the century. The thorns brought great suffering to the railroad construction workers, many of whom worked barefoot, and the thorns caught and tore the skin of their arms. The wounds then became infected. Undoubtedly the land since 1900 has been subjected to countless slash-and-burn clearings, certainly severe droughts, and overgrazing by both domestic and wild animals—all of which have lessened the ferocity of the virgin land that Preston called the Taru Desert.

MacKinnon Road: It is at MacKinnon Road that the route carved out by the Imperial East Africa Company met the old slave caravan route. It is a very well-kept station, and we enjoyed our visit with the stationmaster. Don't overdrive the entrance as we did.

Voi: Drive on to Voi; the town now lies within a horseshoe bypass of the highway. The right-turn entry to the town is clearly marked. Follow the horseshoe around until you see the yellow sign on the left denoting the railroad station. Immediately opposite the sign is Voi Cemetery, where the veterans of several wars are buried.

Voi station is large and well kept, and there is ample parking. Lock the car and walk around. There is an interesting huge old baobob tree with countless initials scarred into its bark. You may want to introduce yourself to the stationmaster; his office is well marked. The staff here are responsible not only for operating the Mombasa-Nairobi line but also the Taveta-Arushua line.

Leaving the station, turn right and drive slowly so as not to miss (on your left) the sign for the "Voi Entrance" of Tsavo East National Park. (You passed it on your right going in.)

There is a charge to enter, and you must sign your name in a ledger. Follow the road to the left and wherever there is an alternate road, *keep to the left*. The lodge will be seen in just under 2 miles.

The lodge is the ideal place to have lunch. You may want to take it in the bar instead of the dining room. Here, for the first time, we felt the immensity of the task that lay ahead of the railroad builders as we saw from this vantage point the seemingly endless stretch of empty space that builds to the horizon.

The recent history of wildlife conservation at Tsavo East has been a sorry one. British and White Kenyan conservationists became embroiled in personal squabbles during the 1970s about how best to preserve Tsavo East wildlife—particularly the elephant and rhino. Kenyan Somali tribesmen had a field day killing the animals, taking their ivories and horns, while the "experts" argued. The result is that there is little wildlife of the "big five" variety to be seen today at Tsavo East. (For details, read Ian Parker's *Ivory Crisis*, Chatto & Windus, London, 1983; and Esmond Bradley Martin's *Run Rhino, Run,* Chatto & Windus, London, 1982.)

We met a young Englishman who had been traveling in a rented car with his parents in Tsavo East. They got stuck in mud up to the axle and it was two nights and a day and a half before they got out of their predicament. No wardens were patrolling the park in their vicinity. No one came to search for them, despite the fact that the purpose of the ledger at the main gate is to keep track of visitors. They had reservations at the self-service cottages and when they did not arrive, no one queried it or checked the ledger. They had no food and were out in the vast plain with nothing in sight. Zebra stopped by, but that was all they saw during their imprisonment. They kept believing a game warden or other tourists would come. They didn't. On the morning of the third day they got out and walked—although walking in the game parks is strictly prohibited because of wild animals—to the self-service cottages only to be told that their cottage had been given to someone else, and because the cottages were "self-catering," there was no food for them. This surely has to be the all-time low in the Kenyan Park Service relations with tourists.

Obviously the game wardens' morale is low because so few tourists visit Tsavo East. The moral of the story is don't drive around Tsavo East to look at wildlife. Much more abundant game may be seen in other parks on the *Lunatic Express* itinerary, so don't get stuck in this park. Make sure you take a left turn after you enter through the Voi entrance gate; keep to the left, and go around, not through, any mud. However, you're unlikely to encounter mud along this particular 2 miles to the lodge.

Maps of the park are available either at the gate or in the lodge bookshop. For railroad enthusiasts they are an interesting addition to a *Lunatic Express* collection.

Voi is 94 mi (149 km) from Mombasa. If you left Rabai around 11 a.m., this should put you at Tsavo East Lodge at Voi for lunch about 1:30. Try to leave by 2:30. Return the way you came. Turn right after the gate onto the horseshoe bypass until you reach the highway. Go right. Some 30 miles ahead, on the right, is the yellow railroad sign for Tsavo railroad station. (About 300 yards, on the left, is the Mobil Maneaters gas station. If you pass this you know you've gone too far. Turn around and go back onto the rough road that leads to the station. It's only a track, not a real road.)

You will want to spend some time at Tsavo Station, which is famous for the man-eating lions. Today it's a lonely, quiet station since it isn't a stop for passengers, only freight. Philip Njenga was the new stationmaster when we visited in 1984. We hope he will be there when our readers visit. His enthusiasm and knowledge can make this a delightful experience. Mr. Njenga appears a bit hesitant at first. This is deceptive. His mind is racing ahead, wondering what facet of his work or his station you would most appreciate. He quietly, and with a slow smile, asked us, "Would you like to see how the signals work?" Upon confirmation that his sixth sense had been accurate, he led the way. We are very conscious of being women in a man's world when it comes to railroads, and never in our wildest dreams did we expect to be permitted inside that most holy of holies—the signal tower. He explained in detail the safety features of the signal levers as he pulled the shining brass handles and urged us to watch the signal 200 feet away move its "arms." Mr. Njenga is unassuming, patient, and extremely polite; readers are cautioned not to interrupt him, as a Kenyan of his character would form a poor opinion of the visitor. Mr. Njenga is an excellent example of Kenya's large cadre of skilled people. Such people are not often encountered by tourists, and if you approach your meeting with Mr. Njenga with a certain amount of sensitivity, the reward will be an accurate picture of a modern Kenyan.

It was high noon during our visit, but I was eager to see Patterson's bridge up close. Mr. Njenga and I walked down the track, leaving Leah (who had more sense) in the shade. He countered my complaints that it was a long walk for an old woman by assuring me that "healthy exercise is very good for the elderly." It is a beautiful little bridge, and Mr. Njenga can point out where Patterson laid his rails to bring the stone from the quarry he found while out hunting for guinea fowl. (See *The Maneaters of Tsavo,* by J. H. Patterson, 1907, reprinted 1979 by Fontana Books.) The land is dry, slightly rocky, but covered only with light brush—quite different from the description given by Patterson and Preston at the time of the railroad's construction.

Walk along the tracks, noticing how perfectly the stone chippings bordering the rails lie in a perfect straight line at the outer edge. These chips are regularly raked with a plumb line. Ask Mr. Njenga about the maintenance routine for the rails.

Behind Tsavo Station is a European grave marked by a now broken cross and a surround. The inscription reads:

VERITE __ARD

Elle etait de ce monde on les plus douces __nt
le pire dest.

"She was of this world where the sweetest things
have the worst destiny."

The Granth Sahib, the holy book of the Sikhs whose temple is a few miles on up the road, has a verse which reads:

See how sugar-cane is cut down and made into
    sheaves after the stalks are cleaned.
The laborers put it into a press and squeeze it.
Having expressed the juice, they put it into
    a pan, and it groans as it burns.
The residue is collected and put into the fire
    beneath the pan.
Nanak, sweet things are thus ill-treated, come
    and see, O people!

Who was the lady buried at Tsavo Station? How did Death come to take her in this barren land? Did a Sikh railroad worker console her loved ones with the sentiment expressed in his holy book? Or was this simply coincidence?

Drive back to the highway, Mobil's Maneaters gas station is a reminder of home and worth a stop for a cold Coke. While wandering around, look down at the rails in the grass under the open stairs leading to the upstairs dining room. We thought, when we first saw them on an earlier drive to the coast, that these were Patterson's quarry rails. They were laid in the 1970s, however, when some enterprising Kenyan government employees decided that a hotel-cum-motel along the road at Tsavo would be a tourist attraction if old refurbished sleeping cars were used for rooms. To add authenticity, they laid the rails and purchased the cars from the railroad for a mere 1000 shillings each (US$74). The newspapers in Nairobi found out about it, a hue and cry went up from the public, the would-be entrepreneurs lost their government jobs, and their brilliant moneymaker never came to fruition. Presumably Mobil bought the site, and today instead of a colorful sleeping-car motel we have an antiseptic white concrete facade and a typical American gas station.

Makindu: Leaving Maneaters behind, drive to Makindu. On the right is a sign to the railroad station just as you approach the town. The actual village of Makindu is farther in from the road and cannot be seen. There is a small administrative complex near the Makindu railroad station consisting of a police headquarters and barracks with a canteen, a post office and radio-call public phone; and a hospital. Everyone was very friendly and we had a Coke at the police canteen.

As it is by now about to turn dark (and remember, it does so very quickly), we suggest staying the night at the Sikh temple (Sikh Gurdwara), an ornate, pastel-colored building of Indian architecture on the main highway just after the railroad station sign and Twenty Second Boarding and Lodging, Hard Life Bar and Restaurant, and Road Side Butcher (their fronts painted brilliant red and white courtesy of Coca-Cola).

There are two other places to stay in the vicinity: Hunter's Lodge about 7 miles up the road, and Tsavo Inn. Hunter's Lodge caters to tour groups, and we consider it a ripoff for the independent traveler—unappetizing food and too-high prices. Tsavo Inn is all right and its food is quite good, but it is too far away to include in the *Lunatic Express* itinerary. In any case, spending a night at a Sikh temple is not something every tourist gets to do, and the experience will add to an appreciation of the men who built the Uganda Railway.

There was no ethnic recording of the Indian labor force brought to Kenya to work on the railroad, but the majority were from Gujarat and Punjabi Sikhs. The Sikhs were not the "coolies" so often referred to but semiskilled and skilled metal workers. They stayed on in East Africa after the completion of the track laying to man the workshops and engines of the Uganda Railway for 60 to 70 years. India has many religions, but the largest are Hindu, Moslem, and Sikh. The British never did manage to make the distinction between Sikh and Hindu throughout the colonial history of India. This is the source of today's problems in India over the desire for Sikh autonomy.

The Sikh religion began as a reform of the Hindu and Moslem religions plus the philosophy of the first Sikh teacher, Nanak, born in 1469. Nine other teachers followed him down to the year 1708, the last teacher being Gobind (born 1666). Nanak had taught peaceful reform, but the violent zeal of Moslem evangelists proved this to be impractical if the Sikh religion was to survive. Gobind instituted a form of adult baptism in which Sikhs were to distinguish themselves from Hindus and Moslems by (1) not cutting their hair, (2) wearing undershorts so as to be always ready to defend themselves (as opposed to the loose "dhoti," or skirt worn over bare skin throughout much of India), (3) carry a knife or sword, (4) wear a turban as a form of helmet, and (5) wear a steel bracelet to remind them to put their faith in steel, not gold. Gobind also gave the name "Singh" (meaning "lion") to men to further identify themselves. "Kaur" is used by women.

The Sikh religion has no idols and believes God to be an indefinable life force incomprehensible to man. All religions are believed to be equal; each person perceives God as God wishes. Sikhs are forbidden to evangelize and no one will discuss religion with you if you stay at the gurdwara. In their gurdwaras only the holy book (Granth Sahib) containing the written teachings of their ten teachers is on the altar. Any Sikh may conduct services; there are no learned priests, only caretakers (gyanis) of the building. Women, from the time of Nanak, have always been equal with men. Work and the perfection of skills is an integral part of Sikhism. However, higher university learning is not encouraged as much as the trades: military, metalworking, carpentry, and farming. Loyalty to one's political master is considered virtuous. For this last reason, and because Gobind foresaw the coming of the English, the British when they conquered India found the Sikhs to be the most tractable of all Indians and used them as soldiers, policemen, skilled carpenters, and metalworkers. Their home state is the fertile, well-watered Punjab where their farms produce an abundance of staple crops for all of India. An English translation by Max Arthur Macauliffe of the Granth Sahib (Oxford University Press, 1910) is available in reprint from a publisher in India (See "Annotated Bibliography.") The Makindu Gurdwara is the central temple for all of Kenya. Mt. Kilimanjaro can be seen on the far horizon from the turrets.

At one time the railway workshops were located at Makindu and there was, therefore a large concentration of Sikh metalworkers whose families living in Mombasa or Nairobi would come to visit on weekends. Thus the Makindu Gurdwara developed in a comparatively unpopulated area. There is a legend popular among modern Kenyan Sikhs that one of the railway workers, while working at Makindu, "had a vision" and "heard a voice," telling Sikhs to build a gurdwara at Makindu. (See "Kenyan Accommodations.")

The market immediately outside the Sikh temple sells fruits and vegetables. An old woman sells some of the nicest hand-carved wooden kitchen spoons, ranging in size from standard (10 to 12 inches long) to long (24 to 28 inches). Her prices are absurdly cheap and too low to bargain over without feeling you are exploiting her.

A Moslem mosque, just farther on, was under construction during the time we were in Kenya. We look forward to its completion.

Day 4: Next morning, after breakfast, drive to Nairobi. On the outskirts of the city the signs point to the Industrial Area, the airport, and the city center. Disregard the first two and continue straight as the road becomes Uhuru Highway. Follow the Nairobi city map to the Hilton. There is valet parking, so pull up at the entrance. For a description of the Hilton International Nairobi, see "Kenyan Accommodation."

After you're settled into your room call Avis and ask that they arrange for you to have a driver the next morning. Suggest that he meet you in the Hilton lobby at 9:15. Driving in Nairobi is terrible; there are no predictable traffic patterns; drivers lack common courtesy; there are unmarked one-way streets. All and all, Nairobi driving is a frustration, so ask for a driver.

Night 4: Overnight at the Hilton.

Day 5: The Railroad Buff's Nairobi. The first stop today is the Railway Museum. There is a small entrance fee. A printed guide can also be purchased for a few shillings. The indoor displays exhibit early maps, equipment, dining-car furniture, utensils, and anything concerning the Uganda Railway.

The outdoor museum has the following preserved locomotives on display: Beyer Peacock Ltd., Manchester, England, 49.8-ton, Class DL Tanzanian Rail-way locomotive used from 1923 to 1973; Kenya, Uganda Railways, and Harbours "F" Class locomotive built in 1897; Kenya, Uganda Railways, No. 1 "Kilifi," later 28 Class "2801" locomotive; the last Vulcan Foundry, Manchester, England, 50.7-ton "26" Class saturated steam locomotive; and the following locomotives used by East African Railways—"12" Class, "13" Class, "26" Class, "29" Class, "31" Class, "54" Class, "58" Class, and "60" Class.

The museum has collectors' items for sale. Inquire at the director's office. *Permanent Way,* the official history of the railroad, can also be purchased.

After visiting the Railway Museum, drive to Nairobi Station and have lunch at the Station Restaurant—one of the best places in Nairobi to eat, and without question they brew the best pot of tea.

We suggest the afternoon be spent at the Railway Training Center and Railway Workshops, and we have given the name of the person to call confirming the time you will be there in ''Plan Ahead'' at the end of this itinerary.

It's a long time until dinner, so after seeing the training center and workshops have the driver take you to the Norfolk Hotel. Try to beat the rush-hour traffic that starts about 4:20.

The Norfolk is the most historic hotel in Kenya, and we describe it in ''Kenyan Accommodation.'' Tea or a beer on their terrace passes a pleasant hour. Go into the garden to see the old automobiles and wagons, and have a glance at the Pioneer Room photographs.

After 5:45 (when the traffic will have died down) return to the Hilton; let the Avis driver park the car at the Hilton, and unless you want him for the evening, tell him to return at 11 the next morning. A good meal in the Hilton's Amboseli Grills rounds off a good day. (They usually have a live band and dancing.)

Night 5: At the Hilton.

Day 6: In the morning plan to take it easy until about 11. You might want to go to Select Bookshop, just a block away from the Hilton, and get a copy of *Steam in Africa* by A. E. Durrant, et al. (Hamlyn: London and New York, 1981).

At 11 meet your Avis driver and have him drive you to the suburbs, where he can leave, as you can drive the rest of the route. You want to get onto the Limuru Road to arrive at Kentmere Club in time for lunch. Look for the sign ''Kentmere Club'' just after passing the turn to Nazareth Hospital. The sign is on the right and hangs high along a 6-foot fence. Park, lock the car, and check in. Settle in your room or cottage, and after lunch spend the afternoon exploring the station at Limuru and the huge open market, and photographing the Rift Valley from the Lookout Point at the Escarpment.

Limuru: The Limuru railroad station sign is on the left-hand side of the road going into the village, after leaving Tigoni, and just before the Bata Shoe Factory entrance. Pull into the yard and have a look. When you've finished, drive to the entrance to the shoe factory, park and lock the car, and walk up into the market. We drove through, but the donkey carts, matatoos, and farmers loading and unloading in the single lane ''passage''—it cannot by any stretch of the imagination be called a road—can try one's patience.

Don't be intimidated by the crowds. The people are kind and helpful, but they are country people and may be a bit shy. Here in the market is the place to purchase blackened, handmade, clay cooking pots such as the people use every day over charcoal fires and which look so exotic outside Africa. If, when you get Kisumu, you buy a basketweave ring, which the lake women use to carry burdens on their heads, you can stand the round-bottomed Kikuyu pot on it and use it as a vase. The medium size, about 3 quarts, costs 9 shillings (67 cents); the large ones, one gallon or more, are 12 shillings (about 89 cents). It will cost you twenty times that much to get one of them home unbroken unless you carry it in your hand baggage on the plane and pack its spacious inside with smaller souvenirs.

Limuru is where, for the first time since starting to build the railway, the workers and engineers were free from sickness. Driving around the area you'll see why. The climate is almost alpine; fires are needed at night; mosquitoes are few; Limuru is a thousand feet higher than swampy Nairobi. At Limuru the railmen's wounds healed, their lungs were freed from hacking coughs, and their malarial fevers subsided.

We suggest readers ask permission before taking pictures of the people in the market.

You should be finished with the market and Limuru station by 3:30, so there is plenty of time for the drive to the Lookout Point for the Escarpment. Today drive only as far as the Escarpment Lookout. It is a marvelous place to take pictures, and you will want to bring all your photographic equipment, including a tripod if you brought one, to photograph the magnificent scene. From the Lookout Point, scars in the rock (to the left) mark where the steep inclined tracks (by which trains were raised and lowered by pullies) were set. There is a definite break in the tree line; the trees beside the inclined track are more mature and taller than the volunteer seedlings that have taken root since the tracks were removed. Today's trip should end at the lookout. Return to Kentmere for dinner and an evening in the Kentmere bar.

Night 6: At Kentmere Club. Before you turn in for the night ask that early morning coffee or tea be brought to your room or cottage.

Day 7: Explore the floor of the Rift Valley and the stations there. Retrace your steps to the Escarpment Lookout but don't stop; continue on. Follow the new highway to the turning, on the left, for Naivasha. Continue until the remnants of the old Nairobi-Nakuru road are seen. This is a tarmacked road but is not kept in repair. Turn left onto it, missing the town of Naivasha, which would be straight on. You may want to see Naivasha Station, but we found the people not too helpful.

The lanes (a more accurate word than roads) to the stations on the Escarpment floor became obvious, as there is nothing along here but the stations. Just after going onto the old road—about 2 miles—is Lake Naivasha Hotel. We're sorry not to be able to recommend it because it would be a convenient place to stop, and the setting is very beautiful. If an emergency should arise, we feel certain the staff at the hotel would be helpful, but other than that, and until standards improve (everything is very confused, service absolutely hopeless and slow), there is no reason to stop.

Longonot Station: Stands at the foot of Longonot Crater, a volcanic Rift Valley hill whose crater is a mile wide. The surrounding area is now a national reserve. Although climbers walk up to the crater, we suggest readers not do so as it is lonely and thieves may be about. In any case, readers will primarily be interested in the station.

Kijabe Station: This location is now best known as the headquarters and main school of the African Inland Mission (AIM). This is a Christian American evangelical group, very well established since the early days of missionary work in Kenya, and you may want to stop in for a visit.

We suggest you use the new road down to Naivasha and the old road back for several reasons: (1) driving back you will be on the left-hand side of the road nearest the cliff (remember, in Kenya they drive on the left); the right-hand side has some sheer drops with no guardrails; (2) the old road follows the railroad track, and the new one is a long way up and away from them; (3) we think you will enjoy exploring the floor of the Escarpment after seeing it from above.

After Kijabe is a small stone church, which was built by Italian prisoners of war who were in Kenya during World War II. It is beautiful in its simplicity, and is well tended, with fresh flowers on the altar in tin can vases. There is a place to pull off the road while you look at the church. The view of the Escarpment floor from the churchyard is well worth studying.

Immediately opposite the church is a dirt road. Drive down this road, looking back at the Rift cliff faces. We saw over 20 Grant's gazelle and African guinea fowl and zebra among grazing cows. In 1984 this area was gazetted by the Kenyan government as a national game reserve, and it may be under their care when you visit. In this case, there may be more game and probably a fee to pay somewhere.

Night 7: Kentmere Club. Plan to make an early start the next morning for the drive to Kericho via Nakuru.

Day 8: Nakuru station and Kericho. Give the town of Nakuru a miss, except for the railroad station. Nakuru has some great public relations people working on publicizing the town's beauties, but we have yet to identify what they are and the inhabitants are not very hospitable. However, the staff at the railway station, like all their colleagues along the line, are very helpful.

Apart from the Station Restaurant, Nakuru boasts two hotels where a foreign visitor might stop: the Stag's Head and the Midland. We recommend neither.

Another reason to dislike Nakuru is the town's predisposition to put huge speed bumps in the street without adequate warning signs that are clearly visible to drivers in both directions. Crack your car's drive shaft on one of these and see if you don't share our opinion that Nakuru should be given a miss except for the railroad station.

> **AUTHOR'S NOTE:** *The only thing you want out of Nakuru is gas (petrol). Don't, whatever you do, forget to get gas at Nakuru, because the next gas station is in Kericho, and the car takes more than the usual amount of gas to get around the hills in third gear (see below).*

Park the car in front of the station (disregard the 20-minute parking notice), and enter through the main entrance. On the far wall is a huge ethnocentric mural. In the center of the mural is a train winding its way through the Rift Valley. The male figure of a White settler dominates the picture. Immediately to his right, on horseback, is his fair-skinned wife (?). (It is difficult to make assumptions on their relationship: the settlers swapped wives as other people trade stamps, so the lady may be someone else's wife. Be that as it may, the artist obviously meant to convey that there were females in supporting roles; all the same, she is no "Madonna of the Trail.") To the left foreground of the mural is Kikuyu warrior in full tribal dress. The remainder of the mural is filled with landscape. The message of the mural seems to be the heroic settlement of the Rift Valley, that responsibility for the existence of the railroad is due to the energies of the White settler, and that the Africans were happy to see the "iron snake" (as the Masai called the train) churn up their land. The assertion that the mural is ethnocentric comes not so much because the artist depicted all of the local tribes as Kikuyu, but for the omission of any reference to the 32,000 Indian workers who laid the tracks for the railroad. Certainly no White settlers were even hanging around the Rift Valley, waiting on horseback or otherwise, for the plate-layers to complete the job. The only British were Preston and his surveyors and a few other hard-working construction engineers. Nothing we can write can more adequately convey the racist attitude of the majority (not *all*; there are always some liberals everywhere) of Kenya's White settlers than this Nakuru Railway Station mural.

A wide staircase leads to a second-floor (first floor in British counting) restaurant. Through the doors, on the right, is an innocent mural by the same artist. It is of African wildlife. We make no criticism. The restaurant is well laid out; the tables are covered with starched white tablecloths and railway-heavy, hotel-grade silver. Service is excellent. Three-course meals are very good and tea or coffee is served, again, from heavy railway silver pots.

You may want, after lunch or before, to introduce yourself to the station-master whose office is on the ground floor. He will give you a warm welcome and answer any questions you may have.

Drive on to Molo. The village itself is rather tatty, but the Highlands Hotel just outside of town is nice for a stop.

Once at Mau Summit the weather becomes cooler than down on the floor of the Escarpment, the air freer of dust, and the vegetation green. Look for the turning to Kericho. This road (it is tarmac) goes south of the railroad tracks, but we want readers to see beautiful Kericho. The road climbs and drops, and driving is completely different than it was two hours earlier. We shifted to second gear on the turns for easier maneuverability. This helps when trucks come barreling around the curves crossing over the median line. By all means swear at such drivers, but it is up to you to take evasive action. It's your neck. They don't seem particularly worried about theirs.

Mau Summit: As you drive up the Escarpment it is seen in all its beauty. Mau Summit is only a wide place in the road, but it presents a forecast of the breathtakingly beautiful scenery that you will see on the road to Kericho. The station itself is made of corrugated iron sheets, and while not the original station, it is very old. Before you reach Kericho the tea estates come into view. Their trimmed Nile-green bushes contrast with the forest green of the tall pines, all set under a brilliantly blue sky, where one beautiful panorama follows another. The first indications of "tea country" are the small cement houses on the left-hand side of the road. These belong to the tea pickers. They will be followed by signs indicating that you are approaching Kericho. Drive on until you see the "Tea Hotel" sign.

Kericho: At Kericho the impression is of order and cleanliness. Buildings are well maintained, lawns cut, and signs exist to inform the newcomer of the whereabouts of various services. The Tea Hotel is described in "Kenyan Accommodation."

Night 8: Tea Hotel, Kericho.

Day 9: Kericho to Kisumu and Sunset Hotel. After breakfast, leave the Tea Hotel, turning left onto the Kisumu road. The scenery changes as, after climbing steep hills with Devil's Horseshoe turns, the descent to Lake Victoria begins. The Nandi Hills are pale blue far off to the right, and one waits expectantly for the first sight of Lake Victoria. Moisture from the lake, dust from secondary roads (the route we follow is on tarmac), or smoke from slash-and-burn culti-vation can be held in suspension above the lake and at the base of the hills, preventing that first glimpse of Victoria. But on a clear day it is seen in all its majesty. When you reach Kisumu, take a left-hand turn to the Sunset Hotel. Check into the hotel and ask for a room on one of the upper floors (they have a better view); all rooms face the lake and have sliding glass doors from floor to ceiling and wall to wall. A description of the Sunset Hotel is in "Kenyan Accommodation."

The hotel is very close, 500 yards at most, to the lake's shore and is rightly named—the sunsets are magnificent. The railway enthusiast wonders if Engi-neer and Mrs. Preston took time, at the end of the day, to watch the sun go down over the lake. We would think they did. They seem, through the pages of his diary, to be a very human couple; he left the last spike in the track for her to hammer home; their domesticity was enhanced by their little dog and Mrs. Preston's insistence on wearing the clothes, in the midst of literally un-charted wilderness, that Victorian women in cooler, more genteel climates wore. Only when she drove home the spike did she hand over her parasol, which shielded her from the ravages of the African sun. The Prestons stayed on in Kenya after the completion of the railroad. He wrote his diary into a book and, always a friend to the Indian community in Kenya, he edited *Oriental Nairobi,* which describes the activities of Hindu, Moslem, and Sikh peoples in building that city. Their son, Vic Preston, was one of the earliest competitors in the East African Rally (now the Marlboro Safari Rally) and owns a large automobile dealership in Nairobi.

Kisumu Town: After settling into the Sunset Hotel, drive a few miles back into the city center of Kisumu. Kisumu proves that not all Kenyan towns—apart from Nairobi and Mombasa—must be sidewalkless. Additionally, the entire in-dustrial area—where the vehicle repair and wholesale merchants are—is paved, which is certainly not true of any other Kenyan town. What a difference it makes to the quality of life for everyone, especially for the people working there. Kisumu also proves life is possible in Kenya without billowing clouds of dust and shows what city pride can do. The town is clean, the buildings well maintained, and it is a pleasure to walk along the streets, peering into shop windows that display a multitude of merchandise.

Stock up on spices at Nyanza Trading Company, where they are sold by the kilo (or fraction thereof) at prices that make you recognize that importers of spices in our home country must be just as wealthy as were those who brought spices from the east by camel caravan.

More important, however, than the physical attributes of Kisumu is the hospitality of the people.

Night 9: Sunset Hotel.

Day 10: Have breakfast early and visit Kisumu City Market and the mu-seum before driving back to Nairobi. It is possible to drive straight through to Nairobi from Kisumu in 6–7 hours if stops are not made (except for gas and a meal).

A drive into town is well worthwhile to visit Kisumu City Market. The market is very clean. We had expected better baskets than we found, but other things made up for this disappointment. Let us preface our comments by saying that every seller in the market understood everything we said in our American

English. This is such a change from having to resort to pidgin English in the Nairobi area. Our first comments were on the high chairs used by the sellers themselves behind the counters. There are two styles: wrapped papyrus and natural bentwood. They can be made to order for 50 Kenyan shillings each. If you're looking for a comfortable chair for your bar, these chairs may just be the answer, although how much it would cost to get them home is another matter. They are not collapsible. The vegetables and fruits are beautifully laid out, and the sellers do not hassle you to buy once you tell them you are living in a hotel with no kitchen! Clay pots, not quite as nice as at Limuru, are stacked in tall piles. We liked the 6-foot-long drinking straws, which are used for communal sipping of local beer. One end of the straw has an infinitely fine sieve, woven of split reed, to catch any sediment. These would look attractive pinned to a wall alongside a few Masai spears. Macrame hanging plant holders made from locally produced sisal are also sold. Kenyans hang the macrame, or a similar braided string holder, from the rafters in their homes to keep food away from dirt and animals. Hanging pots are less expensive than storing food in a meat safe (a wooden cupboard with screened doors) and save space.

The Kisumu Museum is just on the immediate outskirts of Kisumu. It is a very original museum; there are few glass-encased exhibits, but the full-scale typical Luo village is a one-of-a-kind exhibit for any country. Rarely does a visitor, or even an expatriate resident, have the opportunity to go inside a real African mud-and-thatch home. The day we visited Kisumu Museum was very hot. Walking into the house is like going into air conditioning. Naturally cool, dark, the roof shades the doorway so that no streak of sunshine heats the room. Your eyes grow accustomed to the dark, and you realize that it isn't dark, it is merely shadow in which everything can be seen. There is an incline made of mud that is worn smooth and used for a bed. Pots hang from the rafters, and if this were a lived-in home, they would contain food and milk. The floor is also worn smooth from the grass brooms that seek our every crevice. When the house was originally built, the clay was packed hard by countless short steps. Outside the house the daily sweeping makes the immediate surroundings as clean as the inside floor. A cluster of homes comprise a family grouping. The architecture is marvelously practical for the climate, because almost every day is sunny. Housing is needed for privacy, to store personal belongings, for protection from wild animals at night, and for shelter from the rain—although many times shelter from the weather is taken in a community shelter so that conversation can continue.

Several locally found snakes are housed in tanks in the museum building, as well as some stuffed animals and exhibits of tribal dress, spears, and tools. Altogether a memorable exhibit.

Night 10: Sunset Hotel.

Day 11: We have not listed the sights to be seen in Kisumu in order, believing that you'll want to arrange your own schedules, but Kisumu Railway Station is a must whether it is visited at the start of your visit to Kisumu or at the end of the visit. We strongly suggest that you go to the stationmaster's office and ask that either he, or one of his staff, show you around the station, and perhaps drive with you to the harbor area. In this way you'll have a better appreciation of the rationale for building the *Lunatic Express:* the harbor provides easy access for cargoes and passengers into central Africa by steamer.

Night 11: Sunset Hotel.

Day 12: Drive back to Nairobi after breakfast. Drive straight through—not via Kericho—to Limuru and stay overnight at Kentmere Club. Confirm your train tickets for Mombasa when you arrive at Kentmere.

Night 12: Kentmere Club.

Day 13: After breakfast at Kentmere, late in the morning drive to Nairobi and have lunch, if you like, in the Tate Room at the New Stanley Hotel. The food is excellent. Use the Avis to go to the station and pick up your tickets for the night train. Return the car and settle your account. Undoubtedly, if you ask, they will give you a driver and car to take you to the station. The train leaves at 7 p.m., and it's best to be there 45 minutes before departure. Your name and the compartment assigned to you will be chalked on the board on the platform.

Night 13: On the overnight sleeper train to Mombasa.

Day 14: We have designed the *Lunatic Express* itinerary to fit into a two-week vacation. However, if time permits, there are several excellent beach hotels on the south coast. We highly recommend the Sheraton Golden Beach at Diani Beach (see "Kenyan Accommodation").

PLAN AHEAD: All reservations can be made, without charge, through Meri-kani Hotel Reservations Service. They do not charge for obtaining visas; they only charge for the actual cost of the visa plus registered, return-receipt postage, if hotel reservations are made through them. Merikani offers these services to all our readers regardless of where they live. Their address is P.O. Box 53394, Temple Heights Station, Washington, DC 20009, tel. (USA) 301–530–1911. However, we have provided all the necessary information to make your own reservations.

The following needs to be done before departure: Check the "Basic Information Checklist" at the beginning of the "Background Information" section for necessary travel documents; make hotel reservations—numbers and addresses are given in the headings preceding each hotel's description; make airline reservations for international flights using the routings we suggest at the beginning of the itinerary; reserve an Avis car where needed; purchase SOS insurance (see "Travel Documents"); purchase traveler's checks; write, but do not send money, to Kenya Railways for a reservation on their overnight sleeper train Nairobi-Mombasa (details in "Transportation"). Write to Public Relations Officer, Kenya Railways, P.O. Box 30121, Nairobi, Kenya, to make a date to visit the Railway Training Center and Railway Workshops. You may want to take a small gift for the stationmaster at Tsavo Station—pictures of your hometown, something to do with railroads, etc.—nothing elaborate. If you use de-caffeinated coffee, take some with with you as there is none in Kenya. Remember to take plenty of film and perhaps a tripod to take pictures of the engines in the grounds of the Railway Museum.

Accommodation recommended in the *Lunatic Express* itinerary: (all in Kenya)—Mombasa: Outrigger Hotel; Makindu: Sikh Temple; Nairobi: Hilton International; Rift Valley: Kentmere Club; Kericho: Tea Hotel; Kisumu: Sunset Hotel. Stop at Diani Beach on the south coast: Sheraton Golden Beach.

Estimated Budget

Lunatic Express Itinerary

Does not include airfare to Mombasa, Kenya

	US$	
	1 person	2 people
Arrive Mombasa: Avis agent meets plane		
10 days' rental of class A or B unlimited mileage with full insurance and driver for Nairobi	$797	$797
Gas (petrol)	100	100
Outrigger Hotel, Mombasa, 2 nights, includes breakfast and taxes, $36 single, $56 double	72	112
Meals: lunch $7, dinner $10 = $17 × 2 days	34	68
Candy (sweets) for children at Rabai Primary School	3	3
Donation to Rabai Mission Building Fund	10	20
Lunch at Tsavo East Lodge at Voi and park entrance fee	10	20
Donation to Makindu Sikh temple; no charge for meals at temple	4	8
Hilton International Nairobi, overnight	89	110
Pick up Avis driver; tea at Norfolk Hotel	7	14
Meals: dinner evening of arrival in Nairobi $8, breakfast next morning $6	14	28
Drive to Kentmere Club, 3 nights, includes breakfast and taxes $30 single, $50 double	90	150
Meals: lunch $10, dinner $12 = $22 × 3 days	66	122
Lunch Nakuru RR Station	8	16
1 night, $42 single, $74 double, includes breakfast and taxes	42	74
Meals: dinner on evening of arrival $7, picnic lunch for drive the following day $4	11	22
Sunset Hotel, 2 nights $34 single, $60 double, includes breakfast	68	120
Meals: dinner on evening of arrival $20; lunch $7, dinner second day $10	37	74
Picnic lunch to take on drive to Nairobi	6	12
Arrive Nairobi: check into Hilton for overnight, return Avis	89	110
Meals: breakfast $6, lunch $8, dinner on evening of arrival $12	26	52
Taxi to railroad station	3	3
Night train to Mombasa, first-class single plus dinner, breakfast, early morning tea served in compartment and bedding	46	92
Day room at Castle Hotel, Mombasa	24	37
Lunch	7	14
Taxi to airport	4.50	4.50

	US$	
	1 person	2 people
Departure tax	10	20
SOS Insurance, $15 a week, $45 a month	30	60
15% tips to waiters/waitresses on all meals	35	70
Gratuity to housekeeping staff, $1 a night for 1 or 2 persons	11	11
Tips to bellmen/porters/train stewards	26	26
Total:	**$1779.50**	**$2369.75**
Cost per person sharing:	**$1184.75**	

Paupers *Lunatic Express* Itinerary

Making economies for the *Lunatic Express* itinerary is difficult, apart from the obvious choice of cheaper accommodation. The trains operate only twice a day, within 2 hours of one another, and the most interesting station, Tsavo, has no accommodation nearby and is not a passenger station. Therefore, a rental car is almost a necessity.

The purpose of using the Outrigger Hotel in the itinerary is that it is at the Kilindini Harbour, where the railroad started. Many young people use a hotel in Mombasa called the Hydro. There are some other equally disagreeable flophouses in Mombasa, and neither Leah nor I recommend them. The New Palm Court didn't have locks on the doors when we were there, and only recently has an "Oriental masseur" taken down her shingle in one of the rooms. The Lotus Hotel in Mombasa is recommended, but it is not near the harbor.

If, repeat if, you have a rental car, the Church of the Province of Kenya (C.P.K.) has a guest house at Likoni, immediately after the ferry, which is extremely reasonable and includes three meals and afternoon tea, and has clean rooms. We stipulate that readers have a car because we have heard of a number of muggings between the ferry and the guest house. Once in the guest house there is no problem. Nor is there a problem within the lights of the ferry—only that strip in between, which is dark and allows muggings to go unseen by the public (who, incidentally, will always come to the rescue of a victim). C.P.K. Likoni is the same price as C.P.K. Nairobi: see hotel rates.

	US$	
	1 person	2 people
Arrive Mombasa: Avis agent meets plane; 10 days' rental of class A or B, unlimited mileage with full insurance and driver for Nairobi	$797	$797
Gas (petrol)	100	100
Outrigger Hotel, Mombasa, 2 nights, includes breakfast and taxes, $36 single, $56 double	72	112
Meals: lunch $7, dinner $10 = $17 × 2 days	34	68
Candy (sweets) for children at Rabai Primary School	3	3
Donation to the Rabai Mission Building Fund	10	20

	US$	
	1 person	2 people
Lunch at Tsavo East Lodge at Voi and park entrance fee	10	20
Donation to Makindu Sikh temple; no charge for meals	4	8
Methodist Guest House, Nairobi, 1 night, includes full board	17	34
Pick up Avis driver. Tea at Norfolk Hotel	7	14
Drive to Kentmere Club, 3 nights, $30 single, $50 double includes breakfast and taxes	90	150
Meals at Kentmere Club: lunch $10, dinner $12 = $22 × 3 days	66	132
Highlands Hotel, Molo, $23 single, $31 double, includes breakfast, 1 night	23	31
Meals: dinner $8, picnic lunch for drive to Kisumu $4	12	24
Budget Hotel in Kisumu, 2 nights, allow $17 single, $20 double, includes breakfast and taxes	34	40
Meals: dinner on evening of arrival $7, lunch $5, and dinner the second day $7	19	38
Picnic lunch for drive to Nairobi	5	10
Arrive Nairobi: check into Methodist Guest House for overnight stay. Full board included.	17	34
Next day, return car, and although lunch is included in rates at Methodist Guest House, have lunch at Nairobi Railway Station dining room when purchasing tickets for the evening train	8	16
Night sleeper train to Mombasa, second class, includes bedding, breakfast and evening meal	35	70
Arrive Mombasa: Depending on your flight home, either leave your baggage in Left Luggage at the RR station, or go to Moi International Airport. Walk to Castle Hotel from the RR station and have lunch.	6	12
Kenya Airways bus to airport	2	4
Departure tax	10	20
SOS Insurance, $15 a week, $45 a month	30	60
15% tips to waiters/waitresses on all meals	26	52
Gratuity to housekeeping staff, $1 a night for 1 or 2 persons	9	9
Total:	$1446	$1878
Cost per person sharing:	$ 939	

ANGOLOPHILIA:
FLAME TREES OF THIKA

BY
ELSPETH HUXLEY

WILLIAM MORROW
& CO., NEW YORK
1959

This African version of *Little House on the Prairie* describes the pioneering life of Ms. Huxley and her parents in pre–World War I Kenya. The story was adapted for television and shown in a 13-part series not only in the United Kingdom and North America but in many other countries throughout the world. The story is based on actual events that happened to the author's family along with incidents that were gossiped about among the White community at the time. She has followed *Flame Trees of Thika* with *The Mottled Lizard* (London: Chatto and Windus, 1962), which continues the semi-fictitious family history upon their return to Kenya after World War I.

Nellie: Letters from Africa (London: Weidenfeld and Nicholson, 1980) are the actual diaries and letters of her mother, Nellie ("Tilly" in *Flame Trees of Thika*). These letters cover her life: her youth in England; marriage; pioneering in Kenya; World War I in England; her return to Kenya during the Roaring '20s, and comments on the Happy Valley Set. (For a more in-depth discussion of the Happy Valley Set, see *White Mischief* [London: Jonathan Cape, 1982 and New York: Random House, 1983].) Her letters continue with a most interesting account of her experiences and reactions under the Mau Mau during the 1950s. She then discusses the adjustments she had to make under Black rule after Kenya's independence in 1963. Fans of *Flame Trees of Thika* will want to read all three volumes.

We have selected the following places mentioned in *Flame Trees of Thika* for the itinerary: Norfolk Hotel, Ruiru, Thika town, Chania and Thika Falls, Blue Posts Hotel, Mt. Kenya, Archer's Post, Samburu Plain, Meru, and the train to Mombasa.

Travelers will need a car—with or without an Avis driver—to follow this route, although we have also outlined a cheaper itinerary.

Tilly and Elspeth arrived in Kenya at Kilindini Docks after their voyage from England. Mother and daughter had come out to Kenya on a P&O liner from England's Tilbury Docks. The ship came through the Mediterranean and down the Suez Canal into the Red Sea, stopping at Aden and Mombasa, then usually going on to India.

I took that same route to Bombay in 1947 on the P&O's *Empire Windrush*. Our ship unloaded cargo and passengers at Mombasa, but I had been so disappointed with hot, dusty, boring Aden a few days earlier that I concluded the same would be true of Mombasa and stayed aboard ship. It is ironic that places that are of no consequence at one period in life can become of momentous importance later. Twenty-five years later when General Amin started making things hot for Americans in Uganda, where I had been teaching, we went to Mombasa. The ocean promised safety after the claustrophobic tensions of land-locked Uganda. We have returned many times since 1962 and learned to love

A cartoon in an 1892 issue of the British magazine Punch *depicted Cecil Rhodes, leader of the southern African gold rush, in a posture that exemplified his driving ambition—to subjugate Africa from "Cape to Cairo" to the British crown.*

Mombasa. However, tourism and the establishment of a U.S. submarine base have seen a deterioration in the services the city once enjoyed, and her streets have become unsafe to walk at night except in Old Town. Old Town is inhabited by a closely knit Moslem community where everyone knows everyone else and life is governed by the disciplines of the extended family.

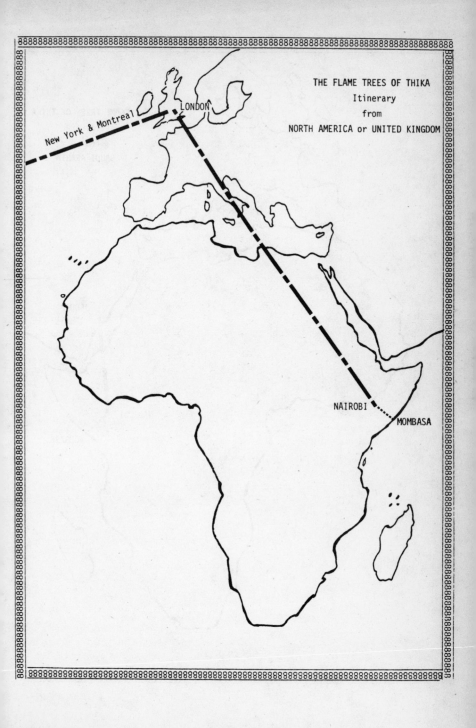

THE FLAME TREES OF THIKA
Itinerary
from
NORTH AMERICA or UNITED KINGDOM

New York & Montreal

LONDON

NAIROBI
MOMBASA

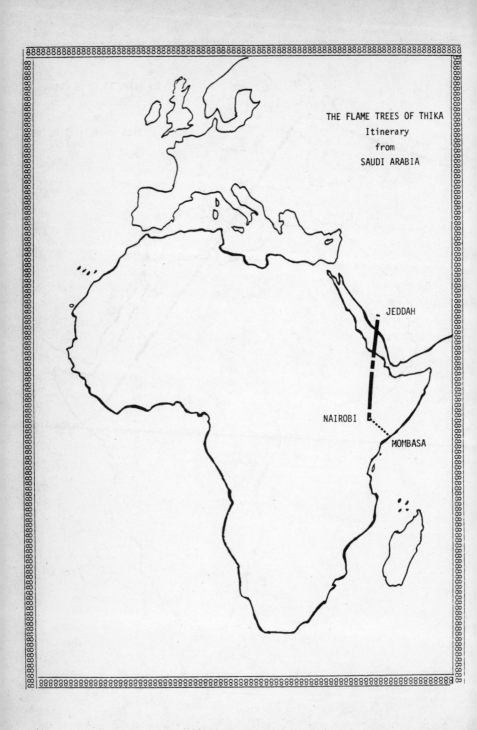

THE FLAME TREES OF THIKA
Itinerary
from
SAUDI ARABIA

JEDDAH

NAIROBI

MOMBASA

THE FLAME TREES OF THIKA
Itinerary
from
AUSTRALIA or NEW ZEALAND

SYDNEY

AUCKLAND

BOMBAY

NAIROBI

MOMBASA

Flame Trees of Thika Routing from North America

Pan American—New York or Montreal-London
Kenya Airways—London-Nairobi
Avis—Land travel in Kenya
Kenya Railways-Nairobi-Mombasa-Nairobi
Kenya Airways—Nairobi-London
Pan American—London-New York or Montreal

Flame Trees of Thika Routing from the United Kingdom

As above but, naturally, starting with the Kenya Airways flight from London.

Flame Trees of Thika Routing from Saudi Arabia

Kenya Airways—Jeddah-Nairobi
Avis—Land travel in Kenya
Kenya Railways—Nairobi-Mombasa-Nairobi
Kenya Airways—Nairobi-Jeddah

Flame Trees of Thika Routing from Australia/New Zealand

Qantas or Singapore Airlines—Sydney-Bombay
Kenya Airways—Bombay-Nairobi
Avis—Land travel in Kenya
Kenya Railways—Nairobi-Mombasa-Nairobi
Kenya Airways—Nairobi-Bombay
Qantas or Singapore Airlines—Bombay-Sydney

The Flame Trees of Thika Itinerary

Our itinerary starts at Nairobi, as P&O have long since abandoned this route and most airlines come into Nairobi, not Mombasa. In *The Mottled Lizard,* Ms. Huxley describes the journey up from the coast to Nairobi and has an interesting description of the stop at Voi. In *Flame Trees of Thika*, descriptions start at the Norfolk Hotel. At the conclusion of the itinerary we suggest you spend an additional week at the Kenyan coast. In which case we take the same train ride, albeit in modern cars, Elspeth and her mother took to Nairobi and again at the end of the book when they returned to England at the outbreak of World War I.

We follow the route exactly as it is in the book up to Thika. After that, the route we suggest is around the western side of Mt. Kenya. (When Tilly went off hunting with Ian Crawford, Lettice, and Hereward Palmer to Samburu, they went around the eastern side of the mountain. This can be done, but there are not as many interesting places to stop as going via the west side.) The Thika-Nyeri district on the west side was the region where their homes were located, and the many unidentified sites in the book are on the western side of the mountain. The original house is up a road on a commercial coffee plantation to the west of the Thika flyover. An elderly White Kenyan makes the house his home, and it is not open to the public. Nor would it be kind to attempt entry, as the gentleman in residence is in such advanced years.

Molo is mentioned a great deal, but Molo today is not a very nice place; in the *Lunatic Express* itinerary we have recommended the Highlands Hotel, which is in the suburbs, in the event a stopover must be made. However, for the *Flame Trees of Thika* itinerary the Rift Valley can be seen by returning to Nairobi via Limuru. There is no need to go to the far side of the Rift, where Molo is located. Nor is it worth your time to go to Nakuru, which was at one time the country town for many of the White settlers in the "White Highlands." Detailed comments on both Nakuru and Molo can be found in the *Lunatic Express* itinerary.

Reservations for the entire itinerary may be made, without charge, through Merikani Hotel Reservations Service (P.O. Box 53394, Temple Heights Station, Washington, DC 20009, tel: (USA) 301–530–1911).

Days and Nights 1 and 2: Arrive at Jomo Kenyatta International Airport and take a taxi to the Norfolk Hotel. The Norfolk has constantly enjoyed popularity both among resident Kenyans and overseas visitors for 80 years. Unlike some successful enterprises, a substantial percentage of profits have found their way back into maintenance and renovation. The hotel sparkles and everything is immaculate.

The walls of the Pioneer Room, used for conferences and banquets, are hung with sepia enlargements of the early White settlers—with their dogs, wagons, pith helmets, and parasols. These are tremendously interesting, especially in comparison to early pictures of the North American West. The pictures reinforce the feeling that the Norfolk Hotel was the focal point for the life Elspeth and her parents knew. Men who were called back into the services at the beginning of World War I met at the Norfolk for sundowners, roomed their families, said their good-byes before going back to England or, more frightening to wives and mothers, to battle the Germans at Taita Hills along the Kenya-Tanganikya border. We were at the Norfolk when Apple Computers was holding an exhibit in the Pioneer Room. The contrast of those sleek computers near the large pioneer photographs taken just over 50 years ago was entertaining.

The Norfolk today is patronized by a broad cross section of Kenyan society and many prominent overseas visitors. We found the atmosphere very egalitarian. It is located near the University of Nairobi and a ballet school, and many of the students stop after classes to have a soft drink on the terrace, as well as judges and executives after leaving their offices and courtrooms.

On the afternoon of Day 2 call Avis and ask that the car be brought to the Norfolk the next morning. Check your cash and make certain you have at least the equivalent of US$50 each in Kenya currency as it will be difficult to get money changed between Nairobi and Mountain Lodge.

Day 3: Drive to Thika. Check out of the Norfolk after breakfast. Ask the Avis driver to drive the car through the city center and to put you onto the road to Thika. (You can then drop him and he can take a bus back into town.) The highway to Thika is new and tarmacked—it is being repaved and enlarged. No billowing red clouds will impede your progress as Tilly and Elspeth experienced. The present road goes through Ruiru, which is vastly different from the few stores and washed-out road described in the book. Ruiru today is becoming an extension of Nairobi's commerce, has flyovers and, as mentioned in the

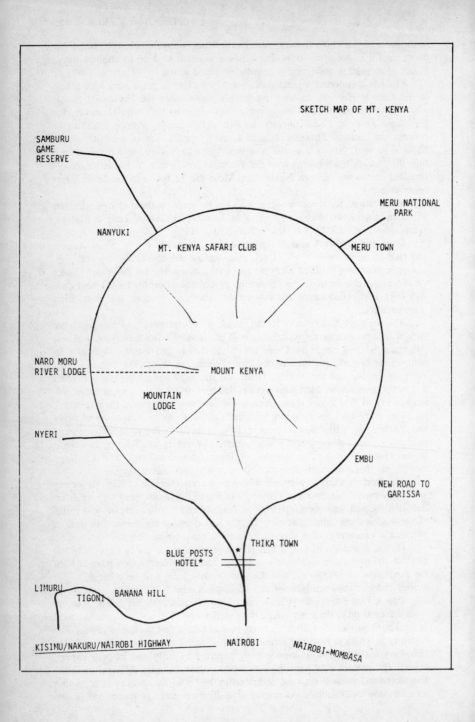

SKETCH MAP OF MT. KENYA

SAMBURU
GAME
RESERVE

MERU NATIONAL
PARK

NANYUKI

MERU TOWN

MT. KENYA SAFARI CLUB

NARO MORU
RIVER LODGE - MOUNT KENYA

MOUNTAIN
LODGE

NYERI

EMBU

NEW ROAD TO
GARISSA

THIKA TOWN

BLUE POSTS
HOTEL*   *

LIMURU   TIGONI   BANANA HILL

KISIMU/NAKURU/NAIROBI HIGHWAY   NAIROBI   NAIROBI-MOMBASA

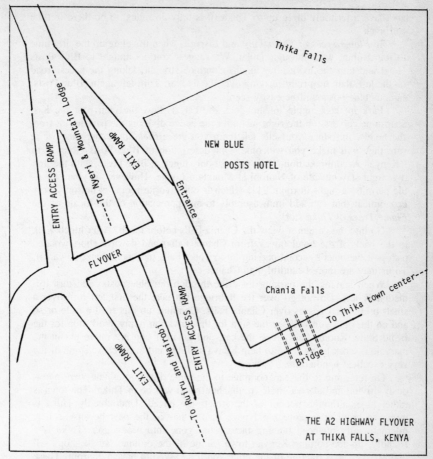

THE A2 HIGHWAY FLYOVER
AT THIKA FALLS, KENYA

closing pages of *Flame Trees of Thika,* has a railway siding. At one time this line carried passengers, but now it is used only for freight. It may be that it will again reopen to passengers because of the increased industrial development planned for Thika in the immediate future. Up until now, agriculture has been the main source of employment. In the early days of White settlement many crops were tried throughout Kenya. Farmers coming up from South Africa attempted and were sometimes successful with direct transfer crops such as wheat and barley, although yields have never reached those of North America. Sisel was grown, and along the coast it sometimes succeeded. Cotton never really produced as well as it did in Uganda. For each crop it was a matter of trial and error, with light conditions, elevations, and soils presenting totally unique problems. Coffee was introduced by the Catholic White Fathers, and as readers of *Out of Africa* will know, this was a very sensitive crop. Today Kenya exports fine Arabica coffee, in addition to tea, both of which combine to be the major foreign exchange earner.

We hope readers will start out from the Norfolk immediately after breakfast and have a leisurely drive up to Thika (it is only 35 miles) to be there in time for lunch.

In *Flame Trees of Thika* Tilly and Elspeth, when traveling up the first time to join Robin, went through Thika. We suggest you go straight to Blue Posts Hotel and tour the town after lunch. Continue straight, taking the access road on the left; then turn right, driving over the flyover. Turn left again. Blue Posts' famous blue posts will be easily seen.

Park in their ample lot and lock the car. Follow the path past the Kisi soapstone carvers (on the right just after the hedge dividing the parking lot from the hotel). Introduce yourself, tell them you are a *Fielding* reader, and we're sure they will make you welcome. Our description of Blue Posts Hotel is in "Kenyan Accommodation." We suggest only lunch at Blue Posts, with the first overnight stay outside of Nairobi at Mountain Lodge. However, if your schedule permits, a night in room 211, which is our favorite room, is not only very economical, but can add immeasurably to an appreciation of the locale of the *Flame Trees of Thika* story.

Go into the garden to view the Chania Falls before lunch. After lunch walk to the back of the hotel (away from Chania Falls) and down a short wooded path past the hotel's second parking lot to Thika Falls (not more than 500 yards). To us they are more beautiful than Chania.

When leaving the parking lot drive through the blue posts, and turn immediately left. Do not go over the flybridge but take the first left turn over a small bridge that passes over Chania Falls. Continue up this road a mile or so and on the right you will see the sign for the Salvation Army Workshop for the Blind Show Room. Park, lock the car, and go in if you are interested in the marvelous work being done to help Kenya's blind, and to purchase some of the very excellent handicrafts.

On returning to the car, continue in the same direction as you were previously driving and after a circle (roundabout) you will be in Thika. The town is rather nice, although not all of the streets are paved. Undoubtedly Thika is going to grow at a more rapid pace than it has in the past because a new internationally financed tanning factory has gone into production. Thika is a friendly, up-and-coming Kenyan town. Some of the ordinary small shops sell plain baskets at a fraction of the price you'll be asked to pay in Nairobi. These are the baskets the people use, and most are neutral in color, without trim.

Drive back the way you came, over the small bridge, and turn right. Blue Posts will be seen ahead of you. Turn left (before Blue Posts) and cross the flyover, then turn right immediately after crossing, onto the access road for the main highway.

You should be on the A2 highway. Continue driving for 70 miles until you see signs for Nyeri. You do not want to go into Nyeri. Not for any special reason (it is a nice little town) except that it will be getting late, and you want to get to Mountain Lodge before dark. Just past the Nyeri sign on the right is a sign that reads "Mountain Lodges," which is confusing when you are looking for only one lodge). Here, you continue on a very good paved road for a few miles. A not so good but nevertheless paved road continues on to the turning marked "Mountain Lodge, AT&H." The AT&H (abbreviation for African Tours and Hotels) distinguishes the lodge we recommend from the "State Mountain Lodge" used by the government for their executives. Now begins a hardcore, single-lane, class D road, which is in good condition until about 4 miles from the lodge, where the surface becomes a challenge, with numerous potholes.

Elephants freely roam over Mt. Kenya.

Still, the Avis Mazda did just fine and four-wheel drive was not necessary, even though it had rained the day before.

We want to emphasize that this drive is beautiful; the road is bordered by pines (which grow much more quickly in Africa than in temperate zones) and eucalyptus trees, so often cited in *Flame Trees of Thika*. Small homesteads and plots of healthy potato patches interrupt the forest. The climbing road, to 7200 feet, is not inordinately steep. Everything is green and lush, and the red tropical clays of exposed soil identify the scene as Africa.

Keep climbing. As you do you may see, as we did, mounds of freshly dropped elephant spoor. This may petrify you, as it did us, but we drove on—perhaps a bit faster than we should have—until a high bamboo circular fence enclosed us. This is the parking lot for Mountain Lodge. The entrance to the lodge is not impressive. Follow a wooden walkway and at the end you will see the words "Mountain Lodge" above the doorway. Through the doorway on the left is the reception desk, where absolutely no one stops, as some 15 feet ahead is a huge floor-to-ceiling picture window through which can be seen an immense watering hole and at least one African animal at any time of the day or night. Mountain Lodge is no disappointing anticlimax in the visitors' search for wildlife. The animals you see here are much the same as those that Lettice, Ian, Hereward, and Tilly saw when they went on their safari over Mt. Kenya. (To include the plains animals a visit to Samburu, and Meru also forms a part of this itinerary.) Tearing yourself away from the window, present your voucher (confirmation slip for your reservation) to the receptionist and check into your room.

The steep ascent of Mt. Kenya is directly behind the waterhole, and although it's covered in cloud most of the day, its snow-covered peaks can be seen after midnight and for an hour or so after sunrise. Elspeth mentions this in the book.

Animals seen at Mountain Lodge (copied from the log book): Elephants (smaller than Tsavo West or Meru), Black Rhino, African Buffalo, Giant Forest Hog, Bushpig, Bush Squirrel, Large Spotted Genet, Tree Hyrax, Greater Galago, Syke's Monkey, Abyssinian Black and White Colobus Monkey, Spotted Hyena, Leopard, Red Duiker, Bush Buck, White-tailed Mongoose, Large Gray Mongoose, Black-tipped Mongoose, Suni, and Aardvark.

Birds include: Hartlaub's Turaco, Bronze-napped Pigeon, Golden-winged Sunbird, Streaky Seed-eater, Cinnamon-crested Bee-eater, Pied Wagtail, Augur Buzzard, and Red-headed Parrot.

Mountain Lodge has a subterranean dugout for those who want to get closer to the animals. The dining room is attractive, the food plentiful, and the service good. What more can you ask? Full description in "Kenyan Accommodation."

Night 3: Mountain Lodge.

Day 4: Drive to Samburu Game Reserve. Leaving Mountain Lodge after breakfast, go back the way you came to the main A2 highway. Turn right and follow the signs to Nanyuki. It's nice, during this drive, to stop at Naro Moru River Lodge for a late-morning coffee. The lodge is the official base camp for climbing Mt. Kenya and is set in a lovely garden by the river. The staff are hospitable. The turning is at the left 21 mi after you come onto the A2 from Mountain Lodge. The sign for Naro Moru appears to read 15 km when in effect it should read 1.5 km. The road is not paved and it was raining the day we drove it. I almost gave up as the car slid around but found I was being unduly alarmed. We give a full description of Naro Moru Lodge in "Kenyan Accommodation."

Continue on the A2 for 14 mi (23 km) until you reach the outskirts of Nanuyki. As you approach you will see a sign marking a road on the right to the Mt. Kenya Safari Club. We suggest you visit the club on the way back, but the sign coming from the north is almost unseen, so make note of it when you drive from the south.

The drive to Block Hotel's Samburu Lodge goes through the beautiful sheep ranching country on the northwest slope of Mt. Kenya: rounded, low hills that dip dramatically down onto the Samburu plain. The plain contrasts sharply with the green hills; a harsh woody vegetation replaces the Welsh-like grass where sheep thrive.

Leaving Nanyuki, go directly north to Isiolo. The road is very good. There is a checkpoint manned by the Kenya Army where you get out of the car (we make a point of this because we sat in the car thinking the soldier would come to us. He didn't. The system is you go to him in his sentry box.) Give your name and license plate number. While you are doing this the other occupants of your car will be enduring a state of siege as sellers of brass and copper jewelry push merchandise under their noses, imploring that they buy. Tell them to haggle. Quarter the price and you'll have a good buy. After you return to the car prices drop significantly as you rev the engine, threatening to drive off. We drove past the checkpoint at about 2:30 p.m. on a December day. No more paved roads. Drive carefully; the sun beats down on the loose gravel that has been spread over the corrugated hardbed dirt road, causing the gravel to shift under the car's tries. Too much speed (40 mph) finds you and the vehicle on the other side of the road or in a dry ditch. The road to the lodge is very well marked. There is another lodge along the same route with a similar name, so keep your eye on "Block Hotels" as the magic password here and you won't go wrong.

A cement entrance—actually quite attractive when you get used to it, as its shape carries through the lines of the rounded hills just behind—signals the entrance to Samburu Game Reserve. A fee is charged. There are also immaculately clean flush toilets and wash basins.

Signs warn you to stay in your car and that a game warden should travel with you if you wish to go sightseeing. These gentlemen can be found in a cluster around the entrance of the Block Hotels Lodge. The air becomes drier; the bush harsher. The road is nothing that a rural West Virginian can't take in stride, but for others from less wild, wonderful places, the numerous 20-foot washouts in the road can be a challenge. Again, take it easy. Drive in third gear and shift to first for the gullies. Keep your camera at the ready; we came within 10 feet of zebra, oryx, and ostrich.

Night 4: Samburu Lodge. The river, Uaso Nyiro, muddier when we saw it than the Mississippi and about as wide as the Potomac at Harper's Ferry or the Wye at Ross, is a welcome sight after driving through terrain one becomes convinced God created when He ran out of water. Don't be surprised if the river is low; though it was high and rapidly flowing when we saw it, that isn't the case year round. A huge conical thatch roof shades tables and chairs where afternoon tea, and very excellent tea it is, accompanies thin cucumber, tomato, or cheese bridge sandwiches—all a reminder that the British way of life is still much admired, as is Queen Elizabeth, here in the heart of Africa. When Queen

Crocodiles laze by the river in Samburu Game Reserve.

Elizabeth visited Kenya in 1983 an American reporter was intrigued by a young Kenyan he interviewed during her Nairobi "walkabout," who told him that the Queen was "our mother." When the reporter pointed out that Kenya had been independent for 20 years, the young man said, "Mothers never die—she will always be our mother" (*Executive Magazine,* Nairobi).

After a wash, and something to quench the thirst, or a swim in the pool, there is time for a rest before 6:30 when the crocodiles slide up from the river to within 6 feet (a low stone wall divides you from them) for their dinner. They slide up to lie with open jaws, waiting for an evening feed of beef provided by a member of the lodge staff. Dinner—for you—is in a lovely, open dining room, still within close view of the river, and it is served to the sound of chattering monkeys saying good night to one another in the trees on the far side of the river.

Day 5: The melodies of birds wake you in the morning—not harshly, but in a series of subdued tones until, without rancor, sleep departs. Early-morning tea or coffee can be brought to your room and is included in the rates but must be requested the previous night.

Walking to breakfast, you'll see the ornithological orchestra composed of innumerable species being fed crumbs by a member of the hotel staff; crumbs are spread on stone pedestal tables alongside similarly constructed bird baths. The trees near the dining room have become grandstands for scores of monkeys that wait for the end of the first human meal of the day. They wait to receive their toast and fruit skins. Sometimes, as happened to Leah, the wait becomes too unbearably long and a monkey will rush to a breakfast table and snatch a piece of toast from your hand. Birds, monkeys, crocodiles lazing in the river, and monitor lizards on the bank fill the grounds outside the dining room with the sounds and movements of Africa.

Day and Night 6: Meru Mulika Lodge and Meru Game Reserve. Drive back from Samburu to where the highway joins up with the junction to Meru. Go left until you reach the turnoff (again, to the left) for the gate to Meru Mulika Lodge (see map). If you prefer to use Leopard Rock Self-Catering Cottages, stop in Meru and buy a few groceries before entering the park, or meals can be taken at the lodge and the cottages used just for sleeping. Next morning, as early as possible, check out and take a picnic lunch with you to tour the park. The elephant here are particularly large. If you leave the park not later than 4:30 p.m. there should be enough time to drive to Mt. Kenya Safari Club, Nanyuki, before dark (6:15).

Night 7: Mt. Kenya Safari Club, Nanyuki. Drive through Nanyuki and at the outskirts look for the sign "Mt. Kenya Safari Club." It will now be on the left. We suggested earlier that you make a note of the sign; now you'll see the reason why. The one on the left is turned away from you and the one facing you is obscured by a tree branch. Go slowly and hopefully you'll see the sign with the arrow pointing up a hardcore dirt road. Follow the arrows, which now can be clearly seen, until you arrive at the entrance with a barrier and guard. You must show him the voucher (confirmation slip) for your reservations.

The hotel, or club, as they prefer to call it, is a short distance ahead on the left. To stay at Mt. Kenya Safari Club guests must become temporary members, and the membership fee is included in the rates.

Day 8: Spend a relaxing morning, swimming in the pool (although the water is cold), putting a few golf balls, taking a rod out to fish, or horseback

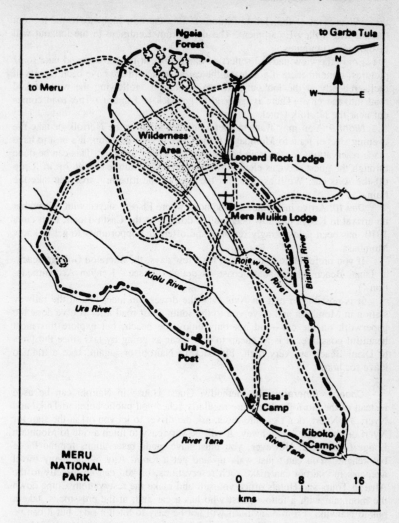

riding. After lunch drive to Banana Hill for an overnight stay at Kentmere Club, 20 mi from Nairobi and near the Rift Valley Lookout Point.

Retrace your steps to Thika and on to Ruiri. At Ruiri leave the A2 and go over the flyover. The road going due west of town will lead to Banana Hill and Limuru. Drive slowly after Banana Hill and stop at Kentmere Club; the sign is on the right (see "Kenyan Accommodation"). You don't want to go as far as Tigoni or Limuru, so if you see those signs, turn back and start again from Banana Hill. This drive from Thika to the Kentmere Club should take no more than an hour. Allow 2½ hours from Mt. Kenya Safari Club to Thika.

Night 8: Kentmere Club.

Day 9: Check out of the Kentmere Club after breakfast, then continue on the road in front of the club to Limuru to join the new highway to the lookout for the Rift Valley Escarpment. The drive from Kentmere to the lookout will take about 30 minutes.

Enjoy the view and the sellers of handicrafts at the lookout and take some pictures, remembering if you leave the car to lock it (there have been reports of thefts recently at the lookout). Return to Nairobi, following the well-marked road into the city. (There is no need to go back to Limuru.) This road comes out near the Norfolk Hotel.

Night 9: You may want to spend another night at the Norfolk or take the evening sleeper train to Mombasa. If the latter is your decision, it's best to have made reservations for the train before the start of the itinerary. This can be done through the guest services clerk at the Norfolk. The train leaves at 7 p.m. Drop off the Avis car. We'll assume, for the sake of the itinerary, that you take the train.

Day 10: Arrive in Mombasa. The hotel where Elspeth stayed with her mother on arrival in Kenya has now been pulled down, but the Castle Hotel, built circa 1910, has been painstakingly restored and offers the opportunity to get to know Mombasa.

If you prefer to go to the beach for a few days, the Sheraton Golden Beach, at Diani Beach on the south coast, is delightful (see "Kenyan Accommodation").

It is possible to rent an Avis car—the driver can meet you at the railway station in Mombasa and drive you to the south coast road after you've done the paperwork on the car—and not only enjoy the beach, but explore this most beautiful coastline. It is as cheap to rent a car as going by taxi since the fares to Diani Beach are very high. Fly back to Nairobi or, again, take a train to leave for home.

Cheaper Itinerary: The Methodist Guest House in Nairobi can be used instead of the Norfolk. There are regularly scheduled public buses to Thika and Nyeri. At Nyeri, don't go into town; ask the driver to let you off at the sign for Nyeri on the main A2 highway. It will be very easy to hitch a ride to Mountain Lodge from there. However, you must have made reservations for the lodge beforehand. You can't just walk up and get a room. Any of the many travel agencies in Nairobi can make such reservations, or you can go directly to the African Tours and Hotels office yourself and make the reservation. Come down the mountain with a fellow guest who has a car and, at the crossroads, take a bus to Nanyuki. From Nanyuki it will not be easy to hitch a ride, but it can be done to get to Samburu. There is camping in the reserve, but if you don't have a car you're not going to see much. You must be in a vehicle to tour the reserve. Animals don't come in numbers to the camping grounds as they do to the lodges, where they are fed daily. Meru presents more difficult problems as a drive is absolutely necessary to appreciate the park—there is no waterhole or central viewing area as at the other two parks. Instead of staying at Mt. Kenya Safari Club, Nanyuki, there are bunkhouses at Naro Moru River Lodge, where you can walk up to the first stage of the mountain. This takes only half a day. Instead of using Sheraton Golden Beach, try Dan Trench's campsite (see "Kenyan Accommodation").

PLAN AHEAD: As mentioned at the start of the itinerary, all reservations can be made through Merikani Hotel Reservations Service, without charge. Nor do

The Somali pony Ian Crawford gave Elspeth.

Comparing the romantic heroes of *Flame Trees of Thika* and *Out of Africa* raises more questions than answers. (Readers will note that the first title was published in 1957 and the second in 1937.) Both authors use a dashing Englishman with Somali connections as their romantic lead; both authors use a shooting scene with lions to climax the romantic involvement of their characters. Was *Flame Trees'* Ian Crawford *Out of Africa*'s Denys Finch Hatton? Perhaps, as Ms. Huxley's book is part fiction he is, but the use of the lions is merely coincidental.

    Denys Finch Hatton most certainly could have been the lover of the aristocrat's wife, Lettice, as well as Karen Blixen, as the "me too" inference coming from Beryl Markham, another White Kenyan whose autobiography (*West With the Night*) adds to Kenya's colonial literature, implies Denys was true to Karen "in his fashion."

they charge for obtaining a visa (only for the actual cost of the visa plus return-receipt registered postage for your passport) if hotel reservations are made through them. However, we have provided all the necessary information to make your own reservations. The following needs to be done before departure: check the "Basic Information Checklist" (see "Background Information") for necessary travel documents; make hotel reservations—numbers and addresses are given in the heading preceding each hotel's description; reserve an Avis car for the up-country leg as well as the coast (see "Transportation"); purchase SOS Insurance (see "Travel Documents"); purchase traveler's checks; start taking malaria tablets 2 weeks before departure.

    Once in Kenya, have the guests services staff at the Norfolk Hotel reserve a berth for you on the overnight sleeper train to Mombasa. Decide if you will fly back to Nairobi from Mombasa or take the train again and have the Norfolk staff make that reservation as well.

Nothing special is needed in the way of clothing—remember beach wear for Diani Beach. Decaffeinated coffee is not available in Kenya and you may want to take a supply, as well as plenty of film, as it is expensive in Kenya. The Estimated Budget follows.

Accommodation recommended: Kenya—Nairobi-Norfolk Hotel; Mt. Kenya—Mountain Lodge; Samburu Game Reserve—Block Hotel's Samburu Lodge; Meru Game Reserve—Meru Mulika Lodge; Mt. Kenya—Mt. Kenya Safari Club, Nanyuki; Rift Valley—Kentmere Club; Mombasa-Castle Hotel.

Estimated Budget

Flame Trees of Thika Itinerary

(10 nights)
Does not include airfare to Nairobi, Kenya

	US$	
	1 person	2 people
Arrive Nairobi: taxi to Norfolk Hotel	$ 15	$ 15
Norfolk Hotel, 2 nights, $113 single, $125 double	226	250
(Note: When Norfolk rates are quoted they do not always include the taxes; therefore, the price quoted here may differ from that provided by other sources.)		
Meals: breakfast $5, lunch $8, dinner $12 = $25 × 2 days	50	100
Avis Toyota Corolla station wagon, includes insurance, and unlimited mileage	407	407
Gas (petrol)	53	53
Arrive Thika: lunch at New Blue Posts Hotel	7	14
Mountain Lodge, Presidential Suite, 1 night, half board (includes dinner that evening and breakfast the next morning and all taxes)	162	182
Picnic lunch prepared by Mountain Lodge Chef	7	14
Tea or soft drink at Naro Moru River Lodge	3	6
Entrance fee to Samburu Game Reserve (includes also charge for car)	12	16
Block Hotel's Samburu Lodge, 1 night, half board, includes taxes	122	174
Entrance fee to Meru Game Reserve	12	16
Meru Mulika Lodge, 1 night, half board, includes taxes	85	109
Mt. Kenya Safari Club, Nanyuki, full board, includes all taxes	131	169
Kentmere Club, lunch	12	24
Evening train to Mombasa, return ticket first-class, includes dinner, bedding, early-morning tea, and breakfast	92	184

	US$	
	1 person	2 people
Avis, 2 days, limited mileage, full insurance, allowing 200 km	137	137
Gas (petrol)	10	10
Likoni ferry toll	2	2
Sheraton Golden Beach, 2 nights, including taxes, single or double $104	208	208
Meals: breakfast $5, lunch $8, dinner $12 = $25 × 2 days	50	100
Train to Nairobi (paid when return ticket was purchased)		
Taxi Nairobi RR station to airport	15	15
15% tips to waiters/waitresses	31.50	63
Gratuity to Housekeeping staff, $1 a night for one or two people	8	8
Tips to porters/bellmen/train stewards	34	34
SOS Insurance, $15 a week or $45 a month	30	60
Departure tax	10	20
Total:	$1931.50	$2390
Cost per person sharing:	$1195	

Paupers *Flame Trees of Thika* Itinerary

17 nights
Does not include airfare to Nairobi

Arrive Nairobi: Kenya Airways bus to city center	3	6
Methodist Guest House, 3 nights, full board, $17 single, $34 double	15	102
Public bus to travel back and forth from the house to city center for 3 days	4	8
Public bus to Thika	2	4
New Blue Posts Hotel, 1 night, includes breakfast and all taxes	13	19
Dinner at hotel on night of arrival	12	24
Bus from Thika to Nyeri	2	4
Mountain Lodge, standard room, 1 night, half board (dinner that evening and breakfast) includes all taxes	86	137
Lunch at Nyeri in a local cafe	3	6
Naro Moru River Lodge, shared accommodation in the bunkhouse, 3 nights, $3 a night	9	18
Allow for groceries cooked in the communal kitchen	20	40
Methodist Guest House, 1 night, full board	17	34
Public bus fares in Nairobi	3	6
Night sleeper train to Mombasa, return ticket, second class, $17 plus bedding, dinner and breakfast	29	58
Taxi from Mombasa RR station to Likoni ferry	3	3
Bus fare to Diani Beach	1	2
Dan Trench's Campsite, 6 nights, $3 per person	18	36

	US$	
	1 person	2 people
Meals and food purchased	60	120
Bus fare to Mombasa	1	2
Taxi to Mombasa RR station from Likoni ferry	3	3
Train fare (paid)		
Kenya Airways bus from city center to airport	3	6
15% tips to waiters/waitresses	19.50	39
Gratuity to housekeeping staff, $1 a night for one or two people	9	9
SOS Insurance, $15 a week or $45 a month	45	90
Departure tax	10	20
Total:	$426.50	$796
Cost per person sharing:	$398	

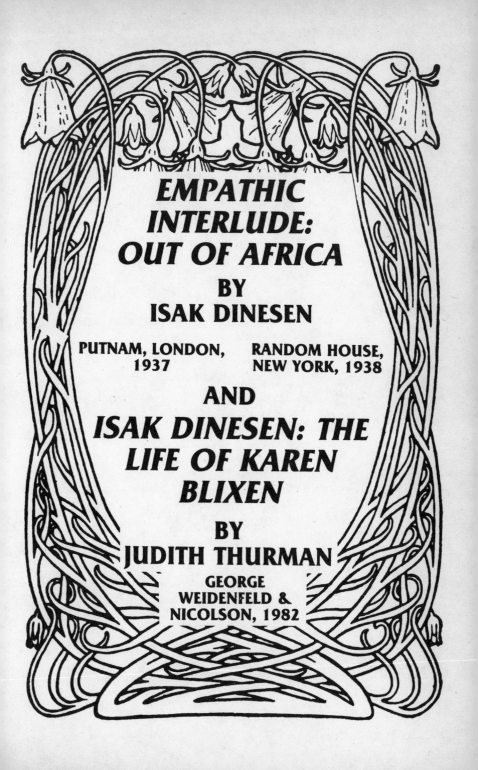

EMPATHIC INTERLUDE: OUT OF AFRICA

BY
ISAK DINESEN

PUTNAM, LONDON, 1937   RANDOM HOUSE, NEW YORK, 1938

AND

ISAK DINESEN: THE LIFE OF KAREN BLIXEN

BY
JUDITH THURMAN

GEORGE WEIDENFELD & NICOLSON, 1982

The film *Out of Africa* is based not only on the book of the same title but also on several biographies of its author, Karen Blixen. We found Judith Thurman's *Isak Dinesen: The Life of Karen Blixen* insightful. Ms. Thurman was an official adviser to the filmmakers.

A wealth of British fictional, biographical, autobiographical, and documentary colonial literature has developed over the past 80 years. It was a natural outgrowth of the accounts reported in the "From Our Correspondent" columns in the London *Times* and the serialization of explorer and missionary journals printed by Victorian weeklies. Some of this literature has been adapted to the movies and television. In *Out of Africa,* director Sidney Pollack succeeded in bringing the beauty of the Rift Valley to the audience by using 70mm film. Leah and I know every blade of grass that the camera pans. Pollack occasionally

A lion and his mate were often seen sunning themselves on Denys Finch-Hatton's grave.

substituted terrain—e.g., the Chuluyu Hills for the Ngong—but the Chuluyu range is the more beautiful. The camera is taken down—during the hero and heroine's flight in a light plane—over a composite landscape: the flamingoes of Elementia and then, in too short a time span, the wildebeast migration at Masai Mara/Serengeti Plain. There is no harm in this as long as one realizes that Pollack took poetic license to produce the effect he desired.

Areas of the combined story line (*Out of Africa* and Thurman's biography) have also been altered. Lord Delamere, whom Ms. Blixen disliked intensely along with the Happy Valley Set that he led, is depicted in the film as her strong British brick. Judith Thurman's biography identified Lord and Lady MacMillan to be her local British support. The director chose one central theme to bring to the audience: possession—of a woman who had everything then lost all. And he wrapped this moral in a romantic aura, as Ms. Blixen saw herself when she reflected on her time in Kenya. Ms. Thurman modifies her book's title by the phrase "biography of a storyteller"; the art of the storyteller is embellishment.

Sidney Pollack's *Out of Africa* will probably increase Kenyan tourism, but, naturally, the past 50 years have brought changes. The Kikuyu tribe today dress as shown in the film, only for tourists, just as at Williamsburg, Virginia, people dress for their sightseers. The Kikuyu are now in every phase of business, academia, and civil administration. Nairobi today has tall buildings and is a modern city with all the attendant problems of big cities. The Nairobi shown in the film was reconstructed in a field on the outskirts of the city by erecting false-front Hollywood sets. Today Kenya's trains are diesel-powered and sleek steel, not the wooden cars lent by the Railway Museum for the movie.

In our itinerary we direct readers to the authentic sites that remain. These are extremely interesting; if readers realize that, as we have written in our intro-duction, Africans have adapted Western lifestyles at greased-light speed, they will not be disappointed in the *Out of Africa* itinerary.

Readers are encouraged to read *White Mischief* by James Fox, as well as Judith Thurman's biography, before starting on the *Out of Africa* itinerary. *White Mischief*, although of a slightly later period, spells out all the juicy tidbits about pre-World War II Kenyan society that Judith Thurman is too scholarly to men-tion. Another title of interest is Errol Trzebinski's *Silence Will Speak: A Study of the Life of Denys Finch Hatton and His Relationship with Karen Blixen* (Chicago: University of Chicago Press, 1977 and 1985). The biography is a rather uncritical study. Trzebinski lived in Kenya for some years in the Nairobi suburb of Karen. This is a somewhat unreal world—as many suburbs are—and while her actual writing is strong and her research impeccable, rubbing shoul-ders with her neighbors over an extended period of time seems to have dulled her appreciation for the implications of her text. For example, she quotes a story about Finch-Hatton: ". . . once, when he was on safari in the very farthest, wildest regions, many days' march from contact with mails and telegraphs, a cable from London forwarded by relays of runners with cleft sticks, caught up with him in the bush. Its content was brief: 'Do you know George Robinson's address?' Back went the reply as it had come, by relays of runners travelling for weeks with cleft sticks. It was even briefer. 'Yes.' "

These were and are the type of practical jokes that White Kenyans find amusing despite the hardship they bring to the Africans whom they have im-pressed with the seriousness of their social intercourse. It never crosses their mind to identify with the hardship they impose in their zeal to score a point with one another. Today their conduct when dressing down waiters or making scenes in the Norfolk Hotel is a carryover from the White settler "gay banter" and "sharp wit."

Misfits that the White settlers were, Kenya molded rugged individualists, and a rich literature by and about them has been published, a literature richer than that of any other Commonwealth country except perhaps India.

Out of Africa Routing from North America or the United Kingdom

SAS Scandinavian Airlines—New York-Copenhagen
SAS Scandinavian Airlines—London-Copenhagen
Taxi—Tour to Karen Blixen's home
SAS Scandinavian Airlines—Copenhagen-Paris
Avis—Travel in Kenya
Kenya Railways—Nairobi-Mombasa
Avis—Travel at the coast
Kenya Airways—Mombasa-Nairobi-London
Pan Am—London-New York

Alternate route;
Kenya Airways—London-Nairobi
Avis—Travel in Kenya
Kenya Railways—Nairobi-Mombasa
Avis—Travel at the coast
Kenya Airways—Mombasa-Nairobi-London

Out of Africa Routing from Jeddah

Kenya Airways—Jeddah-Nairobi
Avis—Travel in Kenya
Kenya Railways—Nairobi-Mombasa
Avis—Travel at the coast
Kenya Airways—Mombasa-Nairobi-Jeddah

Out of Africa Routing from Australia/New Zealand

Qantas or Singapore Airlines—Sydney-Bombay
Kenya Airways—Bombay-Nairobi
Avis—Travel in Kenya
Kenya Railways—Nairobi-Mombasa
Avis—Travel at the coast
Kenya Airways—Mombasa-Nairobi-Bombay
Qantas or Singapore Airlines—Bombay-Sydney

The visit to Denmark to see Karen Blixen's home can, of course, be done but it adds considerably to the price of the itinerary. We suggest a trip to Denmark when readers are on a visit to England using the special tariff charged by Qantas to the United Kingdom and a return ticket from London to Copenhagen.

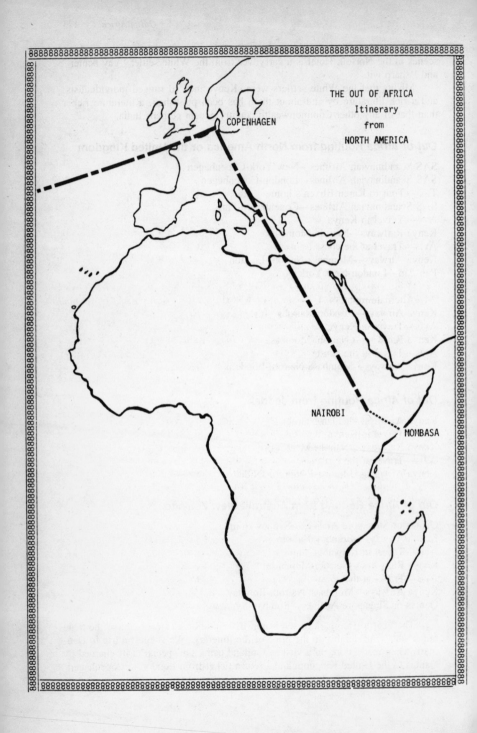

THE OUT OF AFRICA
Itinerary
from
NORTH AMERICA

COPENHAGEN

NAIROBI

MOMBASA

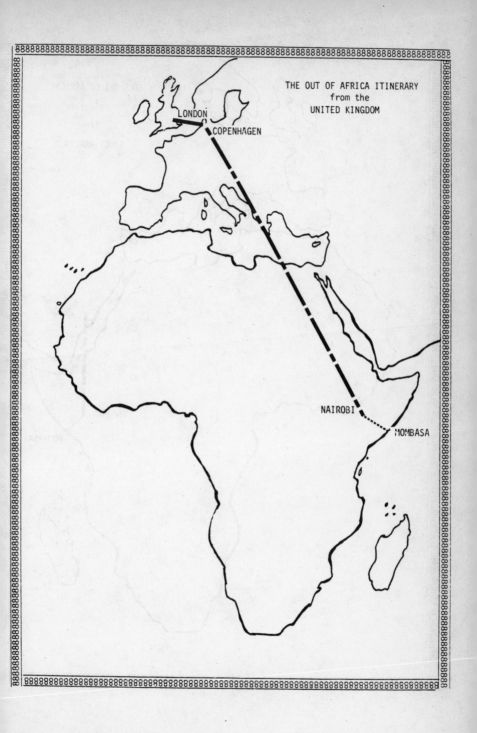

THE OUT OF AFRICA ITINERARY
from the
UNITED KINGDOM

LONDON
COPENHAGEN

NAIROBI

MOMBASA

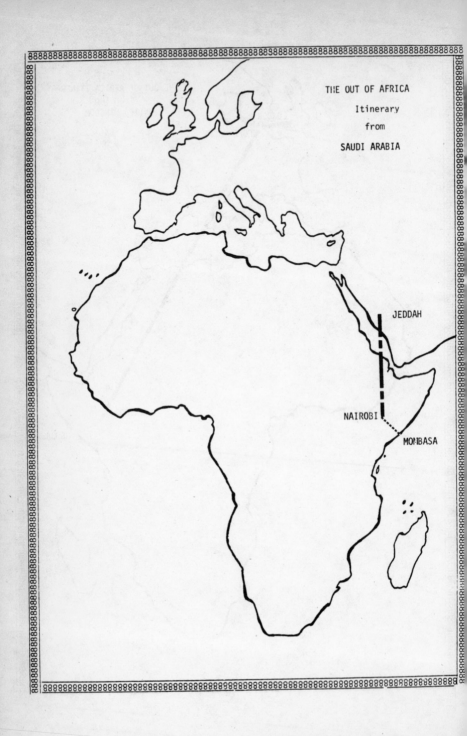

THE OUT OF AFRICA
Itinerary
from
SAUDI ARABIA

JEDDAH

NAIROBI

MOMBASA

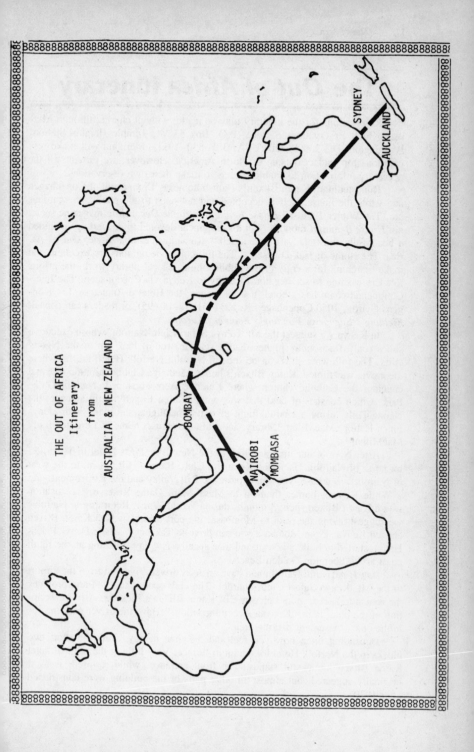

THE OUT OF AFRICA
Itinerary
from
AUSTRALIA & NEW ZEALAND

SYDNEY

AUCKLAND

BOMBAY

NAIROBI

MOMBASA

The *Out of Africa* Itinerary

Reservations for the itinerary may be made, without charge, through Merikani Hotel Reservations Service (P.O. Box 53394, Temple Heights Station, Washington, DC 20009, tel: (USA) 301–530–1911). Merikani will make reservations for readers outside of North America. However, we provide all the necessary information to enable readers to make their own reservations.

Rungstedlund, Karen Blixen's Danish home, is 15 mi north of Copenhagen and while the house itself is occupied and not open to the public, the gardens are. The Winter 1986–87 *House Beautiful's Home Decorating* magazine (note: not *House Beautiful* monthly, but a supplement devoted to decorating) included a beautifully illustrated article entitled: "Romantic Personal Style: Out of Africa: The Home of Isak Dinesen." The full-color photographs are excellent and make searching for a copy of the publication at a local library worth the effort. Readers wishing to see her home can fly to Kenya via Copenhagen. The Inter-Continental chain has a hotel in Copenhagen, the Hotel d'Angleterre (34 Kongens Nytrov, 1050 Copenhagen K, tel: (451) 12–00–95), or readers can consult *Fielding's Europe* or *Fielding's Economy Europe*.

In Kenya we suggest the Mt. Kenya Safari Club, Nairobi, whose executive suites (only fractionally higher than a standard room) look out at the Ngong Hills. The following sites can be seen in Nairobi: Norfolk Hotel; the set where the movie was filmed; Karen Blixen's home; Muthaiga Club; exhibition of tribal dancing; the Catholic church where Karen Blixen worshiped; Nairobi Game Park, which consists of land that was within Karen Blixen's farm acreage; the Ngong Hills, using a charter flight to relive the flights she made with Denys Finch-Hatton; MacMillan Library; and Chiramo House, home of Lord and Lady MacMillan.

After Nairobi our itinerary goes to the New Blue Posts Hotel in Thika, 35 mi north of Nairobi. Using the Kentmere Club, Banana Hill (14 mi to the west of Nairobi), as a base, you can explore the Rift Valley and the Escarpment, and a White Kenyan home, then on to Masai-Mara Game Reserve, the location where Karen Blixen spent 3 months during World War I. Returning to Nairobi, we suggest taking the train to Mombasa, the port through which Karen Blixen entered Kenya. From Mombasa you can drive to Takaungu, where Denys Finch-Hatton started to build a house, and then spend a few days relaxing on the south coast at the Sheraton Golden Beach.

Day 1: Arrive in Nairobi and have an Avis driver drive you from the airport to the Mt. Kenya Safari Club, Nairobi. The club opened in 1984 and provides the romantic backdrop and elegance of Karen Blixen's lifestyle. A full description of the hotel is in "Kenyan Accommodation." Have the driver park the car in the club's basement parking area.

Depending upon how you feel and the time of day, walk the short two blocks to the Norfolk Hotel for tea on its terrace. Very little of the original hotel Karen Blixen knew still stands. The front entrance, while restored, is as it originally appeared, but almost all other parts of the building were constructed after 1930.

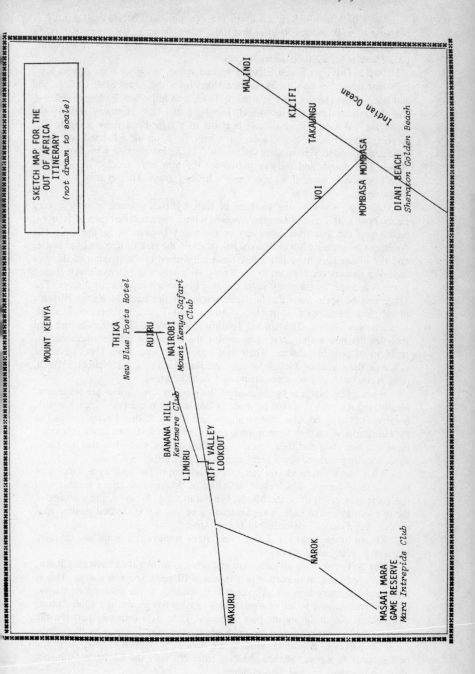

SKETCH MAP FOR THE
OUT OF AFRICA
ITINERARY
(not drawn to scale)

MOUNT KENYA

Indian Ocean

MALINDI

KILIFI

TAKAUNGU

VOI

MOMBASA MOMBASA

DIANI BEACH
Sheraton Golden Beach

THIKA
New Blue Posts Hotel

RUIRU

NAIROBI
Mount Kenya Safari Club

BANANA HILL
Kentmere Club

LIMURU

RIFT VALLEY
LOOKOUT

NAKURU

NAROK

MASAAI MARA
GAME RESERVE
Mara Intrepids Club

Walk back to Mt. Kenya Safari Club, Nairobi, well before 5:30 p.m.; it is not wise to walk the streets after that time. Have dinner in the club's Kirinyaga Restaurant. Or, if you're tired, in the room. The club's room service is luxurious. There is no additional charge.

Day 2: Drive to Karen Blixen's second home, using an Avis driver. Karen's first home became the Westwood Hotel (now the Army Staff College and not open to the public). If you want to drive, turn left when leaving the club at the circle (roundabout). Go around, leaving it at Uhuru Highway. Follow the signs for "Wilson Airport," and bear off to a right-hand road going to that airport. Several miles along, look for a large field, on the left-hand side, with a beaten-up round sign reading "Fairview" at the intersection with Coronation Road. The church and railway station for the film were erected in this field. Don't be disappointed if all you see is a field of grass. The set may have been taken down.

Our map showing the location of Karen Blixen's house is only a very general one and it should be supplemented with a more detailed map of Nairobi, which you can purchase from any of the many bookstores in the city. The American Women's Club of Nairobi has taken on the task of restoring the house, and the filmmakers have left a few furnishings used in the making of the picture. We have never been up to the Ngong Hills where the Denys Finch-Hatton grave is located, as for many years the area has been a hideout for thieves. The grave can be seen from the flagstone terrace at the back of Karen Blixen's house. She mentions this in *Out of Africa,* and Thurman describes how the location was chosen. The United Touring Company (UTC) offers a tour that includes the house and grave; presumably the large tour groups overcome the problem of possible attacks. Their tour starts at 2 p.m. from UTC's Nairobi office (at the corner of Muindi Mbingu and Kaunda streets, tel: Nairobi 331960). This is the only way we recommend you visit the grave.

We suggest lunch at the Horseman Restaurant; reservations are necessary. Ideally, the reservation should be made before leaving home (see "Plan Ahead") because it is very popular. Meryl Streep and Robert Redford often lunched at the Horseman when they were filming *Out of Africa.* Next door to the restaurant there is a nice shop that sells "tack"—saddles, bridles, etc.—but also has packaged, locally produced dried herbs that make nice gifts.

After lunch return as you came. Stop and enjoy the traditional dancing at the Bomas of Kenya, which starts at 2:30 p.m. Make reservations for this with the guest services staff at the Mt. Kenya Safari Club, Nairobi, the morning of the day you intend to visit. Your visit will give you a good, albeit modern idea of the "Big Dances" described in *Out of Africa.*

Return to the hotel for dinner. The club's Kirinyaga Lounge is extremely nice for a drink before dinner.

Day 3: Try to make an early start and drive to St. Austin's Catholic Church, which played such an important part in Karen Blixen's years in Kenya. This is a particularly interesting site. The church is original, as the cornerstone shows, and it is encouraging to see how much this mission has grown into a full-fledged independent parish during the past 70 years. There is a cemetery between the church and the students' playing field where priests and nuns who have dedicated their lives to educating Africans are buried. St. Austin's, now one of the best schools in Kenya, attracts students from not only the Christian faith, but also Hindu, Moslem, and Sikh children.

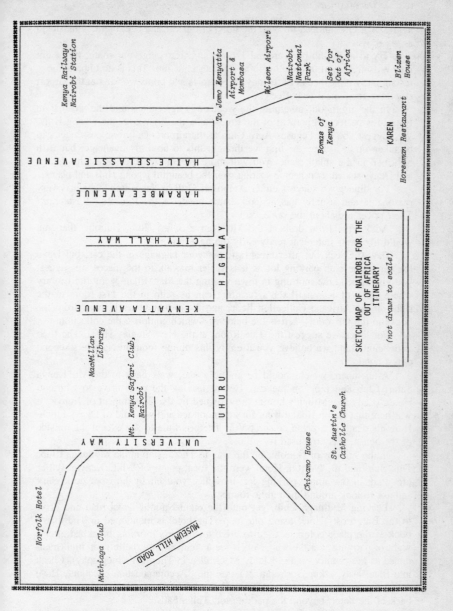

SKETCH MAP OF NAIROBI FOR THE
OUT OF AFRICA
ITINERARY

(not drawn to scale)

Continue down Uhuru Highway, along the same route taken yesterday, but instead of going to the suburb of Karen, enter Nairobi Game Park (the entrance is on the left). Part of the Blixen estate now belongs to the park. All of the Karen suburb was her farm, and you can get an idea of what the land surrounding the estate must have been like years ago. Take a camera; the animals are quite tame and readily seen. Do not get out of the car: The baboons can be aggressive. One jumped up onto the hood of our car and beat on the windshield as we drove.

Try to leave the park around 1 p.m. and, retracing your route, turn right into Wilson Airport to have lunch at Dambusters Club. This is an unpretentious restaurant, with a special of the day. Mechanics and pilots working at the airport stop here for a meal or coffee.

In the afternoon, assuming the weather is agreeable—and the weather in Nairobi is perfect 98 percent of the time—take the flight over the Ngong Hills. We suggest you use Pegasus Aero Club at the airport. Only one passenger can be taken up at a time. At first we thought this to be a disadvantage, but with only two in the small plane, you will more accurately experience what Karen and Denys shared: two people soaring over the beautiful Ngong Hills and plains.

For dinner we suggest either Amboseli Grill at the Hilton, which is very reasonable and usually has a good dance band, or the Red Bull Restaurant. Their prices are about the same.

Advise the front desk at the Mt. Kenya Safari Club, Nairobi, that you would like your statement ready early the next morning.

Day 4: Check out after breakfast, put your baggage in the car, but leave the car in the club parking lot as it is easier to walk to the places we suggest you visit. Spend the morning in town visiting the MacMillan Memorial Library where some of Karen Blixen's furniture can be seen in the first room to the right on the Africana Collection floor, and try to tear yourself away from the books in the far room—across the balcony—which comprise the collection.

For lunch we suggest the Tate Room at the New Stanley Hotel. The food is delicious, and we believe you'll enjoy this dining room in Nairobi's second oldest hotel.

After lunch, which should be an early one, walk back to the Mt. Kenya Safari Club and pick up the car. Before leaving the city, drive to Chiramo House (Lady MacMillan's home), now owned by the Government of Kenya. It was here that Karen Blixen went for afternoon tea and was told of Denys Finch-Hatton's death in a plane crash at Voi. There is little to see except the outside of the house; it is now used for offices.

In the suburbs of Nairobi, on the way to Thika, stop at the Muthiaga Club. This club, and the Norfolk Hotel were the focal points of White Kenyan settler life. Park in the ample parking lot; introduce yourself to the front desk clerk and ask to look around the public rooms

Leaving Muthiaga Club, get onto the main Nairobi-Thika road and drive to the Blue Posts Hotel using our map. The hotel is mentioned in Thurman's book as the place colonials used to drive to for early-morning breakfast after a night of partying. On the way, you'll see a signboard on the left for Juja (mentioned as the country estate of Lady MacMillan in Thurman's biography). Check into Blue Posts, asking for room 211 (see the "Accommodation" section). Have tea in the garden and look at Chaina Falls, facing the garden, and around the back of the hotel, beyond the parking lot, Thika Falls.

The original Blue Posts was composed of six African rondavels with thatch roofs. In the early days of White settlement, Thika was about halfway between Nairobi and the land that many settlers purchased on the slopes to the east and west of Mt. Kenya. After World War II the rondavels were demolished and the building to the right and back of the main kitchen was built. In the early 1950s the building across the driveway, on the left, was constructed.

There is little to do at the New Blue Posts in the evening; if you drink you'll enjoy the bar. Somehow we're never bored and believe an overnight stop will give readers a good insight into present-day Kenya. One thing's for sure; you won't be tripping over other tourists. When the hotel was sold to African owners, the adjective *new* was added to the name; however, most people still refer to the hotel simply as Blue Posts.

Day 5: Make an early start from Blue Posts and drive back to Ruiru, taking the road into town and then turning onto the beautifully scenic route to Kentmere Club. Slow down after passing the sign for Nazareth Hospital on the right, as the driveway for Kentmere Club is only denoted by a rather small white sign along a 6-foot-high fence. Make Kentmere Club your base for exploring the Rift Valley in the afternoon. (You will have passed—and disregarded—a sign reading "Kentmere Estate" on the left.)

After lunch drive to Limuru and get onto the main Nairobi-Navisha road (see map). Stop at the lookout for a magnificent view of the Rift Valley Escarpment.

To return to Limuru and Kentmere Club, take the old road, along the valley floor, driving until you see a small stone church on the right of a hairpin turn. This church was built by Italian prisoners captured in northern Kenya and Somalia by the British during World War II. Southern Somalia was at that time Italian Somaliland. It is a lovely little church now tended by a local man.

The Escarpment lookout, and the drive along the Rift Valley floor covers some of the region described in "A War-time Safari" in *Out of Africa.*

Stop for afternoon at Mrs. Mitchell's home, overlooking her tea estate. Get directions from the front desk at Kentmere before you leave in the morning.

Return to Kentmere Club for dinner and the night. Again, there is little to do but enjoy the beautiful publike bar and the company of local people who stop in for a drink, and, if you're lucky and he's free, the general manager, Paul Landuyt—one of our favorite people.

Day 6: Drive to Keekerok Lodge in the Masai-Mara Game Reserve. Next morning, check out of the Kentmere Club after breakfast, then drive along the new Nairobi-Naivasha road (passing the lookout) and take the left turn for Narok. (Narok is mentioned in *Out of Africa.*) The road is paved as far as town.

In the rainy season, from mid- to late March until August, this road is impassable without a four-wheel drive vehicle. You can get advice on road conditions at any time of the year from the Kenya Automobile Association in Nairobi (tel: 742926) and the many truck drivers parked at the junction of the Narok-Masai Mara roads. Readers who want to take this itinerary during the rainy season can always fly to Masai Mara. Express Kenya (American Express of Kenya, Consor Box 40433, Nairobi, Kenya, tel: Nairobi 334722) can arrange this, or Merikani will do it for you when making reservations for the hotels and Avis car.

Day 7: Tour Masai Mara. There is a local map available and game scouts will accompany you if you would like. Their charge is very reasonable.

Day 8: Make an early start for Nairobi. Overnight at Mt. Kenya Safari Club, Nairobi.

Day 9: Spend the day resting and shopping. Depending upon what time you booked the Avis, turn the car in, remembering to arrange for another Avis

TENTS
FOR THE COLONIES.

Fitted with VERANDAH, BATHROOM, &c.

As used by most eminent Travellers, and supplied to H.M. Government for East, West, Central, and South Africa, &c.

SPECIAL TENTS FOR EXPLORERS & MOUNTAINEERING

COMPLETE EQUIPMENT.
CAMP FURNITURE WITH LATEST IMPROVEMENTS. AIR AND WATERTIGHT TRUNKS. UNIFORMS AND CLOTHING OF ALL KINDS.

"Consult with Messrs. Silver & Co., who know exactly what is needed for every part of the Globe."—*Extract from "Notes on Outfit," by the Royal Geographical Society.*

car to meet you in Mombasa. Take the sleeping-car overnight train to Mombasa, which leaves at 7 p.m. (see "Plan Ahead"). Take a taxi from the hotel to the station around 5:45 p.m. Karen writes about this train and the journey in *Out of Africa*.

Day 10: Arrive in Mombasa, arrange for Avis to meet you at the station. Check into the Castle Hotel. Spend the day using the Avis driver to see Old Town, Mombasa, Fort Jesus, and to shop. Descriptions of these places of interest can be found in the *Lost Cities of Africa* itinerary Kenyan Swahili sites. Keep the driver, as parking is difficult in Mombasa. Alternatively, you could walk, but it gets very hot walking.

Day 11: Check out of the Castle Hotel. Decide if you want the Avis driver again today, or drive yourself, now that you're familiar with the town (it's a small one). Drive to Takaungu, using our map of Mombasa Island, going over New Nyali Bridge and continuing past a small toll bridge.

Takaungu has never been developed and there is little to see except the Indian Ocean from the same locale that Karen did, and which she found so rewarding. Leave Takaungu and have lunch at the Mnarani Club, just south of Kilifi.

The Mnarani Club was once a private hotel where the international Pan Am deep-sea fishing contest was headquartered. It is now operated by the German tour company African Safari Club, which caters primarily to their own clients. Guests are welcome for lunch. The food is excellent; German dishes with tropical fruits served buffet-style. The great attraction is the dining room, which overlooks both Kilifi Creek and the Indian Ocean. Trellised bougainvillea frame the scene. It was from Kilifi Creek that Swahili merchants unloaded and loaded dhows from the Persian Gulf 1000 years ago.

After lunch drive back to Mombasa, crossing the Nyali Bridge, going through the town, and keeping straight until Likoni Ferry. After crossing the ferry continue for 23 miles until the sign "Diani Beach" is seen on the left. Turn into the T-access road, and at the end, go left. Continue to the Sheraton Golden Beach. The beach starting at the Sheraton Golden Beach and running southward for several miles is the one shown in the low-flying scene in the film. Readers of *White Mischief* will remember the interview the author had with Dan Trench. Mr. Trench can usually be found, as the *White Mischief* text informs, just down the beach from the Sheraton at the Trade Winds Hotel bar.

Night 11; Days and Nights 12 and 13: We are going to assume readers will round off the itinerary to two weeks and in the budget allow three nights at the Sheraton, keeping the Avis, and returning to Mombasa's Moi International Airport on the morning of the 14th day to connect in Nairobi with a flight home.

Cheaper Itinerary: The cost of the *Out of Africa* itinerary can be cut considerably using public transportation and the Methodist Guest House as a base instead of the Mt. Kenya Safari Club, Nairobi. There are public buses, which are recommended instead of matatoos (see "Transportation") to Karen. Getting around the game parks—either Nairobi City Game Park or Masai-Mara—is impossible without a car, as foot traffic is not permitted, and the recourse here would be to take a tour. Muthaiga Club can be reached by public bus, and the MacMillan Memorial Library and Chiramo House are within walking distance to Nairobi city center. There is a public bus to Thika and the rates at Blue Posts Hotel are very reasonable. The Kentmere Club part of the itinerary would have to be deleted as a car is essential. For young readers we believe the cheaper itinerary is a valid alternative—the main problem is having enough time to carry it out. Once you're in Nairobi, arrangements for tours can be made through Express Kenya (Consolidated House, Standard St., P.O. Box 40433, Nairobi, Kenya, tel: Nairobi 334722).

PLAN AHEAD: As mentioned at the start of the itinerary, all reservations can be made through Merikani Hotel Reservations Service, without charge. Nor do they charge for obtaining application forms for a visa (only for the actual cost of the visa) if hotel reservations are made through them. They will also send the recommended maps with the confirmation of your hotel reservations. These

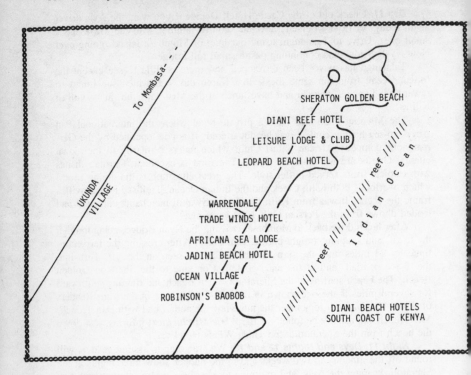

SHERATON GOLDEN BEACH
DIANI REEF HOTEL
LEISURE LODGE & CLUB
LEOPARD BEACH HOTEL

To Mombasa

UKUNDA VILLAGE

WARRENDALE
TRADE WINDS HOTEL
AFRICANA SEA LODGE
JADINI BEACH HOTEL
OCEAN VILLAGE
ROBINSON'S BAOBOB

reef ///////// reef ///////// Indian Ocean

DIANI BEACH HOTELS
SOUTH COAST OF KENYA

are charged at the price quoted on the maps. Merikani offers these services to our non–North American readers as well as Americans and Canadians. Their address is P.O. Box 53394, Temple Heights Station, Washington, DC 20009, tel: (USA) 301–530–1911. However, we have provided all the necessary information to make your own reservations.

The following needs to be done before departure: check the Basic Information Checklist for necessary travel documents; make hotel reservations (the numbers and addresses are given in the heading preceding the hotel descriptions in "Kenya Accommodation"); make your airline reservations; write Pegasus Flyers Ltd. (c/o Aero Club, P.O. Box 40813, Nairobi, Kenya, tel: Nairobi 501772) for time and date for your flight; write to the Horseman Restaurant for a lunch reservation; purchase maps (see "Bye-the-By"); start taking malaria tablets two weeks before departure; purchase SOS Insurance (see "Travel Documents"); purchase traveler's checks; and write, but do not send the money, to Kenya Railways for overnight sleeper reservations—pay when you pick up the tickets.

Once in Nairobi, have the guest services staff at the Mt. Kenya Safari Club: confirm your rail tickets, and if you prefer to fly back to Nairobi, have them reserve a seat for you on the Mombasa-Nairobi Kenya Airways plane; and get a ticket for the Bomas of Kenya afternoon dance performance. Reservations are not necessary for the Mnarani Club.

In the way of clothing, nothing special is needed—remember beach wear for Diani Beach. A pair of binoculars may be useful to see the Finch-Hatton memorial from the terrace of Karen Blixen's house and for game viewing in Masai-Mara. Decaffeinated coffee is not available in Kenya and you may want to take a supply, as well as plenty of film, as it is expensive in Kenya.

Accommodation recommended for the *Out of Africa* itinerary (all in Kenya); Mt. Kenya Safari Club, Nairobi; New Blue Posts Hotel, Thika; Kentmere Club, Banana Hill; Keekorok Lodge or Mara Intrepids Club, Masai-Mara; and Sheraton Golden Beach, Diani Beach.

Estimated Budget

Out of Africa Itinerary

14 nights
Does not include airfare to Nairobi, Kenya

	US$	
	1 person	2 people
Arrive Nairobi: Avis agents meets flight		
Mt. Kenya Safari Club, Nairobi, 3 nights, executive suite $132 single, $148 double, includes all taxes	396	444
Meals: breakfast $5, lunch $8, including picnic lunches prepared by club's chef, dinner $12 = $25 × 3 days	75	150
Select option (a) or (b)		
(a) Avis rental car for 9 days, driving to Masai-Mara, with driver in Nairobi for 2 days, but self-drive once out of that city (allow 896 km and full insurance) $557 + gas (petrol) $56	————	————
(b) Avis rental car for 7 days, flying to Masai-Mara with a driver in Nairobi, but self-drive once out of that city (allow 266 km and full insurance) $460 + gas (petrol) $17	————	————
Tea at Norfolk Hotel	7	14
Entrance fee to Bomas of Kenya	15	30
Entrance fee to Nairobi Game Park (also for your driver) $4 per person plus charge for the car	16	20
Flight over Ngong Hills in private charter plane, maximum	150	300
Lunch, Tate Room, New Stanley Hotel (Nairobi)	12	24
Dinner at New Blue Posts Hotels	12	24
New Blue Posts Hotel, overnight, includes breakfast	13	19
Kentmere Club, 2 nights, includes breakfast, $30 single, $50 double × 2	60	100
Meals: lunch $10, dinner $12 at Kentmere Club × 2 =	44	88
Tea and tour of Masai village at Mayar's Farm	16	32
Select option (1), (2), or (3)		
(1) Self-drive to Keekorok Lodge (cost of Avis shown above), full board, $136 single, $179 double, × 2 nights $282 and $368	————	————

	US$	
	1 person	2 people
(2) Self-drive to Mara Intrepids Club (cost of Avis shown above), full board, $240 single, $300 double × 2 nights (includes escorted drives in park) $480 and $600	———	———
(3) Fly Nairobi-Masai-Mara-Nairobi as part of a tour group. Keekorok Lodge, full board, includes escorted drives, 2 nights $500 and $1000	———	———
Day room, Mt. Kenya Safari Club, Nairobi	66	74
Night sleeper train to Mombasa, first class, includes bedding, dinner, early-morning tea and breakfast	46	92
Arrive Mombasa—met by Avis agent; limited mileage for 4 days using driver for first day only, allow 200 km	229	229
Gas (petrol)	10	10
Castle Hotel, Mombasa, includes breakfast and all taxes, $43 single, $66 double, 1 night	43	66
Meals: lunch $8, dinner $12	20	40
Entrance fee to Fort Jesus	2	4
Toll bridge fees	2	2
Likoni Ferry charge for car	2	2
Sheraton Golden Beach, 3 nights, single or double $101	303	303
Meals: breakfast $6, lunch $10, dinner $15 = $31 × 3	93	186
Lunch in Mombasa day of departure for home	12	24
Departure tax	10	20
15% tips to waiters/waitresses on all meals	50	100
Gratuity to housekeeping staff, $1 a night for 1 or 2 persons	13	13
Tips to bellmen/porters	32	32
SOS Insurance, 2 weeks	30	60
Total option (a) and (1):	$2674	$3483
Total option (a) and (2):	$2872	$3715
Total option (b) and (3):	$2756	$3979
Cost per person sharing: options (a) and (1):	$1746.50	
Cost per person sharing: options (a) and (2):	$1862.50	
Cost per person sharing: options (b) and (3):	$1994.50	

Paupers *Out of Africa* Itinerary

14 nights
Does not include airfare unless otherwise stated

	US$	
	1 person	2 people
Arrive Nairobi: Taxi to Methodist Guest House	$ 15	$ 15
Avis rental car for 5 days self-drive except first day in Nairobi when driver is used, unlimited mileage and full insurance	409	409
Gas (petrol)	17	17
Visit Karen Blixen's home, passing lot where movie was filmed; lunch at Horseman Restaurant	10	20
Entrance fee to Bomas of Kenya	15	30
Avis driver drives to MacMillan Library, then to Norfolk Hotel for afternoon tea	7	14
Blue Posts Hotel, Thika, 2 nights, $13 single, $19 double includes breakfast	26	38
Dinner at Blue Posts	12	24
Lunch at Blue Posts (sandwiches)	5	10
Drive to Nyeri: afternoon tea at Outspan Hotel	5	10
Kentmere Club, Banana Hill, 1 night, $30 single, $50 double, includes breakfast	30	50
Lunch at Kentmere Club	10	20
Mayer's Farm, Masai Village and afternoon tea	16	32
Drive to Nairobi and join tour to Masai-Mara, includes flight to Masai-Mara, 2 nights at Keekorock Lodge, full board, and escorted drives in reserve	258	516
Night sleeper train to Mombasa, second class, includes bedding, dinner, and breakfast	46	92
Arrive Mombasa: Take public bus to Likoni Ferry, walk across ferry, take public bus to Diani Beach, getting off at Dan Trench's Campsite	1	2
Dan Trench's, 5 nights $3 per person per night	15	30
Meals: Allow $10 a day × 5 days	50	100
Take bus to Mombasa and spend day looking at Fort Jesus, and having a drink on Castle Hotel Porch	7	14
Night train to Nairobi	46	92
Arrive Nairobi: airport bus to Kenyatta International Airport (can be picked up at any of the big hotels, which are within walking distance of railroad station)	5	10
Departure tax	10	20
15% tips to waiters/waitresses on all meals	10.20	20.40
Gratuity to housekeeping staff, $1 a night for 1 or 2 persons	6	6
SOS Insurance $15 a week, or $45 a month	30	60
Total:	$1061.20	$1651.40
Per person sharing:	$ 825.70	

THE JUNCTURE:
THE AFRICANS

BY DAVID LAMB

REVISED EDITION

**VINTAGE BOOKS,
RANDOM HOUSE,
NEW YORK
1985**

Readers who have an interest in visiting Africa to see for themselves the international media's concern during the last few years about the continent will find that following an itinerary based on David Lamb's insightful *The Africans* will provide an opportunity to assess the problems and discuss them with Africans and expatriates. David Lamb strikes a compromise between Leah's feelings and mine on the subject of Africa: He details the thousands of stupid occurrences that take place on that continent and at times falls into despair for Africa's future. That is Leah's view. He also points out that historically speaking African countries have come a very short way down the road to nation-building and that it is too soon to judge. This is my view.

International concern focuses on Africa primarily because, as David Lamb writes, "the continent is not catching up with the rest of the world, it is falling further behind. Africa is no longer part of the Third World. It is the Fourth World." This, in spite of the fact that:

> It has 40 percent of the world's potential hydro-electric power supply, the bulk of the world's diamonds and chromium, 30 percent of the world's gold, 90 percent of its cobalt, 50 percent of its phosphates, 40 percent of its platinum, 7.5 percent of its coal, 8 percent of its known petroleum reserves, 12 percent of its natural gas, 3 percent of its iron ores, and millions upon millions of acres of untilled farmland. There is not another continent blessed with such abundance.
>
> *The Africans*

There is no single cause why Africa is falling behind and only by seeing the countries at first-hand and talking to those living and working in Africa can the complexity of the issue be realized. A major component, however, is African leaders' preoccupation with domestic politics. Today Africa is at a juncture and must decide which road to take: to get on with the job of development or continue to live day by day, relying on assistance from industrialized nations when crises occur.

Another component of the problem lies with the economic and cultural ties African countries continue to maintain with the governments of their former colonizers. Thirty years after independence Europe continues to directly influence the economies and attitudes of the new nations. For this reason we hope our readers following the itinerary for *The Africans* will have previously traveled in England, France, and Italy. Travel in Portugal would normally also be of value, but we are not advising travel in that country's former colonies at this writing. Germany's African possessions were turned over to other European powers to administer after World War I and for that reason German influence is not strong. However, both East and West German governments today provide substantial amounts of aid, loans, and technical personnel to various African countries. In doing so, from our observation, they do not attempt—the West Germans at least—to impart cultural values, nor is the funding of the West Germans particularly tied to their national economies. Not so in the case of the British, who have major investments in Kenya. The French export commodities to Africa that they find difficult to sell on the competitive world market. Italy continues to monopolize the Somali import and export market. If one sees at first-hand the high unemployment in England, France, and, Italy by traveling to those countries, it becomes apparent that they cannot afford to lose their African markets or encourage African self-sufficiency. These economic and cultural ties to the former colonizer produce a "company store" syndrome.

Nor should the cultural ties be overlooked; as David Lamb writes, these are stronger in the French colonies than in the British. In fact, we found that the French were successfully indoctrinating Africans to be contemptuous of non-French foreigners. This is more evident among the semi-educated Africans than the peasants. In countries such as Mali, where the national character is strong and the French were unable to control the desert peoples, their current efforts are meeting with little success. But at airports and hotels the contempt for the non-French person is abundantly evident.

Our other itineraries are designed to be "fun itineraries"; this one is intended to be a "learning experience." We have set no time frame for this itinerary, but it cannot be reasonably done in less than three months. Readers who have responsibilities at home will be unable to follow it exactly. But for those who are retired, students on a summer vacation, or graduate students taking a prolonged trip overseas before settling down to pursue a career, it will be time well spent. In the coming years an understanding of the problems of Africa will become increasingly important. David Lamb gives several reasons why non-Africans will find that the continent has a direct impact on their lives:

Humanitarian: "To be oblivious to the problems of Africa is to promote more international misery, hunger, instability—and to increase the threats to peace in the world."

Ideological: ". . . to let Moscow take Africa piece by piece, exploiting the fragility of individual countries and choosing Communism for these people, who would not have chosen it for themselves."

Commercial (in this quote he is referring to the post-independent period, but his remarks are as true today): "Its [Africa's] growing markets were absorbing billions of dollars in foreign goods every year and demanding more; its untilled farmlands were fertile and huge, a potential breadbasket for millions of people at home and abroad . . . from Moscow to Washington, from Rio de Janeiro and Havana to Paris and Tokyo, governments jockeyed for influence, for a stake in the future of this continent, which twenty or thirty years from now might carry the weight to tip the world's balance of power, one way or the other. The first 'scramble for Africa' occurred a century ago when the European powers met in Berlin to carve up the Dark Continent for themselves. This new 'invasion' was more subtle but its aims were similar: economic and strategic domination."

Because *The Africans* itinerary has specific goals—learning from Africans and expatriates working in Africa—we take the liberty of offering advice on how to approach them. Appearance means a great deal in Africa. A certain mind-set must be absorbed by our women readers if they are to get the most from their travels. We also have a few gems of advice for our male readers.

Women's dress: In Africa women are expected to be ladies in the old-fashioned meaning of the word. For a woman traveler to assume any other guise will mean she will not be exposed to the inner thinking of the Africans with whom she comes in contact. A woman's views and thinking are respected, and outsiders who write that women have no voice in national or domestic affairs in Africa are basing their judgment on their own country's means of expressing equality. Each person in Africa has a very definite role; African society shuts the door to those not playing their role.

To define "an old-fashioned lady," think of the 1940s when hems touched just below the knee, breasts were held in position by bras, hair was combed and neatly styled, eyes were lowered and did not meet a man's gaze as he passed, the body was kept clean at all times, the clothes were appropriate to the occasion—sunback dresses for sporting occasions, shorts worn only at the beach, and T-shirts were for male garage mechanics.

Remember, the clothes most East Africans wear are the cast-offs of the 1950s given to charitable agencies by generous friends in North America, Britain, Australia, and New Zealand. Africans pay for those clothes, and they work hard to earn the money to buy them. They take pride in the way they look. For foreigners, whom they know to be capable of buying whatever they want, to dress sloppily sends the message that the visitor has no respect for the host/hostess.

Attire in West Africa differs from East Africa. Some West African women change back and forth between traditional and Western dress. The traditional dresses are gorgeous: the colors, the materials, and how they drape! In Senegal the neckline is cut wide to show the collar bones, but ladies always manage to let the neckline slip so that one shoulder is bare—purely unintentional, they would have the viewer believe! In Somalia and Mali women wear only traditional styles. In Mali the neckline is cut smaller but the arm holes are wider. The women have a habit of readjusting the garment at the shoulders as they converse, allowing an interesting view of breast contours. In Somalia the traditional dress is a body-fitting, slinky, floor-length dress with a piece of the same material—usually tissue-thin nylon—used as a shawl over the shoulders and, sometimes, the head. The shawl is often used as our grandmothers used a fan—to tease, to imply. African women are usually terrible flirts—but there is an elegant and a crass way to flirt, and they manage to be very elegant.

My personal sin (not Leah's—she always wears 3-inch heels) is to wear flip-flops in Africa. Shoes are a status symbol (that's not why Leah wears heels; she wears them because she's short and has beautiful legs). Bata, that famous Third World shoe company, has made a fortune selling flip-flops, which are the first rung on the ladder in the progression from bare to shod feet. The more covered the foot, the more respected the wearer. So, on the subject of shoes, my advice becomes one of "do as I say, not as I do." It doesn't particularly matter if the shoes you wear are old, just so they're kept polished. Find something comfortable and covered and you'll merit respect. Stockings need not be worn.

Cosmetics: If you are used to wearing makeup, you may want to think of applying a bit less and developing a simpler style for your safari. Excessive perspiring, dust, and sand can wreak havoc on the more complicated styles. Cold cream will prove invaluable in removing not only cosmetics but any accumulated grime. Mascara has a way of streaking and streaming in the humid tropics, so give your makeup some thought before you leave.

Men's wear in Africa: A shirt, no matter how patched or torn, is better than no shirt in the eyes of most African men. While jeans are envied and acceptable in some places, men should plan to take along a few different styles of trousers. Businessmen do not wear jeans and a pair of lightweight, no-iron slacks will be useful for many occasions. If readers make Kenya the start of their trip, they can have a safari suit tailor-made in a few days. This is not the military version of a safari suit, but a suit made from a wide choice of light-weight suiting materials, fitted to the body, with four patch pockets. Usually short-sleeved, it is worn without a shirt. We are told it is comfortable and cool, and we know it to be acceptable in both East and West Africa for almost any occasion. Many hotel workers' uniforms are made on this same pattern; they are usually of a solid color and, of course, seldom fit as the tailor-made suits fit. Select a more expensive cloth—even so, it will not be expensive by our standards—and you won't be mistaken for a bellhop. When ordering your safari suit pay only a small deposit, and pay the balance on delivery; that's the secret of having it completed on time. Do not pay the initial deposit by credit card. Pay it in cash, and when you pick up your suit ask that it be refunded and pay the total amount by credit card if you want to do so. A safari suit is acceptable for all but the most formal occasions—a jacket and tie can be left at home if you plan to purchase a good safari suit. Avoid military-appearing clothing— shorts (Bermuda length, hitting midway down the thigh) in white and worn with a white cotton shirt are acceptable, but avoid Hawaiian shirts; leave T-shirts for the tennis courts or other sports, and those God-awful jogging shorts at home. Socks should be worn, knee-high with Bermuda shorts, regular socks of a dark color with safari suits. Leather moccasins (kept polished) are a good all-around choice of shoes, although they will identify you as a North American immedi-ately. Italian-made soft black leather moccasin-style shoes are generally worn by middle-class African and expatriate men. Well-fitting leather sandals can be worn quite appropriately with the knee-high socks.

A well-trimmed beard will not meet with protest by immigration officials, but a let-it-all-hang-out hippie beard will. Both beard styles will soon meet a razor blade in Tanzania or Malawi (also possibly in Burundi). No matter how tired, avoid a 5 o'clock shadow and keep shaved if it is your practice to shave.

Tourists' dress: You will see many women tourists walking the streets of African capital cities in shorts and halter tops. They not only look comical to us, they look comical to Africans. You will also see, if you patronize tourist hotels in West Africa, topless women. These are usually from Europe, including Britain. Considering the marvelous figures of most African women, the sagging bosoms must appear pitiful to most African waiters who serve at poolside.

The Africans Routing from North America and the United Kingdom

This is a very special ticket requiring the patience and attention of a res-ervationist extremely well versed in how to write it to the passenger's best advantage. Otherwise, a great deal of money can be wasted. We strongly rec-ommend that readers contact Merikani Hotel Reservations Service and let them know the cities they particularly wish to visit. They will work with their airline contacts who are familiar with African routings and who know what we want

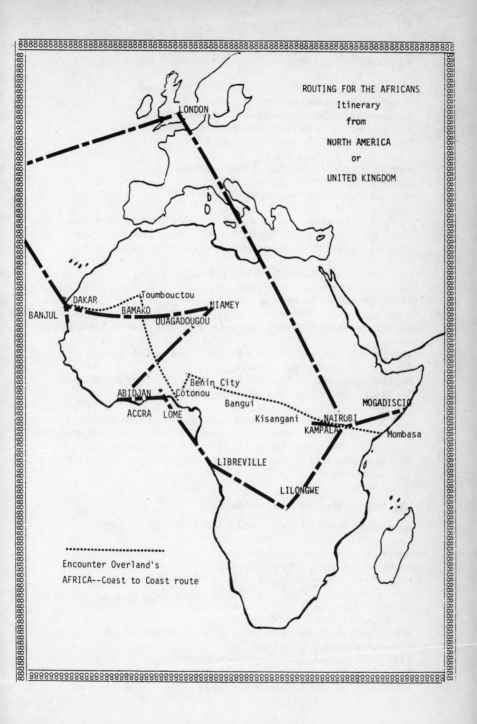

ROUTING FOR THE AFRICANS
Itinerary
from
NORTH AMERICA
or
UNITED KINGDOM

LONDON

Toumbouctou
DAKAR
BAMAKO
NIAMEY
BANJUL
OUAGADOUGOU

Benin City
ABIDJAN
Cotonou
Bangui
MOGADISCIO
ACCRA
LOME
Kisangani
NAIROBI
KAMPALA
Mombasa

LIBREVILLE

LILONGWE

···········
Encounter Overland's
AFRICA--Coast to Coast route

for our readers, namely, the most cities at the most reasonable cost. The following is a suggested routing:

Air Canada or Pan American—Montreal/New York-London
Kenya Airways—London-Nairobi (Kenya)
Kenya Airways—Nairobi-Mogadiscio (Somalia)-Nairobi
Kenya Airways—Nairobi-Entebbe/Kampala (Uganda)-Nairobi
Uganda Railways—Kampala-Jinja-Kampala
                                    or
Kenya Railways—Nairobi-Jinja (Uganda)-Kampala
Kenya Airways—Entebbe (Uganda)-Nairobi
Kenya Airways—Nairobi-Lilongwe (Malawi)

A second ticket is written when purchasing the first ticket for the remainder of this route, indicating that the journey originated in Lilongwe, Malawi. This takes advantage of the more favorable Malawian foreign exchange rates.

UTA-Air France—Lilongwe-Libreville (Gabon)
Air Afrique—Libreville-Lome (Togo)
Taxi-Lome-Accra (Ghana)-Lome
Air Afrique—Lome-Abidjan (Ivory Coast)
Air Afrique—Abidjan-Niamey (Niger)-Ouagadougou (Burkina Faso)-Bamako (Mali)
Mali Railways—river steamer-taxis-Bamako-Koulikoro-Dire-Bamako
Air Afrique—Bamako-Dakar (Senegal)
Nigerian Airways/Ghana Airways—Dakar-Banjul (The Gambia)-Dakar
Air Afrique—Dakar-New York/Montreal

Remember that all African airlines do not have a reputation for reliable departure times *or* dates. We suggest avoiding Air Tanzania and domestic flights of Air Zaire. When using Ghana Airways or Nigerian Airways from Dakar to Banjul take only hand baggage, as we had items taken from our bags that went into the cargo bay.

The Africans Routing from Jeddah

Saudia-Saudi Arabian Airlines—Jeddah-Nairobi (Kenya)
Kenya Airways—Nairobi-Kigali (Rwanda)-Nairobi
Kenya Railways—Nairobi-Jinja-Kampala (Uganda)
Airline bus—Kampala-Entebbe (Uganda)
Kenya Airways—Entebbe-Nairobi-Lilongwe (Malawi)
Avis—Land travel in Malawi
UTA—Air France-Lilongwe-Libreville (Gabon)
Air Afrique—Libreville-Lome (Togo)
Avis—Travel in Togo in connection with the "Volunteer's Safari"
Taxi—Lome-Accra (Ghana)-Lome
KLM-Royal Dutch Airlines—Lome-Kano (Nigeria)
Taxi—Kano
Saudia-Saudi Arabian Airlines—Kano-Jeddah

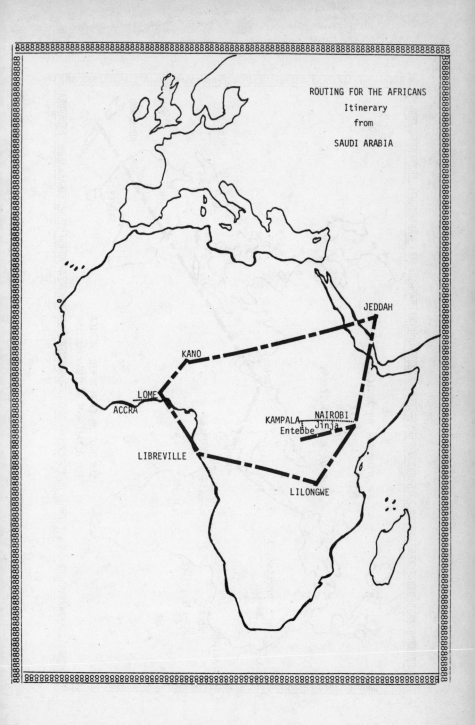

ROUTING FOR THE AFRICANS
Itinerary
from
SAUDI ARABIA

JEDDAH

KANO

LOME
ACCRA

KAMPALA   NAIROBI
        Jinja
    Entebbe

LIBREVILLE

LILONGWE

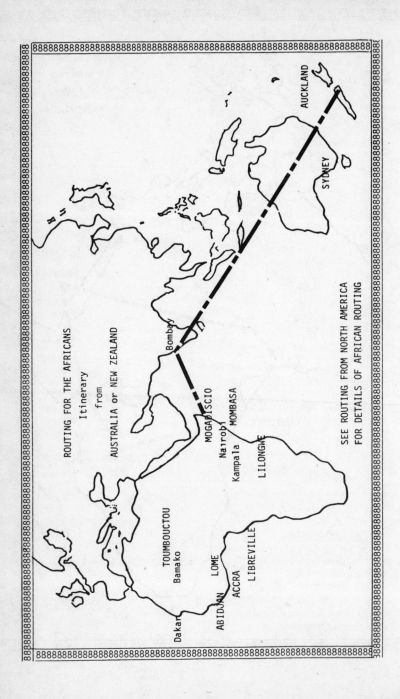

ROUTING FOR THE AFRICANS
Itinerary
from
AUSTRALIA or NEW ZEALAND

SEE ROUTING FROM NORTH AMERICA
FOR DETAILS OF AFRICAN ROUTING

We have deleted the Bamako-Naimey section of the route since readers who live in Saudi Arabia will probably have an understanding of desert life.

The Africans Routing from Australia or New Zealand

Qantas offers many concessional fares, and these should be studied before deciding on a definite itinerary. The following is a suggested routing:

Qantas—Sydney-Bombay (India)
Kenya Airways—Bombay-Nairobi (Kenya)
Kenya Airways—Nairobi-Mogadiscio (Somalia)-Nairobi
Kenya Airways or Kenya Railways—Nairobi-Entebbe/Kampala-Nairobi
Kenya Airways—Nairobi-Lilongwe (Malawi)
Avis—Travel in Malawi
Air Malawi—Lilongwe-Lusaka (Zambia)-Libreville (Gabon)
Taxis—Travel in Libreville (see also Transgabonais Railway in "Transportation")
Air Afrique—Libreville-Lome (Togo)
Avis—Travel in Togo
Air Afrique—Lome-Abidjan (Ivory Coast)
Air Afrique—Abidjan-Dakar (Senegal)
Encounter Overland—"Coast to Coast" expedition: Dakar-Toumbouctou (Mali)-Cotonou-Benin City-(Benin)-Bangui (Central African Republic)-Kisangani (Zaire)-Mbale-Nairobi-Mombasa (Kenya)
Kenya Railways—Mombasa-Nairobi
Kenya Airways—Nairobi-Bombay
Qantas—Bombay-Sydney or Auckland

Pan Am no longer operates via West Africa. Only Ethiopian Airways now crosses the continent. Their flights all route through Addis Ababa, Ethiopia, which substantially increases the fares. Kenya Airways sometimes offers a special fare, Bombay-Nairobi-London, which is very cheap. Inquire if this is being offered as it could make tying in a trip to London very economical.

The Africans Itinerary

Airline reservations: We have outlined a flight itinerary at the beginning of this section. We preface the routing with remarks we feel might save readers money. The "Transportation" section will also be of interest. European tariffs are under review and it may be that if a free market is established for European fare pricing, this will affect prices charged on African routes. Readers planning to purchase their tickets ahead of time (meaning not at discount or "bucket" agencies) should watch for news of these negotiations and ensure that if prices fall, the ticket they purchase is eligible to receive a refund reflecting the changes. Merikani Hotel Reservations Service (P.O. Box 53394, Temple Heights Station, Washington, DC 20009, tel: (USA) 301–530–1911) will be happy to work with our readers, wherever they may live, to pick the routing they particularly want to follow at the most reasonable rates.

Hotel reservations: Again, the staff at Merikani will be more than willing to discuss your itinerary with you and answer any questions you may have, but making firm hotel reservations, except for the first stop, is really not practical. We hope readers following this particular itinerary will be flexible and even follow the path that new friends may suggest.

David Lamb was based in Nairobi, Kenya, and from there during his four years in Africa fanned out, visiting other countries. He had a home and an expense account; our readers will have neither in Africa, and we have tried to expose them to as much as is practical, keeping in mind that money can be a constraint. We believe more will be learned about African problems by meeting people, and in the itinerary we try to suggest places where this can be done.

For men traveling alone or together, we suggest staying at the United Kenya Club in Nairobi, Kenya, at whose bar they will most certainly strike up many acquaintances. Ladies don't hang around bars in Africa; in fact, we're not sure ladies are allowed in the United Kenya Club bar. They are allowed on the terrace, but we've stayed up to six weeks at the club and no one (apart from the staff) has spoken to us! Female guests are wives of members and visiting academicians. A full description of the club is in "Kenyan Accommodation."

A man and woman traveling together can use the United Kenya Club if the female partner is prepared to sit on the terrace while the male partner chats up the boys in the bar. If everything goes well, the boys will probably join her on the terrace.

A woman or women traveling on their own would do better to use the Church of the Province of Kenya (C.P.K.) Guest House. Everyone talks to everyone and many good contacts will be made, which will provide an insight into current Kenyan problems and, more than likely, an invitation to visit fellow guests' homes. Again, C.P.K. is described in "Kenyan Accommodation."

Kenya is the only country that we will discuss in the itinerary where we separate the sexes: just remember, however, that anywhere in Africa ladies do not go into bars on their own. What will happen if they do? Well, either no one will speak to them or they will be deluged with hard-luck stories told by young men who want to go to their home country. If readers tend to think we are fuddy duddies on the subject, let them read Shiva Naipaul's *North of South: An African Journey.* Mr. Naipaul discusses his bar room encounters in some detail. Apart from his passages about bars, his is an excellent book to read before starting this itinerary. David Lamb writes about the Asian community in Africa. (We prefer to call them the "Indian community.") Shiva Naipaul's views (he is of Indian origin but from the Caribbean), as might be expected, contrast with those of Mr. Lamb and will make interesting reading for those who intend to stay at the United Kenya Club, as they are certain to meet Indian as well as African members.

Both the United Kenya Club and C.P.K. Guest House are relatively inexpensive and we suggest staying two weeks in Nairobi getting to know the city and its people.

Somalia: Unless our readers speak Italian, a visit to Somalia will not provide an insight into the country's problems or her people. If they do, Mogadiscio is only an hour's flight from Nairobi and a few days here will give an impression of what we found to be a truly delightful country. Behind the Juba Hotel is a large garden, which is patronized by many Somalis from early morning until late in the evening where they sit drinking coffee, tea, or soft drinks

*The late Jomo Kenyatta, first president of Kenya and the doyen of African lib-
eration leaders. He is seen here waving the traditional badge of a chief. Under
President Kenyatta, Kenya moved forward into the modern world of high technology without abandoning African culture. (Courtesy the Museum of African
Art, Smithsonian Institution, Washington, DC.)*

and gossip. The garden is crumbling and overgrown, but the traditional dress of
the patrons and their elegant, studied movements make the scene exotic. The
Somali language was not written until recently, but its oral use is a sophisticated
art. True, you will be speaking in Italian; however, it is wise to study the
movement of the conversation and to be led by the Somalis. The pattern will
be recognized as going around the barn before coming to the point—in the case
of well-bred Somalis the point may not be reached for several hours.

There are plenty of taxis in Mogadiscio, and they can be hired to go to the
beach to the south of the city—where it is not wise to swim because of sharks.
There is a government-operated Mercedes bus that goes to Kisimaio once a
week. You might strike up an interesting acquaintance on the bus, but again
chances are you will not find an English-speaker.

The United Nations Club and American Club, side by side on the beach at
Mogadiscio, are run-down, dreary places. We found many of the expatriate
community in Somalia to be sensationalists, and we suggest taking what they
say with a grain of salt.

Uganda: You can go to Uganda from Nairobi either by air or by train. The
train is very interesting and, of course, unlike flying one can see a great deal of

the country. The train runs straight through—there was a time when it was necessary to get off the train at the border and walk or take a taxi to board the Ugandan train, but this is no longer necessary. It's best to travel first class in Kenya. In 1981 the Ugandan trains were all the same class, but this may have changed back to the three-class fare system. It is possible to break up the trip at Jinja, and we believe readers will find this an interesting small town—very clean, palm-lined boulevards and gracious people. The Crested Crane Hotel is comfortable and we discuss it in the "Accommodation" section.

Jinja is famous as the place where John Hannington Speke identified the source of the Nile. There was a plaque to denote his finding it, but Uganda's President Yoweri Museveni recently had it taken to Kampala to have the lettering reworded. He resents giving Speke credit for "discovering" the source of the Nile when the local people and Arab traders knew decades before Speke arrived that the location was the Source of the Nile. In any event, the actual spot Speke identified has become part of the hydroelectric dam—Owen Falls. This is a short taxi ride just on the immediate outskirts of Jinja along the Kampala road. The falls can be seen only from the bridge—walking along the banks to the falls is not permitted. A day in Jinja is enough, and the train can be reboarded for Kampala.

Actually, the train operates all the way to the Rwandese border, but until the rural areas are brought under control we advise against going that far. If you want to go to Rwanda, it's better to go by air (see below).

Entebbe was the colonial capital of Uganda; Kampala was the seat of government for the kabakas (kings) of Buganda. Today the international airline destination city is Entebbe, and Kampala is the nation's capital.

We suggest staying at either the Kampala Sikh Gurdwara or the International Hotel. Unless you're inordinately shy, within three days you'll probably know half the people living in Kampala wherever you stay. Ugandans are a very outgoing, refined people, anxious to make visitors welcome. Go to Makerere University's art department and ask to see some of the work being done by young Ugandan artists. Makerere is the hub of intellectual life, and the faculty and students are very approachable.

All the same, conditions in Uganda are still unsettled and will be for some time to come. We suggest staying within the city limits and traveling after dark only in the car of a well-known friend—don't take taxis or walk the streets once the sun goes down just after 6.

An insight into the effect the last 20 years of political unrest has had on the youth of Uganda can be gained from the responses I had from 144 of my St. James Secondary School students when I gave them an essay assignment in 1981. The classes totaled 107 boys and 32 girls of Protestant, Roman Catholic, and Moslem faiths and represented 18 tribes. I asked them to write an essay discussing: (1) What will Uganda be like in the year 2000? Will it be better or worse than it is now? (2) How will it get that way? (3) What part will you play in making it happen? 60% said Uganda would be better; 27% said it would be worse; 8% gave a qualified answer: better "if," worse "if"; 2% did not venture a guess; 1% said the end of the world was coming in the year 2000 so it really did not matter.

Over half the students—both better and worse—mentioned that the fantastic inflation rate Uganda had experienced (sugar was $50 a kilo; bread, when it could be found, was $10 a loaf; a bar of laundry soap $44), and the open black market (Magendo) were the major problems to overcome.

The most interesting information to emerge from the essays was that none of the young people were looking to direct outside financial aid to help their country rejoin the community of nations.

Of those who thought Uganda would get better, the majority identified the *presidency*, the *government*, and *civil service* as the key to rehabilitation: They think the answer lies in "better cooperation between the people and the government"; "by enforcing existing laws"; "under the good leadership of President Obote."

Second among the optimists was *development* of Uganda's *industries* and *natural resources* (coffee, copper, etc.). The third largest group believed progress could only come about through a better *educated* electorate and thus put an end to dictatorships. A minority of the optimists laid the problem at the doorway of *all* the people: "Conditions would get better through personal changes on the part of individual Ugandans." However, many thought that natural historical progress would bring about change for the better (paraphrased): "Look where the cave men were, where we are now, then by the nature of human societies, things must get better." "Unity" and "hard work" were mentioned by two students and one student wrote "Ugandans need to forget the past."

Only 21 felt *foreign influence* was needed to put Uganda back on the road to progress: "Uganda must cultivate better relationships with neighboring countries" (especially Kenya, as the port of Mombasa is vital for the shipment of Ugandan imports/exports). "Advice, technicians, academic exchanges and expatriate teachers are necessary." "Europeans and Americans living in Uganda should vote in Ugandan presidential elections along with Ugandans and this would effect (good) change." "Europeans or Americans should take over the leadership of Uganda." "The United Nations should come and straighten things out." One student wanted a return to Colonialism or foreign rule.

Three students truly believed that we would all be better off once the end of the world comes and that this would happen in their lifetimes. One student believed if Christian evangelism was encouraged this would lead to progress. Another said development could come if "People put God back in their life."

Of those students who thought Uganda would get worse, one pathetic statement succinctly expressed the insight into their own character that so many Ugandans have. He said Uganda would get worse because "Uganda is a confused country." But again, the majority felt the problems revolved around the *presidency, government,* and *civil service:* "There will be continual dictatorship/bad/cruel rule"; "Lack of leadership will continue"; "Instability of government will continue."

Two students predicted President Obote (the ruler at that time) and his followers would continue in office and this would be bad. One student cited the lack of freedom of speech as the inhibitor to progress; another felt that Uganda needs to be "liberated again," but "probably won't be." Another felt conditions would worsen unless a Muganda (a member of the largest tribe) were elected president and that this was unlikely to happen. (The inference here is that without proportional representation by tribe the major tribal group would stir up trouble.) One of the pessimistic young people caustically wrote "Government continues to fail in tackling present problems," another student that "Uganda is led by greedy people," and the last student who felt the presidency, government, or civil service would be responsible for worsening conditions in Uganda wrote "the present rulers are tired people."

On the subject of exploiting *industries* and *natural resources* some felt starvation and famine (in northern Uganda) would spread in the years to come to the now fertile south because of climatic changes and another believed that agricultural production would be low, resulting in a lack of foreign exchange earnings and consequent inability to import necessities to develop industries and natural resources. Very pointedly, one student blames successive governments' emphasis on "guns not tools."

As to *foreign influence* some students felt Uganda would get worse because: "Uganda has made many enemies because of wars"; "There will continue to be wars''; "Uganda's lack of cooperation with neighboring countries." Three students felt their country would continue to get worse, "unless a European or American comes to lead Uganda."

As religion influenced the thinking of those who believed conditions would get better, religion also influenced the thinking of the pessimists: One student cited the biblical prophesy "that God will punish sinful people," and so Uganda will be punished. On a plaintive note one student feels "God has forgotten Uganda."

The subject of *education* was mentioned frequently; education coupled with references to the black market and homicides that continue throughout the country. These topics crossed over the positive and negative attitudes about Uganda in the year 2000: "Educational standards will continue to go down." "Young people are being killed so there will be no educated young people to take over the leadership." (Students at Makerere University and high school students were frequently used for target practice by soldiers.) "The population of educated people will decrease because they are being murdered." Ironically, two students felt "more people will be educated and education has brought unrest, so conditions will get worse."

But the negative group had the most to say about the fault being with *all* the people: "Ugandans will return to traditional lifestyles rather than make the necessary personal changes needed for development." "Ugandans will continue to fight one another." "It is impossible for the people of Uganda to unite." "Ugandans in exile will continue to come back to Uganda bringing armies with them to overthrow the government." "Overpopulation" will be an inhibitor to development." (It must be said that every woman, young or old, in Uganda appears to be pregnant.) "There is too much self-interest among the people." "Everyone will be dead by the year 2000 because Ugandans will have continued to kill each other."

Malawi: Kenya Airways flies to Lilongwe from Nairobi and a visit to Malawi is interesting as South African influence has strongly affected the personality of the people. Only once did we hear a word of contradiction during the entire time we were in Malawi. In Kenya it seems everyone always has an opinion on some aspect of domestic or international life. We're always happy to be in Kenya with the outgoing Kenyans. Malawians, in general, are always differential to Whites, which makes us uncomfortable. In fact, the trait upset Leah so much that we cut short our stay in Malawi by a week.

Malawi is one of the most beautiful countries in all of Africa. There are many very cheap government-operated guest houses in national parks where you can meet Malawians. Following the Wildlife Safari we wrote for *Fielding's African Safaris* will provide you with opportunities to get to know Malawi and her people. We give the itinerary as a part of the budget; it appears with the other budgets for *The Africans* itinerary.

Zimbabwe: We do not suggest going to Zimbabwe. The president there has grown unpredictable since David Lamb wrote of him. Five tourists were killed in Zimbabwe several years ago. It was difficult to obtain the cooperation of the government in recovering their bodies. They were located two years after the killings. The president and cabinet ministers of Zimbabwe have been outrageous in their verbal abuse of the United States, at the same time sending their envoys to Washington to ask for increased aid. You will see tours to Zimbabwe advertised and the occasional glowing report as a result of their tourist department's promotional efforts, but the situation, in our opinion, will continue to be volatile for some years.

Zambia: The government is outspoken in their criticism of South Africa and western countries who have not imposed economic sanctions on South Africa although Zambia continues to do a brisk trade with her neighbor to the south. Mismanagement, corruption, alcoholism, and declining copper prices— formerly Zambia's main export—bankrupted the country's economy after independence. Zambia's government has seen fit to point an accusing finger at South Africa for her economic predicament but, in reality, her troubles are of her own making. Zambia's human rights record is not good, and expatriate Europeans and Africans have shared cells with Zambia's citizenry during the past few years. In our opinion travel in Zambia will continue to be dangerous and untenable for all foreigners for some years to come.

The Kenya Coast: If you return to Kenya because of flight routings you may want to take time out to relax, and the Kenya coast is one of the best places in the world to do so. Take the night sleeper train to Mombasa and, once there, stay either in town or go down to the south coast. The Castle Hotel in town is very comfortable and the "Castle porch" is a good place to meet people, but most will be foreigners like yourself. The Lotus Hotel is a bit cheaper and caters to Kenyan businessmen; over breakfast you may make a few interesting contacts. At the south coast, for the budget-minded, we suggest Dan Trench's Campsite (which has accommodation and is not strictly a campsite) or Trade Winds Hotel.

West African Jaunt: West Africans have turned the Air Afrique plane that flies Dakar, Senegal/Abidjan, Ivory Coast/Lome, Togo/Libreville, Gabon, into a country bus. Anyone who believes African women are not in charge of the commerce of Africa need only fly this route. "Mammas," which is a respectful name given to market women, pile into the plane with everything from large cardboard boxes of okra (Lady Fingers to our English readers) to bolts of cloth and newly woven baskets. The airline cabin crew helps passengers to push and shove chattels and baggage tied in sheets under the seats and into overhead racks. What's left over is thrown onto the last four seats on the starboard side and the merchandise piles up. If you think we exaggerate about how much is brought on board as "hand luggage," remember Africans are very adept at carrying things on their heads and the merchandise comes on board not only in the hands and over the arms but also on the head. One lady sitting next to us had hung a number of new towels (which she obviously intended to sell once she arrived at her destination) over a belt under her voluminous traditional West African dress. Having eaten her airline meal with her fingers, she proceeded to stuff the plastic cutlery, plate, and glass down her ample bosom. She also took the clean linen cloth. No one said anything.

But if a tourist enters the cabin, the stewardess will promptly tell you that whatever it is you're carrying—a magazine and your purse, a cat in an official under-the-seat carrier, whatever—is over the weight limit.

Senegal: Plan, even if it isn't necessary—meaning even if there is a connecting plane within an hour or two—to stay over a couple of nights in the hotel at Dakar's international airport. This is an education in itself. Go into Dakar, remembering that almost everyone fights with the taxi drivers outside the airport. Downtown Dakar is interesting for an afternoon, but we found little to sustain interest and seemed to fight with everyone from waiters to the street vendors. (Apparently, that's par for the course in Senegal.) The Catholic cathedral opposite the Embassy of Mali where you get your visa for that country if you didn't get one earlier, is unusual and the rotunda painting outstanding for an African church.

The Gambia: In Banjul, the capital city, the people are laid back, hospitable, and polite, and the nearest to Ugandans you're going to find in West Africa. Stay at the Apollo Hotel, which is dirt cheap and clean, but leave the bulk of your baggage with the man back in Dakar Airport's Left Luggage room. He is absolutely trustworthy. Things have a way of disappearing at the Apollo; we lost a cheap transistor radio. (Note: Banjul is not on the Air Afrique route and it is necessary—at this writing—to fly to The Gambia and return to Dakar, Senegal, before going on to other West African cities. It takes only 20 minutes to fly from Dakar to Banjul.)

Go to Juffure to see the village that Alex Haley believes his ancestors came from, and don't fail to look up our friend Mr. Chum, Senior Tourist Officer, whose office is immediately next door to the Apollo Hotel.

Cote d'Ivoire: This is the only country where you need to be certain that you have advance hotel reservations. Be sure to make reservations at the Hilton International because their driver will meet you at the airport and see you through the formalities. This is very necessary; Ivorian immigration officials have short fuses. They pack a revolver on their hip, and in our opinion, are totally unprofessional.

It's really impossible to walk around Abidjan and meet the people because obvious newcomers are the targets of street crime. The only purpose, as far as we are concerned, in visiting the city is to see at first-hand the great leap forward the Ivory Coast has made under their intellectual president, who has chosen to let the French guide him and his nation's development. Sadly, they have done no better here than they have in metropolitan France. True to form, emphasis has been on lavish cathedrals instead of clean water for the masses, but the tragic aspect of Ivory Coast development is that upward mobility for Africans has been checked by the presence of French expatriates. Personally, we thought Ivory Coast to be a sad commentary on African development—it has many of the vices of Western big cities. Armed soldiers stood on each side of the highways every 50 yards when we drove out of the capital to the Club Med on a Sunday. Was the president to pass? Were they expecting a coup? We received no answers as to why there were so many soldiers. On the way into town from the airport (we had not been told to let Hilton know the arrival time of our plane) our taxi was stopped by soldiers with machine guns and the trunk of the cab was searched. Even in Uganda, at the worst of times, soldiers were not so lavishly provided to guard the country roads.

The Hilton driver will go back to the airport with you to put you on the plane. Abidjan airport is again full of chattels, merchandise, pushing, and shoving Mammas and traditionally dressed, haughty West African men—who always go first.

Togo: Poor Togo; a little slice of a country that never should have been. Created by Whites from afar, today Togo has all the development problems described in Third World handbooks. Readers may want to follow our "Volunteer's Safari," published in *Fielding's African Safaris* and reprinted here.

The American Peace Corps in Togo is one of the most successful Peace Corps programs and seems an ideal vehicle to use in demonstrating the problems of those who would affect development in Africa. Peace Corps staff are in the travel business only so far as travel is pertinent to getting volunteers and staff from point *a* to point *b* to carry out Peace Corps projects. They haven't the time or manpower to arrange travel for visitors. We have made it clear that Merikani will coordinate all arrangements after the Peace Corps Country Director in Togo supplies them with the names of Peace Corps volunteers willing to offer hospitality to our readers.

Although we have used the Peace Corps, an American volunteer agency, to demonstrate the spirit of volunteerism in Africa, readers should not assume that only American visitors would be welcomed; quite the contrary—we're certain the volunteers would be thrilled to have visitors of other nationalities visit them.

The emphasis of the 105 Peace Corps volunteers in Togo has been shifted from the field of academic education which, when the Peace Corps began working in Togo in 1962, consisted of 80% of the programs. Today, self-help projects to increase rural income, for instance fish farming and the use of draft animals, are stressed. Cooperative village businesses and energy conservation projects encourage rural people to raise their net income. Eighteen volunteers concentrate on teaching agricultural education courses and are establishing 4-H–type clubs. In the field of health, 17 volunteers work to raise awareness of better sanitation practices in the villages. Since 1966, by organizing rural people to work together, 1200 primary-school classrooms have been built and over 100 bridges constructed on farm-to-market roads throughout Togo. Medical dispensaries have also been built through Peace Corps volunteers' joint efforts with others concerned in care for the sick and expectant mothers in remote villages.

Readers should first write to Merikani Hotel Reservations Service (P.O. Box 53394, Temple Heights Station, Washington, DC 20009) for a list of Peace Corps volunteers in Togo willing to offer accommodation. Along with their names will be a short description of the work they are doing, their location, and the date their Peace Corps service will terminate.

Readers will select three (3) names from the list, ensuring that the time they plan to travel to Togo is within the time frame of the selected volunteer's service. Upon receipt of this information, Merikani will contact the volunteer and confirm that the dates selected are agreeable.

Readers then make their own airline reservations. However, Friends of Togo, a nonprofit association composed of former Peace Corps volunteers to Togo with offices in North Carolina, organize two trips a year to Togo for their members. These flights are at group rates, and our readers are invited to join the group by becoming members of the Friends of Togo. Dues are U.S.$20. The charter flight is considerably less than the normal fare. Charters usually leave in June and December, but dates vary from year to year; the group stays in Togo two weeks—the same length of time as our itinerary.

Day One: Arrive Lome, the capital of Togo, Overnight Hotel du 2 Fevrier. (See "Togolese Accommodation" for a description of the hotel and reservations information.)

Day Two: Relax by the hotel swimming pool and recover from any jet lag. Meet with Avis Rent-a-Car representative and arrange for a car next morning with a driver to take you to the city limits, leaving you to self-drive the itinerary unless you prefer to have the driver drive. The roads are good and traffic is not too heavy; each reader will want to make this choice depending upon their personal preference.

Visit the Peace Corps office in Lome.

Day Three: Drive to the first Peace Corps Volunteer's residence. Route will follow from south to north. Remember, no night driving, so an early start will probably be necessary. Allow for 40 mph average; although most of the time you will be driving at 55 or 60, with stops and passing on single-lane roads, the average will be 40 mph.

Night Three, Day and Night Four and Five: At the residence of the first Peace Corps Volunteer.

Morning of Day Six: Depart and drive to the residence of the second Peace Corps Volunteer.

Night Six, Day and Night Seven and Eight: At the residence of the second Peace Corps Volunteer.

Morning of Day Nine: Depart and drive to the residence of the third Peace Corps Volunteer.

Night Nine, Day and Night Ten: At the residence of the third Peace Corps Volunteer.

Morning of Day Eleven: Depart and drive to Lome. Return Avis. Choice of accommodation either at the Hotel du 2 Fevrier or in a self-contained house on the grounds of the Assembly of God's West African School of Theology. (A full description follows this itinerary.)

Night Eleven, Day and Night of Day Twelve: Visit the **Catholic Relief Services warehouse** where food paid for by U.S. federal funds is stored for distribution to the needy in Togo. Shop at the German-sponsored **Handicapped Shop** located at the junction of the main beach road (this road is referred to sometimes as Marinia road, Corniche road, or the road to Ghana). Ask the front desk clerk at Sofitel 2 du Fevrier to tell a taxi driver where you want to go. The shop sells some nice handmade toys and other goods, nice tie-and-dye, tablecloths, T-shirts, some rather crude pottery (perhaps the quality will improve), etc.

While driving to visit the three Peace Corps volunteers there will be an opportunity, at some juncture to be determined according to the route, to visit a large ongoing project being conducted by the Togo Baptist Church under the guidance of Reverend Gerald Bond.

The American Baptist Church has established, for one facet of their missionary effort, the **Baptist Rural Development Program.** Baptists in Tennessee have worked and financed a project in Burkina Fasso (a country just north of Togo), Georgia Baptists have undertaken work in Liberia (to the west of Togo), and North Carolina Baptists have been concerned with a project in Togo. Although Reverend Bond uses the adjective "modest" to describe the Togo Rural Development Project, we tend to disagree. Having chosen for the site of their project one of the most isolated areas of Togo, their first step was to overcome the obstacle to development, which was the lack of a bridge to connect the region with the remainder of Togo. Ardent as Togo government officials and wellwishers were to see a bridge built, the general feeling was that bridge-building is really beyond the competency of missionaries. Such doubting Thomases had not figured on North Carolina volunteers from all walks of life coming forward and offering their expertise and skills. Because of this volunteer effort on the part of North Carolina Baptists the bridge—halfway through the three-year project in 1986—has concrete piers and buttresses made strong by Mississippi steel.

A small village of mud huts has been established near the construction site where the North Carolina volunteers, who pay their own way to Togo, live while they provide a month's labor on the construction of the bridge or other projects necessary to the development of the project. These mud huts will be housing for representatives from villages throughout this once isolated region who will come to the center to attend adult education classes. These classes will include all aspects of rural life development: livestock husbandry, sanitation, arable crop production, harvest storage, nutrition, water supplies, etc. The Rural Training Center is the long-term interest of the North Carolina Baptists—the bridge the means of developing the center and ensuring that an infrastructure is in place that will permit communication with the outside world.

The Baptists, having studied the Togo government's development plan, designed the overall plan that would address some of the priorities listed, and in addition to this long-term commitment, they built, again with North Carolina Baptist volunteer labor, 15 ponds of 3 to 6 acres in size, which they stocked, and instructed the local people in the practice of fish farming. They will have drilled some 100 wells in 60 villages going to a depth of 120–150 feet to reach a good flow. These wells have been fitted with locally manufactured pumps and there is now a clean water supply for families who before the establishment of the wells took water from polluted streams.

Readers who would like to see the bridge and visit the Rural Training Center should, when they write Merikani, indicate they would like to do so, and we will (1) send them information on how to get to Moretan (where the village is located), (2) let them know how best to combine their Peace Corps visits with a visit to the Togo Baptists' project, and (3) inquire and confirm the dates for a visit.

Of course, in addition to providing the physical assistance to the villages in the Moreton region, the North Carolina Baptists also minister to their spiritual needs. Togo is predominantly a nonreligious nation. Never before had we realized the urgent need of formalized religion in African life. Along the west coast of Africa the traditional religion has been corrupted by superstition and mysticism, so finding the route back to the essentials of African traditional religion had become a near impossibility. Without the discipline of a valid religion that centuries have proven to point the way to a useful, healthy life, people remain confused about how their societies should be regulated. Historically, the Catholic Church prevented, by means of boundaries, other Christian religions from evangelizing in French politically controlled areas. A portion of Togo was, at one time, under the Germans, and did have a Protestant influence. However, that influence was weak primarily due to the devastating toll tropical diseases took on missionary lives. Ghana, Togo's neighbor, was strongly evangelized by British Protestant missionaries and the result is obvious today. Ghana has a far higher rate of literacy, political consciousness, and overall sophistication. Benin, Togo's other immediate neighbor, was French-controlled, and her people received little education. Where the Moslem religion has penetrated in Africa a basis of morality has been laid through the teaching and imperative to read the Koran in Arabic. Once religious Moslems come in contact with Western societies, Islam is weakened. This is unfortunate but true in our observations. A case in point is Morocco. We feel strongly that the evangelization of Togo is an absolute necessity if the country is to develop.

Readers, who will all be passing through the town of Atakapama as it is on Route One, the main road to the north of Togo, may wish to stop in for a visit with Msgr. Philippe Fanoko Kossi, under whose guidance a cathedral is now being constructed to serve the large Catholic population resident in the Diocese of Atakapama. Msgr. Kossi has been to the United States and is always happy to talk to visitors.

Readers can be certain of light refreshment being offered and a tour of the work underway on the St. Famille (Holy Family) Cathedral. Readers may want to buy a few of the building blocks as a form of donation to the building of the cathedral; not everyone can say they paid for part of an African cathedral.

A Britisher, Peter Delahey, is in charge of the United Nations children's program in Togo. He was away from Lome during our visit, but readers may want to visit a UNICEF project, and Merikani will have the information if visits can be arranged.

The Assembly of God's West African School of Theology is located on lovely grounds in the immediate outskirts of Lome. The school accepts mature African students from all over West Africa for advanced study. Prospective students must have five years demonstratable religious work experience and study before applying to the School of Theology in Lome. The enrollment is small, allowing for personal and thoughtful assistance from the American teaching staff. The representatives from the American founding church are dedicated not only to their task but also to bringing Christian teaching to Africa.

The supervisory committee has generously offered to provide our readers following the Volunteer's Safari with self-contained accommodation in one of their three guest houses on the schoolgrounds. These are basically furnished and have a nice kitchen where readers can make their own breakfast. For other meals the staff of the school would welcome them in their homes (neighboring the guest houses) for lunch or dinner. Everything necessary to prepare breakfast can be purchased in shops near the school.

We feel that our readers of the Pentacostal churches would thoroughly enjoy the experience of actually living for a day or two with co-religionists and learning from the most hospitable missionaries of their daily lives in Africa; the problems and the triumphs they experience.

For the cost and method of payment for the itinerary see "Estimated Budgets."

Travel: Direction to the Baptist Rural Training School and the bridge: Take highway (Route) One from Lome north. Proceed from Atakpame for 60 km (note km, not miles—Avis car will be in km). Upon reaching Nyamasilla, go right or east. Carry on 13 km, which will be the Mono River. Just beyond the bridge is the village of Kpessi. Continue a further 11 km east to the village of Moretan. The Rural Training Center is a further 1 km east.

▶**Note:** After Nyamasilla the road is not surfaced but it is well used. Four-wheel-drive is not necessary. The road is open October–May. From June to September take the diversion via Anie on Route One through Elevangon, then on to Moretan.

Plan Ahead: It may be helpful to list the steps necessary in making preparations for this rather unusual safari:

(1) Decide if you wish to join the Friends of Togo charter flight or fly to Togo independently. If going with the charter, the dates you will be visiting Peace Corps volunteers will start from the date the charter flight arrives in Togo. If you travel independently, select your own starting date.

(2) Write to Merikani Hotel Reservations Service for a list of Peace Corps volunteers willing to extend hospitality.

(3) Return to Merikani your choice of volunteers and the dates you will be in Togo. We will contact the Peace Corps to confirm the dates, then Merikani will let you know.

(4) Make a reservation at the Hotel du 2 Fevrier for the first night of your visit to Togo. This can be done through Merikani if you like.

(5) Mail a check to the Friends of Togo (P.O. Box 666, Durham, NC 27702) for U.S.$225 or its equivalent as a donation in exchange for volunteer's hospitality. Send a check either to the Sofitel du 2 Fevrier or Merikani as your deposit on the hotel room.

(6) Send a copy—a copy, not the original, which should be kept for your records, as the donation is tax deductible—of their receipt to Merikani and they will confirm your hotel reservation and the volunteer's hospitality.

(7) Purchase an international postal money order for your donation to the Scholarship Fund of the Assembly of God Seminary in return for their hospitality. Take this postal money order with you to Togo and present it at the time of your visit to the seminary. Alternatively, this donation can be paid in Togolese money. The point is that a check is not useful because the scholarship fund is not set up to take foreign checks.

(8) Send your deposit for your hotel room, which should also be a money order, to Merikani Hotel Reservations Service.

Lastly, purchase small gifts for hospitality offered at the Assembly of God School of Theology, and little gifts of appreciation for the Peace Corps volunteers; special foods would be especially welcome.

Nigeria: The devil we know, in this case Uganda, is always preferable to the devil we don't know. Although we are glad that we were not deterred from going to Somalia because of the stories we heard about that country—which we found to be totally without foundation—we are hesitant about going to Nigeria because of the bad reports we've heard. Such information is given substance in our particular case because of two close encounters we've had with Nigerian taxi drivers in our home town of Washington, DC, where some of them are becoming notorious. Readers unfamiliar with our city may be surprised to learn that one out of every ten people living in the greater Washington area is a refugee, and there is an even higher ratio, when the totals are combined, of foreign students. Somehow, they end up driving taxis. Usually nothing more devastating happens when one gets an African driver than that he gets lost or overcharges. Many Nigerian drivers, however, are something else again, and

Leah and I have had two nasty scenes where the driver has become violent and actually taken hold of us.

We have touched down at Lagos international airport about a dozen times but have never gone past the transit lounge. David Lamb doesn't have very pleasant things to say about Nigeria and we feel that our readers can realize many of Nigeria's problems on a smaller scale but in greater safety by visiting Togo. However, Lome is not overpopulated like Lagos and in using the comparison, readers should realize that Togo's problems are compounded a thousand times over if the development literature on Nigeria is accurate.

Gabon: We were in Gabon as world oil prices began to fall; they felt it was a tragedy when Reuters wire services showed U.S.$18 a barrel on the hotel television screens. Forty thousand French and other expatriates were working in the country, their salaries paid from the proceeds of Gabonese oil sales. A rail line was being extended to the interior city of Franceville at an astronomical cost per mile. Prices in Gabon were so high we stayed only a short time. Unless by the time our readers arrive in Gabon the economy of the country has crumbled and prices have dropped as a consequence, we suggest they follow our example. Two or three days will give you an opportunity to walk around Libreville and, if you speak French, to get a feel for the problems. The airport-incoming processing is really a show in itself. Everyone is very good-natured and nonthreatening—colorful, chaotic, comical, interesting, and the only West African country we visited where the Africans were less excitable than the French who chased around in top gear.

South Africa: Without diminishing from the entire text of *The Africans* we feel David Lamb is at his best when he writes of South Africa. We have never been to that country, but we have been in situations similar to the train journey he took from Mozambique into South Africa. Situations where at one moment the surroundings were just as he described the railroad station and exit procedures on the Mozambician side of the border, and suddenly, crossing into the neighboring country, all is changed—order and efficiency prevail.

We called the U.S. Department of State asking them how Black Americans are treated in South Africa. The reply given was that they "had no problems" and because they were tourists "are treated like other tourists"—meaning, presumably, that, as David Lamb describes, ethnic and racial origins can be suddenly changed by the stroke of a South African White's pen.

We do feel that our White readers who hold strong opinions on the South African question should visit South Africa. By doing so we believe they will discover that solutions to the problem are not simplistic. There are many, many ramifications to any solution. How they travel to the country will depend upon conditions at the time they plan to go. Whatever, make sure that South Africa is the country last visited in the itinerary because most African countries will not allow a person who has been in South Africa to enter their country (see "Travel Documents"). Black readers will probably want to take along a good supply of tranquilizers, and the decision to go or not will be a personal one.

Mali: The people bordering the Sahara (interestingly called the Wisahara) are entirely different than the West Africans. However, these former French colonies (Mali, Niger, Chad, Central African Republic, and Burkina Faso, formerly Upper Volta) do share the same inflated consumer prices of all other French-dominated African economies. Mali can be seen, without breaking the bank, when the Niger steamer boat is operable. Its operation depends on the flooding of the river; the river is usually in flood stage from the end of July to early December. *However,* and this is a big however, the rains do not always come when they should. Some years they do not fall heavily enough to raise the river sufficiently to let the boats operate. For this reason it's best to plan to go to Mali well into the season, say September or October, and to check with someone—Merikani Hotel Reservations Service, your embassy in Mali, or the Sofitel hotel chain—to find out if the river steamer is operating. Except in the case of Merikani, a prepaid reply cable should be sent at the time of the inquiry. Ordinary air mail takes a very long time.

It is possible to camp almost anywhere and we suggest readers consider taking along a tent. We have a beautiful, stand-up tent made by Hiliary measuring 11 by 13 feet, with a floor and netting that keeps out mosquitoes yet lets breezes ventilate the sleeping area. It weighs 15 pounds with poles and tent pegs. We used it in Malawi and thoroughly enjoyed having it. Naturally, you won't want to carry a tent around everywhere. United Kenya Club and C.P.K. Guest House have storerooms where the tent can be left while you go off to Somalia or Uganda. There is no charge at United Kenya Club, but we always give the housekeeper, Mary, something. A small charge is made at C.P.K. When traveling in West Africa before going to Mali, the tent can be stored very safely with the young man in the left luggage storeroom at Dakar airport. (We mentioned him when discussing the trip to The Gambia.) There is a charge for this storage, about the equivalent of US$1 a day. Taking a tent with you is not really a hassle. Once out of Bamako, it will save you from having to look around for a place to stay or paying the very high rates charged by the hotels in Mopti or Toumbouctou. We felt very safe in Mali and slept in the car after driving up to a village and introducing ourselves to the local headman.

We had the good fortune of visiting the Africare field staff at Dire, a small town 35 mi SW of Toumbouctou, just at the beginning of the Sahara. We fell in love with it, and dream of going back. The people were very hospitable. We not only met the Africare field staff but also the perfectly charming staff of UNICEF, a beautiful young woman from the Tuareg tribe—the nomadic peoples of the Sahara—and her co-worker, an equally beautiful young woman from the Mandingo tribe. They work under the supervision of a young French woman who is charming and sincere in her work to help the infants and children of Mali toward a better life. She has worked in Mali for a number of years for UNICEF and was transferred to Dire in 1986. There is also a CARE office in Dire housed in a huge, newly painted building. We were told by a staff member that he would have to have clearance from the country director (an American woman) in Bamako before he could give us any information concerning the work CARE-Dire was carrying out with our and your donations. Maybe he had had enough of American women. If this was all done to avoid unfavorable publicity, they missed the mark. If you've got a tougher skin than we have, or if you stop in at the CARE office in Bamako before you leave for Dire, you may be more successful in finding out how CARE is administering relief work.

Dire also has an Italian-staffed hospital. The doctor was away in Dakar at the time of our visit, but we were told he is very approachable.

Take a little gift for the young ladies at UNICEF and a large quantity of boiled Kenyan candy to give to the village children. Set up your tent wherever the mayor or his equivalent suggests you do, and look forward to the experience of a lifetime as you share a few weeks of your life with the people of Dire on the edge of the Sahara. There are ample food supplies and mineral water can be purchased in the local shops.

A reservation for the Sofitel l'Amitie in Bamako can be made by the reservationist at the Sofitel Teranga in Dakar, Senegal, before you board your flight. On arrival you'll be met by a very charming hotel hostess who will see you through formalities and onto a Sofitel bus that will take you, without charge, into town. Plan to spend a few days in Bamako, getting your visa extension (see "Travel Documents"). Make your train reservations and confirm your cabin on the steamer, which must be made four weeks before departure date. Travel from Bamako to Koulikoro by train and take the steamer disembarking at Dire. Once in Dire, ask where the mayor's office is and tell him you would like to set up your tent. On the reverse side of the tourist card you will have been given in Bamako is a short note to officials asking that they make you welcome. We're sure they will, but it is important that the first thing you do before tenting anywhere is check in with the local officials.

Niger, Chad, and Zaire: Traveling in central Africa is best done with an overlanding group such as Encounter Overland or Gerba. There are buses (see "Transportation"), but they are few, unreliable, subject to delays during the journey due to breakdowns, and very uncomfortable. If your money—although their rates are very reasonable because overlanding is strictly a "no frills" trip—and time have held out, you may want to see Niger, Chad, and Zaire, land of the Pygmies.

Much as we encourage overlanding for those in good health, we feel our readers who want to follow this itinerary will not be content solely with an overland trip despite the fact that such trips cover a lot of ground for little money. We all have very strong opinions that we do not hesitate to share. Leah has admonished me to keep this itinerary to an outline. She has not been entirely successful, but let's say that I've tried to write a cursory itinerary and at the same time tried to warn against possible misfortune. If you travel in the company of "an old hand" such as the driver-guide of the overlanding truck, you're going to be influenced by that person. New eyes see things in new ways. Valid learning is self-taught; if you first travel alone, there will be time to examine your first impressions, examine their validity, accept and elaborate on a certain perspective, or reject it if you are either alone or in the company of other newcomers to Africa. When you return home books and media reports on Africa will mean a lot more to you because you've traveled the continent and formed your own impressions. By all means, at the end of your itinerary join up with an overlanding group if you have time. Overlanding has a lot to offer and the driver can handle the many, sometimes troublesome officials met in lonely outposts, such as those along the borders of the Saharan nations.

We have provided a "worksheet" instead of an actual budget for this itinerary since it is more practical for readers to pick and choose the countries they wish to visit. The air fare is going to be the single largest expense. If, after contacting Merikani or your local airline company, you feel it's beyond your budget, think about reading through *Fielding's African Safaris*, where we budget to the penny backpacking down the Nile and detail other cheap trips that might be combined to overcome the all-air itinerary we have given on the worksheet.

PLAN AHEAD: We have discussed at length what to wear for this particular itinerary on previous pages. Keeping that advice in mind, the travel writer's classic admonition to travel light can justifiably be given. Rotating back and forth between two safari suits, in the case of men, or two shirtwaist dresses can work well. Although we have yet to lose anything on an African airline; keeping baggage down to one suitcase plus one carry-on bag containing your camera and film has many advantages. Readers planning to join an Encounter Overland or Gerba expedition should know that either group allows only one "duffel bag" and one hand bag. The safari suit/shirtwaist apparel will not be suitable for overlanding, and both men and women should follow the advice the expedition operators provide (jeans, shirts, etc.), when reservations are made.

Decaffeinated coffee is generally not available in Africa apart from at a few Hiltons, so if you use it plan to take some. It is always reassuring to have a small first-aid kit along—not only for your personal use but to use in case of accident to an African. (I remember getting into a matatoo with Leah and noticing a young, barefoot girl whose foot was cut and bleeding. The only things we had were our khangas. We tore a strip off one and bound her foot to keep out the dirt and stop the bleeding. I was annoyed at myself for not having a small bottle of Dettol, which would have washed away the existing dirt and killed any bacteria.) When you're packing think about what you could use in case of minor accidents. (The strip of khanga was perfectly acceptable as a bandage, and it could have been used as a tourniquet had it been necessary.) You don't want to go to extremes, but do a few mental exercises asking "What could I do to help if . . . ?" Safety pins, a hotel-provided sewing kit, disinfectant, tweezers, a few drops of oil in a tiny bottle, a cigarette lighter, aspirin are all small things that are easy to carry but can, should an occasion arise, be helpful.

If you accumulate too many souvenirs and intend to join an overlanding tour, you can air cargo the excess home. KLM has an excellent reputation in this respect. You may want to plan to send your package from Abidjan, Lilongwe, or Nairobi—these are all KLM destination cities.

Dark glasses are going to be an absolute necessity.

Plan out the countries you intend to visit, then check the "Basic Information Checklist" to decide what visas you'll need. Some visas are only valid for a certain period, so you will want to determine from the visa application form which visas you can get before leaving home and which visas you'll need to get as you travel. When you discuss your flight arrangements with Merikani Hotel Reservations Service ask them to send you the application forms. Merikani will get the visas for you without charge. They charge only for the actual cost of the visa and registered, return-receipt postage. Look at the "Basic Information Checklist" to see what immunizations you'll need for each country you plan to visit. Merikani will reserve an Avis car for you if you feel you're going to want one, although we have not suggested a vehicle apart from Togo. Apply for SOS insurance; purchase traveler's checks. You can make rail reservations for Uganda once you're in Kenya by going to Nairobi Railway station a few days before you plan to leave for Uganda. Remember that airline reservations must be reconfirmed 48 hours before departure time in the case of Kenya Airways, and 24 hours ahead in the case of Air Afrique. This can sometimes present a problem if you're traveling, so keep it in mind. Write to the United Kenya Club or to the C.P.K. Guest House for accommodation. The latter is going to be quite full during Christmas, Easter, and school summer break (August) so if you're planning to stay at C.P.K. don't ask for those dates. It is really not practical to make hotel reservations for the other cities ahead of time as you will want to stay flexible. However, the exception to this is Cote d'Ivoire. Telex the Hilton two weeks before you anticipate arriving in Abidjan. Use a telex, as ordinary air mail takes some weeks. Most hotels have a telex you can pay to use. If not, all post offices offer telex services. You can telephone Kampala from Nairobi for a room at the International the day before you leave the latter city. If you plan to do the "Volunteer's Safari" in Togo you will need to contact the Peace Corps through Merikani and follow the other steps given in the itinerary. The Capital Hotel in Lilongwe can be full at times, and it's best to telex them a few days ahead of your expected arrival. The rest houses in the Malawian game parks usually have rooms and you needn't worry about making reservations. However, to take the car on the *Ilala* steamer, you will need to make arrangements, and the way to do this is explained in "Transportation" under "Lake, river and ferry schedules." The same applies to the Mali steamer. To reserve a seat on an Encounter Overland or Gerba expedition truck you will need to enter into a contract with them before you leave home and must make your itinerary fit their departure dates. Brochures and application forms are available from Merikani (P.O. Box 53394, Temple Heights Station, Washington, DC 20009, tel: (USA) 301–530–1911).

Accommodation recommended in *The Africans* itinerary:
Kenya: United Kenya Club.
Somalia: The Juba Hotel in Mogadiscio.
Uganda: Sikh Gurdwara in Kampala or the International Hotel. In Jinja, the Crested Crane Hotel.
Malawi: On arrival at the Capital Hotel, Lilongwe, thereafter at the government rest houses provided in the wildlife itinerary (shown in budgeting worksheets for this itinerary).
Senegal: Aerogard Hotel at Dakar International Airport.
The Gambia: Apollo Hotel, Banjul.
Cote d'Ivoire: Hilton International Abidjan.
Togo: On arrival, at the Sofitel 2 du Fevrier in Lome, then following the suggested itinerary for the "Volunteer's Safari."
Gabon: The Oukume Palace in Libreville or the Sofitel Dialogue.
Mali: Sofitel l'Amitie, Bamako, thereafter camping.
Sahel and Central Africa: Overlanding tour's tented accommodation.

Estimated Budget

The Africans Itinerary

Nairobi, Kenya Portion (21 nights)
Does not include airfares unless otherwise stated

	US$	
	1 person	2 people
Arrive Nairobi: Taxi to club or guest house	$ 15	$ 15
Select option (a) or (b)		
(a) United Kenya Club, full board, weekly rate, $308 single, $370 double × 2 weeks = $608 single, $740 double. Drinks in club and Hilton bar etc., allow $70 for 1 person, and $140 for 2. Total: $678 single, $880 double	————	————
(b) Church of the Province of Kenya (C.P.K.) Guest House, full board, weekly rate $92 single, $184 double × 2 weeks = $184 single, $368 double. Hospitality offered to fellow guests, allow $70 for 1 person, and $140 for 2. Total: $254 single, $508 double	————	————
Spending money	85	170
Taxis around town	30	30
Books, newspapers, magazines, maps	36	36
Expenses for an invitation extended by a newly made friend, allow for transportation, gift to the host/hostess, and incidental expenses (approximately $200 a week); for budget purposes one week is shown	200	400
Taxi to airport	15	15
15% tips on meals to waiters/waitresses at club or for staff donation box at the guest house	18.90	37.80
Gratuity to housekeeping staff, $1 a night for 1 or 2 persons	14	14
Tips to porters and bellman	8	8
Departure tax	10	20
SOS Insurance 3 weeks, using montly rate $45	45	90
Total option (a):	**$1154.90**	**$1715.80**
Total option (b):	**$730.90**	**$1343.80**
Option (a) cost per person sharing:	**$857.90**	
Option (b) cost per person sharing:	**$671.90**	

Mogadiscio, Somalia portion (3 nights)

Arrive Mogadiscio: Taxi to Juba Hotel	$ 10	$ 10
Juba Hotel, 3 nights $84 single, $108 double	252	324
Meals: continental breakfast $5, lunch $10, dinner $25 = $40 × 4 days =	160	320
Taxis around town	40	40

	US$	
	1 person	2 people
Coffee in Juba Garden and hospitality offered to new friends	20	40
Taxi to airport	10	10
Gifts to take home	50	100
15% tips to waiters/waitresses on meals	24	48
Gratuity to housekeeping staff, $1 a night for 1 or 2 persons	3	3
Tips to porters and bellman	8	8
SOS Insurance $15 for 1 week, proportion for 3 nights	6	12
Total:	$583	$915
Cost per person sharing:	$457.50	

Kampala, Uganda portion (6 nights)

Arrive Entebbe (the international airline destination city): airline bus to Kampala	$ 10	$ 10
Select option (a) or (b)		
(a) Kampala Sikh Temple, donation of $10 a night for 6 nights = $60 single, $120 double		
(b) International Hotel, $90 single, $110 double for 6 nights = $540 single, $660 double		
Meals (not served in this gurdwara, so price for meals, regardless of which accommodation is used, will be the same): breakfast $8, lunch $10, dinner $15 = $33 × 6 days =	198	396
Taxis around town	40	40
Spending money, including souvenirs	200	400
Taxi to airport	10	10
15% tips to waiters/waitresses on meals	29.70	59.40
Gratuity to housekeeping staff, $1 a night for 1 or 2 persons	6	6
Tips to porters and bellman	8	8
SOS Insurance, $15 for 1 week	15	30
Total option (a):	$576.70	$1079.40
Total option (b):	$1056.70	$1619.40
Option (a) cost per person sharing:	$539.70	
Option (b) cost per person sharing:	$809.70	

Malawi portion (21 nights)

Arrive Lilongwe: Pick up Avis at airport. Avis Class B unlimited mileage, full insurance and taxes for 3 weeks	$ 721	$ 721
Gas (petrol) for the entire trip, allowing 3100 km or 1937 miles with gas priced at $5 a U.S. gallon	242	242
Capital Hotel, 2 nights (includes Continental breakfast) $84 single, $94 double	168	188
Meals: lunch: $7, dinner: $8 = $15 × 2 days	30	60
Kasungu National Park entrance fee, $6 a day for car and $2 per person for 3 days	24	30

	US$	
	1 person	2 people
Lifupa Lodge, bed and breakfast for 3 nights at $20 single, $25 double, $30 triple, $35 quad	60	75
Meals: lunch: $6, dinner: $8 = $14 × 3	42	84
Mzuzu Hotel (includes Continental breakfast) 1 night	62	73
Meals: lunch: $6, dinner: $8	14	28
Entrance fee to Nyika National Park (same as for Kasungu), 3 days	24	30
Rest House in park, $27 a day for up to 4 people, 3 days	81	81
Food brought from home supplemented by locally purchased foods, allow	30	40
Mzuzu Hotel, bed and breakfast, 1 night	62	73
Meals: lunch: $6, dinner: $8	14	28
Capital Hotel (includes Continental breakfast)	84	94
Entrance fee to Liwonde National Park (same as for other parks), 3 days	24	30
Mvuu Camp, $8 a day × 3 days per person	24	48
Food brought from home supplemented by locally purchased foods; the higher figure for 1 person includes staples	15	20
Boat trip up Liwonde River	125	125
Shire Highlands Hotel, Limbe, bed and breakfast, 1 night, after-breakfast departure	40	50
Entrance fee, Lengwe National Park (same as for other parks)	24	30
Rest house for 3 nights, $27 a day for up to 4 people	81	81
Food brought from home supplemented by locally purchased foods	15	20
Mwabvi National Park, entrance fee, 2 days	24	30
Accommodation: Personal tent brought from home		
Food brought from home supplemented by local purchases	15	20
Capital Hotel (including Continental breakfast), 1 night	84	94
Meals: lunch: $7, dinner: $8	15	30
Drop Avis at airport upon departure		
15% tips for waiters/waitresses	24.75	49.70
Gratuity to housekeeping staff, $1 a night for 1 or 2 persons, $2 for 3 or 4	18	18
Bellmen/porters and game park staff	32	32
SOS Insurance, 1 month (safari lasts 3 weeks: SOS insurance $15 a week or $45 a month)	45	90
Total:	$2263.75	$2614.50
Cost per person sharing:	$1307.25	

Senegal portion (1 night)

Arrive Dakar International Airport: Check into airport hotel in same building, overnight, same price double or single	$ 44	$ 44
Meals: continental breakfast, $6, lunch $10, dinner $12 =	28	28

	US$	
	1 person	2 people
Taxi to Dakar: $4 each way	8	8
Spending money	25	50
15% tips to waiters/waitresses on meals	4.20	8.40
Gratuity to housekeeping staff	1	1
Tips to porters and bellman	4	4
Proportion of SOS Insurance	1	2
Total:	$115.20	$145.40
Cost per person sharing:	$72.70	

Gambia portion (3 nights)

Arrive Banjul: Taxi to hotel	$ 15	$ 15
Apollo Hotel, 3 nights, includes continental breakfast, $22 single or double	66	66
Meals: lunch $15, dinner $15 = $30 × 3	90	180
Taxis around town	40	40
Boat fare to Juffure	10	20
Hospitality shown to new acquaintances	50	100
Spending money, including souvenirs	30	60
Taxi to airport	15	15
15% tips to waiters/waitresses on meals	14.40	28.80
Gratuity to housekeeping staff, $1 for 1 or 2 persons	3	3
Tips to porters and bellman	8	8
Proportion of SOS Insurance	6	12
Total:	$347.40	$547.80
Cost per person sharing:	$273.90	

Cote d'Ivoire (4 nights)

Arrive Abidjan: Hilton car will meet those with reservations and will return you to airport without charge		
Hilton International Abidjan, $111 single, $131 double for 4 nights =	444	444
Meals: breakfast $6, lunch $10, dinner $17 = $33 × 4 =	132	524
Taxis around town	25	25
Spending money	50	100
15% tips to waiters/waitresses on meals	19.80	39.60
Gratuity to housekeeping staff, $1 a night for 1 or 2 persons	4	4
Tips to porters and bellman	8	8
Proportion of SOS Insurance	8	16
Total:	$690.80	$1160.60
Cost per person sharing:	$580.30	

Togo portion (15 nights)

Arrive Lome: Taxi to hotel	$ 9	$ 9
Hotel du 2 Fevrier, 2 nights (including taxes), $82 single, $90 double	164	180

	US$	
	1 person	2 people
Meals: breakfast $4, lunch $8, dinner $10 = $22 × 2	44	88
Avis car for 11 days, allowing for 625 miles and full insurance	814	814
Gas (petrol)	125	125
Peace Corps volunteers' homes for 8 nights, donation to the friends of Togo @ $25 a night	200	400
Meals at Peace Corps volunteers' homes at $7.50 a day × 8	60	120

Select option (a) or (b)

(a) Return to Lome: 2 nights at Assembly of God cottage, donation to Scholarship Fund $25 a day per person

    Meals: self-catering and by invitation at seminary, allow for groceries $20 for 1, $30 for 2

(b) 2 nights at Hotel du 2 Fevrier, $82 single, $90 double Meals at hotel or Lome restaurants, allow $44 for 1, $88 for 2

Taxis around town	11	11
Taxi to airport	9	9
Gratuity to housekeeping staff in hotels	4	4
Tips for porters/bellmen	20	20
15% tips for waiters/waitresses	13.20	26.40
SOS Insurance, 2 weeks @ $15 a week	30	60
Total option (a):	$1573.20	$1996.40
Total option (b):	$1711.20	$2134.40
Cost per person sharing (a):	$998.20	
Cost per person sharing (b):	$1067.20	

Gabon portion (3 nights)

Arrive Libreville: Taxi to hotel	$ 5	$ 5
Sofitel Dialogue, 3 nights, $77 single, $86 double	231	252
Meals: breakfast $8, lunch $25, dinner $25 = $58 × 3 =	174	248
Taxis around town	30	30
Taxi to airport	5	5
15% tips on meals to waiter/waitress	26.10	52.20
Gratuity to housekeeping staff	3	3
Tips to porters and bellman	8	8
Proportion of SOS Insurance	6	12
Total:	$488.10	$615.20
Cost per person sharing:	$307.60	

Mali (7 or 12 nights)

Arrive Bamako: Sofitel bus meets flight, no charge		
Sofitel l'Amitie, 3 nights, $89 single, $98 double	$ 267	$ 294
Meals: breakfast $6, lunch $10, dinner $15 × 3 days =	93	186
Taxis around town	40	40

	US$	
	1 person	2 people
Charges to extend visa and obtain a permit to photograph	10	20
Select option (a) or (b), depending on time of year		
(a) Tour to Mopti through SMERT, $330 or $660	_____	_____
15% tips to waiters/waitresses on all meals: $32.55, $65.10	_____	_____
Gratuity to housekeeping staff at l'Amitie, $1 per day for 1 or 2 people × 7 days	_____	_____
Tips to bellman/porters, $16 for 1 or 2	_____	_____
SOS Insurance, for 1 week $15/$30	_____	_____
(b) Steamer Bamako-Dire-Bamako, luxury cabin, round trip, $626/$1252	_____	_____
Taxi fare to station: $6 for 1 or 2	_____	_____
Train fare to Koulikoro to board steamer: $20/$40	_____	_____
Disembark at Dire: Taxi to mayor's office and to site he suggests you camp: $8 for 1 or 2	_____	_____
Camping in Dire, food, personal expenses, hospitality, allow $14 a day per person × 10 days (the number of days used for budget purposes) = $140 or $280	_____	_____
Taxi to port at Dire: $6 for 1 or 2	_____	_____
Embark on steamer to Bamako (charged above)		
Train fare to Koulikoro to Bamako: $20/$40	_____	_____
Taxi from station to hotel: $6 for 1 or 2	_____	_____
15% tips to waiter/waitresses on meals: $18.60/$37.20	_____	_____
Gratuity to hotel and cabin housekeeping staff, $12 for 1 or 2	_____	_____
Helper at camp, $3 a day × 10 days: $30 for 1 or 2	_____	_____
Tips to bellman, porters, and boat crew: $24 for 1 or 2	_____	_____
SOS Insurance, $45 a month, $45/$90	_____	_____
Sofitel l'Amitie, 1 night	89	98
Meals: breakfast $6, lunch $10, dinner $15 =	31	62
Sofitel bus to airport, no charge		
Total option (a):	$930.55	$1478.10
Total option (b):	$1491.60	$2531.20
Option (a) cost per person sharing:	$739.05	
Option (b) cost per person sharing:	$1265.60	

			US$	
	1 person	2 people	per person sharing	per day per person sharing
Grand total option (a): 84 days	$8723.60	$12,268.20	$6134.10	$73.02
Grand total option (b): 89 days	$9478.65	$13,627.30	$6813.65	$76.55

Paupers *The Africans* Itinerary

The budget for *The Africans* is the most expensive of all the itineraries. Our readers are going to come upon travelers in Africa or returned travelers who will tell them that they "did Africa" on far less than we suggest. Undoubtedly, they are telling the truth. However, neither Leah nor I are prepared, as responsible travel writers, to provide the names of flophouses and greasy spoon restaurants. We've seen too many really ill travelers to do so. Also, the Africans who have a say in African politics and economies do not hang around flophouses and greasy spoon cafes. To appreciate contemporary Africa and her problems and to meet people in responsible positions means staying in good hotels, clubs, etc. However, if you haven't a lot of money we believe there is no better route to discovering what makes modern Africa tick than by becoming a volunteer. We have provided information in "Bye-the-By" on how to get a teaching job. Additionally, there are several international agencies looking for volunteers. Africa is full of unqualified, unskilled Africans wanting jobs, and to get service with a volunteer agency requires either academic qualifications or trade skills. Readers may want to contact the following international agencies: United Nations (Bureau of Technical Assistance Operations, New York, NY 10017); OXFAM (274 Banbury Rd., Oxford, OX2 &D2, England, tel. (865) 56777); and Catholic Institute for International Relations (22 Coleman Fields, London, N.1, England, tel. (1) 354 0883; volunteers need not be Catholic).

At the national level, readers should apply to their government volunteer agencies as well as volunteer programs connected with professions and religious programs. In the United States there is an umbrella organization that publishes a directory specifically for work in Africa, *Diversity in Development: Africa* (2 volumes), which provides a description of not only the agencies sponsoring development work in Africa, but also the projects themselves. Readers will be able to self-screen and approach the agencies where they feel they are qualified to help. The price is US$20 plus $3 for postage and handling within the U.S. Write: American Council for Voluntary International Action, or Inter-Action (200 Park Ave. South, New York, NY 10003, tel. 212–777–8210; or 2101 L St. N.W., Suite 916, Washington, DC 20037, tel. 202–822–8429). The directory can be studied in the Washington office, but must be purchased through the New York office.

Another exposure to Africa can be obtained through international study programs. However, these tend to be expensive, although a limited number of scholarships are offered. Inquire through your nearest major university. African universities offer a few places for undergraduate foreign students. Inquiries should be made directly to the university, whose address can be obtained from their embassy.

For American readers, the following titles may prove helpful: *The Young American's Scholarship Guide To Travel and Learning Abroad* (Intravco Press, Suite 1303, 211 East 43rd Street, New York, NY 10017, $12.95) and *The Teenagers Guide to Study, Travel and Adventure Abroad* (Council on International Education Exchange, 809 United Nations Plaza, New York, NY 10017), although information in either title on African opportunities is limited.

Assistant professorships are offered by some African universities. The cost of transportation to the country is usually not included, but if applicants state they are willing to cover this cost, the chances of obtaining a position are enhanced.

Anyone with a TOEFL (Teaching of English as a Foreign Language) certificate will find employment in most major cities and capitals of African countries. Africans are very keen on certificates, and recognize an official TOEFL certificate. Training to be a TOEFL instructor does not require a bachelor's degree, but be sure the institution that teaches the TOEFL method is accredited by the headquarters in Chicago, IL. Once trained, and once in Africa, it is only necessary to place an advertisement in the classified columns and wait for potential students to call you.

Readers who are skilled mechanics, plumbers, carpenters, masons, etc., are sorely needed in Africa to teach their skills every bit as much as academicians, and if they are sincere in wanting to understand Africa, they should search to find agencies who can employ them.

The teaching of first aid in villages is in demand. The St. John's Ambulance Corps has trained volunteers who attend public gatherings in Kenya, but the need at the village level for basic first-aid instruction is tremendous. Unfortunately, we know of no agency anywhere—including the International Red Cross—who will sponsor someone willing to teach first aid. Another very great need is for swimming instructors and lifeguards.

Organized sports instruction is in limbo in Africa. Although one country (which will remain unidentified) appropriated money for the training of their boxers, an investigative reporter of a local newspaper found that the money had been diverted to coaches' pockets and the athletes were being fed on an all-starch diet. Most Africans who compete in the Olympics do so having undergone great privations—or have trained at their own expense. Nutrition, professional training, and facilities need foreign assistance. Again, we know of no international organization willing to fund such work.

Youth for Understanding (3501 Newark St., N.W., Washington, DC 20016, tel: 202–966–6800) sponsors exchange visits. Canadian and American 4-H'ers can take advantage of their very reasonable rates for escorted travel to Africa, write: National 4-H Council, International Programs (7100 Connecticut Ave., Chevy Chase, MD 20815).

BYE-THE-BY

Health Precautions in Remote Areas

Much of this text will not concern readers who are following the *Lunatic Express, Flame Trees of Thika,* or *Out of Africa* itineraries as they take place entirely in Kenya, where travel presents no more danger than that in the western United States. The piped water in the larger cities is safe, and the hotels we recommend have catered to foreign visitors for many years and are prepared to meet their needs. Nor will the following information be of more than passing interest to readers following the *Livingstone* itinerary, except if they decide to drive into Zambia, where standards are not as high as in Malawi or Kenya. However, for readers following the *Lost Cities of Africa, White Nile,* and, especially, *The Africans* itineraries, the information should prove helpful and, if heeded, will lead, we hope, to trouble-free traveling insofar as health is concerned.

Rule number one, for everyone, is don't eat or drink anything in Africa you wouldn't eat or drink at home—meaning, if you see a cafe that is obviously dirty, don't patronize it any more than you would your neighborhood greasy spoon. Don't eat suspect, possibly spoiled, food any more than you would eat less than fresh food at home. Curiously, travelers sometimes do such things, believing they are "becoming one of the people," when in effect all they are doing is becoming ill.

Outside of the big international hotels, do not drink local milk unless you see that it has been produced by a commercial pasteurization plant. Milk sealed in commercial dairy packages is safe to drink; milk served in little pitchers in small cafes is highly suspect.

Most African countries import dried powdered milk from Europe, and in Kenya, the Nestle company has a plant. This milk is usually full-cream milk and very good. Make certain to distinguish between infant formula milk and ordinary dried milk powder. Every major African city has a supermarket that may not be like the supermarket you know at home but tries to be. If you fail to find dried milk in smaller stores, ask where the supermarket is located. Beware of dried milk powder sold in other than a sophisticated container. Local shopkeepers sometimes decant milk powder intended for calf feeding into small bags and sell it. Undoubtedly, the milk was sterile when sealed in the 50-kilo bags at the point of manufacture, but the repackaging done by African shopkeepers is not always sanitary, and there certainly is no supervision to ensure

226

This Victorian sedan chair was fabricated in Britain and sold by outfitters to clients "taking up a posting" in West Africa. Demeaning as it may appear to the bearers, knowing Africans' wonderful sense of humor, they must have had a giggle at the inability of the frail White men to put one foot in front of the other.

that flies don't settle on the open bag causing contamination of the milk powder. Evaporated canned milk is also available, but is a little awkward to carry around when traveling once it's been opened.

Coca-Cola is available even in the smallest villages, as are other flavored soft drinks. Fanta, made by Coca-Cola, is especially popular. In Uganda and other countries where imports are tightly controlled, some shopkeepers have their wives and daughters squeeze oranges and lemons early in the morning, mix the juice with water, and pour it into used Coke or Fanta bottles. These are usually easy to spot as they do not have a cap; a piece of paper is twirled and pushed down the neck of the bottle as a substitute. Needless to say, steer clear of such drinks.

There are commercially bottled beers in many countries, and these are safe to drink. Remember, African beers generally have a higher alcoholic content than most American beers, and it's better to experiment with your tolerance level before drinking as much as you would at home. We have tasted the locally made beer when a friend made it for us under absolutely sterile conditions. It is usually sipped from a common pot through a long reed (straw) passed from one friend to another. To us it tasted like dishwater—slightly oily, with the same color and consistency. Not recommended from the standpoint of either hygiene or intestinal health.

Tea and coffee are your best friends in supplying the liquids needed when clean water is not available. The tea water undoubtedly has been kept on the boil for hours. Tea bags are an alien concept—loose tea is used. Properly brewed tea, if not strained, has tea leaves that sink. When water heated to less than boiling is used the leaves float. Therefore, you can be almost certain that water intended for tea-making has been boiled. Coffee is usually preferred strong, and this means it has been boiled with the roughly ground beans for a long time.

If ice is available, it probably has been frozen—outside of the major cities and chain hotels—using unclean water, so it's best to confine the use of cold drinks to those in bottles that have been chilled in a refrigerator or *on* ice.

We have discussed liquids and their availability at length because the chances of becoming dehydrated are greater than coming down with any exotic African disease.

Dehydration

During a long flight the body becomes dehydrated; if the passenger steps out into the tropics, the stress and heat can combine with the damage done during the flight to cause dehydration. Most doctors recommend taking dehydration salts. Sachets or envelopes can be purchased in most good pharmacies in African capital cities. Otherwise, North American readers may want to take Gatorade crystals with them. Specific symptoms of dehydration are constipation that cannot be relieved by taking a laxative, and a headache that does not respond to aspirin or the usual headache remedies. Taking salt tablets can make matters worse; the body needs all the minerals replaced, not simply salt (sodium chloride, potassium chloride, sodium bicarbonate, and glucose).

Allergies

One of my sons is allergic to Elephant Grass, but then, he's allergic to the exhaust fumes that pollute Washington, DC, air.

The air is certainly cleaner in Africa than in most industrialized countries. There is less pollen because many plants are regenerated by root or tubular propagation. In our opinion, readers prone to allergies are less likely to suffer in Africa than at home.

Bites and Stings

The usual precautions about spiders, scorpions, etc., apply, and you can fit out your first-aid kit with a label on the inside cover giving antidotes just as you would for a camping trip in the western United States or Australian outback. But on the subject of African bees, the case is not the same as for other countries.

The recommendation to stay perfectly still if you are attacked by a swarm of bees is not valid for Africa. In Africa the advice is to run until you outrun them or can get inside somewhere and close them out—including into water, such as a pond (in which case you can decide whether you want to contract bilharziasis or suffer multiple stings). African bees simply settle and sting. *Under no circumstances ever throw a stick or stone at a hanging bee hive.* You may want to ask your doctor for a prescription medicine just in case you are unlucky enough to meet up with a swarm.

Mombasa Trains are small cigar-size black millipedes that will not hurt you. They leave behind a defensive brown juice if they happen to use a part of your skin for tracks and this can irritate, but washing the juice off with soap and water cures the problem.

Hollywood has made a fortune from films depicting soldier ants eating all in their path. In our experience, when we have stepped into a convoy of them, all that happens is a very sharp pincer pain where they have dug into the skin. In some cases, though, soldier ants do eat as they go, as described by Elspeth Huxley in *Flame Trees of Thika,* when Tilly's baby chicks were eaten by them.

Chigoes, often referred to as "chiggers" or "jiggers" are not the same little insects that may rise from the grass when we're walking across a lawn. Rather, the chigoe is infinitesimally small and penetrates human skin to lay its eggs. Most commonly found along dry footpaths, chigoes are never encountered along city sidewalks. After penetrating the skin, they usually establish themselves on the toes, near the nail, and proceed to lay their eggs, increasing their sac as they do until it is about the size of a pea.

The first indication that a chigoe has found a home in your foot will be your waking at night with an uncontrollable itching at the site of the penetration. Seldom can an inexperienced eye detect exactly where the chigoe is located. Every night, until the chigoe is taken out of the toe, the sufferer will be awakened by itching. Ultimately, it becomes impossible to go back to sleep because of the increased presence of the chigoe and its eggs. If the sac is broken in trying to remove it, the eggs will scatter and imbed themselves in other parts of the foot, ready to start new families. *The sac must be removed in its entirety without breaking it.*

The wise thing to do is to take care of the chigoe the morning after the first itching starts. African mothers, who generally are very relaxed about disciplining their children, beat them if they fail to report the presence of a chigoe in their foot. As a result, even small African children are expert in the removal of this annoying flea. And do have an African remove the insect from your foot—not another non-African. Sterilize the point of a safety pin in a match flame. Sit wherever circumstances dictate, and prop your foot up in full light. Hold very, very still—if you move, even the most expertly manipulated safety pin will miss the mark. Remain perfectly still, until your benefactor triumphantly raises the flea and her egg sac out of your foot and shows it to you.

You may wish to reward your benefactor, but, traditionally, the removal of the chigoe flea is a duty, an obligation each does for another. It would be better to give him or her some small present at a future time so that your gratitude is not directly linked to the removal of the insect. It certainly is in order to verbally express your relief and appreciation, and to wonder at the size of the sac and how clever the benefactor is to have removed it intact.

Precautions against malaria, which is carried by the mosquito, should be taken before leaving for Africa. Start taking the malaria prophylactic prescribed by your doctor two weeks before your intended departure date. (Note: In the United States malarial prophylatics are available only by doctor's prescription. In England they can be purchased over the counter, as they can in Africa). The drug used will depend upon your destination, and readers planning to travel through several regions of Africa will want to take the drug that will cover all areas. The "Basic Information Checklist" has information on whether the malaria found in a country is resistant to chloroquine-based drugs. If you start taking the prophylatic a good two weeks before arrival in Africa, you should have absolutely no problem, and it is highly unlikely you will contract the disease. However, in some areas there is a very strong strain of maleria that requires extra precautions.

During the course of your travel in Africa, local people may ask you for malaria tablets. It is kinder to go with them and purchase locally manufactured drugs than to give them one or two of yours. Tablets administered to Africans are generally stronger than those prescribed strictly as a preventative. Africans do not take prophylactics for malaria; they simply cannot afford the cost of the medicine. It is felt by some medical authorities that they will eventually build up an immunity to the disease. Apart from the suffering and pain they experience from continual bouts of the disease, the number of man-hours lost due to it is incalculable. For this reason attempts by economists to measure African labor productivity against productivity in industrialized, temperate-zone nations is unrealistic. Many infants and small children die from malaria in Africa. We advise caution about giving your tablets to African babies. If you are concerned about the child brought to you, take the baby and the mother to the nearest clinic or hospital. Sometimes these are miles from the patient and the temptation to try to affect a cure with a simple tablet is great. But, remember, this can backfire on you. The child can die because the tablet is too strong or was given too late, or because, although the complaint looked like malaria, it was something else. In either case, if you give the tablet, some of the blame for the death may rest on your shoulders. Conversely, if the baby dies and you didn't give a tablet, you may get the blame. You're going to have to use your own judgment. Such cases are going to arise if you travel off the tourist circuit. When poor Africans see foreign faces they associate them with knowledge. This is part of the colonial heritage, and no matter what your personal political persuasion, the fact remains that Africans feel this way. It is an inherited responsibility that comes with being a foreigner.

While mosquitoes are present during daylight hours, they bite at night. Do not be deceived by the comparatively (to North American) small size of African mosquitoes. It is common to wake next morning to find exposed skin covered with small bites. This is totally unnecessary. Always, if the room is not air conditioned, sleep covered by a mosquito net and check that there are not holes in it. As with nylon stockings, very small holes can be repaired with fingernail polish. For larger holes, take a handful of the netting over the hole and knot it on itself.

Spray exposed parts of the body with insect repellent before sitting outside in the evening. Try to stay in areas where there is a cross breeze as mosquitoes prefer still, quiet places.

Stagnant water or even small pools of water are breeding grounds for mosquitoes. Don't make camp near puddles, ponds, or lakes. If small pools of water cannot be drained or avoided, oil poured into the water will rise and float, causing conditions that deter mosquitoes.

Really bad mosquito bites can be treated with bicarbonate of soda made into a paste with boiled water and then lightly bandaged. Unless they have been unduly scratched, this should not become necessary. Bourbon, after-shave, or eau de cologne are all good disinfectants and tend to stop the itching.

Sandfly fever (Phlebotomus fever) is found not only in Africa but in most tropical and sub-tropical countries. The insect is very tiny and grayish in color. It can pass through mosquito netting, but its bite is most commonly received when walking through dusty or sandy markets with unprotected ankles and legs.

The incubation period is 4 to 7 days from the time bitten. Any of the following are symptoms of Sandfly fever (all need not be present): swollen face, eyes extra-sensitive to light, severe frontal headache, pain at the back of the eyes, and, most common, a stiffness and aching at the back of the neck. Sandfly fever is common in all Mediterranean countries, the Middle East, northern Sudan (especially Khartoum), and in Egypt at railway stations and car and taxi parks. There is no treatment; the symptoms disappear in three days, during which time overexertion should be avoided. Cases lasting longer than three days should be examined by a doctor.

Tick bite fevers differ from relapsing fever in that the vector is the tick, not the louse. Ticks climb on grasses or pass from animals onto humans; the actual tick is not always found on the body. (Similar to Rocky Mountain Spotted Fever, common in the United States during certain times of the year.) The lymph gland nearest the bite swells and the bite forms a small sore. Ten days of fever, headache, stiff neck, and sore eyes is the norm, and a rash appears on the fifth day. Prevention involves examining the body carefully for tick bites (although not all tick bites carry the fever) after walking through tall grasses or in farm areas where livestock can be carriers. Monitor any bites to determine if there is an enlargement. Suspect fever if the nearest lymph gland becomes swollen. The fever needs professional treatment and prescribed antibiotics.

Tsetse fly fever should not be a problem to our readers as we have not mentioned, except in the case of Malawi, game parks in Kenya where the tsetse fly is found. (In most of the famous parks, tsetse flies are under control.) We did experience tsetse flies in Kasungu National Park, but only for a short distance along the road. Rolling the car windows up solved the problem. We also encountered them in Somalia when our driver stopped to help a camel herder pull a camel that was down out of the mud with the winch of the Land Rover. Readers should be prepared to recognize a tsetse fly by knowing that it is larger than a horsefly and is always brown.

The bite is painful at the time and two or three weeks later erupts into a sore. The sore opens and the nearest lymph gland swells. Medical attention should be sought, as the disease can be cured with modern drugs.

Trematodes (flukes) are the carriers of schistosomiasis or bilharziasis and are always found in water. The flukes are picked up on the skin—for instance, a hand dangling over the side of a rowboat—and a small raised rash *may* be noticed at the time of contact. The flukes are found in lakes, ponds, and puddles where human beings carrying the disease have urinated. The disease is difficult to cure and has a long recuperative period. Prescription drugs are administered under a physician's supervision. The incubation period can be 3 months to 2½ years. Early symptoms are painful urination and spasmodic pain between the ribs and pelvis. Leah and I have traveled extensively in Africa and have never contracted schistosomiasis, but have been extremely careful to avoid swimming in the great lakes or any standing water. We really feel that if readers take similar precautions and discount anything that local people—White or Black— say about the safety of swimming in anything other than chlorinated pools or the ocean, they will have no problems.

Some Washington, DC, summers see a high incidence of rabies from animal bites, and we are warned by public health officials not to touch the raccoons that sometimes find their way into our backyards. The same advice applies to touching sick or dead animals in Africa, who may be carriers of disease. Don't be tempted to touch the skin without taking extreme care—rubber gloves and strict sanitation. Think of disease before deciding to cut out a set of attractive horns as trophies. Bats, of which there are many in certain parts of Africa, also carry disease. Leave them alone and they'll leave you alone.

We've seen more snakes in West Virginia than in Africa. They are there, however, and the usual precautions should be taken about avoiding them when camping. They are not found in the cities, and most African villagers keep the areas surrounding their homes swept clean as a deterrent to snakes.

Internal Parasites

Intestinal worms are one of Africa's major problems; many Africans eat with their hands, and in the absence of strict religious taboos and rituals that insist that the hands be washed before eating, the problem of infestation is compounded. Graphically illustrated patent worm remedies are sold in every small shop in Africa. These are seldom effective as (1) changes in sanitation and eating habits must be made to prevent reinfection, (2) there is no single drug effective for all types of worms, and (3) patients may require protein supplements, rehydration therapy, and care for secondary complications. Undercooked meat, dirty hands, dirty bed linens, improperly washed vegetables grown in soil where human excreta is used as fertilizer or where the vegetable garden is used as a toilet, dogs and cats, bare feet (hookworm), and food prepared by people who have worms can all transmit intestinal worms.

There are times when it is almost impossible to refuse hospitality in conditions that may be suspect. In these cases bread is usually the safest food. Offer many compliments on how appetizing the food looks, but unfortunately you are not feeling well—never say you don't feel hungry, as this will merely make your host/hostess more insistent that you eat. You can also get around the problem by asking that you be allowed to take some food home to eat later. This will save your face and make them happy.

The symptoms for worms are not necessarily that one begins eating like a horse and becomes thin. Many cases have no prelmininary symptoms. Advanced cases have symptoms ranging from personality change (tapeworm), apathy, diarrhea, fever, cough, stomach pain, and bleeding from the lungs.

If you feel you've been exposed, give a stool specimen to your doctor when you return home.

The ameba is the simpliest of organisms. Amebic dysentry—entamoeba histolytica—is the type that breaks down human body tissue. Food handlers infected with the disease can transmit dysentery, as can flies that land on food and unsterilized water. Amebic dysentery is very prelevant along the Nile— especially in Egypt. Hilton Hotel employees in Africa are screened for amebic dysentery by Hilton physicians, and stool specimens are examined in Hilton laboratories. There is a lucrative black market in clean stool samples, which are sold to potential servants and restaurant workers who know they have the disease. Locally conducted medical examinations should always be suspect. Actual transmission is by ingestion of feces that are carried on dirty hands that handle food.

Symptoms are foul-smelling bowel movements that contain mucus and traces of blood. The stomach is painful; there is a mild fever and tenderness on the right side of the abdomen above the appendix. Dehydration comes about through frequent bowel movements.

Prevention is by paying strict attention to how food is prepared in areas where the disease is rampant. It can be cured by prescribed drugs under a physician's supervision. Leah nor I have had a problem, but we make very certain we eat only at the Hilton in Cairo or purchase imported foods from local grocers. Bananas can be eaten with safety.

Other Health Problems

Swimming off the Kenya coast in certain locations can lead to cuts—usually on the legs—made by coral in the water. Many buildings are constructed of coral block and many paths are lined by coral rock. Tripping, as Leah once did, and cutting oneself can be not only painful at the time, but the cut can become deep and ulcerate the surrounding flesh. See a local doctor, who will be able to prescribe a cream to stop the cut running its full course.

Prickly heat is best avoided than cured: Wear only all-cotton clothing. Even 50 percent polyester can produce an almost spontaneous case of prickly heat given the right conditions. Drinking hot fluids aggravates prickly heat. Do not use soap when taking a bath unless the soap is specifically made for the treatment of prickly heat (contains oxymercuriotoluylate of sodium). Keep body parts that touch one another powdered with specially prepared prickly heat powder (equal parts boric acid, zinc, and cornstarch). Some people feel that applying a lanolin-based lotion to the body weekly helps to prevent prickly heat.

Pregnancy

If a woman becomes pregnant while traveling in Africa it is advisable to consult a doctor at the earliest opportunity as malaria prophylactics *may* have an effect on the child. It is wise to take advice from your doctor at home at the time he prescribes your malaria tablets concerning the possible affect the malaria drug may have on the fetus.

Immunizations

Information on immunizations required by the World Health Organization is given in the Basic Information chart.

Famine in Africa

In *Fielding's African Safaris* we discussed this topic at length. Suffice to say here that the famine areas are not in any of the countries that we recommend and there is plenty of food for both visitors and local people.

In Case of Accident or Illness

Kenya: Our advice for Kenya is different than the advice we give for other African countries. In Kenya we always feel we get better medical attention than we do at home. A visitor to Kenya is always treated like a VIP, while here at home, we are just another patient. Services in Kenya are excellent, even for heart patients. Dr. Silverstein in Nairobi is an American heart specialist and we cannot praise him too highly.

Religious hospitals are usually staffed with professionals (European, American, Indian, or African) trained abroad. The nursing staff will usually be African under a head nurse who is an expatriate. In general the standard of care is first class and the cleanliness excellent. Their equipment, if not ultra high tech, is usually adequate.

Nazareth Catholic Hospital outside Nairobi; Aga Khan Hospital in Nairobi and in Mombasa; Mombasa Hospital (formerly Katherine Bibby; not Mombasa General Hospital, which is government operated).

In Africa it is the custom for patients' relatives to come along and stay at the hospital with the patient. This may or may not be permitted in a religious hospital.

Religious hospitals charge all patients a fee for services and medicines. This differs from a government hospital where services and medicines are free under the national health insurance deducted from wage-earners. Most local people, whether they are Christian or followers of traditional religions, prefer the religious hospital even if they have to pay. No discrimination is made by the staff of religious hospitals because of the patients' religious affiliation.

The medicines at religious hospitals are generally subsidized by the church or, in the case of the Aga Khan hospitals, by that community. Where there is a shortage of medicine, and this is often due to transportation difficulties not to lack of funding, you may be using medicine paid for by a donation intended for an African. For this reason we suggest that you take along certain antibiotics so that if there is a shortage and you need antibiotics you will not be taking medicine that rightfully should be given to a local. Alternately, Lord's Pharmacy in Nairobi always has adequate supplies of antibiotics at reasonable Kenya market prices. Of course, it goes without saying that emergencies are emergencies and you will be given antibiotics, but a little forethought can ease the conscience.

Government hospitals and clinics, in our opinion, are not up to the standard of the religious health-care facilities. Bureaucrats are the same everywhere, and the amount of paperwork they require means ample opportunity for foulups. Civil-service discipline doesn't seem to compare to the religious hospitals'. Nevertheless, you will be treated as a special patient and will probably be put at the head of the line. There is little attempt, that we have observed, at triage scheduling; the system is more first come, first served.

Doctors in private practice: Most Kenyan towns have doctors working in private practice; some are African, others Indian or European. In our experience they are excellent. Their charges are low when compared to the outrageous prices we pay in the United States. Failing a religious-operated emergency room, we would go to a doctor in private practice. Their names and locations in the rural areas can be obtained from the local police station.

Egypt: We have had very adverse reports on Egyptian hospital care and suggest, in cases of severe illness, that an expatriate nurse be employed. The primary problem, we understand, is from poor nursing (seeing that the IVs don't run dry, etc.). Contact your embassy for advice.

Gabon: Several expatriate doctors practice in Libreville and your embassy can supply their names and numbers.

The Gambia: We have no first-hand knowledge and advice should be taken from embassy personnel.

Cote d'Ivoire: There is a Canadian-administered hospital in Abidjan, but we were told by the Club Med staff that they rely on SOS Insurance and have seriously ill patients flown directly to Europe.

Malawi: There is a Catholic hospital in Lilongwe, and we strongly advise readers to use it if needed.

Mali: The medical situation in Mali is very, very bad. There is an Italian-operated hospital in Dire that is reportedly quite good, but in the Bamako area, and in the south generally, the situation is very poor. Call SOS in case of emergency and they will arrange for a charter flight.

Morocco: Medical care is very, very poor, and SOS Insurance should be contacted immediately. Contact your embassy for advice.

Senegal: We have no first-hand knowledge of conditions; there is a strong Catholic presence in the country and presumably they operate medical facilities, but as these are probably along French lines (our experience with French-African hospitals is not good), we would rely on advice from embassy staff.

Somalia: There is an Italian hospital for emergency cases in Mogadiscio, but after receiving immediate care the patient should be flown to Nairobi. Special charter flights can be arranged. The flight is only 45 minutes.

Sudan: Contact your embassy, asking their advice on the best course of action to take in the event of illness.

Togo: The drinking water is not safe, and the sewer system in Lome is not adequate. Bottled mineral water should be used. The hospital care is poor, and readers should ensure they have SOS Insurance when traveling in Togo.

Uganda: The Catholic hospitals pre-1971 were excellent; the government hospitals were chronically understaffed even then. Several Indian doctors are in private practice in Kampala. We would suggest flying to Nairobi as soon as possible; it is less than an hour's flight. Take antibiotics with you, as there have been severe shortages.

Suggested items for a first-aid kit for remote areas

Antifungal ointment
Antibacterial ointment
Prescribed pain killer (2 doses)
Periactin (cyproheptadine hydrochloride)
Eyedrops—cleansing
Malaria prophylactic
Malaria curative drug (this may be different than the prophylactic but not necessarily)
Individually packaged alcohol swabs
A medicine you know works for you in event of diarrhea
A laxative
Course of tetracycline tablets

Course of penicillin tablets
Aspirin (although available locally even in small shops)
Baby oil
Antiseptic
Peroxide
Dehydration salts (these may be bought in Africa, as they are difficult to find in the U.S.) or Gatorade crystals
Sunscreen 15 lotion
Sunscreen 15 lipstick
Mint Lifesavers or other candy (sweets) that can be thirst-quenching

Tweezers
Small magnifying glass
Scissors
Thermometer
Needle & spool of white thread (cotton)

Bandages/tape
Men's white handkerchief (2)
Short length of clothesline rope
Small ball of string
Recently published first-aid manual

AIDS

The following information on this subject is strictly hearsay, but it would seem that the present level of knowledge even in the medical world is so unscientific that anyone's opinion is as good as anyone's. We first heard of what was called green monkey fever in 1979 when we were in Kenya. An Indian driver, whose route was into Zaire, died of unknown causes in a Mombasa hospital. The disease was supposedly contracted in eastern Zaire, but we had also read of it in southern Sudan. We aren't saying there's no such thing as a "green monkey," but we haven't seen one. The incidence of AIDS in Uganda, reportedly (*New African*, no. 226, July 1986, pages 30–31), is reaching the same level as AIDS in New York and San Francisco (80 to 90 people per 100,000 in the latter, 100 to every 100,000 in Uganda, Zaire, Zambia, Rwanda, Burundi, and Tanzania). Seldom do Africans engage in homosexual activity and beyond question the spread of the disease in Africa is through heterosexuals. In Uganda AIDS is called "slim," meaning the disease that makes the patient lose weight.

Venereal diseases, generally, are very high in Africa. A hundred years ago the kabaka of Uganda, Mutesa I, died of syphilis. General Idi Amin Dada contracted syphilis during training as a young man in Israel, according to some of his biographers, and we were told by an expatriate nurse, who was a longtime member of a hospital staff in Uganda, that he had undergone treatment for chronic syphilis. Some of his actions during the time he ruled Uganda would appear to be a direct result of this affliction.

Engaging in sexual activity throughout the world seems to be becoming more charged with danger than ever before. Whether AIDS can be contracted apart from sexual contact remains controversial. French testing recently showed that the virus could live even though it had been dried over a period of weeks. Whatever, it would seem to us that risks are no higher in Africa than anywhere else.

In August 1986 Middlesex Hospital in London demonstrated in a study conducted on 225 British homosexuals that there is a possible correlation between AIDS and persons carrying the parasite entamoeba histolytica.

Some people to whom we have spoken, who have not seen a case of amebic dysentery, have a rather cavalier attitude about our cautions to eat only at the Hilton in Cairo and, if away from that hotel, to eat picnic foods purchased from local grocers. They seem to confuse amebic dysentery with other less dangerous types of dysentery, and seem to feel we exaggerate. The little parasite now appears to be more dangerous than we thought, and we cannot stress too strongly that readers should exercise great caution when traveling along the Nile.

The rumor that AIDS is carried in Africa by insects is totally without foundation. An American study conducted in conjunction with the government of Zaire in 1986 demonstrated that although living in cramped, unhygienic conditions, the families of AIDS victims did not contract the disease unless they were sexual partners. If insects carried AIDS, everyone in Africa would have it, including us, and any other returning expatriate. This simply is not the case and the rumor should be laid to rest.

The relatively high incidence of AIDS in Uganda is attributable to the large numbers of men who have been soldiers in one army or another during the past

15 years. These men have been living totally disrupted lives, away from their villages and the social constraints of village life; they have engaged in sex *ad libitum*. In doing so they have spread the disease.

Serendipity versus Coincidence

"**serendipity**—the faculty of finding valuable or agreeable things not sought for"

"**coincidence**—to occupy the same place in space or time; to occupy exactly corresponding or equivalent positions on a scale or in a series; to correspond in nature, character, or to be in accord or agreement."

Webster's Seventh New Collegiate Dictionary

There is, then, a difference between coincidental and serendipitous events; a subtle difference that dictionary definitions do not quite make clear when experienced in the African context.

Serendipitous always means something good. And serendipitous things are always happening in Africa. Maybe it's no more than a thought or a wish that's so ridiculous you don't even want to mention it. Out of the blue, a few days later—two weeks at the most—that thought or wish is mated to a serendipitous occurrence.

This is not to say deliberate wishing will come true. It's nothing like that. Serendipitous events are not something you can program. It's as though there's a psyche somewhere in the vicinity that becomes aware of your psyche and, with a fickleness understandable only to itself, selects certain of your thoughts or wishes and causes them to materialize.

Nor has serendipity anything to do with mysticism or the occult. Being scientifically inclined, we reject belief in such things.

We tell you about serendipitous happenings in Africa so that after you start putting things down to coincidence and then find coincidence isn't quite the right word to describe what has happened, you'll have a word to use to express yourself.

Handling Unpleasant Incidents

Everyone, of necessity, must pass through various forms of officialdom when traveling in Africa. At the minimum there will be the airport officials who process immigration, customs, and public health documents. In countries led by former military officers there may be countless roadblocks where passports must be shown.

Many times officials serving the tourist industry are civil servants as their facilities are government-owned. It is highly unlikely that an official serving in the tourist industry will take a stand opposing that of a more formal, easily recognizable government official. Nor is running to a policeman for help, in all but accident cases or for directions, going to solve a problem with a tour guide, hotel manager, or airport official. The policeman will either remain neutral or take the side of your opponent.

Asking to see your adversary's supervisor is not really practical unless one is familiar with the personalities involved. The higher authority may very well be the father of the official about whom you are complaining. (At minimum he will be a second cousin.)

What all this means is that you are going to have to rely solely on your own finesse to extract yourself from unpleasant incidents should they arise. We offer a few tips:

1. Remember you are approaching the situation with certain preconceived ideas. The African(s) are relating to you with certain preconceived ideas. Neither of you know what those ideas are; therein lies the major obstacle to relating to one another when a problem arises.

2. Much of Africa has a sensationalist press. A news item that appears in a daily paper on the day your problem occurs can alter the African official's perception of that problem. If a headline that day read "American Sailor Kills Mombasa Girl" (which it did on one occasion), you can bet your bottom dollar Americans in that Kenyan port town are not going to be too popular that day. If, on the other hand, the headline read "U.S. Provides $1 million in Aid," and you happen to be American, a potential crisis may be smoothed over without incident.

3. The golden rule when a problem arises with an African official is that good manners always pay off. Doing absolutely nothing is always better than doing something that may offend. No matter how exasperating the situation, never raise your voice. Speaking softly is a sign of respect in Africa; the more softly one speaks the more respect one shows. The very act of raising the voice is an automatic signal of disrespect. No matter how hurried you are, move slowly and with deliberation. Think before you allow yourself to show agitation. Acting gruffly will only aggravate the situation. Deliberately wind yourself down to a dead-slow pace and pattern of speech.

4. Make the official with whom you've encountered a problem feel that he or she is important, a "big man." Address the official as "sir" or "madam." Genuinely compliment them on their country, on the kindness you've received, the beautiful weather, etc. In other words, be the total diplomat.

5. Self-effacing humor is the best weapon; making a joke of your lack of understanding, even adopting (regardless of your sex), a helpless attitude and looking wide-eyed at the official is a valid tactic that works.

The above is certainly much easier to write than to practice. I personally have a short fuse and it has proven to be dangerous at times. After realizing what I've gotten us into, I've successfully (to date) extracted us from a bad situation by getting myself under control and doing absolutely nothing. The onus is then on the official to take action. He/she will either suggest a solution, offer a compromise, or haul you off to jail. Seldom does the latter happen if he/she is given a face-saving way out.

We have never offered a bribe or paid a bribe, but then we avoid those countries where bribery is a way of life—namely, West Africa and Zaire. An old hand told us that in those areas he places a few bills (notes) in among the clothes in his suitcase in an obvious but concealed place. He then suggests that the official look through the case and if a bribe is in order, the official takes the money. In this way offering a bribe is avoided. Such an offer can lead to trouble if a bribe is not the root of the problem.

Airport and Border Departures

All of the countries we discuss have restrictions on taking their currency in and out of their countries. At departure time this can prompt an official to ask to "see your money." Show him *only* the currency of his country. Do not show him your dollars, pounds, francs, etc. How much you have of those is your business, but he may attempt to make it his business and relieve you of some or all of it. If he persists and insists on seeing your "hard currency," as freely exchanged money is called (and over which there are no controls), stall by saying that you spent everything in his country because it has so many things to buy, or that you have only traveler's checks left. He's not going to ask you to stand there in front of everyone and sign your traveler's checks over to him. He may take the local currency you have, which should be less than the equivalent of US$5 if you've planned things right. We refuse to given even that small amount, but you may find it expeditious to do so. Officially, despite the regulations about exporting local currencies there is nothing against taking "souvenir" money out of the country if it is less than US$5.

There should, however, be a bank in the airport prepared to convert your excess local money back to hard currencies. You are asked to show your Currency Declaration form, which itemizes the amount of hard currency you brought into the country. (*x* number of $100 dollar bills, *x* number British pound notes, *x* number francs, etc.). Provided that you do not request to take out more than the total you brought into the country, the conversion will be made. However, it is recognized that you will have spent some money in the country, and so the amount requested to be converted back to hard currency should always be proportionate to the number of days you've spent in the country. Otherwise, it will be suspected that you've been changing money on the black market. The exception to this is winnings at the casinos. It may be that lady luck is on your side, and that after an evening gambling in one of the licensed casinos (say, in Nairobi) that you've won a lot of money. This has definitely been known to happen. You then request from the casino management an official document that states your winnings. This is shown at the time of departure to the airport bank clerk and the conversion will be unhesitatingly given.

Malawi is the exception to this: It is impossible, in our experience, to have excess Malawian kwatcha converted to hard currencies. If the situation does arise, they will transfer the money to your bank through the Bank of Malawi. This takes some weeks and arrangements must be made before you leave Malawi. The rule in Malawi is to exchange only what you think you'll spend. This presents difficulties because, once into the rural areas, it is difficult to have foreign money changed. (It is even sometimes difficult to get smaller denomination kwatcha.)

Also at departure times, customs officers may suggest they will not search or inspect your baggage if you give them something. We never have an objection to our baggage being searched, and smile and suggest that we open the bags for them. As the plane is waiting and there's generally a long line behind you, it is rare that he will continue with his blackmailing tactic. We have listed in detail the items that can and cannot be taken in and out of the various African countries we discuss in the Basic Information Checklist, so none of our readers should find themselves in awkward positions that will lay them open to blackmail.

Game Parks

   Kenyan Ministry of Wildlife game scouts are available at every game park and will accompany visitors through the parks for a small charge. A self-drive car does not mean that you cannot have the services of a professional guide. In fact, the tour guides get their information about where the game are on any particular day from the game scouts. There are always plenty of scouts available.

   There is a charge to be paid when entering a game park—a charge for the car and each occupant. The prices are always clearly signposted at park gates.

   Dogs, cats, etc., are not allowed in the parks; neither are motorcyclists and bicyclists. Due to the danger from wild animals, walking in the parks is not permitted; travel must be done via a closed vehicle.

Languages of Africa

   There is a popular misconception that Swahili is the language spoken throughout the African continent. In fact, Swahili is spoken primarily in Kenya and Tanzania and to a lesser degree as far west as eastern Zaire. Lingala is the language spoken by people living on the banks of the River Zaire. Bantu roots form the basis for some African languages but by no means all. There are several hundred distinct African languages that make their speakers unintelligible to one another. For this reason at independence most African countries adopted the language of their former colonizer as their national language. A few countries have changed their policy and adopted a major African language, making the European language a second language. However, in today's technological world this places such countries at an economic disadvantage. Inevitably foreign words must be incorporated into the African language, adulterating the purity of that language.

Interacting with Africans

Almost without exception, everyone wants to be liked—to be thought well of. From infancy our personalities develop toward finding acceptance among our peers. It's generally true to say that the nicer our character, the more we are anxious to please. This instinct is in part molded by our individual cultures and the norm of the societies into which we have been born or have chosen to live. All this is a preamble to an understanding of interaction with many African peoples.

1. It should be sympathetically understood that a negative attitude is at the opposite end of respect.

2. African societies place a high regard on showing respect to others.

3. Respect is acknowledged by agreeing with others. Therefore, Africans many times will give an affirmative reply to a question or an invitation although they know full well there is no possibility of their being able/capable of upholding that affirmation.

"Will you come to my home for tea at 4 p.m. on Saturday?" To most Africans the answer must be yes, although they know that they must be at home, at work, in another city on Saturday. "Will you get the tickets and bring them to my hotel?" Again, a promise will be made despite the fact that the African may not understand what tickets, which hotel.

Westerners accustomed to people "keeping their promises" can find interacting with the majority of Africans infuriating. Judging Africans by their own mores, they may believe most Africans to be liars, undependable, etc.

To overcome the impasse, try to word your conversation in such a way that you avoid a yes or no reply. "What are you doing Saturday afternoon? Are you going to the football game on Saturday?" Question by beating around the bush until you have ascertained if it would be feasible to meet at 4 p.m. on Saturday.

If an African does let you down, know that he or she is simply totally unable to say no or deny a request and still show you the respect he or she feels you deserve.

Camera and Film Care

Extra care must be taken of exposed and unexposed film. The film and the camera must be protected from not only heat but dust and sand when in rural areas and from high humidities in truly tropical areas and lake shores. For those on beach vacations, there are the usual cautions about salt air.

We suggest the more expensive, larger size of anti-X-ray carrying pouches, and then putting this into a vinyl, shockproof bag manufactured only—that we know of—by Voyageur's (P.O. Box 409, Gardner, KS 66030). Aluminum and black-fitted cases will soak up the heat and are not absolutely airtight. Voyageur also sells a very light but durable aluminum blanket. Wrap the Voyageur air-tight, moisture-proof vinyl bag, with the camera inside, in the aluminum blanket. The insulating properties of the blanket will keep the camera and film cool if the packing was done in a cool room and if during the journey it is kept in the shade. Conversely, if the camera is wrapped in the insulating Voyageur bag and wrapped in the blanket in the heat, it will keep hot.

When traveling allow air, despite the fact it may be warm air, to flow around the bundle. Don't pack other things over or near it.

When the camera is needed to take pictures, find the coolest place to keep it between shots. We find this to be, strangely enough, in Japanese-made rental cars, the open glove compartment. Carried on our lap we throw a khanga (an African sarong—see "Shopper's Safari: Kenya") over it to shade it from the sun coming through the car windows.

Overheated film makes for yellow pictures, and worse yet, heat can melt the gel coating and ruin the film. Leave any film not absolutely necessary in the hotel. Carry only what is intended to be used that day, as described above, for best results.

Bring extra batteries for your camera. It is all lies that under African conditions a one-year battery will hold up. Change the battery at least once a month and always start out with a new one.

The Case for African Polygamy

Several years ago I reviewed *Polygamy Reconsidered: African Plural Marriage and the Christian Churches* by Eugene Hillman, C.S. SP. (Orbis Books: Maryknoll, NY, 1975) for the University of Denver's School of Race Relations' "Africa Today." In an effort to stimulate interest on the part of our readers to do as Father Hillman asks—to reconsider the case for African polygamy as a legitimate social practice—we reproduce that review here.

Eugene Hillman, C.S. SP., assumes the role of the mother who agrees her daughter may go swimming but cautions her, "don't go near the water" as he concludes *Polygamy Reconsidered*. Having made, through scholarly research, perceptive analysis and first-hand observation, the case for African polygamy, he suggests further study into the advisability of accepting polygamists into the Catholic Church, "along the lines already tested by the Lutheran Church in Liberia. Persons who have previously entered polygamous marriages, in good faith, and according to the socially accepted practice of their time and place in history, should not be prevented from participating in the sacramental life of the Church. As part of their normal instruction in the faith however, it should be made clear to them that no additional polygamous marriages are permissible once they have entered the Christian community through baptism."

Beyond question, Hillman realizes the limit to which he can, with profit, make his case to the hierarchy of the Church, but having embarked on the task, one would feel happier had he grasped the nettle firmly and rejected such a compromise, however handy and convenient. Apart from the turmoil such teaching would create within the children and within the family, when would such teaching be contradicted by the truths Hillman puts before us?

1. Monogamy was a pagan Greco-Roman practice which the apostles (who were members of a polygamist-tolerant society) accepted in order to spread the gospel along the Mediterranean basin.

2. Jesus at no time spoke against polygamy.

3. The Western view of polygamy is ethnocentric to the point of irrationality.

4. Polygamy does not bar equality for women: "Have women always been treated as equals, and not as inferiors, in monogamous societies? Is it always and only among polygamists that women are degraded and children neglected?"

5. The concomitants of legal monogamy historically have been concubinage, prostitution, and divorce.

6. The practice of polygamy does not produce more children than monogamy; a woman can have only so many children. In the polygamous marriage the husband usually does not sleep with a wife while she is nursing a child—usually two years. A child is born every three years as a general rule—not every year as in the case of some monogamous marriages.

7. Did Christ mean a man should abandon the mother of his children if he is to receive the sacraments?

Hillman does not explain why he continues to champion monogamy and it is here he makes himself vulnerable to those who would attack him. More's the pity.

Successfully he repudiates the concept that polygamy is based on insatiable lust but he is a trifle naive in supporting the patriarchal image of the polygamous husband—in this polygamist's wives have hoodwinked him as well as their husband—for polygamous societies tend to be woman-dominated in decision-making; wives gang up on the husband; they are not divided, hapless daughters—not possessive clinging vines as some "My Man" Western women.

Hillman is at his best when he illustrates the ethnocentricity of Western thought, (which is better—simultaneous polygamy or consecutive (divorcing) polygamy?) and in pointing-up the male chauvinism of some revered theologians (including saints). However, he is on sticky ground when he argues acceptance of polygamy because of pre-Christian cultural practice.

Hillman has said with courage many things which have needed saying. Practical application of Catholicism in Africa by African priests is apt to overtake any Vatican-directed studies the books' publication may instigate. For, if Hillman and expatriate clergy have been reluctant to take hold of the nettle, their African colleagues cannot do likewise if the Catholic church is to survive on that continent. There is no possibility Africans can totally adopt the nuclear family system. In the absence of spectacular industrial growth, as the West continues to fail Africa, as the beautiful bubble of nationalism bursts, African peoples, and no less the African church, must find African solutions to African problems. If the name of the game is survival, the institution of polygamy and the extended family, upon examination, will have been found to have served Africans well. Africans will realize this, even if the Vatican doesn't.

Apart from polygamy in Africa, I personally find it of intellectual interest to speculate on how the Supreme Court of the United States may rule in coming years when the topic is challenged by, say, a Moslem American citizen. Of course, the Mormons challenged the American concept that only monogamy was acceptable to American society in the last century and lost. The fact that the Supreme Court has consistently allowed state governments to enact laws that they believe to be harmful to the community notwithstanding that such legislation is in contradiction to the First Amendment of the Constitution: "Congress shall make no law respecting an establishment of religion, or prohibiting the free exercise thereof," etc., does not mean they will continue to do so. The present judges on the Supreme Court are conservative constitutionalists. The 1986 ruling on homosexuality stated that there was no constitutional impediment to states' legislating against the practice; the court did not rule on the subject of homosexuality per se. Homosexuality is not a recognized religious practice—polygamy is and has centuries of history to prove its acceptance as a valid social practice. Can the Supreme Court, ruling as conservative constitutionalists, logically determine that polygamy is harmful to the community and divorce is not?

Architecture and African Nationalism

Africa has presented unique challenges to international architects since the 1960s as former European colonies became independent nations. Unlike North and South America where new nations were created by the invaders and the resulting architecture patterned on remembrances of Europe, African land was returned to the indigenous peoples.

Pre-colonial African Architecture

Much of traditional African construction is designed as temporary shelter. Impermanent structures served Africans well. There is no need to describe the advantages of portable housing for the nomad. For the settled agriculturalists the nonpermanent structure meshed with social and political practices as well as the climate. Africans, like Californians, spend much of their time outdoors because the climate is perfect. It was an accepted social practice among most societies to burn a house in which a person had died. Politically, a king routinely moved his court to maintain control over all of his kingdom, or, as Hamo Sasson suggests in the information we have quoted in *The White Nile* itinerary, "One of the reasons for the frequent changes of capitals must have been the need for firewood." The fact that traditional construction was not intended to be permanent does not imply that it was necessarily crude. In the case of the Kabakas of Uganda, the structures were exemplary in their height and number of labor-hours needed to construct them. The roof of ordinary people's homes in the Tororo district along the Kenya-Uganda border are delicate and reminiscent of pagoda roofs albeit made from reed.

Throughout Africa unbaked earth was used in the construction of buildings for every purpose. However, the unbaked earth structures found in countries bordering the Sahara Desert are the more sophisticated and aesthetically pleasing. These buildings can rise up to 40–50 meters high. While unbaked earth construction may be considered impermanent by some standards, the fact remains that such buildings have stood over centuries. It is true that the exteriors have to be touched up each year, but this is true of all but concrete and stone constructions.

Down to Earth: Adobe Architecture—An Old Idea, A New Future is a well-illustrated book based on an exhibition at the Centre Georges Pompidou in Paris, conceived and directed by Jean Dethier, published by Facts on File, Inc. (460 Park Ave. South, NY 10016). It makes the case for unbaked earth construction as used in England—the traditional country cottage with thatch roof—and France, as well as in Africa and Saudi Arabia. The myriad forms and shapes possible are graphically depicted, but what the book cannot convey is the comfort and happy marriage these buildings maintain with the climate—in the tropics or temperate zone, in summer or in winter. The author also stresses the energy conservation possible in the building of the structures, which do not rely on imported materials, and in their maintenance. He makes the point that one third of the world's population live in unbaked earth homes. By including photographs of luxury adobe buildings in contemporary New Mexico immediately next to traditional, centuries-old African buildings, the on-going validity of African traditional architecture is proven.

Colonial Architecture

Prior to the 1960s European colonizers constructed utilitarian buildings for their civil servants' homes and offices. In former British colonies, from Singapore to Accra, the single-story bungalow with wide covered veranda was adapted, country by country. Charles Allen, editor of *Plain Tales from the Raj,* recounts that when British wives moved from one part of India to another, they knew the floor plan would be exactly as the one they were leaving. The British were not unimaginative because they believed theirs to be a temporary condition; quite the contrary, the Empire colonizers believed they and their children would remain for generations to come in the colonies. Apparently, sticking to a style of architecture that worked was simply a total lack of imagination on the part of Colonial Office engineers and architects.

Office buildings, both in British and French Africa, especially those designed for use by their proconsuls, were designed to be more impressive, but the long verandas and clinical lines contributed little of artistic merit.

Private construction during the colonial period was slightly more adventurous, and Kenya's White Highlands has settler housing built from local stone in architectural styles duplicating that of Gloucestershire and Sussex. Only colonial hotels, and then only a very few, commissioned architects to blend European amenities with local cultures. One of the best examples of this is the newly restored Castle Hotel, Mombasa, Kenya, circa 1910, where Swahili arches form the facade, and high English ceilings and hardwood floors form the interior.

Post-independence Architecture

In some African countries the colonizers erected national buildings, which were later used by African leaders, but in most cases the new leadership chose to establish debating chambers and presidential residences to their own design.

African impermanent architecture provides a strong embroynic resource that architects, had they been free from the pressures of designing solely for nationalistic symbolism, could have called upon for inspiration in designing African national buildings. At independence African leaders did not choose to instruct architects to draw on these resources. In all probability, it is doubtful that such a thought would have entered their considerations. Architects were directed to

The concrete and glass Hilton International in Nairobi, Kenya; one of the first major buildings constructed after Kenya's independence.

produce Western cities but to deny resemblances to the colonizer's influence on the new nation. No Roman columns, not because they are Italian, but because Trafalgar Square is full of them. No domes, not because they are Greek, but because Thomas Jefferson had already nabbed them as a symbol for the United States, and St. Paul's and the Vatican also have domes. No Gothic spires, because they are reminiscent of Paris. No rococo, no gargoyles, or flying buttresses to remind one of Europe's past dominance. Instead, what has been alluded to as "international architectural style," or more aptly "speculator architecture," was employed. Bigger was always better; taller asserted dominance and luxury. (There certainly was and is, plenty of land—to build upward is pure luxury in Africa.) Slabs of concrete went up with straight, sharp lines, devoid of adornment, accompanied sometimes by shiny chrome trim and sparkling plate glass, and sometimes made bearable by a bas relief concrete mural of a stylized African design. The emphasis was always on concrete, as if that material was either totally culturally neutral or indigeniously African.

All great nations have great buildings; buildings, to African eyes, are indispensable to nationhood. Impressive buildings were an absolute necessity to consolidate the leaders' legitimacy and impress the populace. That Western development planners did not always agree to the necessity of a Hilton accompanying a debating chamber and taking priority over a network of rural clinics became the topic of jokes among foreigners as towers rose beside shanties.

Some pretty trashy stuff went up on virgin African lands between 1960 and

1980 as money and power plays were realigned using architectural chess pieces. But to fail to understand the role the architect has had on African nationalism is to fail to understand the social and political pressures, both external and internal, at work on African leadership.

Future Architecture in Africa

Twenty years down the road the spurt of energy, and more significantly, money to finance architectural innovation in Africa has been drained. The capital city buildings are in place, except when a leader such as Hastings Banda of Malawi decides to move a capital city and start again. There is still the magnetism of being an Organization of African Unity (OAU) convention city and until each of Africa's 51 countries has had a turn, peer group pressure will divert resources to the building of conference halls and luxury accommodation for OAU delegates. Then, too, there is always the dream of an African city becoming the venue for the Olympic games.

For the most part, in the latter half of the 1980s new construction is in the hands of the private commercial sector. This usually means hoteliers.

Hotel construction since 1960 has been for several purposes; initially, to accommodate donor aid representatives and business travelers, later for tourist accommodation. It is the hotels constructed for the latter purpose that are show-

The huge concrete and glass Kenyatta International Conference Centre in Nairobi, Kenya built as a venue for an Organization of African Unity Conference.

ing the most promising designs and may be the forerunner of a genuine African modern architecture based on traditional design. Outstanding examples are Jadini Beach Hotel and Two Fishes Hotel on Kenya's Indian Ocean south coast, and the Relais Kanaga, Mopti, Mali. Unfortunately, the interiors of these hotels do not carry through their exteriors' aesthestic promise, and the actual rooms are not creatively decorated and are merely boxes. But let's be thankful for small departures from the norm and hope that, as a middle class develops in Africa, as much by circumstance and necessity as by conscious forethought there will be a call on the beautiful lines offered by African traditional architecture.

As for the question of who gets the commissions, up until now they have been given to international architects, not African architects. The devastation that has caused a need for new buildings in Kampala, Uganda, and the strong College of Art at Makerere University in that city may provide the opportunity young African architects have been waiting for. Let us hope they will have sufficient confidence in their own genius to turn the new city of Kampala into something other than a concrete jungle.

Suggested reading: *African Traditional Architecture: An Historical and Geographical Perspective* by Susan Denyer (Africana Publishing Company, NY) and the previously mentioned title, *Down to Earth*.

The Application of Western Educational Psychology in African Schools

For those not in the teaching profession, let me provide a very brief, thumbnail sketch of today's Western educational psychology.

A child's physical development from infancy is presumed to follow a certain pattern, which has been observed by researchers over time among a sufficient number of children to provide a norm. A child's mental development is the subject of study and sequences of learning or readiness to learn increasingly difficult material. Curriculum and teaching methods are designed on this information. Using such guidelines the child moves from kindergarten to high school. The child's ability to move with the norm, tested by examination, becomes report card information.

Until recently the norms were established on a relatively small number of child subjects. For instance, the internationally acclaimed educational psychologist Piaget studied his own children and produced his widely accepted theories on physical and mental development. His theories have been tested against large numbers of children in the Western world and proven to have sufficient validity to the satisfaction of educators, if not parents. The criteria he and other specialists in educational psychology define are used as the base in educating the masses. It has been assumed that the sequences of attaining certain functions, both mental and physical, are invariable and hold universal truth.

The observations on children, which established measurement criteria, have, to my knowledge, been made using White children as subjects. (There are isolated studies where a classroom has been composed of both Black and White children, but no attempt was made to racially measure the observations.) The mental development of the Black child has never been scientifically observed in isolation from White children over a projected period of time. The assumption has been that all children develop the same way. The reluctance to initiate studies is based in part on that assumption and in part on unscientific studies done by White racist researchers in the past. Liberal educational psychologists disassociate themselves from such research and use the panacea "all people are the same" or "everyone is equal." This inhibits serious research. Ironically, it has been proven beyond controversy by scores of responsible human development researchers that African babies are born and remain more advanced than White babies for the first two years of their life. The reason why remains, at this stage of our knowledge, unknown. A few African educational psychologists have started to examine the mental development of African children. As they have the marvelous advantage of understanding local languages and cultures as well as having been educated in Western educational psychology theories, this avenue of research is the most promising. Unfortunately, such researchers obtain little funding for their work.

The one common denominator in American, British, and African educational systems is that they pattern their curricula on the findings of research done on White children. This may be very unfair to the African students. Black children in the U.S., Britain, Canada, and Africa successfully graduate from schools in those countries. However, many do not. It is my contention that those who do are adept at rote learning or force themselves to conform to the superimposed pattern to learning. In doing so, I believe, their creativity is stifled. The free thinkers that Black societies so desperately need do not, in the majority, make it to graduation.

The replies to "What Will Uganda Be Like in the Year 2000?" could not have been, in my opinion, as creatively and farsightedly answered by students enrolled in the schools of any other African country where expatriate teachers and Western educational psychology is applied. Ugandan education has been without expatriate teachers and dependent upon untrained African teachers for the past 10 years. Ugandan parents consider this to be a tragedy. I consider it to be a blessing in disguise. The students educated comparatively free from the imposition of White educational psychology standards appear to be far more mature than their counterparts in other countries.

Research needs to be conducted on the Black child in isolation from White children if the Black race is to be allowed to develop to its potential without constantly being hamstrung by White constraints.

African Agriculture and African Health

We in the industrialized nations have become so specialized in our own disciplines we sometimes are blinded and do not see the whole picture; in this context I have reference to the obvious relationship between farmer health and agricultural productivity.

In 1980 when Leah and I returned to Uganda the Catholic Cardinal of Uganda asked that we go to the former U.S. Agency for International Development ranching project in central Uganda and report to him our recommendations for revitalizing the ranch after the years of neglect suffered under the rule of Idi Amin. (Early in his administration his soldiers had slaughtered the breeding cows to provide beef for the army.) In 1980 the Cardinal had received donations of cattle from parishioners throughout the diocese and was attempting to reestablish the ranch as a cooperative venture.

Readers will not be interested in a livestock report; suffice to say that at the end of the three weeks, our recommendations were to immunize the cattle against the standard tropical diseases, change the personnel herding the cattle, and request technical assistance from overseas to teach recordkeeping.

The cattle without exception suffered from TB, brucellosis (*Brucella melitensis* and *Brucella abortus*—known in Britain as Bang's disease), Trypanosomiasis (tsetse fly fever), and worms. They were being dipped, when the insecticide was available, for tick fever.

Nomadic tribesmen were employed to tend the cattle and they worked on a schedule of two days sleep and one day work. Nomadic peoples traditionally drink the milk of their cattle as their main source of nourishment and deny milk to calves, which are only allowed to suckle after the cows have been milked. They are not the best people to put in charge of a commercial herd of beef cattle. Needless to say, we recommended getting rid of the nomads as protectors of the herd as the few calves there were grossly undersized.

Technical assistance from overseas could have established a recording system to ascertain which cows were producing, which were barren and the latter culled, and calf records and weights could be maintained. Such records would also have placed a check on "accidents" and resulting deaths of cows due to "broken legs." Meat from broken-legged cows found a ready cash market in the nearby village.

We lived on the ranch during our three-week study and every morning milk was brought to us for our use. We were assured that it had been boiled. After leaving the ranch, back in Jinja, we came down with undulant fever, the human form of brucellosis.

It is remarkable how expert one becomes about a disease when one's own body serves as its host. Leah and I became experts on brucellosis: back pain, insomnia, low-grade fever, tremendous lethargy, lack of stamina, continual tiredness, coupled with the invariable secondary disease always present in the tropics, malaria.

Heavy doses of tetrycacline taken religiously every 6 hours over a period of three weeks can arrest the disease, but such drugs are rarely available in African rural areas and certainly the nursing care necessary to ensure that the drug is taken as prescribed is not available. Even with treatment, the disease often leaves the sufferer with an inability to engage in prolonged activity.

We realized the herdsmen, children, women, everyone who drank the supposedly boiled milk, probably suffered from TB, undulant fever, and, of course, malaria. When we reconstructed our observations about the milk having been boiled, Leah recalled seeing the woman who was boiling it pour cold milk into the boiling cauldron so that the milk would not overflow and put out her charcoal fire. She had not returned the milk to the rolling boil.

Any recommendations I might naively give on livestock management could not be implemented because the people were so chronically ill.

In recent years donor aid nations have provided grants and assistance primarily to subsistence farmers to increase their production, but unless such assistance is given with intense medical care, the situation will not markedly improve. In addressing the problem of African agricultural productivity, the farmer's health must be addressed concurrently with farmer education. This is simply not possible because of the shortage of qualified staff and money.

The number of professional agriculturalists and public health workers willing to go to Africa and work at the grass-roots level is exceedingly small. The prospect of recruiting them is even slimmer when the salaries offered are uncompetitive with the private sector in their home countries. The religious denominations have, up until now, supplied the largest contingents of expatriate personnel. Peace Corps and other voluntary agencies recognize the need and try to meet it, but they have difficulty in attracting experienced working farmers to work in Africa and are always chronically short of medical personnel.

Even when qualified people are induced to give their services, impediments are many times placed in their way by local African politicians who resist changing the status quo. Handling and overcoming bureaucrats is a full-time job. The problem is too complex for amateurs.

Both Leah and I have come to believe that African agricultural productivity can only be significantly raised by the introduction of vertically integrated corporation farming. Workers would work a 40-hour week and their health would be maintained by a company health clinic. Qualified technical staff can be found in agribusiness, and corporate negotiators have enough clout to handle the political and bureaucratic impediments. In the African tea industry corporate agribusiness works. However, the American rubber companies in Liberia have created many problems; when we watch the pictures on American television of corporate-run banana plantations in the Philippines we realize that weak Third World governments cannot control corporate abuses. It would have to be a very special kind of corporation that could tackle—in fairness to the worker and shareholder alike—agribusiness in Africa. The good, reputable corporations earn high enough profits without venturing into high-risk enterprises.

And risk is something Africa has in abundance. Three weeks after we left the ranch, before I could finish typing my recommendations, the new president's (Obote) soldiers came to the cardinal's ranch, burned down the buildings, and took away the cattle to slaughter. We can only hope the soldiers became chronically infected with TB, brucellosis, and malaria.

Former Names of African Colonial Territories

Present name	Colonial name or region and colonizer
Algeria	Algeria—French
Angola	Angola—Portuguese
Benin (earlier Dahomey)	Part of French West Africa
Botswana	Bechuanaland—British

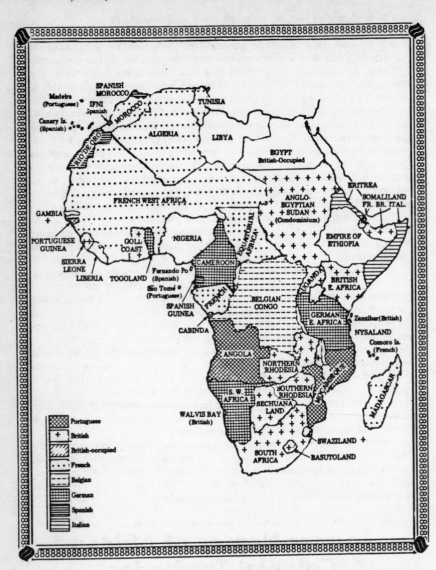

Present name	Colonial name or region and colonizer
Burkina Faso (earlier Upper Volta)	Part of French West Africa
Burundi	Ruanda-Urundi—German up until WWI, then Belgian.
Cameroun	German up to 1914, then divided between British and French in 1919, which became mandates in 1922. In 1946 became UN trust territories. The French portion

Present name	Colonial name or region and colonizer
	became independent in 1960, joining with the southern portion of the British sector to become, as it now is, the United Republic of Cameroon. The northern portion of the British-administered territory voted to become part of Nigeria. Also on old maps shown using the German spelling *Kamerun*.
Canary Islands	Canary Islands—Spain
Central African Republic	Part of French Equatorial Africa—Ubangi-Shari
Chad, Tchad	Part of French Equatorial Africa—Tchad
Comoro Islands	Anjouann—Comprises four islands. Anjouann is often mentioned in explorers' diaries concerning men from the islands used as porters—French
Congo-Brazzaville	Boundaries are slightly different today than during colonial times. A corridor connecting French Equatorial Africa known as the Middle Congo.
Djibouti	French Somaliland, Afars and Issas
Egypt	The former Egyptian boundary extended into Libya—British
Equatorial Guinea	Spanish Guinea, Fernando Poo. The present country includes the mainland territory of Rio Muni, and the island of Fernando Poo and Annobon—Spain
Eretria	Italian East Africa, which also included Somalia in 1936, prior to that time an Italian colony.
Ethiopia	Independent kingdom. Claimed by Italians in 1889. Coastal region made an Italian colony, Eritrea, in 1890. Recognized as a kingdom in 1906. Italians claimed it as part of Italian East Africa 1936–41.
Gabon	The southern portion of French Equatorial Africa.
The Gambia	Gambia—British
Ghana	Gold Coast—British. Ghana incorporates a portion of what was formerly Togoland.
Guinea	French West Africa
Guinea-Bissau	Portuguese Guinea
Ivory Coast	French West Africa
Kenya	British East Africa Protectorate (not including the coastal 10-mile-wide area from the Tanzanian border to the river Tana, just above Malindi, and the island of Zanzibar). These were the Kenya Protectorate. In 1920 they all became Kenya Colony.
Lesotho	Basutoland—British
Liberia	Liberia. The separate republic of Maryland was incorporated into Liberia in 1857. Under U.S. protection after 1911.
Libya	Italians occupied Libya in 1914.
Malagasy Republic	Madagascar—French
Malawi	Nysaland 1893–1907. British Central African Protectorate until 1891.
Mali	Upper Senegal-Niger until 1920 in French West Africa.
Mauritania	Part of the Roman Empire, which at that time included Morocco. In the European colonial period Mauritania was a part of French West Africa.
Mauritius	Ile de France, Islands of the Mascarene Islands. British from 1814.

Present name	Colonial name or region and colonizer
Morocco	Most of Morocco was held by the French after 1912 with the capital at Rabat; the northern coast was held by Spain with the capital at Tetouan. Tangier became an international city in 1923, administered by an international commission by agreement with France, Spain, and England. Ifni (Sidi Ifni) in the south was held by Spain from 1934 to 1969.
Morocco (disputed territory)	Rio de Oro, Western or Spanish Sahara. From Cape Bojador to Cape Blanc relinquished by Spain in 1975 and divided between Mauritania and Morocco. The former country gave up claim to the territory in 1979 but there is a section of the populace who wish to form a separate state. Held by Morocco along the coast, but the Saharan boundary is unstable.
Mozambique	Portuguese East Africa
Namibia	South West Africa. Formerly German (prior to WWI), mandated to South Africa in 1919. A 1966 UN resolution declared the mandate terminated but South Africa disagreed.
Niger	Part of French West Africa
Nigeria	Colony and Protectorate of Lagos, Oil Rivers Protectorate, Protectorates of Northern and Southern Nigeria in 1899, and Colony of Nigeria in 1914. British.
Reunion	Bourbon, also Bonaparte Island—French
Rwanda	Ruanda-Urundi—German until WWI, then Belgian.
Sao Tombe and Principe	Portuguese
Senegal	Protectorate until 1920, afterward a colony under the French.
Seychelles	Crown colony under the British.
Sierra Leone	British
Somalia	Divided into northern Somaliland, which was under the British with capital at Hargeisa, and southern Somaliland under the Italians. After WWII the British administered Italian Somaliland until 1950, when the UN made it a trust territory administered by the Italians. The present country combines what was British and Italian Somaliland.
South Africa	Dutch then British. After their defeat the Dutch moved inland (1936) and formed the Orange Free State, Federal union in 1910 under the British.
Spanish Sahara	(See Morocco—disputed territory)
Sudan	Anglo-Egyptian Sudan. Administered by the British and Egyptians. Equatoria referred to southern Sudan, whose capital was at Juba.
Tanzania	German East Africa up until the end of WWI. This included what is now Rwanda and Burundi, which were put under Belgian supervision after WWI, and the remaining territory under the British, who changed the name to Tanganyika. Independence in 1962 under that name, but when they took over the island of Zanzibar they changed the name to Tanzania.
Tunisia	French

Present name	Colonial name or region and colonizer
Uganda	British East Africa in some references after WWI meant to include Uganda/Kenya/Tanganyika/Zanzibar, but the more usual is Uganda Protectorate.
Zaire	Congo Free State—Belgian Congo
Zambia	Northern Rhodesia. Federation of Rhodesia and Nyasaland (Zambia/Zimbabwe/Malawi). British.
Zimbabwe	Southern Rhodesia (see preceding entry)

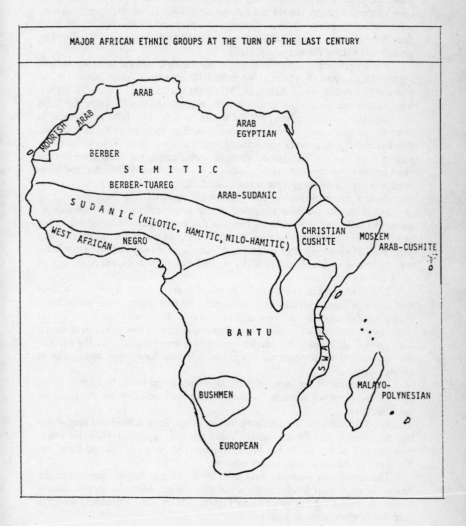

MAJOR AFRICAN ETHNIC GROUPS AT THE TURN OF THE LAST CENTURY

Maps

Our maps are not what we would wish them to be; nor are they what maps must be in order to allow readers to locate all of the places we discuss. The reasons are several: (1) We are citing locations that, in many cases, have never been highlighted as tourist sites. Therefore, there has been no commercial demand for maps of those places. (2) Although Africa is a large continent, it has been charted. Readers should not assume otherwise. However, many maps remain on cartographers' shelves waiting to be prepared for the public. (3) More than these reasons is the fact that a map reduced to the page size of a Fielding guide cannot show the necessary detail.

We are providing some basic maps, but the most helpful thing we believe we can do is to give the name of Rochelle Jaffe, owner of Travel Books Unlimited (4931 Cordell Ave., Bethesda, MD 20814, (USA) tel. 301–951–8533), who studied our manuscript before it went to press and has identified the maps that she believes will be most helpful to our readers. Ms. Jaffe is prepared to offer this service to our overseas readers as well as those from North America. Readers making their hotel reservations with Merikani Hotel Reservations Service can ask that the appropriate maps be sent along at the same time as their hotel reservations are confirmed—Bethesda is a suburb of Washington and Merikani will send a messenger, at no additional charge to readers, to pick up their maps before they mail out the confirmation for the hotel.

In our travels we have identified certain maps and have given this information to Jaffe, but it sometimes happens that better maps are available either in Europe or North America than in Africa and our travel has, at times, been frustrated. We strongly urge readers to obtain the necessary map(s) before leaving, as arrival in the destination city to find that local booksellers are out of stock can ruin the vacation.

Jaffe will reply at her own cost to inquiries from North America; she asks that inquiries from overseas be accompanied by two international postal reply coupons (obtainable at any post office) to cover the cost of her reply via air mail. Her prices are extremely competitive; the service she offers in devoting her personal attention to our readers' requests is immeasurable, as she has had the opportunity to question us where our text may have been ambiguous in giving directions.

As the name of her store implies, Jaffe sells travel books and has in stock most of the titles we mention, including the great books that are the basis for the itineraries.

The first map that is a necessity for our itineraries is a Michelin map showing the *general* area of the safari. There are three pertinent Michelin maps: Number 153 Africa North and West, Number 154 Africa North and East, and Number 155 Africa Central and Southern.

Throughout our guide we have used the spelling or transliteration from the Arabic as shown on Michelin maps for city names. Michelin shows country names of former French colonies in French, and in these instances, we have used the English name as follows:

English spelling we use	Michelin
Algeria	Algerie
Angola	Angola
Botswana	Botswana
Burkina Fasso (formerly Upper Volta)	Haute Volta
Burundi	Burundi
Cameroun	Cameroun
Canary Islands	Islas Canarias
Cape Verde	not shown
Central African Republic	Centrafique
Chad	Tchad
Comoro Islands	Comores
Congo	Congo
Djibouti	Djibouti
Egypt	Egypt
Equatorial Guinea	Guinea Ecuatorial
Ethiopia	Ethiopia
Gabon	Gabon
The Gambia	Gambia
Ghana	Ghana
Guinea	Guinee
Guinea Bissau	Guine Bissau
Ivory Coast	Cote d'Ivoire
Kenya	Kenya
Lesotho	Lesotho
Liberia	Liberia
Libya	Libya
Madagascar	Madagascar
Malawi	Malawi
Mali	Mali
Mauritania	Mauritanie
Mauritius	Mauritius
Morocco	Maroc
Mozambique	Mozambique
Namibia	Namibia
Niger	Niger
Nigeria	Nigeria
Reunion	La Reunion
Rwanda	Rwanda
Senegal	Senegal
Sierra Leone	Sierra Leone
Somalia	Somalia
South Africa	South Africa
Sudan	Sudan
Swaziland	Swaziland
Tanzania	Tanzania
Togo	Togo
Tunisia	Tunisie
Uganda	Uganda
Zaire	Zaire
Zambia	Zambia
Zimbabwe	Zimbabwe

This map drawn in 900 B.C. depicts Africa (Libya) as it was then thought to be.

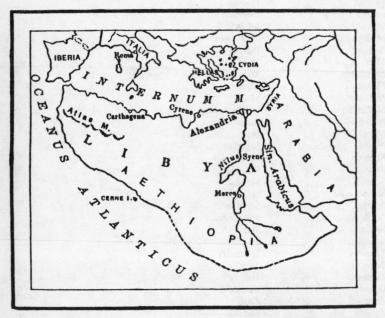

Libya, as Africa was then called, surrounded by oceans, is illustrated on this map circa 200 B.C.

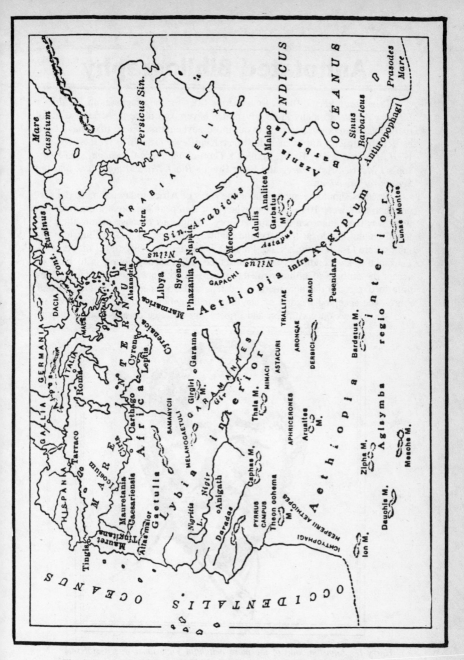

The famous second century A.D. map drawn by Ptolemy, in which Livingstone placed so much trust, shows the waters of the River Nile rising in the Mountains of the Moon (Lunae Montes). Only two small lakes are shown—neither of which could be construed to be Lake Victoria. As the entire scale is wildly inaccurate, Livingstone could allow his imagination full play and in his later years looked for the Source of the Nile in present-day Zambia.

Annotated Bibliography

It has been very difficult to select the titles for the itineraries in *Fielding's Literary Africa;* so many great adventures have taken place in Africa; so many marvelous writers have written about those adventurers. These titles have been especially difficult not to include: Mary Kingsley's *Travels in West Africa* and *West African Studies,* H. M. Stanley's *Through the Dark Continent,* Osa Johnson's *I Married Adventure,* and Peter Brent's *Black Nile: Mungo Park and the Search for the Niger.*

Readers should be aware that some areas of Africa today are more dangerous than they were 100 years ago when first European explorers journeyed into what was then unknown African territory. Dangerous because of unsettled political conditions; local thievery and highway holdups, as in traveling to Marsabit where Osa Johnson's Lake Paradise is located; and any travel that crosses Tanzania where conditions are so unsettled. Most disappointing is to have to accept the attitude of military-ruled, soldier-enforced laws that one must penetrate to overcome the bureaucratic red tape and documentation in Nigeria and Zaire—the accepted method of handling such gentlemen being bribery. Whatever your views on corruption and bribery, the practice permits abuses of per-

Harry H. Johnston, one of the more delightful Victorians, was a statesman, author, botanist, and amateur geographer; the list could go on and on. His British Central Africa, *published in 1897, has been reprinted by the Negro University Press. His biography, is amusing and interesting, and* The Story of My Life, *is in print (published by Arden Libraries).*

sonal rights for local people and visitors alike. Where the law does not work, other forces that do work can lead to dangerous situations from which no amount of pressure by the visitor's embassy can extract the victim. In all our years in Africa we have never offered a bribe. Experienced African hands will say we are naive. That may be so. But neither of us are interested in the hassle and loss of dignity that African officials generate when bribery is a way of life. We avoid those countries where the only way to travel is by bribery. Nor do we believe such a system should be rewarded by a flow of tourist dollars coming into a country that brings such humiliation on their people.

We have sincerely tried to show our readers Africans at their very best and where we feel this is not possible, we have modified our descriptions to indicate that problems can be expected.

We did make strenuous efforts to include the above titles, but at this writing, for the reasons given, we have not traveled the routes. We are prepared, if readers will write us, to provide the travel information we have available, but if they take up the challenge, they do so without our recommendation.

In providing a reading list we have, in some instances, provided the full address of the publisher; we find booksellers today reluctant to special order titles and readers may want to go ahead and order the book directly from the publisher. (See also "Maps," where we mention that Travel Books Unlimited stocks most of the following titles and the books that are the basis for the itineraries.)

For those interested in contemporary African-authored titles, we provide the following:

Things Fall Apart, Chinua Achebe. Astor-Honor, Inc., 48 East 43rd St., NY 100017, 1959.

Cry Sorrow, Cry Joy: Selections from Contemporary African Writers, edited by Jane A. Moore. Friend Press, 1971.

Tell Me Africa: An Approach to African Literature, James Olney. Princeton University Press, 1973.

Poems from East Africa, David Cook and David Rubadiri, editors. Heinemann Ed, 1971.

African History

Africa: History of a Continent, Basil Davidson, original edition published in 1966 by George Weidenfeld and Nicholson Ltd., London. Revised editions, 1972 and fourth impression 1978, by the Hamlyn Publishing Group Ltd., Astronaut House, Feltham, Middlesex, England. A gorgeous, beautifully illustrated (many in color) art book on Africa that can form the basis for the budding Africanist's library. Although the text cannot, because the topic is so broad, treat historical events in depth, it is nonetheless helpful for an overview of Africa's history.

The African Dream, Brian Gardner. Putnam, NY. We feel this to be the very best introduction to Africa.

The River Congo: The Discovery, Exploration & Exploitation of the World's Most Dramatic River, Peter Forbath. Harper & Row, NY. 1977. A work entailing precise research on a topic where resource material is difficult to come by. A classic study yet written in highly readable style. Unlikely to be surpassed for some years to come.

The Student Africanist's Handbook: A Guide to Resources, G. W. Hartwig & W. M. O'Barr. N Halsted Press, div. of John Wiley & Sons, Inc. NY, 1974.

East Africa Through a Thousand Years: AD 1000 to the present day, Gideon S. Were and Derek A. Wilson. Evans Brothers Ltd., Montague House, Russell Square, London, WC1, England. The accepted high school history textbook in Kenya is easy to read and is a good beginning survey of East African history devoid of colonial jargon.

Periodicals Covering Current Events in Africa

New African
IC Publications Ltd.
69 Great Queen St.
London WC2B 5BN, England

(a monthly)
annual subscription:
overseas (from U.K.) U.S.$40; U.K. 20 pounds

Africa Today
School of Race Relations
University of Denver

(a quarterly)
annual subscription: U.S.$30

Azania
British Institute in
  Eastern Africa
P.O. Box 30710
Nairobi, Kenya

Membership in the Institute
includes a subscription
to the journal: U.S.$16
annually

Lost Cities of Africa Itinerary: Meroe (Sudan)

Meroe: A Civilization of the Sudan, P. L. Shinnie. F. A. Praeger, Division of Holt, Rinehart & Winston/CBS, 383 Madison Avenue, NY 10017. 1967. As far as we can determine this is, at this writing, the definitive study on Meroe. Invaluable, and an absolute necessity for readers planning to take the Sudanese portion of the Lost Cities of Africa itinerary.

The Peopling of Ancient-Egypt and the Deciphering of Meroitic Script, proceedings of the symposium held in Cairo Jan. 28–Feb. 3, 1974. 136 pages. Published in 1978 by UNESCO. Copies cost U.S.$9.50 from any UNIPUB office (in U.S. at 10033-F King Highway, Lanham, MD 20706-4391; add U.S.$2.50 to cover postage and handling). Information on this title came from UNESCO too late for us to order and read the publication before our deadline, but in the case of writings on Meroe, with the scarcity of information, everything is welcome.

Greene, David L. *Dentition of Meroitic X-Group, and Christian Populations of Wadi Halfa, Sudan* (Nubian Series No. 1), reprint of 1967 edition (ISBN 0-404-60685-7). AMS Press, Inc., 56 East 13th Street, New York, NY 10003, telephone (212) 777-4700.

Dunham, Dows. *Royal Cemeteries of Kush,* 5 vols. incl. vol. I *El Kurru,* 1950. (ISBN 0-685-72186-8) vol. II *Nuri.* 1955. vol. III *Decorated Chapels of the Meroitic Pyramids at Meroe and Barkal.* Chapman, Suzanne E. 1952 (ISBN 0-87846-041-1). vol. IV *Royal Tombs at Meroe and Barkal.* 1957. (ISBN 0-

87846-043-8). vol. V *The West and South Cemeteries of Meroe.* 1963 (ISBN-0-87846-043-8) (illustrations). Museum of Fine Arts, 465 Huntington Avenue, Boston, MA 02115, telephone (617) 267-9300.

Lost Cities of Africa Itinerary: The Swahili City States: Somalia

"An Archaeological Reconnaissance of the Southern Somali Coast," *Azania,* no. 4, H. N. Chittick, 1969. This is the single most important publication to have in following the *Lost Cities of Africa* itinerary in Somalia. The major sites are covered by Neville Chittick who was, before his death in the summer of 1984, the authority on the area between Kismaio and Mogadiscio. Available in reprint from the British Institute in Eastern Africa (P.O. Box 30710, Nairobi, Kenya). Send the equivalent or U.S.$5 in the form of an international postal money order to cover the cost of the reprint and air mail postage.

"Archaeological Remains on the Southern Somali Coast," *Azania,* no. 18, Hilary Costa Sanseverino, 1983. A companion to the above paper with pictures and drawings, equally important to an appreciation of the itinerary. Also available from the British Institute in Eastern Africa (see above) at the same cost of U.S.$5.

"A Visit to the Banjun Islands," *Journal of the African Studies,* no. 25, J. A. G. Elliot, 1926. One of the early surveys of the Swahili sites south of Kismaio. Available on inter-library loan through your local library.

Lost Cities of Africa Itinerary: The Swahili City States: Kenya and in General

East Africa and the Orient: A Cultural Synthesis in Pre-Colonial Times, H. Neville Chittick and Robert I. Rotberg, editors. Africana Publishing Co., 101 Fifth Ave., NY 10003. One of the most valuable texts for the study of Swahili culture; it is a compilation of papers prepared by specialists on the region under the guidance of Neville Chittick, recognized as one of the foremost authorities on the Kenya-Tanzanian-Somali archaeological ruins.

Swahili Houses and Tombs of the Coast of Kenya, James de Vere Allen and Thomas H. Wilson. Art & Archeology Research Papers, 102 St. Paul's Rd., London, N.1., England. 1979. A study primarily for the architect and researcher interested in the graphic arts of Kenya's Swahili settlements. Beautifully produced in black and white.

Men and Monuments of the East African Coast, by James S. Kirkman. Letterworth Press, Wilmer Bros. & Harm Ltd., Birkenhead, Cheshire, England. This is the reference work used by all Swahili scholars; although much of the information is outdated, it remains an invaluable tool.

Kenya's Coast: An Illustrated guide, Simon Mollison. East African Publishing House, Uniafric House, P.O. Box 30571, Nairobi, Kenya, 1971. Intended originally as a tourist guide to the Kenya coast, the title remains the most useful detailed guide to the coastal area of Kenya and includes the sites of Swahili ruins among the very detailed sectional maps of the shoreline. Information on hotels is out of date; much new construction has taken place and new highways built, but by using a more recently published maps it is possible to find the secondary roads that lead to many of the ruins. Also useful on the sea life found along the beaches.

Al-Inkishafi: Catechism of a Soul, Sayyid Abdalla Bin Ali Bin Nasir with a translation and notes by James de Vere Allen. East African Literature Bureau, P.O. Box 30022, Nairobi, Kenya. 1977. The classic poem rivals *The Rubaiyat.* The text is given first in classic Swahili followed by an English translation. We quote a part of the work in the Swahili portion of the Lost Cities of Africa itinerary.

Swahili Culture: A Bibliography of the History and Peoples of the Swahili Speaking World, Richard Wilding. The Lamu Society, P.O. Box 45916, Nairobi, Kenya. 1976. This title would have been more helpful had it been annotated, nevertheless, it makes a valid contribution to the literature.

Wedding Customs in Lamu, Francoise le Guennec-Coppens. The Lamu Society, P.O. Box 45916, Nairobi, Kenya. 1980. Intended for tourists and well illustrated with line drawings, the booklet is the result of a French graduate student's research conducted while living with a Lamu family. A better appreciation of the wedding exhibits in the Lamu Museum is formed by reading this short study.

A Lamu Cookbook, Fatma Shapi and Katie Halford. The Lamu Society, P.O. Box 45916, Nairobi, Kenya. 1982. A short booklet providing basic Swahili recipes, which will be of interest to readers who enjoy the cooking of the Kenya coast. The recipes are provided using the basic method of preparation but also using commercially prepared products sold by American and European grocers.

Chinese Porcelain in Fort Jesus, the Museums of Kenya. Mombasa, 1975. Available at Fort Jesus or by mail from the Museum Bookshop, P.O. Box 40658, Nairobi, Kenya.

Jumba la Mtwana Guide, the Kenya Museum Society and the Friends of Fort Jesus. Kenya Museum Society, P.O. Box 40658, Nairobi, Kenya. 1981. A detailed guide to the ruins at Jumba la Mtwana—absolutely invaluable for an understanding and appreciation of the site.

Lamu Town, James de Vere Allen. Rodwell Press, Ltd., P.O. Box 90252, Mombasa, Kenya. An explicit guide and plan of the town; well illustrated and providing a wealth of information.

Lost Cities of Africa Itinerary: The Swahili City States: Madagascar

Les Echelles Anciennes du Commerce sur les cotes nord de Madagascar, Tome I, Pierre Verin. L'Universite de Paris I, October, 1972. In French with maps showing ancient Swahili settlements on the northern Malagasy coast.

Lost Cities of Africa Itinerary: The Swahili City States: Tanzania

Kilwa, An Islamic Trading City on the African Coast (2 volumes), H. N. Chittick. The British Institute in Eastern Africa, 1974. Write to Eva Ndavu, editor, the *Azania* journal, at the British Institute, P.O. Box 30710, Nairobi, Kenya, inquiring if copies are available and the price.

Lost Cities of Africa Itinerary: Toumbouctou (Mali)

The Strong Brown God: The Story of the Niger River, Sanche De Gramont. Houghton Mifflin Co., 1976.

The Golden Trade of the Moors, E. W. Bovil. Oxford University Press, 1958.

The Heart of the Ngoni: Heroes of the African Kingdom of Segu, Harold Courlander with Ousmane Sako. Crown Publishers, Inc., One Park Ave., NY 10016. 1982. Segou (Michelin spelling) was the capital city along the River Niger of the 17th-century kingdom that included the region of Bamako and Toumbouctou—and, of course, Djenne. The French used this ancient town as their capital during the colonial period.

Livingstone Itinerary

Stanley: An Adventurer Explored, Richard Hall. Houghton Mifflin & Co., Boston, 1975. An excellent, insightful view of Stanley with information not previously found in other biographies.

Dark Companions: The African Contribution to the European Exploration of East Africa, Donald Simpson. Paul Elek Ltd., 54–58 Caledonian Rd., London N1, England. 1975. A long overdue title; beautifully and objectively written. An absolute must for readers following the Livingstone itinerary. Well illustrated with reproductions of not often seen photographs taken at the time of the explorations.

Tim Jeal has provided an extensive bibliography of the classic titles on Livingstone and we urge readers to consult his list. Please remember too, the titles mentioned in the itinerary available from the Mangochi Museum in Malawi.

Faith and the Flag: The Opening of Africa, Jeremy Murray-Brown. Allen Unwin, P.O. Box 978, Edison, NJ, 08817. Sensitively written account of all the major faiths' efforts to evangelize in Africa during the early years of exploration. A book to read and read again.

White Nile Itinerary

Africa: The Nile Route, Kim Naylor. Roger Lascelles, 47 York Rd., Brentford, Middlesex TX8 OQP, England. First published 1982, reprinted 1983, which is the edition available in the U.S. in 1986. A modern guidebook to backpacking down the Nile. Excellent, although minor portions are now out of date. We would prefer our readers take our advice on health matters to that given by Kim Naylor, much as we admire him in other ways, because we have seen young people clutching his guide and their stomachs at the same time—not everyone has a constitution of iron as he has. Apart from this, the book is excellent and provides information on travel south of Khartoum, which, as we write, is not permitted; but should the area open up again, Kim Naylor's guide would be helpful.

Alexandria: A History and a Guide, E. M. Forester. Anchor Books, Doubleday & Co., Inc., Garden City, NY. 1961. Although the majority of the information is totally out of date the title still makes interesting armchair reading because of its author. Also, *Selected Letters of E. M. Forester: Volume One* (edited by Mary Largo and P. N. Furbank, Harvard University Press, 1983) treats in part Forester's stay in Alexandria.

Alexandria Quartet, four novels by Lawrence Durrell. Dutton, New York, 1961. This title should be read if for no other reason than the entire expatriate population presently living in Alexandria has read it and one feels rather out of it in not being able to intelligently discuss its characters.

Morning Star: Florence Baker's Diary of the Expedition to put down the Slave Trade on the Nile 1870–1873, Anne Baker. William Kimber, London. The text is taken from Florence Baker's diary and has some excellent illustrations.

Lovers on the Nile: The Incredible African Journeys of Sam and Florence Baker. Random House, 400 Hahn Rd., Westminster, MD 21157. 1980. An excellent description, written much as a novel, of Samuel and Florence Baker's African travel, life in England, and how Sam "bought" Florence at a slave market in the Balkans. (The slave trade was not confined only to Africa and the Black race, but also flourished in southern Europe during the 19th century.) Richard Hall is also the author of the book on Stanley, which we list in the Livingstone itinerary suggested reading. One of our favorite authors.

The Baganda: An Account of Their Native Customs and Beliefs, John Roscoe. Reprinted from the 1911 edition, available from Biblio Distribution Centre, 81 Adams Drive, Totowa, NJ 07512 (tel. 201–256–8600), is a masterpiece of early anthropological studies. Another title, *Northern Bantu*, by the same author, reprinted 1966, is available also from Biblio. Their catalog will be sent upon request and is worthwhile obtaining as the Centre holds many African titles that may be of interest.

John Roscoe also wrote *Bakitara of Banyoro: The First Part of the Report of the Mackie Ethnological Expedition to Central Africa* reprint of the Cambridge, 1923 edition, and *Reports of the Mackie Ethnological Expedition to Central Africa, Parts 2 and 3*. The Banyaakole are covered in part 2, and the Bagesu in part 3. Both books are available from Humanities Press, Inc., Atlantic Highlands, NJ 07716 (tel. 201–872–1441).

Greenwood Press at 88 Post Rd. West, P.O. Box 5007, Westport, CT 06881 (tel. 203–226–3571), has Roscoe's *Soul of Central Africa: A General Account of the Mackie Expedition*, reprint of the 1922 edition, and *Twenty-five Years in East Africa*, a reprint of his 1921 edition.

The Rubaga Diary, 1878–82; series C13 and C14; letters and journals of the White Fathers, 1878–97 are held in their Archives, 269, via Aurelia, Rome, Italy.

Great Ages of Man Series: African Kingdoms, Basil Davidson, Time-Life International, 1975 reprint. Interesting for the reproductions of exhibits in the Sudan National Museum.

Two Kings of Uganda: Or, Life by the Shores of Victoria Nyanza. Being an Account of a Residence of Six Years in Eastern Equatorial Africa, Robert Pickering Ashe with an introduction by John Rowe. Frank Cass & Co. Ltd., 1970. Reprint of 1889 edition. Order from Biblio Distribution Centre, 81 Adams Drive, Totowa, NJ 07512. A critical study and account of the momentous years in the 1880's when Christian churches met opposition from the court of the kabaka of Uganda.

So Abundant a Harvest: The Catholic Church in Uganda 1879–1979, Yves Tourigny, White Fathers. Darton, Longman & Todd, 89 Lillie Rd., London, SW6, England, 1970. Church histories when authored by adherents to the faith about which they are writing are inclined to do so as if they were wearing blinders; Father Tourigny has done his best to be objective, but quite naturally, the viewpoint of the Church is presented. Our readers interested in the early history of Christian evangelization in Uganda should read the title mentioned above (Two Kings of Uganda) as well as *A. M. Mackay: Pioneer Missionary of the Church Missionary Society of Uganda,* which he wrote and first published in 1890. Available in reprint from Biblio Distribution Centre, 81 Adams Drive, Totowa, NJ 07512 (publisher F. Cass Co.), to come to a semi-objective assessment of the conditions that prevailed between the two faiths.

The Church in East Africa 1840–1974, W. B. Anderson. Uzima Press Ltd., P.O. Box 48127, Nairobi, Kenya, reprinted 1981. This title covers not only Uganda, but Kenya and Tanzania as well.

The Kings of Buganda, M. S. M. Kiwanuka. East African Publishing House, Nairobi, Kenya. 1971. This may be hard going for all but the dedicated Africanist, yet it provides an African perspective on the kingdom and the kabakas.

The Missionary Factor in East Africa, R. Oliver. Longmans, Green, London, 1952. Concerned more with Kenya than Uganda, this Protestant-written text keeps an even keel in navigating religious waters.

The History of the London Missionary Society. 2 volumes. London, 1899. (Obtain on inter-library loan.) Not so even a keel is kept in this text, but of great interest to readers wishing to probe deeper into the early history of East Africa.

East Africa and Its Invaders, Russell and Russell. Oxford, 1956 and 1965. Additional background reading covering the political scene as well as religious. Slightly slanted.

Lunatic Express Itinerary

The Man-Eaters of Tsavo, J. H. Patterson. A reprint paperback edition published by Macmillan. Sold in most Nairobi and Mombasa bookshops. If readers have difficulty obtaining a copy outside of Kenya, write to Select Bookshop, P.O. Box 40683, Nairobi, Kenya. Patterson was a railroad director who was in many respects a "Johnny come lately" by comparison to Chief Engineer R. O. Preston who had started at Mombasa with the line. Patterson was undeniably English, unlike Preston whose lineage was not absolutely known by the White Kenyan community, and as a result Patterson was allowed more of the limelight than Preston who was the actual hero in the building of the Uganda Railway. Nonetheless, the account, replete with Victorian prose, is interesting.

Descending the Great Rift Valley, which consists of excerpts and pictures from Chief Engineer R. O. Preston's diary kept while he was in charge of building the railway, *The Genesis of Kenya Colony,* and *Oriental Nairobi* (the latter title discussing the Asian—subcontinent of India—contribution to the building of the capital city of Kenya), again authored by Preston, are all out of print and difficult to obtain. If readers will write to us we will see if we can put them in touch with someone who might have copies (P.O. Box 53394, Washington, DC 20009).

Permanent Way, M. H. Hill. East African Railways & Harbours, 1949. The official story of the construction of the Uganda railroad with later information concerning the operation of the lines that went into Uganda. Available in the Railway Museum in Nairobi or from Select Bookshop, P.O. Box 40683, Nairobi, Kenya.

The Sikh Religion its Gurus, Sacred Writings and Authors, 3 volumes, translation by Max Arthur Macauliffee. Oxford University Press, reprint S. Chand & Co., Ram Nagar, New Delhi 110055, India (150 Indian rupees plus postage;

approximately U.S.$20). As the Granth Sahib is the holy book of the Sikhs, these three volumes, while they do contain all the verses of the actual holy book, have the legends of the Sikhs interspersed with the verses. The verses themselves when bound singly constitute the Granth Sahib and must be kept in a reverent manner. In order to assure the Sikh community that no disrespect would be shown, the Oxford University Press and the author, agreed to combine legend and verse so that the volumes are not solely·the verses from the Granth Sahib.

Steam in Africa, A. E. Durrant, C. P. Lewis, and A. A. Jorgensen. Hamlyn Publishing Group Ltd., Astronaut House, Feltham, Middlesex, England. A title that lives up to its name—not an African country where rail lines were laid and steam engines run is neglected. A beautifully produced book with many full-color pictures, art book in size.

Out of Africa and *Flame Trees of Thika* Itineraries

We Made It Our Home. East African Women's League, Nairobi, Kenya. This hardcover book compiled from remembrances, photographs, and clippings by the members of the East African Women's League is a study in nostalgia and a charming look back at a life that was. The text documents the daily life of average settlers. Probably available only on an inter-library loan.

Kenya Chronicles: A Colony in the Making, Lord Cranworth. Macmillan, London, 1912. Difficult to obtain except, perhaps, on an inter-library loan from a major library. As one might expect from the author's affiliation to the aristocracy, the text is inclined to be pompous, but nonetheless his views were typical of his time.

A Guide to the National Parks of East Africa, J. G. Williams. Collins, St. James's Place, London. An invaluable guide to the national parks with maps and detailed lists of the animals to be seen in each park. Some of the information is a bit out of date but not to the extent to invalidate the title as a necessary companion when driving through Kenya. The Ugandan and Tanzanian information is no longer correct.

African Game Trails, Theodore Roosevelt. Scribner, NY. What big game hunting was really like—many interesting pictures and the text primarily concerns hunting in Kenya. Not a title the average person would want to purchase but interesting to look through if it can be, and it probably can—there are a lot of copies around—borrowed on inter-library loan.

The Masai, Their Language and Folklore. Oxford University Press, Clarendon Press, 1905. Another title probably obtainable only on inter-library loan. Good background reading for anyone traveling to Kenya.

My African Journey, Winston Churchill. Hodder and Stoughton, London, 1908. Interesting to read in view of what the author became in later life. He mentions in this book that he shot a lion near Chania Falls at Thika during this trip through East Africa.

Ivory Crisis, Ian Parker with photographs by Mohamed Amin, and *Run Rhino Run,* Esmond and Chryssee Bradley Martin, both published by Chatto & Windus Ltd., 40 William IV St., London WC2, England. 1982. Both these titles attempt to explain what has happened to Kenyan wildlife. Personally, we found the bickering among wildlife lovers as recounted in the texts, a sad commentary on the ability of man's ego to superimpose self on good common sense.

In the Shadow of Man, Jane van Lawick-Goodall. Collins, St. James's, London, 1971. While neither of the itineraries recommends travel to Tanzania, far less to Gombe National Park where Jane Goodall conducted her research, she had much to do with the Kenya National Museum, and her book is of interest to wildlife lovers.

The Africans Itinerary

The Tropical Traveller, John Hatt. Pan Books Ltd., Cavaye Place, London, SW10, England. Distributed in the United States by Academy Chicago, 425 North Michigan Ave., Chicago, IL 60611. A valuable addition to the information we have provided on how to care for your health when traveling in the more remote areas of Africa. Highly recommended and a book we consider a must.

Facing Mt. Kenya, Jomo Kenyatta. Vintage Books, Box 16182, Elway Station, St. Paul, MN 55116. Written in the 1930s by the man who was to become Kenya's first president, *Facing Mt. Kenya* is an insight into the idealism young African nationalists felt before independence. His discussion of Kikuyu traditions is very much of interest.

A Plague of Europeans: Westerners in Africa since the fifteenth century, David Killingray. Penguin Education, Harmondsworth, Middlesex, England. A book we have read and read again and find a marvelous source for easy reference to African events during the colonial period. Illustrated by using old photographs of pompous Europeans weighted down with the task of picking up and carrying the White man's burden. Sad and humorous at the same time.

Tales from the Dark Continent, Charles Allen. Futura Publications, Maxwell House, 74 Worship St., London EC2A 2EN. 1982. The reminiscences of former British Colonial Office personnel stationed in Africa before African nation's became independent the book is easy, can't-put-it-down reading. While entertaining the text offers much factual information concerning the everyday happenings of British families.

Assault at Mogadishu, Peter Koch and Kai Hermann, translated from the German by John Man. Corgi Books, Century House, 61-63 Uxbridge Rd., Ealing, London W5, England. A fast-paced account of the marvelous cooperation the West Germans received from the Somalis when a Lufthansa flight was hijacked in 1977.

Ghosts of Kampala: The Rise and Fall of Idi Amin, George Ivan Smith. St. Martin's Press, Inc., 175 Fifth Ave., NY 10010. Of the many titles that have been written about Uganda since 1972, this is, in our opinion, the best. We do not agree totally with all George Smith writes, but on the whole, the book is well balanced and simply reports events that other writers have tried to sensationalize and exploit to sell their book.

Torture in the Eighties, an Amnesty International Report. Available from their office at 1 Easton St., London WC1X 8DJ, England, or 705 G St., S.E., Washington, DC 20003. Read it and weep. Especially interesting to check on some of the stalwart African leaders' human rights record. Not a pretty picture considering what they mouth about other countries' records.

Travels in West Africa and *West African Studies,* both by Mary Kingsley and available from Biblio Distributers Centre, 81 Adams Drive, Totowa, NJ 07512 (F. Cass Co. publisher). Born in 1862 in England, Mary Kingsley nursed her ailing anthropologist father as a dutiful Victorian daughter should until he died. Dressed in dark taffeta, floor-length dresses, and a prim bonnet she explored the swamps and hinterland of what is now Nigeria and Cameroun. When her small savings ran out she traded with the chiefs, had no time for Christian missionaries, and was admired by the rough, tough "factors" who kept the port of Liverpool busy handling African imports. Always factual, always balanced, Mary Kingsley is the woman Leah and I most admire. These two titles provide wonderful insight not only into her character but also the societies that she visited during her travels and trading in West Africa.

The Roots of the Blues: An African Search, Samuel Charters. Perigee Books, G. P. Putnam's Sons, 200 Madison Ave., NY 10016. Charters' descriptions of The Gambia and Sierra Leone provide an intimacy into the lives of the people difficult to capture. A modern book, well written and of special interest to Black Americans, although Charters is a White writer.

Domestic Slavery in West Africa, John Grace. Frederick Muller, Ltd., London NW2 6LE, England. 1975. Surprising to learn from the text of this title that domestic slavery in West Africa did not officially end until as late as 1927. A factual, dispassionate work on a sensitive issue.

The Royal African Company, K. G. Davies. Longman Group, Ltd., 1957, and reprinted by Atheneum, NY, 1970 as part of the series "Studies in American Negro Life," August Meier, general editor. Obtainable from the Scribner Distribution Center, Vreeland Ave., Boro of Totowa, Paterson, NJ 07512. The bottom line in opening up Africa was business and commerce; the chartered companies were the vehicle used to do so and this title discusses exports, both human and agricultural, from West Africa. Very readable and fascinating. Essential for an understanding of West Africa today.

Staying On

Living in Retirement

Before investigating the regulations governing living in retirement in an African country, and despite the fact that you may have fallen in love with that country, retirees should make a list of the plus and minus marks they apportion to various basic requirements.

First and foremost of these is adequate medical service or easy access to such treatment. This requirement immediately disqualifies certain countries as a site for retirement living. Of the African countries we discuss in this guide, only Kenya qualifies for consideration as a country that has adequate medical services immediately available.

Eastern Africa: Countries that can provide easy access to good treatment by flying to Kenya are: Somalia—the actual climate is marvelous—and Nairobi is less than 45 minutes' flying time from Mogadiscio, less from Kismaio. If Uganda stabilizes there is no more beautiful country in all of Africa and while the climate is tropical, it is healthy. Again, Nairobi is within 45 minutes' flying time. Before Idi Amin's rule we had good medical services in Uganda and these may return once the country is settled. Rwanda is at very high elevations where healing is a problem. Neighboring Burundi is generally unhealthy. Tanzania, of course, is out. Although close to Kenya the constant shortages of gas (petrol) make getting to an airport unreliable, and unless the plane originated in Nairobi, shortages of aviation fuel prevent charter planes from being a viable consideration.

Southern Africa: Medical facilities are limited and the expatriate communities in these countries (Zambia, Zimbabwe, Malawi, Botswana) used to use South African hospitals for medical treatment. We have heard good reports concerning the Catholic Hospital in Malawi, but to what extent they could be relied on for having high-tech equipment, which older people many times require, is questionable.

West Africa: Apparently none of the West African countries have the standard of medical services to offer in the private sector that Kenya offers. There is a Canadian hospital in Abidjan, Ivory Coast, but the Club Meds in that country fly their guests directly to Europe using SOS Insurance (see "Travel Documents"). We doubt they would do so if services in the capital city were adequate. Gabon might be the one exception in West Africa where adequate services are available, and we understand there are several private clinics and physicians practicing in Libreville. Still, the climate is not all that wonderful.

North Africa: Retirement living in Morocco is very tempting, but medical services are totally inadequate. Flying time to Geneva, Switzerland, is 3 hours. All drugs are available, and except in cases needing diagnostic treatment or emergencies, the pluses might outweigh the disadvantages.

Tunisia is a very attractive option for retirement, and the U.S. Department of State's "Background Notes" advises that medical services are adequate. Rome is just a short hop over the Mediterranean, and the Tunisian climate is excellent.

Egypt is another matter. The Nile's contamination with ameobic dysentery is a constant health hazard and the standard of cleanliness in Egypt generally is poor, due more to overcrowding than to lack of personal hygiene. Although Cairo's hospitals feel they are adequate, the many reports we have had indicate that the standards of care are below those of industrialized nations.

Saharan Countries: Mali and Sudan (although the latter is not strictly a Saharan country, it is placed here as latitude's agree) are both totally inadequate in providing sophisticated medical services. Basic care is available in both countries, but in southern Sudan (which is now closed to travel, excluding it from consideration) even basic services are provided only by Christian mission clinics. Such things as broken arms, because of the climate, can become gangrenous. There is an Italian hospital in Mali at Dire, which, we understand, provides good if not sophisticated treatment.

The second basic requirement in considering a country for retirement living is its overall political stability and security for the noncitizen.

Overall Political Stability

Neither Leah nor I are crystal ball readers, and our personal appraisal of political conditions in any given country would be based on our knowledge of past events, keeping abreast of African current events by reading *The New African* magazine, and gut instinct. The latter is not a reliable tool. While we will not directly comment on political stability country by country, the following are some *un*helpful guidelines.

Because a country has been stable for a number of years, it does not necessarily follow that it will remain so. African politics can be compared to gambling where, sooner or later, a number is bound, by the law of averages, to come up. Even today's industrialized countries experienced traumatic unrest— the American Civil War, the French Revolution, the Repeal of the Corn Laws. In the modern world where events appear to be condensed and time accelerated, African countries run the gamut of their histories at a much faster pace. Alternately, because an African country has been *un*stable since independence, it does not necessarily follow that it will continue to be so. In fact, Leah feels that Uganda and Nigeria, two countries plagued by unrest since their independence, will ultimately become the most stable countries in Africa and that Sudan will lead the continent culturally.

Security for the Noncitizen

As for an expatriate's personal security—in countries such as Zimbabwe, where the head of the government is openly hostile to Americans in particular, and to a lesser extent Britishers—security is very questionable. Personal security can also be a problem where a small, radical faction in an African country attempts to score a point with the government in power by harassing expatriates. A case in point is southern Sudan, where the people certainly present no security problem to expatriates but where the rebel forces have kidnapped expatriates to express their unhappiness with the government in office.

Personal security from the standpoint of street crime and home burglaries is still another consideration. In this respect Kenya is very bad. Were we to live in Kenya we would live only in Old Town Mombasa, where security is excellent. Street crime in Mombasa and Nairobi has become a problem, and we have heard many adverse reports in the past year. Unless Kenya addresses this problem positively and ceases to believe that it will not affect her tourist industry, there will be a considerable drop in tourism except for tour group travel, where the visitor is shrouded in a protective cocoon, and the revenues are half those received from independent tourists.

We have never felt safer anywhere in the world than in Mali, Somalia, and northern Sudan. West Africa, except Gabon, suffers from high-crime incidents. Morocco is, we understand, bad because of pickpockets; Egypt is the same. Tunisians appear, from what we understand, to have the situation of crime under control, and we have not heard any adverse reports about that country. Undoubtedly, there are exceptions. Malawi is very safe, although we were told there was a certain amount of waylaying of bicyclists in the rural areas, and stealing from them. For this reason, although Malawi is otherwise an ideal country for backpacking and cycling, we did not recommend that country in *Fielding's African Safaris* for those sports.

We will use Kenya, which is probably the country most of our readers will be attracted to as a possible retirement site, for the outline of plus and minus requirements that should be considered in selecting any country

The plus side: The official language of Kenya is English, although Swahili is stated to be of equal importance. Nevertheless, after elementary or grade school, teaching is conducted solely in English, and all government offices use that language. This means that most people reading this guide will know what is going on all the time through the press and radio, and can easily communicate with almost everyone in the country.

Rental housing is good, reasonably priced and available. US$200–450 a month, with an average rental at US$260. Food is of good quality and reasonably priced: US$30, at most US$35, a week for two people.

There are no taxes on money brought into the country. Taxes may be payable on income in the home country. This should be investigated with your internal revenue departments or ministries.

Excellent hospitals and doctors are available near the major towns. Private rooms in those hospitals are very reasonable. Professionally trained registered nurses are available for home or intensive hospital care at reasonable prices. Medicines and drugs are available, and are considerably cheaper than in the United States.

Direct-dial telephone service is available *from* overseas countries and can put friends and relatives in touch with retirees living in Kenya in a matter of minutes. While direct-dial service is not available for calls originating in Kenya, the operator service is good.

The climate is marvelous. Depending upon where you live it can be 55–70°F in the Nairobi and Mt. Kenya areas or 80–98° with a constant breeze at the coast.

Housekeeping help is well trained if they have been working for other expatriates or Indian families, and can be hired for 30 Kenya shillings (at present exchange rates this is just under US$2) a day for a maid responsible for cleaning the house, and up to US$70 a month for a driver or experienced houseman. Jobs are usually split and a gardener does not work in the house, or a houseman in the garden. Some rental houses have servant's quarters in which case these are provided, but this is not always the case. Unless the retiree lives in an apartment complex (block of flats) a security guard, known as an askari, is employed and his wages can run US$70 a month. On the average, the number of servants employed by people living in a house with a garden is four. This should be added into the budget. Write to your embassy in the country you are considering and ask the normal scale of wages. Embassy and diplomatic personnel usually pay above going wages, so this will be an outside figure.

The minus side: Kenya is a minimum 14 hours' flying time from North America; 8 hours from Europe, and even longer to Australia or New Zealand. This will mean that getting home in an emergency can present delays.

Burglaries are common in Nairobi suburbs; not so common along the coast, but common enough to justify keeping guard dogs. These can be purchased from any of the excellent pedigree breeders of German Shepherds, Dobermans, or Labradors to be found in Kenya.

Television is only broadcast in the evening and programs are nonprofessional and locally produced or reruns of shows from Western English-speaking countries. Videos can take the place of television and there are many good film rental shops.

Moving household goods to Kenya will cost around US$3000 from North American or European ports using container shipment. Household goods enter duty free. However, if you're moving from your present home to a retirement home, the cost to Kenya will not be that much more and will probably be compensated by the cheaper cost of living in the first year.

A car is an absolute necessity. Locally purchased second-hand cars are not excessively priced, but they are usually in bad shape and are not a good value. Your own car can be brought into Kenya duty free if you place a bond not to sell it for two years.

The electric current is 220 volts, meaning Americans will need a transformer to operate U.S. appliances. Cosmetics and luxury goods are subject to high import duties, making them expensive to purchase. Antimalarial tablets must be taken weekly.

Of course, there is the adjustment and adaptation to a new country to be made, but such adaptation will be far less than in non-English speaking countries if you are mono-lingual. The general atmosphere in the expatriate communities tends to be very British, and people who have had contact with the British way of life will adapt quickly. There is a sizable American community in Nairobi, but unless retirees plan to live in the suburb of Karen, they would not find Nairobi city life conducive to enjoyable living. Karen rentals are above the figures we have quoted. There is little commercial entertainment, although at the coast the hotels always welcome local residents, as, of course, do the hotels in Nairobi. There is a growing Italian community at the coast, which is tending to thaw the British atmosphere, and for those readers who speak Italian, friendships will be made quickly.

Notwithstanding our comments in the text concerning working in Kenya, there are many useful jobs to be done by older people on a voluntary basis— the Red Cross, active Lions and Rotary club projects, and church-sponsored efforts. Additionally, there are flower and agricultural shows, as well as dog and cat clubs where all entires are welcome.

A visa to reside in Kenya is available upon payment of a bond, which would be used if you were unable to pay your fare home; it is refundable when you leave. Tourist visas, if requested, are issued for 3 months, and these can be extended for an additional 3 months. During such a 6-month period it would be possible to decide if Kenya is the country for your retirement. (This applies to any other country, as well, although the length of tourist visas will vary.)

Apart from year-round retirement living, shorter periods can be considered using any number of self-catering rentals available by the month during the low and mid seasons at the coast. Temporary rental housing is more difficult to obtain in areas away from the coast. Household storage charges for the months away from Kenya are very reasonable. Mwani Cottages at Tiwi Beach, on Kenya's south coast (P.O. Box 96024, Mombasa, Kenya), are excellent, security is good, and only one person is needed to do the cooking and housecleaning. Place an advertisement in either of the national newspapers for rental housing other than at the coast (*Daily Nation,* P.O. Box 49010, Nairobi; *Standard,* P.O. Box 30080, Nairobi, Kenya). *Coastweek* (P.O. Box 87270, Mombasa) is a good paper in which to place an ad for a house at the coast.

Investing in a Business

Most African countries welcome, and make substantial concessions, to persons wishing to establish a business. The International Monetary Fund and the World Bank have helped the countries to prioritize their needs for business investment. Usually, if the investor wishes to develop a business that comes within these guidelines, there is no problem other than the usual red tape and bureaucratic chain of command. Details can be obtained from the commercial attache at your embassy located in the African capital city.

The government of The Gambia is eager to identify an entrepreneur who will operate a regular service on the River Gambia. Before it caught fire, a steamer operated on the river and did excellent business, as there is a strong tourist as well as local demand.

The government of Somalia is actively interested in working with investors who wish to develop the country's tourist industry. There is a need for every type of tourist service and facility. While the government is willing to make land available or to turn over existing hotels after negotiation, there is no cash forthcoming from the Somali government and investors must be prepared to provide all the necessary capital.

Working in Africa

Every African country suffers from high unemployment rates and usually jealously guards each job vacancy. Apart from the unemployment problem, many of the jobs in the past could be held only by Whites. The Africans are proving they can do the job. Even voluntary work may take paid work away from Africans. However, where there are shortages of qualified Africans the governments are prepared to issue work permits. This usually includes the medical profession—both physicians, technicians, and nurses—and the teaching profession.

In Kenya doctors are required to work three years in a Kenyan government medical facility before they can take up a private practice. Additionally there is an annual fee to pay, once the practice is established. Nurses must pass a Kenyan government examination.

Bachelor-degree graduates are welcome to work in rural schools of Kenya if (a) they are prepared to pay their own way to and from Kenya, (b) work at local level salaries—about US$200 a month for a B.A. or B.S. increasing, in the case of trained teachers, by the number of years' experience. Housing is provided, but it is very basic and not to be compared to the rental housing we have described in "Living in Retirement." A teacher's salary will provide grocery money and a part-time servant, but not too many nights out at good hotels. However, the rewards are great both as a learning experience and for the appreciation students have for good teachers.

How to Get a Teaching Job

First of all, you must speak the language of the country where you would like to teach. All former British colonies use English in their schools.

Unless you go with Peace Corps, VSO, or some other organization, it is practically impossible to get a job without going to the country. The school terms differ but generally run from January to December with short breaks at Easter, in July, and at Christmas. Vacancies are advertised just after Christmas and in early January. (They are advertised between terms as well, but these are few—teachers try to complete the school year before resigning.) Bring along some neatly typed resumes, which, in addition to your academic background and any teaching experience, indicate the games and sports you played and the clubs you belonged to in college. Delete any work history of jobs you did while in college or high school not strictly of an academic nature. List any paid or voluntary teaching work. The salaries, as we mentioned above, are based—after the basic, minimum wage—on the number of years' experience in teaching. This means an experienced teacher costs more. This can work to the detriment of your application because a headmaster on a tight budget watches every penny.

It is only the private schools that are prepared to cough up more for experienced teachers. So if you have more than two years' experience, cut it back on the resume and show that you did some other kind of work. Send your resume, along with *copies,* not originals, of your B.S. or B.A. degree to the school's headmaster at the address given in the classified advertisement. Write a cover letter, in your own handwriting, saying why you came to Kenya with the goal of teaching and what subjects you are qualified to teach. These naturally should be the same as advertised, but sometimes high school headmasters expect a teacher to teach two subjects. In all cases you can say you also, or are prepared to, teach English. If English is your mother tongue this will probably give you an edge over local applicants. There is usually a small charge for a work permit, which the school usually pays—but they may ask you to do so or deduct it from your first month's salary.

The most sought after subjects are science and math. Try not to get stuck with one of the schools run for profit. Conditions are not usually very good. Ask any educated African friend whether the school you are considering is government aided or a religious school. If it is not, don't apply. There are very few exceptions to this because the demand for schools who will take students who failed promotional exams is tremendous, and there are many opportunists willing to take advantage of parents who urgently want an education for their children even if that education is of poor quality.

End your cover letter, saying you are prepared to accept local level salary and a probation period. Curricula are based on the British system in former English colonies and on the French system where that country colonized. The grading is also different than that used in the United States. A guide book is not the place to explain this, but once with other teachers you'll catch on.

Apart from teaching jobs and work in the medical profession, there are genuine needs for mechanics—particularly tractor mechanics. There's a crying need for agricultural extensionists, first-aid teachers, public health workers, and homemakers to demonstrate good nutrition and baby care. Where the infrastructure is that which will enable a non-African to meet these needs, even at local level salaries, we do not know. Some African governments (note we say governments, not people) fear a White invasion. Coupled with this is their insistence that they are capable of managing their problems alone. How long this will continue remains to be seen; the present economic chaos that typifies African nations' dependence on outside financial assistance may be brought into perspective by donor nations. In former French colonies there are high concentrations of French people working in jobs that rightly should be done by Africans, so we can appreciate the reluctance of former British colonies to take on outside workers. However, most—indeed many—educated Africans do not want to work at the village level where the need is the greatest. There is a difference between Whites taking the plush jobs as in French Africa and denying jobs to Whites in the villages. Unfortunately, African governments sometimes fail to make the distinction.

Making a Job for Yourself in Africa

Expatriates who are willing to bring into a country even small amounts of cash that will provide employment to Africans, theoretically are welcomed by African governments. Unfortunately, so many impediments are put in the path of small entrepreneurs, most get discouraged and abandon the effort. Most readers who travel in Africa will immediately see opportunities. In fact, the opportunities that present themselves are so abundant it becomes almost sickening. If you have a slow fuse and plenty of patience, and believe one is not supposed to do good with the hope of reward, investigate the possibilities. The Indians we have met who once had businesses in Uganda and were forced to leave that country by Idi Amin, have told us never again would they put up with the hassle of trying to do business in East Africa. Most of them, although they started literally with nothing, established businesses in Canada and the United Kingdom where the law is the law, and running a business is predictable.

Numerical Miscellany

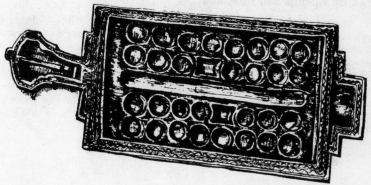

While it is true that Black Africa had no counting system as we understand counting, they did count as evidenced by their proficiency at playing Mancala or Ubao. In this game pebbles, or other small objects, are moved around the board and it is necessary to count before each play just how many objects are in each well if the player is to win. Other evidence of African traditional arithmetic is given in Africa Counts, *by Claudia Zaslavsky (Lawrence Hill, 520 Riverside Ave., Westport CT 06880, tel. 203–226–9392).*

Counting in Swahili

1 moja, 2 mbili, 3 tatu, 4 nne, 5 tano, 6 sita, 7 saba, 8 nane, 9 tisa, 10 kumi, 11 kumi na moja (10 + 1), 12 kumi na mbili (10 + 2), 20 ishirini, 30 thelathini, 40 arubaini, 100 mia moja.

When Africans do not speak one another's language they may indicate numbers through finger displays. It should not be assumed that showing nine fingers on two hands will be interpreted as 9. The method of displaying certain fingers varies across the continent. Numbers higher than three are usually denoted by combinations of fingers or the entire hand, which add up to the higher number. Thus, the number 9 can be expressed by holding the four fingers of the left hand in the grasp of the right hand or, among Nilotic people, by holding the forefinger of the right hand to the thumb. Simply putting up *x* number of fingers does not guarantee that your meaning has been accurately conveyed!

It is always bad luck to name the number of living things. For example, do not ask how many children a person has, or how many farm animals.

Swahili Time

The time of day in Swahili is told according to the hours that have passed since the sun rose or set. In Uganda and Kenya, which are along the equator, the sun rises and sets within 15 minutes throughout the year. 7 a.m. is 1 o'clock, 9 a.m., 3 o'clock, and so on. However, it is unlikely that readers will find the need for expressing the time of day in Swahili except occasionally in Mombasa or rural areas.

Swahilil Weights and Measures

ounce—aunsi, kilo—kilo, pound—ratli, 2 liters—pishi, ½ liter—kibaba, 4 gallons—debi, yard—yadi, foot—futi, inch—inchi, tape measure—futikamba (literally, a foot rope), mile—maili.

Roadside stands and market people usually sell either by "piles," as in the case of tomatoes, or use a dried, split gourd as a measure. Look around the market before you start to buy and count how many of each item of produce comprises a pile. A debi is a universal measure throughout Africa. A debi is a can (tin) (that usually originally contained oil) that holds 4 gallons.

BACKGROUND INFORMATION FOR SELECTED AFRICAN COUNTRIES*

Carved column from a Yorouba temple. Reproduced courtesy Air Afrique.

Factual information and maps for "Background" section courtesy of the U.S. Department of State's "Background Notes."

	EGYPT	GABON
When to go	Nov thru Feb	June thru Aug
Visa required for Australian citizens? Canadian citizens? New Zealand citizens? Saudi Arabian citizens? United Kingdom citizens? United States citizens?	Y Y Y N Y Y	Y Y Y Y Y Y
Immunizations required	Ch,YF	YF
Immunizations recommended (all childhood diseases plus)	Tetanus in case of accident, and Cholera	
Country is in a malaria area?	Y	Y
Immigration procedures	G	G
Customs prohibitions	YC	YC
Permitted Duty Free	S	S
Currency Control?	Y	YCFA
Monetary unit (abbreviation)	Egyptian pound (EG)	CFA franc (AFR)
Exchange rate as of May 27, 1987	2 rates official/ tourist	
Australian $	.50(o) 1.55(fm)	216.12
Canadian $	.52(o) 1.61(fm)	225.25
New Zealand $	.41(o) 1.26(fm)	176.55
Saudi Arabian Riyal	.18(o) .56(fm)	79.14
British pound	1.13(o) 3.53(fm)	493.12
United States $	.70(o) 2.18(fm)	304.4
International airline arrival city	Cairo	Libreville
Departure tax? U.S.$ Equiv. Exit Permit?	none	none

(o) official, (fm) free market
*In all official publications, such as foreign exchange rates, etc., the Ivory Coast, by presidential order (1987) is listed as Cote d'Ivoire. The English translation "Ivory Coast" is no longer acceptable to the government.

THE GAMBIA	IVORY* COAST	KENYA	MALAWI	MALI
15 Nov to 15 May	Jan & Feb	1 Dec thru 31 Mar	Please see each safari	Not Feb Mar–Apr
N N N Y N Y	Y Y Y Y N Y	Y N N Y N Y	N N N Y N N	Y Y Y Y Y Y
YF	YF	YF	YF	Ch.YF
Tetanus in case of accident, and Cholera				
Y	Y	Yr	Yr	Y
G	C	G	G	G
YC	YC	YC	YC	YC
S	S	S	S	S except allow 1,000 cigs
Y	YCFA	Y	Y	YCFA
Gambian dalasi (GAD)	CFA franc (AFR)	Kenya shilling (KES)	Malawi Kwacha (MWK)	CFA franc (AFR)
5.38 5.61 4.40 1.97 12.28 7.58	216.12 225.25 176.55 79.14 493.12 304.4	11.46 11.95 9.37 4.20 26.16 16.15	1.59 1.66 1.30 .58 3.64 2.25	216.12 225.25 176.55 79.14 493.12 304.4
Banjul	Abidjan	Nairobi	Lilongwe	Bamako
3	none	10	6	4

	MOROCCO	SENEGAL
When to go	All year; avoid summer	Too cold for the beach Dec–May
Visa required for Australian citizens? Canadian citizens? New Zealand citizens? Saudi Arabian citizens? United Kingdom citizens? United States citizens?	N N N N N N	Y Y Y Y Y Y
Immunizations required	None	YF
Immunizations recommended (all childhood diseases plus)	Tetanus in case of accident, and Cholera	
Country is in a malaria area?	Y	Y
Immigration procedures	G	G
Customs prohibitions	YC	YC
Permitted Duty Free	S	S except no free alcohol
Currency control?	Y	YCFA
Monetary unit (abbreviation)	Moroccan dirham (MDH)	CFA franc (AFR)
Exchange rate as of May 27, 1987 Australian $ Canadian $ New Zealand $ Saudi Arabian Riyal British pound United States $	5.86 6.11 4.79 2.15 13.38 8.26	216.12 225.25 176.55 79.14 493.12 304.40
International airline arrival city	Casablanca	Dakar
Departure Tax? U.S.$ Equiv. Exit Permit?	none	none

SOMALIA	SUDAN*	TANZANIA	TOGO	UGANDA**
mid-May to December	Dec–Jan–Feb	Travel recommended only for a one-day safari see Background	Year round	Year round
Y	Y	N	Y	N
Y	Y	N	N	N
Y	Y	N	Y	N
Y	Y	N	Y	Y
Y	Y	N	N	N
Y	Y	Y	N	Y
Ch,YF	Ch,YF	Ch,YF	YF	YF
TY, TYP, Tetanus in case of accident, and Cholera				
Y'	Yr	We do not recommend travel to Tanzania because of the virulent strain of malaria.	Y	Yr
Chaos	G	C	C	G
YC	YC	YC	YC	YC
S	SX: no alcohol	S	S except only 100 cigs.	S
Y	Y	Y	Y	Y
Somali shilling (SOM)	Sudanese pound (SUL)	Tanzanian shilling (TAS)	CFA franc (AFR)	Ugandan shilling (UGS)
85.34	1.74(o)	44.05	216.12	42.60
88.95	1.81(o)	45.91	225.25	44.40
69.72	1.42(o)	35.98	176.55	34.80
31.25	.64(o)	16.13	79.14	15.60
194.72	3.97(o)	100.50	493.12	97.20
120.20	2.45(o)	62.04	304.40	60.00
Mogadiscio	Khartoum	Dar-es-Salaam	Lome	Kampala
5	8	10	none yes	2

*Sudan: operates 3 exchange rates—financial rate, agricultural products, and official (o).
**Uganda: new shilling introduced 18 May 87. 1 new shilling = 100 old shillings.

Background for Egypt

PROFILE

People

Nationality: Noun and adjective—Egyptian(s). **Population** (1984): 47 million. **Annual growth rate:** 2.7%. **Ethnic groups:** Egyptian, Bedouin Arabs, Nubian. **Religions:** Sunni Muslim 90%, Coptic Christian. **Languages:** Arabic, English, French. **Education:** Years compulsory—ages 6–12. Literacy—44%. **Health:** Infant mortality rate—69/1000 (1983). Life expectancy—57 yrs. **Work force:** Agriculture—50%; services—26%; industry—13%; trade and finance—11%.

Geography

Area: 1,001,258 sq. km. (386,650 sq. mi.); slightly smaller than Texas, Oklahoma, and Arkansas combined, a little larger than British Columbia, over 4 times the size of Great Britain, a little larger than South Australia, and over three times the size of Southern Yemen.

Cities: Capital—Cairo (pop. over 11 million). Other cities—Alexandria (3 million), Aswan, Asyut, Port Said, Suez, Ismailia. **Terrain:** Desert except Nile River valley and delta—desert, wasteland, urban (96.5%), cultivated (2.8%), inland water (0.7%). **Climate:** Dry, hot summer, moderate winters.

Telecommunications: Telephone service can be erratic. Delays are frequent, even on local calls. International service and reception vary with demand and atmospheric conditions. Telegrams can be sent from the main post office and hotels, and telex service is available. Cairo is 2 hours ahead of Greenwich Mean Time; 3 hours ahead in summer.

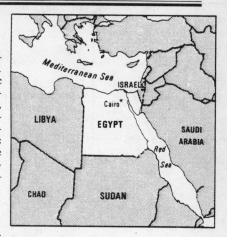

Official Name:
Arab Republic of Egypt

Transportation: Domestic and international airlines serve Cairo. Domestic air service from Cairo to Alexandria, Aswan, Luxor and Hurghada, and the Sinai is available but, reportedly, flights are not kept to schedule. Rail service, which is good and reliable, is available from Cairo to Aswan and Cairo to Alexandria. There are excellent long-distance buses. Misr taxis or limos are the most pleasant to use; ordinary taxi drivers, many times, drive unroad-worthy vehicles and are rude.

National Holidays: Unity Day: Feb. 22. Sinai Day: April 26. Labor Day: May 1. Evacuation Day: June 18. Revolution Day: July 23. Armed Forces Day: Oct. 6. Suez Day: Oct. 25. Victory Day: Dec. 23. plus Muslim religious holidays.

Arrival in Cairo

We've heard some rather startling stories about the chaos at Cairo International Airport, but we arrived at 3 a.m. and, apart from a few other eccentric passengers who chose to arrive in Egypt during the early hours of the morning, we were processed immediately. The airport was totally lit—so many times airports reduce illumination after the onslaught of the peak traffic—and every

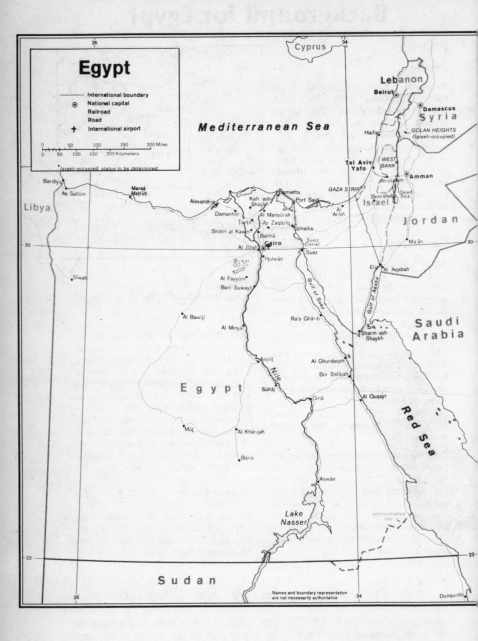

facility was open. The drive into town was pleasant. All in all, our experiences contrasted greatly to those that we have read concerning conditions in Cairo Airport when it is crowded. The moral of the story is, try and arrange to arrive on a late flight.

Background

If you have not been to Egypt before, you will want to purchase a good guide to the ancient monuments and combine seeing these with your itinerary for the *White Nile* and for the *Lost Cities of Africa,* if you elect to stop over in Cairo on the way to Khartoum. Baededker has published a new edition of their famous guide to Egypt. A copy can be purchased by writing to Travel Books Unlimited (4931 Cordell Avenue, Bethesda, MD 20814).

Egypt is one of those countries one becomes nostalgic about after you've left the country; this has happened to me on the two occasions I have been in Egypt and it has happened to Leah. In all fairness, Leah enjoyed Egypt more than I did this last time. She was full of anticipation about the Pyramids, the Sphinx, and King Tut's treasures. But, as she says, that isn't Cairo. Cairo is buses emitting foul smoke, honking taxis driven by incredibly rude, spitting drivers, people living on roofs, and dirt.

The people living in Cairo today are not responsible for the culture of the ancient kingdoms of the pharaohs; they are a mixture of southern Europeans with only a hint now and again of Arab blood. On the whole they are gracious, helpful, and hospitable. How they manage to keep their optimism, which admittedly is tempered with a good helping of fatalism, is difficult to understand, because the cancer that has eaten at Egypt throughout her modern history— Egyptian business practices—is enough to discourage a saint. The bad guys always seem to win and only very slowly do things get better. The sad part about Egypt is that the average Egyptian knows—recognizes—corrupt practices, whereas, in some other countries (India comes to our mind) corruption has become respectable and an accepted method of doing business.

Egypt is now experiencing an economic recession brought about by several causes: The slump in oil prices and inability of the OPEC countries to hold together has seen a decline in the number of workers needed in Saudi Arabia and the Gulf oil producing states. Many of these workers were Egyptians who regularly sent money home to Egypt. Not only have those remittances stopped, but the worker has returned to join the ranks of Egyptian unemployed.

Tourism, which was a major source of revenue for Egypt, has drastically fallen since the terrorist attacks in the eastern Mediterranean. If the truth be known, tourism numbers had dropped months before those incidents and tourist occupancy was running about 40% in the high season. The blame for the drop in tourist numbers, therefore, cannot entirely be blamed on international terrorism. Egypt has gone along for many years riding on King Tut's coattails. Tourism could be diversified if efforts were made to do so, as Egypt does not get the lucrative repeat business that many other tourist-oriented countries have. Once the Pyramids have been seen, tourists are not made aware of the other potential recreational facilities Egypt has to offer. The reason for this is that tourist operators are intent on hussling tourists in and out of Egypt as quickly as possible. The concept of service and a personal interest in each guest is totally alien.

The last economic arrow Egypt has suffered has been a reduction in American aid to the country. Under the Carter administration money poured into Egypt—so much that Egypt couldn't assimilate it all. Quite unfairly, today, many Egyptians blame President Mubarak for a failure to ingratiate himself with President Reagan and keep the money coming.

There is a strong undercurrent of Islamic fundamentalism at work in Egypt and President Mubarak has been courageous in tackling these elements, which were responsible for the assassination of his predecessor. On the whole his is not an easy task, and it is made more difficult by an intractable business community on which Egypt's economy pivots.

As Leah says, Egypt is a country to go back to once the preconceptions have been shed. For my part, Egypt is a country to reminisce about as only the good experiences tend to be remembered. Whatever, it is an experience not to be missed at least once in a lifetime.

Cairo

David Lamb has written *The Arabs,* and his chapters on Cairo are excellent. We strongly urge our readers to purchase a copy of *The Arabs* before visiting Egypt.

In their own inimitable fashion the French are digging a subway (tube) for the Cairenes. They scoop down to the subsoil, bring it to the surface, and then leave it there, beside the hole. Perhaps they are hoping to rival the ancient Egyptians and construct modern pyramids, but as fast as they heap the piles, so the gentle breezes carry off the dirt to infiltrate the nostrils of passers-by, cover vehicles, buildings, and rise above the city and the River Nile to form a polluted haze that effectively blocks the sun's rays.

Driving is not a pleasant pastime in Cairo, as can be seen from the windows of guests' rooms in the Hilton International. Drivers do not keep to lanes, the streets are totally incapable of handling the volume of traffic, and drivers are not the least bit considerate of one another or pedestrians. Nor are the taxi drivers, who spend their driving time swearing at their foreign passengers (because they want to pay the regulated fare) in Arabic. Car hire in Egypt is a disaster, and we are sorry not to recommend even Avis. Misr Limos (Mercedes saloon cars, not proper limos) are government owned and the best way to get around the city. While the doormen at the Ramses Hilton prefer to put you into an ordinary taxi, insist on a Misr. The price will be the same, and you'll suffer no abusive comments from the driver.

By our inclusion of Egypt in general and Cairo in particular in our remarks on health in ''Bye-the By,'' readers will realize that although Cairo appears to be a modern city, many of the ancient illnesses persist. Care should be taken about where you eat and drink. We have also discussed Cairo in more detail in the *White Nile* itinerary. However, it bears repeating that we found the Cairenes very helpful when we asked directions of them; many times they would go out of their way to put us on the right street, or, if they did not know where a place was, to find a policeman and translate his information.

Alexandria, Port Said, Ismailia, Aswan, and Suez

Egypt has proper small cities apart from the capital city; this is unusual for Africa. Many times the names of places, other than the capital, are internationally known, and one is disappointed when the visual image is nothing more than a small town. Not so with Egypt.

Alexandria puts one in mind of the housewife/mother who languishes over what might have been: "I could have been a great opera singer/ballet dancer/movie star if I hadn't given up my career to marry." In the case of Alexandria it is difficult to pinpoint the juncture where all was forfeited and the city failed to emerge as a sophisticated metropolis.

From ancient times Alexandria has started on promising careers, but looking at her now, at the end of the 20th century, only her aborted starts at greatness are seen. Developers are starting yet again, leaving behind along her seafront and harbors the tawdy remembrances of past failures. They are erecting speculator cement architectural monstrosities a few miles inland instead of renovating the old (a real money-maker for the foreign developers who import materials from their own countries, as well as personnel, instead of utilizing Egypt's craftsmen skilled in less modern construction practices). Perhaps it is the transient nature of Alexandria's power brokers that makes her play the role of the unwanted stepchild, but without Cinderella's happy ending—never finding a prince who will protect her virtues.

During our research we came across British-conceived plans for the city's development. Those plans were overtaken by the advent of the second World War 19 years later, which brought alien armies to Alexandria's doorstep. After the war Alexandria became influenced by the slightly seedy international set (before the war, they had been genuine). Nationalism overtook the city until a gentleman from Plains, Georgia, and a gentleman from Ismailia (see below) determined she should become the dumping ground for those in search of "free port" commerce and factories producing cheap goods to challenge Taiwan in the eastern Mediterranean.

For all that, Alexandria has charm, and we personally like the city. It's a place one could live in retirement and enjoy. Historically, throughout many periods, Alexandria has much to offer the visitor.

Port Said: I first saw it in 1947, and in all honesty it had more going for it then than now. It was only a small port town; today it has become a free port and many new buildings, to the extent that the old section is virtually unrecognizable. Unlike Alexandria there is an openness to the sky and the people are very friendly. We enjoyed the time we spent in the town.

Ismailia: It never pays to go back, and going back to Ismailia, where I had lived for two years in the 1950s, was no exception. Ismailia was President Anwar Sadat's hometown, and he diverted many U.S. dollars to the city. More concrete jungle, more half-done, unfinished streets and parks. The locals say this is because when Sadat was killed the money ceased to come. That may be, but there are many things that could have been completed with elbow grease. We're more inclined to think the cause is a predisposition to leave things unfinished.

Ismailia is suffering, as is much of Egypt today, from high unemployment. In the case of Ismailia the people have been spoiled by too much money too quickly received, and the adjustment to a post–Jimmy Carter economy hurts. Our readers will have no reason, insofar as the itineraries are concerned, to visit Ismailia, and the city is mentioned here only in passing.

Aswan: When the Aga Khan used this section of the Nile as a home, it must have been very beautiful. Today, although his widow lives in seclusion on the western shore of the River Nile, Aswan is pretty much a tourist town, even though it has been difficult for commercialism to mar its charm. Life is slower at Aswan than to the north, and, again, it is a place we enjoyed. Details are provided in the *White Nile* itinerary.

Suez: So vital in Victorian and colonial times, because it was at the southern end of the Suez Canal, Suez has in the nuclear age diminished in strategic importance, but her role as a center of Red Sea commerce remains. Once the Middle Eastern question is settled, Suez will also become a gateway city for tourism along the Red Sea coasts.

Communications

Egypt is served by sophisticated satellite telecommunications services, and cable, telex, and telephone service is good. However, overseas telephone calls are subject to delay; the situation is not as bad as it was in the early 1980s.

Radio and television broadcasting is in Arabic, but the news is televised in English and French at certain times of the day. Consult the program schedule provided by the Hilton.

There are several daily newspapers; these are printed in Arabic. We found *Arab News,* published in Saudi Arabia, which was put under our door by the Hilton, to be the best way to keep up with daily happenings.

Business Hours

Shops and offices are open from 8:30 a.m.–7 p.m., but there can be 2-hour breaks for lunch, Saturday through Thursday. However, some stores close on Sunday, while others are open; some stores are closed on Friday, while others stay open. Reportedly, the museums only close for a long lunch on Fridays. Within the grounds of the Nile Hilton International there are many branch offices of major businesses. Rather than chase around downtown trying to find the main office, it will save time to check with the Hilton to determine if you can do your business there. In either case, call the office or store you are intending to visit to ensure they will be open.

Banking is undoubtedly the thing the Egyptians do best. Misr (incidentally, the word is the Arabic for Egypt) Bank in the lobby of the Ramses Hilton International is open very late at night. They are extremely efficient, pay the correct rates, and a joy to patronize.

Religious Services

While the major religion of Egypt is the Moslem religion, there are a substantial number of Coptic Christians, and a history of the Roman and Greek Catholic Churches in the country as well as Anglican houses of worship. Check with guest services at the Ramses for the time and nearest church or mosque to attend services of your choice.

Languages

Arabic is the official language of Egypt, and for many years Cairo was the center of Islamic learning and Arabic scholars. French is the preferred non-Arabic language, with English second. Most of the staff of the major hotels speak English, as do guides, vendors, and shopkeepers.

Geographic Description

We all remember from our childhood geography lessons that the River Nile is the lifeline of Egypt. The vast majority of the population is established along the river. From ancient times the flooding of the river—when the snows of Zaire, Rwanda, and Uganda melted and trickled down the mountains to form streams that converged and made their way to the river bed—the people of Egypt had been totally dependent upon this act of nature. With the building of the Aswan Dam, or Lake Nassir Dam, that dependency has lessened. However, the sediment that used to provide a natural fertilizer for Egyptian crops now stays and settles at the bottom of the dam, and new problems have been presented to agriculturalists.

The land to the east and west of the River Nile is arid, becoming true desert in southwestern Egypt. For the most part this land is flat, with only the occasional small hill to break the monotony. Oil has been a productive income earner, but the wells are not as lucrative as those in Saudi Arabia and the Gulf States.

Tribes and Ethnic Groups

It would take a professional anthropologist to examine each and every Egyptian to determine their tribal and ethnic origins. The people one sees in the major Egyptian cities and towns are certainly more European looking than Arab. The "typical" Egyptian one stereotypes—lean, small, dark curly hair, brown eyes—becoming rotund in middle age, is, from our observations, now in the minority. The French were in Egypt a number of generations and the people appear more Mediterranean than they do any other single physical type. This is not so true in the rural areas. To the south, once at Aswan, complexions become darker, and true black-skinned Nubians are seen. Greeks, too, have played a major role in Egypt's business life, as have Lebanese and Libians.

The people wear European dress primarily, but caftans and *djibban* are commonly seen. The fez is going out of fashion.

Social Customs

Each ethnic group—Greek, Lebanese, Turkish, Balkan, and Egyptian—subscribes to its traditional social customs when it comes to the rituals of birth, marriage, and death, but in the main, the social customs one experiences in everyday travel are similar to those found in Europe.

Shopping in Egypt

The country has had so many tourists that souvenirs have become rather cheap and nasty. There are a few nice alabaster pieces, but it's better to purchase reproductions of objects from ancient Egypt through the New York Metropolitan Museum's catalog than in Cairo.

Hotel and Restaurant Food

For reasons that we have discussed at length in "Egyptian Accommodation: Ramses Hilton International," the *White Nile* itinerary, and "Health Precautions," we recommend eating only at the Hilton Internationals in Cairo, or at the Ramada Renaissance in Alexandria. We also found the cooked food at the Holiday Hotel in Port Said acceptable. We do not recommend eating at the Oberoi Spa Hotel in Aswan as we have no information that their food handlers are checked for amebic dysentery. In Aswan readers should purchase sealed groceries at local stores and picnic.

Background for Kenya

PROFILE

People

Nationality: Noun and adjective—Kenyan(s). **Population** (1981 est.): 17.5 million. Annual growth rate (1982: est.): 4%. **Ethnic groups:** African—Kikuyu 21%, Luhya 14%, Luo 13%, Kalenjin 11%, Kamba 11%, Kissi 6%, Meru 5%, non-African (1%)—Asian, European, Arab. **Religions:** Indigenous 26%, Protestant 38%, Roman Catholic 28%, Muslim 6%. **Languages:** English, Swahili, and many tribal languages. **Education:** Years compulsory—none, but first 7 yrs. of primary school are provided free by government. Attendance—83% for primary grades. Functional literacy in English—25%. **Health:** Infant mortality rate 83/1000. Life expectancy (1977)—men 51.2 yrs., women 55.2 yrs. **Work force** (1.1 million wage earners); Agriculture—17%; industry and commerce—18%; services—13%; public sector—47%.

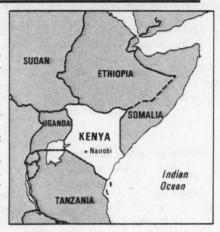

Official Name:
Republic of Kenya

Geography

Area: 582,646 sq. km. (224,960 sq. mi.); slightly smaller than Texas, a little smaller than Alberta, about 2½ times the size of Great Britain, 2¼ times the size of New Zealand, and a little larger than Bahrain.

Cities: Nairobi (pop. 959,000 in 1978). Other cities—Mombasa (401,000), Kisumu (115,000). **Terrain:** Coastal area—tropical, north—arid and semi-desert, central and west—mountainous and savanna.

Telecommunications: Kenya is connected with the U.S., Canada, and the UK by direct dial *from* those countries, but it is not possible to direct dial *out* of Kenya. International telephone services are available all over the world from Kenya. These calls can be booked from any hotel, and there is a special international or overseas call box in the main post offices of most cities. An excellent telex service allows replies to the public number. All these services utilize a satellite. The VOK (Voice of Kenya) radio broadcasts in English as well as Swahili, as does the VOK TV.

Transportation: Many international airlines serve Nairobi. Most major towns are linked by Kenya Airways flights, good passenger train services, and intercity bus service. Charter aircraft available. Kenya is 3 hours ahead of Greenwich Mean Time.

National Holidays: New Year's Day: Jan. 1. Labor Day: May 1. Madaraka Day: June 1. Kenyatta Day: Oct. 20. Independence Day: Dec. 12. Christmas Day and Boxing Day: Dec. 25 and 26. Plus Easter Monday and some Muslim holidays.

Arrival in Kenya at Nairobi

Most visitors arrive in Kenya at Jomo Kenyatta Airport (Kenyatta was the first president of Kenya). This is a magnificent new airport but unfortunately it does not have the facilities to trundle a disembarkation ramp to the door of the airplane. This means that passengers first go down a gangplank of steps, walk

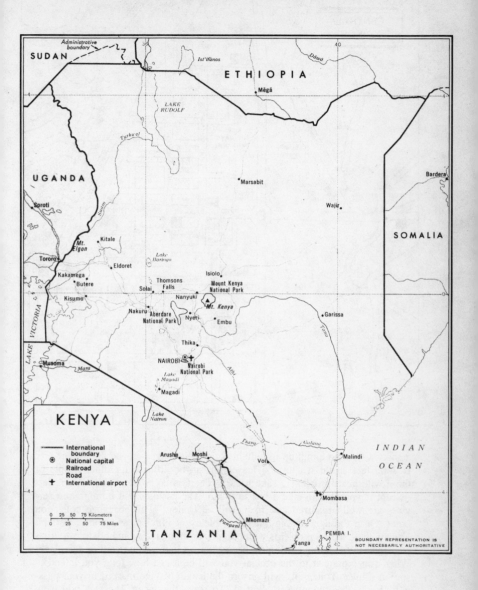

SUDAN

ETHIOPIA

Administrative boundary

Ist'ifānos

Dāwa

•Mêga

LAKE RUDOLF

Turkwel

UGANDA

•Marsabit

Bardera•

•Sproti

Wajir•

Kitale•

Mt. Elgon

Tororo•

SOMALIA

Kakamega•

Eldoret•

Lake Baringo

Isiolo•

•Butere

Solai•

Thomsons Falls

Mount Kenya National Park

Kisumu•

Nanyuki

▲*Mt. Kenya*

Nakuru•

Aberdare National Park

Nyeri•

•Embu

Garissa•

LAKE VICTORIA

Thika•

Musoma•

Mara

NAIROBI ⊛✚

Nairobi National Park

Lake Magadi

•Magadi

Lake Natron

INDIAN

OCEAN

KENYA

——— International boundary
⊛ National capital
········ Railroad
········ Road
✚ International airport

Arusha• Moshi•

Tsavo

Galana

•Voi

Malindi•

0 25 50 75 Kilometers
0 25 50 75 Miles

TANZANIA

Pangani

Mkomazi•

✚Mombasa

PEMBA I.

BOUNDARY REPRESENTATION IS
NOT NECESSARILY AUTHORITATIVE

Tanga•

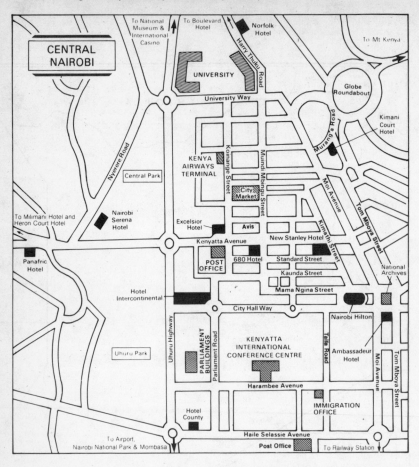

a short way, then climb up two flights of steps arranged as one flight. The city is 7000 feet above sea level. This climb can be difficult for older people or those with heart problems. Take it easy. There is no problem about being last (except if you plan to take a bus to town). The customs and immigration services are well organized and there will be trolleys at the baggage collection point. Once through customs there are plenty of efficient and honest porters. Usually there are no problems with customs or immigration and obvious tourists pass right through. You will have been given an immigration card on the plane. When you present it to the official you will be asked how long you intend to stay in Kenya. Your reply will govern the length of time marked in your passport. Up to three months is allowed. To make this clear: The visa you were issued by the embassy or high commission for Kenya does not (usually) have a time limit; it simply states "Good for single journey to Kenya within six months of date hereof if passport remains valid." The immigration officials set the time limit; therefore it is important to cover the time period you intend to stay when you give your reply. If you run over this time, or if the time is longer than three months—the maximum the official can give—then it becomes necessary to go to an immigration office and get an extension. There is nothing difficult in this, but knowing exactly what you want when you make your reply and allowing a week either way can save you this inconvenience.

Immediately upon clearing customs, health, and immigration formalities you pass into the lobby of the airport. Here you will find Avis, if you have reserved a car, and the driver will be waiting as you come through the doors holding a placard with your name on it. In the lobby there are banks (open 24 hours a day), Kenatco taxis (most reliable and we recommend), private taxis (whose touts will descend upon you), and a Kenya Airways airline bus. The latter is inclined to take off before all passengers have been cleared, so if you want to go into town by bus disregard our earlier advice about being last coming off the plane. The bus, if you catch it, stops at the major hotels and is, of course, cheaper than the taxis.

The airport is about 10 mi from city center, a 20-minute drive (although we have made it in 12 when rushing to catch a plane).

There are telephones in the airport waiting room if you need one. However, they take only Kenya shillings, so a visit to the banker's window is a necessary first stop.

We have found the information clerks to be totally useless. Don't waste time making inquiries of them. Instead, even if you haven't rented an Avis, ask the gentleman in the familiar red coat your questions.

Nairobi

Nairobi has tall buildings, paved streets, streetlights, and all the conveniences of a Western city. The slums are on the outskirts of town and are seldom seen by tourists. These are not as bad—all slums are bad, but even slums can be measured by degrees of deprivation and misery—as those of West Africa.

Occasionally there are electric power failures, but these are becoming less frequent. The water supply is good and pure. There may be water shortages in times of drought, but this is not for lack of planning.

Nairobi has every conceivable type of store except a street of porn shops, as this type of literature is prohibited (see the "Basic Information Checklist"). In general there is an air of a population getting on with the business of catching up with the 20th century.

Although dress is not as varied as that seen in Mombasa, Nairobi is a mixture of many peoples and cultures. They tend to keep to their separate enclaves in the city, but there is more interaction across cultures in Nairobi than in Mombasa.

Because Nairobi is so westernized, street crime can be a problem after dark. Use a taxi door to door after nightfall.

The effects of Nairobi's altitude seem to hit most people about the third day after arrival: shortness of breath and tiredness after brief exertion. It can take awhile to adjust unless you come from a city located at an equally (7000 feet) high altitude.

Rains, when they do occur in the high season, are brief, and readers should not feel that a safari is going to be spoiled by rain. During certain months, however, rain can be a major problem, making roads in the game parks impassable. All the roads between major towns are paved.

Nairobi is a modern city, which came about with the construction of the railroad linking Kenya's coast to Lake Victoria. Africans living in the region prior to the coming of the British lived in small settlements scattered around Mt. Kenya. The city of Nairobi was a swamp—like Washington, DC—which local people avoided. Nairobi has come a long way in 85 years.

Mombasa

The first British consul to eastern Africa was headquartered on Zanzibar Island off the coast of what is now Tanzania. The sultan ruled the islands and a 10-mile-wide coastal strip along the Kenya coast. When the British started developing their own commerce into eastern Africa, they selected the ancient port of Mombasa as the entry point.

Mombasa, naturally, is at sea level. Although efforts are being made to make it modern by tearing down lovely old buildings and replacing them with ugly office towers of concrete, Mombasa still has charm. The "Old Town" remains but is quite small and likely to be swamped eventually by the concrete towers.

The city water is pure and thanks to assistance from the U.S. Agency for International Development, a constant supply is provided. Electric power supplies can be erratic, especially in the smaller coastal towns to the north and south of Mombasa Island, particularly during the Moslem fast of Ramadan.

Again, like the other major towns of Kenya, the stores supply a variety of goods and Central Pharmacy's staff in the city center is always very helpful in filling prescriptions, and the pharmacy has a good display of toiletries. Bishara Street, like the street of the same name in Nairobi, offers all manner of African textiles and souvenirs.

There is always a breeze off the ocean, caught more in alleyways than by streets, and while temperatures can be hot, a cool place can always be found.

Fishing is an interesting possibility for those who have a few days to spend at the coast, and we suggest readers who are interested in doing so contact Bharai Club, which is located just after the New Nyali Bridge north of the city.

Diani Beach

This is the best beach in Kenya, located on the south coast. Other beaches tend to have ugly outcrops of coral or low water that prohibits swimming, or are banked by inferior hotels patronized by cheap European tour groups. Readers will undoubtedly hear about the coastal town of Malindi, but it is a sad comment on what crass commercialism can do to a once enjoyable stretch of beach. In any event, the beaches were never as good as Diani, and Malindi was more a gathering spot for the White Kenyan settlers than a viable beach resort.

There are a number of good hotels along Diani Beach, which we have described in "Kenyan Accommodation." Reference is also made to Diani Beach in the *Out of Africa* and *Flame Trees of Thika* itineraries.

Communications

Kenya Posts and Telecommunications is extremely efficient. There is no home or office delivery; patrons collect their mail from boxes at their nearest post office. For this reason the box number given in an address must always be used; the street address may eventually get mail to the addressee, but not always. Many small post offices, short of individual boxes, keep mail for collection with the postmaster, and patrons request their letters at the counter.

For tourists and visitors, the Poste Restante system operates. A letter is addressed preferably as follows:

> JONES, Mary
> Poste Restante
> GPO
> Nairobi, Kenya

Mary Jones can be written as Miss or Mrs. Mary Jones, but it is wiser to put the surname first. There are Poste Restante windows in all major post offices. Behind the counter the clerk stands in front of a number of pigeon holes marked with letters of the alphabet. An interestingly attired group of foreign visitors usually lines up in front of the clerk and as their turn comes, each gives his/her surname. The postal clerk removes, in our case, all the mail in the *T* slot. Slowly, letter by letter, the face of each envelope is shown. When a letter addressed to, in our case, a *Taylor* appears, the initial or Christian names are checked, and if correct, the letter is passed from his or her hand to ours. The display is resumed until the pile of *T*s is exhausted. All this takes considerable time, especially if one gets behind a person whose name begins with an *M* or a *B*. Poste Restante offices are found throughout Africa.

American Express also accepts mail if you're traveling with them or have purchased their traveler's checks. However, we have not found them to be as efficient, and certainly not as courteous, as post office employees.

Hotels also hold mail addressed to their guests. This can be hit or miss, and readers should ask the front desk clerk to look through *all* the mail at the front desk, not merely that filed under their surname. The mail is not automatically put in your box even when you're registered and actually occupying a room. Guests must ask for it.

Most hotels either sell stamps at the front desk or at a shop in their lobby. Hilton Communications Centers operate cable and telex services, but regretably, we have not found them to be too helpful, as the English of the staff manning these facilities is not always good. Cables and telegrams can also be sent from post offices. In Kenya, when the post offices are closed a Telecommunications Center, located in a building separate from the post office, and many times in another part of the city, is used for cables. For telexs, there is a "public number," which can be used for replies to you. Ask the clerk what that number is if you wish a telex reply.

Whatever problems Americans may have with cables being delivered quickly rests not at the African end, but with the policy of delivering cables with the next day's mail in the United States. Tough luck if it's a Saturday, your cable isn't delivered until Monday. Domestic telegrams and cables addressed to people in Kenya are delivered immediately, as they are in most other African countries. However, in this case, when immediate delivery is required remember to use the street address as well as the post office box number.

Express Mail is a service offered in Kenya for overnight deliveries to major Kenyan towns. The charge is very, very small. Mail must be taken to the post office and handed in before 10 a.m. for delivery the same day between Mombasa and Nairobi, and vice versa. Deadlines vary from town to town, so it's best to inquire.

Three national tabloid-size dailies are published in Kenya in English: *The Daily Nation, The Standard* (formerly the *East African Standard*), and *The Kenya Times*. All are morning papers, published seven days a week. There is a weekly newspaper of interest to those visiting or living at the coast, *Coast Week*, published in English with feature pages in Swahili and German.

Many magazines are published locally: *National Review* (political), *Executive* (business), various homemaker and sports periodicals. *Time* and *Newsweek* international editions are regularly available. An interesting magazine for the visitor is the East African Wildlife Society's *Swara*, which invariably has interesting articles on the wildlife in all of East Africa, not simply Kenya.

Telephones also come under the Ministry of Posts and Telecommunications. In our opinion the "good workman" can blame his tools with justification: The phone system and equipment is British. Patience and engaging operators in personal conversation is the best method of getting calls through. There is direct dial for most cities and towns in Kenya, but not for overseas calls. The latter go through fairly quickly (5–10 minutes), depending upon the traffic. Time and charges can be requested if using a friend's phone. Services can be station-to-station or personal and can also be timed by the operator.

Once outside a hotel room, getting at a public phone is a major undertaking. Hotel lobbies, restaurants, drug stores, shops, etc. do not have public phones. The Nairobi Hilton International had a bank of phones in the lobby but took them out because of the nuisance caused to guests by people (especially pickpockets) coming into the lobby to use them. The only public phones are housed in cast-iron, fireman red phone booths (call boxes). These are located outside post offices with long lines of people waiting to use them. There are special overseas telephone boxes inside the main post offices that are open during normal working hours. Except for radio call phones in certain remote areas, all phones have dials, none are touch tone.

On the whole, Kenyan phones are something to be endured. For local calls it is many times quicker to go and see someone than try to get through on the phone. Reportedly, the Japanese are installing new equipment in Kenya and this may improve matters.

Hotels add a surcharge to calls made from the rooms. Mount Kenya Safari Club, Nanyuki, charged us 100 shillings for a 90-shilling call to Washington. Inquire what the surcharges are before placing a call. Rates for overseas calls are the same at all hours of the day or night.

The Kenyan government owns and operates the radio stations. Schedules for programs appear in the daily newspapers. The BBC Overseas Services broadcasts its world news at 10 nightly. Reception is good even on cheap radios. The Voice of America, the Canadian Broadcasting Service, the South African World Service, and, of course, the Soviets broadcast to East Africa.

The Kenyan government also owns and operates the one television station. Programs are generally shown only during the evening hours and provide a combination of locally produced dramas and old television programs from Western countries.

Video tapes are available cheaply and may be rented from many stores. Videos are very popular.

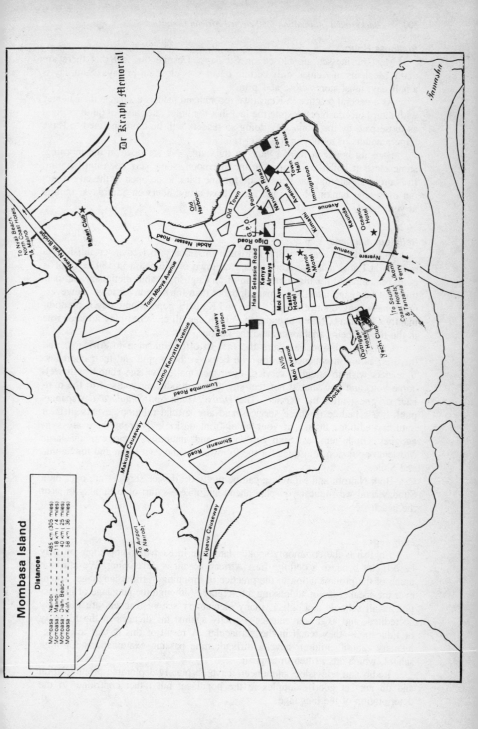

Mombasa Island

Distances

Mombasa - Nairobi - - - - - - 485 km (305 miles)
Mombasa - Malindi - - - - - - 118 km (74 miles)
Mombasa - Diani Beach - - - - 40 km (25 miles)
Mombasa - Kilifi - - - - - - 58 km (36 miles)

Dr Kraph Memorial

Tanzania

To Nyali Beach,
North Coast Hotels
& Malindi

New Nyali Bridge

Bahari Club

Abdel Nasser Road

Old
Harbour

Old Town

Police

Fort
Jesus

Nkrumah Road

Town Hall

Avenue

Immigration

Avenue

Kilindini Avenue

Kenuka Avenue

G.P.O.

Digo Road

Oceanic Hotel

Nyerere Avenue

Tom Mboya Avenue

Haile Selassie Road

Kenya
Airways

Manor
Motel

Moi Ave.

Castle
Hotel

Ukonu Ferry

To South,
Coast Hotels
& Tanzania Ferry

Railway
Station

Jomo Kenyatta Avenue

Lumumba Road

AVIS

Moi Avenue

Outrigger
Hotel

Yacht Club

Docks

Shimanzi Road

Makupa Causeway

Kipevu Causeway

To Airport
& Nairobi

Business Hours

Most businesses are closed on Sundays. Despite the fact that there are many Moslems in Kenya, only certain businesses close on Fridays. Saturday is a half day; most stores close at 1 p.m.

As a general practice in Kenya we recommend readers exchange their money with their hotel cashiers despite the fact that the hotel rates are not quite as good as those paid by the banks. By doing so readers will be more inclined to leave large amounts of money in the hotel safe.

Banking hours in Kenya vary by the bank. All are open in the morning; some close at lunch and reopen in the afternoon, some stay open until 2 p.m. In Nairobi an attempt has been made for one bank to be open in the city center out of regular banking hours and for at least a few hours on Saturdays. Inquire at your hotel.

Religious Services

Johann Krapf was the first Christian missionary to Kenya, establishing a mission at Rabai near the Kenyan coastal town of Mombasa in 1842. Krapf is more remembered for his compilation of an English-Swahili dictionary and putting that language into the Roman alphabet than for his conversions. However, much has changed since Krapf's time and Kenya's population today is predominantly Christian. Church attendance is high and all churches play a major role in the life of their parishioners and the nation.

Christian missionaries were the first to offer education to Africans, and there is, as a consequence, a close tie between the people and their churches. If readers wish to attend a service, even the smallest village church will welcome you, and you should not feel shy about introducing yourself to the minister or priest after the service. The *Daily Nation* and *Standard* newspapers publish a schedule of those services and any special religious events in their Saturday editions or ask at your hotel front desk. In Nairobi there are synagogues, Hindu temples, Sikh gurdwaras, and, naturally, because of the large Moslem population, mosques for the followers of the Aga Khan and for Sunnie and Shite.

Both Nairobi and Mombasa can be pretty dead once services are over on a Sunday, and we suggest you plan ahead and take a safari on a Sunday or visit the beach.

Languages

English is the commonly spoken language in Kenya. Comprehension may be difficult because a definite East African accent is developing. We attribute much of the pronunciation to the practice of dropping in tribal languages whenever the speaker is not addressing a foreigner. Although the language of instruction in all schools is English, many elementary school teachers are not fully accredited, and as a convenience—strictly against the dictates of the Ministry of Education—they teach in the vernacular. A result of this is that many elementary school children have a difficult time passing examinations for high school, which are written in English.

Radio and television announcers have absolutely deplorable pronunciation and do not set good examples to the populace, but rather contribute to the deterioration of the language.

Swahili is spoken at the coast and in rural areas to a greater or lesser degree depending upon the location.

Geographical Description

The coastal belt of Kenya is tropical with coconut palms bordering the beaches. (It is interesting to note that coconuts do not grow north of the Banjun Islands in Somalia for reasons that are not known.) Much of the actual ground is coral, with only a slight covering of soil. However, the entire area is very fertile and lush.

The area between Nairobi and Mombasa is very dry and supports only thorn bush vegetation and little else. To the northeast of Nairobi, up to the banks of the Tana River, the terrain is much the same. Along the river heavy tropical vegetation is seen, but once away from the life-supporting stream, arid lands again take over.

The Mt. Kenya region is fertile and small farms are interspersed with pine forests. North of the mountain the land again becomes, very quickly, dry and arid. The Rift Valley floor running west of Nairobi is dry, but at higher elevations—known as the "White Highlands"—there is good wheat country, and higher still, dense forests and tea plantations. Approaching Lake Victoria the land again becomes tropical until, at the Uganda border, in the south, almost any tropical crop can be successfully grown.

Kenya receives much of her electric power supply from Owen Falls in Jinja, Uganda, and a new power plant along her own Tana River. Her mineral and energy resources, as the government has not seen fit to utilize solar energy, are much smaller than those found in many other African countries. Exploration for oil has taken place in the north, but to date no commercial reserves have been identified.

Tribes and Ethnic Groups

Kenya, before British colonization, was not a country or a series of large kingdoms such as found in Uganda. Rather, Kenya was composed of many divergent tribes, and modern Kenya has tried hard to subdue tribalism and bring the geographic area within her borders into a cohesive group. The coastal area during the early colonial period came under the administration of the sultan of Zanzibar, and the people along the Indian Ocean littoral differ in character from the "up-country" people: Life on the coast is slower; the people are predominantly Moslem and speak grammatical Swahili, while people in other parts of the country speak their own tribal languages, although Swahili is officially the national language along with English. Coast people wear traditional dress more often than European styles; their diet is based on rice not cornmeal; and they are less anxious to move into Western lifestyles than other Kenyans.

The Nairobi area and the Rift Valley to the west is inhabited primarily by members of the Kikuyu tribe. This is now the single largest tribe in Kenya. They differ ethnically from the nomadic, pastoral peoples such as the Masai, Turkana, and Samburu, as they were agriculturalists when the colonizers arrived. The Luo live along the shores of Lake Victoria as do the Luyha; traditionally they are farmers and fishermen. The Kamba live to the east of Nairobi; their main center is Machokas. Intelligent and good hunters, they were much liked by the British, although preference was reportedly given to the Luo.

The first president of Kenya was a Kikuyu and the present vice-president is from that tribe. President Daniel arap Moi is a Kalejin, a very small tribe from the Lake Baringo region.

The Kikuyu have aggressively pursued Western lifestyles and are in influential positions in both the government, civil service, and business. The Masai have resisted change, as have the Turkana and Samburu, although there are some extremely interesting university-educated members of those tribes, most particularly the Turkana.

To the trained eye there is a marked distinction in the appearance of people belonging to each tribe and as intermarriage is not really popular, the distinctive characteristics will probably continue to be apparent for some years to come.

Joy Adamson's *The Peoples of Kenya* details the customs and traditional dress of all of Kenya's tribes, and her work provides marvelous paintings of typical members of each tribe.

Social Customs

Kenya is racing pell-mell into the 21st century hoping to catch up with the technological world. As a result very few genuine traditional customs remain. Witchcraft is a practice punishable under the criminal code. Polygamy is legal but "Letters to the Editor" columns in national papers decry the practice and the payment of dowries. Scarification is to be seen only on the elderly. Traditional dancing is reserved for tourist performances and occasions when either the president of Kenya or a visiting dignitary arrives at the international airport. A modern African society is evolving founded on British customs and the influence of the American media. For these reasons Kenya is a good introduction to Africa because the break with Western culture is not extremely alien.

It should be noted here that one custom has not died, and that is mob justice. Take care in sounding the alarm if your purse is snatched. Passersby more often than not will descend upon the thief and beat him to death with their fists or whatever is handy. Police, when they arrive, must concern themselves with saving the thief from the mob, and many times there are just too many in the mob for them to do so.

On the whole the people are courteous, and the courtesy and charm increase as the traveler leaves Nairobi and goes further into Kenya. Every tourist we have spoken to never fails to remark on the courteous service in the hotels. Mombasa is much slower paced, and the people in the lakeside city of Kisumu are a delight.

The visitor may encounter "Uncle Tomism." Ingratiating oneself is the accepted route to ripping off the foreigner. Very few hard-luck stories have valid substance in Kenya. Medical services are free; there are many excellent charities offering subsistence wages in return for work, but some Kenyans have their sights set higher and see life in Europe and North America's fast lane as the way to go. The truth is that education has outstripped white collar opportunity; agriculture is without status for the high school graduate. Nor are the street beggars in need of your charity. If you wish to help Kenyans in genuine need, step into the nearest church and drop a donation in the poor box. That way you'll know your gift is helping to answer a genuine need.

The initiate to Africa will enjoy Kenya; we consider it our second home, and perhaps one is always hardest on those they know best. The country has been politically stable since independence if for no other reason than the British have invested heavily in Kenya. In 1987 an undercurrent of political unrest began to surface again (there was a 2-day coup that was aborted in 1981). It is sincerely hoped by all friends of Kenya that wise counsel will prevail and that President Moi can address the problems with finesse—which has always been his strong suit. However, Kenya has been very vocal in her opposition to South Africa and the Soviet Union, and these two powers have it in their vested interest to foment unrest. Coping with foreign-financed dissenters in an African country where many of the populace are illiterate is not always conducive to the exercise of human rights—unpalatable as that may be to some.

Shopping

Nairobi City Market is one of the best places to shop—with a bit of bargaining prices will drop dramatically. There is a wide choice of items of every description. Kenyan women bring their sisal baskets (so popular in Western countries) to this particular market.

Mombasa City Market is due to be rebuilt. When it is we hope it will improve. At the moment the only offerings are fresh vegetables and fruits. The basketsellers immediately outside the market charge exhorbitant prices and exploit the weavers. Buy your baskets in Nairobi.

Bishara Street (Market Street) in either Nairobi or Mombasa has a multitude of shops specializing in everything conceivable. It is on these streets that you'll find the greatest choice of khangas and African prints as well as souvenir items. Usually the prices are clearly marked.

Old Town Mombasa, as we have mentioned in the *Lost Cities of Africa* itinerary, can offer some unusual items.

Bookstores in Nairobi and Mombasa many times have titles on African subjects that are almost impossible to find elsewhere in the world.

On the main Nairobi-Mombasa highway—about midway—the Kamba Carvers Cooperative has sale rooms. The construction was financed through a grant from the government of Norway. Some excellent, but not collector's quality carvings can be purchased.

Good European antiques can be purchased from the Antique Gallery, Ltd. (Consolidated House, Kuanda St., P.O. Box 47616) and the Antiquity Shoppe (Nairobi Hilton International Arcade, P.O. Box 32182), both in Nairobi, and from Hassanali Abdulhusein (Nkrumah Rd., P.O. Box 82959) and Gallery Ghalia Ltd. (Rex House, Moi Ave., P.O. Box 80654), both in Mombasa.

Precious stones are always a risky purchase unless one knows the seller is absolutely reputable. In Kenya we know this to be true of Chandu Pattini (Hamilton House, Wabera St.) in Nairobi and Ahmed Haji Elyas (Digo Rd., P.O. Box 81419) in Mombasa. Their telephone numbers are Nairobi 337675 and Mombasa 24092 respectively.

Hotel and Restaurant Food

Make up your mind from the start that eating in Kenya is not going to be any great culinary experience. With the exception of the few places we have listed at the end of this section, the food the average tourist encounters in Kenya is edible and plentiful but not great. Chefs who were once house cooks to British families now cook in hotels and restaurants for tourists, and although

Leah and I personally prefer British cooking to many other ethnic foods, it has seldom been internationally acclaimed. The Kenyan government-operated Utali College in Nairobi produces younger chefs under the tutelage of Swiss instructors, but what do the Swiss know of tropical foods?

Meat is undoubtedly the biggest problem. Unless the cut is the filet mignon, the meat is tough and inclined to stringiness. Pork is good but usually dry and overcooked. Ham is good. Lamb is tough and dry. Rubbing the meat with juice from the locally grown papaya—the same ingredient in Accent meat tenderizer—could help. But a milch cow will always be a milch cow and trying to turn her, once she has passed her lactations, into prime beef can't be done. But prices reflect this more cheaply produced meat on the menus so there is compensation.

Tropical fruits are plentiful in Kenya but chefs have yet to learn that cold food needs to stay under refrigeration at least, if not twice as long, as hot foods need to stay in an oven. Consequently, what could otherwise be a glorious tropical dessert is a tepid, gagging-to-the-American palate mish-mash.

Forget, too, those great Hawaiian and Caribbean bars where tropical fruit courts alcohols to cumulate into perfect pina coladas, margaritas, banana, lime or pineapple daiquiris. Your best bet is the national drink, Export or Tusker beer. Coca-Cola and Pepsi are cheap and available everywhere, but trying to get enough ice to drink them really cold is another matter. Scotch—no bourbon or rye—gin, vodka, Bacardi, European wines, and a local reisling are available at all the resort and Nariobi hotels and restaurants. Asking that they be mixed with anything other than Schweppes tonic, ginger ale, or soda is to ask for disappointment, even at the Hilton.

Cadbury, the English chocolate manufacturer, produces the same high-quality products in Kenya as they do in the UK and U.S. Other locally manufactured candies are colored sugar syrup boiled to rock hardness. But Kenyan children love them, and we take two or three 2-kilo packs along with us when driving to rural areas to throw out to the children from the car or train windows.

Bakery products are unbelievably terrible, from California Cookies to the cakes served at tea time—unless homemade. The Hilton pastry chef is the exception, but even he has failed to continue the practice of his predecessor and serve the pastries really well chilled.

The national dish of Kenya, which was most certainly not always so, is boiled white cornmeal served in a huge mound with a soupy sauce of beef or chicken and diced vegetables. Nice to try.

Swahili cooking, when the recipes are read, sounds terrible, as coconut juice or coconut milk is used in virtually everything. To us, Swahili dishes are delicious—the milk seems to heighten and give body to otherwise mild flavors. Hot spices are not used in Swahili cooking, only cardomon, fengreek, vanilla, Zanzibar black pepper, and cloves. Chilis are used very sparingly. It is difficult to find Swahili restaurants, but if you do happen on one that looks reasonably clean, don't hesitate to try it along with the ones we recommend.

Seafood is plentiful in Kenya, but refrigerated trucks are not. Much as we love seafood, we avoid it when traveling in Africa.

The following, in order of merit by our judgment, are our recommended Kenyan restaurants:

Kentmere Club (Banana Hill, 20 mi west of Nairobi). European/British cooking. Vegetables picked from their own garden the day they are to be used. Beautifully set tables, in an old English cottage type setting. Outstanding service. Reasonably priced 3-course dinner under $25.

The Horseman (Karen, a suburb of Nairobi). Reservations required. Unlike many other restaurants of its caliber around the world, the prices do not reflect the high reputation this restaurant has earned. Each dish is prepared daily as the chef cooks only to reservations held. European food. Set in a converted stable loft with all the trimmings of British hunt country inns: shining horse brasses, Liberty print slip covers, rubbed mahogany tables, Sanderson wallpaper, and muted pastels against white frame Tudor beams.

Tamarind Restaurant. Although there is one Tamarind in Nairobi and another in Mombasa, we prefer the latter, whose dining room and terrace look out over the old harbor. Exotic tropical and European dishes. Expensive for Kenya but under $40 for a 3-course meal.

Tate Room (New Stanley Hotel, Nairobi city center). Their lunchtime buffet is very attractively presented, especially the roasted cold meats. Salads, desserts, including cakes, and excellent service. Very reasonably priced at under $15 for an all-you-can-eat lunch.

Leopard Beach Hotel Dining Room (Diani Beach, Ukunda, South Coast). Impeccable service; the evening meal is a delight as the dining room overlooks the Indian Ocean. European dishes with a slight Italian accent.

Mnarani Club (on the south side of Kilifi Creek, north coast). A buffet lunch is served of primarily German dishes and desserts. The view of the creek and ocean in a magnificent garden setting is one of the rare opportunities the north coast offers. Lunch under $13.

Outrigger Hotel Dining Room (Mombasa). Although not sharing the luxury decor of the preceding restaurants, the chef's Swahili chicken and coconut is perfect. He also has a way with vegetables and uses only butter to complement them. Lunch or dinner under $13.

Manor Hotel Dining Room (city center, Mombasa). Although serving just plain British cooking and a few Kenyan dishes, the dining room is a lovely, cool place to spend the 2-hour lunch break when shopping in Mombasa. Service cannot be faulted. Lunch under $7.

Bush Baby (opposite the entrance for Jadini Beach Hotel, Diani Beach). This little open-air cafe is primarily for employees of the hotel, but all are welcome. Their kebabs are marvelous. Very reasonable.

In the same lovely alpine setting as the Kentmere Club is the home of a White Kenyan tea planter, Mrs. Mitchell. She opens her home to the public every afternoon for a traditional English high tea. Directions and arrangements can be made at the Kentmere Club.

Background for Malawi

PROFILE

People

Nationality: Noun and adjective—Malawian(s). **Population** (1980 est.): 6.3 million. Annual growth rate: 2.9%. **Ethnic groups:** Chewa, Nyanja, Tumbuka, Yao, Lomwe, Sena, Tonga, Ngoni, Asians, Europeans. **Religions:** Protestant 55%, Roman Catholic 20%, Muslim 20%; African traditional religions are also practiced by some members of these groups. **Languages:** Chichewa and English are official. **Education:** Years compulsory—none. Attendance—45%. Literacy—25% (age 15 and older). **Health:** Infant mortality rate—14/1000. Life expectancy—47 yrs. **Work force** (360,000 paid): Agriculture—45%; industry and commerce—17%; services—18%; government—20%.

Geography

Area: 118,484 sq. km. (45,747 sq. mi.); about the size of Pennsylvania, twice the size of Nova Scotia, slightly less than half the size of Great Britain, half the size of Muscat and Oman, and a little larger than New Zealand's North Island.

Cities: Capital—Lilongwe (pop. 130,000). Other cities—Blantyre (250,000), Mzuzu (20,000). Terrain: Plateaus, highlands, valleys. Lake Malawi is about 20% of total area. Climate: Predominantly subtropical.

Telecommunications: Good long-distance radiotelephone service is available. Telegraph services connect Malawi with the U.S. and Europe. Lilongwe is two hours ahead of Greenwich Mean Time.

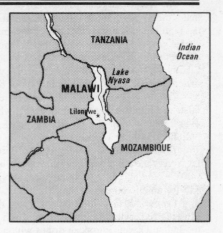

Official Name:
Malawi

Transportation: Several international airlines serve Malawi's Kamuzu International Airport a few miles outside Lilongwe. There is rail service between Lilongwe and Salima and from Salima to Nsanje via Blantyre-Limbe. This line connects with the train to Mozambique and the port of Beira but is slow and unreliable. The government operated steamer on Lake Malawi carries the major portion of traffic and cargo.

National Holidays: New Year's Day: Jan. 1. Martyrs' Day: March 3. Kamuzu Day: May 14. Republic Day: July 6. August Day: 1st Monday in Aug. Mother's Day: Oct. 17. Christmas and Boxing Day: Dec. 25 and 26. Plus Good Friday, Easter and Easter Monday. Particular attention should be paid to national holidays as the country literally closes down in observance of them.

Arrival in Malawi

Everything is squeaky clean at the new international airport 7 mi from Lilongwe. Few tourists visit Malawi, and after the expatriate residents have passed through immigration and customs, visitors are processed. Malawi has a dress code—no jeans and slacks for women, only dresses; men's hair must be cut short on back and sides—in addition to a control on pornographic and revolutionary literature, and once the customs officers have satisfied themselves

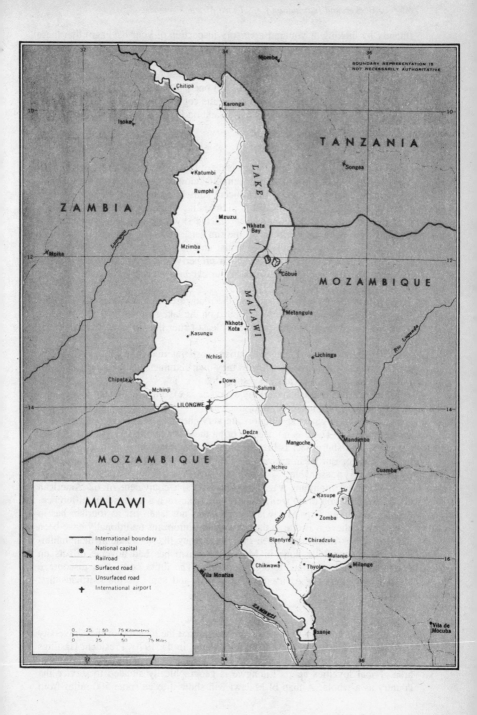

BOUNDARY REPRESENTATION IS
NOT NECESSARILY AUTHORITATIVE

Njombe

TANZANIA

Chitipa

Karonga

Isoka

Songea

ZAMBIA

Katumbi

Rumphi

Mzuzu

Nkhata
Bay

Mpika

Mzimba

Côbué

MOZAMBIQUE

Metangula

Nkhota
Kota

Kasungu

Lichinga

Rio Luangwa

Nchisi

Chipata

Dowa

Mchinji

Salima

LILONGWE

Dedza

Mangoche

Mandimba

Ncheu

Cuamba

Kasupe

Zomba

MOZAMBIQUE

Blantyre

Chiradzulu

Mulanje

Vila Moatize

Chikwawa

Thyolo

Milenge

ZAMBEZI

Nsanje

Vila de
Mocuba

MALAWI

	International boundary
	National capital
	Railroad
	Surfaced road
	Unsurfaced road
	International airport

0   25   50   75 Kilometers
0   25   50   75 Miles

(merely by looking at you and a cursory inspection of your baggage) that these conditions have been met, visitors are passed on through. If you have reserved an Avis car there will be an agent of the company to meet you, which will facilitate matters, but we had no problems and were handled efficiently.

The drive into Lilongwe is a beautiful one along flowering, tree-lined roads, and even for a driver who has not been in the country before, very easily driven. There is little traffic on Malawi's roads, and once into Lilongwe the way to the Capital Hotel is well marked.

Background

Malawi skies are sky blue—the shade of blue in African skies changes with the latitudes—and ever-changing cumulus clouds move across the country throughout the day. Perfectly magnificent sunsets occur every evening—not in the classical sense, as in Mogadiscio in Somalia, where a great fireball descends over the horizon, but Malawi sunsets fill the sky with pink and lavender that becomes more intensely brilliant as the sun sets.

The country is scenically spectacular and immaculately clean.

Personal security is good, although property security can present a problem. We had the gas syphoned out of our car in a hotel (not recommended in our list) parking lot.

There are very few tourists, and the roads are practically devoid of traffic since most cargo north to south is shipped on the lake steamer instead of tractor-trailers. Driving is, if not hassle-free, at least better than in most African countries.

The Malawi Department of Tourism posts internationally illegal disclaimers of responsibility on the properties they own and manage. Whatever happens, for whatever cause, they are not responsible.

The level of English spoken by everyone is excellent. The people are helpful, friendly, good mannered, and gracious.

All imported wines and liquors are very cheap; in some cases cheaper than duty-free prices. There is no need to bring these with you. The same is true for cigarettes. Carlsburg beer is brewed under license in Malawi.

Canned or European grocery food is expensive. Meals in the recommended hotels are very reasonable.

The daily minimum wage in Malawi is the equivalent of 62 American cents. We urge you to tip well; so little can make such a tremendous difference.

In examining why Malawian tourism has not taken off as tourism has in Kenya, we believe it is due to the dress code. Europeans traditionally have been the tourists to Africa, and when they travel they like to abandon their inhibitions. This cannot be done in Malawi. Tourism has had adverse effects on Africa as well as earning foreign exchange. The dress code does discourage tourists who come to Africa for "sex, sand and sun" as the Germans first advertised Kenya.

Lilongwe

Zomba, a town to the south of Lilongwe and the location of the University of Malawi, was the colonial capital of Malawi. In the 1970s President Hastings Banda decided to move the capital to Lilongwe, which was located in his tribal area. Tribal loyalties apart, Lilongwe is geographically situated to service the country as a whole. A map of Malawi will show it to be some 500 miles from

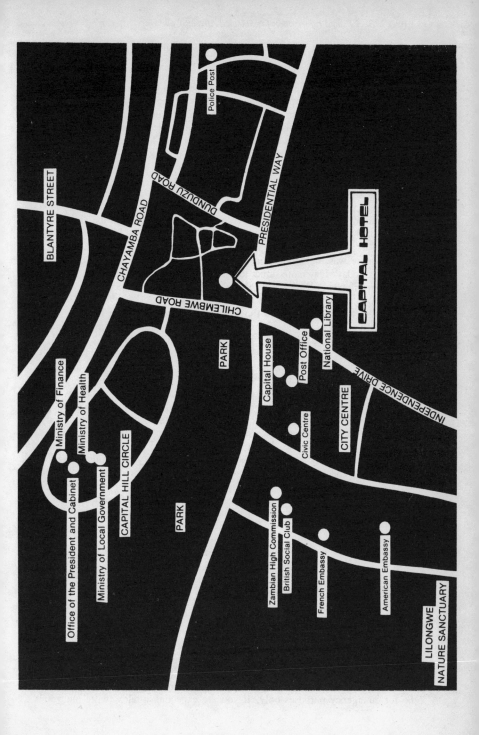

north to south and, at its widest point, 100 miles. Lilongwe is midway between the north and south.

The city has been laid out by architects unlike most cities that simply "grow." The government buildings are concentrated in an area known as Capital Hill, the modern shops and stores are in a type of "mall," and the hotels are set out in grassed lawns. There is an old part of Lilongwe, and this is where the market is located. While there are a few multistoried buildings, the effect is that the city blends in with the lush green parks and flowering trees that make up so much of the town. There is absolutely not one piece of trash (rubbish) to be seen anywhere.

Zomba, Blantyre, and Limbe

These are towns to the south of Lilongwe. As mentioned above, Zomba was the former capital and has some colonial buildings as well as the university. It is situated at the foot of Zomba Plateau, which we describe in the *Livingstone* itinerary.

Blantyre was the commercial capital of Malawi and remains a center for commerce today. It is more direct to drive to Lusaka in Zambia from Blantyre than from Lilongwe. During the colonial period, Northern Rhodesia (as Zambia was known) and Nyasaland were economically tied.

Limbe was the location of the international auction houses that marketed Malawi's tea, tobacco, and cotton. Today, while a number of small factories are located in Limbe, the auction house activity is much reduced.

None of these Malawi cities are larger than big towns; all are very clean and well administered. The visitor does not see the slums and poverty that is so common in other African towns.

These brief descriptions make Malawi seem rather bland—Malawi is very low-key, very organized, and very quiet. We like it; it is the perfect country to vacation, where the visitor appreciates having the time to follow an itinerary without hassle or pressure. If we saw a policeman in Malawi, it was so infrequent as to make us feel we didn't see any. Contrasted to other African countries, such as Ivory Coast, where there were soldiers every 500 yards lining the highways and checkpoints in and out of the airports and main cities, the absence of uniformed personnel gave a feeling of relaxation, which can never be compensated for by the existence of massive "holiday and resort facilities" such as those the government of the Ivory Coast has been at such pains to erect.

Communications

The front desk at the Capital Hotel is very well organized (except for the cash drawer, where the bills are just dropped in without being divided by denomination—however, this may be just a hang-up on our part as they make change very quickly), and mail addressed in care of them, we feel, will be delivered to their guests. Mail can be addressed to Poste Restante, at the general post office, Lilongwe, as we have described in "Background for Kenya: Communications." However, unlike in Kenya, mail takes a very long time in and out of Malawi, and we believe readers will be better advised to use telex services. If you're renting an Avis car, give your emergency number as their telex number. Their staff are very conscientious, and if you let them know which itinerary you are following, they can try to get the message to you. This should be for emergency purposes only. If you are expecting a telex, write out your itinerary for the Avis manager and make a point of seeing her personally. There is an English daily newspaper run by the government. This has mostly local news. *Time* and *Newsweek* are available in the Capital Hotel lobby newspaper shop, as are other non-Malawian periodicals.

Radio is, again, controlled by the government and programs are broadcast in English. The BBC Overseas Service has programs directed to southern Africa and reception is good after dark.

Business Hours

Stores open at 9 a.m., close for a 2-hour lunch, and reopen for the afternoon until 5:30. The market is open on Saturday afternoon, but most stores close half day and all day Sunday. We had money sent to us from England through the bank and found the services efficient. Banks are open in the morning and for a few hours in the afternoon. Hours depend upon the bank—ask at the Capital Hotel front desk.

Religious Services

While there are a number of churches in all the major towns, we were not overly impressed, as in Uganda, with the devotion of the Malawian people to their churches. We were told that religious affiliation is taken quite casually, and when a woman marries she follows the religious persuasion of her husband without hesitation. Despite the fact that Malawi was one of the earliest countries to be evangelized, a certain amount of traditional religious influence is felt and has not died.

There are Roman Catholic churches and churches of every Protestant denomination in most towns. Make inquiries as to the times of their services; everyone's English is so good, you'll have no problem.

Languages

The official language of Malawi is English, and the level spoken, as mentioned above, is so high, even in rural areas, that it is a pleasure to move around the country.

The Shire River is pronounced as though the word was spelled *Shiri*.

Tribal languages are spoken, of course (Cinyanja in the south, Citumbyk in the north), but not to the extent that they are in eastern Africa. We have not traveled in Malawi's far north, and it may be that in this more remote region near the Zaire border, English is not as commonly used. On the whole, it is a relief to travel where everything one says is understood *the first time*.

Geographical Description

Malawi's boundary includes the greater portion of Lake Malawi, although Mozambique has some rights to the lake. The sand along the lake's shore is a light brown, and the water itself is not particularly beautiful in color. However, the views of the lake with the low hills of Mozambique on the far shore and the formation of clouds that are always present are beautiful. Malawi is more reminiscent of Scotland than any other African country, yet it is known as "The Warm Heart of Africa" because of the genuineness of her people.

Malawi is a chain of plateaus forming the most southerly end of the Great Rift Valley. The British colonizers, preferring the cooler climates, away from malarial zones, settled the plateaus. It can become quite chilly even in the daytime, because one has not adapted to cooler temperatures if time has been spent at the lakeshore.

The northwestern boundary between Malawi and Zambia is not too well defined, and visitors to Nyika Plateau can be in Zambia without realizing it. In view of Zambia's hypersensitivity to possible "South African agents" entering their country "from the north," readers would be wise to ask local park wardens what the situation is before wandering too far. The *Livingstone* itinerary does not go as far as Nyika Plateau, but readers who have a copy of *Fielding's African Safaris* may want to extend the itinerary to include this beautiful park.

The Shire River is a very difficult one to trace on a map, and we have yet to identify a map that really enables one to do so. It flows from the southern end of Lake Malawi through Liwonde National Park, after passing through Lake Malombe, then flows southwest to Matope, where navigation becomes impossible because of the Kloombidzo Falls, continues south to Tedzuni Falls/Nkuld Falls; more southerly are Hamilton Falls and Kapichira Falls. The Shire dissipates after turning eastward through Elephant Marsh, and reforms as a river at Chiromo to flow south to Nsanje and Ndinde Marsh to empty into the Zambezi River.

Climate in Malawi: The rainy season starts in November and continues until the end of March. The rains completely alter the vegetative cover of the land. During the rains the country is green and lush. There are fewer flowers than in Kenya, but by comparison to temperate climates, there are profuse bursts of color especially from the flowering trees. The yellow blooms that line Lilongwe's streets are especially striking. It is during the rainy season that the wild orchids are to be found on mountains and plateaus. (See *Fielding's African Safaris,* "Orchid Hunter's Safari.")

Since the rains do not fall around the lakeshore as intensely as they do at the higher elevations, it is almost certain that the rainy days experienced between November and March at Blantyre and Limbe can be escaped by driving to the lake.

In either case, except at elevations of 7000 feet and over, the temperature hovers at 70°F and the rainwater is warm to the touch.

Golfers complain that plastic tees melt and bend and wooden tees splinter and break when an attempt is made to put them in the ground during the dry season. Then August–September and April–May, the grasses wither and the dust billows behind cars and trucks. There are no orchids, but game viewing is better as animals search out water. Again, the temperatures stay around the 70-degree mark but afternoons can be hot.

A wind comes off the lake near the shore, from an easterly direction, and is more noticeable along the western shore of the lake (Selima) than where the shoreline is sheltered in areas such as Makokolo and Nkopola.

Tribes and Ethnic Groups

There are a number of tribes, all of Bantu origin, in Malawi. They offered severe resistance to early explorers as the territory had been savaged by Arab slavers for many years. Slaves were taken to Kilwa and Zanzibar Island for shipment to North and South America.

While descendants of Arab traders continue to do business in Malawi, their interests are primarily in small shops and the single largest minority ethnic group are the British. The latter control much of Malawi's agricultural exports and British investment in Malawi is considerable.

Social Customs

Malawi is primarily an agricultural country, and there is not the concentration of population in the cities as in African countries that have tried to establish light and heavy industries instead of agriculture. The effect of this on the social customs is that life is followed at a more leisurely pace typical of country people the world over.

We found a few Malawians, who have had the benefit of an education, who were rude, obviously lording over their compatriots what they feel should be the attitude of educated people, and forgetting, when they speak to a foreigner, that they too are educated. A case in point is the civil servant who administers the survey office where maps are sold in Blantyre. If he gives any trouble, treat him firmly and put him in his place. We did, and cooperation was forthcoming. However, in contrast to many West African countries where rudeness is part and parcel of interacting with Africans except those in the employ of the Hilton International Abidjan, the Malawians are ever courteous and helpful.

Tipping is not expected, but we always tip and found that this was much appreciated by the people whose daily wage is the equivalent of 62 cents in the U.S. More than money, clothing is appreciated, and if readers have room in their incoming baggage for a few clothes that they would normally give to a local charity (for either men or women) to give to room stewards, etc., they will be much appreciated.

Shopping in Malawi

The Department of Wildlife and Forestry annually crop elephant, and ivory is sold as handcrafted objects with the tusk number on each item. Whatever your feelings about the sale of ivory, the fact remains that southern Africa has large herds of elephant because their numbers are kept in proportion to the food available—unlike Kenya, where conservationists have argued while Kenyan elephants died of hunger or at the hands of poachers. The price of ivory objects in Malawi is very low, and the quality excellent.

Ebony carvings are well done and original in design. Masks are carved from a soft wood, with the exception of some outstanding ironwood examples.

Perhaps the most beautiful of all Malawian crafts are the wooden chests, carved more intricately than Swahili chests and left unvarnished and unstained. They come in all sizes from jewelry boxes to hope chests. Not a nail is used, and it is virtually impossible to identify joins. They have, of course, cedar interiors and some have a tray. The owner/manager of Serendipity, a shop in the lobby of the Mount Souche Hotel in Blantyre, has an empathy with the carvers. As a result, the most outstanding examples are to be found in her shop.

We found the lobby shops in the Capital Hotel in Lilongwe very attractive and fairly priced.

Hotels and Food

Hotels are not to be found in every town and it will be necessary to plan ahead if readers depart from the day-to-day itineraries we have outlined. Remember, it is always possible to park in a police station compound and sleep in the car overnight in case of emergency.

The hotels we have recommended will be found clean and the service good. The Mount Souche Hotel in Blantyre is government owned and there is a problem receiving replies to inquiries for reservations—this is why we have not recommended it.

We did not care for Ryall's Hotel, which is just across the street. The food made us ill, and we preferred driving the short distance to Shire Highlands Hotel in Limbe, which we found excellent, if not modern.

The Grand Hotel, again government owned, near Salima on the shores of Lake Malawi, is not recommended, although you can park the car in their adjacent campsite in case of emergencies.

Restaurants that we found particularly good are: Pioneer Room, Mount Souche Hotel, Blantyre; Hotel Training Dining Room, Blantyre (reservations must be made the day before, ask the Avis agent to use her influence to get you a table); dining room of the Shire Highlands, Limbe (exceptionally good service and food); and dining room of Club Makololo, southern shore of Lake Malawi.

Distances in Malawi

First, know that all mileages given on any map, Michelin or those issued by the Malawian government's Department of Surveys, are totally inaccurate in the distances stated. Second, know that the colored road designations used by cartographers of Malawian maps have absolutely no correlation to road conditions. A main (M) road, a heavy red line on Department of Surveys maps, may be the only road. Main road does not necessary mean tarmacked. Although a road may begin at point *a* tarmacked, then suddenly a few miles on become a dirt road, the entire length of the road is colored red.

On Michelin's map, Afrique Centre et Sud Madagascar, the legend indicates that red roads bordered in black are "two or more surfaced lanes." Gross hallucinations must have overtaken their informants. The road Salima to Balaka, which is full of potholes and patches, is a case in point. On the other hand, Michelin's yellow road bordered in black, indicating it is a "one surfaced lane," is in reality a two-lane, newly black-topped road between Lilongwe and Kasungu.

There is no Malawi Automobile Association to advise on road conditions. At one time Malawi's road services were combined with Zimbabwe's. Take it all in stride. If you bog down, there are usually many friendly hands to manhandle you out of the mud.

Swimming in Lake Malawi

Despite the Malawi government's assurances to the contrary and that of some local people, there is bilharzia in the water of Lake Malawi, and it is spreading. Readers should not swim in the lake, no matter what the public relations people or old-timers say.

Foreign Exchange

Credit cards are honored by the major hotels.

Once changed to Malawian kwatcha foreign currency is virtually impossible to convert back to dollars, pounds, or francs. Exchange only what you know you will need. If you have money cabled to you, insist that it be paid to you in dollars, pounds, or francs because—despite what it says on the official papers—you will not get kwatchas exchanged at the airport or anywhere else at the time of departure.

Background for Mali

PROFILE

People

Nationality: Noun and adjective—Malian(s). **Population** (1983 est.): 6.9 million. Annual growth rate: 2.7%. **Ethnic groups:** Mande (Bambara, Malinke, Sarakole) 50%, Peul 17%, Voltaic 12%, Songhai 6%, Tuareg and Moor 5%. **Religions:** Islam 90%, indigenous 9%, Christian 1%. **Languages:** French (official) and Bambara (spoken by about 80% of the population). **Education:** Attendance—28% (primary); 9% (secondary). Literacy—10%. **Health:** Infant mortality rate—152/1000. Life expectancy—45 yrs. **Work force** (3.5 million): Agriculture—73%; industry and commerce—12%; services—16%.

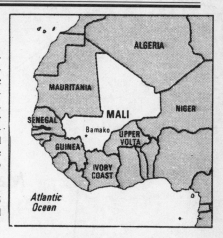

Official Name:
Republic of Mali

Geography

Area: 1,240,000 sq. km. (478,764 sq. mi.); about the size of Texas and California, a little larger than Quebec, nine times the size of England, half the size of Saudi Arabia, and a little smaller than the Northern Territory of Australia.

Cities: Capital—Bamako (pop. 620,000). **Other cities**—Segou (65,000), Mopti (54,000), Kayes (45,000), Gao (37,000). **Terrain:** Savanna and desert. **Climate:** Ranges from semitropical to arid.

Telecommunications: Long-distance telephone service is often unsatisfactory. Local telegraphic service is unreliable. Mali is on Greenwich Mean Time.

Transportation: Privately owned automobiles are the principal means of transportation in Bamako. Taxis are available at stands and fares are inexpensive. The road between Bamako and Mopti and those branching south to Bougouni and Sikasso are paved. Other roads are of laterite and usually passable in the dry season without 4-wheel drive.

National holidays: New Year's Day: Jan. 1. Army Day: Jan. 20. Labor Day: May 1. Day of Africa: May 25. Independence Day: Sept. 22. Liberation Day: Nov. 19. Christmas: Dec. 25. Plus Easter Sunday and Monday and all Muslim holidays.

Arrival in Bamako

By air: Dakar, the city from which most passengers arriving in Mali will have come, is apparently always slightly overcast. The first impression when alighting from the Air Afrique plane at Bamako's Senou International Airport, 9 mi from the city center, is one of open spaces, light, and a definite increase in temperature. The air is dry, and the sun really hot.

Coming into the shade of the airport, a Sofitel kiosk is seen ahead of any

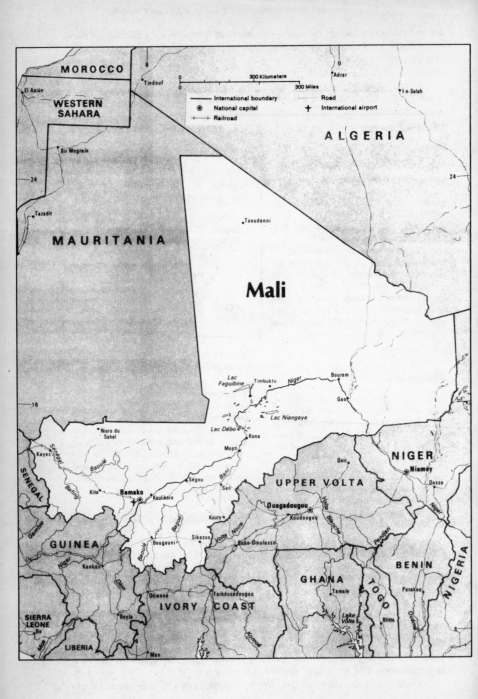

government processing procedures, and if you have reservations at the Sofitel l'Amitie in Bamako, the procedure is to give your passport and WHO health card to the hotel representative at the kiosk. The rest is simply going through the motions of collecting baggage, which is brought into the customs area not by conveyor belt but by human hands. (Note: We did get a sizable oil stain on one of our suitcases between the time we handed it over in Dakar and when we saw it in Bamako. The oil was similar to car oil, and we had our doubts about the condition of the contents of our case. Everything was fine; the oil did not penetrate. In Africa it pays to carry well-made, reinforced luggage.)

Visitors are directed to a waiting Mercedes bus, and the driver appears once all the passengers booked into the Sofitel l'Amitie have been cleared. The drive into Bamako is exotic; overblown sand rises from the road when the driver follows too closely behind a vehicle ahead. However, the road is paved all the way.

We recommend that all our readers stay at the Sofitel l'Amitie; even though you could save money by staying at other hotels, the hassle of getting around Bamako from them is really a case of "penny wise, pound foolish." All of the hotels are overpriced; a few dollars more isn't going to make that much difference.

To travel in Mali once away from Bamako-Segou is to go back in time. Not to biblical times, because the culture is not reminiscent of the Middle East despite Islamic influences, but back to one's own earliest fantasies of the exotic, romantic Sahara Desert. The flowing robes, caparisoned horses, and camel caravans are ordinary sights. We had a glimpse of just how exotic Mali can be when, on the road from Dire to Toumbouctou, a short, very black, naked woman carrying a child on her hip, darted, like a frightened animal, across the road in front of the Land Rover. There was no settlement for miles, and she obviously lived as would a wild animal in the barren landscape that verged the high dunes of the desert. Her hair was matted, her eyes wild, and she reminded us more of the Australian aborigine illustrated in *People of the Dreamtime* (D. Baglin and D. R. Moore, Walker/Weatherhill, NY and London, 1970) than any African we had previously seen. We felt many more such surprises, perhaps of a different nature, awaited the traveler in Mali. We'll definitely be going back.

Mali is the stuff dreams are made of; it can also be the stuff nightmares are made of. Make certain you have SOS insurance and are in good health; it's a long way back to civilization from Toumbouctou.

Bamako

Spread out—they've got plenty of room—Bamako is another large town, not a city. There are a few multistoried buildings, but on the whole the buildings are single-story, at most two-story. The sand blown up from the unpaved side roads carries a light coating to the buildings, people, vehicles, and animals so that the color of Bamako is all a slightly yellow-brick shade.

Presumably the former French colonizers decided with Gaulist logic that as it seldom rains in Mali, street drains were an unnecessary expense, and while there are no torrential downpours that need sluicing, the problem of where the sand goes needs answering. As things are now, the slight winds blow it back and forth, piling along curbs (kerbs), until the next gust of air finds it a new resting place.

Trees have been planted, and they are now of good size, but they seem overwhelmed by the dry air. Instead of their leaves glistening in the sunlight, they hang rather forlornly, trying to be a crowning glory but succeeding only in giving the appearance of a wispy hairnet on an aged lady.

For all that, Bamako has charm, and it certainly does not suffer from more than a token European influence. We predict that even that token influence will recede within a few years, allowing Bamako to become a genuine African town like her smaller sister cities along the River Niger.

Segou, Mopti, Dire, and Toumbouctou

Segou was the colonial capital of Mali and has a good percentage of French colonial style buildings. The trees are very large and border the streets, providing more shade and coolness than those in Bamako. The lifestyle is based on peasant markets and truck-stop commerce.

Unfortunately, very unfortunately, we did not get to Mopti because we went to Toumbouctou turning west at Segou. Mali is one of our favorite—in fact is is now Leah's very favorite—African countries, and we plan to return very soon. And visiting Mopti is the top priority. The mosque there is beautiful and of classic Malian architecture.

Dire is a small town on the western side of the River Niger about 50 mi before Toumbouctou. We stayed there a week and found the very wide streets, the people, and the general atmosphere engaging. There is a small market at Dire, and a number of international charitable agencies are located behind the 7-foot-high adobe walls that enclose the houses, and an Italian-staffed hospital, but when you've listed these, you've said it all. Essentially, Dire is another reality; there could be no place that contrasted more greatly with the background from which we come than Dire. There are no hotels or places for visitors to stay—at least not foreign visitors—and we suggest readers who wish to spend some time in this small Malian town bring their own tent and set it up, after asking permission of the officials.

We have described Toumbouctou in the *Lost Cities of Africa* itinerary.

Communications

There is a main post office in Bamako. The post office is a rather chaotic affair and undoubtedly things, including mail, do get sorted out eventually. However, it is an unnerving system, and we suggest readers rely on telexing in emergencies. If you're planning to be in Mali long enough to go to Toumbouctou, stop in at your embassy and let them know you're in the country. Canadians can, of course, use the office of the British Consulate, as can Australians and New Zealanders. The British embassy representation is served from Dakar, Senegal, with only a consulate at Bamako. However, this, provided you obtain their telex number, will serve as a contact. The American Embassy has a large staff in Mali, and the marines hold a "happy hour" to celebrate TGIF (thank God it's Friday) from 5 to 7. Marine House is rather difficult to find, and it's best to go along to the embassy earlier in the day, speak to the marine on duty, and ask him to send a taxi driver to your hotel to pick you up about 4:45.

Radio broadcasting is in French; the BBC Overseas Service can be picked up after dark.

Telephone service in Bamako is reasonably good, especially from the Sofitel l'Amitie or the Grand Hotel.

Business Hours

Hours Monday–Thursday and Saturdays are from 7:30 a.m. to 2:30 p.m., and on Fridays 7:30–12:30.

We found the Bank of Mali very helpful and friendly; their filing system is unbelievable, but they seem to have few problems sorting things out. They have unusual hours—as we remember they close at 2—but check before going. As the hotels charge such a high price to change foreign money, we used the Bank of Mali—there is absolutely no danger of pickpockets when carrying money as there is in Kenya.

Religious Services

Mali is a predominantly Moslem country, with a minority Christian population of which the majority is Roman Catholic. Inquire at the hotel's front desk where the nearest church is and the time of their services.

Languages

French is the official language of Mali. Readers who have no working knowledge of that language would do well to memorize the basic tourist phrases.

The vast majority of Malians speak Bambara, which means that there is less tribal rivalry than in many other African countries. The nomadic peoples historically resented intrusion by governments into their way of life, but since independence they are beginning to develop a feeling of loyalty to the republic.

Geographic Description

It is not until one travels up to Toumbouctou that the utter vastness of Mali is realized. The northern part of the country reaches into the Sahara Desert, and as writers of the North African campaign described the fighting in World War II, the desert is like a vast ocean. No army held or controlled any location. As soon as the tanks moved out, the desert swallowed up all trace of human habitation. Like the ocean, nature was the master—not man.

The task of patrolling Saharan borders quite apart from controlling the nomadic peoples, who make the desert their preserve, can really only be realized when standing from a vantage point such as Toumbouctou. As far as the eye can see, there is nothing but space. Adventure tales have been written about the old French Foreign Legion patroling from their garrisons the Saharan borders, but in reality they were ineffective.

When it floods the River Niger irrigates (anytime between the end of July, and the flow continues until November—occasionally until December) the southern regions of Mali: Bamako, Segou, Mopti, Dire, Toumbouctou, and on to Gao. The irrigation is natural; only at Niono, where the French established artificial canals and irrigation trenches, has the river been commercially utilized. The river gradually recedes until by February its bed is totally exposed, and there is only a hint of the vast amount of water that previously rushed to meet the Atlantic by such a torturous route. With its marvelous climate and sunshine, Mali could be an exporter of tropical crops if common sense was employed to conserve water. Yet Mali is almost totally dependent upon outside assistance to feed her people.

The perennial range grass is high in protein, and we saw exceptionally beautiful cattle that had lived through the previous year's drought. The dry climate does not harbor as many cattle diseases as the more humid southern regions of Africa.

Tribes and Ethnic Groups

The nomadic peoples of Mali—the Tuaregs and Moors—are related to the Berbers found in the central and northern areas of the Sahara Desert. The River Niger between Gao and Bamako is the home of the Songhai, who farm the shores of the river and fish its waters. Southwestern Mali is inhabited by the Bambara, Malinke, Sarakole, and Voltaic, who are also farmers. The traditional fishing tribe of the Bozo earn their livelihood from the Niger.

We found the Malians exceptionally beautiful people—their skin color ranges from the very fair to jet black; they are graceful and elegant in their national dress of flowing robes.

Social Customs

We found the people very hospitable, refined, and gracious. There is no need to worry about personal security, and Mali is one of the few countries in the world where we would never feel afraid. The people are very, very poor, but, like those in Somalia, they have no criminal intent toward those more fortunate. They are proud of their heritage and wear traditional dress, except when a uniform is in order in the military or hotel and service industries.

We did tip, as usual, and this seems to be an accepted and expected practice.

Shopping in Mali

In the center of Bamako is an artisan's center where handmade jewelry, woven blankets, sculptures, and leatherwork can be purchased. There is also some nice tie-and-dye, and local tailors can make up the fabric. It's important to sort the strictly commercial stuff from the more genuine, as well as to bargain hard once something is chosen. Prices drop tremendously when a serious effort is made at bargaining.

Apart from the artisan's center, good buys of unusual but primitive objects are found in most village markets.

Hotels and Restaurant Food

The food generally was good, but terribly, terribly expensive, just as in the rest of French West Africa. Nothing we ate made us ill, except the prices.

For lunch try the Swimming Pool Snack Bar at Sofitel l'Amitie Bamako (there is a salad buffet that is very nice); the Sofitel Dining Room (passable, but the waiters are hopeless); the Grand Hotel Dining Room has a very restricted menu, which was a bit too French for us; service very, very slow.

The water is not pure, and only bottled water should be used. The hotels charge a high price per liter, and the brand AWA, bottled in Senegal, is every bit as good as the imported French water. There is a supermarket in town, where it can be purchased. Even if you take a taxi coming and going, it will be cheaper than paying the hotel prices.

Background for Somalia

PROFILE

People

Nationality: Noun and adjective—Somali(s). **Population** (1982 est.): 6,124,000. Annual growth rate: 3.5%. **Ethnic groups:** Somali 98.8%, Arab and Asian 1.2%. **Religion:** Muslim 99%. **Language:** Somali. **Education:** Years compulsory—12. **Attendance**—primary 50%, secondary 7%. Literacy—5–10%. **Health:** Infant mortality rate—150/1000. Life expectancy—43.9 yrs. **Work force** (2.2 million): Agriculture—82%; industry and commerce—13%; government—5%.

Geography

Area: 686,803 sq. km. (246,000 sq. mi.); about the size of California, a little larger than Manitoba, 2½ times as large as Great Britain, twice the size of Southern Yemen, and more than twice the size of New Zealand.

Official Name:
Somali Democratic Republic

Cities: Capital—Mogadiscio (pop. 600,000 est.). **Other cities**—Hargeysa (100,000 est.), Kisimaio. **Terrain:** Tropical at the River Juba south to the Kenya border along the coastal area, desert and rocky to the north of Mogadishu. **Climate:** Hot and dry with seasonal monsoons.

Telecommunications: Mogadiscio has an automatic telephone service. Long-distance calls may be placed to Europe and the U.S. at any time through the Ministry of Posts and Telegraphs. (More expensive than if booked from Europe or the U.S.)

Telegraph service is available 7 p.m.–11 a.m. A telex service is available at the Croce del Sud Hotel. Radio broadcasting in Somali and Arabic; English language news at 2–2:30 p.m. shortwave. Weekly English-language newspaper.

Transportation: Mogadiscio is served by several international airlines. No trains but a bus service between Mogadishu and Kisimaio weekly. Good taxi service.

National holidays: New Year's Day: Jan. 1. Labor Day: May 1. Independence Day for the Northern Region: June 26. Independence Day-Somali Republic: July 1. Revolution Day: Oct. 21–22. Plus all Muslim holidays.

Arrival

See the *Lost Cities of Africa* itinerary, Swahili City States: Mogadiscio.

For the purpose of researching Somalia we were the guests of the Democratic Republic of Somalia's Ministry of Tourism. Before this time we had not visited the country. We wish to thank Mr. Ahmed Hagi Mohamud Juma, director of Planning and Tourism Promotion, and his staff, and Mr. Leno Marano of the pioneering firm of MAHI for their generous efforts to provide us with an enjoyable two weeks' traveling in Somalia.

We were in much the same position as most of our readers in that our only knowledge of Somalia before the visit was the basic data given in certain official publications, encyclopedias, and histories. More often, our preconceptions were

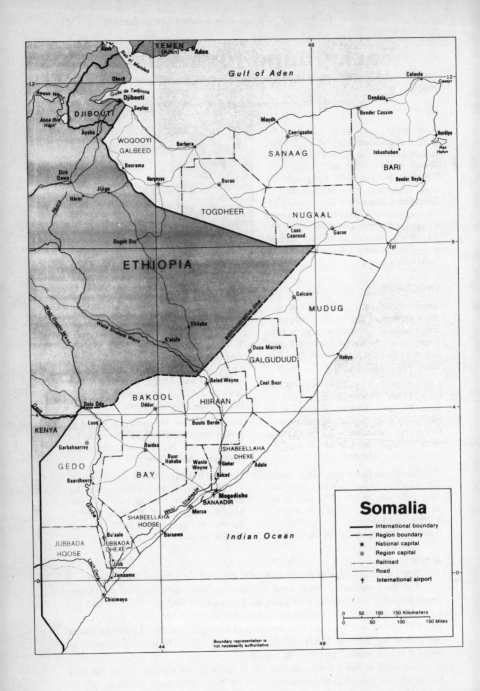

formed by the negative verbal descriptions given by Americans and Britishers who had either worked in Somalia or visited Mogadiscio on business. To say that these plus television reporting of the refugee situation have given Somalia a bad press must certainly be one of the major understatements of all time.

Looking at Somalia through the eyes of a tourist we found the country to be one of the most spectacularly beautiful ones we had ever seen. Only the American southwest deserts could be used as a point of reference, but Somali deserts are pastels, not harsh oranges, and it is only the expansiveness of nature that Somali north of Mogadiscio shares with Arizona and New Mexico. Southern Somalia has a varied landscape, becoming very tropical the farther one travels to the south.

Colonial History

The cake-cutting that took place with the signing of the Treaty of Berlin in 1886–87 has been the originator of many of today's African problems. Perhaps the Somali slice will be the most persistent cause (even to the year 2000) for international concern of all the ill effects that have come about because of that treaty.

The signators agreed to lines drawn latitudinally across the map of Africa. From these lines the signators were entitled to colonize an undetermined distance inland. As no one knew how far "inland" was, this was a rather ambiguous point.

The French concentrated on penetrating the continent from west Africa to the east. The British concentrated on penetrating from south to north. The Portuguese held on to what they had in southern Africa, but were thwarted by the British in joining Angola to Mozambique. The Germans, as traditionalists, tried a pincer movement from their latitudes. Italian explorers had been in the minority during the preceding 30 years, and Italy more or less had to be content with the crumbs that fell from the cake.

In eastern Africa the slicing was refined by the complex question of access and control of the Suez Canal. That access, vital to the lines of communication in a world without airplanes, radios, or satellites, was the economic lifeline of Europe. The British and French jointly administered the actual canal. Aden, the coaling station for ships, was in British hands and Djibouti, which was opposite, became French. But to keep an eye on them the British took the northern littoral of the Horn of Africa. The Italians were allotted the lower portion of the Horn. The Sultan of Zanzibar leased to Italy the fertile Juba River Valley in 1905. However, Italian control was established along the coast well before this date, and the town of Lugh upriver was founded by Captain Bottego in 1895.

The British and the French got on with the job of moving inland; the British took Kenya and Uganda and then from the north formed their Cape to Cairo axis by indirectly administering Anglo-Egyptian Sudan. Stanley claimed Zaire for Belgium, which rather interrupted the cross, but nothing daunted, they picked it up again at Rhodesia and Nyasaland (Zimbabwe-Zambia-Malawi). The story continues with the French in Niger, Mali, Senegal, Dahomey, with Algeria forming a Mediterranean access. The French had tried to continue eastward from Chad to Djibouti, but they were stopped by the British at Fashoda on the Nile in Sudan.

Naturally, the Italians interpreted the wording concerning penetration inland the same as those of the other signators to the treaty only to find the British and French opposed to their annexation of Ethiopia. After the excitement died down their western Somali border line was left in limbo and to this day is identified on maps as "disputed territory." Britain and France did take the precaution of landlocking Ethiopia, and this is the source of the fighting we read about today in the Ogodon and Eriteria.

The cake-cutting had split the Somali people: Somalis are Somalis; there are clans among them, but not tribes because they are all one tribal group. The Kenyan northern boundary split one part of the Somalis and, naturally, the division of northern Somalia to the British and the midsection to the Italians repeated the offense. To no avail the Somalis tried to reclaim their brothers in northern Kenya, but have now given up the effort. At the decade of independence for African countries, British Somaliland and Italian Somaliland were joined to form what is now Somalia.

Academicians may be dismayed at the above thumbnail, highly subjective sketch of 100 years of political turmoil, but we justify the exercise by believing that the average English-speaking reader has even a more garbled version of Italian colonization than we have given.

Bad press has made international public opinion believe that it was Mussolini who first used aerial bombardment against African peoples when in actuality Italians *and British* jointly used air power to subdue followers of the Somali national hero, Mohammed Abdille Hassan (who died in 1920) some years prior to the Italian effort in Ethiopia. The one-sided air war failed to dislodge Hassan from his mountain stronghold, and defeat came in the form of a smallpox epidemic, not from British and Italian bombs. Yet in 1935 Pathe News, reporting on the Italo-Ethiopian war and Haile Selassie's impassioned speech at the League of Nations, accused only the Italians of first using air power in Africa.

The Horn of Africa has undergone a series of small turmoils for many years. During those years people of all nationalities have been living and working in Somalia. The traveler to Somalia in the 1980s can move about with greater personal and property safety than anywhere in North America or Europe. As our guide told us when we asked why there was no crime in Somalia: "Stealing and murder for gain are the hallmarks of civilized society. Where the people are primitive, rural, and poor, it doesn't happen."

To conclude these comments on Somalia's colonial history, we quote from *The Geographical Journal* (vol. LXXXIII, no. 2, Feb. 1935, p. 38) an article entitled "The Somali Coasts: An account of the T. A. Glover Senegal-Somali Expedition in the Somalilands and Eritrea: A paper read at the evening meeting of the society on 4 Dec 1933 by Captain R.B.W.G. Andrew," Royal Geographical Society, London:

Somaliland is one of the most interesting countries with which we at the Colonial Office have to deal. We are able to maintain only a skeleton administration there, and it is instructive to consider exactly what we hope to accomplish and how we are attaining our object in contrast with other nations. Next door to us there is Italian Somaliland. Italy, having few colonies and being prepared to spend plenty of money on those she has, runs her part of Somaliland on a scale of expenditure with which it is impossible for us to compete. The Chancellor of the Exchequer would be horrified if we wanted to launch out on the same scale of expenditure as Signor Mussolini.

The Italians had good relations with the Somalis; they intermarried with them, laid out beautiful towns and roads, boulevards lined with trees, and today evidence of this is not only to be found in the physical amenities they left behind, but in the interaction of Somalis and Italians living today in the country.

Mogadiscio

The natural harbor at Mogadiscio has provided a site for dhows and ships for over a thousand years and a settlement at Mogadiscio is shown on ancient maps. Today, the harbor has been developed and while buildings still stand that are of ancient origin, the majority of the city dates from Italian colonial occupation to the present. Trees line the wide streets, paved sidewalks front the buildings, and the infrastructure necessary for nationhood is being put in place. The pace is relaxed—as much due to Somali character as Italian influence and the intense midday heat. Hire a taxi to take you on a tour of the city; there are several outstanding national monuments and the drive along the Indian Ocean shore is beautiful.

Merca, Brava, Kismaio

These coastal towns are ancient cities where the Italians salvaged what was worth saving and superimposed grid-aligned streets and avenues over traditional winding Arab alleys. Brava is particularly beautiful when seen from the elevation of the main Mogadiscio-Kismaio highway, her white buildings gleaming in the sun with the blue Indian Ocean as a backdrop. More old buildings have been left standing at Merca than at Brava, and Kismaio is essentially a small, modern port town. Behind these coastal cities the population is primarily nomadic, although Gelib, just north of Kismaio, is the market town for the extensive banana plantations in the surrounding area.

The banks of The river Guiba are very fertile, and lush vegetation is in stark contrast to the desert, which soon takes over away from the nourishing waters. Irrigated farming is practiced to increase production.

Communications

We found the telephone service in Mogadiscio to be good despite the apparent antiquity of the instruments. International cable service is available. Radio broadcasting is in the Somali language, with English speakers relying on the BBC Overseas Service and the Voice of America.

There is a weekly English-language newspaper that is not easily obtainable as it appears to circulate on subscription.

Business Hours

Shops and banks are open in the mornings until noon and reopen about 4 p.m. for the evening. The official holiday is Friday, with all Moslem holidays observed throughout the year.

Religious Services

There are two Roman Catholic churches in Mogadiscio, an Episcopalian service is held once a week on Saturdays in one of the Catholic churches, and an Interdenominational Lay Worship service is held on Sunday evenings in the American School Library. Latterday Saints (Mormon) services are also held in the library on Friday mornings.

Mogadishu

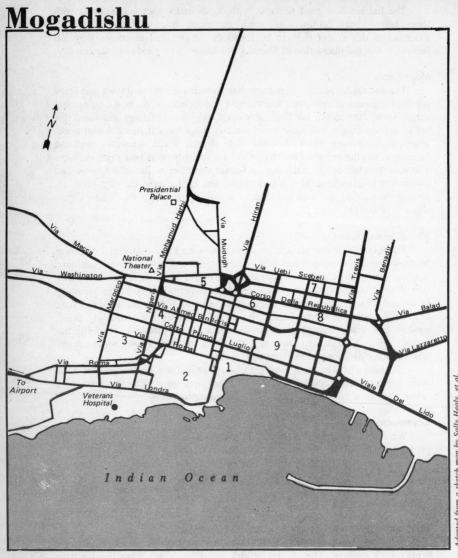

Adapted from a sketch map by Sally Healy, et al.

1. Original museum (next door to Al Aruba Hotel).
2. Mogadiscio Great Mosque, 13th century
3. Benadir cloth weavers
4. Open air markets and goldsmiths
5. Craft shops for ivory/wood carvings/ meerschaums and embroidered dresses/shirts
6. Grocery stores
7. Post office
8. Juba Hotel
9. Shingani Old Town
Banks on via Hiran at via Ahmed Bin Idris and Corso Primo Luglio

Languages

Somali is a highly complex and intricate language that was not written prior to 1971. Many Somalis are poets, and the use of the language greatly influences social interactions. Italian is spoken by most educated Somalis and is the language of instruction in institutions of higher learning. Peace Corps teachers were in Somalia during the late 1960s, and many of their students have continued to use English. We found we could usually locate an English speaker to help us with basic necessities. Arabic is taught in the schools at elementary and high school levels.

Geographical Description

Northern Somalia is hot, dry, rocky, and sometimes mountainous. From Mogadiscio south the land becomes less arid along the coast until the banks of the Giuba River, which nurtures tropical growth.

It is interesting to note that coconut trees do not grow along the Somali coast, and agriculturalists seem unable to provide a reason why this is so.

The rains bring a burst of light vegetative cover in May, but these tidbits are soon cropped back by goats and sheep. It is amazing how much verdant cover can spring up from what appeared to be only a very light rain. The wildflowers such rains encourage are particularly beautiful.

Tribes and Ethnic Groups

The Somalis are quite distinct from other African peoples. Invariably, the true Somali is light skinned and very thin—wispy. Their facial features are rounded and smooth. When this is not the case the particular person may have Swahili or Italian blood running in their veins.

The Banjunis live south of Kisimaio and are of Bantu origin. The tribe extends all the way south into Kenya at Lamu and Pate.

Social Customs

Like most desert people, the Somalis are extremely hospitable and generous with what they have. They are a refined people and their aloofness hides an inherent dignity. Once this is overcome one cannot ask for more congenial hosts and hostesses.

Taxis

Be sure to negotiate the price of the ride with the driver before getting into his vehicle. We found the standard of driving to be very good; the drivers were courteous and obeyed the rules of the road.

Money

Although Somalia, at the suggestion of the World Bank, has devalued her currency since we were in the country, prices, when money is exchanged at the official rates, are still high. We suggest that readers avoid the temptation to use the black market, as problems could arise that would be difficult to settle.

If readers will bring along the items we suggest in the following pages, there will be little to spend money on except the hotel bill and meals. The hotel prices are government controlled and the meals we found to be reasonable.

Cash in multiples of $100 and not more than a hundred (or its equivalent) at a time. Get small change not in coins (they are practically worthless) but in 5, 10, and 20 shilling notes, not in silver because once out of town it is difficult to get change.

Health Conditions

We felt better in Somalia than in any country we visited; even our U.S. sinusitis and allergies disappeared. That early-morning tired feeling so common in Nairobi was nonexistent, and the climate was invigorating and perfect.

Swimming at the Beaches

The Soviet Union built a slaughterhouse for the Somalis in Mogadiscio at the northern end of the beautiful harbor. The offal and blood from this enterprise empties into the bay, making swimming anywhere along the Somali coast impossible; sharks from as far away as the China Seas head straight for the Horn of Africa to feast on the slaughterhouse discharge.

Hotel and Restaurant Food

Azan serves nice lunches downstairs and offers an extensive buffet on their rooftop restaurant nightly from 7 p.m. It is advisable to go early for dinner to avoid the crowd and assure yourself of the range of dishes.

Capucetto Nero serves Italian-style food and offers lunches and dinners at moderate prices.

Croce del Sud Hotel Dining Room is located in a very pleasant courtyard with piazza tables and chairs surrounded by shady trees, with a collection of local cultural items gathered by the owners. The menu is varied enough to include octopus and lobster. Be warned, however, not to be in a great hurry to order, eat, and run when dining at the Croce. Patience and the company of a good conversationalist are essential for proper dining there.

Syrian Sandwich Shop offers hot beef sandwiches (roasted on a spit) served on pita bread at very reasonable prices.

Jumbo Ice Cream Parlour provides ice cream served up to the music of Bob Marley.

Hong Kong Restaurant is another good place to eat.

What to Take to Somalia

We cannot reliably predict what can be purchased in Somalia, as the situation changes so frequently, but we found taking the following with us to be useful:

Crackers, potato sticks, corn chips, any kind of snack food. Cookies, especially the Danish butter cookies that are sold in a can (tin). Decaffeinated coffee if you use it; tea if you prefer British tea, as Somali tea is not quite the same, although their cinnamon tea is excellent. One pound of white sugar or sugar cubes; Somali sugar is coarse and brown and can be laxative. Any type of meat paste, Vienna sausages, Smithfield ham spread, corned beef, cheese in cans or jars that do not require refrigeration. Alcoholic beverages are available but are very, very expensive. You may want to ask when you obtain your Somali visa if bringing in a bottle of alcohol will be acceptable. Toothpaste, all the toiletries you normally use, Kleenex to use instead of the toilet paper supplied, Kotex, etc. Off or other brand of insect repellent. Individually wrapped alcohol swabs, Murine, or other eye wash. Absolutely everything needed for photography, including more film than you believe you'll use. Butter if you can purchase it in a can—this can be done in Kenya. Cigarettes if you smoke. I paid a ludicrous $20 a pack to keep myself in the filthy habit the day before we left as I had run out!

Somalia is a country where you will want to have a few small gifts to give instead of money. We had purchased some inexpensive machine-crocheted shawls, and these were well received by the housekeeping ladies who cleaned our room. Cigarettes, as can be imagined from their price—although that price was before Somalia devalued her currency and it should be better now—are very much appreciated. Use your imagination and take a collection of items under $5 to give to those who perform small services for you.

Background for Sudan

PROFILE

People

Nationality: Noun and adjective—Sudanese (sing. and pl.). **Population** (1980 est.): 18.5 million; 23.9% urban. Annual growth rate (1980 est.): 2.8%. **Ethnic groups:** Arab-African, Black African. **Religions:** Muslim 70%, indigenous (southern Sudan), Christian 5%. **Languages:** Arabic (official), English, tribal dialects. **Education:** Years compulsory—9. Attendance—50%. Literacy—20%. **Health:** Infant mortality rate—141/1000. Life expectancy—47 yrs. **Work force** (1982 est.): 5.7 million. Agriculture—78.4%; industry and commerce—9.8%; government—6%, nonmilitary sector.

Geography

Area: 2.5 million sq. km. (967,500 sq. mi.); almost one third the size of the continental U.S., twice the size of Ontario, 10 times larger than Great Britain, 1¼ times larger than Saudi Arabia, and a little smaller than western Australia.

Cities: Capital—Khartoum (comprising Khartoum Omdurman and Khartoum North, pop. 784,000, 1973 census; 1.1 million, 1975 est.). **Other cities**—Port Sudan (133,000, 1973 census), Kosti (65,000, 1973 census), Juba (67,000, 1973 census, 100,000, 1979 est.; capital of Southern Region). Populations of all cities, especially Juba and Kosti, have grown rapidly since the 1973 census. **Terrain:** Desert and semi-arid in the north, moun-

Official Name:
Democratic Republic of Sudan

tains in the east and west, and tropical/savanna in the south. **Climate:** Dry and hot in the north, humid and tropical in the south.

Telecommunications—Limited international and telegraph service is available in Khartoum and Port Sudan. Khartoum is 2 hours ahead of Greenwich Mean Time.

Transportation—Sudan is connected by international airlines with Europe, Saudi Arabia and some African countries. There is a domestic airline service. Train service connecting Wadi Halfa to Khartoum via Atbara Khartoum and Port Sudan, Khartoum and Khartoum-Kosti-Wau with a

branch line at Babanusa to Nyala. Taxis in Khartoum and good connections by rural taxi from Wadi Halfa to the embarkation port for the Lake Nasser steamer to Aswan.

National holidays: New Year's Day: Jan. 1. Unity Day: March 3. Revolution Day: May 25. Republic Day: Oct. 12. Christmas: Dec. 25. Plus all Muslim holidays. Easter is also observed by Christians.

Arrival

We entered Sudan overland at Wadi Halfa and departed from Khartoum airport; in both cases the processing was efficient and professional. We do feel one's appearance is important in Sudan and we urge readers who want to be treated respectfully by officials to dress conservatively and appear well groomed. The Sudanese are a very proud people and a couldn't-care-less look is an affront to them.

It should be realized when traveling anywhere in Africa that the local people believe you to be a wealthy person. Your protestations to the contrary will do nothing to change their opinion. The very fact that you had enough money to purchase an airline ticket makes your protestations lies in their eyes. The major airlines advertise in African newspapers and many times include the price of fares to London, New York, etc., in their ads. The amount shown can equal the average African's wages for several years. Refusing to dress tidily when it is apparent by your presence in Africa that you can afford clean, well-fitting clothes does nothing to endear you to your hosts/hostesses. This is especially true of Sudan.

We fell in love with Sudan as we did Somalia and Mali, and look forward to the day when we can make another visit. Sudan holds many unexpected surprises, more by way of the contacts made than physical characteristics, although the walk along the Nile from the Hilton into town, the aged trees shading the paths, is unforgettable. The star on the Christmas tree for us was the customs officer at the Khartoum airport who asked us, since we came from Washington, DC, to give his best regards to President Reagan. We did by means of a letter to the White House when we got home. It's nice to travel in a country where one is liked. That may seem a trite observation to make, but Leah and I had enough of the antagonism we found in French-African countries (with the exception of Mali), so that when people were openly friendly, we relaxed and enjoyed the country. Never, at any time, no matter how far we were from civilization, did we feel worried in Sudan.

We found the taxi drivers fair, although most did not speak English. We managed to explain by speaking slowly where we wanted to go. Failing that, we would ask the front desk clerk at the Hilton to write the address in Arabic and then give this to the driver. Taxis are difficult to obtain after dark, and the charges are doubled.

The expatriate population in Khartoum must make their own amusements as Khartoum is a devoutly Moslem city (see "Social Customs" in this section). There is an American Club, the Sudan Club (British), and various sports clubs, but there is little purely commercial entertainment outside the major hotels. The American Club has no residential facilities, unlike the Sudan Club, but visitors of any nationality, including Sudanese, are welcome. The Hilton has tennis courts, which are open to the general public, and on the subterranean level there is a bowling alley with automatic equipment. Polo is played weekly at the Racing Club.

The cost of living is high for the expatriate community and rents are exhorbitant. Khartoum is considered to be a "hardship" station by the U.S. Department of State, but to our way of thinking it seemed delightful.

In addition to the Khalifa's House Museum and the Sudan National Museum, there is the Ethnological Museum, which exhibits many tribal artifacts.

Young graduates from Cambridge University in England were the chief administrators of Sudan when it was under British rule. The boast was often made that "2000 Blues" ran the entire country. With the coming of independence the northerners (being better educated) soon returned to exploiting the peoples of the south. During the interim, missionaries had traveled down the Nile and begun conversions. This had infuriated the Moslem northerners, and a civil war raged for 15 years once the British were out of the country. In the early 1980s, under former President Nimeri, Islamic law was legislated that would govern not only the Moslem north but also the south. This has been strongly resisted. American oil companies that were exploring for oil in southern Sudan have pulled out of the country, and life has reverted to a backwater existence for the people. The leaders of the southern guerrilla movement have been as merciless as were the northern slave traders of a century ago to the people whom they purport to wish to save. They have refused to allow international relief agencies to airlift food to the people of the south, believing that their northern adversaries will take the opportunity to send troops along with the food. As a result, many, many southerners have died of starvation.

Sudan should have been two countries—the differences are too great to overcome without a capitulation of the rights of the southerners or many more years of bloodshed.

Sudan is a very large country and it is safe to travel in the north, but under no circumstances should you be tempted to travel south or talk politics.

Khartoum was planned by the British General Lord Kitchener opposite the old city of Omdurman, across the River Nile. Government buildings have been situated along the river bank and the streets are tree lined—although we noticed that some of the trees were being felled, we hope only because they were diseased and not for any other reason. The modern part of the city consists of some multistoried buildings, but for the most part, low, single-story buildings are in evidence. The city is very clean.

Juba is the administrative capital of southern Sudan and this city, along with Wau, is not open, at this writing, to unauthorized foreign travelers because of political unrest. However, the many villages along the Nile between Khartoum and Wadi Halfa are open.

Communications
Cables and telex services are available, but hours of service are limited. Radio broadcasting is in Arabic, and English speakers rely on the BBC Overseas Service or the Voice of America. We found the telephone service in Khartoum to be very good.

Geographical Description
The north is dry and desert, becoming part of the Sahara to the west. The south, by contrast, has such dense tropical vegetation that the River Nile is blocked by papyrus and water lilies. Sudan has the potential to become "the

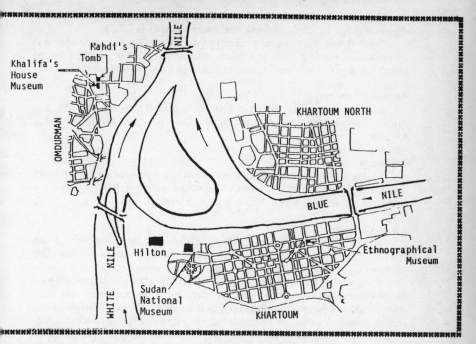

breadbasket of the Middle East'' and there are plenty of mouths to feed, which now are nourished by imports from halfway around the world. If only political conditions would stabilize and the secret of valid development for Sudan unfold, the Sudanese people would quickly emerge from poverty.

The White Nile runs from south to north, dividing Sudan, and is joined at Khartoum by the Blue Nile, whose waters are fed by the mountain streams of Ethiopia.

Tribal and Ethnic Groups

The diversity of the people in what constitutes the modern nation of Sudan has been the cause of trouble and civil war since it gained independence. The people of the north are of Arab origin, while the peoples of the south are Nilotic and Bantu. Historically, because they were pagans, the northerners felt the southerners were fair game for the slave trade and merciless, bloody sorties were made by slavers into the deep reaches of southern Sudan. It was to put down the final vestiges of the slave trade in British Africa that Gordon was sent to that country. That success did not come until General Kitchener arrived 15 years after Gordon's death with an army gives an indication of the obstinancy of those who persisted in the trade.

Business Hours

National Museum is open Sunday through Thursday 8 a.m.–noon. City Market and the nearby Gold and Silver Market are open mornings or after 5:30 p.m. Bookshops are open 8–11:30 a.m. and 5:30–7:30 p.m. Post office is closed 12:30–5 p.m.

Generally, banks are open to customers daily 8:30 a.m.–noon except Fridays and public holidays. Citibank's telephone number is 76654.

Note: Beside the room telephones in the Hilton International Khartoum is a booklet on opening hours and other valuable information prepared by the general manager, which can be used to supplement this information.

Religious Services

There is an Anglican church in Khartoum, as well as Greek Orthodox and Roman Catholic, and the Sudan Interior Mission (Protestant) also holds weekly services.

Language

Arabic is the national language and is spoken throughout the north, with English being the legacy of Sudan's British colonizers. Tribal languages are spoken in the south although Arabic is used in commerce.

Social Customs

Alcoholic beverages are stricly illegal in Sudan and the Hilton International has concocted some perfectly marvelous tall, cool fruit drinks to take the place of American cocktails. Men and women are not permitted to use the same swimming pool at the same time, and the Hilton has compromised by allowing the morning hours to the ladies and the afternoon to the gentlemen. The strict interpretation of Islamic law that was practiced during the last years of former President Nimeri's rule has been relaxed, but there is a strong Moslem fundamentalist movement in Khartoum that cannot be ignored by the present, more liberal government.

We found the people to be very friendly and helpful, and while some may feel that women are relegated to second place in Moslem society, we did not find this to be the case in our interactions with Sudanese.

Most Sudanese in the north pray five times a day, do not eat pork, eat with the right hand, etc.—in other words, are traditional Moslems and hospitable hosts/hostesses.

The following is from *Shopper's Guide to Khartoum* written by Carol Correira for the Family Liaison Office, American Embassy in Khartoum in 1983:

I found shopkeepers to be very friendly and helpful. Many people spoke English, but when they didn't, I managed to get by with a few numbers in Arabic, hand gestures, and politeness. It would be a good idea to carry the numbers in Arabic with you.

It is advisable to bring as much change as possible when shopping at the souk (market), even at some stores. Be patient if a shopkeeper asks you to wait while he gets change. I have, without exception, found people to be honest and trustworthy.

Once in the souk you will have plenty of help. The "bag boys" trail you around hoping you'll give them the job of carrying your purchases. Many boys will also translate for you. It has been my experience to either be very firm at the beginning and say no, or choose a particular boy to carry the basket and let him be responsible for discouraging others from following you. After a few regular visits to the souk, you may find the same boy searching for you. You may wish to pay your help 50 piasters or one pound depending on the load and amount of time spent shopping.

Please remember to dress modestly when in public. Avoid sundresses, shorts, tight-fitting trousers.

Rental cars: Blue Nile (tel. 75452); Auto Rent Company (tel. 81098); or Enterprises (tel. 72355). Speed limit in Khartoum is 30 mph.

Beauty shops: Grand Hotel, Nile Avenue (tel. 72782); Hilton Hotel (Nile Ave., tel. 74100); and Chloe (Street 43, New Extension, tel. 43141).

Barber shops: Grand Hotel (Nile Ave., tel. 72782); Hilton Hotel (Nile Ave., tel. 74100).

Boat rental: River Transport Corporation (tel. 33471 after 10 a.m. and ask for "Fati"). To get to their offices, which are in *North* Khartoum, leaving Khartoum proper, take the road leading to Friendship Palace Hotel. Turn left just before the hotel entrance. There will be a sign that says "River Transport." Go down to the river and turn right, park, and enter the building on the west side. You must give at least 18 hours notice that you want to rent a boat. You can rent a large boat carrying 160 people for Sudanese pounds 20 an hour. Be careful in July and August when the Nile is high. Smaller boats are also available (25 people). Prices vary.

Arabic Words and Phrases for Use in the Souk

Here are a few English phonetically spelled Arabic words to get you around town in a taxi. (The phonetics are based on an American accent.) Phonetic sounds are *not* the correct spelling of the Arabic transliteration.

Please	min fudluck
Thank you	shukran
You're welcome	afwan
Straight ahead	tawally
(to the) right	yameen
(to the) left	shamell
Stop here	agaffeena, or bas hinna
How much?	be kam?
Hotel	finduk (Hilton, etc)
American embassy	Safara Amrikiya
Hello	ahlen
Goodbye	maa salaama
Yes	eye-wah
No	la

Numbers

1	2	3	4	5	6	7	8	9	10
١	٢	٣	٤	٥	٦	٧	٨	٩	١٠

Examples:

17	29	38	41	57	89	177
١٧	٢٩	٣٨	٤١	٥٧	٨٩	١٧٧

247	540
٢٤٧	٥٤٠

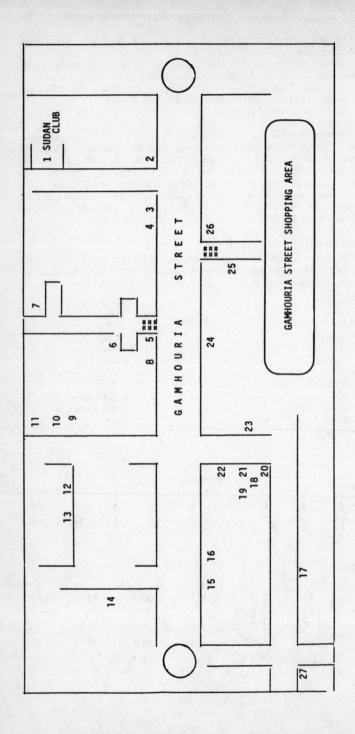

Gamhouria Street

1. Sudan Club
2. Anwar Electrical
3. Central Stationery Bookshop: stationery/toys/newspapers
4. Kamal Mohamed Saddler: suitcases/cases/handbags/trinkets
5. Almasarra Textiles and Haberdashery: beautiful fabrics
6. Slimming: handicrafts/water colors/T-shirts/stationery/dietetic items
7. Gazas: housewares
8. Dilka: perfumes/colognes for men and women/hair and hand care products/ladies lingerie/cosmetics
9. Mourad: handicrafts/paintings on fabric
10. Mora: handicrafts/Egyptian items/Saudi headdress/papyrus
11. Stationery supplies
12. Jacky's: handicrafts
13. Repair shop: watch repair
14. Sudan Folklore: handicrafts/jewelry/brass and copper pots and trays/drums
15. Excelsior Hotel
16. Sahara Hotel
17. Lussinian Goldsmith: reliable jeweler; the place to purchase gold necklaces with name in Arabic
18. Dinder Bazaar: beautiful lizard purses
19. African Folklore: trays/unique carvings/handicrafts/ostrich eggs
20. Stationery store
21. Annette: sewing thread/trims/elastic thread
22. Adwa Sahara: electrical appliances/gas burners
23. Fabric store: will take orders for jellabiyas (Sudanese national dress similar to a caftan)
24. Gamberts: large selection of housewares
25. Jewelry store
26. Jewelry store
27. Khartoum Bookstore

The main shopping area of Khartoum is located on Gamhouria Street. There are numerous stores supplying a variety of items, including clothing (locally made and imported), perfumes (mostly imported from France but bottled in Sudan), and cosmetics.

Souvenirs, particularly gold and silver jewelry and local handicrafts, can also be purchased in the same area. Many of these shops are located in the Sahara Hotel arcade and in the square across Gamhouria Street. The same things may be cheaper in the Omdurman souk.

15th Street Extension: Walking west from the junction of Middle Road and 15th Street there is (starting on the west corner) a general store, which sells hamburger, canned (tinned) goods, detergents, and soap. On the next corner Stella's also sells canned goods, cleaning supplies, and cheese. Farouk's on the opposite west corner is probably the best stocked grocery store in Khartoum: canned goods, Pepsi, candles, postcards, cheeses, ice cream, sliced meat (packaged), cleaning supplies, etc. Rimonda, on the same side of the street and a few doors down, sells sewing supplies and embroidery thread. In the next block, still on the same side of the street, El Hawi sells ice cream, cheeses, peanuts, candy, canned foods, as well as medicine. Family Pharmacy on the next corner, same side of the street, has a very good selection of beauty products as well as medicine, paper doilies, baby clothes, and disposable diapers. There is a general store a few doors down that has a variety of canned goods, cheeses, and yogurt.

Going south at the junction of Middle Road and 15th Street, take the very first street to the right (you'll know if you're going in the right direction, as there is a Bata Shoe store on the corner). There are a good fruit and vegetable stand, a butcher, and a cobbler, who sits on the corner and will repair minor problems immediately—very reasonably priced.

Riyad: Next door to the Chinese Embassy there is a good butcher who sells beef, lamb, and veal. Go early in the morning. You may leave an order and pick it up later. Closed on Wednesday. The fruit and vegetable stand next to this butcher

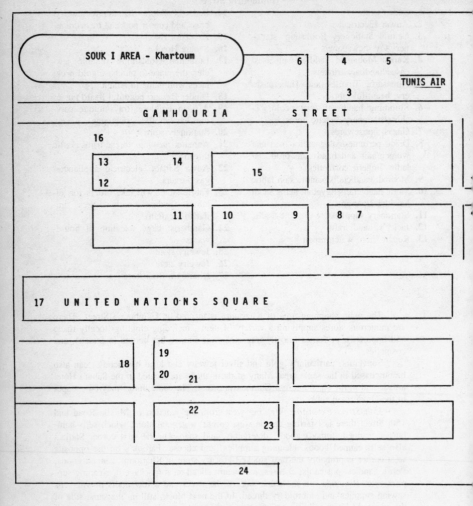

SOUK I AREA - Khartoum   6   4   5

TUNIS AIR

3

G A M H O U R I A   S T R E E T

16

13   14

12   15

11   10   9   8   7

17   **U N I T E D   N A T I O N S   S Q U A R E**

18   19

20   21

22

23

24

Souk I Area

1. Gumuchian Housewares: lots of plastic wares/buckets/pitchers/containers/trays/ashtrays/reasonable prices
2. Araak Hotel
3. New KGS: toys/wrapping paper
4. KGS: school/office supplies/Christmas decorations and lights/greeting cards
5. LEGO Shop: variety of LEGO and other toys/darts/dart boards
6. Sudan Bookshop: books/magazines/wrapping paper
7. Modern butcher
8. Felari butcher
9. Fowl
10. Spices
11. Fruits
12. Fresh fish
13. Vegetables
14. Spices
15. Meat
16. Straw baskets/pottery/food covers
17. United Nations Square

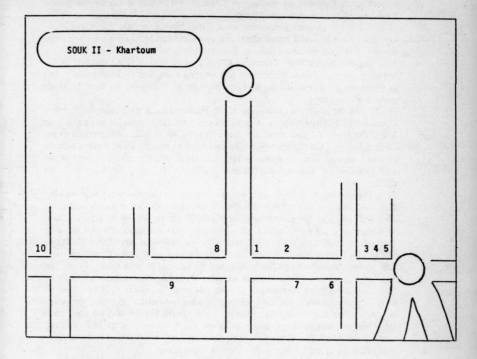

Souk II

1. The Korea Restaurant
2. Hardware/paints
3. Meat/fruit/vegetables
4. Flowers: Mrs. Renata Abdel Massih will prepare floral bouquets and arrangements upon request. She needs at least a 24-hour notice. Look for the green brick "planters" in front of her house.
5. Pizza take-out
6. Meat/fruit/vegetables
7. Pharmacy
8. Fruits/vegetables/canned (tinned) goods
9. Miscellaneous
10. Dr. Assadour Ekmejian's clinic

18. Sewing thread/embroidery thread and hoops/trims/crochet thread and hooks
19. Electrical store
20. Housewares and fabric
21. Fabric stores
22. Fabric stores and seamstress
23. Perfume shop
24. Housewares shops: good selection of glass/metal and plastic items

is very good. Opposite the embassy is Saudi Market, which stocks canned goods, fresh vegetables, ice cream, and bread.

A few blocks away (ask directions at Saudi Market) is Zaki Florist and Nursery. They have beautiful potted plants and customers can bring their own pots to be planted. Cut roses are also available. Reasonable prices.

The Omdurman Souk: Remember to put a jug of cold drinking water in the car before every trip. [Note: We also suggest wearing knee-high socks or boots as this is where we got a case of sand fly fever from the fleas jumping up from the sandy paths in the market.]

Cross the bridge to Omdurman at the Hilton. Take a right after the People's Council Hall (a large building on a right-hand corner). Remain on this road, bear left at the first "Y" (the right turn runs along the River Nile), and proceed to the "Eiffel Tower." Go slightly around the circle and go straight ahead north. Continue on this road until you see arches facing you. There will be a circle in front of the arches, and a bus stop and taxi stand to the left of the circle. Park on the main street.

The tour begins from the traffic circle. The path is rough so wear good walking shoes and pause to look up now and then to see where you are. It's easy to become confused. The souk has several sections and similar items are loosely grouped, such as housewares, souvenirs, spices, etc. With the traffic circle and the taxi stand on your left, walk into the souk, which now stretches all around you. Ahead about two blocks you can see the end of the street. At the first main intersection turn right. This street is also about two blocks long and the end can be seen ahead of you. The first block has many goldsmiths and souvenir shops. A favorite technique is to go from shop to shop for comparisons in both this street and the ivory alleys, then go back to purchase when you have an idea of what is available and what the prices are. At the first corner, turn right into the alley. On the left you will see some shoe shops and two narrow alleys, almost hallways. Go down one, out the other end and back up the other. This is what is called the ivory section where you will find ivory being carved and sold, silversmiths, ebony carvings, etc.

Baskets, foodcovers (these are made of basketweave with leather trim and very pretty), handicrafts, can be found by returning to the street of goldsmiths, turn right and continue toward the end. On your left you will come to a large parking lot with four long sheds. In these sheds are women selling handicrafts of every sort from straw sleeping mats to coffee pots. There is a wide assortment of food covers with the most expensive coming from El-Fashir. In nearby alleys are cloth merchants and spice sellers, etc.

Camel-hair rugs, saddles and knives can be found close by. Go back to the main intersection where you turned into the goldsmiths' street. Turn right (left would bring you back to the traffic circle), and to to the end of the street. The last shop on the left is that of a shopkeeper with rugs, saddles, swords, etc. Turn the corner to the right, and in the first alley on the right you can watch camel whips being made. The man on that corner will hail you to come see his wares, piled unbelievably to the roof.

Souk el Shaaby: Cross the bridge from the Hilton to Omdurman. Continue on the main road toward the Omdurman souk. Turn left at the Eiffel Tower. Watch for a Pepsi-Cola sign in the center of the boulevard. After you see this sign, there will be a large mosque on the left. Look for a road on the right opposite the mosque and turn right in front of the building with green shutters. Follow that road north until it bends to the left. You will see rows of small buildings, which are the Souk el Shaaby. If you were to take the right curve you get into the pot factories. Souk el Shaaby offers fabrics, pots, pans, tea kettles, spices, and robe material.

Ms. Correira includes other very useful information for expatriates planning to make Khartoum their home: an English/Arabic vocabulary of words to do with grocery shopping, a table giving not only the names for fruits in the two languages, but also their seasons in Sudan, as well as a similar table for vegetables. Most helpfully she has provided an index at the end of the guide by item, cross-referencing what you're looking for and where to find it. Our readers who plan to live in Khartoum should, whether they are American or not, contact the Family Liaison Office at the American Embassy for a copy of her guide.

Hotel and Restaurant Food

The cautions about eating other than at the Hilton in Egypt apply pretty much to eating in Khartoum. Amebic dysentery is still a problem because the city is on the River Nile. We feel that the Sudan Club is perfectly safe as well, but having said this, we suggest eating only packaged, imported foods and picnicking in your room or one of the many parks in the city.

Background for Uganda

PROFILE

People

Nationality: Noun and adjective—Ugandan(s). **Population** (1980): 12,630,076. Annual growth rate: 2.9%. **Ethnic groups:** African 99%, European, Asian, and Arab 1%. **Religions:** Christian (majority), Muslim, traditional. **Languages:** English (official); Luganda and Swahili widely used; other Bantu and Nilotic languages. Health: Infant mortality rate—120/1000. Life expectancy—53 yrs.

Geography

Area: 235,885 sq. km. (94,354 sq. mi.); about the size of Oregon, the size of Great Britain, and three-fourths the size of Southern Yemen.

Cities: Capital—Kampala (pop. 331,900). **Other cities:** Entebbe, Soroti. **Terrain:** 18% inland water and swamp; 12% national parks, forest, and game reserves; 70% forest, woodland, grassland. **Climate:** Varies—in the northeast, semiarid with rainfall less than 50 cm. (20 in.) or more. Two dry seasons—Dec–Feb. and June–July.

Telecommunications: Telephone and telex services generally are available to North

Official Name:
Republic of Uganda

America and Europe. Kampala is 3 hours ahead of Greenwich Mean Time.

Transportation—The international airline destination city is Entebbe not the capital city of Kampala. (Entebbe was the British capital of Uganda.) Airlines run buses from the airport into Kampala. Train service connecting Kenya through Jinja, and a rail service from Kampala to Kas-

ese. Rail service Tororo-Mbale-Soroti was freight service only, at present. Steamer service *was* operative on Lake Victoria, at present. Roads in a state of disrepair for lack of maintenance but pre-Amin were good and hard surfaced.

National holidays: New Year's Day: Jan. 1. Republic Day: Jan. 25. Labor Day: May 1. National Day: July 10. Independence Day: Oct. 9. Christmas and Boxing Day: Dec. 25 and 26. Plus all Christian and Muslim holidays.

Arrival in Uganda

By air: Entebbe, on a promontory that extends into Lake Victoria, was the colonial capital of Uganda. Kampala, surrounded by hills, is the capital of independent Uganda, and the area was the traditional capital of the kingdom of Buganda.

The airport procedures have been good in the past, and even when the Indian community was given a 90-day notice to leave in 1972 and scores of multicarrier flights descended unscheduled on Entebbe, the authorities and staff managed efficiently and professionally.

Previously, Uganda was a partner in East African Airways. When the community broke up, each of the three countries formed their own airlines. Air Tanzania was unreliable from the start and today is hopeless due to ground-based and maintenance problems more than to in-flight inadequacies. Uganda Airways managed to keep going throughout Idi Amin's tenure and up until about 1982–83, but was then forced to close down for economic reasons. Kenya Airways has gone from strength to strength and services now both Uganda and Tanzania with flights radiating from Nairobi.

There will be an airport bus at Entebbe to take passengers directly to Kampala. It may or may not have the Uganda Airways logo. It will let you off in the city center or at the International Hotel. If you can handle your baggage and it is daylight, and if you're planning to stay at the Sikh Gurdwara you can ask the driver to let you off at the main post office and then walk from there to the temple. Of course, if you're planning to stay at the International, the airport bus will take you to the door. Readers who don't want to walk to the temple can go to the hotel, and from there catch a taxi. We strongly urge readers to use only the airport bus and not be tempted to take a taxi from Entebbe as a number of robberies of single car vehicles have taken place along this particular road.

By rail: The train station is in the center of Kampala, and there are usually taxis waiting. The ride from Jinja to Kampala will have been a slow one, as the train stops at virtually every stop. There is no refreshment car on the train; however, during stops there are usually vendors selling fruits. Try the very small Uganda desert bananas; they are very sweet. Soft drinks are usually sold; be sure they have been factory capped.

Pre-Amin Uganda Railways had three classes just as Kenya Railways does; when the new Uganda Railways cars arrived from India sometime in the late 1970s, tickets offered were one class only. If the train is crowded Ugandans will insist on giving their guest in the country a seat. This should be accepted graciously; everyone in the compartment will be offended if it is not. You could offer a Coke to the person who gave up his or her seat when you stop at a station if you'd like to return the favor.

Kampala

Kampala is not a big city but a spread-out, large town. Since her political troubles during the past 17 years, buildings have been bombed and not rebuilt. The International Hotel is about the tallest building, made more so by being constructed on a hill. Most buildings are not more than five stories high.

Kampala gets its water from Lake Victoria, where it is pumped into a system on the outskirts of Kampala that purifies it. In 1980 the British took on the job of restoring the lakeside pumps and the Americans the piping and sewers of Kampala. During all the years of Idi Amin's rule not one shilling had gone toward maintaining the city's water supply. Pipes corroded and became clogged. The resourceful citizens of Kampala utilized the locations where pipes burst as standpipes and went back to fetching and carrying water to their homes in buckets on their heads. Enterprising small businessmen rigged up empty clean oil drums and started delivering water to the more affluent Kampala homes where they would—for a charge—fill household tanks on a regular weekly basis. Reportedly, the Kampala city water system is working again and things are better than in the early years of this decade.

Most of the services visitors need are within a short walking distance to the accommodation we've recommended. The Speke Hotel, near the International, used to serve delicious midmorning coffee and afternoon teas on their arched brick terrace at street level. When we looked in one morning in 1981 the lobby was full of Ugandan army officers, and unlike the International, where the civil service was billeted, there was a tense atmosphere. The Speke Hotel used to have one of the most sophisticated cocktail lounges and bars in Africa, but field-promoted officers not quite comfortable with the authority their newly acquired brass bestowed could make problems. We decided not to push our luck and had our tea and coffee at the International. Things may be different today, and if so, the Speke has a great deal of charm.

Behind the International Hotel are the government buildings, including the parliament; down the hill is the city center and a multitude of small Indian-run cloth shops; to the west is Makerere University and to the east, the Industrial area. The shops used to stock everything and anything; after Amin was sent packing, the government of India encouraged small—very small—Indian businesses to go to Uganda to sell cheap nylon fabrics, which the Indian mills churn out and can sell nowhere else. One occasionally meets Indians, particularly in the International Hotel, who were once citizens of Uganda and who formed part of the "Exodus of the Asians" in 1972. They have returned to Uganda strictly (for the most part) for a visit and to file a claim for the property they left behind, which was confiscated without compensation by Idi Amin's government. Some may have intentions of installing a relative from the subcontinent of India in a reclaimed business, but none that we have met have any desire to return to Uganda despite the hardships they endured during the early years of adjustment in the UK or Canada.

The government of Uganda under Milton Obote advertised and actually contacted by mail former Ugandan businessmen of Indian descent, hoping to attract them back to the country. One very wealthy Sikh lumberman told us he had told the authorities he would take his mill back when it was "returned to me the way it was turned over to you." Needless to say, all businesses and factories had become derelict and inoperable.

Jinja

Uganda has many small towns apart from Jinja, but we shall confine our comments to Jinja, as it is the only town where we have personal knowledge that conditions are returning to normal.

Jinja is the town built around the place that John Hanningston Speke identified as the source of the River Nile. Since that time his actual siting has been replaced by a huge hydroelectric dam, Owen Falls. Jinja has palm-lined boulevards, low buildings reminiscent of many Indian towns, and a lovely botanical garden. (There is another botanical garden at Entebbe where one of the Tarzan films was made.) The sugarcane factory at nearby Lungazi was the source of much of Jinja's wealth in addition to small factories and coffee marketing.

We have recommended staying at the Crested Crane Hotel; a description is given under "Ugandan Accommodation."

Communications

Mail can be addressed in care of Poste Restante, General Post Office Kampala, just as described in "Background for Kenya: Communication." The postal services in Uganda were very reliable and, as we understand, continue to be. This does not apply to gifts or parcels sent through the mail, and caution should be exercised in sending anything of value.

Cable and telex services are good, and as in Kenya, they are under the auspices of the government. There are telecommunications offices in the post offices.

Newspapers in Uganda have followed a yo-yo pattern in the past 17 years; there is now a government-operated newspaper in English, but the most independent and reliable paper is *Munno,* published by the Catholic Church. Journalists, both Ugandan and expatriate, have been imprisoned during the political upheavals, and it is hoped that there will be a sincere return to freedom of the press once Uganda settles down.

Certain issues of *Time* and *Newsweek* can be censored in East African countries, but many times issues containing controversial (to local political events) reports are not withdrawn. It depends on the mood of the moment.

Radio, also, is under the control of the government. African radio broadcasting stations are considered of great political importance, and they are always the first buildings to be commandeered when a coup comes. Most people rely on the BBC Overseas Service; reception is best once the sun goes down.

Locally produced television has been affected by the unrest as well as other facets of Ugandan daily life. General Amin liked *Sesame Street* so much that at times only that program was broadcast. It goes without saying that there are no independent companies and what is available is under the sponsorship of the government.

Business Hours

Stores are closed on Sundays, and half day on Saturdays. Sundays can be pretty dull, and it is wise to accept invitations to private homes on this day, as there is little else to do but visit the museum.

Throughout the week the stores open around 8 a.m.—although some of the smaller shops are open at sunrise to accommodate the needs of working people who are in the habit of purchasing cigarettes, etc., on their way to work. They close at 12:30 p.m.—again, the exception is the small kiosk type of shop that caters to working people and stays open during the lunch hour—and reopen at 3, closing about 7 p.m.

Banks are always open in the morning—usually after 10—and may or may not be open for certain hours during the afternoon. Ask at the front desk. The major British banks are represented in Uganda; Barclays has more branches in the smaller towns than other banks.

Taxis

In pre-Amin days there was a system of licensing taxi drivers just as there is in any other country. Since the collapse of political institutions and the Ugandan economy, this system, too, has disappeared. Do not assume that simply because a man is driving a taxi he can be trusted. Travel only in daylight and within the city limits of Kampala. Establish a fare before you get in and, if at all possible, travel with another person—not alone.

Religious Services

The people of Uganda are very devout Christians: 31% are Church of Uganda (Church of England or Episcopalian), 29% Roman Catholic, and 7% Moslem. The remaining observe traditional religions and are usually found in the northern part of the country.

There are two cathedrals in Kampala—one Church of Uganda and one Catholic—plus many smaller churches of these faiths in addition to Baptist, Methodist, etc. churches. General Amin started the construction of a beautiful mosque on a hill to balance the cathedrals, each of which are set on a hill, but we don't know whether it has been completed. It was under construction in 1981 when we were in Kampala. Needless to say there are other smaller mosques that are open for worship.

There are Hindu temples and the Sikh gurdwara; the latter we have described under "Ugandan Accommodation."

Hours for the services can be obtained from the front desk staff at the International Hotel or are posted in front of the churches.

Languages

The official language of Uganda is English. Luganda is widely spoken in the south, but seldom is a Swahili speaker met, despite the widely held belief that Swahili is the lingua franca of Africa. In actuality, while there are a few speakers in Uganda, and while some of the words can be understood by, say a Luganda speaker, apart from Ugandans who have lived in Kenya, Swahili is not understood by most Ugandans.

If you have an American or Canadian accent, Ugandans are going to have a difficult time with it. When I first started teaching in Jinja in 1981 my students asked me to say something in American. They thought I was speaking English with a foreign accent. Go slowly, be patient, and if they smile, know that it has been a very long time since most of them have heard American accents. New Zealanders and Australians may have an equally difficult time. However, Ugandans are polite, and it is unlikely that they will comment on your accent or let you know it sounds strange to their ears.

Geographical Description

Much of Uganda is covered by water. The land in the south is very fertile, and literally any tropical crop will grow. Fingers of rivers and small streams provide ample water for irrigation, and are supplemented by short-lived, predictable rains. The northern part of Uganda becomes very dry, semi-arid, similar to the land to the east in northern Kenya. Western Uganda becomes alpine until in the far west the Mountains of the Moon rise to over 16,000 feet.

Tribal and Ethnic Groups

There have been settlements along the banks of Lake Victoria for several thousand years. The climate, vegetation, and abundance of water made the region attractive to prehistoric man. The great Bantu migration into central Africa from the western part of the continent established peoples of Bantu origin around the lake. Nilotic peoples had migrated down the River Nile and they, too, settled in what is now Uganda. The Bantus established sophisticated kingdoms and forms of government—the Nilotic peoples remained primarily nomadic.

Today the Buganda and the Busoga inhabit the shores of Lake Victoria within Uganda's boundary; the Ankole are found in the western part of the country to the Rwandese border, and the Lango and Acholi in the north. A primitive tribe, the Karamajong, live in northeastern Uganda along the Kenyan border. In addition, there are a number of minor Ugandan tribes, including the peoples of West Nile province, which was the homeland of General Amin.

Tribalism is an important factor in Uganda's contemporary politics, and rivalries have been the cause of near genocide in certain parts of the country during the past 20 years.

Social Customs

As our readers will be visiting primarily Kampala and Jinja, we will confine our remarks on social customs to the people in those regions—the Baganda and the Busoga. Uganda is comprised of many tribes, and each of them have particular social customs that may or may not be practiced by a neighboring tribe.

Both the Busoga and the Buganda have been exposed to foreigners over decades and adroitly move from traditional to western social customs. However, the demarcation is not always totally distinct and if a western practice conflicts strongly with a traditional practice—the traditional practice wins. A case in point is the Buganda and Busoga practice of greeting one another. There is a long exchange of conversation on the topic of personal health, the health of one's immediate family, and the health of one's in-laws. A simple "How are you?" is not so much rhetoric. An answer is expected; you are expected to ask about the other person's health, and to only gradually work up to the main topic of conversation. Americans especially are criticized for being too blunt. Despite the fact that the person with whom you are in contact is wearing a western suit or dress, take time to make preliminary inquiries about how they are, etc. Naturally, you do not know their relatives, but you can change the topic for the introductory preliminaries to the weather, to something you particularly like about the country, etc.

It is the custom for people to kneel when speaking to someone whom they greatly respect. If a woman does this to you, you can offer your right hand and gently pull her up, indicating that there is no necessity for such action. Diverting the eyes is often practiced, and because someone fails to look you straight in the eye does not necessarily mean they are shifty characters. Speaking very softly is another sign of respect; it goes without saying that shouting or loud voices are unacceptable. Always go to someone's home through the back door— not the front, unless you know them to be well-educated, westernized people. Younger people always carry parcels and packages for their elders. You may be surprised when a younger person, without comment, rushes up and takes whatever you are carrying. Sometimes this extends to your handbag and, if you know the child, give it to them to carry without worrying that the contents will be tampered with.

Having said all this, you should be aware of a phenomenon that occurs not only among the Buganda and Busoga but other African tribal groups (not, however, in Kenya). A mass hysteria can overtake people—not mob hysteria, because the participants may not necessarily be in a group at the time the hysteria occurs. They may be in their homes, in their places of work, in the fields, anywhere. Say there is a car accident and someone is killed. From out of nowhere people rush to the vehicle and beat the driver, whom they consider to be the instigator of the accident, to death. No time is taken to determine if the pedestrian walked out into the road, creating an unavoidable accident, etc. Another example: say a burglar is heard attempting to break into someone's hut or home. A high-pitched vocal sound will be made by the person who first hears the burglar. This call will be picked up by a neighbor—then the next neighbor and the next. They will move inward toward the original voice, forming a closed circle as they do. The burglar is entrapped and beaten to death. This phenomenon is totally unpredictable and may occur for any number of reasons. Newcomers to Uganda are always warned not to stop to assist anyone who has been hurt beside the road. This advice holds good whether they or another car hit the victim. When I have questioned Catholic priests about this advice I've been told that suicide is the greatest sin and to stop is to voluntarily commit suicide. It goes without saying that it is always best to employ a driver in Uganda rather than drive yourself.

It is illegal to carry firearms in either Uganda or Kenya, but a panga— similar to a machete—can inflict terrible wounds and is the weapon of choice of criminals. They inflict a stroke of the panga between the neck and shoulder of their victims. As in Kenya, pickpockets, if caught in the act, are beaten to death there and then.

The Buganda and the Busoga are complex societies. Good manners will see you through most situations, and if you hear that high vocal call—you'll never forget it.

Health Conditions

Uganda's climate, in the Kampala-Entebbe-Jinja area, is hot and humid. This naturally favors the growth of bacteria and provides a perfect environment for infections to live year round without a killing frost or an extremely dry season. Children should be urged to wash their hands frequently as, should they put them in their mouth, stomach upsets can occur from germs picked up on the hands. There is a high incidence of malaria in Uganda because of the prevalence of water—in the lakes, rivers, and ponds. In pre-Amin days we had a most efficient public health service that sent officers routinely to our homes to check for any standing water in the gardens, etc., which could be breeding grounds for mosquitoes. These niceties have gone, as has the once effective control in the rural areas for tsetse fly. Be certain to use mosquito nets at night if there is no air conditioning in the room, which permits the windows to be kept closed after the room has been sprayed; coat the exposed portions of the body with insect repellent if you plan to be outdoors once the sun has gone down, and take immediate, repeat immediate, care of even small cuts, which can turn into infected sores in a very short time. A small tube of antiseptic ointment carried in a purse or pocket is not out of place under present Ugandan conditions.

Notwithstanding the foregoing remarks, we always feel marvelous in Uganda, but we have had our share of illnesses when in that country.

Swimming in Lake Victoria

Under no circumstances swim in the lakes or rivers of Uganda as there is a high infestation of bilharziasis in the waters. Don't even trail a hand in the waters when boating.

Hotel and Restaurant Food

Kampala used to have marvelous restaurants; now it is a case of patronizing whatever is available. We ate in the International Hotel and had no ill effects. However, be on your guard, be suspect of dirty conditions, and stick to plain simple foods without mayonnaise or dressings. Do not eat raw vegetables or fruits that cannot be peeled before consuming.

Street vendors sell deep-fried cassava chips, and these can make a reliable and very satisfying snack food.

Shopping

On leaving the International Hotel and turning right there is a Ugandan-government-operated craft pavillion two blocks down the road. This is without doubt the best place to purchase gifts as prices are strictly controlled. The variety is excellent and the quality of a high standard.

The city market has little to offer apart from fruits and vegetables; however, Leah and I always enjoy making a few purchases from the medicine men.

BACKGROUND INFORMATION FOR WEST AFRICA*

Mask from the Congo River basin.

There is a saying that those accustomed to east and southern Africa can never adjust to West Africa. We would agree, although we have trouble in adjusting to lifestyles a lot closer to home as well. Analyzing our maladjustments, the single common denominator would appear to be our aversion to filth and dirt. My mother used to say "Nothing is beautiful, not even a diamond, if it is dirty." West Africa is dirty—east and southern Africa, what we've seen of it— is clean. The exception that proves the rule in this case is downtown Nairobi. Standard Street and Kaunda Street are particularly bad. Garbage containers overflow for days on end, attracting flies and rats. The sidewalks (pavements) are seldom swept by the owners of stores that front these streets. They let Nairobi down badly.

*Factual information and maps for "Background" section courtesy of the U.S. Department of State's "Background Notes."

Much of the problem of West Africa is that urban infrastructure has not kept pace with rural migration to the city. There are pockets of slums in east and southern Africa, but in West Africa the entire city in any given area is without adequate piped water, sewers, street lighting, and even paved streets. The Gambia is probably the cleanest, but The Gambia is also very poor. Poor people have little to throw away. Sierra Leone, of the countries we've seen, is undoubtedly the worst. Garbage is piled, without exaggeration, two stories high on the corners of Freetown streets, when it could be thrown in the ocean only a stone's throw away. Senegal is fairly clean, but we have seen only the downtown area and the strip of highway between the airport and Dakar. Judging from the airport hotel, which is swept but not scrubbed, we imagine there are grim areas outside the showcase tourist paths. Togo is not as bad as Sierra Leone, but multimillion-dollar national buildings are set within streets where there is no piped water and sewers for the houses. Togolese compensate for this by using the beach as a public latrine. Gabon—what we saw of it—while certainly short of civic pride in Libreville, suffers more from poor access roads to the capital and broken pavements than from actual filth.

The people of West Africa differ dramatically from the people of southern and eastern Africa. Traditional dress is worn in West Africa, while in Kenya, Tanzania, Uganda, and Malawi, European dress is generally seen. West Africans are, from our observations, more emotional, have a lower boiling point, are more aggressive and less disciplined. They do not understand the meaning of the word queue or line, or turn-taking, because a small bribe inevitably can put one ahead. Except for the Gambians, a smile does not come quickly; this is one reason why the cheerfulness of the Gambians is so noticeable. These commentaries are strictly our observations and subjective opinions, and readers will, of course, find exceptions. Even on a one-to-one basis, however, we could not strike an accord with most West Africans outside of The Gambia. Part of this may be our color; we found a great animosity toward Whites, except among educated Nigerians. Our color, plus the fact that we do not speak French, made us the subject of abusive treatment by airline personnel, both on the ground and in the air, hotel staff, and, of course, taxi drivers. (We assume everyone has problems with the latter.) All in all, traveling in West Africa is not a "fun experience."

We have one regret: We did not visit Ghana. Getting to Accra from Lome in Togo is simply a matter of taking a taxi; we have many Ghanain friends in Washington whom we admire greatly, and both Leah and I are enamored with Flight Lieutenant Jerry Rawlings, the leader of Ghana. So, why didn't we go? At the time of our visit to Togo, the Ghanian cedi was at an artificially high rate on the legal market. Prices were astronomical, and for that reason we did not feel Ghana would be a country we could recommend to readers. Now the exchange rate has been lowered, and Ghana is making a serious attempt to attract tourists. Readers following *The Africans* itinerary may want to ask about rates and taxi fares and discover Ghana for themselves.

Benin, Togo's other neighbor, suffers from high crime, and we really do not recommend a visit to that country, unless perhaps you are part of a tour. Benin has, in our opinion, nothing to offer that can't be seen elsewhere, and the government's human rights record is deplorable.

We did not encounter any reason to bribe in Senegal, The Gambia, Togo, or Gabon. Ivory Coast presents problems, and we have discussed these in our description of *The Africans* itinerary. Ivory Coast was comparatively clean and we cannot fault the country on that score. The lagoons that surround Abidjan are used by some resort operators along the coast, but appeared to us to be polluted, and we would not want to swim in them.

In *Fielding's Literary Africa* West Africa is mentioned only in *The Africans* itinerary. We want our readers following this particular itinerary to make up their own minds about Africa as a whole. For this reason, only very general information is provided for Cote d' Ivoire, Gabon, The Gambia, Togo, and Senegal.

Background for Cote d' Ivoire *

PROFILE

People

Nationality: Noun and adjective—Ivorian(s). **Population** (1982): 8.6 million. Annual growth rate (1980): 3.5%. **Ethnic groups:** More than 60. **Religions:** Indigenous 63%, Muslim 25%, Christian 12%. **Languages:** French (official), tribal dialects. **Education:** Years compulsory—none. Attendance—75%. Literacy—24%. **Health** (1980): Infant mortality rate—127/1000. Life expectancy—47 yrs.

Geography

Area: 322,500 sq. km. (124,500 sq. mi.); slightly larger than New Mexico, four-fifths the size of Newfoundland, a quarter more than the size of Great Britain, 21,000 sq. mi. larger than New Zealand, and a sixth the size of Saudi Arabia.

Cities: Capital—Abidjan (pop. 1.1 million; 1977 est.). **Other cities**—Bouake, Daloa, Gagnoa, Korhogo, Man. **Terrain:** Mostly flat. **Climate:** Tropical.

Telecommunications—Local phone service is adequate. International calls can be dialed directly to the U.S. and many other countries. Ivory Coast is on the same time as Greenwich Mean Time.

Transportation—Abidjan is served by several international airlines. Air Ivoire serves the country's principal cities, and small planes are available for charter. Air fares are expensive. The railroad runs be-

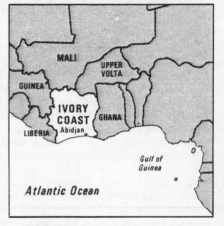

Official Name:
Cote d' Ivoire

tween Abidjan and Ouagadougou, Burkina Fasso. Most Abidjan roads are paved, and several fine macadam roads lead to major towns within 300 km. (190 mi.) of the capital. All unpaved roads are dusty during the dry season. Heavy-duty 4-wheel drive vehicles are essential for trips into the more isolated areas. Metered taxis, with low fares, and rental cars are available.

National holidays: New Year's Day: Jan. 1. Labor Day: May 1. All Saint's Day: Nov. 1. Independence Day: Dec. 7. Christmas Day: Dec. 25. Plus Easter, Ascension Day, the Feast of the Assumption, and Whit Monday. Muslim holidays are also observed.

*In 1987 the government proclaimed that all references to the "Ivory Coast" in foreign publications should be changed to the French name for their country.

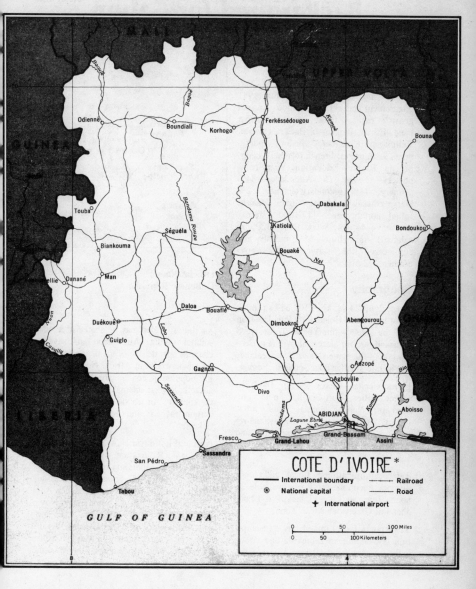

MALI

UPPER VOLTA

GUINEA

Bafoué

Boé

Odienné

Boundiali

Korhogo

Ferkéssédougou

Komoé

Bouna

Bandama Rouge

Dabakala

Bondoukou

Touba

Séguéla

Katiola

Biankouma

Bouaké

Nzi

Danané

Man

Daloa

Bouaflé

Dimbokro

Abengourou

GHANA

Sassandra

Duékoué

Lobo

Guiglo

Cavally

Nzon

Gagnoa

Adzopé

Bia

LIBERIA

Divo

Agboville

Aboisso

Bandama

Komoé

ABIDJAN

Fresco

Lagune Ebrié

Grand-Bassam

Assini

Grand-Lahou

San Pédro

Sassandra

Tabou

GULF OF GUINEA

COTE D'IVOIRE *

— International boundary   ·-·-·- Railroad

⊛ National capital   ——— Road

✝ International airport

0   50   100 Miles

0   50   100 Kilometers

*Formerly known in English language publications as Ivory Coast.

Background for Gabon

PROFILE

People

Nationality: Noun and adjective—Gabonese (sing. and pl.). **Population** (1981 government census): 1.2 million. **Annual growth rate:** 1.08%. **Ethnic groups:** Fang, Eshira, Bapounou, Bateke, Okande. **Religions:** Christian, Muslim, indigenous. **Languages:** French (official), Fang, Myene, Bateke. **Education:** Years compulsory—to age 16. Attendance—84% primary, 14% secondary/technical, 2% higher education. Literacy—65%. **Health:** Infant mortality rate—117/1000. Life expectancy—44 yrs. Work force (120,000 salaried): Agriculture—65%; industry and commerce—30%; services—2.5%; government—2.5%.

Geography

Area: 266,024 sq. km. (102,317 sq. mi.); about the size of Colorado, a little less than half the size of the Yukon Territory, 8 thousand sq. mi. larger than Great Britain, about the same size as New Zealand, and a little smaller than Southern Yemen.

Cities: Capital—Libreville (pop. 180,000). **Other cities**—Port-Gentil, Franceville. **Terrain:** Narrow coastal plain; hilly, heavily jungled interior; some savanna regions in east and south. **Climate:** Hot and humid all year with two rainy and two dry seasons.

Telecommunications: Local and long-distance telephone service is available 24 hours. Telex and cable. Libreville is 1 hour ahead of Greenwich Mean Time.

Transportation: Limited bus transportation is available in Libreville and erratically in some of the larger cities of the interior. Taxis are plentiful along the ma-

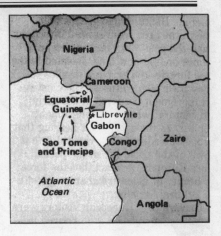

Official Name:
Gabonese Republic

jor routes. Rides may be shared at a substantial saving. Air Gabon and several charters operate one of the densest domestic air networks in Africa. Nearly all major population centers are linked by jet aircraft. Several international airlines serve the country. Air Gabon offers discounts for certain travelers; inquire when purchasing tickets.

National holidays: New Year's Day: Jan. 1. Jour de Renovation: March 12. Labor Day: May 1. Liberation of African Continent Day: May 25. Feast of the Blessed Virgin Mary: Aug. 15. Independence Anniversary: Aug. 18. All Saint's Day: Nov. 1. Christmas Day: Dec. 25. Also the movable holidays of Easter Monday, Youth Day (the second Sunday in May), Ascension Day, Whit Monday, and the Muslim holiday Eid el Fitr.

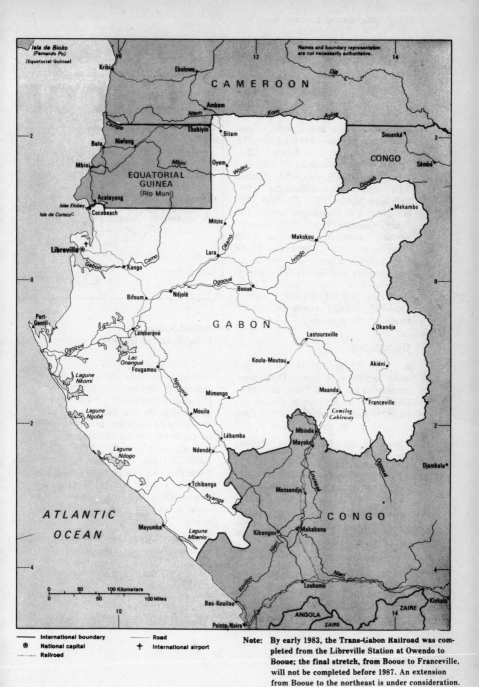

Isla de Bioko
(Fernando Po)
(Equatorial Guinea)

Names and boundary representation
are not necessarily authoritative.

CAMEROON

Kribi · Ebolowa · Dja · Ambam · Kom · Ayina ·
Ntem · CONGO
Campo · Ebebiyin · Bitam · Souanké · Sémbé ·
Bata · Niefang · Oyem · Woleu ·
Mbini · Mbini · Djouab ·
EQUATORIAL GUINEA (Río Muni) · Mekambo ·
Islas Elobey · Acalayong · Mitzic · Makokou ·
Isla de Corisco · Cocobeach · Ivindo ·
Lara · Okano ·
Libreville ✚ · Kango · Como · Ogooué · Booué ·
Gabon · Bifoum · Ndjolé · Okandja ·
Port-Gentil · GABON · Lastoursville · Akiéni ·
Ogooué · Lambaréné · Koula-Moutou ·
Lac Onangué · Fougamou · Moanda ·
Lagune Nkomi · Mimongo · Franceville ·
Ngounié · Comilog Cableway ·
Lagune Ngobé · Mouila ·
Lébamba · Mbinda · Djembala ·
Lagune Ndogo · Ndendé · Mayoko ·
Louessé ·
Tchibanga · Mossendjo · CONGO ·
ATLANTIC OCEAN · Nyanga · Ogooué ·
Mayumba · Lagune Mbanio · Kibangou · Makabana ·
Niari ·
Bas-Kouilou · Loubomo ·
Koulou · Niari · ZAIRE · Kinkala ·
Pointe-Noire · ANGOLA · ZAIRE ·

Scale: 50 · 100 Kilometers
0 · 50 · 100 Miles

— International boundary   —— Road
⊛ National capital   ✚ International airport
·-·-· Railroad

Note: By early 1983, the Trans-Gabon Railroad was completed from the Libreville Station at Owendo to Booue; the final stretch, from Booue to Franceville, will not be completed before 1987. An extension from Booue to the northeast is under consideration.

Background for The Gambia

PROFILE

People

Nationality: Noun and adjective—Gambian(s). **Population** (1980 est.): 619,052. Annual growth rate (1980–81 est.): 2.8%. **Ethnic groups:** Mandinka 37.7%, Fula 16.2%, Wolof 14%, Jola 8.5%, Serahuli 7.8%, other 5.3%, non-Gambian 10.5%. **Religions:** Muslim 85%, Christian 14%, indigenous 1%. **Languages:** English (official), Mandinka, Wolof, Fula, other indigenous languages. **Education:** Years compulsory—none. Attendance—14.2% (ages 5–19). Literacy—12%. **Health:** Infant mortality rate—217/1000. Life expectancy—men 32 yrs., women 34 yrs. Work force (378,850, 1980 est.): Agriculture—75%; industry, commerce, and services—18.9%; government—6.1%.

Geography

Area: 11,295 sq. km. (4,361 sq. mi.); about four-fifths the size of Connecticut, about twice the size of Prince Edward Island, and twice the size of Devon, five times the size of Australian Capital Territory, and half the size of Kuwait.

Cities: Capital: Banjul (pop. 40,000). **Terrain:** Savanna. **Climate:** Subtropical.

Telecommunications—Telex service is available to the U.S., Europe, and Dakar in neighboring Senegal. Radiophone service operates to the U.K., most of Europe, and the west coast of Africa. Satellite telephone service is available to Europe and the U.S. Banjul is on the same time as Greenwich Mean Time.

Transportation—Banjul is 25 minutes by air from Dakar, Senegal, where world-

Official Name:
Republic of The Gambia

wide air connections are frequent and excellent. The international airport is Banjul (Yundum International), 29 km. (18 mi.) southwest of the city. Taxis are available. Banjul can be reached by road from Dakar by the Trans-Gambia Highway 482 km. (300 mi.) or the car ferry from Barra to Banjul 321 km. (200 mi.)—days only. Collective taxis can be hired from Barra to Dakar. Car hire possible. Roads in and around Banjul in general bitumized. Unsealed roads often impassable in the rainy season.

National holidays: New Year's Day: Jan. 1. Independence Day: Feb. 18. Labor Day: May 1. Christmas: Dec. 25. Plus movable Christian holidays. Also observed are Muslim holidays.

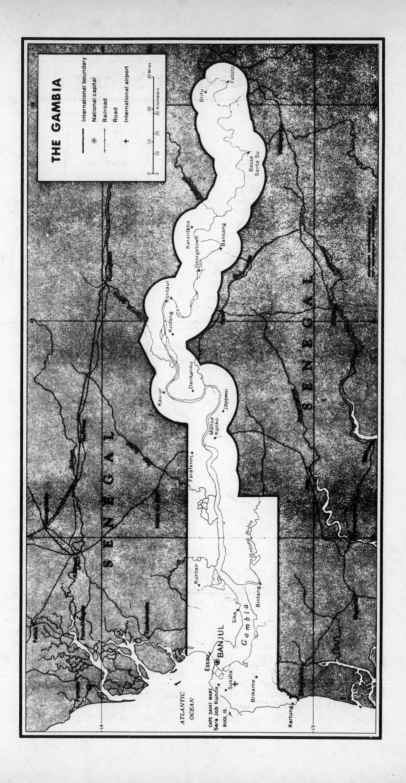

THE GAMBIA

International boundary
⊙ National capital
Railroad
Road
+ International airport

30 Miles
30 Kilometers

Fatoto
Brtu
Basse Santa Su
Bansang
Karantaba
Georgetown
Kuntaur
Kudang
Dankunku
Kau-ur
Jappeni
Mansa Konko
Farafenni
Kuntair
Njntung Bulun
Bintang
Sika
Gambia
BANJUL
Essau
Sara Job Kunda
Sukuta
Brikama
Kartung
CAPE SAINT MARY
BIJOL IS.

ATLANTIC OCEAN

S E N E G A L

S E N E G A L

-14
-13

Background for Senegal

PROFILE

People

Nationality: Noun and adjective—Senegalese (singl. and pl.). **Population** (est.): 5.6 million. Annual growth rate 2.3%. **Ethnic groups:** Wolof 36%, Fulani 17.5%, Serer 16.5%, Toucouleur 9%, Diola 9%, Mandingo 6.5%, other African 4.5%, other 1%. **Religions:** Muslim 75%, Christian 5%, traditional 20%. **Languages:** French (official), Wolof, Pulaar, Diola, Mandingo. **Education:** Attendance—53% primary, 11% secondary. Literacy—5–10%. **Health:** Infant mortality rate—158/1000. Life expectancy—44 yrs. **Work force** (1,732,000): Agriculture—70% (subsistence). Wage earners (175,000)—private sector—40%; government and parapublic—60%.

Official Name:
Republic of Senegal

Geography

Area: 196,840 sq. km. (76,000 sq. mi.); about the size of South Dakota, half the size of Newfoundland, slightly smaller than England and Scotland, three times the size of Tasmania, and the same size as the Yemen Arab Republic.

Cities: Capital—Dakar. **Other cities**—Thies, Kaolack, Saint-Louis. **Terrain:** Flat or rising to foothills. **Climate:** Tropical.

Telecommunications: Excellent long-distance telephone service is available by ra-dio link. Cable and telex services are available. Dakar is on Greenwich Mean Time.

Transportation: Dakar has excellent and frequent worldwide airline connections. In the city, metered taxis are available, but the drivers are very argumentative. Make sure to settle on a price before putting baggage in the taxi.

National holidays: Muslim holidays. Independence Day is April 4.

Background for Togo

PROFILE

People

Nationality: Noun and adjective—Togolese (sing. and pl.). **Population** (1979 est.): 2.4 million. Annual growth rate (1966–79): 2.6%. **Ethnic groups:** Ewe, Mina, Kabye. **Religions:** 60% indigenous, 20% Christian, 20% Muslim. **Languages:** French (official), tribal dialects.

Education: Attendance—50% of age groups 5–19 enrolled. Literacy—10% est. **Health:** Life expectancy—40 yrs. **Work force:** Agriculture—78%; industry—22%.

Geography

Area: 56,600 sq. km. (21,853 sq. mi.); slightly smaller than West Virginia, a little smaller than New Brunswick, or Scot-

Senegal

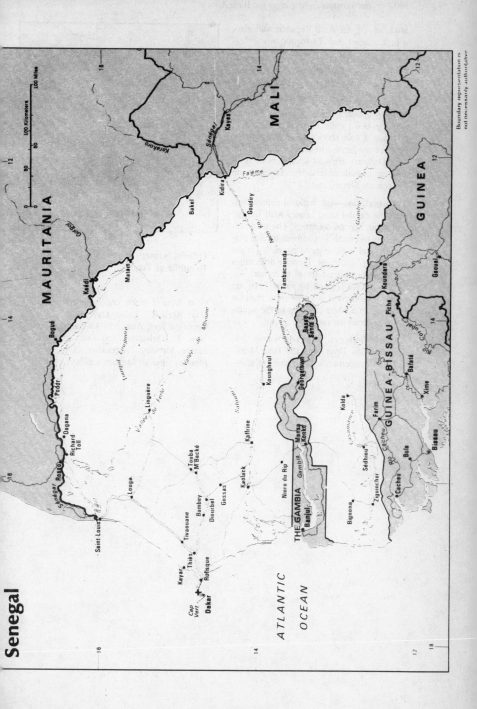

Boundary representation is not necessarily authoritative

land, or Yemen Arab Republic and also, a little smaller than Tasmania.

Cities: Capital—Lome. **Other cities**— Anecho, Atakpame, Kande. **Terrain:** savanna and hills. **Climate:** Tropical.

Telecommunications—A radiotelephone systems operates between Lome, Europe, and the U.S.; calls must be arranged in advance. Cable service is adequate. Both services are limited to certain hours of the day. Ordinary air mail letter service is liable to considerable delay. Lome is on Greenwich Mean Time.

Transportation—International airlines connect the capital city, Lome, with Europe and other African countries. The road network to the north is confined to one macadam road with spurs of passable (in the dry season) dirt roads. Frontier difficulties can complicate road travel to Benin. Access to Ghana is good by road. Taxis are available and good in Lome. Rail travel is confined to a short distance in the southern portion of the country.

National holidays: New Year's Day: Jan. 1. Liberation Day: Jan. 13. Jan. 24 and Feb. 2 commemorate the president's sur-

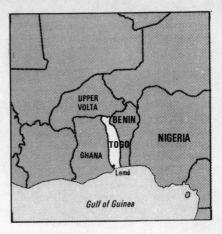

Official Name:
Republic of Togo

vival from a plane crash. Independence Day: April 27. Labor Day: May 1. Assumption Day: Aug. 15. All Saint's Day: Nov. 1. Christmas Day: Dec. 25. Also Easter Monday, Ascension Day, Whit Monday, and all Muslim holidays.

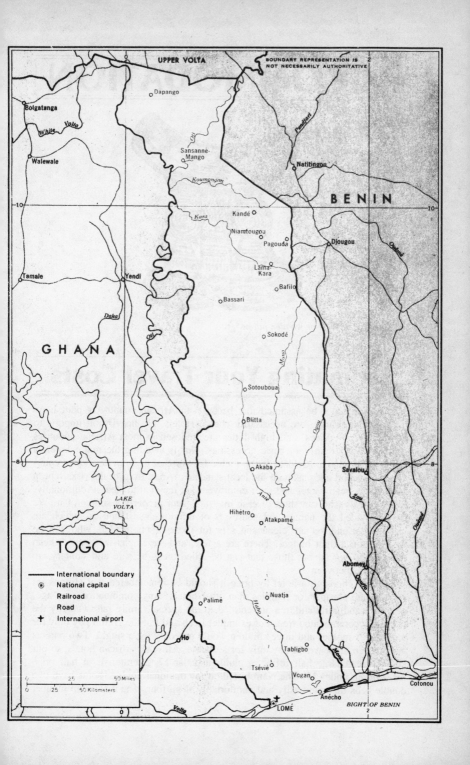

UPPER VOLTA

BOUNDARY REPRESENTATION IS
NOT NECESSARILY AUTHORITATIVE

Dapango

Bolgatanga

White Volta

Walewale

Sansanne-
Mango

Koumongou

Natitingou

BENIN

10

Kandé

Kara

Niamtougou

Pagouda

Djougou

Oudrei

Tamale

Yendi

Lama-
Kara

Bafilo

Deka

Bassari

GHANA

Sokodé

Mono

Sotouboua

Blitta

8

Akaba

Savalou

Zou

LAKE
VOLTA

Hihétro

Atakpamé

Anié

Abomey

Oueme

TOGO

— International boundary
⊛ National capital
  Railroad
  Road
✛ International airport

Palimé

Nuatja

Haho

Ho

Tabligbo

Tsévie

Vogan

Cotonou

Mono

0   25   50 Miles
0   25   50 Kilometers

Volta

LOMÉ

Anécho

BIGHT OF BENIN

2

ACCOMMODATION

Angoni head-rest or wooden pillow

Estimating Your Travel Costs

It should not be assumed that because an African country is poor hotel rates in that country are necessarily cheap. Hotels rely heavily on imports to provide their services, and high duties are imposed in most African countries on items other than very basic necessities. Nor is avoiding the major hotels a practical alternative. Seldom is it possible for those of us from developed countries to function adequately at the local standards. Apart from health risks, cheap hotels pay cheap wages and their employees are tempted to steal. Additionally, fellow guests who run short of cash may find your property a source of it. We have provided the names and addresses of religious guest houses, which are inexpensive and yet are clean and safe for those of our readers who will be traveling on a tight budget. There are a few, and we emphasize a few, cheap commercial hotels, but those that can be relied on to be safe and sanitary are few and far between.

When choosing a hotel by price it should be remembered that Hiltons invariably are cheaper for families than other hotels. Any combination, any age, of parent and child/children are entitled to the special family rate whereby the child is accommodated free. For example, Leah and I at the Hilton pay only for a single. A mother and three children would pay only for a single. Two parents and four children would pay only for a double. All other African hotels, to our knowledge, charge half price for children under 17 (Sheratons), or half price for children under 12. The Nairobi Hilton International double rooms have two double beds that can easily and comfortably sleep four. The maximum number of people allowed in each double room, however, is five (they will put in a rollaway bed). Suite prices, for larger groups (unrelated) can also be more economical than separate double/single rooms.

Apart from accommodation, food will be the largest single expense for the vacationer. Africa, unlike some other continents, is not a place where Westerners can survive over a period of time on traditional dishes. Usually these are too high in fiber and as a result can cause digestive trouble. The exception to this (of the countries we discuss) are parts of West Africa and Somalia, where rice forms the staple food. East African diets where corn (maize), cooked green banana, millet, and sorghum are the staples take a lot of getting used to before they can be tolerated over a period of time. This is not to discourage readers from trying local dishes when they are offered on reputable hotel or restaurant menus. No problem will be encountered. But over a period of days the western stomach rebels. The cheaper establishments (usually street stalls) patronized by local people present a health risk to those not accustomed to unsanitary conditions. However, on the whole, menu prices in reputable hotels and restaurants are below those in comparable hotels in western cities. Economies on food can certainly be made by purchasing factory-packaged foods from local grocers, supplementing these with fruits that have a skin that must be peeled before eating. Picnic lunches are a viable way to reduce food costs safely.

Shopping for souvenirs in Africa is always a pleasure and inevitably unusual, inexpensive, non-commercial gifts can be purchased in central markets if one shops around.

Trying to stretch money by seeking out a black market operator dealing in hard currency is a temptation to avoid. Many are the tourists who have been given a sealed envelope purportedly containing their Kenya shillings (or other African currency) only to find, when the envelope is opened in the privacy of their hotel room, that it contains neatly cut-up newspaper.

An Avis rental car is not a necessity and public transportation can be used, but when time is a factor this will be found to be very slow. Economizing on transportation is one of the more practical economies for those not confined by dates as public services are very cheap. Taxi fares, even in expensive Gabon, are certainly cheaper than in most developed countries if you bargain.

Perhaps the feature that makes traveling in Africa most enjoyable is the abundance of willing, honest hands ready to help with baggage in return for a small tip. Traveling without tipping for services in Africa is really unconscionable, and no matter how tight the budget, vacationers should plan to tip at least modestly.

Insurance is an absolute necessity and we have provided in "Travel Documents" a source of inexpensive yet totally reliable insurance coverage.

Making Hotel Reservations

As readers will know, most of the large chain hotels that we recommend have reservations offices throughout the world. However, when it comes to some of their African hotels, their reservations clerks have difficulty with the countries and the cities. With the exception of Restinger, a reservation service for an association of smaller French hotels, we have found the service to be indifferent and unprofessional.

Many of the hotels that we recommend that are not affiliated with chains do not have an international reservations service; to make reservations, travel agents, especially the larger travel agents, charge US$25 for each reservation made.

Lastly, it is difficult to identify reservations clerks, working either for travel agents or chain hotel reservations offices, who have actually stayed in the hotels they book.

These three factors, and our desire to markedly increase tourism to Africa have prompted us to go into partnership for the sole and exclusive purpose of making reservations *only* in the hotels we recommend in our Fielding guides. This partnership is Merikani Hotel Reservations Service, Inc. (P.O. Box 53394, Temple Heights Station, Washington, DC, 20009). The 24-hour telephone number is (USA) 301–530–1911. This is not a toll-free number, but we feel that readers sincerely wanting to go on safari will not hesitate to telephone during cheap rate hours if they know that the reservation clerk at the other end of the line will have answers to any questions they might have concerning our recommended hotels.

As we have mentioned in the guide, Merikani will also obtain African visas for readers who have made hotel reservations through them. There is no charge for this service, only the cost of the visas asked by the respective embassies.

There is no reason why readers should not make reservations directly with the hotels or the international reservations offices. For hotels that do not have international reservations offices, we have given a cable address (if possible) preceding the description of the hotel. Additional information for Kenyan hotel reservations precedes their description. Where no cable address is given use the mailing address on your cable or letter.

U.S.A. and Canada

HILTON INTERNATIONAL	Ask the 800 operator (800–555–1212) for the HI Reservations Office in your area.
HYATT	800–228–9000
INTER-CONTINENTAL	(USA) 800–327–0200 (Canada) 800–268–3708
MERIDIEN	(USA) 800–223–7385 (Canada) 800–361–8234

United Kingdom

HILTON INTERNATIONAL	(London area) (01) 631–1767 (remainder of the country) Freefone 2124
HYATT	(01) 580–8197
INTER-CONTINENTAL	(01) 491–7181
MERIDIEN	(01) 491–3516

Saudi Arabia

HILTON INTERNATIONAL	(Jeddah) (02) 6824432 (Riyada) (01) 4789578
HYATT	(Jeddah) (02) 6519800 (Riyada) (01) 4771111
INTER-CONTINENTAL	(Riyada) (01) 4655000
MERIDIEN	(Jeddah) (02) 6314000

Australia

HILTON INTERNATIONAL	(Adelaide) 08–217–0711 (Melbourne) 419–3311 (Perth) 321–4088 (Sydney) 02–267–6295 (remainder of the country) 008–22–22–55
HYATT	(Sydney) 02–357–3919 (remainder of the country) 008–22–21–88
INTER-CONTINENTAL	(Sydney) 02–232–1933 (Melbourne) 637–219
MERIDIEN	(Sydney) 02–612–235

New Zealand

HILTON INTERNATIONAL	(Auckland) 9–775–874
HYATT	(Auckland) 9–797–220
INTER-CONTINENTAL	(Auckland) 9–793–800
MERIDIEN	none

Confirming Reservations

There is a hotel reservation system in Kenya known as the voucher system. It is the same thing as a "confirmation slip," but the word *voucher* is used so often that it sometimes startles the uninitiated to be confronted with a request for "your voucher" by desk clerks, and in the case of Mt. Kenya Safari Club, Nanyuki, by the guard at the gate to the club.

If you have made advance reservations you should have in your possession before leaving home vouchers or confirmation slips with the correct date of your reservation, and notations either that your credit card is to be billed or that you have paid or partially paid in advance. If you have made reservations through a travel agent or tour operator and paid for the entire safari, your individual hotel reservation confirmation slips or vouchers should indicate that the accommodation has been paid in full.

The absence of an indication that payment has been made in full or in part is a trick used by some travel agents—mostly those based in Kenya but sometimes overseas—so that clients arrive at a hotel without written evidence that they have paid the travel agent in full or in part for the accommodation reserved. The reservation may be at the hotel's front desk, but in lieu of some form of written evidence, you will be asked to pay again.

Your confirmation slips or hotel vouchers are as important as your airline tickets.

Canceling Reservations

The penalty for canceling reservations varies by hotel but most follow the usual practices, dependent upon how much advance notice of a cancelation is given. Cancelation fees are government-regulated in Kenya; city hotels cannot charge as much as game lodges. Detailed information can be obtained when making reservations.

Dishonored Reservations

In the hotel business when a reservation is not honored, it is said that the guest has been "walked." Yes, the reservation was received; yes, it was guaranteed by a credit card or the travel agent, but no, there is no room. This happens more in the U.S. than in Africa. We have advised the hoteliers we recommend that if a reservation made through Merikani Hotel Reservations Service is dishonored it will be the last reservation Merikani will make for their hotel.

Methods of Payment

The credit cards accepted by the hotel are shown at the end of our description of the hotel.

If payment is made in cash in Kenya the guest should be prepared to show the receipts received either from local banks or from hotel cashiers for the foreign exchange transactions they had made. In some cases in Kenya payment for hotel accommodation can only be made directly in foreign currency cash or traveler's checks; receipts showing foreign exchange transactions are not acceptable. You may want to inquire about this when checking in; however, it is simple to keep back traveler's checks or cash for the purpose of settling a hotel bill. Alternately, the payment may be by credit card.

Under no circumstances pay hotel bills in Egypt using a credit card. Hilton accepts prepayment before arrival in Egypt and the usual cancelation charges for Hilton apply—there is no advantage in waiting—and quite a marked difference in billings if payment by credit card is made in Egypt. One way it is at the official rate, the other at the tourist rate. See Egyptian two-tiered exchange rates in the Basic Information Checklist. To our knowledge, this two-tier system of credit card charges does not apply in any other country.

Some of the smaller hotels throughout Africa are not authorized to accept payment in foreign currencies and we have noted this at the end of the hotel's description where information on credit cards usually appears. Naturally, they usually do not take credit card charges either.

When traveling in CFA countries any change left from one country, despite the fact that the portraits on the bills (notes) are different, can be used in another CFA country.

Tipping

We sincerely hope our readers will leave something for the housekeeping staff when they check out of a room. The fact that a service charge may be appended to a hotel bill really doesn't mean that the personal care and attention shown by individuals is rewarded. In our estimated budgets we have made provision for this by adding US$1 a day to the budget for *all* occupants of the room. Two people to a room, we suggest US$1; if the room is occupied by one, the same tip.

This may rub British readers the wrong way; they may feel that tipping is not required. All we can say to them is, don't complain if North American, Saudi, and readers from Down Under and New Zealand habitually, as soon as they walk into any establishment, receive better service.

Evaluating Accommodation

The hotels recommended for *Fielding's Literary Africa* usually have a historic association with the book followed in the itineraries. For example, the Norfolk Hotel is mentioned in *Flame Trees of Thika*. Or a hotel may, in our opinion, set the mood for an itinerary. For this latter reason we have chosen the Mount Kenya Safari Club, Nairobi, instead of the Norfolk for *Out of Africa*. Although the club was built during the 1980s, there is an elegance and aura of romance about it that, had she lived to see it, we feel Karen Blixen would have liked. Her cherished Ngong Hills can be clearly seen from the windows of the Executive suites (which are the standard rooms at the club). Another influence in selecting a hotel has been its geographic location for the purpose of the itinerary.

In *Fielding's African Safaris* we developed a 60-point questionnaire to evaluate hotels, and details of each hotel's scoring is given in that guide. When, at the conclusion of a hotel description the phrase ''Criteria scores'' appears, this makes reference to that 60-point questionnaire. The maximum score is 60:

none of the hotels scored above 50, and 40 was not a bad score. However, some hotels we did not mention in *Fielding's African Safaris* appear in this guide, in which case, because they were chosen for the reasons given above, they are not scored.

Hotel Rates

There was a time (1981–82) when hotel rates in Kenya were low enough to offset the higher airfare to Nairobi when compared to travel to Europe or the Caribbean. However, Kenyan hotel rates are rising dramatically and there is a danger of killing the goose that lays the golden egg if increases continue. For the moment, Kenyan hotels are competitive, but they hardly offset the higher airfares. Internationally managed hotels in French Africa are excessively high. The Sudanese Hilton is artificially high due to the exchange rate, apart from the fact that Sudan is not engaged in tourist promotion. Naturally, exchange rates have a direct bearing on hotel rates, and in earlier years, when the dollar was stronger, prices were lower. However, Kenya does not follow the British pound as it previously did, and the rate of exchange at present is 2 shillings better against the U.S. dollar than it was when we wrote *Fielding's African Safaris*. In that guide we quoted the Nairobi Hilton at US$61, $68, and $75. It will be seen that the actual increase ($110–142), despite the more favorable exchange rate, is considerable. However, of the luxury hotels, for families (see "Estimating Your Travel Costs" at the beginning of "Accommodation"), Hilton will prove to be cheaper than most budget or tourist-class hotels.

Cote D'Ivoire Accommodation

Hilton International Abidjan

Location:	*Mailing address:*	*Cables:*	*24-hour Reservations:*
in the city	01 B.P. 2185	HILTELS	(USA) 301–530–1911
center over-	Abidjan	ABIDJAN	
looking the	Ivory Coast		*Local telephone number:*
Blue Lagoon			32.83.22

The HI is a small (241-room) hotel, newly built, that offers very personal attention and care to all their guests. The rooms are well furnished and maintenance is perfect. The coffee shop is the only HI coffee shop in Africa that we have visited that is not a total disaster. This may have something to do with the fact that the general manager, Andre Charriere, takes his lunch in the coffee shop. (GMs in other African HIs please note—Joseph Albrand in Antananarivo excepted.)

The Vista formal dining room offers a French menu that will please gourmets and the cocktail lounge, with a French pianist, provides an element of sophistication difficult to achieve in Africa. The barman shakes an excellent American cocktail and prices are just under the Washington, DC, Vista Hilton International cocktail lounge. (Our references to high prices in Ivory Coast do not apply to the HI; these are very competitive, but outside the Hilton charges are astronomical.)

Before coming to Abidjan make certain HI has your flight number and a representative from the hotel will meet your plane and provide transportation (without cost) into the city.

Rack rates, when compared to value given, are cheaper than other first-class tourist hotels in Abidjan.

Guests are predominantly American businessmen and a few tourists.

Highly recommended; every aspect of the hotel shows TLC, most especially the beautiful menus. Concierage services are excellent.

Rates at the end of this section, Cote d'Ivoire, Abidjan.

Major credit cards and all hard currencies are accepted, as well as CFA francs.

Criteria scores: 48.82 with 13 + s out of a possible 60.

Egyptian Accommodation

El Mehrek Hotel

Location:	*Mailing address:*	*Cables:*	*24-hour Reservations:*
a short dis-	133 El Gueish,	MEHOTEL	(USA) 301–530–1911
tance from	Sporting,		
Alex's city	Alexandria,		*Local telephone number:*
center, nr.	Egypt-4		851008 or 960737
Cleopatra			
Casino			

The front room French doors look out directly onto the Mediterranean and open onto a little balcony. Very clean, medium-size rooms with private bath. Furniture and draperies good quality, actually better than the Ramada Renaissance down the road. We had tea and coffee sent up, but did not try the dining room, and ate in our room or at the Ramada. Breakfast comes with the room. We stuck to breads (there are several kinds) and eggs. Highly recommended for its class.

Very comfortable, with a staff that is hospitable and friendly. Guests predominantly Egyptian and Middle Eastern businessmen.

Rates at the end of this section, Egypt, Alexandria.

Pay only in Egyptian pounds; this is the only thing we had trouble with them about as they are not used to taking foreign currencies. No credit cards. You will need to show your currency declaration form.

Criteria scores: 31.98 + out of a possible 60.

Garden City House

Location:	Mailing address:	Cables:	24-hour Reservations:
near Hiltons in the city center	23, Kamal el Din Salah St. Cairo, Egypt	use address	none
			Local telephone number: information not available

A budget hotel in Cairo that reputedly is reasonably good. Because of this, reservations should be made well in advance. We still recommend eating at the Hilton, which is just south (on the same block).

Rates at the end of this section, Egypt, Cairo.

Pay in Egyptian pounds, having shown the declaration form.

Criteria scores: We did not stay at Garden City House.

Happi Hotel

Location:	Mailing address:	Cables:	24-hour Reservations:
off Cornich el Nil in the center of Aswan	Abtal El-Tahrir St. Aswan, Egypt	none	none
			Local telephone number: not available

A traveler's class hotel. Located a short block from the main street. Happi Hotel is what one might expect from its name. Swept and mopped free of litter and dust but not scrubbed. Each room has a private bathroom with Western toilet, a shower fed by an automatic geyser for hot water, and wash basin. Rooms are very, very small but adequate. Clean white sheets and blanket. Electric fan (although they advertise air conditioned). Happi Hotel definitely not recommended during the summer. However, we slept better than we had for many days. Security good. Fire prevention nil.

Guests predominantly—you name them, they're there.

Rates at the end of this section, Egypt, Aswan.

Pay only in Egyptian pounds after showing, if asked, the currency declaration form. It is customary to pay in advance. No credit cards.

Criteria scores: 16.61 out of a possible 60.

Holiday Hotel

Location:	Mailing address:	Cables:	24-hour Reservations:
in the center of the city	Goumhourea St. Port Said, Egypt	use mailing address	(USA) 301–530–1911
			Local telephone number: Port Said 20710

Tourist class, but the best in town.

We found the staff most helpful. Very clean. Seven stories high with the dining room on the top floor, where we felt the food could be trusted. We had a steak and French fries (Egyptian pounds 4.50), about the most expensive dish. Plenty of fire extinguishers around and every room fitted with a television, video, and mini-bar.

Guests predominantly visitors and business people from all points of the compass.

Rates at the end of this section, Egypt, Port Said.

Plan to pay in Egyptian pounds, although we imagine they are accustomed to taking foreign exchange. Doubtful that they take credit cards.

Criteria scores: We did not stay at Holiday Hotel.

Ramses Hilton International

Location:	*Mailing address:*	*Cables:*	*24-hour Reservations:*
overlooking the River Nile in the city center	1115 Corniche El Nil, Cairo, Egypt	HILTELS RAMSES CAIRO	(USA) 301–530–1911
			Local telephone number: 744400 or 758000 or 754999

The windows of the Ramses Hilton International look out on the River Nile; the pyramids can be seen off in the distance. Wall-to-wall carpets, glass sliding doors onto a small balcony, luxurious bathrooms with instant really-hot water, and a ventilating system that filters out the coarse dust and pollution that hangs over Cairo, all provide a haven of peace in the noisy city center. Rooms are large and all that loyal patrons of Hilton International have come to take for granted.

The biggest bugbear of Egyptian travel is amebic dysentery, which is endemic, but safety avoided by staying at the Hilton because of their high standard of sanitation. We kid you not—eating elsewhere is very risky. We have personally visited the main kitchen of the Ramses Hilton and can verify that (a) salad vegetables are contracted a year in advance from modern farms; (b) the salad vegetables are washed, then soaked in a solution of permonganate of potash; and (c) all food handlers have biannual health checks by Hilton's own doctor and the testing is done in their own laboratories so that the traditional black-market trade in "clean stool samples" is thwarted. Salads can be safety eaten at the Hilton. The food and beverage manager feels there to be more risk of upset stomach from drinking tap water than salad vegetables. The body builds up immunities, he says, to substances that may be harmful and that are encountered in our home environment. New substances, although not unclean, can cause upsets. So he is not guaranteeing no upset stomachs, but he is saying you'll never contract amebic dysentery or botulism poisoning at the Hilton.

Service throughout the Ramses Hilton is prompt and professional, except in the coffee shop. The level of English-language comprehension is a genuine relief after the blank looks from Hilton International Nairobi employees. It takes a day to adjust to talking normally if you come from Kenya, as we did.

The Ramses HI's Falafel Room offers a menu of classic Middle Eastern dishes and a twice-nightly floor show always featuring a classical belly dancer. From a cocktail lounge on the 36th floor the lights of Cairo sparkle across the darkness of the night. The little pastry shop on the lobby floor has excellent

French pastries, kept cold, and replaces the famous Groppi's of Cairo (which we no longer find attractive). Ramses HI coffee shop, Terrace Cafe, suffered from the chronic Hilton coffee-shop syndrome: poor service and arguing waiters-waitresses. We prefer room service, which provides the same menu and saves witnessing their early-morning cat-scratching. French service and excellent food in the Citadel grill. The Citadel was our favorite outlet: really outstanding food.

The Two Seasons nightclub is an experience not to be missed. It does a roaring trade in wedding receptions. We saw four in one 3-hour period. All very ethnic—multi-ethnic. The brides wear *Bride's* magazine white dresses. According to the purse, torchbearers (in pairs of 2, 3, 4, or 6) escort the couple to the table. The table, again, is positioned according to the up-front cash, floorshow level, mid-tier, and upper tier. During the flame procession, "Here Comes the Bride" rings out from the hotel resident band. The couple then dances to Greek-style traditional music as the members of the wedding party encircle them, stomping and clapping.

These entrances are followed by a cake-cutting. The regular Two Seasons floor show fills the remainder of the evening. Gwen Perry, a great American Black singer, backed by an unbelievably bad Egyptian band, constituted the show. We fantasized on the Kenya coast's "Safari Sound" band cavorting with her through "I Will Survive." We give her top marks for good sportsmanship. Her great voice overcame the accompaniment and she was first class.

Ramses Hilton International rates and menu prices are good value. Television, mini-refrigerators, suites have kitchens. All standard rooms have a small sitting room area; telephone; shaver outlets; bath and shower.

The only hotel we recommend in Cairo. There's just so much we'll do for our publishers, and trying out Cairo hotels is not on the list. We are very fond of our digestive systems as they are.

Guests are predominantly the creme de la creme of foreign visitors.

Rates at the end of this section, Egypt, Cairo.

Although major credit cards are taken, the Egyptian government operates two sets of exchange rates, and your payment, if made at the hotel, may be charged to your credit card account at the higher, more expensive rate of exchange. If you pay in traveler's checks you will be paying at the tourist rate—which is the best.

Criteria scores: 49.18 + + − − − out of a possible 60.

English Accommodation

Bed & Breakfasts (private homes)

We have heard good reports about the Worldwide Bed and Breakfast Association, which represents homes offering bed and breakfast in the United Kingdom. As London hotel prices are so high in the Hyde Park area, we investigated WWBBA and found that they list several very nice private homes in the immediate Hyde Park-Kensington area. Write to them providing the following

Readers following the White Nile *and* Livingstone *itineraries may want to visit the Royal Geographical Society in London, England, as well as the other sites we have mentioned in connection with Gordon of Khartoum and David Livingstone. The picture above shows the sculpture of the continent of Africa at the base of the Albert Memorial, which is immediately opposite the society's offices, and a short walk from the Sheraton Park Tower Hotel.* Photograph by Jane and Leah Taylor

information: your name, address and telephone number, if there are children in your party, date of arrival in London, dates of stay in London, the location you desire—in this case it will be Knightsbridge, Hyde Park (south side), or Kensington (near the Albert Hall). Add to this the accommodation required—a single room, twin-bed double room, or a double-bed double room. Tell them you don't want accommodation outside this immediate area (you might as well use the Crichton Hotel, which is near the British Museum and still downtown).

They require a deposit of £3 (US$4.50) per person *per night* reserved. This can be done by personal check or charged to Access, American Express, Master-Card, or Visa credit cards. If using a credit card, in addition to the number be sure to give the expiration date.

Rates are given at the end of this section under "English Accommodation."

Write: World Wide Bed & Breakfast Association (P.O. Box 134, 15 Gledhow Gardens, London SW5 OTX, England, tel. 1 370 7099). You can leave your reservations on their answering machine during cheap long-distance hours or call them during normal British working hours, 9 to 5 weekdays.

Crichton Hotel

Location:	*Mailing address:*	*24-hour Reservations:*
Near Holborn	36 Bedford Pl.	(USA) 301–530–1911
Tube Station	London	
	England	*Local telephone number:*
		(1) 637 3955

A small, newly redecorated, basically furnished hotel very near the British Museum. Television on a meter. The rooms at the rates we give have a private bath. The breakfast is not a full English or American breakfast, but it is better than the continental version of that meal.

Guests are predominantly young people from France and Germany.

Rates at the end of this section, England, London. Pay in English pounds; no exchange facilities available at the reception desk.

Sheraton Park Tower

Location:	*Mailing address:*	*Cables:*	*24-hour Reservations:*
SW city	101 Knights-		(USA) 301–530–1911
center	bridge		
	London SW1X		*Local telephone number:*
	7RW		01 235 8050
	England		

Everyone who has been to London has an area that is their favorite. Knightsbridge holds a lot of happy memories for us, and over the years the once rather upper-crust area has lost its pre-War sedateness and become exciting. The construction of the Sheraton Park Tower at the very center of Knightsbridge has much to do with that excitement. For readers interested in Africa, the Sheraton Park Tower is just a short walk from the Royal Geographical Society headquarters where a statue of David Livingstone is set in an alcove facing the Albert Memorial in Hyde Park. In crossing that park, using Lancaster Walk, you will see a statue to John Hannington Speke. The Sheraton is also convenient for shopping; the famous Harrods department store (where we believe mosquito netting can be purchased by those following the *White Nile* itinerary), is almost next door. Knightsbridge tube station is very close, and many buses pass the hotel going to all parts of London, making the Sheraton an excellent base.

Rates are at the end of this section under "English Accommodation." All good London hotels are expensive for Americans at the present rates of exchange; however, the Sheraton is no higher than its peers and offers 24-hour room service—something not always found in traditional British hotels. This may seem a minor point, but if your plane arrives after 10 p.m. there is nothing more infuriating than not being able to get something to eat or drink until the next morning. Ask about their special weekend rates.

Gabonese Accommodation

Sofitel Dialogue

Location:
2½ miles
from the city
center on the
beach

Mailing address:
B.P. 3947
Libreville
Gabon

Cables:
Use mailing ad-
dress

24-hour Reservations:
(USA) 301–530–1911

Local telephone number:
Libreville (241) 73.20.85

The Sofitel Dialogue faces the bay on which Libreville is situated. We did not find the waters inspiring—the color was rather murky, and the waves neither strong so as to make a surf nor placid. The hotel has a very small private beach and a swimming pool surrounded by unkempt gardens. To compensate for this the front desk staff were welcoming, and the rooms are clean and, if not furnished with panache, comfortable. The Sofitel Dialogue is halfway between the international airport and the city center—the better hotels seem to be out of the immediate downtown area.

The fall in oil prices has brought chaos to Gabon's economy as oil was the country's main export. Dependence on French imports and neglect of Gabonese agriculture compound the country's economic woes. This may or may not affect tourist prices and hotel rates. We would hope the latter will go down as they are not competitive with other African hotels that we describe.

There is a foreign exchange facility at the front desk, and payment can be made in either hard currency or CFA francs. American Express cards are accepted.

Rates at the end of this section, Gabon, Libreville.

Gambian Accommodation

Apollo Hotel

Location:
next door to
the Min. of
Tourism in
city center,
33, Buckle
St.

Mailing address:
P.O. Box 419
Banjul
The Gambia

Cables:

24-hour Reservations:
not available

Local telephone number:
Banjul 8184

A small African hotel located conveniently in the middle of town. The rooms are very basic and comfortable. Air conditioned. If they could put an end to petty thievery in the rooms (we lost a cheap radio), business could develop by catering to budget travelers. Keep everything locked in suitcases and there should be no problem. Staff welcoming and hospitable, but then so is everyone in The Gambia.

Rates at the end of this section, The Gambia, Banjul.

Payment should be made—and it is payable in advance—in either U.S. dollars, British pounds, or local currency.

Criteria scores: 24.49 out of a possible 60.

Novotel Kombo Beach

Location:	*Mailing address:*	*Cables:*	*24-hour Reservations:*
facing the Atlantic in the Tourist Development Area 25 miles from Banjul	P.O. Box 694 Banjul, The Gambia	use mailing address	(USA) 301–530–1911 *Local telephone number:* (93) 24.65 and 24.68

We looked at every hotel in the Tourist Development Area and, like the wine at the wedding of Cana, we found the best hotel at the end of the inspection. The Novotel Kombo Beach would be an outstanding beach hotel anywhere in the world—set down in The Gambia, where the people are so delightful and service so willing, makes it a small miracle. Our good friend, Mr. M. Hakim of Dakar and Dearborn, Michigan, treated us to dinner in the beautifully decorated Rive Gauche a la carte dining room. The food was delicious and we are not admirers of French cuisine. The chefs at the Novotel Kombo Beach were not heavy-handed with the sauces but were generous with the butter, using it instead of oils. The wine selection was excellent.

Not only does the Kombo Beach hotel have a fresh-water swimming pool, it also has lifeguards both around the pool and on the beach. We recommend the suites as they are situated at the end of the building and have marvelous views of the Atlantic Ocean. The rooms are nice as well, but the suites are only slightly more expensive and are, of course, larger than standard rooms.

Apart from the Rive Gauche, there is the main indoor restaurant where guests taking the full-board rate have their meals; the full-board rate can be taken and meals eaten in Rive Gauche for an additional sum. The Kingfisher Bar is near the lobby and the Bellengo nightclub just off the lobby. We enjoyed the latter; it's more a disco than a nightclub. Nothing spectacular by way of lighting, but an interesting crowd dances the night away—aged in their late 20s, with a good mixture of local patrons.

There is a hairdresser, attractive shops, and a short walk away is a little shopping arcade that is a nice objective for an evening stroll. Two tennis courts, children's playground, windsurfing, and sailing. A golf course is nearby and there are excursions into Banjul for shopping.

Very highly recommended; one of the very nicest beach hotels we have seen in Africa.

Rates at the end of this section, The Gambia, Tourist Development Area.

Major credit cards are accepted, as well as British pounds, U.S. dollars, and local currency.

Kenyan Accommodation

Reservations

It is certainly possible to reserve lodge and hotel accommodation once in Kenya, and when it has been impossible to obtain a reservation before arrival there because the hotel or lodge is fully booked, there is a chance of picking up a cancellation. We urge readers to make their reservations directly through the owners of the lodge or hotel. Their addresses are the local ones we provide preceding the hotel or lodge description. It may be useful to know that the following companies own the hotels named, so reservations for those hotels can be requested in the same letter or telephone call.

Castle Hotel is owned by Alliance (see below). Highlands Hotel reservations can be made through AA Kenya; Keekorok Lodge is Block Hotel Management; Leopard Rock Self-Catering Cottages through AA Kenya; Meru Mulika can be addressed to African Tours and Hotels, which are across the hall from them in the same Nairobi office building; Mountain Lodge is owned by African Tours and Hotels; Mount Kenya Safari Club, Nanyuki, is no longer managed by Inter-Continental, so use the address we give preceding the description; Naro Moru River Lodge is owned by Alliance; Norfolk Hotel uses Block Hotel Management; Samburu Lodge, Block Hotel Management; Tea Hotel, African Tours and Hotels.

AA Kenya (Travel) Ltd.
AA House Westlands
P.O. Box 14982
Nairobi
tel. 742926

African Tours and Hotels
Consolidated House
Standard St.
P.O. Box 30471
Nairobi
tel. 336858

Alliance Hotels
College House, University Way
P.O. Box 49839
Nairobi
tel. 337501

Block Hotel Management
New Stanley House
(behind New Stanley Hotel)
P.O. Box 47557
Nairobi
tel. 22860

It is necessary to take a taxi to AA Kenya in Westlands; the remaining offices are within a short walking distance of either the Hilton or Mt. Kenya Safari Club, Nairobi. From the United Kenya Club or the Norfolk it's easier to take a taxi to the city center, although, naturally, reservations for Block Hotel lodges can be made through the guests' services desk in the Norfolk. It is always best to go in person to the offices, and not rely on a telephone call—the reservationist will be more sympathetic to a personal visit than a telephone call when you wish to obtain a cancellation.

When making reservations for hotels owned by African Tours and Hotels a personal check covering half of each day's tariff must be sent in order to obtain confirmations. Alliance Hotels will take a credit card number, as will Block Hotels. A personal check covering half of each day's tariff should also be sent to AA Kenya when making reservations.

Blue Posts Hotel

Location:	*Mailing address:*	*Cables:*	*24-hour Reservations:*
Off the A Highway at Thika between Chaina & Thika Falls. Nairobi, 35 km	P.O. Box 42 Thika, Kenya	Use mailing address	(USA) 301–530–1911 *Local telephone number:* Thika 22589

Leah feels that Blue Posts won't suit everyone so we are recommending it with qualifications.

I love Blue Posts.

Blue Posts has character.

Blue Posts has honesty.

Blue Posts is living history.

Once a posh, up-country inn where Kenya's White settlers took afternoon tea or dined by candlelight and referred to the indigenous population as "natives," Blue Posts now hosts middle-class Black Kenyans and has a swinging—but not boisterous—bar clientele, a great disco on Friday and Saturday nights, and the friendliest service by a staff that has worked at the hotel for years.

Blue Posts is clean and does the best it can with what it has.

Blue Posts has Dutch Boy blue–painted gates hung on Dutch Boy blue posts opening onto the parking lot. Blue Posts has Dutch Boy blue–painted doors and woodwork throughout the residential wing. There are two residential wings; one built circa 1946–47, the other in 1952. The former is better than the latter, and we particularly like room 211. There is plenty of boiling hot water coming through the pipes. The furniture is basic early settler African hardwood wardrobes, dressing tables, and chairs. Everything is spotlessly clean.

The garden flowers are not tamed as they once were into geometric patterned beds, but are left to grow as they will in bursts of reds, yellows, and purples. The waterfalls on either side of the hotel beat down on the rocks from 40–50-foot drops and Blue Posts—as though the stone and mortar from which its buildings are constructed have life—complements the timeless energy of the falls and adapts to the changing humans it houses.

Blue Posts isn't for everyone, but if you view life from the historical standpoint and want to understand "today's Africa"—and provided you're at peace with yourself—you just might enjoy what Blue Posts has to offer.

Guests are predominantly middle-class Kenyan businessmen and women, local people from Thika town, a few expatriate contract workers, and only now and again does a tourist stay overnight, although many stop at the hotel to view the falls.

Rates at the end of this section, Kenya, Thika. Pay in Kenyan shillings accompanied by a Currency Declaration form.

Castle Hotel

Location:	*Mailing address:*	*Cables:*	*24-hour Reservations:*
in the city	P.O. Box 84231	CASTLE	(USA) 301–530–1911
center on	Mombasa	MOMBASA	
Moi Ave.	Kenya		*Local telephone number:*
			Mombasa 23403 or
			21683

Objectively speaking, trash is no stranger to Mombasa streets, nor are broken pavements large enough to trip and break a leg over, nor myriad potholed roads. Objectively, to the unknowing eye, Mombasa appears to be a pitiful municipality; a town poor in taxation resources and economically struggling to function as a large center of human habitation. The main street, Moi Avenue, receives attention from time to time from town council employees, but side streets are no-man's lands, having the same aura of pockmarked earth and scorched vegetation one associates with the Flanders of 1918. Yet millions of dollars come into Mombasa daily; the port serves not only Kenya, but Uganda, Rwanda, Zaire, and southern Sudan. It is the purveyor of supplies for some 40–60 beach resort hotels and the alleys of Old Town are replete with ships' chandlers. Additionally, Mombasa is the collection point for all tropical crops grown along Kenya's coast and the base for many fishing trawlers.

Mombasa is rich, rich, rich and poor, poor, poor in consumer advocates and better business bureaus.

Architecturally little in the past or present has been constructed along other than Spartan, utilitarian lines. The few buildings that had aesthetic appeal have been pulled down (for instance, the original Provincial Headquarters building), are in the process of being eroded away by sea air (the original Swahili-style pre-World War I German Embassy), or are under threat of demolition possibly as a hotel site as historically—catch this—they are not pedantically a part of African culture (Fort Jesus built by the Portuguese in 1599 being the structure in view!).

Only a few buildings, that of the Kenya Commercial Bank at Government Square, the secretarial school also facing the square, and Castle Hotel, have been tenderly and expensively renovated internally and faithfully preserved externally.

It is a reflection on the times that such work has been undertaken by private business—not government.

In 1984 7 million Kenya shillings—half a million dollars—was spent on renovating the Castle Hotel. The exterior remains virtually as it was originally in 1910 but guest rooms, while still having 12-foot-high ceilings are replastered, painted pure Swahili white, fitted with ample hardwood, louvered closets, full-room width sliding glass doors, new air conditioners, and furnished with interior-sprung beds and comfortable, attractive chairs. The bathrooms have all new plumbing and fixtures bearing the imported Armitage hallmark. Each guest room has a balcony.

The famous Castle Porch is one of the gems the dilapidated town of Mombasa has in store for those who will not judge her objectively but who will realize that every corner and crack of the town has a story to tell—because whatever else Mombasa hasn't got, she is full of character and characters and so is the Castle Porch.

There's one law for Castle Hotel guests and another for the porch, bar, and restaurant patrons; residents are family.

Top marks to the attractive head housekeeper—she wears the smartest and best tailored uniform of any hotel employee in our travels and her supervision is impeccable.

The hotel's food is excellent, with three Swahili dishes that the chef describes as those which Mombasa housewives serve to "keep their husbands happy."

Large reproductions of our favorite Henri Rousseau's tropical studies adorn the walls of guest rooms.

There is a small conference room, amazingly quiet when so near the center of town.

Rooms, direct-dial phones, radios and television with video.

The general manager, Pius Gmur, has supervised every facet of the renovation—a real labor of love for generations to come.

The garden at the rear of the hotel is lovely for snacks or a drink.

Very highly recommended. Guests predominantly independent visitors; not tour groups.

Rates at the end of this section, Kenya, Mombasa.

Payment may be made in U.S. or Canadian dollars, British pounds, or in Kenya shillings provided the currency declaration form is shown.

Criteria scores: 44.79 + + + + out of a possible 60.

C.P.K. Guest House—Nairobi

Location:	*Mailing address:*	*Cables:*	*24-hour Reservations:*
Nairobi sub-	P.O. Box 56292	KARIBUNI	none
urbs, on	Nairobi	NAIROBI	
Bishop's Rd.	Kenya		*Local telephone number:*
off 2nd			(unreliable) 723200
Ngong Rd.			

First, a short personal story about C.P.K. The letters stand for Church of the Province of Kenya—which is another way of saying Anglican or Episcopalian. When General Amin pushed us out of Uganda, we went first to the Nairobi Hilton International. The Hilton can become expensive over a period of time, and we looked around for a cheaper place to stay. We learned that most of the major faiths have guest houses in Nairobi. Being a Catholic volunteer, I called Flora Catholic Hostel. Yes, I could have a room—two double rooms? Children? Oh no, children might disturb the other guests! So, we called C.P.K. Yes, we could have a room—would we like the family room that sleeps 6? The irony of the situation has always amused me; the Catholic church staunchly against birth control but unwilling to accept children in their guest house; and the Church of England, without any strong opinion on the subject, willingly providing accommodation, including a nursery and nannies for Christian volunteers' children.

C.P.K. is extremely reasonable. There is one price for missionaries and volunteers, another for those not attached to any church. The rooms are freshly painted, immaculately clean, bright, and airy. Rates include all meals, breakfast, elevenses (coffee at 11 a.m.), lunch, afternoon tea, and dinner. Guests must be prompt for meals; there is one set menu with no substitutions. Plain British cooking.

C.P.K. is a great place to meet people who really know Africa. Most of the guests are missionaries who have lived in Africa over a period of years. They can be very helpful and provide contacts in remote places.

A blessing is said before meals, but apart from this custom, and that all members of the staff have a morning service in the lounge at 8 a.m., nothing sets C.P.K. apart from any other guest house except the very warm welcome and friendliness of other guests.

Washing machines, ironing room, and a playground for children. Communal television in the lounge during the evening. Personal and property security absolute.

C.P.K. Guest House is located within a relatively short walking distance, across Uhuru Park, from the city center. Unfortunately, although the park is open lawns it has become the scene of many nasty, often violent purse snatchings and robberies. During *full* daylight hours such attacks seldom occur, but once dusk falls the park is dangerous. In the very early morning walk to the bottom of the road, turning right from C.P.K.'s front gates, following the path as it turns left, and take a bus into town. Or you can walk to town across Uhuru Park if it's after 8 a.m. If you are returning after 5 p.m., take a taxi back. We have personally known people who have been attacked during the early evening. Believing they'd save a few shillings, they walked back to the guest house only to finish their walk bleeding and bruised and minus their valuables.

Very highly recommended for those who would have an insight into today's Africa.

Guests predominantly British and American missionaries and volunteers, Kenyan clergy, and visitors from Uganda and Tanzania, plus tourists.

Rates at the end of this section, Kenya, Nairobi.

Criteria scores: We do not score religious guest houses.

Dan Trench's Campsite

Location:	*Mailing address:*	*Cables:*	*24-hour Reservations:*
directly behind Trade Winds Hotel on Diani Beach, near Ukunda on Kenya's south coast	Box 1, Ukunda via Mombasa Kenya	not applicable	none
			Local telephone number:
			none

We challenge any travel writer to accurately describe Dan Trench's Campsite, because it is all things to all people. Using our criteria for evaluating hotels—not the questions, but the insistence upon factual, objectively answerable questions, we can start by saying:

Dan Trench's Campsite has been established on approximately one acre of land directly behind Trade Winds Hotel at Diani Beach. The hotel faces the beach, the campsite does not. This plot of land is enclosed on three sides by a yellowing flowering hedge, which Dan ruthlessly hacks back with a panga annually. The hedge has a mind of its own and responds to Dan's onslaught by becoming more vigorous every year. Several shade trees grow on the plot of land, none of which are coconut palms; the palms grow along Trade Winds' beach. At some time concrete was poured in two rectangular 2-foot-high shuttered platforms midway along the length of the plot. The platforms, supposedly, were the foundation for some long forgotten construction. The platforms remain rooted into the soil, absorbing the afternoon sun, and serve only as reclines for nostalgic campers to gaze at the Indian Ocean moon as it slithers across the night sky.

Not far from one platform a 3-sided coral-block shower stall, without curtain (hang a kanga), supports a single ½-inch pipe that allows water warmed by the sun during its passage from the tank to pour down onto a camper's body in such a manner as to impress the camper's soul with disdain for any shower ever taken again anywhere on earth. Perhaps, once inside the Pearly Gates the body will again know such luxury, but only then.

The semiformal entrance to the plot can be recognized by the upright slab of sandstone carved with a symbol not unlike that of an American Indian tepee, and a driveway usually filled by a 1981 white Datsun pickup. This belongs to Dan. When the pickup is there, he is. When it's not, he's out.

To the left of the driveway is a small garden totally enveloped by chicken wire nailed to 2″ × 4″ frames to seal out creatures great and small. The vegetation growing in the garden varies by time of year and Dan's moods: sometimes it is blossoming and full of promise; at other times a Monitor Lizard is imprisoned, having found a way through the chicken wire but not a way out.

(James Fox, in his book *White Mischief,* discussed Dan Trench, describes the campsite, and weaves an interesting story about a murder that took place in Kenya in the 1940s that you may enjoy reading. Published by Random House, NY, 1983.)

After the driveway is Dan's house. This is a 2-room and kitchen affair, made of whitewashed coral block, with a small porch. At the same time as the concrete platforms were poured in the middle of the plot, the remaining concrete was used to pour sturdy cement benches on Dan's porch. Invariably these have slightly soiled cushions in varying states of repair along their seats. Sometimes Dan sleeps on one of these; sometimes in one of the bedrooms. Sometimes, when all other accommodation is occupied, campers sleep on one of these cement, soiled-cushioned benches.

The rental accommodation can be in one of several unique architectural structures.

There is what has come to be known as the "Dog House." This is a building the height of a Great Dane's house, with walls of coral block, which Dan tired of building halfway through the construction process. The Dog House has two cement slabs covered by foam mattresses that are divided by a foot-space some 14″ wide.

There is a large coral-block whitewashed building housing iron bunk beds. Approximately 6 people, of either sex, can sleep in this room; but we have known occasions when, with the addition of bedrolls, the capacity has risen to 14.

Another building houses two rooms joined by an open arch. This was the "Pot Smoking Lounge." The coffee table in the lounge is made from a varnished 2-foot-high tree trunk. In the good old days (not anymore), campers used to leave an opened tabloid newspaper, filled to overflowing with grass, on the coffee table as a sign of hospitality. Leah, being highly allergic to the weed, and I, never having acquired a taste for the product, seldom used the lounge, preferring instead the porch of Trade Winds Hotel, where we could make one Coca-Cola last an afternoon.

Down the campsite plot, near the heavenly shower, is another sleeping structure. This has a cement base (naturally), but the sides are of sawn (at the ends, not across) tree branches. It has a grass roof. Newcomers to the campsite are traditionally put in this house so they can regale fellow campers about the snakes they believe they saw in the roof during the night. (There aren't any.)

The remaining accommodation consists of grassy land where campers may put up their own tent. In the past few years, Dan has had tents to rent.

There are outhouse toilets, one specifically for ladies on which Dan poured the best day's cement he's every poured. It is rondoval in shape, and has a paper holder and saloon doors. Unfortunately, female campers have been unable to keep male campers from using it.

It goes totally without saying that Dan Trench's Campsite is the best place in Kenya to meet people from all over the world. Campers can use all the facilities (dining room, bar, disco) of Trade Winds Hotel without charge.

Highly recommended.

Pay in Kenya shillings, in advance, for the time of the expected stay.

Rates at the end of this section, Kenya, Diani Beach.

Criteria scores: not applicable.

Highlands Hotel

Location:	*Mailing address:*	*Cables:*	*24-hour Reservations:*
in the suburbs of the village of Molo	P.O. Box 142 Molo Kenya	use mailing address	(USA) 301–530–1911
			Local telephone number: Molo 50

A newly renovated hotel just outside the village of Molo. While we did not care for the staring and rather indifferent reception we received when shopping in the village market, we found the Highlands Hotel, which is away from the village, very hospitable. Basic accommodation is offered; the hotel is not used by tour groups but rather by Kenyan business people driving between the western part of Kenya and Nairobi. The setting, in a garden, is lovely, and we feel readers will enjoy their stay at the Highlands.

Rates at the end of this section, Kenya, Molo. Pay in Kenya shillings accompanied by a Currency Declaration form.

Hilton International Nairobi

Location:	Mailing address:	Cables:	24-hour Reservations:
on Watalii	P.O. Box 30624	HILTELS	(USA) 301–530–1911
St. off	Nairobi	NAIROBI	
Mama Ngina	Kenya		*Local telephone number:*
St. and Moi			334000
Ave.			

What do you say about home?

Home is where you go when you're in trouble.

Home is something familiar.

Home is where there is a warm bed, things as you like them, and memories.

Home is also the warts of life.

Home for us—well, a second home—is the Hilton International Nairobi. How can we be critical without being disloyal?

Hilton International Nairobi is where we came, literally without a penny to our name, when Americans had to leave Uganda in 1972. General Amin's soldiers took departing foreigners' money before allowing passage into Kenya. Hilton International Nairobi took my personal check, for 10 days' stay with four children, not backed by credit cards or any ID other than a passport.

Hilton International Nairobi is the center of Nairobi life. The Hilton tower echoes the triumph of Kenya's Kenyatta Conference Center across the park and so similar in architectural design—the trademark of the city of Nairobi. Together they are the symbols of a budding international city. The family at the Hilton, straining at the bit to bring the city into the 21st century, are an integral part of Kenya's daily osmosis.

Visitors pile out of airport minibuses filling the lobby with Grecian gray heads and pyramids of designer baggage, surrounded by the staff of the Hilton. The osmosis progresses a step farther with the arrival of every tour. Visitors are drawn into Kenya's culture within the confines of the familiar. Kenyans become less and less shocked and impressed by the affluence that is the foreign traveler. Rapport begins at the entrance to the Hilton, where the 6'3" doorman in top hat and scrupulously honest bellmen offer broad-smiled, mute hospitality and indicate deep-cushioned sofas waiting to accept weary bodies.

Room service is good and quick. Housekeeping knows its job. The coffee shop waiters behave like incorrigible small brothers driving everyone—including the food and beverage managers—insane with their gross incompetence. Amboseli Grill is reasonably priced and has French-service waiters and a maitre d' who cares about every guest.

We have found that in the coffee shop, in Amboseli Grill, or at the poolside snack bar, the food can be totally trusted not to cause an upset stomach.

The bed linen in the rooms is luxury quality and the views from *every* room—looking out over the city of Nairobi—are excellent.

There's no place like it. Home.

Guests predominantly American and British tourists and executives, international conventioneers, and foreign diplomats.

Major credit cards are accepted as is all foreign hard currency, or Kenya shillings when accompanied by a currency declaration form.

A photograph of the HI Nairobi appears in "Bye-the-By."

Rates at the end of this section, Kenya, Nairobi.

Criteria scores: 45.24 with 7 + s and 2 − − out of a possible 60.

Keekorok Lodge

Location:	Mailing address:	Cables:	24-hour Reservations:
in Masai Mara Game Reserve	P.O. Box 47557 Nairobi Kenya	BLOCOTELS NAIROBI	(USA) 301–530–1911
			Local telephone number: Nairobi 335807

Probably, apart from Treetops, this is the most famous and most patronized of all Block Hotel safari lodges. Keekorok is perfect for early game drives in Masai Mara and for the balloon safari.

The usual good Block Hotel fare; in generous amounts and well cooked.

Guests predominantly tour group participants from all over the world; particularly Americans and Canadians.

Payment can be in Canadian or U.S. dollars or English pounds. Major credit cards are accepted, as are Kenya shillings with a currency declaration form.

Rates at the end of this section, Kenya, Masai Mara.

Criteria scores: We have not stayed at Keekorok Lodge and base our recommendation on the many very favorable reports we've heard from people who have stayed at the lodge. (Each time we've started out for Keekorok, we've left it too late in the season and the road past Narok, which is not hardtopped, has forced us to turn back.)

Kentmere Club

Location:	Mailing address:	Cables:	24-hour Reservations:
14 miles west of Nairobi on the Nairobi-Nakuru Rd. Nearest village is Banana Hill	P.O. Box 39508 Nairobi Kenya	use mailing address	(USA) 301–530–1911
			Local telephone number: 42101/41053

Some English settler, a long time ago, homesick for Cheshire and the Shropshire Hills, built the Kentmere Club as the next best thing to the Tudor black-and-white cottages characteristic of his home. Compromises had to be made architecturally with the African climate and building materials so that dark ceiling beams are backed by papyrus reed instead of lime-wash plaster. The

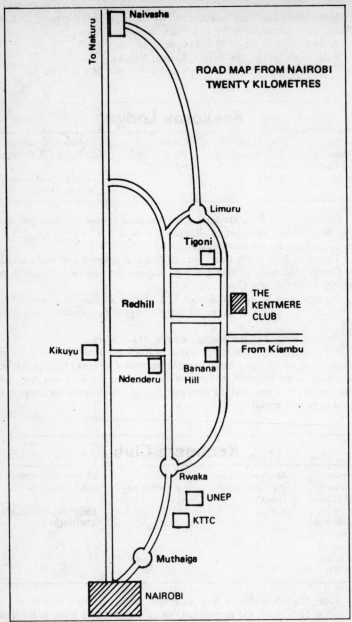

ROAD MAP FROM NAIROBI
TWENTY KILOMETRES

The road marked "From Kiambu" leads to that town and on to Ruiru and Thika. Coming from Thika/Ruira, upon reaching Kiambu town center, turn left— then take the first right following signs for Limuru. (The road running Nairobi-Naivasha runs north-northwest.)

effect is charming. The roof, of wooden shingle instead of slate, nevertheless rises and falls and maintains the illusion of a country cottage.

The garden is full of temperate zone blue hydrangeas and black-eyed Susan daisies. Instead of blooming quietly and modestly, providing only hints of color, at Kentmere Club they misbehave and bloom recklessly in great profusion. Their colors arrest the eye and force the passerby to stop and look. No Hollywood starlet could put on a better show. Here, near Limuru at 8000 feet, everything is green—more green than the forest greens of Mt. Kenya—and the light plays in and out of the mature trees along the hillside to make ever changing patterns.

Kentmere Club has a few simple rooms (complete with fireplaces) and cottages set in these flower gardens beside a path that leads down a hill to the vegetable plots that the Kentmere Club gardeners tend. Their produce becomes perfectly cooked "Vegetables in Season" on the tables of the club dining room.

For years Kentmere Club has had a justifiably famous reputation for good food. We showed up after 3 p.m. one afternoon, asked for lunch, and were the only diners (sensible patrons having eaten at normal hours). No fuss was made because of the hour; half an hour later perfect filet mignon and veal were placed before us, with firm boiled potatoes that had the just-dug taste only really new potatoes can impart. Buttered baby carrots and green beans accompanied them.

The dining room china and silver sparkle, the service is exceptional, and on cold nights the huge stone fireplace adds physical warmth to a hospitable atmosphere.

Guests predominantly the resident foreign community in Kenya.

Since the publication of *Fielding's African Safaris,* Paul Lundyet, the general manager, has written us to say that if our readers turn up at Kentmere's door and their rooms are completely taken, he will contact one of the club's neighbors who can offer accommodation. This is a marvelous opportunity to stay in the home of a Kenyan family.

Rates at the end of this section, Kenya, Banana Hill. Pay in U.S. or Canadian dollars, English pounds, or Kenya shillings when accompanied by a currency declaration form.

Criteria scores: 34.22 + + out of a possible 60.

Leopard Rock Self-Catering Cottages

Location:	Mailing address:	Cables:	24-hour Reservations:
in Meru National Park near the Meru Mulika Lodge	c/o AA Travel P.O. Box 14982 Nairobi Kenya	use mailing address	none *Local telephone number:* Nairobi 742926

The cottages are permanent buildings consisting of a very large room with beds to sleep 4 to 6 people. Outside, on an enclosed porch, is the kitchen. Our most vivid memory about Leopard Rock cottages is that even the slightest bit of food left out on the table—once the cook turns his or her back—becomes a clever monkey's snack. The cottages have electric light and the windows are screened. The furniture is basic and adequate.

There is a security guard on duty and a nice gravel parking space by each cottage. This is one of the loveliest places to have a budget wildlife safari in Kenya.

Rates at the end of this section, Kenya, Meru. Pay in Kenya shillings with a currency declaration form, or with traveler's checks. Payment is in advance.

Criteria scores: not applicable.

Lotus Hotel

Location:	*Mailing address:*	*Cables:*	*24-hour Reservations:*
near government offices and a few short blocks from the city center of Mombasa	P.O. Box 90193 Mombasa Kenya	use mailing address	(USA) 301–530–1911 *Local telephone number:* Mombasa 313207

The Lotus is away from the main thoroughfare yet not difficult to use as a base for visiting Mombasa. Built in the 1940s, it has been totally renovated and refurbished, and is Kenyan owned and managed. The local men's clubs have their monthly luncheon meetings, always a good sign for any hotel, at the Lotus. The rooms are basically furnished and come either with or without air conditioning. Take the air conditioning. The staff in every department is unusually hospitable and conscientious; every detail receives attention.

Breakfast and afternoon tea are especially nice. The menu could have more variety, but Lotus is close enough to other restaurants to overcome this problem. Nothing you eat will make you ill. Personal and property security are absolute.

The Lotus is a very short walk to the Law Courts, government offices, Mombasa (formerly Katherine Bibby) Hospital, and Fort Jesus.

Guests predominantly Kenyan and a few tourists.

Highly recommended.

Pay in Kenya shillings with a currency declaration form. No credit cards. Rates at the end of this section, Kenya, Mombasa.

Criteria scores: 33.14 + out of a possible 60.

Makindu Sikh Gurdwara (Temple)

Location:	*Mailing address:*	*Cables:*	*24-hour Reservations:*
99 mi. south of Nairobi and 208 mi WNW of Mombasa on the main highway	Gyani-in-Charge P.O. Box 43 Makindu, Kenya	use mailing address	none *Local telephone number:* Makindu 11

The Makindu Gurdwara is the pride of the Sikh community in Kenya and its primary purpose is to offer hospitality to any and all Sikhs and non-Sikhs who travel the Nairobi-Mombasa Road as well as a place of worship. A tenet of the Sikh religion is to feed and house travelers.

Reservations are not necessary. To stay overnight, drive through the Gurdwara gates and park. Lock the car and enter the Gurdwara compound. Immediately on the right is a small office usually manned by one of the caretakers. Say that you would like to make a donation of 50 shillings for each person in your party, although *this is by no means required*. The 50 shillings is only a demonstration on your part of respect, and has no relation to the value of the food and accommodation you will receive without cost. Arrange here for a room for the night.

If you go straight out of the office into the courtyard, the dining room is on the left. There are washbasins and towels, and you should wash your hands (for reasons that will become apparent) before sitting down at one of the long tables. Take any place you like—there is no high or low seating.

Without asking, one of the cooks will bring you large, family-style bowls of Indian dishes and *chapatis* (bread). Take as much or as little as you like of everything. It is strictly table d' hote. Wash it all down with Sikh tea, made with milk instead of water, green ginger, crushed cardamon, and plenty of sugar. This is kept on the simmer in huge cauldrons in the kitchen. Spoons are on a table by the door to the kitchen, but most people eat the Sikh way by tearing off bite-size pieces of chapati and using them as scoops to gather vegetables that are then popped in their mouth.

The Sikh kitchen and dining room is open 6 a.m. to 10 p.m., seven days a week, and serves continually throughout these hours.

If you wish to go to the Gurdwara proper, most certainly do. You are asked to remove your shoes and leave them beside the door and to take one of the scarves hanging by the door (this applies to men as well as women; men can use a handkerchief if they prefer) and cover your head. Having done so, enter with your hands in a praying position. Go to the altar, kneel, touch your forehead to the floor; rise, dispense with the attitude of prayer, and sit down on the floor: men to the right side of the room, women to the left. On the altar is the holy book, and someone may or may not be reading aloud from it. Leave anytime you wish; put your hands in the prayer position and nod toward the altar before you go. Do not go to the altar again.

You may now wish to take your things from the car to your room if you did not do so before eating.

The rooms are very plain and usually have more beds than is comfortable to move around. If it is necessary, other people may be put in your room, but this is usually not necessary. The usual pattern is one family, or one party, to a room.

There is little to do except go for a walk outside the Gurdwara. No one is going to bother you in the village, and you may want to walk down and see the tavern and typical African restaurants. These are not always serving food—it depends upon the time of day.

▶ **Note:** It is strictly "No Smoking" in the Gurdwara. A smoke must be taken outside the compound; that's why I spend so much time investigating the serving hours of the Hard Luck Cafe.

Guests are predominantly Kenyan Indians and independent foreign visitors.

Rates: there is no charge for staying at the Temple although we are very

anxious that our readers make a donation to the Sikhs in return for their generous hospitality. Such a donation should be made in Kenya shillings.

Criteria scores: We do not score religious guest houses; they are what they
infer, "guest houses" that accept guests as into a private home.

Manor Hotel

Location:	*Mailing address:*	*Cables:*	*24-hour Reservations:*
City center,	P.O. Box 84851	MANORIAL	none
Nyerere	Mombasa, Kenya		
Ave.			*Local telephone number:*
			Mombasa 21821 or 22

Set in the heart of Mombasa on the second busiest street, the Manor Hotel's lounge has been stripped of its 1930s art deco and rendered contemporary
African through the use of vinyl-based paint, Congoleum, and leatherette easy
chairs. Remembrances of past colonial glory persist: The verandah's high-gloss
enameled wicker chairs—authentic circa 1935—attractively mix with an assortment of chairs from more recent eras. Traveler's palms in huge pots shade
guests sitting on the porch from the heat of late morning as the sun rises behind
the Catholic Cathedral of the Holy Ghost immediately opposite. By noon only
a small sliver of sunlight penetrates the Manor Hotel's high-ceilinged dark dining room where overhead fans slowly move the air.

The buffet lunch at the Manor is one of our favorite Kenyan experiences.
The food is very plain, very British, right down to the rubbery Jell-O with fruit.
The cold beef, pork, and lamb roasts that the chef carves as you put your plate
before him are excellent. Sliced beets, shredded carrots, lettuce leaves, tomatoes, and cold boiled potatoes have no other adornment than your selection of
British-made Heinz salad cream or oil and vinegar. The service, by waiters who
may have been serving in this same dining room since the 1930s, is attentive,
and a patron's face once seen is always remembered on future visits.

The front desk at the Manor is a disaster. Two barely literate-in-English
clerks attempt to function behind the original African hardwood counter beneath
an ancient Boston sea captain's clock. Registrations are entered in Victorian
ledgers that a Dickens' character would have found familiar.

The rooms at the Manor are large, air conditioned for an additional charge,
basically furnished, and those at the back are quiet. The bed linens and towels,
although perhaps not always matching in color, are spotless and invariably freshly
laundered. The front rooms at the Manor are the perfect vantage point from
which to watch the Marlboro Safari Rally, as the route through Mombasa usually passes in front of the hotel. Throughout the year we find the Manor less
hectic than the Castle as a place to have lunch and pass the time until the stores
reopen at 3 p.m.

In a country of immaculate ladies' rooms, the Manor's is at the top of
the list.

Rates at the end of this section, Kenya, Mombasa. Pay in hard currencies, traveler's checks, or Kenya shillings accompanied by a Currency Declaration form.

Mara Intrepids Club

Location:	Mailing address:	24-hour Reservations:
In Masai-Mara National Re- serve	P.O. Box 14040 Nairobi Kenya	(USA) 301–530–1911 *Local telephone number:* Nairobi 335208

Mara Intrepids Club has opened since we were in Kenya, and it is seldom that we include accommodation in our guides that we have not personally visited. However, accommodation in Masai-Mara is relatively limited and the Mara Intrepids Club sounds as if it will handsomely add to what is available. We quote here from an article that appeared in the Kenyan tourist magazine *What's On*, May 1986:

"When one considers that Khaled Khashoggi, son of Arab billionaire Adnan, is on the Board of Directors of the Mara Intrepids Club it is not surprising that the Club, although tented, is elegant.

"Mara Intrepids Camp sits in the heart of the park amid the wild fig trees of a riverine forest about 14 kilometers west of Talek Gate. Despite its central location on the banks of the Talek River the camp manages to stay secluded, poor tracks and black cotton soil keeping out the saloons and mini buses of the hoi polloi. The now lush grasslands which sweep away from the camp are thus unsullied, the game retaining its dominance of this prime slice of Kenya's showplace reserve.

"That Mara Intrepids' 22 accommodation tents rival the best hotel rooms this country has to offer is not an overstatement. The tents are cavernous, probably twice the size of those elsewhere in the park, and the furnishings are lavish almost to the point of incongruity. Attractive ethnic rugs cover the floor and the single (and in some tents, double) beds do indeed have four posts, although these are designed as much for holding mosquito nets as for decoration.

"Richly upholstered chests, a design table, canvas wardrobe and en-suite bathroom/shower complete the interior layout. Outside, on a private paved verandah, table, chairs, and a sun-lounge are provided.

"The public areas comprise a lounge and bar, which would do justice to any gentleman's club in London's West End, and a dining room spacious enough to give each table its privacy while retaining an under-canvas ambience. Food served in the restaurant is exceptionally well prepared and plentiful.

"Intrepids has a swimming pool, a garden bar that overhangs the river, and a small shop which sells safari paraphernalia, souvenirs, and toiletries at not unreasonable prices.

"A few hundred metres from the public area, a large tower has been built on stilts on the edge of the forest. From here one can enjoy an elevated view of the game-laden plains, perhaps over a sundowner cocktail. When dusk falls the game-spotting continues under a massive spotlight which can be swept Colditz-style over the grasslands by guests.

"Tents are grouped into four, six and eight bed units, each with their own mess tent and private barbecue. Individual groups may be assigned their own steward and chef and can practically enjoy a stay at Intrepids without noticing the presence of other guests.

"The Club's fleet of open-topped Land Rovers offers a fair measure of comfort during the dawn, dusk and mid-day game drives which are included in the tariff."

Allowing for the travel writer's superlatives, the club does sound nice, although we have no way of knowing what arrangements they've made for fire-fighting and what fire prevention equipment they have installed. Readers may like to try Intrepids as its credentials are first class.

Rates at the end of this section, Kenya, Masai-Mara. Payment can be made with major credit cards, traveler's checks, or hard currency cash.

Criteria scores: We have not stayed at Mara Intrepids Club.

Meru Mulika Lodge

Location:	*Mailing address:*	*Cables:*	*24-hour Reservations:*
in Meru National Park east of Mt. Kenya	P.O. Box 484 Meru Kenya		(USA) 301–530–1911 *Local telephone number:* Radio call 2204

Meru Reserve has an abundance of elephants and leopards (which have been relocated to this park from farming country), and is the place where Joy Adamson released Elsa the lioness slowly back into the wild from her life in captivity. The reserve has escaped poachers as there is lush vegetation and trees to provide hiding places for the game.

The lodge is very comfortable—the bar well stocked, and the rooms each have a private bathroom. Rates include all meals.

After lunch, have a rest until about 3:45 p.m., then drive around the park and see the animals. There are good maps available in the lodge shop, and the park is well patrolled, so there is no fear that if you get stuck, you won't be located.

Meru is a very underrated game park not visited by the mobs that go to the game parks closer to Nairobi and Mombasa. As a consequence it is possible to drive the well-marked roads within the park without becoming one of a convoy of minibuses all looking at the same examples of African game.

There are also self-catering cottages in the park (see Leopard Rock Self-service Camp). These are cheaper than the lodge, naturally, but we feel the lodge is reasonable compared to some of the other park lodges. Security is excellent, and we found the service hospitable and helpful.

Payment can be made using major credit cards, in Canadian or U.S. dollars or British pounds, as well as in Kenya shillings when accompanied by a currency declaration form.

Rates at the end of this section, Kenya, Meru.

Criteria scores: not scored.

Methodist Church in Kenya Guest House

Location:	*Mailing address:*	*Cables:*	*24-hour Reservations:*
on Oloitoki-tok Rd. in the suburbs of Nairobi	P.O. Box 25086 Nairobi Kenya	use mailing ad-dress	none
			Local telephone number: Nairobi 567225

Large, basically furnished rooms with wash basins, but sharing the bathrooms, the Methodist Guest House makes visitors, missionaries, and tourists alike feel welcome. The guest house is immaculately clean. Meals, served family style, are excellent. As at other religiously affiliated guest houses, there is a set menu and guests are asked to be on time for meals. Smoking is allowed, but no alcoholic beverages. Rates include all meals, plus morning and afternoon tea. Children are welcome.

A comfortable sitting room with well-stocked library shelves and a pleasant garden make the Methodist Guest House another comfortable place to stay for the budget traveler. There are washing machines and an ironing room.

Bus nearby into town; however, the Methodist Guest House is a bit farther away from the city center than C.P.K. Guest House.

Guests are predominantly Kenyan clergy, church workers, and foreign volunteers. A few tourists.

Payment is in advance and in Kenya shillings when accompanied by a currency declaration form.

Rates at the end of this section, Kenya, Nairobi.

Criteria scores: we do not score religious guest houses.

Mountain Lodge

Location:	*Mailing address:*	*Cables:*	*24-hour Reservations:*
on the western slope of Mt. Kenya; nearest town is Nyeri, nearest village, Kiganjo	P.O. Box 123 Kiganjo Kenya	use mailing ad-dress	(USA) 301–530–1911
			Local telephone number: Radio call 3622

Mountain Lodge is, in our opinion, one of the best game lodges in Kenya; however, readers should realize that not all animals will be seen, only those who are comfortable in a mountain habitat. Mountain Lodge is just that little bit farther from Nairobi to be off the beaten tourist path. Its location—up on the side of Mount Kenya—is more natural than many of the other game lodge locations. Mt. Kenya is covered with lush tropical and temperate vegetation at the level of the lodge.

Each guest room faces the waterhole; the rooms are very small but well furnished, with wall-to-wall carpet, and with a private bathroom. There are three "Presidential Suites." These have floor-to-ceiling, glass-enclosed porches instead of the open porch all other rooms have. Consult the hotel rates chart in the "Money" section of our guide and ask yourself if you don't deserve—after coming thousands of miles—the comfort of a Presidential Suite. You can set up your camera, leave it on its tripod as you go in and out of the room and, in the warmth (because it gets cold) of the electric warm air heater, sit in your pajamas photographing the floodlit scene all night and genets that come to take the food put out for them. At sunrise there will be no frantic rush to dress before photographing the animals coming to drink just 30–50 feet below the window. It is the best value in Kenya's game lodge offerings and an experience never to be forgotten.

Ask that early morning tea or coffee be brought to your room; no extra charge. There is a well-stocked small refrigerated mini-bar on the porch of the Presidential Suite. More ice can be had by calling room service. The rates include breakfast and dinner. Lunch is extra and can be, if you like, a picnic lunch to take and eat along the way at one of the many beautiful places around Mt. Kenya.

Very highly recommended.

Guests are predominantly more knowledgeable American and British independent tourists and small, discerning tour groups.

Major credit cards are accepted, as are Canadian or U.S. dollars, English pounds, or Kenya shillings if accompanied by a currency declaration form.

Rates at the end of this section, Kenya, Mt. Kenya.

Criteria scores: 32.99 out of a possible 60.

Mount Kenya Safari Club, Nairobi

Location:	*Mailing address:*	*Cables:*	*24-hour Reservations:*
some 5 blocks from the city center on Koinage St. at University Way opposite U. of Nairobi	P.O. Box 43564 Nairobi Kenya	INHOTCLUB	(USA) 301–530–1911 *Local telephone number:* 330621

With a bit of creative financing "Lillian Towers"—ask not why "Lillian"—that's privileged information—opened in 1984. Inter-Continental Hotels assumed the management.

Lillian Towers—by which name every Nairobite knows the structure—is preferred by their public relations people to be referred to as Mt. Kenya Safari Club, Nairobi. It is run as a club, with temporary membership to nonresidents as a part of the room rates. There are 30 suites, and rates for these are very reasonable compared to standard room rates in North American or European hotels. They are beautifully furnished with classic European furniture. Not a hint of veneer; strictly gorgeous African hardwoods with hand-rubbed finishes. Wall-to-wall carpeting throughout the hotel. Several "outlets": the Brasserie doesn't seem to waste money on their steaks; the Safari Terrace, a bar where locals like to be seen after office hours; and on the third floor the Kirinyaga Lounge, reminiscent of uppercrust London private clubs, complete with over-stuffed leather sofas and chairs and a gorgeous circular library table on which rest the latest issues of European newspapers and periodicals. Then there is Kirinyaga Restaurant, which occasionally has a live band.

There is a health club with sauna, steam and massage room, and a gym the size of a postage stamp. The pool, on this same floor, has a beautiful sculptured mural by a Kenyan artist along the wall that shelters it from the neighboring buildings. The pool itself is quite small.

Like Mt. Kenya Safari Club, Nanyuki, Lillian Towers has "Princess" phones, and it is possible to dial out directly without having to go through the operator; a big plus. The cabinet-model television produces the latest Reuters closing stock market prices as well as videos.

The service throughout the hotel is excellent and cheerful. The food no better and no worse than average in Kenya. The extra touches of a peppermint patty on the pillow after the room steward has drawn the drapes and turned down the bed are engaging. The beautiful bathroom suites are everything a lover of fine plumbing could desire. The view from the sliding picture windows, with Mounts Kenya and Kilimanjaro in the far distance, make for beautiful sunsets. Personal and property security inside the building are excellent, but it is not advisable to walk the streets of Nairobi after 5 p.m., and this is particularly true near Lillian Towers; although it is certainly not in a "bad district," it is in a less trafficked area.

Lillian Towers promises to give the Hilton and the Norfolk competition. It is eminently comfortable and luxurious. Smoke detectors are in the halls but not in the rooms; a pity for a newly built hotel.

Lillian Towers has parking for 40 cars in the basement, but our friend, Dr. Percy Gipson, an American doctor practicing in Nairobi and a member of the club, asks us to caution readers to "Stoop down, and watch your head as you come up the stairs, as the architect forgot most guests are over 5 foot 3 inches tall."

Payment is accepted using major credit cards, U.S. or Canadian dollars, English pounds, as well as in Kenya shillings when accompanied by a currency declaration form.

Rates at the end of this section, Kenya, Nairobi.
Criteria scores: 44.07 + + out of a possible 60.

Mount Kenya Safari Club, Nanyuki

Location:	*Mailing address:*	*24-hour Reservations:*
on the north-western slope of Mt. Kenya	P.O. Box 59749 Nairobi Kenya	(USA) 301–530–1911
		Local telephone number: Nanyuki 2141 to 2144

In Kenya, reservations for the club can be made by telephone Nairobi 335887 or 21318.

The site of the club, exactly on the Equator yet at an altitude high enough to always be cool, was first selected as a place away from the rest of the world by a Mrs. Wheeler of San Francisco who, in the 1920s, intended to build a love nest on the Equator for herself and her fiance. Unfortunately, her lover was killed, and she agreed to sell the site to another American, this time a New Yorker, Rhoda Lewisohn and her French lover, Gabriel Prud'homme. Mrs. Wheeler made one condition: that the ashes of her lost love be scattered over the slopes of Mt. Kenya. Gabriel, a pilot, did so.

Rhoda and Gabriel built the original large country house, and had a year of happiness before the outbreak of World War II. Gabriel left to join the Free French and Rhoda returned to New York. Like so many other people who took part in that war, they grew apart, and after the war could not recapture the happiness they had known at the foot of Mt. Kenya.

The house was sold to the Kenyan company, Block Hotels, and operated as a hotel for some years. William Holden had been among the guests on several occasions; he decided to purchase it in partnership with friends, and once more the house became an integral part of the lives of those who frequent the French Riveria and southern California. Stefanie Powers was going with Bill Holden, and the two found Mr. Kenya Safari Club a perfect retreat. They became interested in wildlife, and he purchased the land adjacent to the Club in order to take a more active role in conservation. Holden met with a fatal accident, and while it might have meant the end of his efforts, Powers shared his interest and the work has continued. Powers formed the William Holden Wildlife Foundation and has succeeded in bringing the foundation to the attention of the international community.

The club has a private stable where horses may be hired by guests. There is also a swimming pool, tennis courts, and a 9-hole golf course.

We recommend visitors reserve one of the separate cottages (not a room in the main block) for their visit. Each cottage has its own garden and is very private. Luxurious beds, Princess phones, a separate sitting room, and fireplace make for comfort and luxury. The bathrooms are outstanding: elegant and large with black-tiled sunken baths/showers.

The dining room is a joy—French service and the best of continental dishes served by candlelight. Breakfast is bright and cheerful with sun lighting the buffet.

Guests are predominantly tourists and Kenyan residents who are members of the club. The club is closed to non-members over the Christmas holidays.

Rates at the end of this section, Kenya, Mt. Kenya.

Naro Moru River Lodge

Location:	*Mailing address:*	*Cables:*	*24-hour Reservations:*
1 mile off the Nyeri-Nanyuki highway on the shores of the Naro Moru	P.O. Box 49839 Nairobi Kenya	ALLIANCE NAIROBI	(USA) 301–530–1911
			Local telephone number: Nairobi 337501 or 337533

The river Naro Moru, artificially dammed to create two 3-foot waterfalls along the hotel frontage, is the focal point of the lodge. And while trout fishing is reportedly fair, the lodge is better known as the base camp for mountaineers who wish to climb Mr. Kenya. In keeping with that sport, the accommodation is of four categories: well-built chalets facing the lawn and river, each with shower and toilet and usually rented with full board; self-service log cabins for 2 to 7 people with cooking facilities and bathrooms, although meals can be taken at the lodge dining room on the days no one wants to cook; bunkhouses with shared cooking areas, showers, and toilets; and a campsite for those who have their own tents. The latter can also use the shared cooking and bathroom facilities.

In all cases the amenities are simple and clean. The public rooms have a rough-and-ready appearance, with stickers and penants identifying the scores of international climbing and mountaineering clubs that have used the lodge as a base camp. There is a rental service where everything needed to climb Mt. Kenya can be rented at a nominal cost. Fishing rods are also available for hire.

The management offers several escorted climbs that are described in detail in their well-prepared brochure. They will also provide food for a picnic or the climb. The mountain can be climbed without an escort, but don't try to scrounge advice; freeloaders are firmly told that advice costs money. As the prices are very, very reasonable and the service first class, we don't blame them.

Guests include expatriates living in Kenya and a few Kenyan mountain club members, but the vast majority are young people from all over the world intent on climbing Mt. Kenya.

Recommended as a base camp for climbing Mt. Kenya and as a lodge for touring the Mt. Kenya area: Aberdare National Park, etc. Readers should know that the lodge offers a very nice half-day trip, with no climbing of the mountain, to the first ascent.

Payment, in advance, in Kenya shillings with a Currency Declaration form. Rates at the end of this section, Kenya, Mt. Kenya.

Criteria scores: (before renovation) 25.04 + out of a possible 60.

Norfolk Hotel

Location:	*Mailing address:*	*Cables:*	*24-hour Reservations:*
Harry Thuku Rd., 15-min. walk from city center	P.O. Box 40064 Nairobi Kenya	NORFOLK NAIROBI	(USA) 301–530–1911
			Local telephone number: Nairobi 335422

The outstanding feature of the Norfolk is the service. Without doubt every employee is proud to be working at this historic hotel. No dead blooms are left in the many floral arrangements that are seen in obvious and also unlikely spots throughout the hotel. Every part of the Norfolk receives the attention of a member of the staff. Nothing is neglected—certainly not the guests. Unobtrusively, meaning they are quietly left on the room balcony exactly at 5 p.m., hors d'oeuvres are brought to guests' rooms to accompany an evening cocktail. Unobtrusively, meaning when you are out of the room, the bed is turned down for the night, the drapes drawn, towels checked to determine if fresh ones are required, and many other small touches set the Norfolk apart for resident guests. Readers will not be exposed to this excellent service unless they are resident in the hotel, as there is one law for residents and another for casual visitors who patronize the terrace, where grills and snacks are available. We've often stopped on the terrace but have always come away less than happy; when we actually stayed in the hotel, everything changed, and we recommend using the formal dining room because the terrace staff can be a bit pretentious and the service is certainly nothing to rave about.

The Norfolk is tied to the history of the White settlers of Kenya although it has been totally remodeled and only the front of the building appears as it did years ago. The hotel is built around a garden in which restored Kenyan pioneer wagons and buggies are parked under flowering trees. In the Pioneer Room are enlargements of photographs taken, as the name implies, during the settlement of Kenya by British and South African farmers. These are of great interest to those, like ourselves, who are interested in the colonial history of Kenya.

There are a number of price categories for the Norfolk rooms, and it is only the more expensive rooms that offer the same facilities as the Hilton or Mt. Kenya Safari Club, Nairobi's standard rooms. For instance, the Norfolk standard rooms are not air conditioned and there is no television or video except by paying an additional charge. For guests not interested in hanging around the Norfolk bar in the evening, and who have taken the warning about walking Nairobi streets at night seriously, this lack of entertainment in the room or the hotel—as there is no nightclub—puts the Norfolk at a disadvantage. However, to get a good night's sleep after a long flight, the Norfolk offers comfort, absolute personal and property security, and "old world" charm, plus the knowledge that—if not under the exact same roof—many of her guests have had a hand in the making of both local and international history.

Recommended. Guests, depending upon what category of room is occupied, are tour group participants, independent tourists, VIPs, and members of the jet set.

Rates at the end of this section, Kenya, Nairobi.

Criteria scores: 38.53 + + + + + − − − out of a possible 60.

North Coast

In the *Lost Cities of Africa* itinerary we have written that while the north coast of Kenya is liked by some Kenyans and visitors, to us it is not as beautiful as the south coast. The beaches are not as safe for swimming because of outcrops of coral, sea urchins, and other, if not poisonous, annoying sea life. Seaweed floats in and out with the tide, covering the beaches at low tide, and throughout the day the water is either too shallow or too rough and deep to swim. Added to this is the chronic problem the north coast has experienced in obtaining an adequate water supply for hotels and homes. Water for Mombasa and the south coast comes via a modern system from Mzima Spring in Tsavo West National Park. The north coast did not tie into this system, and guests in hotels all the way to Malindi on occasion—usually during the high season—are rationed for showers, etc. In a hot climate this can be a real trial.

However, for those interested in historical sites, the north coast is far richer than the coast south of Mombasa, and readers may want to stop overnight.

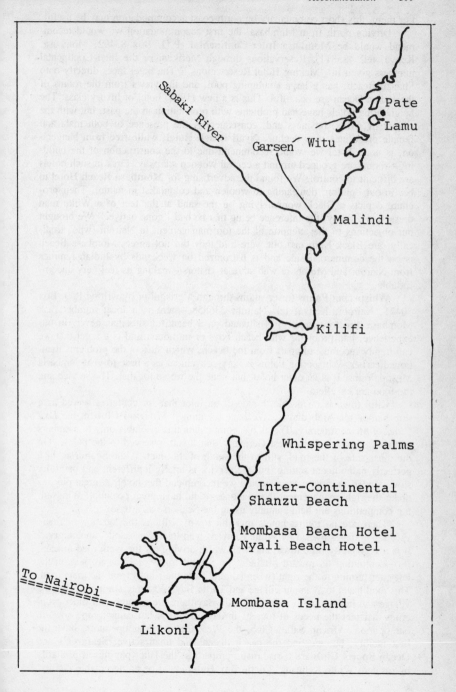

For them, this short commentary on north-coast accommodation may be useful.

Driving north from Mombasa, the first accommodation we would recommend would be **Mombasa Inter-Continental** (P.O. Box 83492, Mombasa, Kenya, tel. 485811). Reservations through Merikani or the Inter-Continental numbers given in "Making Hotel Reservations." The hotel faces directly onto Shanzu Beach, has a large swimming pool, and the views from the rooms of the Indian Ocean are beautiful. This is a new (1985) hotel of luxury class. The neighboring hotels have had problems with prostitution in the past, but with the advent of AIDS, business and, consequently, the presence of both male and female prostitutes may decline. **Nyali Beach Hotel,** while free from hangers-on, is not a hotel we would recommend due to the construction of the building—rooms are grouped around a central wooden stairway. Fires in such hotels are difficult to control. We found the advertising for **Mombasa Beach Hotel** to be, in our opinion, demeaning to women and colonialist in nature. Their brochure depicts a Black woman lying on the sand at the feet of a White man dressed in a kikoy, the inference being that he had "gone native." We brought our objections to the attention of the top management in Nairobi (who, ironically, are Black Kenyans) but were told they did not agree. Mombasa Beach is on the commercial side and is patronized on weekends by Indian families from Nairobi and Mombasa who stare at visitors—making us feel very uncomfortable.

Whispering Palms (reservations through Merikani or by writing P.O. Box 30471, Nairobi, Kenya, tel. Nairobi 336858—there is a local number; ask Mombasa directory inquiry) is situated on a beautiful site, has never, in our experience, had problems with beach boys or intruders, and is a hotel that we can highly recommend apart from the beach, which suffers the problems mentioned earlier. Whispering Palms is very convenient as a base to visit Jumba la Mtwapa ruins. It is an older hotel, but none the worse for that. The service and the food are excellent.

Kilifi town is on the north side of an inlet that for centuries served as a safe harbor for Arab dhows. We have mentioned **Mnarani Club** in the *Lost Cities of Africa* itinerary. The club accommodation is available only to members of tours organized from West Germany, but lunch is served to the public. On the other side of the road, still to the south of the inlet, is the **Seahorse.** In a perfectly magnificent setting, but the service is totally indifferent and painfully slow. Under no circumstances could we recommend this hotel. A great pity, as under the right management the Seahorse would have great potential. Windsailing competitions are held annually using the Seahorse as a base.

There are no tourist hotels in Kilifi town; Kilifi is the location of many vacation cottages owned by White Kenyans who live year round "up country." It is a very pretty little town, and well worth driving off the main road to see.

Continuing on toward Malindi, the Swahili ruins of Gedi are just on the left after turning to the right (when coming from the south) from the main road. This road leads to Watamu village and Turtle Bay. Watamu is a model Giriama village and interesting to visit. At Turtle Bay there are a number of older properties that met the needs of tourists in days gone by, but cannot cope now, in our opinion. African Safari Club, the West German tour operators, have the best facility, but we find the beach dismal and unattractive. **Seafarer's** and **Ocean Sports Club** are basic, rustic properties, the latter patronized primarily by resident White Kenyans. **Turtle Bay Hotel** could be an acceptable facility, but its owners fail to budget for maintenance—the result is an overall shoddy appearance. Turtle Bay itself is the location of a marine reserve, and the tropical fish are supposedly profuse and beautiful. We had a problem with the operators of the glass-bottom boats trying to rip us off, and rather than be blackmailed into paying their outrageous price, gave up.

Malindi itself was the first center for coast tourism and has a number of older hotels that have undergone renovation in the past few years. Whether this will make the town, which we found to be dirty and cluttered with street vendors, more acceptable remains to be seen. Malindi was a center for female prostitution and beach boys until the city council woke up to the fact that the south coast, with its better amenities and control, was taking all the business. The guests in Malindi hotels have been primarily German tourists—some of Malindi's street signs are in German as well as English. Reportedly, **Silversands Villas** (P.O. Box 91, Malindi, Kenya, tel. Malindi 20407) offers excellent food and is well run.

Readers who would like to drive to Lamu—north of Malindi—should realize that in order to do so a diversion from a straight line between the two towns must be made to Garsen. The road is very rough between Malindi and Garsen; and from Garsen to Lamu the road is composed (in part) of black cotton soil that can be treacherous. Allow 8 hours to drive the distance Malindi-Lamu. Cars cannot be taken onto the island of Lamu and there is a safe, secure parking lot at the ferry port, which operates to Lamu island.

Garsen is nothing more than a trading post—no accommodation—but if an emergency arises there is a Catholic mission a few miles along the road to Witu-Lamu where the sister-in-charge is very sympathetic to the problems of travelers in this rather remote area. The night we imposed on their hospitality we made a donation to the clinic the sisters run for local people.

There is a turning to the right off the Garsen-Lamu road that leads to the village of Witu. It was at Witu that the German explorer Karl Peters made his headquarters, hoping to send his forces across northern Kenya into Uganda. His plan was to form a pincer by joining up with German forces in colonial Tanganyika—then force the British out of Kenya. Peters had built a rather elaborate headquarters building, which in later years became a notorious tavern and haven for foreigners who had dallied too long in the midday sun. Witu was a place I had wanted to see for many years. Unfortunately, the people proved to be most inhospitable and we could not locate Peters' former headquarters or even the Swahili ruins that are shown on the map. The word *Witu* has become a standing joke between Leah and me—it took a lot of effort to get to that "historic site" and it proved to be a tremendous letdown. Whenever I suggest a similar remote, unknown destination, Leah invariably remarks, "Another Witu." For the purist, Witu may be of interest, and male readers may have more success than we did in obtaining information from the local people about the historic buildings/ruins in their village.

At Lamu we stayed at **Petley's Inn.** (Write them at Petley's Inn, Lamu via Malindi, Kenya. There is a radio call number, but it is virtually impossible to get through.) Petley's is situated in the center of town. During our stay the inn was under the management of Jambo Hotels. Their management was excellent, and we thoroughly enjoyed the high-ceilinged Swahili rooms, comfortable beds, and views from the balcony that face onto the main street and harbor. The food was excellent. Petley's is almost immediately next door to the museum. However, the general manager warned us about the water shortage experienced during the Moslem month of Ramadan. We hesitate to recommend Petley's since the management changed—it may continue to be excellent, but then again, it may not.

Accommodation in Lamu is also available in private homes; sometimes a room is provided but, more generally, sleeping space on a flat roof is offered. This type of accommodation was extremely popular among hippies during the late 1970s, and provides an opportunity to live with a local family. It should be remembered that the people of Lamu are Moslem, and alcoholic beverage consumption is frowned on. Inquire upon arrival in Lamu, at the museum or at one of the small cafes, where such accommodation or "sleeping space" is available.

In the *Lost Cities of Africa* itinerary we mentioned that it is possible to rent a traditional Swahili house that has been restored and modernized by White Kenyans and expatriates having an interest in preserving Lamu. Contact the curator at the Lamu Museum or write P.O. Box 99, Lamu, or Lamu Historical Society (P.O. Box 45916, Nairobi).

Rates for the north-coast accommodation we recommend are at the end of this section, Kenya, North Coast.

Outrigger Hotel

Location:	*Mailing address:*	*Cables:*	*24-hour Reservations:*
overlooking Kilindini Harbor on Ras Liwatoni Rd. 8–10 min. from city center	P.O. Box 82345 Mombasa Kenya	ALLIANCE NAIROBI	(USA) 301–530–1911 *Local telephone number:* Mombasa 20822 or 20823

Advertised as a hotel "for businessmen and executives," the Outrigger faces the entrance to Kilindini Harbor. The Outrigger is a simple, African-run hotel with no frills except excellent food and interior sprung mattresses (as opposed to kapok in many other tourist-class hotels). Breakfast at Outrigger caters to four nationalities:

English or American: Toast, marmalade, eggs, sausages, bacon, cereal, fruits, juices.

Dutch or German: Ham, salami, cheeses.

Indian: Kababs, bhajia, and curried mince.

African: Mahamri and kaimati.

At lunch or dinner, vegetables and french fries, so often a disaster in Kenya, are perfect. Particularly delicious are celery with baby leeks in butter and the way the chef prepares chopped greens using his own special blend of spices and herbs. His Pepper Steak and Swahili Chicken in Coconut Sauce rank with the best. All very reasonably priced, and too-large helping are given.

There is a nice pool, plenty of deck chairs, and a bar in the garden. The waters of Kilindini Harbor are within 25 feet of the garden and the ships, as they pass, are almost in touching distance.

The approach to the hotel is misleading, going as it does through one or two blocks of shanties, but don't be put off—Outrigger is a little jewel of African hospitality at very reasonable rates. Ample parking space and a taxi stand are at the door.

Guests are predominantly international merchant navy officers and shipping executives, both Kenyan and foreign, doing business at the port.

Payment can be made in Canadian or U.S. dollars, British pounds, or in Kenya shillings when accompanied by a currency declaration form.

Rates at the end of this section, Kenya, Mombasa.

Criteria scores: 38.17 + + out of a possible 60.

Samburu Lodge (Block Hotels)

Location:	*Mailing address:*	*Cables:*	*24-hour Reservations:*
on the banks of the Uaso Nyiro River in Samburu Game Reserve	c/o Block Hotels P.O. Box 47557 Nairobi Kenya	BLOCOTELS NAIROBI	(USA) 301–530–1911 *Local telephone number:* Nairobi 335807

The reception at Samburu River Lodge is a reenactment of a cowboy movie where the highlight of the day in a frontier town is the new arrivals. The game wardens, who lean against the rail fence, are Samburu tribesmen, their loop earlobes now devoid of ornament and their traditional dress replaced by the smart uniforms of the Park Service, equate to the silent cowboys who met the stage coaches.

The check-in by Block Hotel staff is low-key; no hassle. A bellboy is at hand, helpful and eager to please.

Accommodation is in either self-contained log cabins or in an ordinary room in very attractive two-story buildings. All face the river. All rooms and cabins have private bathrooms with a full tub and shower. There are also tents with zippered closings and private flush toilets to the rear of each tent.

(Author's Note: The above is a totally inadequate description of a perfectly delightful lodge. Difficult to describe because the adjective "rustic" is not correct, nor is "chalet type" or "Rocky Mountain style"—Block Hotels' Samburu Lodge buildings are unique and totally compatible with the surroundings yet offer, with simplicity, every convenience one could require.)

Although not air conditioned, the rooms are lovely and cool. There are mosquito nets over the beds. The water pressure in the faucets (taps) is strong and there is abundant (even at night) solar-heated hot water to make a shower or bath luxurious. The public rooms are designed to give maximum views of the river.

We had Sunday buffet lunch at the lodge. The British tradition of Indian curry on Sunday constituted the hot dish, along with quiche. Every type of salad was served, including the best potato salad we have eaten outside of a private home. The cold dishes looked fresh and just out of the garden despite the fact that the chef confided it was always touch and go whether the truck bringing supplies on Saturday night would make it. An outstanding buffet anywhere in the world. The cold food was really cold; the hot food really hot.

Service throughout the lodge very, very good.

Tents numbered 55, 59, and 69 face the river, the others are set back about 150 yards across a trimmed lawn.

Absolutely no flies anywhere despite the proximity of the river. Very highly recommended. Readers are cautioned not to mistake other lodges and camps in Samburu Game Reserve who have adopted a similar name to Block Hotel's Samburu Lodge in order to cash in on the reputation of this very fine lodge. Ensure the right lodge by using the preface, Block Hotels. The road signs after entering the park are all marked "Block Hotels."

Guests are predominantly American, Saudi, and British independent tourists and more discerning tour groups.

Payment can be made with major credit cards, any foreign hard currency, or Kenya shillings when accompanied by a currency declaration form.

Rates at the end of this section, Kenya, Samburu Reserve.

Criteria scores: 38.28 with 10 + marks.

Sunset Hotel

Location:	*Mailing address:*	*Cables:*	*24-hour Reservations:*
shore of Lake Victoria	P.O. Box 215 Kisumu Kenya	SUNSET Kenya	(USA) 301–530–1911
			Local telephone number: Kisumu 41100

Set immediately on the shore of Lake Victoria, the Sunset Hotel, as its name implies, provides uninterrupted views from guests' rooms of sunsets over the lake. We had imagined these would be more spectacular than they are, but it's the fault of the climate, not the hotel, that the mists and light make for rather ordinary sunsets.

The hotel is modern, very clean, air conditioned, well furnished, the bed linens are immaculate, and the bathrooms excellent. However, the service is not up to that found at many of our other recommended hotels, and the dining room—both in respect to food and service—was, when we were there (we read changes were in the air) a disaster. Property and personal security are good. A nice bar and attentive barman.

Rates at the end of this section, Kenya, Kisumu.

Tea Hotel

Location:	*Mailing address:*	*Cables:*	*24-hour Reservations:*
in Kericho, 163 mi. WSW of Nairobi & 52 mi. E of Kisumu	P.O. Box 75 Kericho Kenya	use mailing address	(USA) 301–530–1911
			Local telephone number: Kericho 40

If you think you'll like Kentmere Club, you'll love Tea Hotel. Much, much larger, but still very colonial British. Rooms, cottages, or a suite (we had the "Kericho Suite") are extremely well furnished and immaculately, spotlessly, clean. The weather is cool at Kericho and so there are fireplaces.

Leah, having worked in hotels, has a theory about hotel general managers. With European or American GMs the hotel building becomes an extension of his physical person. Something like the projection psychologists tell us our body assumes in relation to the vehicle we drive so that, after a few hours of driving a new car, we know where the back bumper is even though we can't see it. Adopting this psychological state allows us to park. Leah says that when there is a leak in the ceiling of a room in the west wing of a hotel, the GM feels it. As if his left arm was drowning. The hotel and the GM are one and the same. American and European GMs are in a perpetual state of anxiety. This translates to their staff and in turn to guests. Guests unconsciously brace themselves and become uptight when approaching a front desk clerk in direct proportion to the tension radiating from the GMs. This is especially true in posh hotels: the more posh the premises the more acutely aware is the GM of the perfection expected when his physical person is examined. Whatever warts there may be must be concealed. The chain reaction is to make the staff apprehensive and guests look for inadequacies.

With a prolonged hellava fight and finally achieved only by legislation, Africans have become GMs of Kenyan hotels. As in so many other things, White couldn't believe they could be adequately replaced.

Fortunately, Black GMs did not take on the mantle of neurosis carried by their White predecessors. The Black GM has much too high a regard for the privacy of his body to let it become bricks and mortar. He has a life outside the hotel—a life where he needs his body if he is to participate on a par with the other men in African society. As a result, even a posh hotel under a Black GM is relaxed, the staff and guests are relaxed, and the general atmosphere is more conducive to a carefree holiday than it might otherwise be when everyone is so neurotic.

Tea Hotel knows it looks right, that no petticoat is showing. Therefore it can relax and be charming. Needless to say, its general manager is an African!

Gorgeous gardens overlooking endless tea fields. Sumptuous beds, bathrooms with heaters to dispell any chill, delicious food, impeccable service—we could live in Tea Hotel forever.

Highly recommended. Guests predominantly a very few independent foreign tourists and Kenyan expatriate residents.

Payment can be made in Kenya shillings accompanied by a currency declaration form.

Rates at the end of this section, Kenya, Kericho.
Criteria scores: 36.38 + out of a possible 60.

United Kenya Club

Location:	*Mailing address:*	*24-hour Reservations:*
Just away from the city center on Uhuru Highway	P.O. Box 42220 Nairobi Kenya	(USA) 301–530–1911
		Local telephone number: Nairobi 25638

Sardar Inder Singh Gill, who started his immigrant life in East Africa as a railroad clerk at Kampala Station in the 1920s and who now owns the largest sawmills in Kenya and Uganda, donated the beautiful hardwoods that panel the lounge and dining room of the United Kenya Club. Donated because the formation of the club was, as the name implies, a "united" effort on the part of Whites, Blacks, and Kenyans of Indian descent to establish a social club in their colony's capital city that would welcome all races. Today every race and profession attend the Wednesday lunch when there is invariably a prominent guest speaker to keep members abreast of topical events.

The club is composed of a number of single and double rooms, which are not lavishly furnished but are always immaculate. The bathrooms are particularly nice as there is a plentiful supply of really hot water at good pressure. A lounge, furnished with heavy, well-maintained leather sofas, and low coffee tables, serves not only as a reading room but also for after-dinner coffee. The bar, very much a gentlemen's bar, closes early (11 p.m.) but not before several good debates have taken place between members and their guests. A tiled terrace follows the building and looks out over well-kept lawns, children's swings, and Uhuru Highway at the garden's boundary. From the terrace or guest rooms the city of Nairobi is seen with the university grounds and buildings directly ahead.

The service, by all members of the staff, is impeccable. Most of the staff has been with the club a very long time and know each member. We have never found a reason to fault them.

Guests can request either full board or bed and breakfast rates. Full board is good value, but for our readers who are not enamored of British cooking, bed and breakfast rates might be better. The Sunday lunch is served buffet-style, and always has a marvelous curry—meat or vegetarian—as well as many bowls of salad. Dessert is usually cream carmel or Jell-O with cream. Breakfast is a full English one, although the corn flakes are not to our liking; the juice and sausage or bacon with eggs cooked to order are excellent.

There is a large parking lot beside the garden and the city center is a sometimes hot but short walk. Mt. Kenya Safari Club, Nairobi—Lillian Towers—is the tall white building just beyond the trees, and the Norfolk Hotel huddles low, out of view, among the trees to the left. If it's a hot day, take a taxi into town; many times one is parked in front of the club. The fare is very reasonable.

Guests are predominantly Kenya's business, academic, and civil service communities as well as many overseas visitors. Nonresidents of Kenya are provided with temporary membership as a part of their room rates. Rates at the end of this section, Kenya, Nairobi. Payment can be made by traveler's checks, hard currency cash, or Kenya shillings upon presentation of a Currency Declaration form.

Malawian Accommodation

Capital Hotel

Location:	*Mailing address:*	*Cables:*	*24-hour Reservations:*
Chilembwe	P.O. Box 30018	CAPHOTEL	(USA) 301–530–1911
Rd. near city	Lilongwe 3	LILONGWE	
center	Malawi		*Local telephone number:*
			Lilongwe 730 444

Architecturally, the Capital Hotel blends with the terrain on which it was built, and the interior, of red brick and green accents, reflects the feeling of Malawi. The rooms each have a small private sunbathing balcony, and while the view, abutting onto tree foliage, may not be spectacular, it is pleasant and fresh. Beds are extremely comfortable. Attention to detail has been given to the decor, which although not lavish manages to convey a feeling of comfort and style. Service throughout the hotel is excellent and the rooms are spotless. There is a medium-size pool screened from the gaze of nonresidents—a plus in Malawi, where the dress code does not allow bare knees.

The shops in the lobby are particularly outstanding for a hotel: we found no better ebony and ivory than that in Gangecraft. Although the same company has a shop in Blantyre, we felt the quality in the hotel shop was just a bit superior. And the prices were the same—no higher markups as in so many hotel lobby shops.

The pastry shop sells particularly good Cornish pasties (hamburger in pastry with potatoes and onions), French and Danish pastries, and quiche.

The bus to Blantyre can be booked at a desk in the lobby. Don't believe the fella when he tells you, as he did us, that the bus stops for dinner. It doesn't. The bus leaves at 4 p.m. and arrives in Blantyre at 9 p.m.—take something from the pastry shop.

Two restaurants, both with excellent food.

Capital Hotel, managed by Hotel Management International, can be highly recommended without qualifications. The general manager is William Holdridge.

Guests are predominantly foreign businessmen; the local expatriate resident communities use the hotel as they would a club. We were the only tourists.

Payments can be made with major credit cards, U.S., Canadian, Australian, or New Zealand dollars, or British pounds. Payment can also be made in Malawian kwacha.

Rates at the end of this section, Malawi, Lilongwe.

Criteria scores: 39.55 out of a possible 60.

Chambe and Lichenye Rest Huts

Location:	*Mailing address:*	*Cables:*	*24-hour Reservations:*
on Mt. Mu-lunje	Mulunje Moun-tain Club P.O. Box 240 Blantyre Malawi	to mailing ad-dress	(USA) 301–530–1911
			Local telephone number: none

These are simple overnight rest huts for hikers and climbers of Mt. Mu-lunje. Permission to occupy the huts must be obtained from the Mulanje Moun-tain Club, whose address is given above. The huts are shared; not private.

The huts are available only to members of the club, although we under-stand the members are prepared to make exceptions for overseas guests to Ma-lawi. Nevertheless, the membership dues to the club are very reasonable and we would imagine any reader interested enough to climb the mountain would want to join in the preservation work that the Mulanje Mountain Club under-takes. After corresponding with the secretary of the club, membership dues may be paid to the club treasurer using an international postal money order.

Criteria scores: not applicable.

Chilinda Camp*

Location:	*Mailing address:*	*24-hour Reservations:*
35 miles from the entrance of Nyika Plateau National Park	Dept. of National Parks and Wildlife P.O. Box 30131 Lilongwe 3, Malawi	(USA) 301–530–1911
		Local telephone number: not applicable

*also spelled Chelinda

Chelinda Camp, set in a pine forest, has four chalets, each accommodating four people, and six double bedrooms. All units have hot and cold water. Cots are available for babies. The camp is noncatering, but fully equipped kitchens are provided for each chalet and a dining room for guests occupying bedrooms. Some nonperishable commodities may be purchased at the shop in Chelinda, but in general, visitors should bring all their own food.

There is also a secluded campsite at Chelinda, where visitors may camp using their own camping equipment. There are two shelters, and fireplaces for cooking. Firewood is provided. The camp has pit latrines, and water is supplied from a well by bucket.

At the Juniper Forest there is a tourist cabin with bunk beds for four peo-ple. Kitchenware and some bedding are provided; there is no running water. Vehicles must be left 400 yards from the cabin.

Gasoline (petrol) is normally on sale to visitors at Chelinda, subject to availability. Visitors should ascertain that they will have adequate gas for their return journey.

There is an information center at Chelinda, providing information on the history and ecology of the park.

A variety of wilderness trails have been established, and visitors may walk through the really remote and beautiful areas of the park. Trails range from 1 to 5 days, and involve camping in tents. All groups are escorted by a trained game scout, and porters may be hired if desired. Park transport may be hired to the start and from the finish of the trails, or visitors' vehicles can be driven by a park driver if desired. All camping and other equipment must be provided by visitors.

Trout fishing is available under license in the dams near Chilinda Camp from September to April inclusive, and in the streams throughout the year. One fishing wilderness trail has been established. Details from the Department of National Parks and Wildlife, whose address is given above.

The entrance to Nyika National Park is 42 miles from Rumphi and 84 miles from Mzuzu. The road from Rumphi is dirt and may be in bad condition, especially during the rains, when four-wheel-drive vehicles are necessary. Chilinda Camp is 35 miles from the park entrance. There is a grass airstrip at Chilinda.

A second campsite has just been opened in the Chilinda Forest in Nyika National Park. The site is in an attractive and secluded area on the edge of the forest, looking out onto the grasslands to the south.

At present, there is room for up to eight tents. There are two fireplaces for cooking, and picnic shelters in case of rain. Firewood is provided, and water is supplied from a well using a bucket. There are simple bathrooms and pit latrines. Visitors must bring their own tents, bedding, cooking and eating utensils, etc. Some nonperishable food may be brought from the shop at Chilinda, but in general, visitors are advised to bring all food with them.

Visitors are welcome to build a campfire in the center at the site, but special care must be taken not to cause fires in the forest or grassland around. Pits are provided for the disposal of trash and refuse.

All visitors intending to camp should report to the Chilinda Office of the National Parks and Wildlife Department.

Rates at the end of this section, Malawi, Nyika (Plateau) National Park.

Payment should be made in Malawian kwacha. There is a rest house just over the Zambian border in the park; payment can also be made in Malawian kwacha for accommodation here.

Club Makokola

Location:	Mailing address:	Cables:	24-hour Reservations:
southern shore of Lake Malawi between Monkey Bay and Mangochi	Box 59 Mangochi Malawi	CLUBMAK	(USA) 301–530–1911 *Local telephone number:* 584 228

Club Makokola, owned by an Italian living permanently in beautiful Malawi, is destined to be the pioneer of private beach development along the southern shore of Lake Malawi. Capitalizing on the natural beauty of the area, the club makes available the physical amenities of comfortable tourism to best exploit the environment.

Rooms look out over the lake. Rondovals at beach level. A new block of rooms provides the best views of the lake and the island bird sanctuary just offshore. All have bathrooms and are attractively furnished.

We found the food excellent, and most certainly believe it to be very safe for the digestive system. There is a nice beach bar, and individual tables at the water's edge are shaded by thatch umbrellas.

We still caution, as we have in "Background for Malawi," against swimming in the lake because of the presence of bilharzia, but there is a power boat and many other marine sports to enjoy without the need to swim. The bird life is natural and plentiful and the climate marvelous.

Rates at the end of this section, Malawi, Mangochi (for the southern lakeshore lodges).

Payments should be made in Malawian kwacha.

Criteria scores: 36.43 — out of a possible 60.

Ku Chawe Inn

Location:	Mailing address:	Cables:	24-hour Reservations:
on the south-eastern side of Zomba Plateau; nearest town is Zomba	P.O. Box 71 Zomba Malawi	RYALLS BLANTYRE ATTN DZIKO SAFARIS	(USA) 301–530–1911 *Local telephone number:* 635 935

The lodge is composed of a group of small, one-room bungalows, each with a private bath. All the rooms look out over a beautiful view of the valleys below. Very clean and basically furnished.

When we ate at the inn the food served was perfectly awful, and a small lounge had taped Malawian music at full blast. Very off-putting for what should have been a tranquil sylvan atmosphere.

The view and the setting is truly magnificent and well worth the drive up, but the drive up is quite an experience. First of all, there is no indication that the road is one way, but it is. This would be reassuring to know as the road is a series of repetitive hairpin turns with sheer drops on the left. The road is tarmacked, but not more than 9 feet wide. The road down is not tarmacked but is wider, not as steep, and, if care is used not to go too fast on the slick red mud, is much less dangerous.

Children sell some of the most beautiful little baskets we have seen anywhere in Africa near the gate to the lodge. The adult souvenir sellers who monopolize the porch of the main buildings are a nuisance—they lounge in chairs intended for guests and talk constantly.

Guests are predominantly expatriate residents of Malawi with the occasional tourist.

Payment should be in Malawian kwacha.

Rates at the end of this section, Malawi, Zomba Plateau.

Criteria scores: we did not stay at the lodge.

Lengwe National Park Rest House

Location:	*Mailing address:*	*Cables:*	*24-hour Reservations:*
near the park entrance	Dept. of National Parks and Wildlife P.O. Box 30131 Lilongwe Malawi		(USA) 301–530–1911 *Local telephone number:* not applicable

There are four comfortable chalets at the visitor's camp, each with two double rooms with wash basins. Showers and toilets are in a separate building. Each chalet has a refrigerator. All food must be taken to the park by visitors: there is a cook who will prepare meals using the food brought in. There is no gasoline (petrol) and no shop, although there is a supermarket and gas station at Nchalo, 12 miles from the park entrance. Chikwawa also has a gas station. There is a picnic shelter for day visitors to the park.

During the rains (November to April) daily temperatures in the park usually exceed 95°F. May to August are the most comfortable months in the park, weatherwise. Visitors should come equipped for hot weather.

Visitors may walk anywhere in the park in the company of a hired game scout guide. There is a nature trail near the entrance, which visitors may follow unescorted.

Various artificial waterholes have been opened and game-viewing hides constructed near them, from which visitors can observe and photograph wild animals undisturbed by human presence. This is best during the second half of the dry season.

The park supports a large population of nyala antelope and a variety of other large animals including bushbuck, impala, warthog, bushpig, leopard, spotted hyena, monkeys, and baboons. Buffalo, kudu, sable, reedbuck, and common duiker are present in limited numbers.

Lengwe is rich in bird species, some of which are unlikely to be seen elsewhere in Malawi: crested guineafowl, barred long-tailed cuckoo, black and white flycatcher, and gorgeous bushshrike.

The entrance to Lengwe National Park is 46 miles from Blantyre, the last 5 miles being a dirt road. The park is accessible virtually all year-round. There is no airstrip in the park. The visitor's camp is near the park entrance.

Payment should be in Malawian kwacha.

Rates at the end of this section, Malawi, Lengwe National Park.

Lifupa Lodge

Location:	*Mailing address:*	*Cables:*	*24-hour Reservations:*
9 miles inside Kasungu National Park	Dept. of National Parks and Wildlife P.O. Box 30131 Lilongwe Malawi	use mailing address	(USA) 301–530–1911 *Local telephone number:* none

Set immediately beside a man-made lake that provides water for the park animals during the dry season, Lifupa Lodge consists of a series of rondovals set apart from one another, each having twin beds with room for one more bed or a cot for babies. Each rondoval has a shower, wash basin, and toilet.

The nearby lodge restaurant serves good meals and it's nice to sit on the terrace and watch the activity on the lake either while having a meal or simply relaxing. During the rainy season the animals do not come to drink at the lake and it is necessary to drive through the park. Taking a game warden along will ensure that game is found; they know exactly where to find them.

This is the terrain that Livingstone crossed and found blacksmiths working at their trade. One of these has been restored. There is a 7-mile trail through the park that passes this, as well as some geometric rock paintings. Visitors may walk anywhere in the park as long as they are accompanied by a game warden. The park has a dirt road system that is normally open for wildlife viewing from mid-June to early January. However, the park is open all year except for the month of March. Game viewing vehicles are available for hire, and night game-viewing drives are being organized by the management of Lifupa Lodge, when it is hoped many nocturnal species may be seen.

Seven tents are also available at a campsite, each with three beds and a separate shower room. There are cooking facilities for visitors if they do not wish to use the restaurant.

At Lifupa Lodge there is a swimming pool and a bar, both of which may be used by campsite users, and a small shop with very basic items. Also of interest is a small museum illustrating the history and ecology of the park. Gasoline (petrol) is sold at the lodge subject to availability and readers should ensure they have enough gas to get back to the town of Kasungu.

The park entrance is reached by a good, hard-packed dirt road 24 miles from the town of Kasungu; this road does not require four-wheel drive. Kasungu is on the main Lilongwe-Mzuzu road, a marvelous newly tarmacked one. With a good driver, good time can be made. The distance from Lilongwe to the park entrance is 99 miles. There is a grass airstrip at the Administration Camp, just over 2 miles from the lodge.

We had such a good time at this park, it is one of our happiest memories of Africa. It was in January and we were the only party of tourists in the park. The staff at the lodge was welcoming and interested in making us comfortable; the company was good. There is a problem at one patch in the drive with tsetse flies, and we wished we had taped mosquito net to the car windows before we started on the safari.

Payment should be made in Malawian kwacha.

Rates at the end of this section, Malawi, Kasungu National Park.

Criteria scores: not applicable.

Likoma Island Rest House

Location:	*Mailing address:*	*24-hour Reservations:*
On the beach near the cathedral	District Commissioner P.O. Box 1 Nkhata Bay Malawi	(USA) 301–530–1911

A four-bed rest house especially for travelers visiting the island. There is no unloading facility at Likoma Island for automobiles from the steamer, and if readers plan to stay they would either have to be traveling without the car or leave (and pay the extra charge) the car on the steamer to the turn-around port, then be picked up by the steamer (with the car on board) several days later when it returns to the island.

Rates at the end of this section, Malawi, Likoma Island. Payment may be made in Malawian kwatcha, but readers should be prepared to show their Currency Declaration form if requested.

Criteria scores: not applicable.

Mvuu Camp

Location:	*Mailing address:*	*24-hour Reservations:*
Shire River in Liwonde National Park	Dept. of National Parks and Wildlife P.O. Box 30131 Lilongwe, Malawi	(USA) 301–530–1911
		Local telephone number: not applicable

Accommodation is available at Mvuu Camp, situated in a very attractive setting on the Shire River and offering a quiet stay in the wild. Available accommodation at present consists of six twin-bedded rondovals; this will be increased in the future. There is no running water; water is carried from the river, and the camp has pit latrines. Visitors should bring their own drinking water as well as food, bedding, cooking equipment, eating utensils, etc. Firewood is provided.

Gasoline (petrol) is not available for sale to visitors in the park, but there are a gas station and shops in Liwonde Township, which is only a short drive from the camp.

The park has a network of dirt roads that are *accessible only during the dry season* normally (April to November inclusive). Visitors may walk in the park if they are accompanied by a scout. It is possible to enter the park by boat and travel up the Shire River to Lake Malombe, viewing wildlife on the way. The second half of the dry season is the best time to see animals, both from a boat and from a vehicle, as they concentrate near the river. No fishing by visitors is permitted within the park.

High temperatures are experienced in the park, especially just before and during the rains.

The park is 75 miles from Blantyre, 153 miles from Lilongwe, and 35 miles from Zomba. Access by car is from the M1 road to the south, the entrance gate being 3.75 miles from the turn-off to the park just outside the town of Liwonde. Visitors may also enter the park by rented *boat during the rainy reason* (December to March).

Birdlife is rich and varied, and includes the only Malawi population of Lilian's lovebird.

Payment should be made in Malawian kwacha.

Rates at the end of this section, Malawi, Liwonde National Park.

Criteria sources: not applicable.

Mzuzu Hotel

Location:	Mailing address:	Cables:	24-hour Reservations:
at the town of Mzuzu on the road to the north	P.O. Box 231 Mzuzu Malawi	use mailing address	(USA) 301–530–1911
			Local telephone number: Mzuzu 332 622

Managed by Hotel Management International of London, the same firm who manage the Capital Hotel in Lilongwe, this newest hotel in Malawi has been a much needed addition to the tourist circuit in the country as previously there was no accommodation other than in game parks.

We did not get to stay in the Mzuzu but very much look forward to doing so the next time we are in Malawi. We understand it is a totally modern hotel and extremely comfortable.

It is our loss not to be able to more specifically review the Mzuzu; however, knowing the HMI management, we recommend it without hesitation.

Payment should be made in Malawian kwacha.

Rates at the end of this section, Malawi, Mzuzu.

Criteria scores: not scored.

Nkhata Bay Rest House

Location:	Mailing address:	24-hour Reservations:
Nkhata Bay near the lakeshore	District Commissioner P.O. Box 1 Nkhata Bay Malawi	(USA) 301–530–1911
		Local telephone: Nkhata Bay 7, or Caretaker 551

A 16-bed, government rest house convenient for passengers disembarking with their cars at Nkhata Bay before traveling onward.

Rates at the end of this section, Malawi, Nkhata Bay. Payment may be made in Malawian kwacha, but readers should be prepared to show their Currency Declaration form if requested.

Criteria scores: not applicable.

Nkopola Leisure Center

Location:	Mailing address:	Cables:	24-hour Reservations:
on the southern shores of Lake Malawi near Mangochi town	% Post Office Mangochi Malawi		(USA) 301–530–1911
			Local telephone number: None

This is a Malawi government-operated site situated immediately on the shores of Lake Malawi, immaculately clean and well maintained. There are chalets perched up on the side of the cliff, a few chalets at beach level (stone with modern roof), large plastic tents on cement bases with a cover of thatch suspended over them to keep them cooler, and a tent site. Local expatriate residents also use the site on a permanent basis to park small mobile homes (caravans). These are inconspicuous and do not detract from the natural beauty of the site. There is a standpipe with a table-height cement counter convenient for washing dishes.

We are not recommending the rental plastic tents, although they are large and have nicely made white-sheeted beds, because they are not mosquito-proof. They could be utilized if you carry your own net, but mosquitoes after dark do become a problem, and to avoid them it would be necessary to spend the evening in bed under the net. We appreciated our Hillary tent and did not use nets, as it is completely mosquito-proof. Alternately, a mosquito repellent can be used in the evenings. Kindling and firewood are provided for cooking, but we used Sterno for tea and ate either at the lodge next door (see "Nkopola Lodge") or made do with cold foods. We also tried the bar near the beach. It has an adequate selection of liquor as well as cold Carlsberg beer. Immaculately clean toilets, and showers with hot and cold water.

The site may be inclined to be too heavily used during school holidays, the Christmas and Easter holidays and August.

We were the only visitors during the days we spent at the center. (February to early March).

Payment should be made in Malawian kwacha.

Rates at the end of this section, Malawi, Mangochi (for the southern lakeshore lodges).

Criteria scores: not applicable.

Nkopola Lodge

Location: on the south- ern shores of Lake Malawi near Mango- chi town	Mailing address: % Post Office Mangochi Malawi	Cables:	24-hour Reservations: (USA) 301–530–1911 Local telephone number: None

---

Situated on the other side of the small cover from the Leisure Center, the lodge provides basic tourist-class rooms, has a dining room and bar, darts and Ping-Pong. It is right on the beach. We preferred the Leisure Center because it was quieter, with more privacy and wild birds.

Guests are predominantly White South African tourists.

Rates at the end of this section, Malawi, Mangochi (for southern lakeshore lodges).

Payment should be made in Malawian kwacha.

Criteria scores: we did not stay at the lodge.

Shire Highlands Hotel

Location:	*Mailing address:*	*Cables:*	*24-hour Reservations:*
on Churchill Rd. in Limbe, which is adjacent to Blantyre	P.O. Box 5204 Limbe Malawi	HIGHTEL LIMBE	(USA) 301–530–1911 *Local telephone number:* Blantyre 650 055

Don't be too quick to judge the Shire Highlands. At first impression the post-independence touches jar the nerves, but given time within its walls the glory that once was asserts itself and nostalgia takes over.

Shire Highlands has character. Unlike the Cecil in Alexandria, Egypt, it has not become seedy, but rather shares the same character as Tea Hotel, Kericho, Kenya. While the Tea Hotel treasures remembrances past, Shire Highlands tries to forget. Both are British Colonial. Both have in common the tea-drinking public of Empire. Shire Highlands adds tobacco to tea; it sheltered the doyens of the Imperial Tobacco Company as well as Liptons, Brooke Bond and Mc-Cormick when Malawi plantations were a force in those international trading commodities.

The rooms at Shire Highlands are large. A balcony for each overlooks a garden where tea dances and Chinese-lantern-festooned balls were held under aged, flowering trees—40 years ago. Now black faces are opposite guests at the front desk, where once only Anglo-Saxons took down "particulars." A dowdy exterior (it could do with a paint job) belies the immaculate interior and spotless bathrooms. Service is attentive and probably better than years ago. Guests are fewer; no chortling, giggling English maidens dressed in limpy soft cottons fills the upstairs corridors to descend the grand staircase and float in the embrace of freckle-faced English colonials on the dance floor. All that is gone. The real world of the 1980s, detesting imperialism, produces a vacuum. In a land as yet to be discovered by tourists, the Shire Highlands waits for the influx of gaiety and wealth to once again fill her hospitable walls.

Bring a group with you when you come to Shire Highlands. The management is accommodating, and while there may not be a live band, they need only a gentle push to revive the elegance of former days.

Give the Shire Highlands time to grow on you. If you're alone, without companions to breathe life into yesterday's memories, fantasize on the way it was in the old days.

Anglophiles will love Shire Highlands.

Africanists will learn from Shire Highlands.

Revolutionists will revel in its decadence.

There's something for everyone.

Highly recommended in the preceding context. The food is delicious, the service perfect.

Payment should be made in Malawian kwacha.

Rates at the end of this section, Malawi, Limbe.

Criteria scores: 36.33 + + + +—out of a possible 60.

Zomba Plateau Camp Site

Location:	*Mailing address:*	*Cables:*	*Any questions call:*
on the south-eastern side of Zomba Plateau: access road from Zomba town	no reservations necessary		(USA) 301–530–1911
			Local telephone number: none

Please read the description for Ku Chawe Inn, which adjoins the site for camping.

The campsite is mown grass in the center of a lovely group of tall trees, with one side open to the road. There are permanent shower and toilet rooms, one for each sex, most attractively built of local stone.

The grass, while mown, was some 6 to 7 inches high when we saw the site. This would be inclined to be very, very wet at night, and a very good waterproof tent would be needed to keep out the damp. It also gets very cold—well, maybe not very cold, but cold enough: 35–40°. Good bed rolls, preferably on cots up off the ground, would be necessary for a comfortable night.

There's plenty of wood for campfires and plenty of eager, hospitable hands to help. Fresh water available at the site.

We would imagine that if one of the local people were hired to help with the chores, he or she would also watch any property left in the tents while campers were climbing the plateau. Certainly for personal safety we believe conditions are excellent. Property, in a country as poor as Malawi, could be a temptation, but we feel as we say, that paying a local person well to keep an eye on things would solve the problem. Minimum daily wage in Malawi is 62 American cents. Be extravagant; give the person you hire U.S.$2 and you can explore to your heart's content in the knowledge that everything back at the camp is safe. We have been told that in the South African mines, Malawians are historically the storekeepers; refusing to clock out until every pick and shovel has been turned in. Throughout southern Africa they have the reputation of being reliable workers.

Campers predominantly—although there was no one there when we were—the local expatriate community, and a few people like yourself.

Payment should be made in Malawian kwacha.

Rates are very reasonable; not more than the equivalent of U.S.$7 per person a night—if that.

Criteria scores: not applicable.

Malian Accommodation

Dakan or Les Jardins de Niarela

Location:
in the sub-
urbs of Ba-
mako
Quartier Ni-
arela

Mailing Address:
B.P. 2031
Bamako
Mali

Cables:
not applicable

24-hour Reservations:
not available

Local telephone number:
Bamako 22.36.67

Second-lowest only to the Holiday Inn, Nossi-Be, Madagascar, of all the hotels we've patronized is the Hotel Dakan in Bamako, Mali. Mentioned here only because it is apparently the cheapest yet safest place to stay in Bamako for tourists. Still not cheap, in our opinion. Peace Corps Volunteers, poor dears, many times stay at the Dakan.

Our bed had one sheet, no second, and the sheet on the bed appeared to have been used by the previous occupant.

No toilet seat or toilet tank cover in our room.

Our room had been swept of litter but not washed.

Childishly painted brush strokes cover the glass on windows and doors, apparently an economy in lieu of shades.

No bugs, but mosquitoes at night in our room, nor did we have a mosquito net supplied.

Staff we thought to be utterly hopeless.

Cold water only. Shower. One unbelievably gray towel provided in our room.

Rates at the end of this section, Mali, Bamako.

Payment should be made in CFA francs.

Criteria scores: 13.72—out of a possible 60.

Grand Hotel

Location:
in the city
center

Mailing address:
B.P. 104
Bamako
Republique du
Mali

Cables:
GRANOTEL

24-hour Reservations:
(USA) 301–530–1911

Local telephone number:
Bamako 22.38.47

Rooms at the Grand are superior to those at the Sofitel l'Amitie—the paint is fresher, the rooms cleaner and better kept. The Grand is near the center of town and as such does not have the marvelous view of the River Niger of the l'Amitie. However, the staff at the front desk, the doorman-cum-bellman, are exceptionally professional and gracious. Housekeeping staff are first rate. Air conditioned. Excellent bathroom suites and plenty of hot and cold water.

Rooms are of medium size and each has a large balcony overlooking the street, but the Saharan dust makes keeping the garden below attractive an impossibility. Telephone did not work when we were at the Grand; this may be a temporary condition.

Dining room staff try hard to please but are overanxious, and the chef produces orders at a snail's pace.

Guests predominantly foreign businessmen and donor aid country personnel.

Recommended. Rates lower than the Sofitel l'Amitie but still, in our opinion, grossly overpriced.

Rates at the end of this section, Mali, Bamako.

Pay in any hard currency, or CFA.

Criteria scores: 30.67 out of a possible 60.

Les Hirondelles

Location:	*Mailing address:*	*Cables:*	*24-hour Reservations:*
on the outskirts of Bamako	B.P. 1026 Bamako Mali	none	none
			Local telephone number: 2244–34 or 2244–35

From what we could learn, there are five hotels used by tourists in Bamako. These are in descending order of price and amenities the Sofitel l'Amitie, the Grand, Les Hirondelles, and the Dakan—the fifth is some way out of town and we did not get to investigate it. Les Hirondelles is the most bearable of the two cheaper hotels. The air conditioning works; the toilet in our room was complete and flushed; there was the occasional missing bulb (lamp); the beds were comfortable, sheets and spreads clean and new. The bathroom was clean and there was plenty of hot water. Room service was prompt, the food not bad but extremely expensive, and the Continental breakfast coming as a part of the tariff softened the blow made by the room rates. Security is good.

That's the up side. On the down side a spring cleaning is in order if the fine dust that coats everything is not to impregnate your belongings; the closet shelves last saw a wipe over the day the carpenter finished building them, the floors are swept but not washed, and the drapes in our rooms could function as sandbags. Being housewives at heart, we took the one bath towel supplied and washed everything down, including the floor, and stuffed the drapes in a section of the closet. The room then became liveable.

Taxis are at the door; the fare into town is 500 CFA. The swimming pool, while tended with loving care, was unbelievably cloudy when we were there and functions better as a mosquito breeding zone than for swimmers. We found the service excellent despite the fact that few members of the staff spoke English—only French—and for this reason, enjoyed our stay. No attempt to pad the bill or overcharge.

Guests are predominantly African businessmen, a few Peace Corps volunteers (those who presumably balk at the Dakan), and budget tourists who refuse to pay the high prices charged by the Sofitel and Grand. Even so, we think Les Hirondelles to be grossly overpriced.

Pay in CFA francs.

Rates at the end of this section, Mali, Bamako.

Criteria scores: 20.30 out of a possible 60.

Office du Niger Resthouse

Location:	Mailing address:	Cables:	24-hour Reservations:
in the town of Niono	not available	none	apparently not necessary
			Local telephone number: not available

Jeff Gray, country director for Africare, showed us this resthouse and we stayed overnight on the drive to Toumbouctou. We haven't the details we should have, but include it to let readers know that it exists. It is located on the main road and we're certain anyone in Niono can direct readers to it.

The rooms consist of two iron double-bunk beds with immaculately clean sheets but no pillows—Africans in this part of the world don't use them—and blankets. The room is spotless, has a hand basin and a central electric light and screened but small windows. Mosquito nets are supplied, and there wasn't the hint of a tear in either of ours. The shower is a shared shower room. There is a central Casablanca—although I'm sure they don't call it that—fan in the room.

Office du Niger is the company formed in French colonial times as an irrigation scheme; it is now owned by the government of Mali. It certainly lived up to its name—a resthouse—and we slept like logs because, having left the black-topped road after Segou, the going gets tough. Breakfast can be had nearby.

Rates at the end of this section, Mali, Niono.

Pay in CFA francs.

Criteria scores: really not applicable. With regard to fire it would be very safe (the rooms open out onto a courtyard and from there it's open to the road). Security perfect.

Relais Azalai Hotel

Location:	Mailing address:	Cables:	24-hour Reservations:
overlooking Toumbouc-tou	B.P. 64 Toumbouctou Mali		(USA) 301–530–1911
			Local telephone number: use Sofitel Bamako: 22.33.18

The exterior of the Relais Azalai is a masterpiece of blending contemporary architecture with traditional, and is aesthetically very pleasing. The rooms, however, painted with a water-base sand color paint, a cement floor that once knew Cardinal Red polish, and furnished very basically (although the beds are comfortable), leaves much to be desired. Not a picture or nonessential object is provided. Anything that might have been supplied to make the rooms and lobby other than clinically basic is missing, causing speculation as to where such items went; to the homes of the staff or into the suitcases of guests desperate for souvenirs from Toumbouctou?

One gets the impression that a nonlocal staff has been employed to man the hotel in an effort to ensure no hanky-panky goes on, but the effort to turn a tight ship has been defeated. Front desk reception on the day we signed into the

Relais Azalai was good because the manager personally checked us in; at all other times it was deplorable. Service in every department was performed with a snarl. Hardly a hospitable welcome for those who have journeyed literally to Toumbouctou.

At times travel writing becomes terribly frustrating. When, for example, a hotel that for one reason or another—in this case because of its location—could be a great hotel under proper management and with motivated staff, must be written up as a hotel that provides simply the basics. An inn at Toumbouctou calls for more than the Relais Azalai offers. Perhaps not a reception of hot cookies offered by a homebody in a starched apron, but at least—as the Casablanca Hyatt Regency offers—a glass of traditional tea served upon entering the lobby by a young man in national dress. At the Relais Azalai even an ordinary cup of tea is not available until the mood strikes someone in the far reaches of the kitchen to turn on the generator at appointed meal times.

The water is safe; however, we took the precaution of boiling it. Light in the room from 6 p.m. to 10 p.m. No meals or snacks other than at the usual mealtimes—because, as noted above, the electricity is off.

There is no excuse for these inconveniences—apart from the fact that the Government of Mali continues—"in the French tradition"—as Sofitel advertises their chain of managed hotels—to believe that civil servants can run private businesses. The hotel is a modern building and has every facility; only the fact that the staff are totally indifferent and perform the bare minimum of duties produces the inhospitable atmosphere found at the Relais Azalai

The exchange rate paid for foreign currency is outrageously lower than the bank rate.

A nice shop in the lobby with some modern, recently dug-up African wood carvings. No set price except for the T-shirts carrying the Toumbouctou logo. Meals higher, in relation to quantity and quality, than the Hay-Adams, situated near the White House, which caters to Washington's finest.

Guests predominantly tourists from every corner of the world.

Rates at the end of this section, Mali, Toumbouctou.

Pay in CFA francs. Do not use traveler's checks here because they will use the perfectly fantastic rate of exchange only they quote. Take along enough CFA to pay in cash and for souvenirs.

Criteria scores: 21.61 − out of a possible 60.

Relais Kanaga

Location:	Mailing address:	24-hour Reservations:
Shores of River	B.P. 244	(USA) 301–530–1911
Niger city cen-	Mopti	
ter Mopti	Republic of Mali	Local telephone:
		None listed

Like the Relais Azalai Hotel in Toumbouctou, the Relais Kanaga in Mopti is architecturally very pleasing, designed to compliment the adobe building for which Mopti is justly famous. We have not stayed at the hotel, but imagine that the rooms of the hotel may be disappointing, as were the rooms at Toumbouctou. Spartan and utilitarian.

The Relais Kanaga has 56 rooms with private shower and toilet, and is air conditioned. There is a restaurant and bar, as well as a small drugstore and souvenir shops in the lobby. They also advertise foreign currency exchange, but if they use the same rates as their sister hotel in Toumbouctou, we make an exception in our advice about using hotel cashiers and suggest readers find the nearest bank in Mopti, as the Toumbouctou rates were a scandal.

They also advertise that canoes are available, but we have no first-hand knowledge of this and imagine that our readers would be staying at the Relais Kanaga in connection with a journey on the river steamer, in which case they will have had enough of the river by the time they arrive in Mopti.

Like the Sofitel l'Amitie in Bamako, the Relais Kanaga also operates a free shuttle service from the airport in Mopti to the hotel. Reconfirming reservations can be made from l'Amitie or from the Hotel Sofitel Teranga in Dakar, Senegal.

Pay in CFA, but be prepared to show a Currency Declaration form or the receipt from the bank, if requested. Rates at the end of this section, Mali, Mopti.

Criteria scores: We have not stayed at the Relais Kanaga.

Sofitel l'Amitie

Location:	Mailing address:	Cables:	24-hour Reservations:
business district on bank of Niger River	B.P. 1720 Bamako Republique du Mali	use mailing address	(USA) 301–530–1911
			Local telephone number: Bamako (223) 22.43.21 or 95

Government-owned, operated by the budget tourist-class French management firm of Sofitel, the Hotel Sofitel l'Amitie, as one first sees it when crossing the bridge on the airport road into Bamako, is beautiful and exactly as the company's brochure depicts it to be. On arrival, front desk service is good, there are English speakers among the staff, and the attitude is welcoming.

Sofitel l'Amitie has a desk at the airport ahead of immigration and customs counters, where a hotel hostess take the passports of visitors with reservations at the hotel, and she gets them stamped and processed. It remains only for the traveler to claim his or her baggage—which is not inspected by customs for most tourists—then board the Sofitel l'Amitie bus. A very nice reception. This service sets the Sofitel l'Amitie apart from other Bamako hotels and is very helpful. The bus to the airport is, again, available without charge for Sofitel guests when they leave the country.

The hotel lobby has the atmosphere of a railroad station in miniature and without doubt the l'Amitie is the recognized overnight stay for business and donor aid personnel—the l'Amitie is where the action in Bamako is at.

The rooms are of medium size and have excellent views of the River Niger. Basically furnished, but not as clean as could be were vacuums used instead of brooms to remove the fine Saharan dust that guests and staff bring in on their shoes. Menu prices are, as in all French African hotels, exhorbitant. We feel French African hotels set their room rates by Paris without regard to value. As such, we believe the Sofitel l'Amitie to be grossly overpriced for the standard offered. Still, apart from the Grand, the only hotel with acceptable amenities.

Rates at the end of this section, Mali, Bamako.

Payment can be made in hard currencies or in CFA; the bank rate is better, though.

Criteria scores: 30.49 + + + + + – out of a possible 60.

Scottish Accommodation

Caledonian Hotel

Location:	*Mailing address:*	*24-hour Reservations:*
City center	Princes St.	(USA) 301–530–1911
	Edinburgh	
	Scotland EH1 2AB	*Local telephone:*
		Edinburgh 225 2433

I hate telling readers how long ago it was that I stayed at the Caledonian Hotel in Edinburgh—1947. It is one of the earliest Edinburgh hotels and Edinburgh is an old city. I found it beautiful then, and imagine it is still equally beautiful if one appreciates the old and the elegant. It's located near Edinburgh Castle, and Princes Street is one of the most beautiful avenues in Europe. The hotel itself is quiet, although it has 174 rooms and 36 suites. The hotel has recently undergone major renovations.

There is a full, formal dining room, a circular bar, and the concierge can confirm your train reservations as well as arrange an Avis car with a driver for the visit to Livingstone's village of Blantyre. In Princes Street Gardens, which boasts the first floral clock (planted in 1903) there is a statue of David Livingstone.

My personal experiences with the Scots is that they certainly do not deserve their reputation for being penny-pinchers. The rates at the Caledonian Hotel are an example of this. There is no "high" and "low" season rate—rather a "high occupancy" and a "low occupancy" rate. The hotel usually enjoys a high occupancy rate throughout the late spring, summer, and early fall. During these months the standard rate is charged. However, if they are experiencing a "low occupancy" in April, they continue with the low occupancy rate where normally they would change over in that month to the high occupancy or standard rate. The same is true for the fall months. The Caledonian offers a special winter package for a two-night stay that includes breakfast and an evening meal. This is very reasonable, and as followers of the *Livingstone* itinerary will probably elect to go to Africa during northern-hemisphere winter months, this can make the visit to Livingstone's village more reasonable than imagined.

Rates at the end of this section, Scotland, Edinburgh. Pay with major credit cards, traveler's checks, foreign currency, or British pounds.

Senegalese Accommodation

Aerogare Hotel

Location:
in Dakar's
Yoff interna-
tional airport

Mailing address:
B.P. 8.195
Aerogare Dakar:
Yoff
Dakar
Senegal

Cables:
to mailing ad-
dress

24-hour Reservations:
none

Local telephone number:
20.07.35

Readers may find it helpful to know that this hotel exists as it is inside the airport building in Dakar, and many African flights change planes in Dakar. For early-morning flight departures it is worth putting up with the austere conditions of the Hotel Aerogare rooms in order to be on time for an early take-off. Unfortunately, there is no telex number for the hotel, and in an emergency it would be necessary to telephone. Then, the caller should be capable of speaking French. The hotel is many times fully occupied and letting them know in advance may, repeat, *may* ensure a room.

The hotel is government-owned, on the second floor of the airport: rooms are extremely basic, swept clean but not spic-and-span clean, service, while friendly, is not efficient, and the staff's knowledge of English is very limited. Personal and property security is good, although not absolute for property, and rooms are air conditioned. It's about the cheapest way to layover in Dakar.

There are other hotels, primarily beach hotels, within a mile of the airport, but the prices are very high, taxi fares must be paid to and from the airport, and the standards, while somewhat better than the Aerogare, are not that much better, in our opinion. However, if there is no room at the Aerogare, try the Meridien, which is less than a half mile from the airport.

Pay in hard currencies, CFA, no credit cards or traveler's checks.

Rates at the end of this section, Senegal, Dakar: Yoff Airport.

Criteria scores: 21.89 out of a possible 60.

Somali Accommodation

Croce del Sud

Location:
just away
from the city
center

Mailing address:
P.O. Box 91
Mogadicio
Somalia

Cables:

24-hour Reservations:
none

Local telephone number:
22050 or 23001

We could not stay at the Croce del Sud, reportedly the best hotel in Mogadicio, because we were staying two weeks. Guests at the hotel must vacate their rooms 2 days a week because the rooms are reserved for Alitalia Airline crews. As you can surmise, the hotel is small. Operated by an Italian couple, with good food a standard part of their dining room fare. The rates are no higher than at the other big hotels in Mogadichio, but it is very difficult to get a room.

Mentioned here because readers are sure to hear about the Croce del Sud if they are planning a visit to Somalia.

Guests predominantly Alitalia crew, Italians with contacts, and the odd well-connected European or American.

Rates: not listed.

Criteria scores: We did not stay at the Croce del Sud.

Juba Hotel

Location:	*Mailing address:*	*Cables:*	*24-hour Reservations:*
in the city center on Viale della Repubblica, Mogadiscio	Viale della Repubblica Mogadiscio Somalia	NATSOMALIA ATTN: JUBA HOTEL	(USA) 301–530–1911
			Local telephone number: not available

Although we have never visited the Soviet Union, in the course of our travels we have come upon examples of Soviet development in the Third World. Agreed, the U.S. Agency for International Development has produced some real fiascos, but on balance the Soviets would appear to have outdone USAID in total number of failures. Certainly, the Soviets err more basically, and in the case of the Juba Hotel, built during the time the Soviets were advising Somalia on development, their unfamiliarity with commercial enterprises is demonstrated by the oversize lobbies that, when accounting is done on a square-foot basis, could never make the hotel a paying proposition. The food and beverage layouts in connection with the storerooms and kitchens again make for inordinately high labor costs even in a country where labor is cheap. The government of Somalia owns the Juba, as it does all tourist hotels. They are eagerly looking for entrepreneurs to take over these enterprises and to extract the government from the tourist industry. Unfortunately, to date, the entrepreneurs who have presented themselves have asked for 50% or more investment on the part of the government; the government, at this juncture, does not have money for such purposes. All they have is land and the existing buildings. We sincerely hope that entrepreneurs will be found as Somalia, with her people trained for the hotel industry, is one of the most promising African countries we have visited for tourist development.

Until such time as an angel comes along, the Juba is the best that can be offered. In addition to the answers given in our hotel evaluation criteria questionnaire, we provide the following by way of description:

—96 rooms, tile floors throughout, except for passageways, which are in need of new carpets.

—rooms very high-ceilinged; walls clean and bright waterpaint colors.

—all-tile bathrooms with safe-to-drink water.

—rooms air conditioned, plus a fan. Beds interior sprung on box frames. Basic furniture of good quality hardwoods.

—double rooms numbered 66, 70, and 72 face the harbor, and the view is beautiful.

—each room has a balcony, entered through glass doors, with large windows to either side.

—breakfast is excellent; lunch and dinner menus a bit heavy for our taste, being Italian-Somali style, but nothing made us ill.

Recommended on condition that readers understand that everything is very basic. We thoroughly enjoyed ourselves.

Rates at the end of this section, Somalia, Mogadiscio.

Payment should be made at the front desk in Somali shillings, but hard currencies can be changed in the office behind the front desk. No credit cards.

Criteria scores: 25.53 out of a possible 60.

Safari Inn

Location:	*Mailing address:*	*Cables:*	*24-hour Reservations:*
See below	c/o National Agency for Tourism Mogadiscio Somalia	NATSOMALIA ATTN: SAFARI HOTEL	(USA) 301–530–1911 *Local telephone number:* not available

Conveniently located for a stop for lunch or afternoon tea, on the main Mogadiscio-Kisimaio highway—and also convenient for visits to Brava, which is not more than 5 miles due east of the hotel.

Unfortunately, this is another example of Soviet influence on Somali development, and while the site is beautiful and well laid out, the buildings, which are small, individual rondels, were poorly constructed. The Ministry of Tourism is having a problem maintaining the basic structures. The rondels are very cool and clean. Security is excellent. Rooms are very basically furnished.

Meals are served at a long table, family style, in what was years ago the backyard of an Italian farmhouse. The old house faces the road and is an interesting example of Italian settler architecture—very like Italian farmhouses in southern Italy.

Rates at the end of this section, Somalia.

Payment should be in Somali shillings.

Criteria scores: 20.73 out of a possible 60.

Waamo Tourist Village

Location:	*Mailing address:*	*Cables:*	*24-hour Reservations:*
Kisimaio outskirts, beach ½ mile	Waamo Tourist Village Hotel Kisimaio Somalia	NATSOMALIA: ATTN: WAAMO VILLAGE	(USA) 301–530–1911 *Local telephone number:* not available

Waamo Tourist Village, as the name implies, was another of the facilities constructed for tourists during the period when the Soviets were advising Somalia on development. It consists of a number of rondovals made of cement with permanent roofs, and a large central building incorporating reception, dining room, and bar, all set in an informal garden. The staff are very welcoming and very hard-working.

The food in the dining room is safe to eat but may not be to everyone's taste, and there is a set menu. Somali rice with sauce, and the diner is supplied with a generous hand of bananas to slice over the entree; very popular in Somalia.

A tame, full-grown ostrich roams the garden. She enjoys hand-fed tidbits, which is her purpose in coming to the tables on the porch during meals. Small monkeys frequent the roof of the dining room and also enjoy the odd treat from the tables.

We very much enjoyed our time at Waamo Tourist Village but we are content with very simple and basic facilities if the atmosphere is right—and it's right at Kisimaio; just to be near this beautiful stretch of coast is exciting. However, the tourist village is a good half mile from the beach and to get to the beach you really need a car.

Rates at the end of this section, Somalia, Kisimaio.

Payment should be in Somali shillings.

Criteria scores: 16.40 out of a possible 60.

Sudanese Accommodation

Hilton International Khartoum

Location:	*Mailing address:*	*Cables:*	*24-hour Reservations:*
See below	Mogran	HILTELS	(USA) 301–530–1911
	Khartoum	KHARTOUM	
	Sudan		*Local telephone number:*
			74100 or 78930

Where the Blue and White Nile meet to become the River Nile, the Hilton International has provided their guests with rooms that overlook the merging of the two great rivers. The rooms' decor, utilizing the colors of Sudan, complement the view, and a simple elegance is achieved that validly interprets the visitor's preconceived image of Khartoum.

The hotel is not a towering skyscraper, upsetting the balance of its neighbors, the immediate one being the Sudan National Museum, but houses 291 rooms, 17 one-bedroom and 17 two-bedroom suites. The Presidential Suite is exceptionally well decorated; tomato/orange walls the color of so many Sudanese adobe buildings.

Khartoum HI has had more than its share of coping with political change under the long rule of the now ousted General Numeri. Factions within Sudan, forces outside the country's borders, and Numeri's own neurosis introduced strict interpretation of Islamic law. For the Hilton this has meant—and the new government has continued the same policy—no alcoholic beverages, and that ladies and gentlemen use the swimming pool at separate times (ladies in the morning, gentlemen in the afternoon). The bar, consisting of the right half of the lobby, produces excellent fresh fruit cocktails, beautifully garnished. Our favorite is based on watermelon juice. It angers us that other African-based hotels with every form of alcohol at their disposal make so little effort to produce attractive cocktails, and the Khartoum HI working under difficult conditions does so very well.

Rooms are of medium-to-large size, with full picture windows, beautifully clothed beds, and video for which there are new changes of tapes several times a day, obtained under very difficult circumstances. An information booklet published by the hotel is most helpful for local telephone numbers and opening hours of businesses and stores. The hotel is a short, pleasant walk to the center of town, along the Nile.

We thoroughly enjoyed our stay. Perhaps our awareness of the good things in life had been heightened after three days on an antiquated train through the Nubian Desert, but the Hilton reinforces the preconceived image of Khartoum and all the romantic history surrounding the River Nile.

The food is good; there is a coffee shop and a formal dining room, the Ivoire. The newsstand proprietor was not the most genial of men, and his prices were wildly inflated. The ivory we saw at the boutique-cum-souvenir shop was badly carved.

Service throughout the hotel was very good, particularly the housekeeping department.

Guests are predominantly Middle Eastern, American, and European businessmen and donor aid country administrators. I believe we were the only tourists at the time of our visit.

Highly recommended without qualification.

Payment can be made by major credit card, hard currencies, traveler's checks, and in Sudanese pounds with a Currency Declaration form.

Rates at the end of this section under Sudan.

Criteria scores: 48.35 out of a possible 60.

Sudan Club

Location:	Mailing address:	Cables:	24-hour Reservations:
near the	c/o P.O. Box 801	use mailing ad-	none
Presidential	Khartoum	dress	
Palace city	Sudan		Local telephone number:
center			ask at: 70760

The Sudan Club is the British Club in Khartoum. There is an American Club, but the printed word states that a visitor must know a member to be admitted. The Sudan Club accepts visitors of any nationality.

The club is situated immediately adjacent to the administrative headquarters used by General Gordon. This is now the Presidential Palace and is cordoned off by a high wall and closed to the public. The Sudan Club used to be within the confines of this wall, but as British official presence receded, so did the club's premises. Still, the Sudan Club is in the center of the city and very convenient.

There is a small swimming pool, a nice terrace where light meals are served, and an indoor dining room. The furnishings are basic, with no pretensions to luxury. We found the members to be friendly and welcoming.

There is an information bulletin board on which are advertised not only expatriate property for sale but also jobs. We were tempted. However, housing is so terribly expensive in Khartoum that even the good salaries offered would be spent primarily on rent. We found the prices at the club very reasonable for meals. We did not have the opportunity to stay in one of the rooms, but feel safe in recommending them for those on a budget. Security appeared to be absolute, both property and personal.

Guests predominantly international visitors to Khartoum preferring the intimacy of a small club to that of a hotel, and British and American residents of Khartoum.

Payment should be made in Sudanese pounds accompanied by your Currency Declaration form.

Rates at the end of this section under Sudan.

Criteria scores: we did not stay at the Sudan Club.

Togolese Accommodation

Hotel Sofitel du 2 Fevrier

Location:	*Mailing address:*	*Cables:*	*24-hour Reservations:*
city center in a landscaped park	B.P. 131 Lome Togo	use mailing address	(USA) 301–530–1911 *Local telephone number:* 21.00.03

The 2 Fevrier is one of the very few government-owned hotels that succeeds and can compete with hotels owned by the private sector. Managed, as the name signifies, by the French management chain Sofitel, the service is excellent. Virtually all staff members speak English as well as French; performance in every department is professional and hospitable.

The hotel is 35 stories high, and was constructed to complement the beautiful national assembly convention hall, which rooms 04, 05, 06, 07, and 08 on every floor overlook. The conventional hall is an excellent, aesthetically pleasing example of post-independence African architecture. Clean, modern exterior lines; the interior equipped with the most modern high-tech sound and lighting.

The hotel rooms are of medium size, wall-to-wall carpeting, well and comfortably furnished. A huge picture window of two-way glass frames a scene of Lome: the foreground the conference hall, the background the city. From such a vantage point it is possible to study the mixture of older colonial buildings and the sleek modern city Lome will be in the future.

Television with video movies at 4:30 and 10:30 p.m. Radio brings in the BBC Overseas Service in the early morning and local stations. A very nice swimming pool and a snack bar: again, one of the few poolside snack bars that is not a disaster. Lunch hour in Lome is from 12 to 3 p.m. We fell into a routine of helping ourselves to the all-salad buffet and then a swim and a lie-down before our afternoon appointments. Service exceptionally good at the snack bar and by the pool attendant, who will also look after small children while parents sunbathe.

A French pastry shop on the lobby floor produces delicious morning and afternoon pastries.

Two dining rooms on the 35th floor, we did not particularly care for the food as it tended to be too oily and the meat too strong. Those who enjoy French cooking may want to try these dining rooms for themselves.

Guests predominantly Americans and French and a few government residents.

Payment can be in any hard currency, CFA francs, and with major credit cards.

Rates at the end of this section under Togo.

Criteria scores: 43.65 + + + out of a possible 60.

Ugandan Accommodation

Crested Crane Hotel

Location:	*Mailing address:*	*24-hour Reservations:*
Jinja suburbs	P.O. Box 444	(USA) 301–530–1911
	Jinja	
	Uganda	*Local telephone number:*
		Ask directory inquiry

This lovely hotel, set in beautiful gardens and tended lawns within the city limits of Jinja, Uganda, is a government-owned hotel, which, during Uganda's more settled times, offered accommodation in 24 single or 8 double rooms, all with private baths.

We visited the hotel in 1981. It was as immaculate then as when we had often patronized it in 1970–72. The shelves in the bar held Johnnie Walker Red Label Scotch and nothing else. We asked for tea. A waiter, in a much patched jacket served us just that—there was no milk or sugar available. Only black tea, no cakes or sandwiches. At dinner, only a set, one-plate meal was offered. Still, the service was as charming as ever, the staff as hospitable. Things must be better now; there was little other direction to go but up.

We believe it will be acceptable to pay in Uganda shillings as the number of foreign visitors is so small the hotel probably has not reinstituted foreign exchange procedures. In doing so, be prepared to show your Currency Declaration form or bank receipts. Estimated rates are given at the end of this section, Uganda, Jinja.

Criteria scores: not applicable at this writing.

International Hotel

Location:	*Mailing address:*	*24-hour Reservations:*
city center	P.O. Box 7041	(USA) 301–530–1911
	Kampala	
	Uganda	

We see, when looking up the number of rooms (in the Automobile Association of East Africa's *Official Touring Guide to East Africa 1971–72*) that the International Hotel's official name at that time was Uganda International Hotel. Depending on the whim of the head of government in Uganda, so the name of the hotel changes. We have known it to be the Apollo, then the International, and who knows now what the name is, but everyone in Kampala will know the hotel you mean if you ask for the International.

In the early 1970s it was very sophisticated and very elegant with a night-club called the Leopard's Lair on the roof. Behind the live band a crouching, snarling, stuffed leopard's green eyes caught the light from the mirror balls that hung from the half ceiling. The band was always great, the music went on until 2 a.m., then everyone went to an all-night disco in the suburbs of Kampala. The crowd consisted of every nationality and every age. If ever there was a country that shouldn't have had a race problem, it was Uganda in those heady days of the late 1960s and early 1970s. But it did. The Indian men who were such swingers at the Leopard's Lair were soon put on planes and asked to take up a new life in the gray, cold Midlands of England or under the overcast skies of Vancouver. The balmy, perfect spring days typical of Uganda would be nothing more than a memory; the summer of 1971 saw General Idi Amin's "Exodus of the Asians."

Then there were the Peace Corps, the British VSOs, the Danish volunteers, and the Germans and Norwegians who saved up their pennies and had a fling at the Leopard's Lair at least once a month. The international exchange students from Makerere University and their Ugandan classmates—soon to be shot by Amin in nearby forests—added to the mix. Tall, lanky Watusi refugees sometimes played their Congolese rhythms when the band stepped down for a break. Ankoles from western Uganda and a preponderance of Buganda dancers all mixed with one another and the foreigners. Non-Africans from the embassies and donor aid countries' personnel packed into the Leopard's Lair. From that vantage point the lights of Kampala's streets could be seen as far as the horizon.

In 1981 we went back to the International. The Leopard's Lair had been closed because, we were told, General Amin's soldiers found sport in throwing their girlfriends off the roof after consuming the Scotch whiskey the general had flown in by the crate from Wiltshire every week.

The hotel was open, but we only got a room because some Indian friends doubled-up. This was during Obote's second try at running the country; he had his senior civil service barracked with their families in the International. The hotel is government owned, but even government businesses need payment, and Obote never saw to it that the hotel was paid for the food his civil servants and their children were consuming. Cash to purchase food for meals came from the few paying customers—businessmen like our Indian friends, international journalists, and relief agency personnel. There was a set menu and if it was repetitive, it was filling.

A young Ugandan was general manager and under the circumstances was doing very, very well. This was before the joint U.S.-British effort to restore piped water to Kampala had been completed. Water was available only at night. Before they went down to dinner, occupants would turn on their bathtub faucets (taps) to ensure they got their share of water. Sometimes they would stay downstairs in the lounge for an after-dinner coffee. The water would come on, the bathtubs would overflow, and the water would channel itself out into the corridors of the hotel, and returning to one's rooms at 10 p.m. there would be a squelching underfoot as the extensive underfelt of the carpets was compressed and the water it held was forced through the carpets' tufts to the surface.

Instead of the top 20 tunes filtering through the night skies from the nightclub roof, shots could be heard in the city streets below. Looking down from the windows in daylight, a burnt helicopter was seen parked askew on the lawn.

We have it on good authority that times have changed, that Kampala's city streets are now quiet. What condition the International is in, we don't know. Presumably better than in 1981. Readers can have a look, and fall back on the Kampala Sikh temple if things look too grim. We have estimated the rates for the International. Rates at the end of this section, Uganda, Kampala. Pay in Uganda shillings and be prepared to show a Currency Declaration form or receipts from the bank for money changed.

Criteria scores: not applicable at this writing.

Kampala Sikh Gurdwara (Temple)

Location:	*Mailing address:*	*24-hour Reservations:*
city center	Gyani-in-Charge	not applicable
	Kampala Sikh Temple	
	Kampala	*Local telephone number:*
	Uganda	ask directory inquiry

The Kampala Sikh Gurdwara, located in the center of Kampala, is highly respected by all—Ugandans and expatriates alike—and not to be confused with the Hindu temple, which has had problems. Throughout the "troubles" the Kampala Sikh Temple has never been assaulted and received only one small bomb, which inadvertently fell into the temple compound.

The rooms available to travelers are very, very basic. The temple itself is one of the earliest in East Africa and there has not been a sizable congregation to maintain the upkeep of the temple for 14 years. More than anything, the temple remained open to symbolically demonstrate the permanency of the Sikhs in Uganda. The building consists of a large open compound with rooms off of it, with the place of worship off to one side. The gyani-in-charge lives with his family in an upstairs apartment.

The Sikhs make no charge for providing accommodation to travelers, but we hope that our readers will take along a few presents for the gyani's children, as well as donate to the temple the amount we suggest at the end of this section, Uganda, Kampala. Such donations should be made in Ugandan shillings.

Criteria scores: We do not score religious guest houses.

HOTEL RATES

Expressed in U.S.$ using exchange rates as of May 27, 1987; rounded to the nearest dollar. Double is the total price for 2 people; divide by 2 for the per person rate when sharing.

Y = year-round rate	NB = no board included
H = high-season rate	B&B = bed & breakfast
M = mid-season rate	B&CB = bed & continental breakfast
L = low-season rate	HB = half board (no lunch)
	FB = full board

Season dates are given in country backgrounds.

	Single	Double	Suite
Cote d'Ivoire			
Abidjan			
Hilton International Abidjan	Y$111/121/131/NB	Y$131/141/150NB	Y$233NB*
Egypt			
Alexandria			
El Mehrek	Y$25B&B	Y$25B&B	
Aswan			
Happi Hotel	Y$25NB	Y$25NB	
Cairo			
Garden City House	Y$25NB	Y$25NB	
Ramses Hilton	Y$97/106/123NB	Y$123/134/151NB	Y$235/500/780NB*
Port Said			
Holiday Hotel	Y$25B&CB	Y$25B&CB	
England			
London			
Bed & Breakfast (private homes)	$35 to $50 per person B&B		
Crichton Hotel	Y$34B&CB	Y$60B&CB	
Sheraton Park Tower	Y$209/239NB	Y$230/266NB	Y$486/835NB
Gabon			
Libreville			
Sofitel Dialogue	Y$77/88NB	Y$86/98NB	

*See "Estimating Your Travel Costs."

	Single	*Double*	*Suite*
The Gambia			
Banjul			
Apollo Hotel	Y$22B&CB	Y$22B&CB	
Tourist Development Area			
Novotel Kombo Beach Hotel	Y$72NB	Y$84NB	Y$111NB
Kenya			
Banana Hill			
Kentmere Club	Y$30B&B	Y$50B&B	
Diani Beach			
Dan Trench's Campsite	Y$3NB	Y$6NB	
Sheraton Golden Beach	Y$101/132NB	Y$101/132NB	$19 for a rollaway
Kericho			
Tea Hotel	Y$42B&B	Y$74B&B	$105B&B (double)
Kisumu			
Sunset Hotel	Y$33B&B	Y$60B&B	
Kitale			
Kitale Country Club	Y$25B&B	Y$35B&B	
Makindu			
Makindu Sikh Gurdwara	$5 donation per person		
Masai-Mara Game Reserve			
Keekorok Lodge	H$136FB	H$179FB	
Mara Intrepids Club	Y$240FB	Y$300 (includes escorted game drives) FB	
Meru National Park			
Leopard Rock Self-Catering Cottages	Y$12NB	Y$24NB	
Meru Mulika Lodge	H$85FB	H$109FB	
Molo			
Highlands Hotel	Y$25B&B	Y$34B&B	
Mombasa			
Castle Hotel	Y$43/47B&B	Y$66/74B&B	Y$82B&B (double)
Lotus Hotel	Y$21B&B	Y$29B&B	
Manor Hotel	Y$16/23NB	Y$30/35NB	
Outrigger Hotel	Y$36B&B	Y$56B&B	
Mount Kenya			
Mountain Lodge	H$86HB	Y$137HB Presidential suite— Y$182HB (double)	
Mt. Kenya Safari Club, Nanyuki	Y$131HB	Y$169HB Presidential suite— Y$247/362HB (sleeps four)	
Naro Moru River Lodge	H$66FB	H$93FB	H$147/232FB

	Single	Double	Suite
Nairobi			
C.P.K. Guest House	Y$14FB	Y$28FB	
Hilton International, Nairobi	Y$89/100/ 114NB	Y$110/127/ 142NB	Y$204/300NB*
Methodist Guest House	Y$17FB	Y$34FB	
Mt. Kenya Safari Club, Nairobi	Y$132NB Executive Suite—Y$148NB Presidential suite—Y$404/456NB (sleeps four)		
Norfolk Hotel	Y$113B&B	Y$125B&B	$136/272B&B
United Kenya Club	Y$48FB	Y$58FB	
North Coast			
Mombasa Inter- Continental	H$145B&B	H$165B&B	
Whispering Palms	H$60FB	H$83FB	
Silversands Villas	H$90HB	H$135HB	
Garsen: (emergencies)	Catholic Mission	donation to the clinic	
Lamu: Petley's Inn	H$75HB	H$95HB	
Private homes	approximately $3 a day per person		
House rental	$25 to $30 a day for entire house and servant (no food)		
Samburu Game Reserve			
Samburu Lodge (Block Hotel's)	H$122FB	H$174FB	
Thika			
Blue Posts Hotel, also known as New Blue Posts	Y$13B&B	Y$19B&B	

Malawi

	Single	Double	Suite
Kasungu National Park			
Lifupa Lodge	Y$20NB	Y$25NB	
Lengwe National Park			
Rest Houses	High season: $27 for a house, which sleeps 4, NB Low season $7 per person, NB		
Likoma Island			
Likoma Island Rest House	Y$12NB	Y$24NB	
Lilongwe			
Capital Hotel	Y$84B&B	Y$94B&B	
Limbe			
Shire Highlands Hotel	Y$40B&B	Y$50B&B	
Liwonde National Park			
Mvuu Camp	Y$8NB	Y$16NB	
Mangochi (for the southern lake shore lodges)			
Club Makolola	Y$35NB	Y$44NB	
Nkopola Leisure Center (tent or tent space)	Y$8NB	Y$16NB	
Nkopola Lodge	Y$32NB	Y$41NB	

	Single	Double	Suite
Mzuzu			
Mzuzu Hotel	Y$62B&B	Y$73B&B	
Nkhata Bay			
Nkhata Bay Rest House	Y$12NB	Y$24NB	
Nyika Plateau National Park			
Chilinda Camp	H$27NB, L$7NB per person for up to 4 guests		
Zomba Plateau			
Ku Chawe Campsite	Y$4NB	Y$8NB	
Ku Chawe Lodge	Y$22NB	Y$33NB	

Mali
Bamako

Dakan or Les Jardins de Niarela	$35NB	Y$35NB	
Grand Hotel	Y$55NB	Y$72NB	
Les Hirondelles	Y$48B&CB	Y$62B&CB	
Sofitel l'Amitie	$89NB	$98NB	
Mopti			
Relais Kanaga	Y$50NB	Y$57	$65 (triple room) NB
Niono			
Office du Niger Resthouse	Y$4NB	Y$8NB	
Toumbouctou			
Relais Azalai	Y$50NB	Y$57NB	

Scotland
Edinburgh

Caledonian Hotel	Y$113HB	Y$170HB	Note: Y$108HB double per night, minimum 2-night stay, upon availability

Senegal
Dakar: Yoff Airport

Hotel Aerogare	Y$41NB	Y$41NB	

Somali
Kisimaio

Waamo Tourist Hotel	Y$66NB	Y$82NB	
Mogadiscio			
Croce del Sud	Y$88NB	Y$99NB	
Juba	Y$77NB	Y$88NB	
Mogadiscio-Kisimaio Highway			
Safari Inn	Y$55NB	Y$55NB	

Sudan
Khartoum

Hilton International Khartoum	Y$146/158/170NB	Y$170/182/194NB	Y$362/542/662NB*
Sudan Club	Y$25NB	Y$50NB	

	Single	Double	Suite
Togo			
Lome			
Sofitel 2 du Fevrier	Y$82NB	Y$90NB	Y$228/342NB
Uganda			
Jinja			
Crested Crane	Y$66NB (estimated)	Y$83NB (estimated)	
Kampala			
International	Y$90NB (estimated)	Y$110NB (estimated)	
Kampala Sikh Gurdwara (Temple)	$10 donation per night per person		

TRANSPORTATION

Airlines Serving Africa

Most African countries, no matter how low their GNP, operate an airline to "fly the flag." We have chosen what we believe to be the best carriers. We have selected them because their service is excellent and they fly the routes needed in *Fielding's Literary Africa*. All of them have excellent safety records with no crashes to date. Uganda had an airline, but the political upheavels of the past few years forced it to close down. We look forward to Uganda Airways flying again, as they were excellent.

If you are forced to fly airlines other than our recommended ones, it is always better to fly on one of the European carriers such as KLM, SAS, and Air France rather than use an African airline that is not on our recommended list. However, some European carriers do no have "passenger rights" between certain African cities. This forces the passenger to change to a domestic service. This is not always satisfactory.

British Airways changed from a government-owned company to a privately owned corporation in 1986. They have mounted an intensive advertising campaign in the United States. It is going to take a lot more than a Madison Avenue advertising campaign to overcome the absolutely deplorable service they rendered when they were government owned. If you can avoid using British Airways, do.

Air Mali closed down for a time in 1986–87 after one of their planes crashed near Toumbouctou. The airline computers are showing that Air Mali is flying again. The World Bank recommended that they be taken over—administratively—by Air Zaire. Presumably this has happened and the carrier is again operating. However, it is best to check with Air Afrique before making final plans. It is unwise to rely simply on information in airline computers. Air Afrique's telephone numbers are given in this section.

While African airlines have good safety records, there can be problems when using certain carriers. Vulindlela Kumalo (undersecretary of the Ministry of Finance of Zimbabwe) wrote a letter to the editor that was published in the September 1986 issue of the *New African* that illustrated some of these problems. The undersecretary stated that although he had confirmed his flight on Ethiopian Airlines from Douala, Cameroun, for Nairobi, when he presented his tickets to the Cameroun Airline clerk acting on behalf of Ethiopian Airlines he was told that he could not board the plane unless he presented "a gift as an incentive." When he refused to do so, he had to stay in the transit lounge (because he had no visa for Cameroun) for the next four days until the next Ethiopian Airlines flight came through. We have flown Ethiopian Airlines and found their service excellent; but it sometimes happens, as in this case and in one in New York where Royal Air Maroc has Lufthansa staff process their passengers—the ground staff reflect poorly on the carrier. In the case of Lufthansa, we found them—without exception, the supervisory staff included—to be extremely arrogant. Granted, they did not demand a bribe, but their attitude was infuriating. Readers who are processed at Kennedy in New York by Lufthansa should realize that the service on Royal Air Maroc is very good, and that they are in for a pleasurable flight once away from Lufthansa staff.

Making a reservation for an international flight is easier than for a domestic flight as, on occasion, some local bigwig comes along, puts the pressure on a reservation clerk, and an outsider's name is dropped from the passenger list. For this reason, we have used land travel in cases where one would think flight might be quicker. If a flight is missed, usually there isn't another one until the next day.

Nor do African airline computer banks necessarily show information on all other African airlines. This means if there's a layover between flights and the airline is supposed to pick up the tab for the hotel, your room drops between the slats. If it's not on their computer, the flight doesn't exist. Again, we've tried to avoid such situations for our readers.

If nothing else, African airlines have it all over major international carriers when it comes to keeping baggage intact and where it's going. A Royal Air Maroc porter tenderly affixed a "fragile" label to a parcel of ours in Casablanca, only for us to see it, on arrival at Kennedy, have some huge trunk slammed onto it. Uganda Airlines have held a flight for us until they found a piece of missing baggage. On the down side, Pan Am has lost our baggage so many times and never answered, let alone paid, claims that we do not check our baggage through Kennedy but physically unload it from a domestic Pan Am and put it onto the onward flight to Africa.

Royal Air Maroc, to ensure a total check for explosives when the occasion demands, has passengers individually and personally identify their bags and hand the bags to the cargo porter alongside the aircraft. No midair detonations for them. Most African airlines also have an individual (in a screened-off closet) passenger-frisking routine. Female or male staff do the frisking, depending upon the sex of the passenger. They do not rely completely on the mechanical scanners. As most African countries do not have diplomatic relations with Israel, their national carriers are not as subject to highjacking by Arab terrorists as national carriers operated by countries whose foreign policies support Israel. The exception, of course, is Egypt, which, since the Camp David Accord, does have diplomatic representation to Israel. It is not pertinent here to discuss the reasons why African countries, except for a very few, have broken ties with Israel, but the cause lies in Israel's interaction with South Africa more than for any other reason.

The regard shown by many African airlines for the human condition goes beyond adherence to departure times. Three young Americans had been the victims of a car crash and the American Embassy asked that our flight be held until they could board. The flight was held. Africa is a continent where human compassion ranks above slurs about late arrivals. Delays may not always be because of such an incident, but they don't risk safety in order to keep to flight schedules. The particular flight we mention was with Royal Air Maroc.

Having said this, it is pertinent to add that we have never experienced delays (on the carriers we recommend) such as those currently being reported by passengers on domestic U.S. routes. Never have we circled an airport in Africa waiting to land. The longest delay we have experienced is 30 minutes in taking off. This has usually been made up during the flight so that arrival time is on schedule.

Kenya Airways, that old reliable, is one of the few carriers in the world today showing a profit. Their service is excellent, they keep to schedules—although we think they would hold a plane in an emergency. TWA handles their reservations in the United States and if any problem occurs, it's TWA that's screwed up—most of their reservation clerks are unaware that TWA represents Kenya Airways in the U.S. If there's any confusion, call Kenya Airways' office in New York at 212–832–8810.

Air Afrique flies to some of the most exotic destinations on the African continent; and they fly some of the most exotically dressed passengers in the world. Their trans-Atlantic cabin crews handle what could be a clash of cultures with poise as they pass down the aisles distributing periodicals in French, English, and Arabic. The crews themselves represent the 10 countries who jointly own Air Afrique: the People's Republic of the Congo, Ivory Coast, Burkina Faso, Mauritania, Niger, Mali, Central African Republic, Senegal, Chad, and Togo. Air Afrique connects the capital cities of these countries with New York, Paris, and Jeddah.

In February 1987 Pan Am discontinued its flight New York-Dakar-Monrovia-Lagos-Nairobi as the Nigerians were not, reportedly, allowing them to take revenues from ticket sales out of Nigeria. They now fly to Nairobi from New York via Frankfurt. This is not too interesting a routing and in the itineraries we have used Pan Am to cross the Atlantic, with a change to a Kenya Airways flight in either London or Paris.

Qantas flies to Harare, Zimbabwe, and passengers can connect with Kenya Airways to Nairobi, and of course, Lilongwe is right next door on an Air Malawi flight. They also fly to Bombay to connect with Kenya Airways to Nairobi.

Singapore Airlines has two direct flights from Auckland connecting with their flights to Cairo or Bombay. Air New Zealand International has flights to Singapore from both Wellington and Auckland. Connections can be made to either Nairobi via Bombay, or Cairo, depending on which itinerary you are following.

Making Airline Reservations

The itineraries we have suggested in *Fielding's Literary Africa* are original, and while travel agents and tour operators may use them after publication of the guide, they are not offered by anyone at this writing.

We have worked in close collaboration with the airlines we recommend to work out flight times and routes that will save our readers money. We have found that many airline reservationists do not know the African routes. Also, it appears that they are being monitored during daytime hours to determine how long they take with each call. The late-night operators seemingly have more time and will take more care, but not all airlines have late-night reservations services.

For these reasons we have asked Christine at Merikani Hotel Reservations Service if she will handle the airline reservations for our readers following itineraries in *Fielding's Literary Africa*. Feel free to call Christine at (USA) 301–530–1911 for the information she has on the airline routings and fares, and she will ensure that your reservations are made through our personal contacts with the individual airlines. Incidentally, Christine also knows the best discount fares for more straightforward destinations.

Within Africa, airlines fares can differ because of exchange rates when the potential passenger is paying (as they must almost without exception) in dollars, pounds, or riyals. It is $110 more expensive to fly Lusaka, Zambia, to Nairobi, Kenya, than Nairobi to Lusaka for this reason. Christine knows these variations and also has suggestions for reliably economizing by taking advantage of foreign exchange rates.

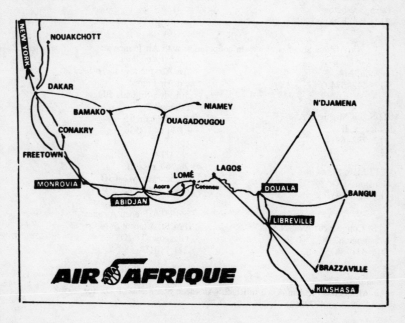

It may sometimes appear that there are more direct routes than we suggest. For instance, between Dakar, Senegal, and Lilongwe, Malawi. "The shortest distance between two points is a straight line" may not always be true, because of the unreliability of connecting airlines.

We really feel we can stand by the airlines we have recommended, and if readers experience problems, we most certainly want them to let us know (P.O. Box 53394, Washington, D.C. 20009, U.S.A.).

AIR AFRIQUE RESERVATIONS OFFICES

Canada
c/o Air France
Librairie 31st Flr.
3321, Place Ville-Marie
Montreal H3B 3N4
514–861–9861

Saudi Arabia
Air Afrique
Shohaddah St.
Medina Rd.
Facing Palestine Bridge Station
Jeddah
66 024 34 or 66 572 69

U.S.A.
Air Afrique
683 Fifth Ave.
New York, NY 10002
(also, see below)
212–758–6300

Australia
c/o UTA
Kindersley House
33/35 Bligh St.
Sydney
2333277

United Kingdom
c/o UTA French Railways House
177 Picadilly
London W.1.
(also, see below)
(1) 221 2101

New Zealand
c/o UTA-Air France
11, Commerce St.
P.O. Box 924
Auckland

U.S.: Air Afrique also has offices in cooperation with Air France at:

601 Boylston St.
Boston, MA
617–242–5740

22 South Michigan Ave.
Chicago, IL
312–782–6111

1212 Main St.
Houston, TX
713–225–1931

1120 Connecticut Ave. N.W.
Washington, DC
202–331–8875

United Kingdom:
Air Afrique also has offices at:
c/o Air France
3rd Flr., Rotunda Bldg.
Edmond St.
Birmingham 3
(021) 643 2556

c/o UTA
70/76 Cross St.
Manchester M2 4 JG
(061) 834 7891–2-3-4

c/o UTA French Airlines
124 St. Vincent St.
Glasgow G1 2DT
221 2101

Saudia Arabia:
Air Afrique also has an office in Riadh (Alavaeen St., Malaz, P.O. Box 20508, 4779835 or 4779862).

Air Afrique Reservations Offices in Africa

▶ **Note:** Reservations must be reconfirmed 12 hours before intended departure or the reservation will be dropped automatically.

Burkina Faso
Ave. William-Ponty
B.P. 213
Bobo-Dioulasso
991 26

Ave. Kadiogo
Ouagadougou
34501

Cameroun
3 Boule. de la Liberte
Douala
42 42 22

Central African Republic
Rue J. Mobutu
B.P. 875
Bangui
61 46 60

Chad
66, Ave. du President Tombalbaye
B.P. 466
N'Djamena
30.00
Offices in Abecher, Bongor, Faya-
    Largeau, Mongo, Moundou, and Pala.

People's Republic of the Congo
Ave. Patrice Lumumba
B.P. 172
Brazzaville

Ave. du General de Gaulle
B.P. 1126, Pointe-Noire
27 31 32

Gabon
Boulevard de l'Independence
B.P. 311
Libreville
2340

Offices also in Franceville, Moanda, and
    Port-Gentil.

The Gambia
c/o Gambia Airways
6, Bukle St., P.O. Box 268
Banjul

Ghana
Cocoa House Building
Accra
283 26

Ivory Coast
3 Ave. J. Anoma
B.P. 1595
Abidjan
32 02 00 or 32 05 00

Office also in Bouake.

Kenya
Total Building
Koinange St.
P.O. Box 30159
Nairobi
33 53 25 or 33 33 01

Liberia
Michlin St.
P.O. Box 327
Monrovia
22 28 99 or 22 25 57

Madagascar
c/o Air Madagascar
29, Ave. de l'Independence
Antananarivo
22222

Mali
Sq. Patrice Lumumba
B.P. 2651
Bamako
22 57 54 or 22 58 02

Mauritania
B.P. 51
Nouakchott
52084 or 52545

Office also c/o Air Mauritania in
    Nouadhibou.

Morocco
After a year's wait Air Afrique have
    been licensed to open an office in
    Casablanca; we do not have the
    address but it is only 3 blocks from the
    Hyatt; ask the concierge.

c/o Royal Air Maroc
Ave. Mohammad V
Rabat
24604

c/o Royal Air Maroc
Pl. de France
Immeuble El Nasr
Tanger
25501

Niger
c/o Air France
Immeuble El Nasr
Niamey
73 33 76 or 73 30 10/11

Offices also c/o Niger Afrique in Agades,
    Maradi, and Zinder; and in Tahoua c/o
    Dan Maradi

Nigeria
Sq. Tafawa Balewa
P.o. Box 1702
Lagos

c/o Nigeria Airways
P.O. Box 11
Bank Rd.
Kano
3891/30101

Senegal
Pl. de l'Independence
B.P. 3132
Dakar
21 25 72 or 61 13 63

Pl. Franchet d'Esperey
B.P. 40
Saint-Louis
21 54 63 or 23 10 45

Tanzania
c/o Air France
P.O. Box 2661
Dar-es-Salam
20356

Togo
12, rue du Commerce
B.P. 111
Lome
21 20 42

Tunisia
c/o Air France
1, rue d'Athenes
24 79 22 or 26

Tunisair also acts for Air Afrique, but we
    found them very difficult.

Zaire
c/o UTA
B.P. 857
Boulevard du 30 Juin
Kinshasa
269 95

c/o UTA
B.P. 3672
1055 Ave. F. Youlou
Lumumbashi
5454

In Asia and Europe, Air France usually
    represents Air Afrique, and Air France
    should be contacted for reservation
    confirmation or schedule information.

KENYA AIRWAYS RESERVATIONS OFFICES

Canada and U.S.
424 Madison Avenue
6th Floor
New York, NY 10017
212–832–8810/13/18

United Kingdom
16 Conduit St.
London, W.1.
409–0277

Saudi Arabia
c/o Attar Centre, Medina Rd.
P.O. Box 11820
Jeddah
6530813

c/o Attar Travel
Alpatha St.
P.O. Box 364
Riyadh
4121704 or 4121678

Australia and New Zealand
Through Qantas or your travel agent.

Kenya Airways Reservations Offices in Kenya

Nairobi
Tourist Information Center
In front of the Hilton International
Nairobi
332750

Main Office
Koinange St.
P.O. Box 19002
Nairobi

Kenyatta International Conference Center
29291

Cargo Reservations
822171

Mombasa
Main City Office
Digo Rd. at Meru Rd.
P.O. Box 99302
Mombasa
21251 or 59

Almost impossible to get through; it's
better to go to the office.

There are also offices in Kisumu (P.O. Box 1427, tel: 2630) and at Malindi (P.O. Box 634, tel: 20237).

Kenya Airways Reservations Offices in Africa

Egypt
Nile Hilton Hotel
Tahir Sq.
Cairo
776771 ext. 14

Ethiopia
Ato Tesfaye Kadjela Bldg.
P.O. Box 3381
Addis Ababa
443018 or 19

Malawi
Development House
1st Floor
P.O. Box 808
620820

Rwanda
Pl. De l'Independance
1 Boul. de la Revolution
B.P. 357, Kigali
3999

Somalia
J.H. Building
Hawatako St.
P.O. Box 2996
Mogadishu
23137

Sudan
El Nazir Building
P.O. Box 1982
Khartoum
73429

Tanzania
Tancot House, 2nd Floor
P.O. Box 5342
Dar-es-Salaam
25352 or 36826

Sonara Building
P.O. Box 3840
Zanzibar
32041 or 42 or 43

KENYA AIRWAYS ROUTE MAP

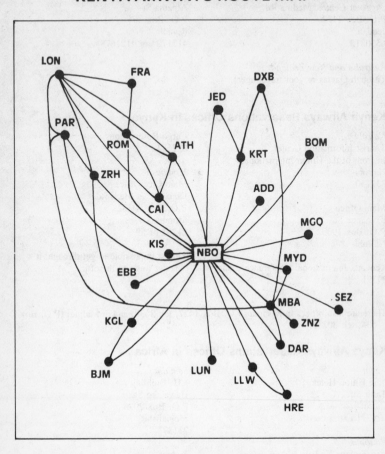

ONLINE STATIONS CITY CODES

ADDIS ABABA	-ADD	KIGALI	-KGL
ATHENS	-ATH	LILONGWE	-LLW
BOMBAY	-BOM	LONDON (Heathrow)	-LON
BUJUMBURA	-BJM	LUSAKA	-LUN
CAIRO	-CAI	MALINDI	-MYD
DAR ES SALAAM	-DAR	MOGADISHU	-MGQ
DUBAI	-DXB	MOMBASA	-MBA
ENTEBBE	-EBB	NAIROBI	-NBO
FRANKFURT	-FRA	PARIS (Orly)	-PAR
HARARE	-HRE	ROME (Fiumicino)	-ROM
JEDDAH	-JED	SEYCHELLES	-SEZ
KHARTOUM	-KRT	ZANZIBAR	-ZNZ
KISUMU	-KIS	ZURICH	-ZRH

Uganda
Apollo Hotel Arcade
P.O. Box 6969
Kampala
59472 or 33068

Zambia
Findeco House
P.O. Box 31856
Lusaka
214569 or 214156

Edinburgh Arcade
P.O. Box 20947
Kitwe
215272 or 215855

PAN AMERICAN AIRLINES RESERVATIONS OFFICES

Canada

Montreal
Reptour-Pan Am (G.S.A.)
1801 McGill College Ave.
514–288–4204

Toronto
Suite 402
80 Bloor St. West
416–368–2941

U.S.

Alaska	800–227–3052	*Hawaii*	800–227–3052
California		*Illinois*	
Beverly Hills/Santa Monica/		Chicago	332–4900
West Los Angeles	274–9935		
Glendale—Pasadena	247-1513	*Maryland*	
Long Beach/Compton	639-7440	Baltimore	685–2115
Los Angeles	670–7301		
Oakland (East Bay Area)	835–2900	*Nevada*	
Orange County	638-8800	Las Vegas	384–2997
Palo Alto/Redwood City	364–1921		
Sacramento	441–7212	*New Jersey*	
San Diego	234–7321	Newark *en espanol*	*643–3172*
San Fernando Valley/			
Van Nuys	787–6100	*New York*	
San Francisco	397–5200	New York City	
San Jose	244–9411	Manhattan/Bronx	687–2600
South San Francisco	583–5632	Staten Island/Brooklyn	
		Queens	625–5555
District of Columbia/		*en espanol*	*986–5940*
(Washington)	845–8000		
		Oregon	
Florida		Portland	227–6671
Fort Myers	334–2141		
Ft. Lauderdale	462–6600	*Texas*	
Miami	874–5000	Austin	476–7511
en espanol	*874–4455*	Dallas	988–0456
Orlando	422–0701	Houston	447–0088
St. Petersburg/			
Clearwater	822–4261	*Virginia*	
Tampa	229–0951	Norfolk/	
West Palm Beach	683–2500	Virginia Beach	627–2391

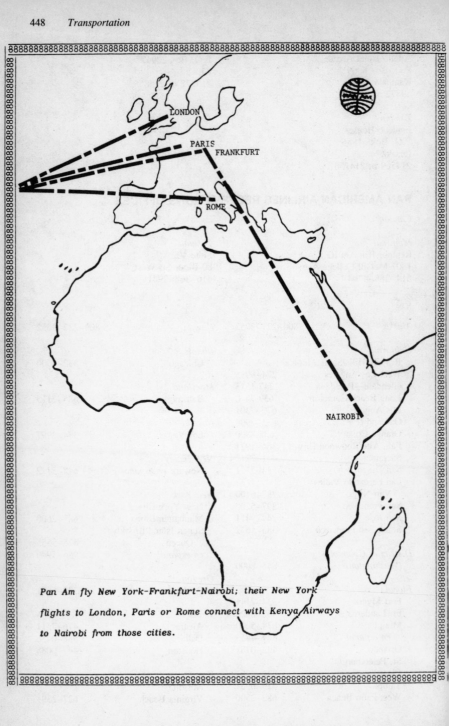

Pan Am fly New York-Frankfurt-Nairobi; their New York flights to London, Paris or Rome connect with Kenya Airways to Nairobi from those cities.

Washington
Seattle   447–9001

United Kingdom

London
193 Piccadilly
14 Old Park Lane
120 Cheapside
(01) 409 0688

Saudi Arabia

Al-Khobar
c/o Ace Travel, 16th & Rahman sts.
894 3122 or 894 2977

Dhahran Airport
P.O. Box 6
894 2977

Jeddah
c/o Ace Travel, Niowi Al Mudun St.
P.O. Box 6152
6533102 or 06

Riyadh
Intercontinental Hotel
4648810

Yanbu
c/o Ace Travel, Ahmed Khalaf Building
P.O. Box 860
322 5663

Australia

Adelaide
Taa Building, 144 North Terrace
512821

For all areas not shown
above   800–221–1111

Brisbane
307 Queen St.
07 221 7477

Canberra
Scott House, 219 London Circuit
489184

Darwin
Ansett Airlines, Mitchell St.
803211

Melbourne
233 Collins St.
654 4788

Perth
178 St. George Terrace
3212719

Sydney
14 Martin Pl.
233 1111

New Zealand

Auckland
3 Shortland St.
793800

Christchurch
Airline International Marketing Services
152 Hereford St.
61736

Wellington
Airline International Marketing Service
26 Brandon St.
720470

Pan American Airlines Reservations Offices

Egypt
EMECO Travel
2 Talaat Harb St.
Cairo
760307 or 757202

Gabon
c/o Air Afrique
Boul. de l'Independence
Libreville
72 17 07

Kenya
Hilton International Hotel Lobby
P.O. Box 30544
Nairobi
23581

Malawi
c/o Air Malawi
Robins Road, Blantyre
633111

c/o Air Malawi
Lilongwe
720966

Morocco
c/o Royal Air Maroc
44 Av. Forces Armees Royales
Casablanca
314141

Nigeria
290 A Akin Adeshola St.
Victoria Island
P.O. Box 2311, Lagos
610706 or 07 or 08

Senegal
2 Pla. de l'Independence
B.P. 480, Dakar
22–57–86

Tanzania
Kilimanjaro Hotel
P.O. Box 1428, Dar-es-Salaam
21747 or 23526

ROYAL AIR MAROC RESERVATIONS OFFICES

Canada
1001 de Maisonneuve Ouest
Suite 440
Montreal, Quebec H3A 3C8
514–285–1619

U.S.
666 Fifth Ave.
New York, NY 10013
212–974–3850 or 974–3853

United Kingdom
174 Regent St.
London W.1.
734 5943 or 54; 439 4361 or 62

Saudi Arabia
c/o Arab Wings
Ibrahim Shakeer Building
P.O. Box 5580, Jeddah
(02) 6446475 or 6447197

c/o Wahat Al Jazira
R. Alabraiin St./Almalaz
Riyadh
01 4789038 or 4789597

Australia and New Zealand
Qantas represents Royal Air Maroc.

Royal Air Maroc Reservations Offices in Africa

Abidjan, Ivory Coast
Immeuble "LA Paris"
Boul. Botreau Roussel
B.P. 2413
32 20 79

Alexandria, Egypt
c/o Agent General de ventes Azzahra
  Travel
26, Alghorfa Attijaria St.
(We had great difficulty with the
Alexandrian travel agent we used to
confirm our Kenya Airways reservations:
"the computer was down" for 3 days;
we advise calling directly to the Royal
Air Maroc office in Cairo—see below.)

Cairo, Egypt
9, Al Boustan St.
74 29 56 or 75 05 61 or 74 03 78

Conakry, Guinea
Av. de la Republique
B.P. 1151 Bis
444 559

Dakar, Senegal
1 Pl. de l'Independence
B.P. 3324
21 37 20 or 223 667

Libreville, Gabon
Hall de l'Hotel Okoume Palace Inter-
  Continental
73 10 25

Malabo, Equatorial Guinea
Av. Independencia No. 20
2000

Santa Isabel
RAM 3121

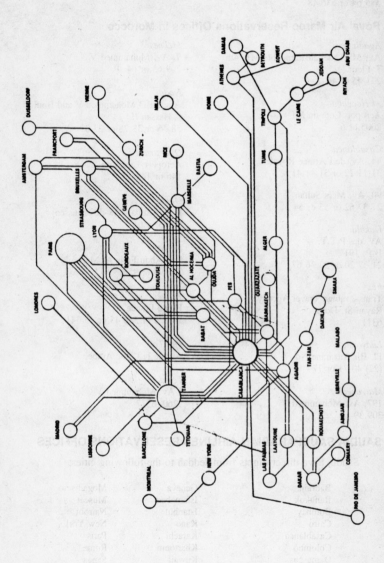

Nouakchott, Mauritania
c/o Air Mauritania
Avenue Gamel Abdel Nasser
Immeuble Smar, B.P. 1190
535 64 or 536 48

Tunis, Tunisia
45 Av. Habib Bourguiba
Le Colisee
249 611 or 249 016

Royal Air Maroc Reservations Offices in Morocco

Agadir
Av. M. Abdellah Immeuble M1, 4th
  Floor
231 45 or 46

Al Hoceima
Aeroport Cote du Rif
2005 or 6

Casablanca
44, Av. de l'Armee Royale
31 11 22 or 31 41 41

90, Av. Mers Sultan
27 37 52 or 53 or 54

Dakhla
Av. des P.T.T.
B.P. 191
21 37 20 or 22 36 67

Fes
Trans-Arabian Travel Agency
Rayan St.-Doha
6311

Laayoune
Pl. Bir Anzarane No. 7
(22) 40 71 or 77

Marrakech
197, Av. Mohammed V
309.39

Meknes
7, Av. Mohammed V
209.63 or 64

Nador
Angle-BD Mohammed V and Boul.
  Hassan II
38 46 or 38 78 or 23 37

Ouarzazate
Aeroport Taouirirte
146 or 148

Oujda
Hotel Oudja (Rex-de-chaussee)
39 63 or 64

Rabat
Rue Abou Faris Al Marini
215 94 or 95

Tanger
Pl. de France
347 22 or 340 45 or 45 341

Tan Tan
Av. de la Ligue Arabe

Tetouan
5 Av. Mohammed V
2260–6577

SAUDIA SAUDI ARABIAN AIRLINES RESERVATIONS OFFICES

Saudia have direct flights from Jeddah to the following cities:

Bahrain	Geneva	Mogadiscio
Bangkok	Islamabad	Muscat
Bombay	Istanbul	Nairobi
Cairo	Kano	New York
Casablanca	Karachi	Paris
Colombo	Khartoum	Rome
Damascus	Kuwait	Sanaa
Delhi	London	Singapore
Dubai	Madrid	Tripoli
El Djazair (Algiers)	Manila	Tunis
Frankfurt		

Saudia offers more gateways to round-the-world travel than any other airline through Frankfurt, Geneva, Istanbul, London, Paris, Rome, Seoul, Singapore, Manila, and New York.

Canada
Use toll-free U.S. number
800–223–0468

U.S.
747 Third Ave.
29th Floor
New York, NY 10017
212–758–4991

New York State: 800–221–6744

2049 Century Park East
Suite 2000
Los Angeles, CA
213–552–9000
California: 800–252–2161
Elsewhere: 800–223–0468

1990 Post Oak Blvd., Suite 910
Houston, TX 77056
713–850–7227

United Kingdom
171 Regent St.
London W1R 7FB
(01) 995 7777

Egypt
Cairo: 741200 or 741999
Alexandria: 807330

Kenya
Nairobi: 334270 or 331456

Nigeria
Kano: 7198

Somalia
via Brava, P.O. Box 2916
Mogadiscio
21028 or 22216

Sudan
Gamhoria St.
Omer a/Salam Building, P.O. Box 2041
Khartoum
80413 or 80416

India
Express Towers
Nariman Point
Bombay, India 400 021
2020049

Saudia Hansalya Building
15-Barakhmba Rd.
New Delhi 110–001
40466 or 40467

Saudia Saudi Arabian Airlines Reservations Offices in Saudi Arabia

Abha
Main St.
224 6666

Abqaiq
c/o Saudi Tourist & Travel Bureau
Alshafi Motel Building
St. number 35
(03) 566 1845

Al-Aflaj
c/o Al Musfar Travel
P.O. Box 8040
Riyadh
(01) 682 0265

Ad-Dillum
c/o Falcon Travel Agency
P.O. Box 14
(01) 544 6600 ext. 265

Al-Ghat
c/o Eastern Travel & Tourism
P.O. Box 35
(06) 442 1818

Al-Hariq
c/o Debbas Tours
P.O. Box 9254
Riyadh
476 2123

Al-Khabra
c/o M.S. Al-Muazzin Tourism & Travel
  Agency

Al-Khafji
c/o G.S.A. Ace Travel Shafi
Shafi Building
Khafji Lane
P.O. Box 92
(03) 766 2304

Arar
Saudi Reservations
P.O. Box 397
Alshadly
662 1888

Baha
Alagig Rd.
(07) 725 2480

Bahra
GSA-Saudia
c/o Saudi Tourist & Travel Bureau
Main Rd.
591 1777

Bisha
622 6262 or 6268

Dammam
P.O. Box 4636
(03) 833 1865

Dhahran
P.O. Box 126
894 3333

Gassim
323 4804
(Buraidah) 323 3333

Hafer-Al-Batin
c/o Najd Travel & Tourism
P.O. Box 196
(03) 722 0024

Hail
532 0105

Hofuf
582 4780 or 582 4660
(King Faisal University) 587 0936

Jeddah
632 3333
(Saudia Plaza office) 642 7836
(Medina Road office) 665 3755 or
  665 3765

Jouf
King Abdul Aziz St.
624 4444 or 624 5555

Jubail
Jeddah St./Jubail St.
361 1925 or 361 0353 or 361 3333 or
  361 0165

Khureis
c/o G.S.A. Saudi Tourist & Travel
  Bureau
Central Province Area
P.O. Box 3519, Riyadh
401 2985

Makkah
Al-Nuzha St.
543 3333 or 544 5121

Medina
King Abdul Aziz St.
836 2222
(Sultana office) 823 3615 or 823 3362
(Islamic University office) 822 4080
(Quba office) 823 3585 or 823 3357

Nejran
Main St., P.O. Box 286
522 3333

Qaisumah
(03) 833 3077

Qatif
Ali Bin Abu Talib Rd.
855 3333 or 855 4114 or 855 5225 or
  855 5555

Rabigh
c/o Arabian Commercial Enterprise
Prince Abdullah, Alfaisal Building
P.O. Box 6152, Jeddah
642 3731 or 643 1151

Rafha
P.O. Box 397
King Soud St.
Al Shadly Building
662 2222

Ras Tanura
Yusuf Bin Ahmedhanoo Travel Agency
Kanoo Building, P.O. Box 711
(03) 667 0388

Riyadh
477 2222 or 477 3333
Reconfirmation: 476 0739

Sabia
c/o M.S. Samara Travel Agency
P.O. Box 065
326 1008 or 326 0356

Safwa
c/o Saudi Tourist & Travel Agency
Main St.
(03) 664 2376 or 664 2380

Saihat
c/o Almuazzin Tourism & Travel Agency
Qatif Rd., P.O. Box 230
(03) 850 0644 or 850 2472

Salboukh
c/o Almuazzin Tourism & Travel Agency
M.S. Al-Ahmadia Est. for Traveling &
  Tourist

Sharurah
532 1665 or 532 1666

Sudier
c/o Alsarh Travel
(06) 432 1051

Tabuk
423 3333

Taif
733 3333

Turaif
(04) 652 1555

Udhailiyah
c/o Al-Jindan Travel Agency
Haradh St.

Wedjh
G.S.A. Saudia, New Market St.
442 1054

Yanbu
Building 3335, Royal Commission
  Compound
P.O. Box 500
(04) 322 4422 or 322 4433

SINGAPORE AIRLINES RESERVATIONS OFFICE

Head offices: SIA Building, 77 Robinson Rd., Singapore 0106, tel: 5456666. Singapore Airlines has direct flights from Singapore to the following cities:

Abu Dhabi	Dubai	Melbourne
Adelaide	Frankfurt	Osaka
Amsterdam	Hong Kong	Paris
Athens	Honolulu	Penang
Auckland	Jakarta	Perth
Bahrain	Karachi	Rome
Bangkok	Kuala Lumpur	San Francisco
Beijing	London	Seoul
Bombay	Los Angeles	Shanghai
Brisbane	Madras	Sydney
Brussels	Male (Maldive Islands)	Taipei
Cairo	Malta	Tokyo
Canberra	Manila	Vienna
Copenhagen	Mauritius	Zurich
Dhahran	Medan	

Singapore Airlines has offices in Egypt at the Nile Hilton Hotel (tel: 762702 or 762492). They also list agents on Cornish El Nil in Cairo, and an agent in

Singapore Airlines Offices and Sales Agents

Canada

Toronto	85 Richmond St. West, Suite 800, Toronto, Ontario M5H 2C9	416-366-7555
Vancouver	P.O. Box 49334, Suite 1994, Four Bentall Centre, 1055 Dunsmuir St.	604-689-1223
	Vancouver B.C., Canada V6X IL4	
	For British Columbia/Alberta	800-663-3046
	For Soskatoon/Manitoba	800-663-1417

United States of America

Atlanta	230 Peachtree St. N.W., Suite 305, Atlanta, GA 30303	800-742-3333
Chicago	6 North Michigan Ave., Suite 1304, Chicago IL 60602	800-742-3333
Dallas	1111 West Mockingbird Lane, Suite 925, Dallas, TX 75247	800-742-3333
Honolulu	Pioneer Plaza, 900 Fort St. Mall, #1110, Honolulu, HI 96813	808-524-6063
Houston	3701 Kirby St., #1290, Houston, TX 77098	800-742-3333
Los Angeles	8350 Wilshire Blvd., Beverly Hills, CA 90211-2381	800-742-3333
Miami	200 South Miami Ave., #286, Downtown Center, Miami, FL 33130	800-742-3333
New York	535 Fifth Ave., Suite 1206, New York, NY 10017	800-742-3333
San Francisco	476 Post St., San Francisco, CA 94108	800-742-3333
Washington, DC	1050 17th St., N.W., Suite 400, Washington, DC 20036	800-742-3333

United Kingdom

London	143-147 Regent St., London W.1	(01) 747 0007
Birmingham	7th Floor, The Rotunda, New St., Birmingham B2 4PA	(021) 643 5171
Glasgow	5th Floor, Stock Exchange House, St. George's Place, Glasgow G2 1BU	(041) 204 0656
Manchester	3rd Floor, Macintosh House, Market Pl., Shambles Sq., Manchester M4 3AF	(061) 832 3346

Saudi Arabia

Damman	GSA—Yusuf bin Ahmed Kanoo, P O Box 37, Damman	864 1992
		894 6814
Dhahran	Kaki Building, Prince Nasser St., P O Box 1760, Alkhobar 31952	864 6025
	Airline Centre, King Abdul Aziz Blvd., P.O. Box 1760, Alkhobar 31952	895 1515
Riyadh	GSA—Saudi Tourist & Travel Bureau P O Box 3519 King Faisal Foundation Building	465 6791
	Oleyya, Riyadh	
Jeddah	GSA—Arab Wings Travel & Tourism Agency Kaki Centre, Medina Rd. North	667 4345
	P O Box 1620, Jeddah	667 1690

Australia

Adelaide	38 Currie St., Adelaide, South Australia 5000	(08) 212 3656
Brisbane	Ground Floor, United Dominions House, 127 Creek St., Brisbane, Queensland 4000	(07) 221 6300
Canberra	Wales Centre, 211-219 London Circuit, Canberra City ACT 2601	(062) 474 122

Hobart	185 Liverpool St., Hobart, Tasmania 7000	(002) 347 955
Melbourne	Singapore Airlines House, 414 Collins St., Melbourne, Victoria 3000	(03) 602 4555
Newcastle	5th Floor, Mercantile Mutual Building, 456/458 Hunter St., Newcastle, NSW 2300	(049) 24511
Perth	Grain Pool Building, 172 St. George's Terrace, Perth W A 6000	(09) 322 2422
Sydney	Singapore Airline House, 17-19 Bridge St., Sydney, NSW 2000	(02) 231 3522
Townsville	350/352 Flinders St., Chit Chat Arcade, Ground Floor, Townsville Northern Queensland	(077) 713171

New Zealand

Auckland	Lower Ground Floor, West Plaza Building, Corner of Customs and Albert sts. P.O. Box 4290, Auckland 1	32129
Christchurch	Ground Floor, A.M.P. Building, Cathedral Square, P.O. Box 78 Christchurch	68099
Wellington	Norwich Insurance House, 3/11 Hunter St., Wellington	739749

Alexandria. However, we will save readers the possible frustration of working through agents. We asked that our tickets be confirmed by the representative (a travel agency) of our airline in Alexandria. After our calling them over a period of three days they sent a note to our hotel saying that they could not get through to the airline. Just another example that if there isn't a direct profit for an Egyptian travel agent most of them don't bother to perform a service.

Readers flying Singapore Airlines changing to Kenya Airways in Bombay may find the address of the first carrier helpful. They are located in the Air India Building, on the ground floor, Naiman Point, Bombay 400021, tel: 2023365. The number at the airport is 6320700, ext. 531.

QANTAS AIRLINES RESERVATIONS OFFICES

Head Office: Qantas International Centre, International Square, Sydney, Australia, tel. 436 6111.

Qantas Airlines has direct flights from Sydney to the following cities:

Adelaide	Denpasar	Nadi
Amsterdam	Frankfurt	Noumea
Athens	Haráre	Papeete
Auckland	Hong Kong	Perth
Bahrain	Honolulu	Port Moresby
Bangkok	Jakarta	Rome
Beijing	Kuala Lumpur	San Francisco
Belgrade	London	Singapore
Bombay	Los Angeles	Tokyo
Brisbane	Manila	Wellington
Christchurch	Melbourne	

Qantas Airlines Offices and Sales Agents

Canada
Toronto	800 Bloor St.W., suite 1704	tel. 800 663 3423 or 922 3593

United States
New York	542 Fifth Ave.	tel. 800 227 4500 or (212) 764 0215
Washington, D.C.	1825 K St.N.W., suite 1210	tel. 800 227 4500 or (202) 223 3033

United Kingdom
Birmingham	36 Paradise St.	
Bristol	36–38 Baldwin St., 1st Flr.	034 574 7767
Glasgow	128 Buchanan St.	(toll free)
Leeds	11 Albion St., 2nd Flr.	
London	169 Regent St.	
	394–405 King St., Hammersmith	tel. 748 5050
	144A Brompton Rd., Knightsbridge	
	Arundel Great Court, Strand	

Saudi Arabia
Jeddah	Attar Travel, Medina Rd.	tel. 651 3541
Riyadh	Riyadh Tours & Travel Services, King Faisal Foundation Complex, Makkah Rd., Aloya	tel. 465 9839

Australia

Adelaide	14 King William St.	
	211 Victoria Sq.	
	Colonnades Shopping Ctr.,	tel. 218 8541
	Beach Rd. Noarlunga Ctr.	
	Parabanks Shopping Ctr.,	
	John St. Salisbury	
Brisbane	262 Adelaide St.	tel. 833 3747
Cairns	13 Spence St.	tel. 008 226 449
		(toll free)
Canberra	Qantas House, 197 London Circuit	tel. 75 5518
Darwin	Bennett St. and The Mall	tel. 82 3355
Hobart	77 Elizabeth Mall-Hobart	tel. 008 11 2121
	Tasmania outside Hobart	toll free
Melbourne	233 Collins St.	
	114 Williams St.	
	Shop 20, Collins Pl., 45 Collins St.	tel. 602 6111
	795 Burke Rd., Camberwell	
	361 Lonsdale St., Dandenong	
	321 Chapel St., Prahran	
Newcastle	400 Hunter St.	tel. 69 0918
Perth	Wesley Ctr., 93 Williams St.	
	Shop 1, McNess Royal Arcade,	tel. 322 0222
	Hay St. Mall	
Palmerston	NZI Building, The Square	tel. 8 6184
Port Hedland	Wedge & Anderson Sts. (AWA)	tel. 73 1777
Sydney	Head office—International Centre—see above	
	Bondi Junction, 237 Oxford St.	tel. 387 7466
	Chatswood, 387 Victoria Ave.	tel. 419 2356
	Hurstville, 247 Forest Rd.	tel. 570 6444
	Liverpool, 255 George St.	tel. 821 1122
	North Sydney, 141 Walker St.	tel. 957 2555
	Parramatta, 248 Church St.	tel. 635 7199
Townsville	280 Finder's Mall	tel. 008 22 6449
		(toll free)

New Zealand

Auckland	154 Queen St.	tel. 79 0306
Christchurch	CML Bldg., Cathedral Sq.	tel. 79 3100
Dunedin	Civic Ctr. Arcade, The Octagon	tel. 77 0742
Hamilton	Regency House, Ward St., Flr. 3	tel. 8 0319
Wellington	Featherstone & Panama Sts.	tel. 73 8378

India

Bombay	Hotel Oberoi Towers, Nariman Pt., HC Level	tel. 202 0343 or
		202 9288

Car Rental

We have made a strenuous effort to write about only those things we have actually done; to review only hotels where we have actually stayed; to recommend only services we have tried. It has not been possible to do this in every case, and on the occasions we have had to simply "report" we have indicated this.

On the subject of rental cars, we prefer Avis because theirs are the only cars we have rented in over 30 years of driving. We confine renting cars to Avis because of their policy of sending a new car out to clients if the original vehicle breaks down. We are not aware of any other car rental agency that follows this policy. We personally have better things to do than sit in a garage all day while a rental car is being repaired. Some agencies want every car out all the time and leave no reserve as backup. It's more profitable to let the client sit in a garage five or six hours and give a discount than have another car idle.

Not all Avis agencies are efficiently run; where we have tried to rent an Avis and found the service unsatisfactory, as in the case of Egypt, then tried another agency, that agency has proven to be equally unsatisfactory. We have therefore come to generalize that when Avis is bad in a country, all car rental in that country is bad. This may be unfair, but that's the way we do it after spending a lot of money on trial and error.

Using smaller, cheaper, local car rental firms can be physically dangerous. There is no way they can compete with the big firms who purchase cars directly from the manufacturers in large quantities. Certainly, readers may have had good experiences with small companies; however, we are trying to give the very best advice we can to a large number of readers. For this reason, we do not feel that the risk of a small company's economies, which may endanger safety, can be taken. Automobile accidents anywhere in the world are terrible experiences; in a foreign country where there is no strong backup of a big company's power to smooth the outcome such an experience can mean a lifetime of regret.

We specify Avis because we mean Avis, not any old rental car. And then, we only recommend Avis in countries where we have had good experiences: Kenya, Malawi, and Togo for self-drive, and in Morocco only with an Avis driver. If loyal clients of other car-rental companies resent our naming Avis, we can only say that we have tried to write only about what we have actually seen and done.

On the downside, a number of people have told us that making reservations for an Avis through the U.S. Avis 800 number is anything but a pleasant experience. We, too, have experienced difficulties. We've asked Merikani Hotel Reservations Service [(USA) 301–530–1911] if they can make Avis reservations in Africa for our readers when they make the hotel reservation; they've agreed.

Our information indicates there to be no one single number in the United Kingdom for Avis, but a multitude of numbers in England, Scotland, Wales, and Northern Ireland. The number in London at Hyde Park Corner is 01–2459862; in Edinburgh it is 031–3376363, in Cardiff 0223–212551, and in Belfast it is 0232–240404. However, check your local directory if you do not live in these cities to find the office nearest you.

For readers in Saudi Arabia Avis has an office in Jeddah where the number is 651168 or 6518152; in Riyadh the number is 4761500, in Al-Khobar 8646085, and in Dhahran 8792202.

Readers in Australia will find over 130 Avis offices they can contact to reserve a car in Africa. The number in Sydney is 517.1055.

In New Zealand there are many local offices. The number in Auckland is 792–545, and in Christchurch it is 793840.

Information on driver's licenses is in "Travel Documents."

Avis in Kenya

In Nairobi there are two offices: (one in the Hilton lobby and the other on Kenyatta Ave., marked on our city map of Nairobi) and are at the airport. Their numbers are: Nairobi Hilton: 29576; Jomo Kenyatta Ave.: 336703 or 04; at the airport: 822186.

At the coast there are Avis offices at Mombasa, again at the airport and in town. Remember that Mr. Hassan, the manager for Mombasa, will always be happy to send the car to you and take you back to the office to do the paperwork if you call from Mombasa city center. (The city office is located on Kilindini Rd.; again, we've marked it on our map.) The relevant telephone numbers are: Mombasa office: 23048; at the airport: 433211.

There is also an Avis office at Malindi, in Sitawi House. The telephone number is Radio call 35 Y 3.

There is a stiff drop-off charge for customers wanting to rent a car in either Mombasa or Nairobi and drop it off in the opposite city.

Unlike Avis rentals in the U.S., it is not necessary to have a credit card to rent a car; a substantial deposit can be made instead—meaning the equivalent of US$300 depending upon how long the car is wanted. Kenya Avis takes the following credit cards: American Express, Diners Club, Air Travel Card, and Barclacard, as well as their own Avis Worldwide Charge Card.

Minimum age for a rental is 25 and the driver must have been in possession of his/her home driver's license for two years.

Avis in Malawi

In Malawi Avis has a rental desk at the international airport in Lilonge, at the domestic airport outside Blantyre, as well as offices in Blantyre. There is a telephone marked "Avis" on the counter at the Capital Hotel Front Desk. When we were in Malawi some creative wiring had been done to make this phone ring an Avis competitor. If you use this phone, which is very convenient, make sure you have truly contacted the Avis office; if another car-rental company's car shows up, don't hesitate to refuse to rent it. See Mr. Holdridge, the general manager of the Capital Hotel, and he'll soon put a stop to any hanky-panky.

Avis Malawi has an excellent Subaru four-wheel drive saloon car that we used. They also have a 12-seater bus that they rent with a driver. There's plenty of room for everyone's baggage and it's practically new. The only fault we'd find with it would be the gas (petrol) consumption, but if a number of people are sharing the cost, this becomes relative. They also have a 4 × 4 Survey Truck that sleeps four.

A cash deposit—the amount is negotiable at the time of rental—is accepted in lieu of a credit card, but the major credit cards are accepted: American Express, Diners Club, and although the brochure does not say so, we imagine Barclacard.

The car, like the cars in Kenya, can meet clients at the airport or hotel. One-way rentals can be arranged, but generally speaking the cars should be returned to the renting station.

We want to assure you that Avis Malawi cars can go into Zambia if the driver so requests.

Avis in Togo

The only office is at 252, Boule. Circulaire, Lome, tel: 21.59.80 or 21.05.82. If your French isn't up to your English, you may want to ask the front desk clerk at the Hotel 2 du Fevrier to call them when you're ready for the car, although there will be an English-speaking agent in the Avis office to complete the form.

We feel the Peugeot 504 or 505 would be the best, most reliable car—these are class D and E cars respectively. Failing these, the Toyota, a class B car. We've observed that in Africa class A and B cars are often interchangeable and charged at the class A price. We don't feel readers will need a driver once they've managed to find the main highway north.

Avis-Togo takes American Express, Diners Club, and VISA.

Shipping Your Car

Unless you intend to spend several months in Africa it is not economic to ship your car and ship it back. There are strict regulations governing the sale of vehicles in most African countries, and while the car most certainly can be sold, there is a lot of paperwork to be done before the sale can be completed. This means chasing around several government offices to obtain necessary clearances, and in many countries there is an import tax to pay before the vehicle can be handed over. Notwithstanding the foregoing, a profit can be made if the vehicle is one that is well known in Africa. This usually means Mercedes, Toyota, Nissan, Subaru, Suzuki, and most popular of all, Peugeot.

A Carnet de Passages en Douances must be obtained before you can ship the car from home. Information on this documentation and all other necessary information can be obtained from your nearest automobile club.

If you do decide to ship your car, make certain that you also ship basic spare parts as they are often in short supply.

You can purchase a car once you've arrived in Africa—a secondhand one—people wait months for new cars—and then sell it when you're ready to leave. In this case the paperwork will have been done by the previous owner. Most people make their money back on the car providing it's been reasonably well treated and not involved in an accident. At the worst, provided you've struck a good deal initially, the price you receive will be only slightly under what you've paid. A good person to "talk cars" to is the driver of your country's ambassador. He's likely to know what's available and to be on your side in any deal.

Taxis

In Kenya and Egypt, where the government is actively involved in the tourist industry, apart from privately owned taxis, the government also operates a taxi service. In both Kenya and Egypt Mercedes cars are used and are referred to as "limos." They are not limos by our definition of the word, but four-door saloon cars.

Egypt: Misr Limos: The fares are controlled and posted at the Ramses Hilton International entrance—unfortunately, only at one entrance when we were in Cairo, so that if you happen to go to the wrong entrance, there's no way to check the fare. The cars and drivers are very reasonable and extremely good. However, should a Saudi sheik want a car, despite the fact that a humbler guest has reserved one for an appointed hour, the shiek gets the car. We hope if we draw this to the attention of Hilton they will straighten this out, as we recommend using only Misr Limos for reasons given in "Background for Egypt."

Kenya: Kenatco: This Kenyan government-owned company has been through some ups and downs but it appears to be leveling out, and our more recent experiences in the past 3 years have been very good. Previously, the drivers were overcharging and were in collusion with some hotel doormen. The Kenatco fares are posted to the left, facing the front entrance, of the Nairobi Hilton just behind a small stand. As prices are just a bit more than private taxis, we suggest using Kenatco whenever a car is available. A Kenatco stand is outside the Mount Kenya Safari Club, Nairobi (Lillian Towers).

Privately operated taxis in Africa are generally held together with bits of binder twine and baling wire. There is absolutely no possibility that a reputable insurance company would insure them. On the whole, the driving is good as much for the reason that the cars simply cannot make high speeds as for the drivers' caution. There is usually a government inspection of vehicles, but as our hometown, Washington, DC, has come under suspicion on the subject of the issuance of stickers to taxis, we have no justification for throwing stones. The bottom line is, however, that should an accident occur in one of these privately operated taxis, there virtually would be no insurance coverage available to passengers. The cars really are in terrible shape and readers are cautioned strongly about using them. It's always much better to (a) walk to your destination, (b) use a government-operated vehicle, or (c) rent an Avis if you're planning to do any running around.

Japanese pickup trucks have been fashioned into "bush taxis" as they are called in West Africa, and "matatoos" as they are called in East Africa. The bed of the pickup is enclosed with a shell; usually made in Africa, not Japan. Along both sides of the bed a strong wooden or metal bench is usually (not always) bolted or soldered to the floor. Such seating can carry 5 people on each bench in reasonable comfort. In practice 8 or 9 people sit on each bench. Some enterprising matatoo operators have had a bar installed bisecting the roof for use as a handrail. Passengers can then crouch in half-standing positions in the tiny aisle between the benches.

We used to ride matatoos regularly, until the evening we missed the last bus to Diani Beach and shared one with 27 other people. Leah has absolutely refused to ride one again. Some of the pleasure of African travel has diminished for me since that day; a matatoo ride, especially if it is a long one, is good fun. We have never had our pockets picked, and Leah has never experienced wandering male hands. As for danger, the risks are incalcuable, they are so great. Matatoo drivers are, generally speaking, notorious daredevils who habitually pass on a hill, on a curve, in the face of oncoming traffic; you name when not to pass, and they do. When a crash occurs—and most often it is between two matatoos traveling in the opposite direction during an overtaking pass—the carnage is exactly that—a slaughter, because so many passengers are involved.

In Kenya there are several companies running combination long-distance taxi-cum-bus services; these make better time than the government-operated buses and are slightly more expensive. Their drivers are usually more cautious, but not always, than matatoo drivers. The vehicles used are especially equipped Mercedes 9-seater mini-buses or Peugeot station wagons (estate cars).

Buses

Most African countries operate government-owned buses that not only drive city routes but also connect major cities and towns. These are like U.S. school buses, but made, in former British colonies, by Leyland.

There is a "bus park" in the center of most African cities where passengers board the bus as well as stops along the way, but for long-distance travel, like our long-distance buses, pick-ups are generally only at major points.

The buses are usually in poor condition and as it appears to us Leyland has never heard of shock absorbers, the ride is inclined to be rough. Still, the drivers are more cautious than matatoo drivers, and on the whole their records are better than the privately owned vehicles, it appears. Where the government-owned buses are a menace is to pedestrians. Never, never believe you'll intimidate an African public bus driver and force him to let his foot find the brake. It won't. They also pull away from the curb without warning, and only the agile should contemplate using them for transportation.

Bus routes in Kenya

Nairobi-Mombasa: The train connects Nairobi with Mombasa but stops for passengers at very few stations. Privately owned buses—the Gold Line, etc— make the journey on a daily basis and the driver will stop and let passengers off wherever they like. The fares are cheaper than by train and the bus trip takes slightly less time than by train. Upon arrival in Nairobi or Mombasa at night the driver usually takes passengers to their homes or hotel. The buses are comfortable but not Greyhound or Gray Lines and have no toilet facilities. Stops are made twice between these two major cities, and passengers are allowed to get out and stretch their legs and have something to eat. All the same, the trip is tiring—the train, if a night sleeper is used, is very relaxing. Mombasa Peugot Service is a privately owned minibus, and despite the name, usually utilizes a Mercedes bus. They go very fast, and numerous accidents have been reported.

Mombasa-Lunga Lunga: A government-owned bus that goes to the Kenyan-Tanzanian border town of Lunga Lunga can be picked up on the south bank of Likoni Ferry. There is a border post with immigration and customs processing. Whether there is a connecting bus on the Tanzanian side depends upon the spare parts and fuel situation in Tanzania at any given time. A visa for Tanzania can be obtained in Mombasa, and it is important that you have a visa before you arrive in Lunga Lunga. Ensure that you have a re-entry visa for Kenya in case you encounter a problem on the Tanzanian side. Take the bus marked Lunga Lunga for any stops south of the village of Ukunda.

Mombasa-Diani Beach Another bus on the southern shore of Likoni Ferry is marked Diani Beach. This turns east at the village of Ukunda and travels the T-access road to the beach hotels.

Either the bus for Lunga Lunga or Diani Beach can be taken to go to Tiwi Beach, but it is dangerous to walk from the main road to the beach—and there is no bus service.

Mombasa: Many buses serve the city's suburbs and rather than list them here, simply ask someone to direct you.

Mombasa-Likoni Ferry: There is a bus that goes directly to Likoni Ferry from Mombasa city center. It is necessary to get off the bus and walk onto the ferry, then catch another bus on the south side.

Mombasa-Malindi: There is a government-owned bus and the Mombasa Peugout Service bus from Mombasa to Malindi. The driver will let you off anywhere along the route you desire.

Mombasa-Malindi-Garsen-Lamu: A government-owned bus operates this route, but after Malindi the going gets very tough. At one time it was necessary to cross the Juba River (after Garsen) by canoe. A ferry is now operating, but the Kenya Automobile Association should always be contacted before planning to take this bus to determine if the river is too high for the ferry.

Lamu: No vehicles of any type are permitted in Lamu. There is a parking lot with a guard where your car can be left before you take the launch to Lamu Island.

Nairobi-Kitale: There is a government-owned bus that goes from Nairobi via Naivasha, Nakuru, and Eldoret to Kitale. This bus connects with another one to Kapenguria and Konyao.

Nairobi-Meru: A bus operates from Nairobi to Meru around the western side of Mt. Kenya, stopping at Muranga, Nyeri, and Nanyuki. There is also a bus that goes around the eastern side of the mountain, but the western route is better.

Nairobi-Thika: A bus operates and can be boarded in the bus park in Nairobi.

Nairobi-Embu: There is service connecting these two towns. Board the bus at the bus parks in the respective towns.

Nairobi-Kisumu: There is bus service to Kisumu, but the train is usually more comfortable although slightly more expensive.

Nairobi-Marsabit: Travel to Marsabit is not permitted except by convoy in private cars. There is no bus service at this writing.

Nairobi-Lodwar: Private buses operate to Lodwar. Inquire at the bus park in Nairobi, but be prepared to be self-sufficient for water and food after Kitale.

Apart from the above, it is possible to get around Kenya, even the more remote places, by private matatoo. It is usually necessary to wait until the driver succeeds in getting a full load of passengers before the vehicle takes off. We use the adjective *full* advisedly, because every possible inch of space will be filled before he's ready to depart.

Bus routes in Malawi

The lake steamer is the most common means of getting around the country.

Lilongwe-Blantyre: There is excellent private bus service between these two cities (a seat can be reserved at the Capital Hotel), as well as a government-owned bus. Both are routed through Dedza, Ncheu, Balaka, and Zomba.

Blantyre-Limbe: These two towns are sister cities and only a few miles from one another. They are served by frequent bus service.

Blantyre-Monkey Bay: The route is Blantyre, Zomba, Liwonde, Monkey Bay.

Monkey Bay-Mzuzu: Via Chipoka, Salima, Nkhota Kota, Nkhata Bay.

Lilongwe-Karonga: Via Rumphi, Mzuzu, Nkhata Bay, Nkhota Kota, and Salima.

Bus routes in Mali

The bus park in Bamako is on the opposite end of the bridge from the Hotel l'Amitie. Buses run from Bamako to Mopti fairly regularly; to Gao less frequently. There are regular buses to Segou, and from Segou buses operate to Niono.

Bus routes in Somalia

There is a twice-weekly Mercedes minibus that operates between Mogadiscio and Kisimaio via Gelib.

Bus routes in Sudan

While there used to be long-distance buses connecting north and south, as we have mentioned, travel to the south is now prohibited.

Bus routes in Tanzania

Service is totally unreliable due to the lack of spare parts to repair buses and gasoline (petrol) shortages.

Bus routes in Uganda

Kampala-Jinja: Even at the worst of times, and sometimes under the worst of conditions, the bus operated between Kampala and Jinja via Mukuno. In the past there have been roadblocks where passengers were asked to get out of the bus and show their identification papers. This may or may not be the case at present.

Kampala-Entebbe: This road has been the scene of attacks on motorists and we feel that it is better to travel it only by an official airline bus.

Two-Wheeled Vehicles

Bicycles, mopeds, and motorbikes can be rented in many African beach resorts—specifically, Diani Beach in Kenya. Ask at your hotel if they're available.

In general bicyclists are dangerous to automobile drivers in Africa more so than in other countries, because many riders do not know the rules of the road. Not all Avis cars are equipped with side rearview mirrors, and if you feel these would be helpful in spotting bicyclists, you may want to bring along two of the suction attached models.

Motorcycles come under the same regulations as four-wheel vehicles.

If you want to ship a bike to Africa, the information in "Shipping Your Car" will prove helpful.

Rail Routes

Egypt

Cairo/Ismailia/Fayid/Suez
Cairo/Benha/El Zagzig/Ismailia/El Qantara West/Port Said
Cairo Pont Limoun/Suez
Cairo Main/Benha/Minuf/Tanta/Damanhur/Kafr El Dawar/Sidi Gaber/Alexandria. These trains run very frequently throughout the day and evening.
Alexandria/Cairo/Damanhur/Disuq/Tanta/Mah Roh/Qalun/Talkha/Kafr El Sheikh/Biyala/Shirbin/Damietta
Ciaro/El Zagzig/El Simbillawen/El Mansura/Talha/Shirbin/Damietta
Cairo Main/El Wasta/Beni Suef/El Fashn/Maghagha/El Minya/Abu Kerkas/Mallawi/ Dairut/Asyut/Sohag/Girga/El Balyana/Nag Hammadi/Qena/Qus/Luxor/Esna/Edfu/Kom Ombo/Aswan/El Sadd el Ali
Cairo/Alexandria/Sidi Gaber/Moharram Bey/El Amriya/El Hammam/El Alamein/El Dabaa/Similla/Mersa Matruh/Similla/El Salloum
Cairo Main/El Wasta/El Faiyum
Cairo/Helwan

Gabon

The Transgabonais Railways had operated only between Libreville and Ndjole until Dec. 29, 1986. On that date, amid much ceremony, the line was opened all the way to Franceville. The 650 km of track had taken 12 years to lay at a cost of US$4 billion. Franceville is the home town of Gabon's President Bongo, but apart from proving his loyalty to his kinfolk, the line will transport Gabon's beautiful hardwoods to the Atlantic Ocean for export. Previously, these had been shipped by road or by river through the Congo's Port Noire. The World Bank had refused to finance the construction of the line and it fell to European investors to find the money. Six million trees were cut to make way for the tracks, which passes through true African tropical forests, swamps, and even over mountains.

At the present time the major population of Gabon is in Libreville and along the Atlantic coastline port cities; it is hoped that the railroad will develop Gabon's hinterland as railroads have done in so many other countries.

The Gambia

There are no rail services in The Gambia.

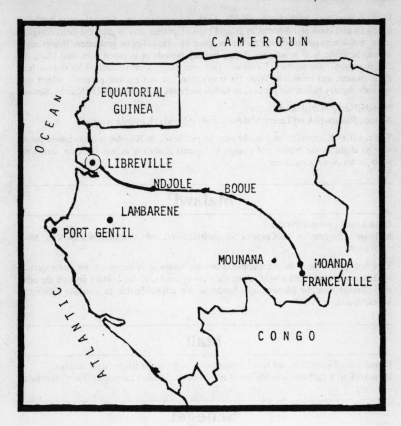

The Transgabonais Railways

Ivory Coast

Treichville / Abidjan / Anyama / Agboville / Dimbokro / Bouake / Katiola / Ninagbo / Tafire / Ferkessedougou/Ouangolodougou/Niangoloko(BurkinaFasso)/Banfora/BoboDioulasso/ Koudougou/Ouagandougou (all Burkina Fasso). First class only is recommended on this train.

Kenya

Nairboi departs 5 p.m., arrives Mombasa 7:20 a.m.   } Daily schedule. 7 days a week.
Nairobi departs 7 p.m., arrives Mombasa 8:00 a.m.   Dining car on the 7 p.m. trains
Mombasa departs 5 p.m., arrives Nairobi 7:50 a.m.   only.
Mombasa departs 7 p.m., arrives Nairobi 8:15 a.m.

First, second and third class available. First and second class have sleeping berths; 2 berths in first class and 4 berths in second class. Families may occupy the same compartment, but otherwise compartments are assigned by sex: ladies or gentlemen. Reservations should be made well in advance during holiday periods or between Nov. and Mar., the "high season" for tourists. First-class fare, one way, approximately US$30 plus bedding, dinner, and breakfast. Write for reservations; do not enclose payment, which may be made the day before the journey, to Kenya Railways (P.O. Box 30121, Nairobi, Kenya).

Nairobi/Naivasha/Nakuru/Kisumu
Nairobi/Nakuru/Eldoret/Leseru/Malaba/Tororo (Uganda)/Kampala (Uganda)

The ticket to Kampala from Nairobi may be purchased in Nairobi; it is no longer necessary to alight at the border and change to Uganda Railways as was the case during the years of Idi Amin's presidency.

Malawi

Entre Lagos/Liwonde/Nkaya
Mchinje/Lilongwe/Salima/Chipoka/Nkaya/Blantyre/Limbe/Chiromo/Nsanje/Vila Nova Fronteria

This last station is at the Mozambique border, where it is necessary for passengers to walk approximately half a mile, along the railway tracks, to the boarder post on the other side. Travel near the Mozambique border is not advisable due to guerrilla fighting in Mozambique.

Mali

Bamako/Koulikoro (this last is the embarkation port for the River Niger steamer)
Bamako/Kati/Kita/Bafoulabe/Medine/Kayes/Ambidedi/Kidira (Senegal)/Dakar (Senegal)

Senegal

St Louis/Louga/Meke/Tivaouane/Thies/Rufisque/Dakar
Dakar/Rufisque/Thies/Drourbel/Touba/Guinguineo/Kaolack/Malem Hodar/Tambacounda/Bala/Kidira (Mali)/Bamako (Mali)

Somalia

There are no rail services in Somalia. Mercedes bus between Mogadiscio-Kisimaio.

Sudan

Atbara/Ed Damer/Shendi/Khartoum Bahri/Khartoum Central
Wadi Halfa/Karima/Abu Haraz/Keheli/Abu Hamed/Dagash/El Karaba/Berber/Atbara/Khartoum

Khartoum Central/Wad Medani/Sennar Junction/Singa/Ed Damazine/Kosti/Tendelti/Umm Rawaba/Er Rahad/El Obeid/Abu Zabad/Babanusa/Nyala/Aweil/Waw
Bus Sudan/Gebeit/Haiya Junction/Atbara/Kassala/Kasham el Girba/New Halfa/Gedaref/Sennar Junction/Khartoum

Togo

Lome/Nouatja/Agbonou/Atakpame/Agbanou/Anie/Blitta
Lome/Amoussoukove/Kpalime
Lome/Port Seguro/Anecho

Uganda

Inquires should be made in person with the station master in Nairobi, Kenya, concerning the advisability of traveling on Ugandan railways before planning a trip to Uganda. The Kenyan station master will have the most up-to-date information available.

Tororo/Mbale/Kumi/Soroti/Lira/Gulu/Pakwach East
Tororo/Busembatia/Luzinga/Jinja/Lugazi/Kampala

Lake, River, and Ferry Ports

Egypt

Red Sea: Suez/Aqaba/Yanbu/Jeddah (Saudi Arabia) Contact: Misr Edco Shipping, P.O. Box 179, Alexandria, Egypt
Jeddah (Saudi Arabia)/Berbera (Somalia)/Hodeidah (Yemen)/Bur Sudan
Reportedly no passenger traffic.

Nile River: Many ships, including ships operated by hotels, sail between Luxor and Aswan/Aswan-Luxor. We recommend only the Hilton International boats as we have no first-hand experience concerning food handling and preparation on other ships. Details from any Hilton reservations operator.

Lake Nassir: El Sadd el Ali (Aswan High Dam)/Wadi Halfa (Sudan) operated by the Nile Valley River Transport Company (7 Atlas Building, Aswan, Egypt, tel: 2300). Tickets *cannot* be purchased in Cairo.

Alexandria: Information concerning ferries from Greece and Italy may be obtained from Menatours (Saad Zaghloul St., Alexandria, Egypt, tel: Alexandria 809676)

The Gambia

Ferry: Barra/Banjul
Gambia River: None (1986). Private charters available.

For details please write to Mr. M.B.O. Cham, senior tourism officer (Apollo Building, Banjul, The Gambia)

Kenya

Lake Victoria: Kisumu/Kendu Bay/Homa Bay/Karungu Reservations: Kenya Railways (P.O. Box 30121, Nairobi, Kenya)
Kisumu/Mwanza (Tanzania)
Lakes Turkana, Nakuru, Baringo, Naivasha: Private hire boats only: Turkana: Lake Na-

kuru inquire Lion Hill Camp (P.O. Box 45627, Nairobi): Baringo and Naivasha arrange for boat hire through Block Hotel's Reservations (P.O. Box 47557, Nairobi).

Tana River: Boat for hire at Baomo Lodge tented camp. Inquire Automobile Assn. Travel Service (P.O. Box 40087, Nairobi, Kenya. Tel. 742926).

Mombasa: Regular services used to ply between Mombasa, other east African ports, the Persian Gulf, and India but these services have been discontinued for some years. It is sometimes possible to hitch a ride on a cement boat; this is entirely at the captain's discretion and very seldom obtained. 8-hour Arab dhow trips along the coast can be reserved through Nilestar Safaricentre (P.O. Box 42291, Nairobi, Kenya) or at their office in Mombasa in Ambalal House Arcade. Fishing boats for hire are given in the fishing safaris. For ocean voyages see "Freighter Passenger's Safari."

Ferry Services: Mombasa Island/Likoni: Operate continuously from 6 a.m. to 1 a.m. and every half hour between 1 a.m. and 5:30 a.m.

Kilifi Creek: Operates continuously; less frequently at night.

Garsen Ferry (for Lamu): Daylight hours only. Subject to flooding Nov.-Mar. Check road conditions with Automobile Assn. Kenya (tel: Mombasa 26778 or Nairobi 742926).

Malawi

Schedule for the *Ilala II* steamer on Lake Malawi: Reservations can be made not more than 2 months ahead. Allow 6–7 weeks for a reply from the date your letter is mailed. Reservations can also be made through Merikani Hotel Reservations Service (tel: (USA) 301-530-1911), who will telex their contact in Malawi.

	Arrives	Departs
Monkey Bay		0800 Fridays
Chilinda (not shown on Michelin; on the east side of the lake)	1000	1030
Makanjila (on the east shore of the lake)	1200	1400
Chipoka (cars can be loaded or unloaded)	1700	2130
Nkhotakota	0500	0600 Saturday
Likoma Island	1230	1330
Chizumulu (not shown on Michelin; an island immediately to the west of Likoma Island)	1500	1600
Nkhata Bay (cars can be loaded or unloaded)	1930	0400 Sunday
Usisya	0630	0730
Ruarwe	0830	0930
Mlowe (not shown on Michelin; just south of Livingstonia)	1130	1230
Chitimba	1330	1430
Chilumba (cars loaded and unloaded)	1600	

Chilumba is the turn-around port; the Ilala II serves the northernmost port of Kambwe, for Karonga, only infrequently.

	Arrives	Departs
Chilumba (cars, etc.)		0400 Monday
Chitimba	0530	0630
Mlowe	0730	0830
Ruarwe	1030	1130
Usisya	1230	1330
Nkhata Bay (cars loaded and unloaded)	1600	0300 Tuesday
Chizumulu	0630	0730

	Arrives	Departs
Limoka Island	0830	1000
Nkhotakota	1600	1700
Chipoka (cars loaded and unloaded)	0200	0800 Wednesday
Makanjila	1100	1200
Chilinda	1400	1500
Monkey Bay	1750	—

Connections can be made (at Chipoka) with the train to Salima, changing for a bus to Lilongwe, and with the train from Chipoka-Limbe, Limbe-Vila Nova Fronteira. (See also train routes for Malawi in this section.)

Approximate fares: Return fares for first-class passengers Monkey Bay to Chilumba 119.99 Kwatcha; Chipoka to Chilumba return 107.81 Kwatcha. Exchange rates given in ''Basic Information Chart.'' Cars are charged according to their weight and the distance between ports. Charges are not excessive.

COMPAGNIE MALIENNE DE NAVIGATION
SERVICE EXPLOITATION
KOULIKORO

Schedule for the weekly packet boat operating between Koulikoro and Gao from mid-Aug. to mid-Nov. The service may operate before mid-Aug. and after mid-Nov. depending upon the depth of the River Niger in which case the public is advised by radio. Reservations for first and luxury cabins should be made 4 weeks in advance; second, third, and fourth class passage, 2 weeks' notice is required for reservations.

Down River

Port	Arrives		Departs		Distances Miles	Kilometers
Koulikoro			Tuesday	2200	0	0
Niamyna	Wednesdays	0400	Wednesdays	0430	56	90
Segou	Wednesdays	1030	Wednesdays	1330	113	180
Markala	Wednesdays	1630	Wednesdays	1700	144	230
Thio	Wednesdays	1800	Wednesdays	1900	150	240
Dioro	Wednesdays	2100	Wednesdays	2130	169	270
Macina	Thursdays	0130	Thursdays	0200	209	334
Diafbe	Thursdays	0500	Thursdays	0530	239	382
Mopti	Thursdays	1330	Thursdays	2000	315	504
Aka	Fridays	0500	Fridays	0530	394	630
Niafunke	Fridays	1230	Fridays	1330	456	729
Tonka	Fridays	1630	Fridays	1700	480	768
Dire	Fridays	2000	Fridays	2300	509	815
Kabara for Toum- bouctou	Saturdays	0500	Saturdays	1100	563	900
Rharous	Saturdays	2100	Saturdays	2200	654	1046
Bamba	Sundays	0200	Sundays	0230	689	1103
Bourem	Sundays	1030	Sundays	1130	758	1213
Gao	Sundays	1800			818	1308

Up River

Port	Arrives		Departs		Miles	Kilometers
					Distances	
Gao			Mondays	2000	0	0
Bourem	Tuesdays	0400	Tuesdays	0500	59	95
Bamba	Tuesdays	1400	Tuesdays	1430	128	205
Rharous	Tuesdays	1930	Tuesdays	2030	164	262
Kabara	Wednesdays	0730	Wednesdays	1500	255	408
Dire	Wednesdays	2200	Thursdays	0100	308	493
Tonka	Thursdays	0400	Thursdays	0430	338	540
Niafunke	Thursdays	0730	Thursdays	0830	362	579
Aka	Thursdays	1630	Thursdays	1700	424	678
Mopti	Fridays	0400	Fridays	0900	503	804
Diafbe	Fridays	2000	Fridays	2030	579	926
Macina	Saturdays	0000	Saturdays	0030	609	974
Dioro	Saturdays	0630	Saturdays	0700	649	1038
Thio	Saturdays	0900	Saturdays	1000	668	1068
Markala	Saturdays	1100	Saturdays	1130	674	1078
Segou	Saturdays	1630	Saturdays	1830	705	1128
Niamyna	Sundays	0230	Sundays	0300	761	1218
Koulikoro	Sundays	1100			818	1308

Schedule for the twice-monthly boat, the *Kankoun Moussa*, operating between Koulikoro and Gao from mid-Aug. to mid-Nov. The service may operate before mid-Aug. and after mid-Nov. depending upon the depth of the River Niger, in which case the public is advised by radio. Reservations for first and luxury cabins should be made 4 weeks in advance; 2nd, 3rd, and 4th class passage, 2 weeks' notice is required for reservations.

Down River

Port	Arrives		Departs		Miles	Kilometers
					Distances	
Koulikoro			Fridays	2200	0	0
Niamyna	Saturdays	0400	Saturdays	0430	56	90
Segou	Saturdays	1030	Saturdays	1330	113	180
Markala	Saturdays	1630	Saturdays	1700	144	230
Thio	Saturdays	1800	Saturdays	1900	150	240
Dioro	Saturdays	2100	Saturdays	2130	169	270
Macina	Sundays	0130	Sundays	0200	209	334
Diafarabe	Sundays	0500	Sundays	0530	239	382
Mopti	Sundays	1330	Sundays	2000	315	504
Aka	Mondays	0500	Mondays	0530	394	630
Niafunke	Mondays	1230	Mondays	1330	456	729
Tonka	Mondays	1630	Mondays	1700	480	768
Dire	Mondays	2000	Mondays	2300	509	815
Kabara for Toumbouctou	Tuesdays	0500	Tuesdays	1100	563	900

Port	Arrives		Departs		Distances Miles	Kilometers
Rharous	Tuesdays	2100	Tuesdays	2200	654	1046
Bamba	Wednesdays	0200	Wednesdays	0230	689	1103
Bourem	Wednesdays	1030	Wednesdays	1130	758	1213
Gao	Wednesdays	1800			818	1308

Up River

Port	Arrives		Departs		Distances Miles	Kilometers
Gao			Thursdays	2000	0	0
Bourem	Fridays	0400	Fridays	0500	59	95
Bamba	Fridays	1400	Fridays	1430	128	205
Rharous	Fridays	1930	Fridays	2030	164	262
Kabara for Toum-bouctou	Saturdays	0730	Saturdays	1500	255	408
Dire	Saturdays	2200	Sundays	0100	308	493
Tonka	Sundays	0400	Sundays	0430	338	540
Niafunke	Sundays	0730	Sundays	0830	362	579
Aka	Sundays	1630	Sundays	1700	424	678
Mopti	Mondays	0400	Mondays	0900	503	804
Diafarabe	Mondays	2000	Mondays	2030	579	926
Macina	Tuesdays	0000	Tuesdays	0030	609	974
Dioro	Tuesdays	0630	Tuesdays	0700	649	1038
Thio	Tuesdays	0900	Tuesdays	1000	668	1068
Markala	Tuesdays	1100	Tuesdays	1130	674	1078
Segou	Tuesdays	1630	Tuesdays	1830	705	1128
Niamyna	Wednesdays	0230	Wednesdays	0300	761	1218
Koulikoro	Wednesdays	1100			818	1308

Senegal

Dakar/Ziguinchor: Our information indicates this route is not operating.
There are regular ferries to Goree Island from Dakar (spelled Ile de Gore on the Michelin map).

Somalia

Only cargo ships call at Somali ports. However, try Somali Shipping Agency & Line (c/o Murtaza Shipping Agency, P.O. Box 81881, Mombasa, Kenya).

Sudan

The Lake Nassir steamer is jointly owned by Sudan and Egypt. For information, please refer to Egypt in this section. The steamer leaves Wadi Halfa for Aswan on Tuesdays and Thursdays.

Dongola/El Goled Bahri/Debba/Korti/Karima (changing at El Goled and Korti)
Kosti/El Jebelein/Renk/Melut/Malakal/Bor/Mongalla/Juba
Kosti/El Jebelein/Renk/Melut/Malakal/Nasir/Jikawo/Gambela

Fascinating as these last two routes are, (a) travel south of Khartoum is prohibited at this writing; (b) when the steamers do run, they do so only when there is sufficient depth of water, and (c) services did operate about every 2 weeks. Reproduced here for dreamers, like ourselves.

Tanzania

It would be interesting to know, if the ferry actually runs, as the schedules say it does, between Dar-es-Salaam and Zanzibar Island. Our information is that like all else in Tanzania, economic conditions and fuel shortages make this service erratic.

Uganda

To our knowledge, the steamer services connecting Kenya with Uganda on Lake Victoria have not been resumed, nor have the Uganda steamers to Tanzania. Inquiries: Kenya Railways & Harbours (P.O. Box 30121, Nairobi, Kenya).

Other Land Travel

Getting around Africa by land today is often a hit or miss business. Either vehicles are not in repair due to the shortage of spare parts or there is no gasoline (petrol) or diesel. For those readers who are anxious to travel by land our best advice is to join an Encounter Overland or Gerba Tours group. Both these British companies have regular, scheduled departures of specially outfitted trucks that cross Africa. Amenities are very basic, but the drivers and guides are experienced and, provided you're in good health, there can be no more exciting experience than to travel with a group of young people (the upper age limit is 40) through territory where the usual tourist never goes. Information on overlanding tours can be obtained by writing to Merikani Hotel Reservations Service, Temple Heights Station, P.O. Box 53394, Washington, DC 20009, tel. (USA) 301-530-1911. The tour prices are very reasonable and usually work out at less than US$25 a day, everything included.

Travel Documents

Always keen on introducing paperwork and bureaucracies, the British instituted in their African colonies the forerunner of South Africa's dreaded "Pass Laws." The travel document was issued in 1926 to "Manyunzu," whose father was "Munnbe." He came from the Kitui district of Kenya, and was a member of the Mkamba tribe. His circumcision age—which equates to a birth date (the boy would have been in his early teens)—is given as the year of the "snake." This may refer to the year the Uganda Railway's tracks were laid through his area as the Africans referred to the railway as the "iron snake." The pass, which was carried in a brass, water-tight case and worn around the neck on a leather thong or on the belt, was required to be carried at all times.

Unfortunately the concept of "one world" is still a long way off when it comes to traveling without documentation as to who one is and the control of contagious diseases. Two documents are always necessary for travel in Africa: an International Health Certificate and a valid passport. A visa may or may not be required, and readers should study the Basic Information Checklist to determine if they will need one.

International Health Certificate

International travelers must have an International Health Certificate documenting that they have received certain vaccinations or immunizations. The requirements vary by country. We have provided this information in the Basic Information Checklist.

The certificates are issued by Public Health authorities and some authorized physicians. They are passport-size yellow booklets with space for the public health worker or physician to certify what immunization was given, the manufacturer and batch number of the serum, and to place an official stamp.

Inquiries should be made at local Public Health offices as to where an approved clinic and/or physicians are located nearest readers' homes.

Although some African countries continue to advise that smallpox vaccinations need to be shown on these official certificates, smallpox has been erradicated. Such information on African visa applications or immigration forms can be safely ignored. Information concerning malaria is not entered on the certificate.

Passports

Readers going overseas for the first time will need to obtain passports. The following addresses and telephone numbers can be contacted to obtain passport information:

Canada: Department of External Affairs (125 Sussex Dr., Ottawa, Ontario K1A OG2, tel: 613–994–3500).

United States: U.S. Department of State Publication 8872, *Your Trip Abroad,* for sale by the Superintendent of Documents, U.S. Government Printing Office, Washington, DC 20402, has helpful and interesting information, apart from instructions on how to obtain a passport.

There are 12 passport agencies, plus the agency in Washington, DC, through which passport applications are processed. Readers should call the agency nearest their home to obtain information on how to apply. These are 24-hour, 7-day-a-week recordings.

Boston: 617–223–3831	New Orleans: 504–589–6728
Chicago: 312–353–5426	New York: 212–541–7700
Honolulu: 808–546–2131	Philadelphia: 215–597–7482
Houston: 713–229–3607	San Francisco: 415–974–7972
Los Angeles: 213–209–7070	Seattle: 206–442–7941
Miami: 305–350–5395	Stamford: 203–325–4401

Washington 202–783–8200

The recording also provides information on the office to contact to obtain emergency passports needed in less than the normal processing time.

United Kingdom: British readers should ask at their local post office for an application form for a passport; on the reverse side of the form will be a list of passport processing offices. Applications will be handled by the office appropriate to the applicant's home address.

Saudi Arabia: Readers who are Saudi citizens should take their birth certificate and the Family Registration Book to the passport office in the Department of the Interior in the city nearest their home to apply for a passport.

Australia: Australian readers should apply to their local post office for information concerning their nearest passport processing office; their post office will also have application forms.

New Zealand: Applications for a visa may be obtained from the Department of Internal Affairs nearest the readers' home; the completed application should then be returned to that office.

Department of Internal Affairs
4th Floor, T. & G. Building
17 Albert St., P.O. Box 2220
Auckland
tel: 31 184

Department of Internal Affairs
2nd Floor, Government Building
Haupapa St., P.O. Box 1146
Rotorua
tel.: 477 680

Department of Internal Affairs
2nd Floor, Local Government Building
114–118 Lambton Quay, P. O. Box 10476
Wellington
tel: 738 205

Department of Internal Affairs
M.L.C. No. 2 Building
159 Manchester St., P.O. Box 1308
Christchurch
tel: 790 209

Department of Internal Affairs
2nd Floor, Public Trust Building
442 Moray Pl., Private Bag
Dunedin
tel: 711 274

These offices are open from 9 a.m. to 4 p.m., Monday through Friday.

Passport Validity

Seasoned travelers will want to glance at their passport to confirm the expiration date goes beyond the period they intend to travel. U.S. citizens returning to the U.S. using a passport that has expired are subject to a fine of US$60. (This is just one of the interesting bits of information provided in the State Department Publication 8872, mentioned earlier.) It is a good rule of thumb to ensure the validity of the passport goes at least 2 months beyond the date of anticipated return.

Lost or Stolen Passports

Certainly no one wants to lose or have their passport stolen, but such an occurrence is not the tragedy it used to be. Readers should make a conscious effort to memorize the number and date of issue of their passport. This can save a lot of aggravation, apart from being useful information to renew a passport and when completing embarkation and disembarkation cards in and out of countries. Failing memorization, put a photocopy of the pertinent pages in the passport in a place other than where the passport is carried. As backup, leave a copy of that information with a contact at home. If your passport is lost or stolen, having this information ready or being able to call home for it, speeds up the process of issuing a new passport.

Identity photographs will be needed as well. These can be obtained in every African capital city, but if you have spare passport pictures, take them with you and, like the information concerning the passport number and date of issue, keep them separate from the passport.

It goes without saying that as soon as the loss or theft of a passport is realized your embassy and the local police should be informed. To determine if your country has diplomatic representation in a particular country, please refer to our visa information by country. For example, if a Saudi reader is interested to know if there is a Saudi embassy in Morocco, reference should be made to "Visas: Morocco." If there is a Moroccan embassy in Jeddah, the reader will know there is a Saudi embassy in Rabat. Nations maintain diplomatic representation on an exchange basis; if there is no representation a friendly nation may act for them. Identifying which country acts for another can also be determined from this page.

Visas

Apart from personal identity, a passport is a request from your government to other governments to allow you to enter their country; a visa, which is stamped in the passport, is their affirmative, conditional response, conditional as it defines the length of stay granted, the number of entries into the country allowed, etc.

Who Needs Them?

In the Basic Information chart we have identified which passport holders need visas for the various African countries. Whether or not a visa is needed is dependent upon what reciprocal agreements your country has with a particular foreign country.

Who Has Problems Getting Certain African Visas?

Africa is a continent where friends are easily made. Our guides are directed (although we are greatly complimented when other nationals read them) to Americans, Canadians, British, Saudis, Australians, and New Zealanders. The information we provide on visas is relevant to those nationalities. If readers are joined by friends of other nationalities apart from those named, it should not be assumed that our visa information is valid for them.

Readers of *any* nationality (including those for whom we are writing) whose passport contains a visa for either South Africa or Israel *may* encounter problems when entering certain African countries regardless of the fact that the passport also contains a valid visa for the country being entered. This is applicable whether or not the South African or Israeli visas are valid or invalid (because they were used at some prior date or have expired). It is against the law to remove pages from any passport, and cutting out a South African or Israeli visa can lead to more trouble than leaving it in. Readers whose passports contain such visas should discuss the problem and their proposed itinerary in Africa with their home country's passport offices *before* leaving for Africa. It may be that obtaining a new passport is the best route to follow.

Travelers holding British passports whose forebearers were/are from the subcontinent of India may encounter difficulties when applying for a visa to certain African consulates, a case in point being Kenya. Before planning a safari they should contact the British Foreign Office or the British Embassy nearest to them for guidance.

Each country, including the reader's own country whatever it may be, has restrictions on the granting of visas. On the whole, genuine tourists will have no problems but an African country's foreign policies are many times reflected in the issuance or denial of visas. Where restrictions exist, most African countries are extremely sensitive on the subject.

How to Obtain Visas

We have found, as a general rule but not an unbreakable practice, that it is best to obtain a visa for an African country in one of their embassies in a Western country rather than to apply for a visa at their embassy in an African country. Processing is usually quicker, and the fee charged more likely to be the authorized one.

Telephone or write to the appropriate embassy for an application for a visa to be sent to you. Potential applicants living in the city where the embassy is located may not receive a response. Some embassies do not mail applications to applicants living in the city where they are located.

On July 20, 1984, we mailed requests for visa applications to 28 African embassies located in Washington, DC. The following is the result of that survey:

Responded by return mail: Gabon, Egypt, Mali, Nigeria, Togo (addressed to Togo Information Office), Tunisia, and Sierra Leone.

Responded within 7 days: Algeria, Cameroun, Upper Volta (now Burkina Faso), Uganda, and Zambia.

Reply received August 14: Zaire.

No response received: Benin, Cape Verde, Central African Republic, Congo-Brazzaville, The Gambia, Ghana, Kenya, Liberia, Malawi, Mauritania, Morocco, Niger, Senegal, and Tanzania.

Of course, staff changes occur and situations change. However, if you live in or near Washington, DC., Ottawa, London, or Jeddah and have not received a response to your written or telephone request for a visa application form within 7 days, there is justification, based on our survey findings, to assume that you are not going to receive one unless you go to the embassy and pick it up.

Once received, the forms are self-explanatory. Study whether multiple entries are permitted or only single entry and what length of stay is offered, and compare this to how long you believe your safari will take. Remember, it is easier to get a longer-term visa at the outset than apply for an extension once in the country. There are exceptions to this, as in the case of Mali, where only 7-day visas are issued and the visitor must, once in the country, apply for an extension.

Most African countries require proof that applicants have either sufficient funds to maintain themselves in the country or an onward or return ticket. A letter, written on the letterhead of a travel agent, confirming such a ticket can be used, or photocopy the tickets—don't send the actual tickets.

Photographs are usually required. These need not be expensive passport photographs but can be snapshots cut to the required size—head and shoulders, full face, posed against a light background.

Lastly, a money order should be sent—checks are not accepted by most embassies, and certainly not credit cards. The form will state how much is required to cover the cost of the visa and the registered, return-receipt postage.

Remember to use only registered, return-receipt rates when mailing your passport to an embassy.

Merikani Hotel Reservations Service (P.O. Box 533394, Temple Heights Station, Washington, DC 20009, tel. (USA) 301–530–1911) will send visa application forms and will obtain visas for our readers who make their hotel reservations through them. There is no service charge—simply the cost of the visa and the registered, return-receipt postage. This service is offered regardless of the readers' nationality or where they live. Using Merikani will save time for readers needing more than one visa, as the passport does not have to go back and forth between the applicant and various embassies.

Where to Write or Call

The following is an international list of the diplomatic representation of selected African countries. Applications for visas should be addressed to the consulate most convenient to you at any given time. Alternately, visas may be obtained through Merikani as detailed in the preceding paragraph.

COTE D'IVOIRE

Readers are strongly advised to obtain visas before arrival as there is no provision for issuance of a visa upon arrival. We had a visa and still had a bad experience with their immigration officers. Readers, we feel, should only enter Ivory Coast as members of a tour group, in which case the tour group leader handles the immigration formalities and customs for clients. Alternately, the Hilton International Abidjan automatically, upon confirmation of a reservation at the hotel, instructs a member of its staff to meet the guest at the airport. Be sure when you make your reservation at the Hilton you provide the reservation clerk with the date, flight number, and time of your arrival in Abidjan.

Embassy of the Republic of Ivory Coast
2412 Massachusetts Ave. N.W.
Washington, DC 20008
202–483–2400

Embassy of the Republic of Ivory Coast
9 Marlborough Ave.
Ottawa K1N 8E6
613–236–9919

Embassy of the Republic of Ivory Coast
2 Upper Belgrave St.
London S.W.1
(01) 235 6991

In Saudi Arabia apply to the French
Embassy in Jeddah.

Readers in Australia should apply to the French Embassy, as should readers in New Zealand to the French Embassy in Wellington.

Ivory Coast also has diplomatic representation in Belgium, France, Federal Republic of Germany, Ghana, Italy, Liberia, The Netherlands, Switzerland, and Tanzania.

EGYPT

Readers are strongly advised to obtain a visa for Egypt before arrival in the country although the official jargon indicates that where Egypt does not have diplomatic representation in the passport holder's country, a visa may be issued at the time of arrival.

Embassy of the Republic of Egypt
2300 Decatur Pl. N.W.
Washington, DC 20008
202–234–3903

Embassy of the Republic of Egypt
454 Laurier Ave.
Ottawa K1N 6R3
613–234–4931

Embassy of the Arab Republic of Egypt
26 South St.
London W1Y 8EL
(10) 499 2401

Embassy of the Arab Republic of Egypt
el Mattar St., El Sharifia
Jeddah
(2) 21011

Embassy of the Arab Republic of Egypt
125 Manaro Crescent
Red Hill, ACT 2603
(062) 95 0394

Embassy of the Arab Republic of Egypt
111 The Terrace, 1
P.O. Box 10-386
Wellington
(04) 725620

Egypt is also represented in Afghanistan, Albania, Algeria, Argentina, Austria, Belgium, Boliva, Brazil, Bulgaria, Burkina Fasa, Burma, Burundi, Cameroun, Central African Republic, Chile, the People's Republic of China, Columbia, the People's Republic of the Congo, Cuba, Cyprus, Czechoslovakia, Denmark, Equador, Ethiopia, Finland, France, The Gambia, Ghana, East and West Germany, Greece, Guinea, Hong Kong, Hungary, India, Indonesia, Iran, Iraq, Italy, Ivory Coast, Japan, Jordan, Kenya, Kuwait, Korea, Lebanon, Liberia, Libya, Malaysia, Mali, Malta, Mauritania, Mexico, Morocco, Nepal, the Netherlands, Nigeria, Niger, Norway, Pakistan, Panama, Peru, Philippines, Poland, Romania, Salvador, Senegal, Sierra Leone, Singapore, Somalia, Spain, Sri Lanka, Sudan, Sweden, Switzerland, Syria, Tanzania, Thailand, Tchad, Togo, Tunisia, Turkey, Uganda, Uruguay, the U.S.S.R., the Vatican, Venezuela, Vietnam, both Yemens, Yugoslavia, Zaire, and Zambia.

GABON

Readers may obtain visas upon arrival in Gabon upon payment of CFA 1500 to CFA 3000, depending upon their nationality. This visa will allow them to stay 72 hours and may be extended at the immigration office in Libreville. The normal tourist visa for Gabon is 30 days. We experienced some "creative financing" on the part of the issuing staff when we obtained a visa for Gabon in an African country. We advise readers to obtain a visa before departing from home or at the airport.

Embassy of the Gabonese Republic
2034 20th St. N.W.
Washington, D.C. 20009
202–797–1000

Embassy of the Gabonese Republic
4 Range Rd.
Ottawa K1N 8J5
613–232–5301

Embassy of the Gabonese Republic
48 Kensington Court
London W.8
(01) 937 5285

Embassy of the Gabonese Republic
P.O. Box 5442
Jeddah
(2) 671 8553

As there is no Gabonese representation in either Australia or New Zealand, readers in those countries may wish to wait until they arrive in Libreville. The only safari we suggest to Gabon is with Jet Tours; ask them about a visa. However, we are certain they obtain visas for the entire group at the time of arrival.

Gabon also has diplomatic representation in Belgium, Cameroun, the People's Republic of the Congo, France, Federal Republic of Germany, Iran, Italy, Ivory Coast, Morocco, Senegal, Spain, Switzerland, and Zaire.

THE GAMBIA

Tourist visas are issued upon arrival in The Gambia and are issued without charge. British, Australians, New Zealanders, and Canadians do not need this visa. The visa is issued on the proviso that the tourist holds return tickets home or onward tickets to another destination. The "Visitor's Pass" is valid for 1 month and there is a small charge for a renewal. This courtesy is not extended to passport holders from any eastern-bloc country nor to citizens of the People's Republic of China—such passport holders always need a visa.

Notwithstanding the above paragraph, visas may be obtained before entry into The Gambia from the following diplomatic representatives:

Permanent Mission to the United Nations
of the Republic of The Gambia
19 E. 47th St.
New York, NY 10017
212–752–6213

Canadians with any questions may
contact the British High Commission
in Ottawa: 80 Elgin St., Ottawa K1P
5K7
613–237–1530

High Commission for The Gambia
57 Kensington Court
London W.8
(01) 937 6316

Embassy of The Gambia
P.O. Box 5458
Jeddah
(2) 653 4233

Australians can also contact the British
High Commission. In Canberra:
Commonwealth Ave., ACT 2600
73 0422

British High Commission
Reserve Bank of New Zealand Building
9th Floor, 2 The Terrace
Wellington, 1, P.O. Box 1812
726 049

The Gambia also has diplomatic representation in Belgium, the Federal Republic of Germany, Nigeria, Senegal, and Switzerland.

KENYA

Kenya will issue visas on arrival, but this is not the generally accepted practice and usually tourists without visas are asked to wait until all other passengers (with visas) have been cleared. Many times a special immigration officer must be brought to the immigration counter; all this can take time. However, we have never experienced anything but courtesy from immigration officials and certainly any thought of a bribe is completely out of the question. In fact, in Kenya this can land the potential giver in trouble.

Embassy of the Republic of Kenya
2249 R Street N.W.
Washington D.C. 20008
202–387–6101

High Commission for Kenya
Gillin Building, Suite 600
141 Laurier Ave. West
Ottawa K1P 5JE
613–563–1773

High Commission for Kenya
Kenya House
45 Portland Pl.
London W.1
(01) 636 2371

Embassy of the Republic of Kenya
P.O. Box 6347
Jeddah
(2) 665 6718

High Commission for Kenya
P.O. Box 1990
General Post Office Canberra
ACT 2601
47 4788

No representation in Wellington; New Zealand passport holders do not require a visa; any questions should be directed to the High Commission in Canberra.

Kenya also has diplomatic representation in Belgium, Egypt, Ethiopia, France, the Federal Republic of Germany, India, Italy, Nigeria, Somalia, Sweden, Switzerland, the U.S.S.R., and Zambia.

MALAWI

The immigration processing at the airport is efficient and professional. Readers are reminded to read the dress code and list of prohibited items for Malawi.

Embassy of the Republic of Malawi
1400 20th St. N.W.
Washington, DC 20036
202–223–4814

High Commission for Malawi
112 Kent St., Suite 905
Tower "B", Place de Ville
Ottawa K1P 5P2
513–236–8931

High Commission for the Republic of
  Malawi
33 Grosvenor St.
London W1X ODE
(01) 491 4172

Saudi Arabian residents may obtain a
  visa for Malawi from
The British Embassy
P.O. Box 393
Jeddah
(2) 665 2000

Australian readers apply to
British High Commission
Commonwealth Ave.
Canberra ACT 2600
73 0422

In New Zealand contact
British High Commission
Reserve Bank Building
2 The Terrace, P. O. Box 1812
Wellington
(04) 726049

Malawi also has diplomatic representation in Belgium, West Germany, Kenya, Mozambique, Tanzania, Zambia, and Zimbabwe.

MALI

We found the immigration procedures well organized; however, the Sofitel hostess met us at the airport as we had reservations at that hotel in Bamako. See "Malian Accommodation: Hotel l'Amitie."

Mali issues visas only for 7 days' validity after arrival in the country. This is because so many visitors travel overland. Compulsory reporting to immigration officials provides a check on the whereabouts of overland travelers if they become lost in the Sahara Desert; if they haven't reported, they're still out there and a search can be mounted.

Embassy of the Republic of Mali
2130 R St. N.W.
Washington, DC 20008
202–332–2249

Embassy of the Republic of Mali
50 Goulburn Ave.
Ottawa K1N 8J4
613–232–1501

In the U.K. apply to
Embassy of the Republic of Mali
89 Rue du Cherche-Midi
Paris 6, France
548 5843

Embassy of the Republic of Mali
P.O. Box 5379
Jeddah
(2) 651 5712

Readers in Australia and New Zealand may wish to obtain a visa either en route through Europe or at the Embassy of Mali in Dakar, Senegal. We did the latter and found the staff very helpful.

Mali also has diplomatic representation in Belgium, the People's Republic of China, Egypt, Federal Republic of Germany, Ghana, Ivory Coast, Lebanon, Senegal, the U.S.S.R., and Yugoslavia.

Full details on the procedures to follow, once in Bamako, to extend visas will be found in "Permits to Photograph."

SENEGAL

On one occasion we went through immigration at Dakar International Airport without a visa and had no problem—the officer simply stamped out passports for a tourist stay in Senegal. Dakar airport, at that time, was starting to be our second home—our faces certainly were familiar to the authorities. At the opposite end of the stick, a Lebanese friend whose flight had been diverted from Monrovia was not issued a visa and could not leave the airport. Like so many things in Africa, it all depends. We feel it is better to ensure there will be no problems and to have a visa before arrival. Visas are not required to transit when changing planes.

Embassy of the Republic of Senegal
2112 Wyoming Ave. N.W.
Washington, DC 20008
202–234–0540

Embassy of the Republic of Senegal
57 Marlborough Ave.
Ottawa K1N 8E8
613–238–6392

Embassy of the Republic of Senegal
11 Phillmore Gardens
London W8 7QG
(01) 973 0925

Embassy of the Republic of Senegal
P.O. Box 1394
Jeddah
(2) 665 4465

Consulate-General Republic of Senegal
15 Fenwick St.
Kew Vic 3101
862 1239

In New Zealand
contact the consulate in Australia.

Senegal also has diplomatic representation in Algeria, Belgium, Brazil, Cameroun, Central African Republic, People's Republic of China, Congo-Brazzaville, Denmark, Egypt, Ethiopia, Finland, France, Gabon, The Gambia, Federal Republic of Germany, Iraq, Italy, Japan, Kuwait, Morocco, The Netherlands, Nigeria, Norway, Sweden, Switzerland, Tunisia, U.S.S.R., and Vatican City.

SOMALIA

Somalia immigration procedures are slightly chaotic but certainly nothing like Madagascar. Strict control (meaning a physical search is made of arriving passengers who have a shabby, unkempt appearance whom the authorities have reason to suspect may be carrying drugs). Otherwise, there is no dress code. At the beach a one-piece swimsuit on women is more acceptable than a bikini. Somali women are not veiled and there is no objection to visitors wearing short sleeves or sundresses.

Visas are not issued upon arrival and should be obtained before departure. Allow three working days to process the visa, plus mailing time.

Embassy of the Democratic Republic of
  Somalia
600 New Hampshire Ave. N.W.
Washington, DC 20037
202–342–1575

Embassy of the Democratic Republic of
  Somalia
130 Slater St., Suite 1000
Ottawa K1P 5P2
613–563–4541

Embassy of the Democratic Republic of
  Somalia
60 Portland Pl.
London W1N 3DG
(01) 580 7140

Embassy of the Democratic Republic of
  Somalia
P.O. Box 729
Jeddah
(2) 267 3903

Officially, readers in Australia and New Zealand are instructed to send their passports to the Somali Embassy in the People's Republic of China to obtain a visa. We would think it easier, and quicker, to obtain a visa en route to Somalia. The Somali Embassy in Nairobi, Kenya, has staff who are extremely nice and very efficient.

Somalia also has diplomatic representation in Algeria, Belgium, People's Republic of China, Djibouti, Egypt, France, Federal Republic of Germany, Democratic Republic of Germany, India, Iran, Iraq, Italy, Japan, Kenya, Kuwait, Libya, Nigeria, Oman, Pakistan, Qatar, Senegal, Sudan, Sweden, Switzerland, Syria, Turkey, Uganda, United Arab Emirates, the U.S.S.R., Yemen Arab Republic, Yemen People's Republic, Yugoslavia, and Zambia.

SUDAN

We found Sudanese immigration and customs procedures very professional and efficient. Under no circumstances will visas be issued upon entry and the Lake Nassir steamer ticket office will not issue a ticket for the steamer unless the purchaser is in possession of a valid visa for Sudan.

Embassy of the Democratic Republic of
the Sudan
2210 Massachusetts Ave. N.W.
Washington, DC 20008
202–466–6280

Readers in Canada should apply to the Washington, DC, embassy.

Embassy of the Democratic Republic of
the Sudan
3 Cleveland Row
St. James's
London SW1A 1DD

Readers in Australia and New Zealand experiencing difficulties in obtaining visas for Sudan may wish to contact Merikani Hotel Reservations Service; however, local travel agents should be contacted before doing so in the event they can offer more immediate assistance. Readers planning to obtain a Sudanese visa in Cairo should allow a week for processing.

Sudan also has diplomatic representation in Belgium, Chad, People's Republic of China, Egypt, Ethiopia, Federal Republic of Germany, France, India (at both Bombay and Delhi), Italy, Kenya, Kuwait, Lebanon, the Netherlands, Nigeria, Pakistan, Somalia, Switzerland, Tanzania, Uganda, the U.S.S.R., the Arab Republic of Yemen, Yugoslavia, and Zaire.

TOGO

Readers should refer to "Background for Togo" concerning our experience with customs at Lome—nothing aggressive, just unprofessional. Visas are not issued on arrival, but many nationalities are exempted from requiring a visa.

Embassy of the Republic of Togo
2208 Massachusetts Ave. N.W.
Washington, DC 20008
202–234–4212

Embassy of the Republic of Togo
12 Range Rd.
Ottawa K1N 8J3
613–238–5916

Charge d'Affaires for the Togolese
  Republic
20 Wellington Court
116 Knightsbridge
London S.W.1
(01) 584 1948

In Saudi Arabia obtain a visa from one
of the Togolese embassies located in
the cities named in this listing.

Toto also has diplomatic representation in the following countries: Belgium, Brazil, People's Republic of China, France, Gabon, Federal Republic of Germany, Ghana, Italy, Lebanon, Libya, the Netherlands, Nigeria, Switzerland, and Zaire.

If you stay in Togo more than 10 days, it will be necessary to obtain a "Departure Clearance" from the police station. This entails completing a form given at the police station and leaving with them your passport and a copy of your flight reservation, which you received upon confirming your return airline reservations. The police will tell you when to return to pick up your passport and your clearance. This is a tiresome formality that serves no purpose for the genuine tourist; there is no charge, therefore no profit to the government. As the Togo government has relaxed restrictions for visas—for Americans and Canadians—and they are not required, it seems a pity to continue this one impediment to becoming more competitive with other African countries encouraging foreign tourists. Anyway, at this writing, it must be done.

UGANDA

When making reference to Uganda we have advised using caution. Travel in the Kampala-Jinja-Entebbe region is now safe, however. Check with your own embassy in Nairobi concerning the issuance of any traveler's warning before going to Uganda. We have also suggested the stationmaster at Kenya Railways Nairobi Station as a good source of information on conditions in Uganda.

Embassy of the Republic of Uganda
5409 16th St. N.W.
Washington, DC 20011
202-726-7100

High Commission for Uganda
170 Laurier Ave. West
Suite 601
Ottawa K1P 5VP
613-233-7797

High Commission for Uganda
Uganda House
58/59 Trafalgar Sq.
London WC2N
(01) 839 5783

Embassy of the Republic of Uganda
P.O. Box 4838
Jeddah
(2) 665 6016

High Commission for Uganda
P.O. Box 342
Dickson ACT 2602
47 2235

The British High Commission—for United Kingdom, Australian, and New Zealand readers—is downtown and the American Embassy is practically next door. The Saudi Embassy is at 7, Kololo Hill, P.O. Box 7274, Kampala—in the suburbs—and the residence is at 5, Summit View, Kampala. Telephone at the embassy is 41983 and at the residence 41112.

▶ **Note:** Tourists, business people, and all non-Ugandans should contact the Ministry of Foreign Affairs in Kampala, as well as their own embassies, upon arrival in Uganda. In this way a monitoring can take place in the event there are security problems. This advice is offered by the Uganda government in order to assist visitors to the country.

Insurance

American Express, Blue Cross-Blue Shield, and a few other companies have started offering overseas accident coverage to their clients. We believe they have taken portions of the International SOS Assistance policy and made a package deal in which they have incorporated parts—not necessarily all—of the SOS original policy. Our best advice is to obtain accident coverage directly from International SOS Assistance, Inc., unless you're prepared to read through all the fine print the others offer to make sure you've got *full* coverage.

So important do we feel accident coverage to be that we reproduce the entire text of the International SOS Assistance brochure below:

International SOS Assistance, Inc. was founded to provide travelers direct access to prompt assistance in the event of a medical or personal emergency while traveling 100 miles or more from home. SOS services are now recognized worldwide as a vital supplement to insurance coverages. These services, ranging from telephone consultation to emergency evacuation are quickly and easily accessible to any SOS member world-wide.

Members are provided assistance after one call to the SOS world-wide, multilingual network of physicians, nurses, paramedics, and other specialists. This network is available 24 hours a day, 365 days a year to render aid in any emergency. International SOS Assistance, Inc. continually monitors facilities and staff to ensure SOS members the best available attention in the event of an emergency.

Each SOS member receives a card which includes a list of SOS Local Medical Centers. When urgent medical advice is needed anytime during travels, a Member may call the nearest SOS Local Medical Center for assistance. SOS maintains Local Medical Centers staffed with multi-lingual medical personnel on 24-hour call, who may be contacted for evaluation and referral to English-speaking doctors in the general area served by the Center.

The Personal Medical Profile Booklet contains SOS membership benefits, charge authorization, as well as pertinent personal information, health insurance and immunization information.

We have capitalized the following paragraphs to arrest readers attention:

EMERGENCY EVACUATION: WHEN ADEQUATE MEDICAL FACILITIES ARE NOT AVAILABLE LOCALLY, SOS WILL PROVIDE EMERGENCY EVACUATION TO THE NEAREST FACILITY CAPABLE OF PROVIDING REQUIRED CARE.

MEDICALLY SUPERVISED REPATRIATION: WHEN THE TREATING PHYSICIAN DETERMINES IT IS MEDICALLY ADVISABLE TO BRING THE INDIVIDUAL TO A FACILITY NEARER HIS PERMANENT RESIDENCE FOLLOWING STABILIZATION, SOS WILL MAKE ARRANGEMENTS AND PAY FOR REPATRIATION UNDER MEDICAL SUPERVISION.

In the two cases where we had received first-hand accounts of this service, the patient was evacuated by a charter aircraft from the African country within 24 hours of the accident's occurrence.

IMPORTANT: SOS DOES NOT EVACUATE OR REPATRIATE A MEMBER WITHOUT MEDICAL AUTHORIZATION OR A MEMBER WITH MILD LESIONS, SIMPLE INJURIES SUCH AS SPRAINS, SIMPLE FRACTURES, OR MILD SICKNESS WHICH CAN BE TREATED BY LOCAL DOCTORS AND DO NOT PREVENT THE MEMBER FROM CONTINUING HIS/HER TRIP OR RETURNING HOME, OR A MEMBER WITH INFECTIONS UNDER TREATMENT AND NOT YET HEALED AND ADVANCED PREGNANCIES OF OVER SEVEN MONTHS.

Note: Insurance purchased by SOS, for its Service Program and Membership Benefits, requires SOS to exclude payment for services when travel is undertaken for the specific purpose of securing medical treatment; injuries resulting from attempt at suicide; suicide; acts of war or insurrections; commission of an unlawful act; or use of drugs unless prescribed by a physician.

Transportation To Join Disabled Member: When a member is traveling alone, and is hospitalized more than 100 miles from home for more than seven days, economy round trip common carrier transportation to the place of hospitalization will be provided to a person chosen by the members.

Return of Minor Children: When minor children named in the application are left unattended as the result of a member's accident or illness, SOS will pay the cost of one way economy transportation by common carrier for return of the children to their place of residence. Qualified attendents will also be provided without charge, when required.

Repatriation of Mortal Remains: In the event of a member's demise while traveling more than 100 miles or more from home, SOS will render every assistance possible and pay for the return of the mortal remains.

US$1,000 In Accident and Sickness Benefits: When the SOS member is outside his/her country of permanent residence and becomes ill or injured, membership provides for reimbursement of medical expenses for accident or sickness up to $1,000 ($25. deductible). This benefit is provided to SOS members under a blanket insurance policy issued to SOS by INA (Insurance Company of North America). The policy does not cover conditions for which a member has received treatment 90 days prior to effective membership date nor conditions covered by Workers Compensation or other group programs.

Hospital deposits: SOS will either guarantee or wire any required hospital admittance deposit up to $1,000.

Charge Authorization: Where accepted for use with internationally accepted charge cards for payment of hospital deposits and other non-covered medical fees.

Emergency Personal Cash Advance: SOS will provide members, when and where possible, an advance of up to US$250 in local currency for personal medical emergencies.

Note: Any emergency hospital admittance deposit or personal cash advance must be repaid within 45 days (without interest).

WHEN AN SOS MEMBER IS TRAVELING OUTSIDE HIS/HER COUNTRY OF RESIDENCE WITHOUT A PLANNED ITINERARY, AND AN UNFORESEEN EMERGENCY OCCURS, UPON NOTIFICATION, SOS WILL PUBLISH THE MEMBER'S SOS IDENTIFICATION NUMBER FOR THREE DAYS IN THE CLASSIFIED SECTION OF THE INTERNATIONAL HERALD TRIBUNE UNDER THE HEADING: SOS CALLING. THE MEMBER THEN CALLS AN SOS CONTROL CENTER FOR THE MESSAGE. SERVICE AVAILABLE FOR EUROPE, AFRICA, AND ASIA.

Travel Interruption: Strike, Weather, Hijack Delay: When an SOS member's air travel is curtailed or delayed subsequent to departure due to an unannounced strike, adverse weather conditions or hijacking, the INA (Insurance Company of North America) will reimburse up to US$200 daily for the non-refundable portion of the SOS member's travel expenses. Benefit is payable (1) provided the delay exceeds 8 consecutive hours, (2) maximum of 3 days.

In addition to the foregoing medical assistance, SOS also provides certain legal assistance. We have initiated correspondence with them to determine their position. This correspondence will take some time and we do not anticipate having their legal adviser's opinion—quite apart from any insurance SOS may or may not consider offering—for some months. Readers particularly interested in this may write to us at P.O. Box 6035, Washington, DC 20005 to monitor the progress of the correspondence.

Under the same membership SOS offers:

> Legal and Bail Bond Services: SOS provides referral to legal assistance for members when required in criminal and civil cases while traveling. The International Legal Defense Counsel, on behalf of SOS, will provide legal consultation and representation throughout the world. If personal presence of attorney is required member will be responsible for fees. SOS will also assist members in obtaining bail bonds where such bonds are customarily issued.

> US$1,000 for Auto Legal Expenses: In the event an SOS member is involved in a traffic accident as a driver, passenger or pedestrian, more than 100 miles from home, SOS will advance up to $1,000 toward the payment of legal fees or fines. (Must be repaid to SOS within 45 days without interest).

Apart from the legal and medical assistance, SOS also provides access to an interpreter at no charge or for a nominal fee if the personal presence of the interpreter is required; SOS Country Profiles—information on many areas of the world concerning health, climate, travel requirements, currency, telephone system, SOS services, holidays, business hours, transportation, embassies/consulates/missions, all cross-referenced for easy access. They also, on the more commercial side, provide discounts on car rentals, including Avis. All this information comes with the application for membership. That application can be obtained:

For readers living in North America, Australia and New Zealand: International SOS Assistance, Inc. Executive and Administrative Offices (P.O. Box 11568, Philadelphia, PA 19116, tel: 800–523–8930; in Pennsylvania or outside the U.S. 215–244–1500; in Canada 800–441–4767).

For readers living in the United Kingdom or Saudi Arabia: International SOS Assistance, S.A. Executive and Administrative Offices (15, rue Lombard, 1205 Geneva, Switzerland, tel: 41 (22) 47–61–61).

Schedule of Fees: For single and/or frequent trips per member (there is no family membership; each person insured must pay a premium):
1–7 days $15
each additional day $2
per month $45
frequent traveler (annual) $195
Payable by personal check, money order, or American Express, Diners Club, VISA, or MasterCard credit cards.

Readers should not rely on their travel agent or the tour operator to provide SOS services; they should have their own personal coverage, because SOS offers a corporate package in which the corporation assumes the responsibility of evacuating members and some of the other services offered by the full coverage that we have discussed. Many times the travel agent or tour operator does not have the resources to cover the deposit necessary before a charter airplane takes off from Europe to come to the assistance of a victim. In this case, it becomes the responsibility of the victim—or relatives—to provide such a deposit. In a case we were told about, the tour operator was a corporate member but could not provide the deposit, and the victim and her fellow tourists had to come up with US$35,000 before the plane could take off for Africa.

So important do we believe it is that our readers carry SOS insurance that we have added the premiums into our estimated budgets. We know some readers will be on a tight budget, but SOS insurance is as necessary as an airline ticket.

In all honesty, International SOS Assistance is not really required in Kenya as that country's medical services are of such a high standard. We discussed this with SOS and they agreed that they would not routinely evacuate a patient from Kenya as the would from, say, Mali. But they advised us that sometimes a patient, for one reason or another (perhaps homesickness), does not make the progress the physician feels he or she should. In such cases, SOS evacuates that patient. We therefore recommend SOS for Kenya as well as the other African countries. The rates, when contracted directly with SOS, seem so reasonable that it appears foolish not to do so.

Driver's Licenses

On the following pages we list a selection of African countries where an International Driving Permit (IDP) is needed to operate a vehicle, and those countries that will accept your home country license. It is not necessary to personally apply for an International Driving Permit or to take a test. Simply contact the automobile club nearest you requesting an application form. Return this with 2 passport pictures and your check—the charge is very reasonable—for processing. Your present license must be valid in order to obtain the international permit; the permit is good for one year. It is not necessary to be a member of an automobile club to obtain an international permit. Applicants must be age 18 or over.

Australian residents apply to: Australian Automobile Association (G.P.O. 1555, 2601 Canberra; offices are located at 212 Northbourne Ave. tel: (062) 477 311, telex: AUSMO AA 62531).

Canadian residents apply to: Canadian Automobile Association (1775 Courtwood Crescent, Ottawa, Ontario K2C 3K2, tel: 613–226–7631).

New Zealand residents apply to: The New Zealand Automobile Association Inc. (P.O. Box 1794, Wellington 1; offices are located at 342 Lambton Quay, tel: (04) 738 738, telegrams: NATAUTO).

Documentation Required to Drive in Selected African Countries; Rule of the Road
(traffic moves on the right or left hand side of the road); and
Distinctive Motor Vehicle Code Letters Internationally Recognized

Country	Visitors may drive using their home country license?	International Driver's Permit (IDP) Required	Rule of the Road	International Code Lettering	Comments
Cote d'Ivoire		Y	Right	CI	Tip "parking boys" in your own self-interest.
Egypt		Y	Right	ET	Driving in Cairo chaotic; once outside the city okay.
Gabon	Y		Right	information not available	
The Gambia	Y		Right	WAG	
Kenya	Y		Left	EAK	Leaving a car double-parked can lead to a ticket.
Malawi	Y		Left	MW	
Mali	Y		Right	RMM	We feel it's best to have an IDP.
Morocco	Y		Right	MA	If an IDP is used it must be accompanied by a home driver's license.
Senegal	Y		Right	SN	
Somalia		Y	Right	information not available	One source states "test must be taken." We doubt this is true for tourists.
Sudan	Y		Right	information not available	License should be presented to the police on arrival for validation.

Tanzania	Y	Left	EAT (or EAZ for Zanzibar)	After crossing the frontier licenses must be endorsed by a revenue officer; home license valid then for 21 days, an IDP for 1 year.
Togo	Y	Right	TG	
Uganda	Y	Left	EAU	

▲ **Note:** An International Driving Permit is very easily obtained and reasonably priced; it is always in the best interest of a driver to have one when driving in Africa. It doesn't matter at all in Malawi or Kenya, but in other countries where the police are not as well educated or do not speak English, an International Permit is much more impressive, in addition to the fact that it is written in nine languages. Military manned and/or police-mounted roadblocks are common in African countries. Drivers should always be prepared to show their license and passport. Under no circumstances lose your temper; always address the men as "sir"; keep cigarettes away from the dashboard unless you're prepared to offer one—or even the entire package; always be willing to allow the vehicle to be searched. This is the way things have been operating for years; don't expect to introduce civil liberties. Kenyan rental cars are clearly marked on the hood (bonnet) that they are tourist vehicles; very little, if any problems will be encountered.

Saudi Arabian residents apply to: Saudi Automobile and Touring Association (P.O. Box 276, Dammam 31411, tel: 83 24 441, 83 29 080, 83 42 053, or 83 41 669; telex: 601259).

United Kingdom residents apply to: Royal Automobile Club (89–91 Pall Mall, London, SW1Y 5HS, tel: (1) 930 2345, telex: rac-club 88 1374 1).

United States residents apply to: American Automobile Association (8111 Gatehouse Rd., Falls Church, VA 22047, telephone: 703–AAA–6778).

Home-country clubs have affiliated services available with some African automobile clubs. We suggest our readers who are planning to drive in Kenya apply for membership in the Kenya Automobile Association. The dues are very small and the benefits—we think—very great. Not only are there the usual automobile club services, routing information, legal advice, etc., but also the Flying Doctor Service is free in case of accident. The charge for the Flying Doctor without membership in the club is equal to the club membership. Readers might as well have the benefit of membership. Malawi does not have an automobile association (they used to share the Zimbabwe Club when Zimbabwe was Rhodesia). However, we feel that the Avis staff in Malawi will be able to provide any necessary information to our readers. The address to write for an application form for membership in the Kenya AA is AA House, Westlands, P.O. Box 40087, Nairobi, Kenya. Specify that you are applying for 6-month temporary membership. The AA Handbook is sent to all members, and is a mine of information.

Automobile clubs also issue Carnets de Passage necessary for overland travel across boundaries, and in some cases are Issuer and Guarantor of Letters of Credit.

Permits to Photograph

Some countries require visitors to obtain a permit before using a camera in their country. Of the countries we discuss in this guide and at this writing, the following countries require such a permit: Mali, Somalia, Sudan, Tanzania (including the island of Zanzibar).

Mali: See full details at the end of this section.

Somalia: A permit to photograph is valid indefinitely and can be obtained in several days with the assistance of the Ministry of Tourism from the Central Censorship Board. The permit authorizes the bearer to photograph historic and cultural places, landscapes, traditional dances, and research areas specifically authorized by the Somali government for scientific purposes. Photographers are reminded that photographing any objects, person or persons that might jeopardize the national security of the Somali Democratic Republic or anything that is contrary to decent behavior or public morality is totally forbidden. All kinds of photographs are subject to censor.

Although the Ministry of Tourism officials told us when we were in Somalia that they wished the need for a permit to photograph would be rescinded, in light of the gross misinformation we were given before arrival in Somalia (see "Background for Somalia"), we can understand the government wanting to retain some type of control. An international charitable agency had been showing films of starving people in the refugee camps on U.S. television, drawing the inference that *all* of Somalia is in such a state. This particular agency was asked to leave the country as their propaganda was damaging Somali's international image.

Sudan: Visitors go to the Sudanese Tourism Corporation or the Ministry of Information & Culture to obtain a free licence to photograph. (See also shopping guide to Khartoum in the "Background for Sudan" section).

Tanzania and Zanzibar: Like everything else to do with Tanzania, a permit to photograph is an on-again-off-again regulation. Readers are advised to ask UTC (United Touring Company) about the need when making their reservations for the tour to Zanzibar.

General restrictions applicable to all countries: The majority of African countries prohibit taking pictures at airports; from the plane window or on the ground—as usually military aircraft share the same field and they do not want it known how many planes they have. The fact that such information is available in internationally available periodicals is irrelevant.

Pictures should never be taken around barracks or other military installations.

Usually it is prohibited to take pictures of the country's president when he passes in his limo or at any function he attends. (It is understood that journalists are exceptions to this and take photographs by prior arrangement with the government of the country.)

Pictures that show a country in a poor light may be objected to by the people in the vicinity where the photograph is being taken. Such an objection can result in the loss of the camera. Discretion should be exercised at all times.

Paying the subject to be photographed: In Kenya the Masai have become so corrupted by tourism that they openly solicit visitors to photograph them, dressed for the part, and demand payment. If you're down on the south coast and are dead set on photographing Masai, the hotels usually have a Masai evening when the warriors come to dance and offer their wares for sale at the conclusion of the performance. During this time it's possible to take their pictures without payment.

Photographing people in Moslem countries: It is naturally only courtesy to ask permission before photographing anyone. In certain Moslem countries, for instance Somalia, women believe it to be against the tenents of the Koran to allow themselves to be photographed. The Koran discourages reproducing the human image in an effort to discourage idolatry.

A telescopic lens can be a way around this, but just as you want your religious beliefs respected by others, so we hope our readers will understand the reluctance on the part of some Moslems not to be photographed. Offering money as an inducement is, from their viewpoint, tempting them to sin.

Although sections of the Malian populace are Moslem, we did not notice the same degree of hesitancy on the part of Malian women, and many quite happily stood, and even posed, to have their pictures taken.

Formalities required of tourists to Mali spending in excess of seven days in the country or wishing to take photographs:

Authority to Photograph

2 pictures	
1 Tourism Card	700CFA
1 Stamp value of	100CFA
1 Stamp value of	2500CFA

TOTAL COST 3300 CFA

Photographic Permit and Extension of the Visa

2 pictures	
1 Form "Demand for Prolongation of the Visa"	
1 Tourism card	700CFA
2 Stamps each of a value of 100 CFA	200CFA
2 Stamps each of a value of 2500 CFA	5000CFA

TOTAL COST 5900 CFA

Visa Extension

2 pictures	
2 copies of the Form "Demand for Prolongation of the Visa"	
1 form (from SMERT) granting the extension of the visa	
1 Tourism card	700 CFA
2 Stamps each of 100 CFA value	200 CFA
1 Stamp value of	2500 CFA

TOTAL COST 3400 CFA

The above formalities are required, in the case of visa extensions, because most tourists enter Mali from the Sahara Desert overland. The requirement to check into police stations provides a check on visitors in the event they are lost in the desert.

We had a difficult time—primarily because we do not speak French—getting to the right place. For the benefit of readers, we provide step-by-step instructions. It is pertinent to add that the Tourist Department of the Government of Mali provides tourist officers in the lobbies of tourist hotels (SMERT), and these people are supposed to help tourists obtain the necessary documents. The system does not work, and while the representatives are physically in the lobbies, they are not, in our opinion, intellectually dedicated to assisting tourists. The exception to this are the young men who staff the central tourist office; they were extremely helpful, spoke English, and were interested in their work. However, it is the task of the tourist to obtain the correct stamps in the correct denominations from the post office; these cannot be obtained at the tourist office. (SMERT is the acronym for that office.)

Go to the main post office in Bamako and purchase the stamps exactly as itemized. There is a special window for this purpose. Postal employees are confused as to which window it is, and several contradictory directions are given.

Enter through the main door at the top of the entrance stairs. *Turn immediately right;* do not go into the post office main room. There are two windows along this passageway. Go to the window nearest the far wall and opposite two public telephones. The window is marked above the opening, "Telephones."

The clerk does not always have the 2500 CFA denomination stamp available but will send for it. This can take 20 minutes or so. Go do some shopping—buy postcards just outside the post office for a quarter of the price charged in the hotels—and come back. The 100 stamps must be two 100s, not one 200.

Take the stamps, two pictures of yourself, and your passport to the SMERT office opposite the Ensamble d'Artizans. They have the forms needed. Complete the forms and obtain the Tourism Card. Take these to Securete Nationale—this is the main police station in Bamako. Leave your passport, the completed and endorsed forms from SMERT, and return for them when you are advised to do so by the officer on duty. We found the police very helpful and courteous.

Reportedly, the procedures are the same in smaller towns: the post office, the local SMERT office, the police.

INDEX